MW01265614

THAT ST. LOUIS THING, Vol. 2

An American Story of Roots, Rhythm and Race

BRUCE R. OLSON

Copyright © 2016 Bruce R. Olson.

Cover art Copyright © 2016 "Louis IX on Art Hill" by Marilyn Ciafone Olson
Index sponsored by Roger Hudson

All rights reserved. No part of this book may be reproduced, stored, or transmitted by any means—whether auditory, graphic, mechanical, or electronic—without written permission of both publisher and author, except in the case of brief excerpts used in critical articles and reviews. Unauthorized reproduction of any part of this work is illegal and is punishable by law.

ISBN: 978-1-4834-5799-4 (sc)
ISBN: 978-1-4834-5798-7 (e)

Because of the dynamic nature of the Internet, any web addresses or links contained in this book may have changed since publication and may no longer be valid. The views expressed in this work are solely those of the author and do not necessarily reflect the views of the publisher, and the publisher hereby disclaims any responsibility for them.

Any people depicted in stock imagery provided by Thinkstock are models, and such images are being used for illustrative purposes only.
Certain stock imagery © Thinkstock.

Lulu Publishing Services rev. date: 09/16/2016

A Note to the Reader

The research for this two-volume story began with interviews with St. Louis musicians and musically connected people conducted during 2012, 2013 and 2014. Information also came from contemporary newspapers and magazines, especially the *St. Louis Post-Dispatch* (P-D) and *The New York Times* (NYT) and also including the *Riverfront Times* (RFT), the *St. Louis Globe-Democrat* (G-D) and the *St. Louis Blues Society BluesLetter.*

Most of the periodical information was obtained in the St. Louis Public Library, the Missouri History Museum and through Internet access to the original items. Some also comes from private collections generously provided by people I interviewed.

I've consulted dozens of books, including first person accounts, diaries, scrapbooks and other sources. I've also used encyclopedias (especially the *Encyclopedia Brittannica, 1971),* catalogues and discography material, much of it accessed in the stacks at the Gaylord Music Library at Washington University in St. Louis as well as in the St. Louis Public Library's St. Louis Room and Special Collections section. Official government data was found on the Internet and in the files at the St. Louis Public Library.

Blogs and Facebook commentary have been pretty much ruled out, but the Internet has been used for access to original sources, especially books and newspapers. I've also used websites posted by musicians and bands, corporations and officials for basic biographical and historical information of a non-controversial nature.

The citations provided at the end of Volume One and Volume Two are intended to give the reader the opportunity for further reading. Everything inside quote marks comes from the above-mentioned sources. Objective truth in history walks along in a context that includes the eye of the beholder. I've tried to keep as much subjectivity out of my story as possible. But sometimes, I can't resist entering the book myself.

Contents

Volume Two:
The Forties to Ferguson

Volume Two:
The Forties to Ferguson

It's always been a polarized town. But people like it like that. North Side, South Side; fine. We'll see you at the club. And we did. White folks would drive to East St. Louis and frequent the black clubs. There was no problem.

-- Jimmy Hinds, St. Louis musician

Prologue: Cultural Diversity and the Burning Fuse

We've got a good scene in St. Louis. In general, we've got a scene that is musician friendly. I hear that from other people who come here. We are just friendly. We are cool about letting others sitting in. Here, we don't have the cutthroat, paranoid attitude that you're going to take away my gig. Everybody knows everybody.

--Rich McDonough, Blues guitarist

St. Louis grew steadily in population and stature from its founding in 1764 into the middle of the twentieth century. As we saw in Volume One, its position at the confluence of the Mississippi and Missouri rivers created an economic dynamo that produced everything from hats to shoes, from airplanes to streetcars, from beer to bricks. Against this growth, the city also saw a cultural cavalcade of musical innovation -- ragtime, blues, jazz -- second to none in America.

But while its factories roared and its coffers filled with cash, political development lagged. Most of the big questions of government were settled by the end of the nineteenth century, its borders firmly drawn, its economic hierarchy entrenched. By 1940, a racial divide between black and white had been carved along the streets of the city. The old lines of the 1916 segregation vote stood firm.

The second volume of *That St. Louis Thing* sees the perpetuation of a governmental system that resulted in a ragged hit and miss pattern of stop and start urban development and the general failure to deal equitably with race relations. At the same time, we still see plenty of progress in the culture -- an increase in quality and quantity. Out of this period comes rock and R&B, two more innovations that add to the city's musical credentials. Here, a music scene second to none in the nation is formed.

In the years after 1940 we can also sense the presence of the fuse of racial conflict burning ever closer to an explosion.

Chapter Nineteen

The Forties: War and Racism

1940-2014

(On the road to Berlin) there were Russians riding in 2 1/2-ton American trucks. There were Russian troops riding in two-wheeled carts, phaetons, in old-fashioned pony carts, in gypsy wagons and surreys with fringed tops . . . The wagons were filled with hay and soldiers rode on top of the hay like an army taking a holiday and going on a great mass hayride . . . the fierce fighting men of the Red Army in their tunics and great boots . . . singing their fighting songs, drinking their vodka.

-- Virginia Irwin, *Post-Dispatch*, April 27, 1945

St. Louis, filled to its boundaries with over 800,000 people by 1940, had taken a severe punch in the Great Depression. The manufacturing level was 70 percent of what it had been when the stock market crashed, well below a national average that had crawled back to 84 percent of the 1929 level. There was a decline in population after 120 years of growth. Where St. Louis was once the fourth largest city in the country it now stood eighth.

But despite the Depression, St. Louis in 1940 was a vibrant, diverse, vital metropolis. Over 200 different industrial classifications were represented in the city's boundaries. It was still the world's largest fur market; it was the biggest producer of brick on the planet and led the world in the production of terra cotta, stoves, sugar-mill machinery, woodenware and hats. It was one of the biggest U.S. grain markets, had numerous shoe and boot factories and retained its central position as the home of Big Beer as well as a major maker of steel, textiles, iron, drugs and chemicals.

In 1940, St. Louis was a mighty transportation hub, served by two dozen railroad lines, 30 bus lines, by airlines and steamboats. There were now four bridges over the Mississippi. No less than 65 hotels served thousands of visitors. There were 90 movie theaters, 13 public swimming pools, a golf course and 116 public tennis courts. Two major league baseball teams shared Sportsman's Park. There were stadiums for college football, midget auto racing and track meets. And there were ice hockey rinks, boxing and wrestling rings, softball fields, handball courts, amateur baseball diamonds, cricket fields, a ski jump, a toboggan slide and 22 picnic grounds.

The city was (and remains) confined in the boundaries established in 1876, about 18 miles from Carondelet north along the Mississippi to the Chain of Rocks Bridge and some seven miles west from the Gateway Arch on the river out to the intersection of Delmar and Skinker at the city line.

Major streets went westerly, like the veins of Marie Chouteau's fan, still following the Osage trading trails and the routes of the initial French trappers. More modern, straighter streets sliced across the city north to south trying to enforce a grid. There were also dozens of "place" developments (Portland Place, Westminster Place), made of large brick and stone houses each sealed off from traffic by a large gate. These were white-only enclaves with many restrictions, cut off from what the rich residents more and more came to fear as "slum" encroachment.

The commercial core in 1940 was much where it had always been, down by the river. Over the years it had moved slightly west and spread north and south, away from the zone that was about to be demolished along the riverfront. Still, the area within a mile or two of the river was packed with large department stores, restaurants and soda fountains. Here were also shoe repair stores, dime stores, wholesale dealers, printers, banks, and professional offices. Tenement housing was interspersed along with saloons and juke joints, especially on the northern edge of this area.

By 1940 there was a new shopping area, the Central West End, featuring expensive imports, toys and unique, handmade clothing, goods that sometimes came from France and England. Another shopping area outside the city center was the Wellston district in the northwest corner of the city, featuring cut-rate products, extending east. Here the middle class could find flowers, vegetables, chicken, geese, fish, clothing, furniture and a host of second-hand items. Its central core was Easton Avenue, crowded with dozens of fortunetellers, astrologers and faith healers. Further south near the city's boundary was the Delmar/DeBaliviere neighborhood of small shops, large supermarkets and restaurants catering to the middle-income residents, black and white.

Black housing ran around and through the central district of the city, both north and south. German neighborhoods, containing half the immigrant population, were also both north and south, next to segregated black areas. South along the river lay the old Soulard district of mixed-ethnic working whites. On the South Side, heading away from the city center, were Czech, Bohemian and Italian neighborhoods.

On the Hill south of Shaw many of the Italians still spoke their native tongue in 1940 and corner taverns were ripe with fresh spaghetti, ravioli and red wine. Not far away north on warm evenings in black districts closer to downtown, residents took to their front stoops or sat in rocking chairs along the street. One guide commented that along Chouteau south of the railroad tracks in Mill Creek Valley, "sidewalk vendors sell spicy chunks of barbecued meat, hot fish or great slices of iced watermelon, and the air is rich with laughter and the soft drawl of conversation."

The end of the nation's economic catastrophe was nearing, but at the start of the forties, America and St. Louis remained in the Depression. The New Deal had run aground on the rocks of Republican opposition and Roosevelt's failed attempt to change the make-up of the Supreme Court from nine to 15 justices.

The 1940 census that showed a decline in St. Louis' population was coupled by news that in the previous five years 80 percent of new construction in the metro area took place in St. Louis County. The population there jumped 12 percent to almost 275,000. Small towns outside the city continued to grow during the war and boomed afterward. Flight away from the city center, by both black and white, was underway.

Planners saw rot in the central district and reacted by backing riverfront demolition, hoping the smoke abatement plan would slow the westward movement. The city decided that the movement to the suburbs was a result of decaying central housing (the worst of the nation's biggest cities) and began thinking of wholesale demolition of the downtown. Developers looked to federal tax subsidies to build large tracks of new housing quickly.

The stage was thereby set for further riverfront clearance in the forties and the demolition of the near North Side and Mill Creek Valley in the fifties. The war, however, delayed the process until late in the decade, except for the riverfront demolition for the Jefferson park, completed in 1942. That area devolved into an empty space of mud and gravel all through the forties and nothing was done at the site until 1950 when Harry Truman dedicated the ground for the new federal park. The city finally managed to plant grass in the mud.

That was all, however, for the riverfront. Another war, this time in Korea, diverted funds. For another 11 years the 40-block area stood empty. Excavation for the Gateway Arch finally began. The giant steel structure was completed in 1965, 30 years after the plan for the Jefferson National Expansion Memorial was first pitched.

Republicans returned to power in City Hall in 1941 and for the next eight years practiced a policy of no change, letting the war economy roll. The city population grew to its high-water mark of 856,796 in 1950. Congestion in the no-loan, redlined black neighborhoods became tighter, with 88,000 families in pre-1900 housing. The Great Migration continued as more and still more southern blacks chased the job opportunities north. Anything was better than the virtual slavery of share cropping in Mississippi, Louisiana and Alabama.

The city made little attempt to improve the housing shortage until 1949, and then the answer involved bulldozers and high-rise apartment blocks. The smoke problem was relieved but that didn't dissuade city residents who could leave from leaving. The county population, 70 percent white, rose faster than ever to 406,349 in 1950. Laws from the nineteenth century made it impossible for the city to annex anything outside the 1876 line. Ideas like new elephant quarters at the zoo and art museum expansion didn't attract many new residents.

Whites were able to get housing loans outside the central city and took advantage of the subdivisions built in the suburbs. Blacks making decent wages in the union organized factories, along with a new class of black lawyers and other professionals, joined them in new, segregated townships. New highways gave them a way in and out to their jobs. The city explained the roads were a way to bring people from the suburbs back downtown, but real estate developers knew full well that these roads also led out of town. After 1950, the draining of city residents increased. Those with good paying jobs and housing opportunity took immediate advantage of the loans and opted to ride the newly elevated highways for free standing homes, a patch of lawn and their own garage.

These trends from the forties live on, and by 2010 the process of white and black flight across the city limits hadn't stopped for six decades. By then, a demographic revolution was a done deal. Many more whites took advantage of their advantages.

Blacks kept the pace of about 25 percent of the growth, not as many could afford the move and the black community crept up to become the majority population inside the city limits, outnumbering whites by over 15,000 by 2010. The black share of the city's population had gone from 12 percent in 1940 to 49 percent in 2010. In St. Louis County the population by then reached just under 1 million with 76 percent white. And in the region, including the nearby Illinois counties and other suburban Missouri areas, the population of Metro St. Louis nearly tripled from 1940, from 921,000 to 2.8 million, with about 77 percent white.

These demographics added up the quiet changes, people packing their furniture for a more pleasant environment, birds and trees instead of decay and broken streets, crime and fear, the byproducts of congestion, corruption and housing discrimination. For those who were handed disadvantages because of their skin color, however, for those whose low pay -- or a myriad of other reasons -- forced them to stay, the numbers spoke a little louder, especially when they ran up against a segregated movie theater, a white-only club, or the small insults and indignities of racism.

These incidents had a wide range -- from forced seating in the balcony to violent death. There was no doubt the treatment of blacks in 1940 had improved from the years following the Civil War, but it is still stunning to find in 1942, just 150 miles to the south of St. Louis, an incident out of the pages of Reconstruction, an incident that jolted any complacency about the fair treatment of a large and diversely talented pool of people.

The shock was one of the last incidents in the long history of the lynching of blacks in the South -- those particularly vicious and incendiary racist killings that left nearly 3,500 African-Americans dead over an 80-year period. This killing took in the town of Sikeston, Mo., a tidy city in a historically volatile area of the state, just above the boot heel where Missouri meets Tennessee, Arkansas and Kentucky, 10 miles west of the Mississippi River.

The town, founded in 1860, had a population of about 8,000 in 1940, some 2,000 black. Early in the Civil War, Confederates planned to link forces in Sikeston and drive up the river for an attack on St. Louis but by 1862 had been thwarted by forces from the Union army contingent active in the area commanded by U. S. Grant. The South tried again to take the town in 1864 but again was thrown back by the Union army.

The Sikeston lynching occurred Jan. 25, 1942, just seven weeks after Pearl Harbor was attacked, bringing the United States into World War II. The victim, Cleo Wright, was not strung up on a tree in the usual style of black lynching but rather his death fit the wider definition of the term. He had been jailed for allegedly assaulting a white woman in her home, but before facing a judge or jury, he was broken out of the jail by a white mob, hauled into the black community and burned alive.

The reaction from black civil rights groups was intense and the lynching led the federal Justice Department to become embroiled directly in such a case for the first time. President Roosevelt, after all, had just entered the war and at least part of his argument against the anti-war isolationists was the necessity to stop Nazi and Japanese aggression against democracy. Protection under of the rule of law – shattered in Europe and Asia -- was at stake in Missouri.

Wright, 26, a black man who worked in the local oil mill, was thought to have broken into the house of the white woman, Grace Sturgeon, 29, who was severely slashed with a knife in the early morning attack. Wright, his pants spattered in blood, was found two miles away by a local policeman, Hess Perrigan. Wright resisted arrest and attacked Perrigan with a knife. Perrigan shot Wright four times before both men collapsed from their wounds and were taken to a local hospital.

Wright was briefly released from the hospital without being charged and went to the home of his in-laws and pregnant wife. But he was soon captured and jailed in the City Hall lockup, charged with the stabbing. About 700 whites gathered in front of the jail, demanding Wright. Just two men, a state trooper and the local prosecuting attorney guarded the jail. They offered some resistance, the prosecutor's ribs were broken, but it didn't take long to get Wright, nearly dead from the bullet wounds, and pull him out of his cell.

His legs were hooked over the rear bumper of a car and dragged for several blocks into the black community, then soaked in gas and burned to death in front of the Baptist church on the block between Lincoln and Fair streets. Grace Sturgeon survived a severe knife wound to her stomach and lived to identify Wright as the attacker.

But while the man's guilt was not in question, the process and violence of the assault came under fierce attack by the NAACP. The injured prosecutor, David Blanton, put the lynching case before a state grand jury but no indictments resulted. The Justice Department then took a historic step to intervene in the case and a federal grand jury also heard the case. But again no indictments were forthcoming. The case was closed and Sikestonians, black and white, attempted to get on with their lives. But the NAACP publicized the lynching across the country. Outrage was felt particularly strongly in the black community of nearby St. Louis.

A *New York Times* editorial published two days after the killing under the headline "Sikeston Disgraces Itself," asked:

> What does it do to the . . . white people who did not act with the mob but who are contaminated by this abuse of justice? What does it do to schoolchildren, who ought to respect human rights? And how sadly do such events tarnish the cause of democracy at war! There are few happenings in the United States that can afford more comfort to the Nazis than evidences of lawlessness.

The federal intervention in the Sikeston case was part of an increasing role by the national government to involve itself in civil rights. Nonetheless, race riots erupted shortly thereafter in Detroit, first in 1942, then in 1943, and again in 1943 in Harlem. There were no riots in St. Louis, but in August 1942, 9,000 people rallied to support desegregation of war plants.

Across the South and in industrial centers like St. Louis, African-Americans workers, always first fired during the Depression, found themselves last hired as war contracts began to revive the economy. Hitler's armies had marched into Belgium in 1939 and even before Pearl Harbor was attacked by Imperial Japan, the United States was getting ready for war.

This war economy began to take shape at places like the Curtiss-Wright Airplane Company, which had combined the fortunes of two aviation pioneers in 1929 and began building fighter planes near Lambert Field in the late thirties. In 1940 the company landed a $16 million contract to build cargo and training planes. American Car and Foundry and St. Louis Car, builders of the city streetcars, received orders for tanks, and Atlas Powder Co. got a deal that soon made it the biggest producer of TNT in the United States, operating in Weldon Springs, 30 miles from the city.

By November 1941, with the U.S. still not officially at war, 60,000 defense contracts had been awarded in the metro area, an outlay of $3 million a month. These contracts meant jobs, but not for black workers, still facing 20 percent unemployment as the Depression began to disappear.

Particularly enraging to black workers was the new factory on the far northwest side of the city, the St. Louis Ordnance Plant at 4300 Goodfellow near The Ville. In December 1940, the government announced plans to build the plant and groundbreaking took place in January 1941 for the 291-acre complex. The cartridge plant became the world's largest producer of the .30-caliber and .50-caliber ammunition for rifles and machine guns. The *Post-Dispatch* showed prescient timing by running a photo spread on the new plant on Sunday, Dec. 7, 1941, the day of the Japanese attack in the Pacific.

Production of ammunition began a week later at the $110 million facility, with only a few black workers. It was open 24 hours a day, seven days a week during World War II. At the peak of production in the summer of 1943, the factory had 35,000 workers in 300 buildings making 250 million bullets a month. The plant produced 1 billion cartridges by October 1942, and its second billion six months later.

St. Louis had been a leading center of the civil rights movement throughout the twentieth century. The movement for black equality dated back to the Civic League reforms in 1910, to the rise of the NAACP following the 1917 race riot in East St. Louis, through the Woolworth lunch counter protests from the Colored Clerks Circle during the Depression. By 1940, Jordan Chambers, the black Democrat, had become a powerful figure in city politics. The war set the stage to take on Jim Crow once again.

In May of 1942, just five months after the Sikeston lynching, the cartridge plant became the focus of one of the first civil rights fights of the forties. Tension had been building at least since January of 1941 when A. Phillip Randolph, the president of the nation's strongest black union, the Brotherhood of Sleeping Car Porters, called for a July 1 march on Washington to demand jobs. The Urban League and the NAACP, two black groups growing stronger as the Depression faded, pledged support. President Roosevelt did not want to see 100,000 marchers in the capitol demanding jobs while he was getting ready for war and agreed to set up a commission to seek the end of segregation in defense plants if Randolph would call off the march on Washington.

The federal Fair Employment Practice Committee was established and set up regional offices, including one in St. Louis, to enforce the ban on segregation. Randolph and his allies started setting up local organizations under the umbrella of the March on Washington Movement. The group in St. Louis included the familiar figures, David Grant and Jordan Chambers, along with other veterans of the civil rights protests in the thirties plus union organizers from the porters union and the new president of the local NAACP chapter.

But neither the federal agency nor the black coalition had much success against the industrialists until the cartridge plant on Goodfellow laid off 300 black workers, including a prominent Communist Party veteran, in May 1942. Of the 20,500 employees at the plant only 600 were black and there were no black women workers at all among the cartridge plant's 8,000 women employees. This was at a time when the company was hiring 1,000 new workers a week.

A month later, on June 20, some 400 protesters, including many unemployed and a large contingent of women, walked silently around the factory's eight buildings for two hours, each carrying a picket sign. A man carrying an American flag led the silent march. Another man carried a sign displaying the Washington March slogan, "Winning democracy for the Negro is winning the war for democracy." The company hired 75 black women the next week and placed ads seeking war production jobs for "colored, male workers." Wages were raised for blacks, those who had been laid off were hired back by July.

The St. Louis Ordnance Plant, unlike many other plants, continued hiring blacks of both genders during the war until it closed June 27, 1945. By then the plant had made 6.7 billion cartridges. It reopened for Korea and Vietnam and in 2014 still housed about 2,000 fully integrated government employees for Social Security, Veterans Affairs and other federal agencies.

The March on Washington Movement did not stop at the cartridge plant. Randolph pushed the coalition's "double victory" campaign across the country, urging the defeat of Germany, Japan and Italy and the end of racial segregation on the job, linking the African-American battle against racism with America's fight against fascism. In New York, 18,000 filled Madison Square Garden, in Chicago 12,000 rallied at the Coliseum. And in St. Louis, one of the strongest movement centers in the nation, 9,000 people packed the Municipal Auditorium Convention Hall for five hours of speeches, music and rousing cheers on Aug. 14, 1942.

In his speech, movement lawyer David Grant reviewed the gains blacks had made during the Depression and the legal status they had achieved. The fight against black oppression was a world-wide one, he said, and the audience passed a resolution supporting Gandhi's rebellion against the British in India as well as his nonviolent approach. Grant also said the Depression had given blacks in America federal protection and a new attitude of being entitled to fair treatment in their demands to end segregation imposed by industrial racists.

At the time of the rally 75 percent of the defense plants in St. Louis had hired no blacks at all. Two weeks after the March on Washington rally, the coalition was back on the streets, this time against the practices of the Carter Carburetor Co., a defense contractor operating on the North Side near The Ville with no black workers among 3,000 employees.

On Aug. 29, 1942, a crowd estimated as high as 500 gathered next door to Sumner High then marched past the tidy brick houses that lined St. Louis Avenue in a working class white neighborhood for five blocks to the Carter plant. The protest failed, however, and the company continued to refuse to hire blacks throughout the war, resisting all legal efforts to change its policy.

The company didn't hire African-Americans for another decade. It went out of business and closed in 1984, leaving a toxic mess. The neighborhood near the plant slowly changed over to mostly black families during the 30 years following the war. These families joined environmentalists during the late eighties to complain about pollution at the property, which was owned by local developers and leased variously to a metal fabrication shop, an auto repair shop, plastics and storage companies. The complaints about pollution grew, however, and the federal Environmental Protection Agency placed the property in the Superfund toxic clean-up program in 1993.

The EPA found 30,000 cubic yards of soil contaminated with cancer-causing PCBs, as well as TCE, a toxic solvent that cleans carburetor parts, and discovered the building materials were laced with asbestos. Neighbors, including the Herbert Hoover Boys & Girls Club, were still waiting in 2015 for a final cleanup. Meanwhile, one of the North Side's most important neighborhoods decayed, its value lowered by an empty industrial giant looming along a major shopping street. The factory became an eyesore, some of its windows smashed and others filled with oddly colored glass.

The American Car and Foundry Co., Carter's parent company after 1922 and the corporation most responsible for the cleanup of the factory, had longtime ties with St. Louis. Based in suburban St. Charles, ACF remained a giant American corporation, controlled by billionaire Carl Icahn. The company built the first New York City subway cars as well as many of the streetcars in St. Louis. The company president was once William K. Bixby, a Gilded Age industrialist who became a full-time philanthropist and rare book collector.

In 1907 he became head of the Missouri Historical Society and in 1909 was the first president of the St. Louis Art Museum when the World's Fair Palace of Fine Arts was taken over by the city. His manuscripts are especially concerned with Jefferson and the Civil War, and remain a core collection of the Missouri History Museum.

In 2013 the EPA announced a five-year plan for finally cleaning up the site. AFC was still liable for most of the $27 million cost. The main manufacturing building was donated to the city by developers Tom and Kathleen Kerr, with the idea they go to the Boys & Girls Club next door. The plan was to demolish the old building and develop the property after the AFC cleanup, probably not before 2021.

Meanwhile, back in 1942, the Washington-March organization was not discouraged by the failure to integrate Carter. It began holding weekly meetings. It staffed an organizing office, gathering complaints it delivered to the federal committee. It peppered city newspapers, getting good response from the two black papers but no coverage at all in the three white dailies, including the liberal *Post-Dispatch.* There the editor, Joseph Pulitzer's son, felt private businesses had the right to hire as they pleased. But the March on Washington Movement (also known as MOWM) did not weaken and Randolph came to St. Louis again, drawing another enthusiastic crowd May 9, 1943.

The next day 30 white women walked off the job at U.S. Cartridge Co., protesting the replacement of several white floor workers with blacks. The company immediately backed down to the whites and removed the black workers. Blacks threatened a strike but agreed instead to meet with management. The company promptly promoted a white foreman ahead of a black worker with more seniority. Confrontation seemed inevitable.

The March-Washington negotiators, led by Grant, urged calm from the work force. But rank-and-file members of the United Electrical, Radio & Machine Workers of America took a different approach and both the midnight and day shifts staged a wildcat strike June 3, getting 100 percent support from the plant's 3,600 black ordnance workers.

The company met again with Grant, MOWM leaders and United Electrical officials and agreed to hold training classes to prepare blacks for foreman jobs. Again, Grant had a found a compromise, one that brought the immediate return of 1,200 strikers. The rest of the workers trickled back shortly thereafter and by month's end 32 black foremen were on the job and the strike was over.

On another front in June 1943, at the Southwest Bell telephone exchange downtown, as many as 300 picketers circled the company headquarters on Pine Street off the Memorial Plaza, asking for more black telephone operators. The protest included a Sept. 18 "pay-in" where 200 members of the MOWM coalition paid their bills by dumping pennies at the Southwest office. After three months of action, the company gave in and hired the operators.

The peaceful St. Louis protests didn't change the world for African Americans in the city that summer and fall, but progress was made, the movement grew larger and companies began watching their practices, even if it was just to give evasive answers to blacks seeking jobs when the companies were advertising for workers.

As the peaceful protests took place in St. Louis, Detroit exploded. There had been a relatively peaceful protest there in 1942, over housing. Whites in the all-white Polish neighborhood stopped black families ready to move into a new federal project. Thousands of police intervened and the families were eventually housed in the project after fights between white and black mobs left 40 injured and more than 100 arrested.

But 1943 brought a very different scenario, a riot about jobs that lasted three days and left 34 dead and nearly 700 injured.

Three weeks before the June 20 riot, 25,000 Packard autoworkers walked off their jobs when three blacks were promoted to work the assembly lines. Over a company loudspeaker came a voice with a southern accent, "I'd rather see Hitler and Hirohito win than work next to a nigger." The tension built, as it had over two years of intense immigration of both black and white into Detroit from the rural South. These were mostly young men without much education looking for war contract work.

Fights between black and white youths started that humid June 20 night before midnight on Belle Isle, an island in the Detroit River where young people partied on an integrated swimming beach. A black man apparently insulted a white sailor's girlfriend and a fight broke out. In the excitement a white youth said he'd seen a black mob throw a mother and her baby into the river. By 4 a.m. whites began beating blacks on downtown streets as they got off streetcars from the park. Looting spread into the black section of downtown, buildings were burned and police began attacking gangs of blacks, killing at least 17 blacks.

Over three days of rioting, 1,800 people were arrested. Federal troops finally brought the fighting to a stop. Eighty-five percent of those arrested were black and police made arrests in only four of the killings of African-Americans.

The riot prompted MOWM to again threaten to make good on its original plan to stage a mass march on Washington, but this time the focus was on civil disobedience training and the slogan "We are Americans, too."

Following the deaths in Detroit, black organizers in St. Louis found that fear of riot dominated the city government's thinking. Republican Mayor William Becker, who won office in 1941, eagerly met with Grant and the other black leaders to try to avert another Detroit. The mayor agreed to establish the city's first civil rights commission to seek peaceful solutions to the city's race conflicts. Both sides agreed this was a step forward. Unfortunately, Becker was unable to take part in the creation of the group.

Becker, born in East St. Louis in 1876, a grad of Harvard and St. Louis Law School, had served for 24 years on the St. Louis Court of Appeals when he was elected. He was the political beneficiary of Barney Dickmann's downfall. Dickmann fell out of favor among business leaders for accepting the influence of Jordan Chambers and his black supporters. City Republicans seized the opportunity, grabbing the "clean government" platform.

Becker won in a rout, carrying all but four wards. But he surprised veterans of City Hall by keeping several Democrats in his administration. He set up a civil service system based on merit and vowed to enforce the smoke reforms adopted under Dickmann. He pushed a merger of city and county. And he was willing to work with Grant and the black coalition on the interracial committee, pledging to promote job desegregation in the war industries.

Roosevelt integrated the Post Office before the Detroit riot and a new set of Fair Practice Enforcement Committees were established to replace the ineffective originals. Left-liberal whites in St. Louis, as elsewhere, pushed for the city committee and the Republican Becker seemed all ready to cooperate. But first he decided to enjoy a Sunday outing at Lambert Airfield aboard an Army glider of the type used in the recent invasion of Italy.

A patriotic crowd of 4,000 people turned out at the airport Aug. 1, 1943, to watch the Army glider perform, waving flags and singing the national anthem. Stunned silence soon replaced the cheers when the glider crashed, killing the mayor and all the other nine people aboard. Among the dead was the president of the St. Louis Chamber of Commerce, the head of the Public Utilities Department, the presiding judge of the St. Louis County Court and the city's deputy comptroller. The pilot and co-pilot of the glider, both Army Air Corps flyers, and the Army commander, also died.

Also killed were the president and founder of the company that built the glider, Maj. William B. Robertson, as well as his chief engineer. The company, Robertson Aircraft, was a St. Louis firm founded in 1918 and Robertson was the first man to land an airplane at Lambert. In 1920, he started the first airmail service between St. Louis and Chicago and employed Charles Lindbergh as a pilot before his New York to Paris flight in 1927.

The glider was built in St. Louis and Robertson and Becker were using the occasion to trumpet the city's crucial role in the war. The tow plane from the 71st Troop Carrier Command pulled the glider up easily on a clear afternoon and circled the airport twice over the heads of the cheering crowd. But when the glider was let go to fly on its own, it was quickly clear that something was horribly wrong.

The wings could not carry the weight of the craft and folded up. There was nothing anyone could do. There was no time to use parachutes as the right wing fell off and the glider plunged straight down 2,000 feet, falling in the middle of the airfield, just short of the crowd.

"At the moment the crowd was absolutely silent," wrote the *Post-Dispatch* reporter. "Then there was a sound it is impossible to describe. It was something between a sigh and a gasp." The craft lay on the ground "a twisted jumble of steel tubing, plywood and fabric." An Army officer ran to the wreckage and said, "they are all gone."

A pair of lucky relatives stood by. Becker's wife had been scheduled to join her husband but because she was a woman was barred by the Army. Robertson's son, a 17-year-boy, had already flown in the glider that morning as the pilot gave it its last test before the fatal failure. He stayed on the ground with his mother.

Less than two years before the crash, Republican Aloys P. Kaufmann, had been elected the head of the Board of Aldermen, his first public office. With Becker's death the 40-year-old political novice suddenly became mayor. On Kaufmann's first day in office, his grief over the crash was brought short by the headline in the afternoon *Post*: "6 Killed in Harlem Rioting." If he had doubts before, he knew civil rights would be on his plate as he filled out the remaining two years of Becker's term. Harlem was the fourth race riot of the year, the second in the North.

Would St. Louis be next? No one could forget blacks hanging from lampposts in East St. Louis during the previous war.

By September 1943 Kaufmann appointed 65 members to the committee Becker had approved before he died, hoping to mollify angry blacks. Grant, Sleeping Car Union leader Tom McNeal, and members of the NAACP and the Urban League were appointed. But whites dominated the Race Relations Committee with a 40-25 majority. Some of the whites were liberal, like Edna Gellhorn, a long-time progressive who had fought to get the women's vote, and Fannie Cook, another suffragette who was active in the fight to get Homer Phillips Hospital located in The Ville. But the less progressive elements of the committee held the majority.

In November 1943 U.S. Cartridge slashed its third shift and Curtiss-Wright cut its black work force by half. In March 1944, white workers at General Cable walked out over the hiring of blacks and white union members at the St. Louis Car Company struck over a non-discriminatory clause in a new United Auto Workers contract. Dozens more strikes and wildcat walkouts, mostly by whites, flared when whites were fired along with blacks to reduce the work force on an equal basis.

War orders were cut all across the nation after massive supplies had been stockpiled for D-Day. Grant estimated that by June 1944 there were 25,000 unemployed blacks seeking jobs in the city. The newly formed federal Fair Employment Practices Committee cited eight firms including Carter Carburetor and U.S. Cartridge, along with big contractors like Wagner Electric, McDonnell Aircraft (which was founded in 1939) and St. Louis Shipbuilding and Steel for discrimination. Workers complained that raises were promised but never given and that the blacks in the big defense plants were assigned only to low-paying jobs as janitors, cooks and maids.

Over 100 workers jammed a courtroom in August 1944. The companies said their policies were simply a reflection of "community patterns;" segregation was needed to avoid trouble and keep the assembly line moving. Black and white activists, however, filed dozens of reports showing animosity between black and white workers was infrequent, especially in the higher paid production jobs. The fair practices committee, finally showing its teeth, told the industrialists they must take "affirmative action" to reverse hiring practices that were the root of the problems. All workers might not have been fully satisfied, but St. Louis saw no running battles in the streets like those in Detroit or New York.

Outside the factories, the Jim Crow system of segregation suffered a series of blows. The Republican mayor proved to be a sluggish ally but an ally nonetheless. Jasper Caston, the first elected black alderman and a friend of Jordan Chambers, held a secret session to discuss a bill seeking desegregation in the lunchrooms of the city courts and City Hall. When the bill was introduced, Pulitzer Jr.'s *Post-Dispatch* called the measure "too hot" to reach a vote. But on April 6, 1944, less than a year after the Detroit riot, the bill passed the Republican controlled board by a surprising 22-4 vote, the first such law in Missouri.

One of those supporting the bill was the first woman alderman, Clara Hemplemann, who said thousands of women working the war factories "are doing things they never had to do before." Women, she added, have "nothing to fear at the hands of the voters." During the war the city saw its first female streetcar drivers, its first women weather forecasters, its first women zoo attendants. By 1943, three-fourths of the workers at U.S. Cartridge were women.

On April 20, 1944, the Women's Ad Club held an event on Hitler's birthday they called the "last birthday ever for Adolf Schicklegruber," mocking the German Fuhrer by the use of his grandmother's name. The club members enjoyed a special Blood and Thunder cocktail (tequila, blood orange juice and dark cherry) and raised their glasses with shouts of "Here's mud in your eye, Adolf!"

NAACP organizer Pearl Maddox was in the audience for the lunchroom desegregation vote along with students from Sumner High and black activists from several organizations. Maddox took the City Hall vote a step further and organized a new coalition called the Citizens Civil Rights Committee (CCRC), aimed at forcing downtown department stores to allow African Americans to sit down at their lunch counters. Maddox had heard the story of a black sailor on leave who had tried to get a spot on a stool at a five-and-dime on Sixth and Washington for a cool drink. Instead, a waitress turned him away. "I've been in three engagements," the Navy vet said before leaving.

That was enough for Maddox and several other women. There was a history of lunch counter protests in St. Louis already -- at segregated Woolworth's counters in the thirties, some 30 years before such protests helped launch the civil rights movement of the sixties.

Maddox stopped writing polite letters to the store on May 17, 1944, and the St. Louis activists began sit down actions, first at Katz Drugstore, then at Stix Baer and Fuller, and at Famous Barr and Scruggs-Vandervoort-Barney.

The visits became routine as the stores still refused to serve blacks. The CCRC women would walk in, sit down, be told to leave, refuse, and then be picked up by the arms by store security and carried out and placed on the street. The stores said allowing black women to order a chicken sandwich in front of white people would hurt business.

Whites joined their black friends, ordered food and gave the African Americans a bite. The stores would then clear the lunch room altogether. This was private property, the owners argued; they could do what they liked. Integration was a good thing, managers said, but could only be allowed after years of education on table manners and proper dress. The black women kept coming to the stores, day after day, month after month. There were no reports in the press that any whites left the stores.

On July 8, 40 black women and 15 white women moved into lunchrooms at three stores. The stores all closed their lunch counters. The *Post-Dispatch*, for the first time since the sit-ins started, covered the women's action, giving the story three inches of space. Maddox owned a house and her bank threatened to foreclose.

In August, the storeowners said they would allow the women to eat in segregated counters in their basements, a move the black women found insulting. The mayor stepped in and said he would use his Race Relations Commission to negotiate between the stores and the CCRC. The women called off the protests but the talks fizzled and it was left to another black organization, the St. Louis Committee of Racial Equality (CORE) to win the lunch counter fight in 1954. And it wasn't until 1961, three decades after the first protests, that St. Louis finally passed a law giving blacks legal access to all public accommodations in the city.

By the last days of the war, as the allies began their final drive in Europe, the civil rights movement, like the St. Louis lunch counter protests, had faded. Winning the fight against Germany and Japan was the overriding concern of all Americans as the civil right actions in St. Louis became part of a "forgotten revolution" of the thirties and forties. The CCRC disbanded. Most of its members joined the NAACP.

By 1944, the March on Washington Movement also wound down. Nearly 20 years passed before the march was fully realized when in 1963 hundreds of thousands of civil rights activists, black and white, stood on the Mall in the nation's capital to hear their new leader, Martin Luther King Jr., remind them that 100 years after the Emancipation Proclamation "the Negro is still not free."

Back in 1944, Mayor Kauffman began planning for the aftermath of war. He and a committee on postwar improvements passed a bond issue -- $43.5 million ($563 million in 2012 dollars) -- aimed at creating jobs for returning veterans on small projects such as street and sewer improvements, three new swimming pools, a viaduct over Mill Creek Valley along Grand Avenue and Art Museum repairs. Ironically, Lambert Airfield was on the bond ballot as well, getting a major expansion from the mayor who had been put in office by the glider crash. No new taxes were required, but the bond money was made under the mistaken assumption that the costs would remain at wartime levels.

By August 1944, the city and the nation realized the war was far from over. By then 748 people from St. Louis had died in battle, in the line of military duty and from disease while in the service. A stiff number indeed, but not as high as the 964 workers who had been killed in industrial accidents in city war plants. Indeed, the national numbers also showed an equally surprising 5,000 industrial deaths above combat deaths.

St. Louis played a major role in the invasion of France by the allies on June 6, 1944. That January orders were especially high for landing craft -- LSTs, LCTs, LVTs, and DUKWs. The city's industries also outfitted the invading soldiers from head to toe, making boots, helmets, jackets, shirts, leggings, sleeping bags and tents. Tanks made at American Car and Foundry and St. Louis Car rolled to Berlin and the ubiquitous bullets continued disgorging from the machines at U.S. Cartridge. The Kilgen Organ Company -- makers of organs (including Carnegie Hall) -- turned its skills to glider manufacture after Robertson gliders were taken out of production.

St. Louis Ship Building and Steel, Stupp Brothers Bridge and Iron, and Mississippi Valley Structural Steel were among the many companies working at a fever pitch to win the war. The DUKW-model amphibious landing vehicles that rolled onto the beaches of Normandy were made at the St. Louis Chevy plant on the North Side. Empire Stove, American Stove and Wrought Iron Range turned from kitchen appliances to bombs. Scullin Steel made giant 12,000-pound bombs dropped by British planes on German cities. Alton Boxboard Co. invented a way to wrap and cushion bombs for transport. Johnson Tinfoil and Metal won awards for its production of parts for the Navy ack-ack guns.

Brown Shoe came up with a new boot that buckled outside the pants and made extra wide footwear for the Russian army so its soldiers could keep their feet warm with extra socks. Landis Shoe invented fast, portable machinery for the shoe repair units that followed the fighters. Rawlings made special helmets for the men in tanks. Angelica Jacket pumped out 25 million combat fatigue uniforms, Foster Brothers made steel cots, Paul K. Weil made parachutes and as D-Day approached several St. Louis companies began making portable bridges for the run to Berlin.

On June 5, 1944 at about four in the morning, Gen. Dwight Eisenhower, the allied commander, sat for five minutes at Southwick House on the south coast of England staring at his staff in silence, then glanced up and said, “Okay. We’ll go.” The invasion was launched that day. The St. Louis made boots hit the French beaches at midnight June 6 – beaches code-named Sword, Juno, Gold, Omaha, and Utah. U.S. troops they flew silently into the French countryside on St. Louis made gliders, they rammed the edge of France in their DUKW vehicles (“Design, Utility, Front Wheel Drive, Two Rear Diving Axles.”)

St. Louis radio picked up the news of the invasion from German stations about a half-hour before the allies announced: “This is D Day.”

Schools held patriotic assemblies, churches gathered the faithful at the Soldiers' Memorial downtown, and two dozen unions began plans for fighting the inevitable layoffs. Predictions for few immediate job losses quickly mounted to 28,000 layoffs, even as the Nazis battled the allies with fierce resistance across France. Three bond drives were held -- the fourth, fifth and sixth of the war. Boy Scout troops went door-to-door looking for money for the last push.

Twice as many Americans died in the Civil War as died 80 years later in the Second World War. And of the 16 million who were in uniform during this most deadly of all wars, the United States saw 300,000 killed with just 9,000 civilian deaths. Russia, in contrast, lost some 10 million in battle and a whopping 7 million civilians, a total higher than all of those who served the United States military.

But the Russian leader Joseph Stain believed it was the American ability to build weapons that made the difference, not its low death count. "Without American production," he said, "the United Nations would never have won the war."

In Western Europe in the summer of 1945 as the allies broke the final German stand, there were many people from St. Louis on the battlefield, including three exceptional examples from the field of journalism -- Virginia Irwin, Joseph Pulitzer II, and Martha Gellhorn. Also, like the millions who worried far from battle, was a writer, Ernest Hemingway, with unusual ties to the city, struggling to work in a bungalow in Cuba while fuming over his highly publicized but fast fading marriage.

Virginia Irwin had been hired as a file clerk at the *Post-Dispatch* in March of 1932, age 24, winner of the Illinois spelling bee in the eighth grade and valedictorian at her Quincy High School class in 1924. By the start of the war she had graduated to a feature writer on the *Post*, one of the best newspapers in the nation.

The boss of the paper, the son of its founder, was Joseph Pulitzer II, a famous liberal who kept his shop closed to women and blacks. The women writers were generally confined to articles about childcare, divorce and household disaster cleanup. Irwin, however, was not content. She was such a sharp writer she was moved to the staff of the feature section, *Everyday Magazine*, and managed to become food editor without knowing how to cook. In 1942 she impressed her boss with an 11-part series on women's roles in the war industries. The series involved a two-week reporting tour around the country and in 1943 she was granted a leave of absence to join the Red Cross, her ticket to Europe.

Irwin knew her stuff and she knew she wanted to be with the invasion of allied troops. By early 1944 she had a job as a Red Cross press relations officer in London and sent stories about wartime conditions in England back to the *Post.* The paper had no foreign correspondent even as the invasion drew nearer. Pulitzer, still wary of a female reporting the news, asked the War Department for accreditation of a member of the Washington bureau and an editor from St. Louis but one of the credentials went to Irwin, who pestered the office in person, with the other card taken by a Washington staffer, Richard Stokes.

Pulitzer did not regret his decision to accredit Irwin, a feisty, curly-headed woman who always seemed to have a big smile on her face. She got along extremely well in England with the Joes waiting for their ride across the channel to France. But in June, when the troops landed, the Army kept her out of the way, forcing her to remain in southern England interviewing wounded GIs returning from the invasion.

On July 11, however, Irwin slipped in with a Women's Army Corps contingent. She wore the regular uniform, looking like "any sad sack in the American army," and crossed the channel. She remembered to bring her typewriter along with 80 pounds of gear and after the liberation of Paris found herself at the Hotel Scribe with the other correspondents. By the start of 1945, Irwin, "itching to see what our Joes were doing" at the front managed several trips out of the hotel, nearly killed during a trip with Judy Barden of the *New York Sun.*

Late in 1944, she hooked on with Gen. George Patton's Third Army and sent back numerous stories still relegated to *Everyday Magazine.* She always included the family names and hometowns of the GIs she wrote about and the soldiers welcomed her with open arms. Pulitzer sent her personal notes, usually warning her not to take chances and telling her not to hesitate to come home if she wanted. But she reached the Rhine with the troops in the spring and went into Nuremberg when it fell to the allies on April 25. She was 5,000 miles from home, but just 275 miles away from Berlin. She talked a soldier into giving her ride toward the front lines. Irwin, the Army driver and a reporter from Boston headed for the German capital.

She and her companions left the 69th American Division behind. They passed through the front at Torgau. She was the "Amerikanski" who had arrived without a map, waving her American flag. Russian infantry in horse drawn wagons mobbed the Jeep, cheering the arrival of the Americans. From there the Jeep traveled north for about 80 miles toward the Nazi capital, moving 10 mph through the war zone.

The three Amerikanskis reached Berlin about eight at night.

> Germans lay dead on the sidewalks, in the front yards of the bomb shattered homes of the suburbs. All streets were clogged with Russian tanks, guns, infantry in their shaggy fur hats and everywhere the horses of the Russian infantry ran loose about the streets.

The three Americans found a Russian command post, a shattered house without electricity or running water. The Red Army Guards-Major was an extraordinary host.

> The minute I arrived he had his Cossack orderly, a fierce Mongolian with a great scar on his cheek, ready with a dishpan of water. After I had washed my face, the Guards-Major produced some German face powder, a quarter bottle of German perfume and a cracked mirror.
>
> I made myself as presentable as possible and sat down to a flower-bedecked dinner. The candelabra was upturned milk bottles and the flower vase was an old pickle jar.

The Russians served their American allies the best vodka and the best food they could find. They ate and drank toasts between courses, served by two women, one a German and the other a Russian. They toasted Stalin, Roosevelt, Churchill and the American Jeep. She asked the Guards-Major if Berlin was his greatest battle of the war. "He smiled and said sadly, 'No there were greater battles. In those we lost our wives and children.'"

The Red Army was in full celebration of their victory. Irwin ate and drank and danced. She learned the knee-bend Russian style acrobatic dance, kicking her feet forward with her hands on her hips. The dinner and the dancing finally ended and Virginian Irwin pulled out her portable typewriter to pound out the copy for the men on the desk back home at the *Post-Dispatch,* 5,000 miles away.

> Artillery roared, the house shook, the candles fluttered. The candles are still fluttering as I write this story, this story of the most exciting thing that could ever happen to a newspaper reporter.

On May 8, 1945, the *Post-Dispatch* ran a triple deck banner:

VICTORY OFFICIALLY PROCLAIMED
WAR IN EUROPE FORMALLY ENDS AT 5:01 P.M. TODAY
POST-DISPATCH REPORTER GETS INTO BERLIN

On the left-hand lead column was another headline that proclaimed Irwin as "One of First Three Americans to Enter Nazi Capital." A two-column picture of a serious Virginia looking over her copy behind her trusty portable typewriter ran about the same size as the signers of the official surrender documents. Over her picture read the headline "She Got to Berlin."

Under the picture ran the caption:

> VIRGINIA IRWIN: Post-Dispatch war correspondent who, when advised by her editors some time ago to return home when she had enough, cabled: "I want to stick it out until I get to Berlin." She made it. A writer for the Post-Dispatch magazine section for 10 years, Miss Irwin joined the Red Cross 22 months ago. After serving in England she rejoined this newspaper as a correspondent and has followed the fortunes of the American Army through France, Holland, Belgium and Germany since invasion day.

The byline on her story: By VIRGINIA IRWIN A WAR CORRESPONDENT OF THE POST-DISPATCH.

The dateline reflected her world scoop as well as the trouble she had getting the story published no sooner than the May 8 edition: BERLIN, Germany, April 27.

Her lead was simple: "I am one of the first three Americans to enter Berlin."

The details of what she saw in the ruined capital following her "fantastic journey northward" from Nuremberg spilled out of her rattling portable. But a furious Eisenhower initially delayed Irwin's story. He promised the Russian invaders of Berlin that the Americans would not enter the city until the Nazi command had surrendered. The surrender had not been completed when Irwin and her two companions crossed into the city.

Indeed, when she arrived, Hitler was still in his bunker, preparing to marry Eva Braun. When Eisenhower heard of Irwin's request to cable back the story he said that it must go through Moscow first, which would have delayed the copy for weeks.

So she went back to Paris where the Army suspended her and took away her press credentials. The Boston reporter was also suspended and did not file a story until later. But Pulitzer stepped in and sent a week of frantic cables to various officials. Irwin was relentless in pressuring the Army, which finally relented and allowed her to cable her copy to New York. From there it was passed on to St. Louis. Though not as early as written, her story still scored its scoop. Her copy was picked up by the Associated Press and sent around the world.

But Irwin never got the credit she deserved for her skill as a reporter or for the bravery she brought to her job. Her suspension was upheld during a wider argument between the Army and the Associated Press. An AP reporter broke an agreement with Eisenhower's staff and sent news of the German surrender a day early. Irwin's story didn't break anybody's embargo, but she was still given a year's suspension from war coverage. The *Post*'s other accredited reporter, Richard Stokes, got the assignment to cover the Nuremberg war crimes trial. Irwin was sent home.

She arrived back in the states on June 4, 1945, and was immediately feted by St. Louis, with honors from the American Legion, the Business and Professional Women's Club and the Women's National Press Club. But she was not invited to the Overseas Press Club dinner honoring war correspondents held in Washington in November 1946.

Back at the *Post* she was given some good assignments and Pulitzer awarded her a bonus of a year's pay, $4,680 ($60,500 in 2013 money).

Stokes, who had been only briefly at the front, was given a bonus of only half-year, but under the newspaper's pay scale, where men made twice as much as women, Stokes' bonus was $5,186. The *Post* official history, published in 1981, doesn't mention Irwin at all. Other books on war correspondents and even on women war correspondents also leave her out.

Perhaps this was because she never achieved fame after the war, going back instead to writing women's features in the nearly all-male newsroom. In 1946, Pulitzer agreed to send her to the New York bureau but her output was not great and when the bureau closed after Pulitzer's death she came back to St. Louis and was relegated to the advice column. He mother died in 1960 and she retired in 1962 at age 55, taking advantage of her own investments until she died in 1980. She was 72.

Pulitzer, the son of the paper's legendary founder, had been in Europe at the same time as Irwin but apparently never made personal contact while there. He was part of a group of 18 editors and publishers invited by Eisenhower to tour the sites of the Nazi atrocities before the May 8 surrender, including the concentration camps of Dauchu and Buchenwald.

Dachau, just south of Munich, was the first such German camp established, opened in 1933 soon after Hitler's rise to power. A World War I munitions factory, it was opened to hold Hitler's political foes, some Jews, some not. Eventually it was expanded and by war's end an estimated 50,000 Jews, Gypsies, homosexuals, Jehovah's Witnesses, and POWs (including several Americans) died there during its 12-year existence. It was liberated on April 27, three days before Hitler's suicide and the same day Irwin entered Berlin.

Buchenwald, near Weimar in east-central Germany, was established in 1937 and liberated on April 15. A variety of medical experiments were carried out there beginning in 1941 by German doctors and scientists, killing hundreds of people. In 1944, experiments on homosexuals were frequent, aimed at "curing" the prisoners through hormone transplants. And there was a special compound at Buchenwald for German political prisoners including Ernst Thalmann, the head of the Communist Party. Hitler's National Socialist German Workers' (Nazi) Party won 14 million votes (38 percent of the total) in the election of 1932 and took control of Germany in 1933.

Pulitizer's articles about the camps began appearing in the *Post* on April 29 and ran until May 27. He organized an atrocity exhibit in St. Louis featuring photographs from the scene, many seen for the first time in the United States, and criticized the War Department for an apparent reluctance to release information about the Holocaust.

On May 22, just home from his trip to Europe, Pulitzer spoke at Carnegie Hall in New York before a meeting of the Society to Prevent World War III and startled his audience by advocating the execution of 1.5 million Germans responsible for the atrocities. He said anyone connected to the camps should be shot, including industrialists, financiers, the military hierarchy and all members of the Gestapo and the SS.

He said trials should be held swiftly and those found guilty "should be put out of this world with Army bullets through their heads."

Pulitzer II, known as Joe or J.P., felt a personal outrage over the Holocaust because of his Jewish ancestry. He was the second son of Joseph Pulitzer, whose father was a Jewish merchant in Hungary. The son and the rest of the family said it felt some ant-Semitism in St. Louis growing up in the twenties, but the city had an established Jewish community and the issue was rarely discussed.

The elder Pulitzer was the founder of the *Post-Dispatch* and the *New York World*, becoming fabulously wealthy before his death in 1911. J.P, his second son, saw great success at the *Post* and was the founder of radio and television stations, including the first postwar TV station.

He lived in St. Louis all his adult life and was the editor of the *Post-Dispatch* for 43 years, inheriting ownership of the paper when his father died. He also took a role in helping oversee the Pulitzer Prize awards established by his father's will, with awards for journalism, literature and education, administered by Columbia University and continuing into the present, now including awards for journalism, literature, drama and musical composition. The elder Pulitzer left $2 million to establish the Columbia School of Journalism.

J.P. was born in New York in 1885 and attended St. Mark's School in Massachusetts and Harvard before coming to St. Louis in 1906 where he took over a paper that had the highest circulation in the city and was considered one of the best in the nation. He fought corruption and led the paper toward a liberal, progressive editorial slant and kept the *Post* a steady leader in the industry until his death on March 30, 1955, suffering an aneurysm in his stomach at his home in the Central West End.

J.P. gave a boost to another young woman writer from St. Louis, the daughter of the city's leading fighter for the woman's vote. This break came in the form of an assignment to the young freelancer, Martha Gellhorn, in 1930, an assignment that sent her to Geneva to write several articles on the most prominent women in the League of Nations. The writer was just 22 at the time, a recent Bryn Mar dropout destined for a journalism career covering the wars of the world from Spain to Vietnam.

She was possibly the greatest journalist ever to come out of St. Louis, author of hundreds of magazine and newspaper articles, five novels, eight collections of stories, a play and her memoir, *Travels With Myself and Another,* published in 1978. Almost all of this writing was based on live reporting from the scenes of the greatest conflicts of the twentieth century. The only thing she missed was World War I, when she was nine years old.

Martha Gellhorn, Marty to her friends, lived nearly 90 years. She grew up on McPherson Street in St. Louis. Her life took her to the White House as a guest of Eleanor Roosevelt and into the arms of Colette's stepson in Paris. And she was with Hemingway in Spain, France, Florida, China and Cuba.

She is the only American woman journalist pictured on a U.S. Postage stamp. She's on the St. Louis Walk of Fame, she was given the O. Henry Award in 1956 and a journalism award was named in her honor given each year to the reporter who does the best job of exposing what she called "official drivel." Winners have included Julian Asante for his WikiLeaks exposes and Chris Woods for revealing drone strikes in Pakistan.

Gellhorn was born Nov. 8, 1908, into one of the leading progressive families in St. Louis. Martha Ellis, her grandmother, had founded the Shelley Club and the Wednesday Club, groups of women who sipped tea and talked atheism and became involved in social welfare, paying attention to the poor and trying to gain equal pay for women. Her mother, Edna Gellhorn, was one of the organizers of the "Golden Lane" women's suffrage demonstration at the 1916 Democratic Convention and later became a leading participant in the earliest downtown lunch counter sit-ins.

Gellhorn's father, George, was the city's first gynecologist. He had left Germany during the rise of Prussian militarism. Martha's childhood dinner table included Herbert Hoover, Woodrow Wilson and others hoping to gain political favor from Edna, who was a founder of the League of Women Voters. Martha attended the private Mary Institute until 1923 when she transferred to a new school founded by her mother, the John Burroughs School, a co-educational, progressive academy run on democratic principles where the students had equal vote on the running of the school.

The school started with 10 teachers and 75 students and in 2014 was considered one the nation's premier private schools with 600 students and 80 full-time teachers. While at the school Gellhorn became interested in writing poetry and after graduating went off to Bryn Mawr, the upper crust private Pennsylvania school her mother attended.

The young Gellhorn was becoming as rebellious as her mother had once been. A classmate found Martha "had a perfect horror of being regimented in any way. She would sometimes defy the rules by smoking where she wasn't supposed to." She grew bored with her classes and quit after her junior year.

She landed a job at the *Albany Times-Union* in upstate New York but after six months decided she was tired of "hobnobbing with odd persons who wore checked loud shirts." She learned at the paper, however, handling the police beat and writing obituaries, the only female on the staff. Tall, blonde and slim, she spent a lot of time fending off her fellow reporters as well as the city editor, a man who was drunk most of the day, slugging whiskey from a bottle he pulled from his desk drawer.

She came back to St. Louis but decided her house was far too upper end for her working class tastes. She left the tidy street near the shining Cathedral that sat a few blocks away on Lindell. Instead she took a $3 room down near the river, applied for work at the *Post* and pounded out stories, going home to her mother for lunch. But she was turned down by Pulitzer and decided she'd had enough of St. Louis. It was 1929, time to head for Paris.

Martha Gellhorn escaped the United States just after the stock crash, arriving in Paris in 1930, carrying two suitcases and her portable typewriter. She told her father she didn't want any money and had but $75 in her pocket when she arrived in France. She, like many young Americans, had read *The Sun Also Rises* in 1926 and discovered many Americans living in cheap Left Bank hotels looking to live the life. She joined in, dancing to *le jazz* in the bistros, seeing another St. Louisan, Josephine Baker, performing in only a pink feather. Chanel was the rage. Ezra Pound, Scott Fitzgerald and Gertrude Stein were in the cafes. She found a room with a mirror on the ceiling and was told it rented by the hour.

Instead of a job at *The New York Times* bureau that she thought was a sure thing, she began work in a flower shop and moved into a new hotel, feeling safe among its homosexual residents. She quit the flower shop and wrote ad copy about bubble bath then managed to land a job at United Press, taking copy from "provincial ragpickers" over the phone, sharpening up her French. But when a South American tycoon favored by the bureau chief made a pass in a cab, she complained to the wrong UP boss and was fired.

She used the few francs she still had to head south to the Mediterranean, thinking if she was going to be broke she might as well be warm. She sat in a hotel looking over the sea, made up an article about men's pajamas and sent it to a French fashion magazine in Paris. She made $25. She lasted five more weeks and went back to Paris. On July 14, 1930, in the office of a journalist, she met Bertrand de Jouvenel, who had once been the lover of the writer Colette, his father's second wife. That affair led Colette to write the scandalous story "Cheri" concerning an older woman's seduction of her stepson.

Bertrand spoke good English, was married, and was very attracted to Martha. She left for Switzerland, but he tracked her down and after much begging and pleading on the part of Bertrand, they began a relationship. But Gellhorn was appalled by her own behavior and escaped out of the hotel window. He followed her, they made up and played near Lake Como for the summer.

Back in Paris she arranged with the *Post-Dispatch* to cover the League of Nation's meetings, stories that marked her first appearance in big-time journalism. Bertrand was editing a leftist paper, *La Voix,* and the couple traveled through Germany working to unite with the German radicals who were trying to stop the rise of the Nazi Party. Gellhorn called Collette a "terrible woman," and the brilliant French writer felt the same about the American. Gellhorn and Bertrand then traveled to St. Louis and through the southwest, but Gellhorn soon tired of him and left him, thankful they never married.

Eleanor Roosevelt, a friend of her mother, in 1934 gave Martha a job in the Roosevelt administration investigating conditions of the unemployed. From there it was back to Paris, then to the United States where in Key West, traveling with her mother, Martha met Ernest Hemingway, whose books she had admired. Then it was on to Spain where she covered the Spanish Civil War, on assignment from *Collier's* magazine, appearing for the time in a popular magazine in July 1937. And there, too, she and Hemingway solidified their romance.

And this was how Gellhorn's life went, moving from story to story, assignment to assignment, love affair to love affair, Spain, D-Day, Dachau, Nuremberg, China, Israel, Africa, Vietnam, Central America, Russia, traveling and reporting until her death in 1997. And she went from man to man -- Bertrand, H.G. Wells, Hemingway, Gen. James Gavin. She married Hemingway in 1940 and divorced him in 1945, then married Tom Matthews, a retired editor of *Time* magazine, in 1954, and divorced him in 1963.

At age 81, in 1989, she covered the U.S. war in Panama for the British magazine *Granta*. Until her mother died in 1974 Gellhorn made yearly trips back to the house on McPherson, especially around Christmas time, then settled somewhat permanently in London.

By February of 1998 she was nearly blind, she had cancer and could no longer work. No more travel either, just her neat flat in London. Twenty-four years had passed since her mother died and over half a century was gone since she last saw Hemingway. Her last article was a piece about the killings of street children by death squads in Brazil for the *London Review of Books* in 1996. It was her last trip, her last attempt to use journalism to arouse outrage over injustice. After the journey she settled quietly in her apartment, reading and waiting to die. But her body was stubborn. Unable to read, she had had enough. She took a pill and died Feb. 14.

About 40 people came to her apartment for the memorial. They laughed and told stories, toasting her life. A few days later her remains were tossed into the Thames along with a few roses. The river picked up the ashes and off she went toward America, toward her old home on McPherson Street.

The street and her house in 2013 were as they were 106 years before, three stories of carefully laid brick behind a round porch where the children played among nine Doric columns; a well-maintained family home in a quiet neighborhood. The house of Martha Gellhorn, war correspondent, bears no acknowledgement from the city.

One can't help but wonder what Gellhorn's first husband, Ernest Hemingway, felt whenever he heard the popular song "The St. Louis Blues" played from a radio or a band in a club. His first three wives, after all, were all from the city, as well as a longtime crony who managed to capture a man said by many to be the greatest novelist of the twentieth century.

When Gellhorn married Hemingway in a Union Pacific dining car parked in Cheyenne, Wyo., on Nov. 21, 1940, she became Hemingway's third and final St. Louis wife. He married once more, eventually winding up in Sun Valley, Ida., where he broke down physically and mentally and committed suicide in 1961. The father of his first wife, the first St. Louis wife, Hadley Richardson, had also committed suicide, as had Hemingway's own father, a Chicago doctor.

Like Gellhorn, Richardson grew up in a big family home in the West End, on Cabanne Place, born in 1891, the youngest of six, the daughter of a banker who had established Richardson Drugs. Hadley learned to play piano at an early age, attended the Mary Institute, the same as Gellhorn, then to Bryn Mawr, where she enrolled nine years before Gellhorn.

After just a year at college she spent a long stint at home, playing her piano, wondering what to do with her life. Her mother became terminally ill and she cared for her until her death in 1920. Soon thereafter she met Hemingway at a party for an old school friend in Chicago. By now she was 28, eight years older than the handsome, witty Hemingway, who wooed her with letters and numerous visits to St. Louis.

She was told constantly that her own health was weak but Hadley didn't feel weak, just bored, and by the time her mother died, she was very ready to get away. Hemingway was 22 and Hadley 30 when they got married at his family summer home in Horton Bay, Mich., in September of 1921.

Three month later the couple was off to Paris. His friend and fellow-budding writer Sherwood Anderson drew Hemingway there with promises of the Bohemian life. There he and Hadley were introduced to such literary lights as Ezra Pound, Gertrude Stein, James Joyce and F. Scott Fitzgerald.

He and Hadley traveled to Spain for the bullfights, the inspiration for Hemingway's *The Sun Also Rises,* the novel that launched his sterling literary career.

By then, however, Hadley was being pushed aside for Hemingway's second St. Louis woman, Pauline Pfeiffer. Born in Iowa in 1895 she moved as a child to St. Louis, where in 1901 her father and his two brothers founded the Pfeiffer Chemical Company. Pfeiffer Chemical bought another chemical company, William R. Warner, in 1908, kept the Warner name, and expanded the company through acquisition.

While Pauline's father became inactive in the management side of the company after 1908, the family kept money in the firm, which after 1955 became Warner-Lambert and then in 2000, Pfizer-Warner-Lambert, the world's biggest drug company. It is the maker of Viagra and maintains 250,000-square-feet of laboratory and manufacturing space as well as 70,000-square-feet of office space in the St. Louis County suburbs of Chesterfield and Weldon Springs.

Pauline attended a private girls school, the Academy of the Visitation, then went to the University of Missouri to study journalism. She hooked on with *Vogue* in New York, then to the magazine's Paris bureau, writing and editing fashion copy. There, Pfieffer launched a campaign that undermined Hemingway and Hadley's relationship. In 1926, she followed him to New York where Hemingway was going over the final version of *The Sun Also Rises.* Hadley had remained in Paris to take care of their new child. By spring the next year his marriage with Hadley was over. He and Pauline were married in 1927 and moved to Key West in 1928.

In 1936, Gellhorn, along with her mother and brother, came for a visit to the Florida Keys and stopped into Sloppy Joe's, Hemingway's favorite bar. There she met the barefoot writer, "a large dirty man" wearing a T-shirt and shorts. Gellhorn was wearing her Chanel traveling dress, the "little black dress" she favored in the thirties.

Edna struck up a conversation and Hemingway said he had known "St. Louis in the days of his youth" and mentioned that both of his wives had gone to school there. Gellhorn sat down next to him and the bartender later told a writer that he remembered the day well -- the couple looked like the "beauty and the beast."

Hemingway and Pauline were divorced by 1940. By then Hemingway had obtained his house on the edge of Havana, Cuba. Pauline kept the Key West house and opened a designer fabric, upholstery and gift store there named the Carolina Shop.

Pauline also maintained an apartment in San Francisco and frequently visited her sister, Virginia Pfeiffer, who lived in Hollywood, with another writer, Aldous Huxley. Pauline died of a brain hemorrhage in 1951 while visiting her sister and was buried in an unmarked grave in the Hollywood Memorial Cemetery.

Hadley stayed in Paris until 1934, living off her inheritance from her father's drug company and the royalties from *The Sun Also Rises*, all of which went to her. In 1933, after five years together, she married Paul Mowrer, a Pulitzer Prize winner who was the foreign correspondent for the *Chicago Daily News*. He became the European editor of the *New York Post* in 1945 until he retired to Chocorua, N. H., in 1948.

There, Hadley was able again to play her piano. After his retirement, Mowrer made a name for himself as a poet, chosen New Hampshire Poet Laureate in 1968 at age 82. He died April 7, 1971, at age 83 while vacationing in South Carolina. Hadley had continued to receive letters from Hemingway, especially during the breakups with Pauline and Gellhorn and they had seen each other shortly before his suicide.

Hadley and Hemingway's life together as members of the twenties lost generation in Paris is recounted in his final book, *A Moveable Feast,* published three years after his death. Hadley lived on until 1979 when he died Lakeland, Fla., at 87.

Hemingway also drew yet another St. Louisan into his life, the writer Aaron Edward Hotchner.

Born in St. Louis in 1920, Hotchner grew up in the Westgate Hotel on Delmar and Kingshighway, where he observed the thirties from his window, observations he published in the charming novel *King of the Hill*, published in 1973. The book told the "memoirs" of a 12-year-old living in the Westgate in 1933 and became a favorite of St. Louisans and a strong national seller, a vivid recapturing of the thirties. Steven Soderbergh made it into an award-winning film in 1993.

Told with great humor and language right out of the mouth of a gentle survivor who always seems to get by, Hotchner captures Depression life in the city better than any journalism or social study ever did. As the review in *The New York Times* said of the book, "if you happened to have missed the Depression, *King of the Hill* can fill that void in your life painlessly."

Hotchner's life seems right out of that novel, always walking the plank blindfolded before finding a Magoo-like saving solution. He went to Soldan High School, then was admitted to Washington University where he earned degrees in both history and law. He wrote a column for the newspaper *Student Life*, edited the literary magazine T*he Eliot*, contributed to the law quarterly, was a member of the debate team and played in student theatricals. He had little money, but managed to hold down a series of part-time jobs, including dressing up as Harpo to promote Marx Brothers movies.

He practiced law briefly before entering the Air Force, but saw no action during the war. Instead he was assigned to make a movie on anti-submarine warfare that put him in Paris, where he ran the European bureau of Air Force magazine. He stayed on in France after the war, telling his law firm back in St. Louis that "I had gone on to bigger and better things."

Two years later, now 28 and out of money again, Hotch came back to the states, landing in New York. He talked his way into a job for *Cosmopolitan* magazine as "a literary bounty hunter"—tracking down former contributors to the magazine to ask for fresh submissions. The names on the list were big -- Dorothy Parker, J.D. Salinger, Sinclair Lewis, Edna Ferber, John Steinbeck -- and Ernest Hemingway.

The two men met in Havana in 1949 and hit it off. Hotchner adapted many of his friend's works for television, stage, and film, and occasionally served as his agent. He helped Hemingway put together *A Moveable Feast,* his last book, published in 1964 and a big seller that recounts Hemingway's days in Paris. Its contents came from an old trunk discovered at a Paris hotel on a day Hotch and Hemingway were having lunch.

Hotchner then wrote *Papa Hemingway*, memories of conversations the two had in bars and on boats. Published in 1966 it became a best seller. *The New York Times* said Hotchner "has moved as close as anyone with a tape recorder can toward defining the intricate character of a man who, for better or worse, was a giant." In 2005, their letters were published as *Dear Papa, Dear Hotch.* Hotchner wrote: "The most resounding thing I learned from him was this: Don't fear failure, and don't overestimate success. It was a tenet he lived by and a legacy I treasure."

In 1976, Hotchner struck again, this time winning a $125,000 libel award against the Doubleday publishing house over a book where a Spanish journalist said Hotchner was "a hypocrite and a rascal" and only pretended to be Hemingway's friend in order to make money.

A few years later Hotchner found another goldmine. He had known Paul Newman since 1955, when they met on a television project and saw each occasionally for a good time. One day in the eighties, he helped Newman mix up a large batch of salad dressing for a party, using a canoe paddle in the movie star's basement. This was the birth of Newman's Own, a line of natural foods that just got more and more popular. Hotchner became director of the Hole in the Wall Gang summer camp for children with life-threatening illnesses.

He has maintained a continued involvement in St. Louis, especially his alma mater, Washington University. There sits the A. E. Hotchner Studio Theatre, a 125-seat state-of-the art theater. It is the home of the annual A.E. Hotchner Playwriting Festival.

Hotchner, 95, in 2015 released the book *Hemingway in Love: His Own Story,* which draws on taped conversations with the novelist, material that recounts the writer's life in the twenties in Paris. Hotchner quotes Hemingway saying Hadley Richardson "was the only woman who mattered in my life."

In March 1945, the American air force began its campaign to end the war in the Pacific with a series of bombings. The start of the campaign was the brainchild of Gen. Curtis Lemay who took over the command of the Army Air Force squadrons after the seizure of the island of Tinian in the Pacific. From there the newly developed B-29 bombers began targeting residential areas and city centers of Japan in a campaign aimed at forcing an imperial surrender.

This campaign quickly shifted to firebombing these civilian targets and on the night of March 9-10, LeMay sent 334 bombers to drop 2,000 pounds of bombs on the center of Tokyo, flying at night and surprising the already depleted Japanese air defense system. The result was horrendous destruction, nearly 85,000 people killed outright, over a million made homeless, over half of the city's residential and commercial center destroyed.

Five months later, after Roosevelt died, the first two bombs were shipped to the Pacific and were dropped on Hiroshima and Nagasaki. A third bomb was in the production pipeline, scheduled for delivery to the Pacific by Aug. 24. The military's schedule called for production and delivery of three more nuclear weapons by September and at least seven more by December.

Col. Paul Tibbetts and his crew took off from Iwo Jima at 2:45 a.m. Aug. 6, 1945, flying the *Enola Gay,* a B-29 named after his mother. He dropped the A-bomb on Hiroshima, killing 130,000 civilians instantly. Two days later 70,000 more people were killed in Nagasaki. Heat from the blast reached several million degrees Centigrade.

The total death toll from these two bombs is hard to calculate, people have continued to die into the present, first from the initial effects over weeks and months, then into years and decades from the long-term effects of leukemia, A-bomb cataracts, and cancers of the thyroid, breast, lungs, and salivary glands. Many more were sickened into the next generation from a variety of birth defects. Other effects include mental retardation and the fear of birth defects in the children of those exposed. Nuclear bombs have never been dropped again.

Five-thousand workers from St. Louis were involved in the project that produced the bombs, which included uranium processing at the Mallinckrodt chemical company's plant on the Mississippi riverfront. The project also used an atom-smashing cyclotron at Washington University in the neighboring suburb of University City.

The waste from the Mallinckrodt uranium has never gone away, still a source for alarm in 2015 for neighbors of the West Lake Landfill near St. Charles Rock Road in Bridgeton, Mo., another nearby suburb.

After the war the government stored the waste near Lambert Airport in north St. Louis County, where it contaminated Coldwater Creek, water that runs into the Missouri River. The government then sold the waste to a private contractor that hauled thousands of tons of uranium waste mixed with dirt by truck further north to the West Lake Landfill during the seventies. In 1990, the site became part of the Environmental Protection Agency's Superfund toxic site program. The EPA in 2008 proposed a plan for putting a soil cap over the waste but the nearby residents in Bridgeton rejected the plan. The EPA promised a revised solution to be announced by the end of 2016.

Meanwhile, in 2010, an underground fire began burning in the nearby Bridgeton Landfill, a facility that is under the direction of the Army Corps of Engineers. A firebreak to keep the fire away from the uranium waste is part of the considerations for the ultimate cleanup of West Lake.

The corps is also responsible for cleanup of the airport sites and Coldwater Creek, said to be the source of radioactive waste found in backyards and parks in Hazelwood, Mo., another north county town.

Residents in the area have also raised concerns about high rates of cancer in North County, concerns that led the state in 2014 to seek federal aid. The company and other companies that used the creek were sued by at least 50 people for disposing nuclear waste in the creek from World War II until the seventies. The lawsuit claims they became sick from contact with the creek water while they were children. A U.S. health agency said in 2015 it would study the possible connection between the cancers and the uranium waste.

Also in 2015, Missouri's two U.S. Senators and two U.S. House representatives forced the transfer of the whole situation out of the hands of the EPA and over to the corps. "The EPA's unacceptable delay in implementing a solution for the West Lake landfill has destroyed its credibility and it is time to change course," Sen. Roy Blunt said of the situation.

In 1945, St. Louis suffered its worst shortages of the war. Beer, cigarettes, meat, poultry, fish, and chicken were affected. A black market developed and flourished through the final months of the war despite pleas from industry and the government to save food for the troops. Coal was also in short supply domestically and out door signs, as well as the lights in stores and theaters were darkened. A midnight curfew was announced but was soon relaxed after numerous violations, especially from nightclubs and bars.

Roosevelt's death in April was mourned by a crowd of 4,000 who stood in the rain at Soldier's Memorial. On May 8, with the victory in Europe proclaimed and Hitler and Mussolini both dead, bells, horns and whistles were heard across the city and a gathering of 5,000 at the downtown memorial attended a prayer service.

By summer, even as the war in the Pacific still raged, layoffs began at the defense plants, the Red Cross blood bank closed, the Office of Civil Defense shut down. At U.S. Cartridge, 4,000 laid-off workers held a protest demanding severance pay and unemployment compensation. The company refused. Curtiss-Wright told 11,000 workers to go home.

That January, Mayor Kauffmann presented a $63 million public works program to be put in effect after the war ended, with a wide agenda including highways, rapid transit, a downtown airport, improvements on the levee, new sewers and other projects to be paid for without raising taxes. There was also an "anti-slum" committee named to seek answers to the wartime crowding caused by the influx of work created by the war.

Talk of these ideas was music to the ears of residents who had seen few improvements during the war years. One study said St. Louis was two years behind the national average in school performance; another found many children underfed.

Business interests jumped on the idea of a new St. Louis, saying the city needed a 35 percent increase in local business to make up for the coming loss of government contracts. For several of the big downtown department stores, their backs against the newly demolished riverfront of mud and gravel, part of the solution appeared to be developments away from the central core in brand new suburban areas called "shopping arcades." There would be plenty of parking and far less traffic. Such developments had been built in Kansas City, Dallas and Houston before the war, but none in St. Louis.

The reunions with soldiers returned from Europe were fine, but following the hugs and kisses came worries about jobs. The government said 10,000 returned vets had obtained work by July, but a need for thousands of jobs was evident.

V-J Day (Victory over Japan) finally arrived. After the surrender terms were reached in Japan Aug. 15 (Aug. 14 St. Louis time) the streets of the city filled with 250,000 people. There were parades on Market, Olive and Delmar, strolling musicians played accordions on the Hill, dancers took to the streets to spin the Lindy hop to the strains of the Russ Davis Big Band that set up in Plaza Square next to the Soldiers' Memorial, a military brass band from Jefferson Barracks played patriotic tunes.

Perhaps the most indelible image from the all-night celebration was an enormous conga line of sailors, soldiers, factory workers and civilians that snaked its way down the middle of Market Street to the river then back up to the plaza, then again and again.

St. Louis almost became the site of the new world organization, the United Nations, which had been formed June 26 by 50 nations that pledged to fight no more wars. Mayor Kauffman, joined by the Missouri governor and the city's Chamber of Commerce, offered the site of the Atlas Powder Co. in suburban Weldon Springs near now-contaminated Coldwater Creek. The UN instead decided to locate in New York and the Atlas site was taken over by the Mallinckrodt Chemical Works, the processors of uranium waste that eventually contaminated the creek.

Since the UN was formed over 150 wars have been fought around the globe, with the United States involved in about 50 of them.

Of the six leaders of World War II, only two were alive on V-J Day. Roosevelt had died from a cerebral hemorrhage April 12, 1945, while sitting for a portrait in his summer home at Warm Springs, Ga., just as the Ninth Army crossed the Elbe River nearing Berlin. He was 63.

Benito Mussolini, 62, the dictator of Italy, and his wife, Clara, were killed on April 28 by Communist Party partisans in Moltrasio, at a farmhouse north of Lake Como. Mussolini was shot nine times by a partisan colonel. Clara died when she grabbed the colonel's gun and was shot once. Mussolini was then taken to Milan, thrown on the pavement, shot five more times. Women urinated on his dead body, and both bodies were hoisted in the air by their feet and hung upside down.

Adolf Hitler was cheered by FDR's death. He sent orders from his Berlin bunker that Germany itself was to be destroyed -- "all resources," the water supply, electricity, transportation, gasoline, railroads, ships, canals, roads, everything was ordered to be blown up. America would not be allowed to profit from its victory.

His staff ignored the orders. A week later, on April 28, he married Eva Braun, his cellmate in the bunker, then on April 30, age 56, he ate a meal prepared by his vegetarian cook. He and Eva went into a small room. She swallowed poison; he shot himself in the head. He was taken to the garden outside the bunker and his body was doused in gasoline and burned.

The Russian leader, Joseph Stalin, made his biggest mark on a war that had devastated his country and its population at a February 1945 conference with Roosevelt and Churchill at Yalta on the Black Sea. Stalin's Red Army was inside Germany moving toward Berlin while U.S. forces stalled at the Battle of the Bulge. At Yalta, Roosevelt convinced him to declare war on Japan but also allowed Poland and Eastern Europe to fall into the Russian sphere of post-war influence. The agreement set the stage for the Cold War. Stalin lived until struck by a heart attack at his dacha outside Moscow on March 5, 1953, age 74. He was buried in Red Square in Moscow near the very spot in 1945 where his victorious army had thrown the shattered banners and torn flags of the defeated Nazis at his feet.

Winston Churchill, the wartime hero and leader of Great Britain, was defeated in the 1945 election following the German surrender, voted out during a wave of reform sentiment and dissension inside his Conservative Party. Defeated in a landslide, Churchill went into shock and depression but recovered and returned to the Prime Minister's post in 1951. He remained in office until 1955 and died a revered statesman in 1965, age 91.

Michinomiya Hirohito, whose imperial reign was called "Shining Peace," surrendered to the United States two days after Nagaski under terms that allowed the imperial office to remain. A week later, on Aug. 8, Hirohito read a surrender speech over Japanese radio, the first time the nation had heard his voice. He lived until Jan. 7, 1989, never admitting accountability for Japanese atrocities during the war. He was given an elaborate state funeral attended by world leaders including George H.W. Bush, the U.S. president. Hirohito was 87. The Big Six were finally all gone.

Chapter Twenty
An Iron Curtain: Shelley, Pruitt-Igoe and the North Side
1945-2015

About 3:30 p.m., Car No. 53 answered a call to meet complainant at 2507 Glasgow Avenue where they were informed by Sherman Lee White, a Negro lad, that at about 3 o'clock while he and a group of other boys were at the swimming pool at Fairgrounds Park, being on the outside of the fence, they were approached by a group of white boys who told them to go home, and suddenly one of the white boys struck him on the head with a stick or piece of small size pipe. The boy was taken to the hospital for treatment.

-- St. Louis Council on Human Relations, 1949

J.D. Shelley and his wife Ethel were part of the Great Migration of 6 million blacks out of the South between 1915 and 1975. Shelley was a gentle man who wanted a quiet life. He had five children, he wanted to feed and clothe them and give his family a warm place to live. His wife was similar, working hard to make her family secure.

In 1939, they lived in Starkville, Miss., 80 miles east of the Mississippi River, the home of Mississippi State University. Ethel had been working as a house cleaner but decided that her children required more of her time and quit her job, recommending a young neighbor woman to the white family she worked for. The young woman was hired. Two days later, when a watch in the family's house couldn't be located, the woman was blamed.

As things went in places like Starkville in 1939, police took the young black house cleaner out of her home, whipped her with a rubber hose and threw her in a ditch. They did this on a Sunday, in the black section, in front of a crowd of churchgoers too afraid to confront the white police. Ethel Shelley heard about the beating, however, and went to the ditch were she rescued the bloodied neighbor woman.

Another two days passed in this southern town where no one had tried to stop this beating of this particular young woman, something not so far out of the ordinary in Oktibbeha County, Mississippi. Then the white woman found her watch. It had slipped behind the bathroom sink.

This incident had an effect on the Shelleys and they decided to join the Great Migration, moving to St. Louis. J.D. went first. He was a laborer who worked in the Starkville sawmill shoveling saw dust from one place to the other, listening to the whine of the saws 10 or 12 hours a day, six days a week. Maybe things would be better in St. Louis, where a couple of other relatives lived.

He soon got a construction job and rented a small apartment on Francis Street just north of what is now called Dr. Martin Luther King Drive. He made enough money to bring the wife and the five kids up from the South, getting plenty of work during the war. In 1945, with both husband and wife working, they had saved enough money to buy a house.

They chose an area to the west of the crowded confines of the downtown and with the help of an elder from their church found a suitable middle class home at 4600 Labadie Ave., about a mile west of Sumner High School just outside The Ville. Significantly, this house was also outside the eight-square-mile area of no-loan "Negro territory" drawn to define the segregated "black zone."

But, no problem, Shelley was told. The churchman worked through a black realtor who used a white "straw party" to buy the house then transfer the deed over to the Shelleys. This was a standard strategy that sometimes worked to get around the web of customs that made segregated housing a reality in the city. The couple moved into the medium-sized, two-story house on Labadie. They were happy homeowners in a house built of tan masonry in a good location not far from the Natural Bridge shopping district and Tandy Park near the high school.

The segregation agreements, called "restrictive covenants" in legal-speak, had been used for decades to keep blacks clamped in an ever more defined area. Under these practices whites had about 85 percent of the land area in the city. Most of the "black zone," the remaining 15 percent, in 1945 was in Mill Creek Valley between Grand and the river, north of Chouteau and south of Cass. There were also swaths of black blocks clumped together both north and south of the zone. While the black population was also about 15 percent of the city at the time, the housing stock where it lived was much older and more densely crowded than that for whites.

The Ville was an exception, a middle class black neighborhood of single family housing north of Cass, just a step away from the affluent Lewis Place, a neighborhood of grand houses recently occupied by prosperous black families. The realtors assured the Shelleys there would be no trouble with their deed, but that was a bit of wishful thinking by an agent who wanted to make his commission. The truth was that a black family moving into the 4600 block of Labadie was a bit bold, representing as it did a western push further beyond Grand than either The Ville or Lewis Place. The Shelleys bought the house in August and moved from Francis Street during the next month.

The Real Estate Exchange, the white board of realtors that controlled land in the city, quickly saw that this purchase meant trouble and on Oct. 9, 1945, the bell rang at the Shelleys' door. A summons was served ordering them to appear in court to defend the title to their new home.

The summons started the ball rolling on the case known as *Shelley vs. Kraemer,* a landmark action that led to a unanimous Supreme Court decision three years later that made housing discrimination illegal in the United States. The Kraemer of the case was a white named Louis Kraemer, who lived down the street from the Shelleys and was working with the Real Estate Exchange. His argument was simple -- by virtue of being black the Shelley family had no right to buy the house.

The case did not come out of thin air. The context was the growing civil rights movement of the forties -- the March on Washington Movement, the downtown sit-ins, the government attempt to desegregate the defense plants, lawsuits filed to desegregate Washington University and the University of Missouri.

Lewis Place had been broken open by black activists who purchased houses in the two blocks of old-stock brick homes built by whites in the eighteen-nineties as a gated community. The neighborhood became contested in 1943 when wildcat black real estate agents, hoping to make fast money and break the segregation system, began selling homes to blacks through the straw-white system. The neighborhood was a place where black families who had done well wanted to move, close to the Finney Avenue shopping district and The Ville and also near several desirable schools and black churches.

A house was sold to a black family in 1943, and then in 1944 and 1945 six more properties were sold to blacks, including at least one sold by a Jewish resident. David Grant's activist law partner Robert Witherspoon and his wife, social activist and NAACP leader Fredda Witherspoon, began to organize homeowners to break the covenants.

Their organizers convinced 49 Lewis Place homeowners, the majority who were white, to sign papers seeking an end to the covenant practice. White families fronting for the white real estate agents filed opposing lawsuits, but with Witherspoon and Grant leading the legal charge, further appeals were dropped. On March 16, 1945, the *St. Louis Argus* reported an integrated, harmonious and orderly meeting of property owners.

The Shelley's story was different. The real estate interests feared no end to the expansion of the black zone and decided to fight for the line north of Lewis Place. Their battle went all the way to the nation's highest court.

Kraemer lost his initial claim in state court in November of 1945 and appealed. The Shelleys saw their case overturned by the Missouri Supreme Court, on Dec. 9, 1946, with an order that the covenant be enforced. The appeal then went up to the U.S. Supreme Court.

Three of the justices on the high court stepped aside in the case, giving no reason. There was speculation one or all of the three themselves owned houses with such covenants or had argued for these cases in lower courts. Two of the three were from the South. The six remaining justices left the bare number for a legal quorum and observers predicted these six were split on the issue.

George L. Vaughn, a St. Louis attorney whose grandfather had been a slave, pointed out in his argument that the black areas of the city contained 117,000 people "living in an area meant for 43,000." He also said the majority of the housing available to blacks could be classified as slums. He said the real estate agreement violated the Fourteen Amendment guarantee to all Americans of equal protection under the law.

Thurgood Marshall, who was the chief counsel for the NAACP at the time, had visited St. Louis many times over the years and spent several months living in the Lewis Place neighborhood researching the facts, helping Vaughn make his case before the Supreme Court. Marshall later became the most renowned black attorney in U. S. history, serving on the court for 34 years.

The court ruled 6-0 on May 3, 1948, that the restrictive covenant was not enforceable. The opinion was written by Chief Justice Fred Vinson and dealt a blow to all forms of discrimination, setting the stage for the ruling that outlawed school segregation in 1954. Vinson, ruling on Shelley, said that restrictive covenants were legally "contrary to the public policy of the United States" and declared the Fourteenth Amendment assures that "all persons, whether colored or white, shall stand equal to the laws of the state, and, in regard to the colored race, for whose protection the amendment was primarily designed, that no discrimination shall be made against them by law because of his color."

By 2010, Lewis Place was 94 percent black, the housing stock on the original two blocks still in reasonable shape, especially compared to the crumbling North City blocks nearby. The area was hit by a tornado on New Year's Eve Day 2010 and suffered damage to several homes. The city promised to help fix the damage, but by 2015 little public money had reached the neighborhood and damage was still evident. Homes on the street were valued far below similar sized properties on the South Side with a six-bedroom, 4,500 square foot brick house selling for $117,000 in 2013. A similar house six blocks south could fetch three times as much.

The Shelleys lived a quiet life after the case was settled, living in their house until 1959. Ethel died in 1983 and J.D. died in 1997 at age 91. Lewis Place was placed on the National Register of Historic Landmarks

Sept. 15, 1980. The Shelley house has a small plaque out front reminding visitors of the case.

While the Shelley case made its way through the courts, a new factor took hold in the American psyche, a factor that complicated race relations for much of the rest of the century -- the Cold War and its anti-communist ideology. Of course, the fear of communism was nothing new, dating back to World War I and even earlier. But the vehemence of its nature and the widespread acceptance of its suppositions grew dramatically in the fifties, starting with a speech given by Winston Churchill in Missouri.

Following his election defeat in 1945, Churchill began considering a visit to the United States. War-shattered Britain needed money and a meeting with a friend, the financier Bernard Baruch, was a step on the road toward that end. He also wanted to see President Harry Truman to discuss what he viewed as a growing threat from the Soviet Union. An additional concern was his health. The old warhorse needed rest and time away from the cauldron of British politics.

That he came to the United States in the spring of 1946 was not so surprising. What was unlikely was that Churchill, one of the most recognized figures of the postwar period, would wind up in a small college in Fulton, Mo. But arrive there he did, with Truman in tow, to deliver what was one of the most important speeches of the twentieth century, a speech that was the opening salvo of the Cold War.

Truman was a haberdasher from Kansas City, selected reluctantly by Roosevelt as his running mate in 1944 and thrust into the White House when FDR died in 1945. He had been kept isolated by Roosevelt during his brief stint as vice-president and when he became president turned to several old friends for advice. Several of these insiders were graduates of Westminster College, a Presbyterian institution in Fulton, located about 100 miles west of St. Louis near Jefferson City, the state capital.

Each year since 1936 the college sponsored the John Findley Green Foundation Lecture as a memorial to a St. Louis lawyer who had amassed a small fortune after graduation from Westminster in 1884. His wife, who had been born in England, arranged the lectures and issued invitations to speakers of international reputation. The lectures had been lackluster during the 1937-1942 years including the Canadian Undersecretary for

Foreign Affairs, a professor of philosophy from Chicago and the former commissioner to the Philippines.

But Truman's Westminster aides decided to shoot for the moon and his old friend and university president F.L. "Bullet" McClure got Truman to endorse the letter of invitation. In October 1945 off went the invitation to London. Churchill accepted in November and delivered the speech March 5,1946, with the title "Sinews of Peace."

After Truman's introduction, Churchill painted a picture of the "awful ruin of Europe, with all its vanished glories" and a world where the "United States stands at this time at the pinnacle of world power." He called for a unified front of Britain and its Commonwealth with the United States to assure peace where once there was war and tyranny. He called on the new United Nations Organization to assure this peace.

But he said:

> A shadow has fallen upon the scenes so lately lit by the Allied victory. Nobody knows what Soviet Russia and its Communist international organization intends to do in the immediate future, or what are the limits, if any, to their expansive and proselytizing tendencies.
>
> From Stettin in the Baltic to Trieste in the Adriatic an iron curtain has descended across the continent. Behind that line lie all the capitals of the ancient states of Central and Eastern Europe. Warsaw, Berlin, Prague, Vienna, Budapest, Belgrade, Bucharest and Sofia, all these famous cities and the populations around them lie in what I must call the Soviet sphere, and all are subject in one form or another, not only to Soviet influence but to a very high and, in some cases, increasing measure of control from Moscow.
>
> The Communist parties, which were very small in all these Eastern States of Europe, have been raised to pre-eminence and power far beyond their numbers and are seeking everywhere to obtain totalitarian control.
>
> Except in the British Commonwealth and in the United States where Communism is in its infancy, the Communist parties or fifth columns constitute a growing challenge and peril to Christian civilization. These are somber facts for anyone to have to recite on the morrow of a victory gained by so much splendid comradeship in arms and in the cause of freedom and democracy;

> but we should be most unwise not to face them squarely while time remains.
>
> I do not believe that Soviet Russia desires war. What they desire is the fruits of war and the indefinite expansion of their power and doctrines. But what we have to consider here today while time remains, is the permanent prevention of war and the establishment of conditions of freedom and democracy as rapidly as possible in all countries.

This analysis, agreed to by Truman and the U.S. military establishment, opened the doors to the buildup of the U.S. security state and its foreign policy goal of containing Communism wherever it appeared. Soon thereafter, in 1947, Truman signed the National Security Act establishing the Central Intelligence Agency. Formerly the Office of Strategic Services, established by Roosevelt as the wartime spy agency, the CIA was given the job of "coordinating the nation's intelligence activities and correlating, evaluating and disseminating intelligence affecting national security."

Domestically, the FBI, led by its anti-communist, anti-black, anti-union director, J. Edgar Hoover, began its campaign of spying and intimidation under Cold War terms, hunting for perceived domestic enemies, aided and encouraged by Sen. Joe McCarthy of Wisconsin. Hoover, politicians from both South and North, and corporate leaders put civil right organizers under the same "subversive" banner as communists. At the same time the United States prepared for all-out nuclear war by producing a massive weapons arsenal, the biggest peacetime buildup of the military in history.

The civil rights movement thus ran up against a wall of southern Democrats and conservative Republicans, FBI agents and racist police that defined as Communist anyone who proposed progressive change during the late forties. The black coalition was upended by charges of Communist Party influence in labor unions and accusations of Red sympathies against those organizing for desegregation of schools, housing and other public accommodations.

The security state, however, did not prove all-powerful. The black movement slowed but did not disappear. The courts provided some relief in cases like *Shelley vs. Kraemer,* the NAACP continued its fight against

Jim Crow laws and many more white liberals joined with blacks in the new environment.

In St. Louis, nonviolent protest continued with demonstrations over seating at the American Theater and protests of a police killing of a black worker, both in 1946. And a group of Washington University students and professors, war veterans, lawyers, postal workers and teachers formed an integrated activist group called the Committee of Racial Equality (CORE) that formed in 1947 around principles of nonviolent protest like those of Mahatmah Ghandi.

Within the Democratic Party, as the 1948 national election approached, Truman spelled out his support for civil rights laws and an end to discrimination. His stand split the party three ways. Southern Democrats bolted into a Dixiecrat faction led by the segregationist Strom Thurmond, Truman led the middle Regular faction and the Progressive Party revived under Henry Wallace.

Jordan Chambers, still the most powerful black politician in the city, rallied support for Truman, appearing on stage with the president at a 1948 appearance at Keil Auditorium. Margaret Bush, a law clerk for David Grant, ran for Congress on the Progressive Party ticket, the first black woman from Missouri to make such a run. She lost her election but Truman carried St. Louis and won the national vote, defeating Thomas Dewey by 3 million votes. Thurmond collected 39 electoral votes in the South with only 2.4 percent of the national tally and the Progressive candidate, Wallace, wound up with 2.3 percent but couldn't carry a state.

The Truman vote in St. Louis set the stage for a razor-thin victory by the Democratic Party in the 1949 city election, a ballot that had deep implications for the future of the city. The victory by Joseph Darst put the Democrats back in City Hall leadership for the first time in eight years. And the victory started a winning streak for the party that has continued all the way to the present, with Democratic wins in 16 consecutive elections through the 2013 fourth- term victory by Francis Slay.

Shortly after the election, St. Louis dodged another civil rights bullet. In the last summer of the decade a disturbance at the Fairgrounds swimming pool threatened to spin into the kind of spark that could have kindled the type of racial conflict seen in cities like Detroit and New York.

But again the city stayed on its road of relative peace, even after its new mayor, Joseph Darst, showed how deep his liberal approach to the race question went.

The Fairgrounds Pool at an old racetrack on the North Side was the city's biggest, one of nine pools across the city, but the most desirable because it was outdoors and very large, perhaps the biggest public pool in the country. It lay just outside the black zone not far from the Shelley house. Following the court decision more black families were on the move north. Many whites were concerned about losing their white-only swimming privileges.

Besides Fairgrounds there was only one other outdoor pool in the city, another white-only pool, at Marquette Park on the South Side. To Darst, under pressure from the civil rights leaders like Chambers and Grant in the Democratic Party and looking squarely at the Shelley decision, it seemed fair to open up the outdoor pools to blacks.

In June, Darst issued an order saying, "If Negroes apply for admission to city pools, they are not to be refused." The order also applied to the 35 city playgrounds of which blacks had been barred from all but eight. "The Negroes pay their taxes," Director of Public Welfare John O'Toole said. "They are citizens and have a right to use public property."

The next day, when the pool opened at 2 p.m. about 35 blacks were admitted through the Fairgrounds gates along with a crowd of white youths. The swim went peacefully enough at first, but a gang of white teenagers surged into the park later in the afternoon, gathering along the fence near the pool.

They began booing and insulting the blacks in the pool, shouting out the usual cliches of racist name-calling. Several blacks left the pool and were attacked with baseball bats. One black teenager was injured before police broke up the fight. A white teen was found with a hunting knife in his belt. Police escorted the blacks to safety.

Darst's liberal spine melted quickly. Hearing about the trouble at the pool, that very afternoon he withdrew the previous day's order, saying he was going back to the city's "time-honored policy" of separate pools for the races so there would be no problems "which would have the effect of destroying the good relationship existing among our citizens."

The order did not have the desired effect. By early evening more than 5,000 people, black and white, gathered at the pool. Darst called out 400 police. Traffic on Natural Bridge between Grand and Vandeventer came to a halt. Skirmishes between blacks and whites broke out in the crowds outside the pool and before the night was over one black and one white had been stabbed and 12 other people were hospitalized with serious injuries.

Seven people were arrested, but the police showed restraint, keeping their tear gas and guns at the ready but unused. By 1 a.m. the area was quiet and the rest of summer saw no more violence at the pool. A few assaults were reported the next few days but only three days later, a baseball game between black and white teams was carried off at the park with good spirit between the two teams.

An independent investigation found that black resentment was directed not against whites per se, but against restrictions that "limit opportunity and freedom of action." The report praised both blacks at the pool and the police for their restraint. Blame for the riot was placed on "a known loosely organized gang of older boys and young men ranging from 17 to 23." There was also sharp criticism of Darst's hasty order rescinding integration.

The report made some generalizations about race relations in St. Louis. It said "white people are very poorly informed regarding the living and economic problems of blacks" and largely "support the idea of racial segregation." Still, "white people, in substantial majority, want to see justice and fair treatment in race relations, but they have no knowledge or experience to help them understand what is involved."

Blacks, on the other hand, "are opposed to arbitrary segregation of public facilities," were very much in favor of opening the pool and opposed to the mayor's rescinding the order. And "a substantial majority feel the police enforce the law in favor of white people."

By the next July, several civil rights groups, represented by the Lewis Place attorney Robert Witherspoon, filed suit against the city for segregation at the pool. On July 17, 1950, a federal judge ordered the pool open to blacks. "No rule or regulation shall be made applicable to the Negro race that is not equally applicable to all other races using the open-air pools," the judge declared.

On July 19, there were eight arrests as two blacks, surrounded by a jeering crowd of 200 whites were escorted into the pool by police. Four of those arrested were said by police to be white ringleaders who planned attacks on the blacks and the other four were charged with threatening the blacks in the pool.

Police remained at the pool over the next few days, arresting four more people on July 22 and three more the next day, but within a week the pool, although far less crowded than usual, was peaceful. The majority of those swimming at the integrated facility were black.

The integration of the Fairgrounds pool as peacefully as it happened could be seen as a victory for those who opposed segregation and Darst's flip-flop on the issue may have been ignored, written off as having to do with inexperience. But behind the scenes, decisions made by Darst and the white leadership of the city were made that would have far-reaching, disastrous, even monstrous results for the black voters who helped put the Democratic Party into office in 1949.

For the election brought with it the implementation of policy regarding public housing that had dire consequences for the black community, consequences shown most vividly in what became known as the Pruitt-Igoe Project.

Pruitt-Igoe became the buildings that provided the poster image in the public mind most closely associated with the failure of urban renewal in major cities across the United States.

Pruitt-Igoe became an icon of failure, the failure of the school of modern architecture, the failure of the Democratic Party and its liberal views, the failure of a city's white leadership to make things right for a hundred years of segregation, the dashing of the hopes of people seeking better lives through better housing, better work and better education.

The buildings stood starkly like Lego toys made of cement -- 33 of them, a wall of apartment blocks 11 stories high holding up 2,870 units. They fell less than two decades after they were built, their 1972 destruction captured on black-and-white film, shown over and over then and into the present. We see the failure of the project in great clouds of dust as the dynamite goes off, the capitulation of a great house of cards; the hope of their planners, their city and their residents sent skyward in a rush of toxic clouds.

These buildings were first conceived in the 1947 city plan that sought the removal of "blighted slums" of "Negro tenements" in the Carr-DeSoto neighborhood on the near North Side. The plan was sharply altered in 1950 under Darst. Ground was broken in 1952 and the project completed in 1956. *Architecture Forum* said they would replace "ramshackle houses jammed with people -- and rats" with "vertical neighborhoods for poor people." The main architect was Minoru Yamasaki, who later designed the World Trade Center in New York City on the LeCorbesier model of Swiss modernism.

Perhaps the concept came from a genuine desire to save the city's downtown, under siege after the destruction of the waterfront for the Jefferson Memorial and the beginnings of white and black flight to the suburbs. Or perhaps the city's real estate interest saw it as a way to keep the growing black population confined in its zone in defiance of *Shelley vs. Kraemer.* There was, after all, only one way to cram more people into an area that already had three times as many people as there was room for -- and that was up.

Earlier plans for two- to three-story public housing projects with nearby parkland and rehabilitated schools would be far more expensive for the city to build than federally-funded high rise blocks. And, with the de facto segregation of swatches of the North Side still in effect, the real estate agents had no desire to run up against white homeowners outside the zone.

The sharp attorneys from Lewis Place had, however, taught the real estate people a lesson. Pruitt-Igoe might have been payback. It would accommodate the same amount of people in its 57 acres of high-rise cement inside the black zone as a posh suburb like Ladue (formed in 1936) could put in 5,472 acres of rolling hills. In the white nightmare of the postwar period, with Communists under the bed and blacks running for office, the desegregation of a place like Ladue was not only possible but also just around the corner.

Joe Darst had the smile, the backslapping confidence of a big city mayor. He was a supporter of Harry Truman. He learned real estate from his father, a 50-year veteran of the business in St. Louis. Joe Darst was born March 18, 1909, in the West End, attended Sacred Heart Convent School, St. Louis University High, and St. Louis University. He survived World War I despite a stint in the infantry in France and came home to sell houses with his father.

Darst supported the Democrat Al Smith in the 1928 race for president and in 1933 became the city's director of public welfare under Mayor Dickmann, a friend and party ally. He later became director of federal housing during the planning for the first developments. He was considered a fair, liberal administrator and built alliances with the black community, rising in the Democratic Party during the Depression and the war. These alliances put him in City Hall in 1949.

Darst carried all the black wards, winning the contest with 54 percent of the vote over his Republican opponent, J. Edward Gragg. The Democrats also won the office of comptroller to give the party a two-to-one edge on the Board of Estimate and shaved off a 15-14 victory on the Board of Alderman.

The GOP did, however, retain control in this post-Shelley environment of 14 wards, all the newer western residential and high-rent wards as well as a swath south of Cherokee and Arsenal. But Darst had enough to win 110,508 to 92,579. By 2015, the Republicans had spent another 66 years looking to get back in the mayor's chair in St. Louis.

"I've lived in St. Louis all my life," Darst said. "I've loved the city and I know how desperately it needs rehabilitation. If, while I'm mayor, I can crack its housing problem, beautify its riverfront and vitalize it with a real spirit of regional bi-state development then I'll go out happy."

Housing was his priority and he pledged he would never forget his responsibilities to the "ill-housed and to those who have what amounts to be no housing at all."

Darst admired New York City Mayor William O'Dwyer, who showed the St. Louis mayor plans for high-rise apartment blocks during a visit to the East. Once back home, Darst pushed for a change in the two-to-three story concept of public housing that had been approved by a 1947 plan.

By 1949, two such low-rise projects were built and a third was proposed as a complex for whites. This project, however, by 1951, was swallowed up by the new fourth city project, called Missouri No. 4 and named the Capt. Wendell Oliver Pruitt Project after a St. Louis war hero.

Pruitt, a Sumner High graduate, was a member of the Tuskeegee Airmen, the Army's first black unit of fliers. He was killed in a training exercise in 1945 after earning a reputation as one of the top airmen in the unit. A middle school on the North Side, the Pruitt Military Academy, is also named after the pilot.

The original Pruitt plan was approved on Jan. 5, 1950, as a $25 million development with 2,490 federally funded, low-rent units and another 750 privately financed units on a 180-acre track bounded by 18th Street and Jefferson, Cass and Franklin (now Martin Luther King).

It was the biggest city development plan in the nation. The original plan included development of 30 acres of parkland within the project, one-sixth of the land, which would be distributed between six- and 13-story apartment blocks.

There was no mention of these buildings being segregated and certainly no talk by the mayor or the planners for an all-black, all-poor enclave. Indeed, these early plans delineated that a majority of the residents be middle-income. But trouble began immediately. The initial bids from contractors came in 60 percent above the national average, far higher than envisioned by the plan.

A battle ensued between the planners and the federal government. The feds wouldn't budge on the subsidy, so Darst raised density and reduced apartment size, knocking the area of the project down by more than two-thirds, packing 33 buildings into 57 acres. The number of apartment units was trimmed only slightly. Parkland disappeared.

Nonetheless, the National Real Estate Association named Darst U. S. Housing Man of the Year for 1951. He said that 90 percent of the bankers, industrialists and real estate men in St. Louis "are with us in our program" of "slum clearance urban development."

He pointed out that the buildings would do more to stop the kind of urban dissatisfaction that bred Communists than anything else government could do. He added that St. Louis was unique among American cities for the breadth of its support for such a project, having won over "business groups normally opposed to them."

These arguments about the shape of downtown housing were also taking place against the template of another federal program that gave post-war loan guarantees through the Veteran Administration. These loans were very difficult to obtain inside the central cities due to redlining by the banks. A stacked rating system put "American business and professional men" at the top of the lists for loans. This system resulted in leaving most blacks without access to the funds.

These loans made it easy for white professionals and high-income wage earners to buy desirable single-family homes lined up in new suburban developments. Builders found it cheap to mass-produce rows of houses on bare land. The old brick neighborhoods in the city were left to decay.

By 1949, the feds put $1 billion into loan funds to help the cities overcome urban crowding. These housing funds funneled through a program called Title 1 that was a bonanza for the real estate industry. The policy allowed cities to buy land, dozer existing housing and sell to developers, with the feds taking the loss. As one New York study showed, this policy gave official federal approval to "uproot low-income people."

In St. Louis this meant clearance of what was termed "blight," first on the North Side for Pruitt-Igoe, then Mill Creek Valley in the central city.

Also, in 1956, President Dwight Eisenhower, the Allied military commander during the war, pushed through what was called the National Defense Highway Act. This program built free-standing "super highways" designed to move military equipment long distances without being slowed by city traffic, paid for by a 90 percent federal contribution and a 10 percent state match. Voila, the Interstate highway system was born.

Eisenhower remembered well his bombing campaigns of German and Japanese cities. He used tax programs to discourage new defense plants inside urban centers. St. Louis factories that had been built for defense contracts during the war had already been reduced and this policy was another blow to employment, especially on the North Side. The remaining plants moved to the suburbs or out of the area all together, to Texas and the southwest. The North Side, again, suffered the most from removal of jobs.

Another factor during the Eisenhower administration came when schools in America were desegregated. After the Supreme Court decision in 1954, blacks, by law, had to be allowed to attend white schools. There was resistance to the decision across the country and while St. Louis saw nothing like the trouble seen in places like Mississippi, Alabama and Arkansas, the effects of the resistance decimated the city's schools over the half-century that followed the decision by the high court.

The city's integrated schools lost enrollment steadily after the decision and a Catch-22 mentality of lost population, declining enrollment and lack of the funding enveloped the city's system to a point where many of the school buildings stand empty. Peak enrollment in the St. Louis Public Schools reached in 115,543 students in 1967. That enrollment in 2015 was about 25,000.

These national developments were met with approval by businesses, the two political parties, newspapers and real estate interests in St. Louis. Darst and the business elite formed a new group, a coalition called Civic Progress Inc., before handing over the mayor's chair to Raymond Tucker in April 1953. Darst announced early that year he would not run for a second term because of ill health and was dead, age 64, three months after the election.

Tucker, an engineer who promoted himself as an expert who remained above the political fray, barely won the primary vote over former school board president Mark Eagleton, a one-time Republican who had switched over to the Democrats during FDR's run for a fourth term in 1944. Eagleton was pro-union and more liberal than Tucker, but was too closely connected to regular party politics to defeat the reform technocrat Tucker.

In the Democratic Party primary conservative Republicans crossed over with enough gusto to give Tucker the South Side and carry the election by 1,600 votes. Tucker easily won the general election and began immediately to expand Civic Progress as his power base, the group that might easily have been called the Big Cinch in 1910 or the One Percent in 2012.

The members in the early fifties included Sidney Baer of the Baer department store; Arthur Blumayer, president of the Bank of St. Louis; August Busch of the beer; Daniel Danforth of Ralston-Purina; Morton May of the May Co. department store; former Republican mayor Aloys Kaufmann; William McDonnell of the aircraft company: David Calhoun of St. Louis Union Trust: Edgar Rand, the king of shoes; Edgar Queeny, whose middle name was Monsanto; Tom Smith, Boatman's Bank (now Bank of America); Powell McHaney of General American Life; Ethan Shipley Washington University chancellor; and Clarence Turley, who in 1956 was president of the National Association of Realtors.

The club worked without staff or representatives. It met weekly during Tucker's three terms, the top men only, in person. This way, according to

Baer, these men, all white, formed a "closely limited fraternity of capable executives, with corporate power behind them (who) could talk to each other in confidence without bombast, or fear of press, and with the knowledge their discussions would not be public property. And if they decided on a course of action requiring money, they could provide it from their own corporate treasures." No blacks, no women, no union members need apply.

Tucker followed their lead. He agreed with their principles and with the 1947 City Plan, the document aimed at wiping "out the obsolescent blighted areas and the costly decaying slums." Away with the old, in with the "New St. Louis." No preservation, no history. Civic progress.

Voters weren't so convinced of the wisdom of this group, however, turning down a bond issue in 1953. But the coalition put the issue back up in May of 1955 and the $110 million measure made it through. The ultimate result was I-64, I-70 and I-44, all part of the national defense system. The Hill was sliced in half. The riverfront was cut away from downtown, preserved for the coming Arch. Soulard was chopped in two. Pruitt-Igoe was well underway and the bulldozers were poised at the gates of Mill Creek Valley where the destruction would begin in 1959, removing 20,000 blacks from their homes.

Loans for suburban housing, especially for whites, were plentiful.

Squabbles over the size of the giant housing project on the North Side ended. Ground breaking at Carr and Jefferson for the first 20 of the 11-story buildings of the Wendell Pruitt project came on May 10, 1952. The first families moved into the project in 1954, quickly filling 80 percent of the apartments.

Reviews by the new tenants were positive. Everything was new and shiny. Plumbing and electricity worked. The final bill by the time the other 13 buildings were finished in 1956 was $57 million, double the original estimate. The second phase of buildings were named after William L. Igoe, a white Congressman from St. Louis who served four terms from 1913 to 1921, a lawyer and head of the city police commission in the thirties. Igoe died aged 71 in 1953 and like Wendell Pruitt never saw completion of his namesake buildings.

By the time all 33 buildings were completed problems began. This housing was nothing like the brick tenements that were dozered out to make room for the modern age. The structures from the mid-nineteenth century lasted 100 years; the life of Pruitt-Igoe was less than 20 years.

The Igoe white-only buildings didn't turn out that way. Since the project was located within the black zone, few whites were willing to move into the imposing apartment buildings. Blacks were the ones losing their tenement apartments to the bulldozers. There were no grocery stores or shopping streets nearby. The project was isolated from the central business district and from industrial jobs.

There were numerous design problems within the buildings, most due to cost saving measures and especially the bizarre feature of having elevators stop on only the fourth, seventh and 10th floors. Mice and roaches driven from bulldozed buildings invaded the buildings. What few green spaces were left were untended by the city and became strewn with garbage. Sewer lines froze. Fires spread quickly before firefighters could respond.

Locks were changed in 1957 because they were so easy to pick. People began to move out in 1960 and rents increased. Couples found that if the man with a job moved out, the woman with her children got a higher subsidy and by 1965, only 7 percent of the men living in the project had a job.

Cramped neighbors became suspicious of each other and grew worn out by constant surveillance by various officials -- police, social workers, project managers, maintenance men. The majority was poor. In 1965, one-third of the families had incomes less than $2,000 a year ($14,000 in 2013). More poor people moved in as the city demolished housing in nearby Mill Creek Valley during the second half of the fifties.

In 1960, the crime rate in the project was lower than that of the city average. But as the buildings decayed, crime erupted. Fights, thefts, attacks ensued. Drug use increased. Vandalism increased. Children, trapped in their apartments, threw things out the windows. There were no bathroom facilities on the first floor. One writer said the project squeezed into one urban area "all of the problems and difficulties that arise from race and poverty and all of the impotence, indifference and hostility with which our society has so far dealt with these problems."

The government gave up. In 1968 residents were urged to find other places to live and on March 15, 1972, the first of two buildings were knocked down as part of a new plan to reduce the density of the project and try to save it. Another implosion took place April 22 and another on July 15. The cameras rolled as the building fell to blasts of dynamite. Clouds of dust billowed into the St. Louis sky.

All plans to rehabilitate the project were abandoned after Richard Nixon became president in January 1973. Demolition was completed in 1976. From then on, the land where Pruitt-Igoe stood was left to its own ends. Woodland took over the spot, leaving a gaping hole on the North Side. Numerous plans were floated over the years. Until, in 2016, a facility for the federal National Geospatial-Intelligence spy agency was approved, ending over 40 years of desolation in a central portion of the North Side.

Several other sixties-style housing developments were built in the city, but all of them failed. The last still standing was the 14-story Blumeyer high rise that survived until 2014 near Grand Boulevard.

Others -- the Darst-Webbe project, Cochran Gardens, Vaughn -- were razed during the nineties and the new century. Blumeyer lasted 46 years and many of its residents moved to new two and three-story buildings that emphasized mixed income residents and open spaces, much like the housing called for by the original Pruitt-Igoe plans.

Looking at the North Side in the second decade of the twenty-first century is to see clearly the catastrophic results of the mistakes made in the late forties and fifties. The housing failures, the loans in the suburbs, the closure of the factories, the building of the raised highways, the empty schools drew the face of today's St. Louis. Crime rose in the empty areas, the crack epidemic wasn't far away. The citizens became nervous and intimidated.

As just about every one in the city is aware, the biggest number for St. Louis population was 1950 at 856,796. Then the cork popped out of the bottle. In 1960 it was down 100,000 to 750,026. Then in 1970 another 130,000 down to 622,236 and by 1980 down 170,000 more to 452,804. After that the flood of lost population became a trickle, losing only 100,000 during the ensuing 30-year period.

The totals put the loss within the city limits at over 400,000 people in the fifties, sixties and seventies, nearly half the population that lived in the city when Joseph Darst was elected.

His inauguration may have been a portent. The last transition of power from Republican to Democrat featured a bizarre donnybrook in City Hall where a dispute during the seating of the aldermen featured shouts and catcalls, insults and booing. The sheriff slugged the parliamentarian. The mayor had to give his inaugural speech outside, away from the raging Board of Aldermen.

The city government did not descend into anarchy. But no matter how hard it tried to save the North Side, things only got worse. The ideas of Civic Progress continued to control the agenda. Opponents to these ideas remained active, but unable to make fundamental changes. The civil rights movement gained momentum in the sixties, but could not stop either the white or black flight.

Many blacks stayed in the city, making up an increasingly large share of the population. The number of blacks also increased in the suburbs, but at a slower rate than whites.

Where the city's black population in 1950 was 153,766, about 17 percent of the total, by the 2010 count it was a bit higher at 156,454, but its share was 49 percent of the total, outnumbering the white population of 140,170. Meanwhile, the population of St. Louis County doubled during the 60 years from 1950 to 2010 from 406,439 in 1950 to 998,954 in 2010. The black population in the county also increased, from 153,766 in 1950 to 235,750 in 2013.

And where the neighborhood Shelley moved into in 1949 was then nearly 100 percent white, in 2015 it was nearly 100 percent black.

Reading this flurry of numbers, of course, is one thing. To take a drive on the North Side of the city is quite another. There is still plenty of life left there, numerous families, a lively population of elderly, church groups and private clubs. But to find that level of normal life takes a little digging, it lies under the surface of a community that outwardly has the look of decline and decay.

J.D. and Ethel Shelley's old house quietly sits as a National Historic Landmark. A small plaque marks its status and it was valued at $45,000 in 2013. It is privately owned and not open to the public.

At Lewis Place the arched gate that once greeted visitors with a grand salute is now locked. To get into the two blocks of houses you drive around the backside of the development, passing two or three other blocks of streets strewn with broken brick and trash, many lots empty of dwellings, many teeth missing from the smile of a neighborhood.

In Lewis Place itself the tradition of proud home ownership lives on. Some tornado damage from 2010 lingers but the houses are intact, several over 120 years old, spared by the various attempts at the final dozer solution. A strong community association and permanent families with adults who hold down steady jobs keep the street together. People help each other out with chores and repairs. Another solid foundation is the nearby Ranken Technical School, a trade school with an enrollment of about 2,500 students.

But nearby there are only a couple of surviving businesses, a couple of stores of the type you see in ghettos all over America, the characteristic barred windows, the shelves half empty or filled with chips and soda, a friendly face behind the counter ready to turn fierce if necessary. A Louisville slugger stands propped against a box of Fritos near the cash register.

Three blocks north of Lewis Place is Dr. Martin Luther King Drive, a six-mile stretch that runs through the middle of the North Side, once the Osage trail west from the river. It was named Easton Avenue in 1881 to honor Rufus Easton, an early St. Louis postmaster. It was renamed Dr. Martin Luther King Drive in 1972 and also covers part of Franklin and a section of Cass. James Earl Ray, an Army veteran born in Alton, Ill., across the river from St. Louis assassinated King in 1968. Some say Ray plotted the killing of King in a South St. Louis bar.

Dr. King Drive looks like many of the more than 900 other such named streets in the United States, centers of the urban ghetto, the "main streets" of a parallel universe in a segregated nation. In St. Louis there is plenty of activity on the street, social clubs, restaurants, churches and rec centers, beauty salons and beauty product outlets. But plenty of empty lots sit between these businesses.

The black comedian Chris Rock has joked, "If a friend calls you on the telephone and says they're lost on Martin Luther King Boulevard and they want to know what they should do, the best response is 'Run!'"

MLK in St. Louis has plenty of broken glass, plenty of lumber awaiting use, plenty of locks, chairs, grates, weedy lots, broken asphalt, hand lettered signs, pawn shops, liquor stores and corner drug markets. There are also a few depictions of the civil rights leader drawn in the rainbow colors of Africa.

There are campaigns to change the street afoot in St. Louis. A postal worker named Melvin White founded Beloved Streets in 2010 and began an attempt to rehabilitate the street. "Dr. King would be turning over in his grave," he says. White developed for a hydroponics factory near his Beloved Streets headquarters to grow lettuce and tomatoes for the Washington University food service supplier.

There was also the controversial $8 billion NorthSide Regeneration plan from mega-developer Paul McKee that included a long stretch of MLK in its two-square-mile footprint. McKee has been buying up property and collecting tax credits beginning in 1999.

The plan has drawn heated comment from supporters (mostly white) who see it as a way to save the North Side and critics (mostly black) who say it has sent hundreds of families packing and done nothing other than create more empty space where houses were bulldozed down, their bricks stolen and sent East for rehabilitation of housing in places like Boston.

Larry Griffin, a handsome white man in his early seventies, tall, fit and well dressed, a working blues guitar player who grew up on the North Side, hasn't ignored his old neighborhood's slide. But, like many thinking people, he doesn't buy the stereotype of the area -- he doesn't see it as a danger zone where white people can enter only at their mortal peril.

Indeed, on Union and MLK near where Griffin grew up, there's nothing particularly ominous to see, just a gas station, an empty lot, a corner shopping strip with a fish market, a beauty supply store, a pawn shop, a car wash across the street. There are some chain link fences to catch the blowing trash, but no reason to expect an imminent drive-by shooting.

Griffin was born in 1944 and well remembers the house his father bought in 1952 on Ashland at the corner of Abner in the 1st Ward. Many of the houses are still there on the quiet street, single-family brick homes, built in the style of the twenties, occupied then by white families, now by black families. His old house is one of them, low slung with a big porch.

This is called the Goodfellow-Wells neighborhood and in 2010 contained 5,745 blacks and 42 whites.

Down the street we see the missing houses, the knocked out teeth. What happened?

> A circle of economic events. You know, jobs dried up, money dried up, people couldn't keep up with payments, couldn't pay the rent, bank foreclosed on the house, house sits vacant, gets condemned, sits vacant for years, can't sell, just sits, too far gone. They just tear it down.
>
> *We drive east over to Union.*
>
> This apartment complex was always here. Johnson's minimart used to be Wally's minimart. Same thing. If you couldn't get something on our block you'd walk over here.
>
> *He points to a garage, car lot and car wash on the corner.*
>
> This has been a body shop all along. My dad used to have his work done here. A landmark.

We find a couple of beauty salons, but across Union sits a rather ominous empty lot, with a lot of unkempt trees and a boarded up building next door to A Touch of Glory, one of the corner's beauty salons. Needles on the ground, trash in the bushes.

Larry points south.

> If you follow Union that way, you get a mile or so, across Delmar, all gentrified. That's where all the nice houses are. Changes completely at Delmar. All the way over until you get there that way it's like this.

North on Union we get to where the giant Chevy plant stood, where no cars have been made since 1981.

The city's auto industry was once second only to Detroit and employed more than 35,000 workers in the region. At the plant at Natural Bridge and Union, Chevy workers banged out 700,000 Corvettes, including every Sting Ray ever made. Over 13,000 worked the plant in the seventies on its 175-acre factory.

> Employed a lot of people, all union labor, I might add. My Dad had a restaurant there, ran 24 hours to feed the workers. They

> made the Corvettes, Chevys and all the frames for any GM car. That's the job every workingman wanted, UAW.

We cross over I-70, one of the highways that cut one side of the neighborhood off from the other.

> Okay, now once you cross the viaduct, you are coming into Walnut Park. This is where St. Louis gets rated with such a high crime number -- recently as the most dangerous city in the country -- is because of the drive-by shootings in Walnut Park. The per capita shooting number is inflated from this area.
>
> *Gangs?*
>
> Some. Or personal, stupid, wanna-be gangs, kids get some money, get a car, put some wheels on it, get a gun, do a shoot, you're a gang. Unfortunately, that's the culture. It's cooled off a little bit, but it doesn't take much to push the statistics up. There's a nice church there. It always amazes me, the faith that African Americans have.

Across the roadway is Bellefonte Cemetery, the huge burial ground for whites that includes many pioneers and many celebrities. All white.

On the other side is still Walnut Park, one of the city's designated crime hot spots. All black.

> Here's a tidy little neighborhood. That's a black neighborhood. There's black neighborhoods here that don't look a damn bit different than they did 40 years ago. This is one. You can drive into this neighborhood and see how people have kept up their houses just like they always were. Walnut Park. They keep them up just as good as any white people in the city. It ain't about that. It's about pride. That place has been a garage since I was knee high to a grasshopper.

We swing back around to his old neighborhood again. I ask about what happened as the whites moved out as he was growing up.

He points to the desegregation of the schools as a major reason, following the *Brown vs. Board of Education* decision by the Supreme Court in 1954.

He said that before the decision his neighborhood was virtually all white, outside the black zone except for one street, Semple Street where the covenant had been broken and had gone all black.

> It had been that way for generations, a black street in a white neighborhood. When we moved in they said it was mixed but this one street was all black and the rest was all white. When they passed Brown vs. Board of Education, we integrated the schools here in 1956-57 then things started changing. The black kids that were on Semple Avenue then started going to what was rightly their neighborhood school, my school, which had previously been an all white school.
>
> Before that they would walk a mile over to Benton School on North Kingshighway that had been built in 1896. My school was right on Semple -- they lived right on the street where the school was -- where they couldn't go to. On Semple, that's where the school was. They couldn't go there. These people could not go to this school that sits right in their back yard. They had to walk a mile. As a young kid I understood how fucked up that was. I had some racist buddies.
>
> *So the whites started moving out?*
>
> It was a gradual thing, from the fifties on. By the late sixties, early seventies the white flight had really set in.
>
> *At first, people didn't notice it was happening?*
>
> Right, it was the racist attitudes. A working class man, say, white, say, he's saying 'I'm working here at the Chevrolet plant; I'm doing good for my family. And now what's going to happen -- the niggers are going to move in -- and there goes the property values.' So whoever gets out first wins and whoever get out last loses -- it's all incrementally a loss for the property holder.
>
> That's how he sees it. 'The longer you stick around the less you're going to have of your American dream. It's time to get out because "here they come." Strictly a racist attitude. And in this town they tore down the ghetto.
>
> *You mean across town in Mill Creek Valley?*
>
> Right, my Dad had another restaurant over there. Burgers, cafeteria line, mashed potatoes and gravy, sweet potato pie, right off the downtown on Jefferson and Olive. Streetcars running both ways, carrying 800,000 people around town, back in the fifties.

Chapter Twenty-One

Jazz in the Forties: Clark Terry, Miles Davis

1941-1950

They take hold of you, they do not lull you. Connecting rod, shaft, spinning top. They beat you, they turn, they crash, the rhythm grips you and shakes you. You bounce in your seat, faster and faster . . . the musicians don't look the same; they speed ahead, they infect each other with this haste, they look mad, taut, as if they were searching for something . . . you have to shout; the band has become an immense spinning top; if you stop, the top stops and falls over. You shout, they shriek, they whistle, they are possessed, you are possessed . . . the whole crowd shouts in time, you can't even hear the jazz,

-- Jean-Paul Sartre, New York, 1947

Clark Terry, a 24-year-old trumpet player from the South Side of St. Louis, was discharged from the Navy June 29, 1945. His war experience involved no danger, no combat, no bombs or guns. Just jazz, high quality jazz, performed with some of the great players in the country, an experience that led to a long and lucrative career, playing on over 900 recordings in nearly 70 years.

The names on this St. Louisan's discography ring out -- Ella Fitzgerald, Oscar Peterson, Dizzy Gillespie, Dinah Washington, Aretha Franklin, Ray Charles, Thelonious Monk, Billie Holiday, Gerry Mulligan, Sarah Vaughan. He performed with the Duke Ellington Orchestra, the Count Basie Orchestra, and the Woody Herman Orchestra.

Terry spent the war at the Great Lakes Naval Training Center, wearing a G-clef on the cuffs of his trim Navy blues, jamming every weekday with other black musicians in a special, volunteer unit organized by a fellow St. Louisan to train thousands of players for swing bands that fanned out to military bases around the country during the war.

On weekends, he'd play Chicago, Milwaukee or Waukegan, in clubs, hotels, on the radio, in concert halls, at outdoor festivals, at ballparks, football fields and along the shores of Lake Michigan. "While bombs were dropping we played our hearts out to keep up morale of our troops," he said of the Great Lakes Experience, joined by "the hippest music with the hottest stars," including visiting players such as Lionel Hampton and Lena Horne. "I couldn't have asked for more."

Terry was an unlikely success. He was born Dec. 14, 1920, into a family of 11 children headed by an abusive father who gave him regular beatings. The family lived in a three-room flat with no electricity or hot water in a strictly segregated black neighborhood near the Mississippi River. His mother died when he was "six or seven." His father worked for Laclede Gas and when union organizers came to his apartment urging him to join a strike he broke out his front window and began firing a shotgun.

As a boy of five, Terry saw a parade in his neighborhood and was mightily impressed with the trumpet players. From then on he battled to make the trumpet his life, overcoming obstacle after obstacle, the first of which was his father, who forbid him to play. But Clark didn't listen to that, instead he heard the sound of jazz coming from the boats on the river, he heard the beat of the rhythms from the neighborhood churches, he listened to a friend's homemade radio -- a primitive crystal set amplified by the echo of a big mixing bowl.

One night, he heard the Duke Ellington band on the crystal set. "I wanted a band like that," he wrote in his autobiography. "Had to have one." He got neighborhood kids together to form a street band. He blew on a kazoo made out of a comb and wax paper, his brother played drums on a bushel basket. Another kid made a tuba out of a tin beer cup and a hose. Another plucked a taut rope tied to an upside down washtub to make the sound of a bass. They played "Tiger Rag" and made fifty cents from a crowd on the Labor Day holiday in 1931. Clark Terry was 10 years old, a paid professional.

By the next Thanksgiving, Terry had moved up from kazoo to trumpet, fashioning his own horn from materials gathered in a junkyard near his house, blowing a lead pipe mouthpiece. A few weeks later his neighbors took up a collection, raised $12.50 and brought the young musician a real trumpet. An older sister was married to a tuba player in a local dance band and when his father was away at work, the musician came to Terry's apartment and taught him how play.

When he was 12, Terry's father, known as "Mr. Son" in the neighborhood, found out Clark had saved money from a paper route and a job collecting ashes and put it toward a bicycle, breaking Mr. Son's decree that all family earnings went to him. Rather than absorb another beating, Terry took his trumpet and rode his bike five miles across town to his sister's apartment. She took him in and he never saw his father again.

As a teenager, Clark Terry was generally on his own. His sister worked in a bar, his brother-in-law, Sy, was often on the road playing music, but when he was home he helped Terry learn the trumpet. Without first realizing it, Terry's move to his sister's house away from the South Side and Mr. Son had put him squarely in the heart of the leading entertainment district in St. Louis -- Mill Creek Valley.

His sister's place wasn't far from Union Station and the Midtown Hotel, a crossroads in the center of the city where the flow of musicians stayed and played in numerous theaters, clubs and house parties at the very center of black cultural life in St. Louis in the thirties, forties and most of the fifties. By 1934, Terry was in the seventh grade at Lincoln Junior High, making new friends, learning more trumpet, listening to the radio and his sister's 78s, and soaking up the neighborhood vibe.

Life was good: "Personal jazz lessons, a comfortable couch to sleep on, and a whole lot of love." And Mr. Son was nowhere around, the beatings were over.

He auditioned for the Tom Powell Post #77 Drum and Bugle Corps, one of dozens of such community bands that dotted the city. The American Legion post dates back to World War I, the oldest black post in the city. The corps practiced on a dusty empty lot and since Lincoln had no music program, this was Terry's first chance to play in an organized band, a band that was soon ready to compete in the state championship competition.

The group marched around the field every Saturday and most Sundays. Terry played a G-note bugle with no values. All the notes came from embouchure -- squeezing his lips together for the high notes and letting them go to blow low. In six months he had learned a lot about breath control and how to use the jaw muscles to play that horn. And by then it was April 1935 and his drum and bugle was on its way to compete in the state Legion championship.

"All us corps boys were lined up as neatly as possible on Market Street at Union Station," Terry remembered. "What a sight we were. Twenty-five colored boys, all sizes, heights, and shades of brown. Teeth were flashing in the sunlight from the big smiles on everyone's face." He'd never ridden a train before. Along side his horn he carried a paper bag lunch of jack salmon sandwich and potato chips.

Tom Powell Post won the competition and brought home a silver trophy. The band tore up the show in Jefferson City, cutting the rug in a more rhythmic style than the competition, "showing off our fancy footwork, cutting sharp turns with abrupt hesitations, up and down the field rapidly, stopping, moving in zigzags, shoving our horn bells high and way down low, high notes screaming in tune, dust flying, sweat dropping." The large crowd surrounding the field cheered and stomped.

Terry was ready for high school when he got back with that trophy, he couldn't wait to enroll in the Vashon High band program. But he was surprised when he found out the principal of the school looked at jazz as the devil's music and relegated Terry to a trombone. The school wouldn't let any student bring their own instrument to class or play jazz in school.

The 15-year-old Terry wasn't about to give up on the trumpet, however. He quickly organized his own band of renegade players to keep up the jazz riffs off campus. They called themselves the Vashon High Swingsters and kept up a campaign to show that there was nothing wrong with jazz. Terry joined the glee club, the debate team and the school newspaper. All summer he cleaned the apartment of the band teacher hoping he would be allowed to play the trumpet in the school band.

He also hooked up with the Sumner High School Swingsters from the other black high school in town, where a more progressive administration let the kids play jazz in the band. Sumner was located in a more affluent black neighborhood, further west and north from Mill Creek, in The Ville. The Sumner band's student leader was Ernie Wilkins, from whom Terry learned to read the big band charts that showed large groups how to play the jazz compositions of composers like Ellington and Basie.

Terry also joined a "scab band" -- outside the musicians union -- called Dollar Bill and His Small Change. Bill set up his piano in the middle of the street and closed off either end for a block party with beer and hamburgers and a long night of jazz music. Bill took the band down to the levee to the dive bars and greasy spoons scattered around the waterfront in the late thirties before the arrival of the wrecking ball.

Terry managed to convince the Vashon assistant principal to let the Swingsters play for the spring dance when he was a junior. By 1939, Terry was ready to graduate with honors from Vashon and go on to college, two scholarships under his hat and the future looking brighter and brighter. Then he and his girlfriend made a big mistake, she got pregnant and Terry found himself at City Hall with his sister and the girlfriend's father taking part in a grim marriage ceremony that included no music, no flowers and no smiles.

The principal of Vashon called him in and expelled him, no graduation, no scholarships, no college. His brother-in-law got him an audition with the highly respected Jeter-Pillars Jazz Orchestra, but he wasn't ready for the complicated charts required in the band. He dropped down another notch and landed a traveling gig with the Reuben and Cherry Carnival. When Terry asked Turk, the band leader, how much the gig paid, the boss, a tall, lighted-skinned man with sideburns, a goatee and 2-inch long fingernails, leaned back and told the fledging trumpet player, "Depends on who comes to the carnival."

Two weeks later Clark Terry was at Union Station at the start of his first professional road trip, waiting amid the crowds of "foxy women, midgets, muscular cats, plain folk and the fattest woman I'd ever seen.

Colored people stood in one area and whites a little distance away." He was decked out in a "hip, black double breasted suit and shiny black McAns," the height of fashion in thirties footwear.

As the train rolled south into Mississippi he met a woman named Ethel Hut, who performed under the name Big Fat Mamma, a motherly sort also from St. Louis who took the teenage Terry under her plentiful wings. She laughed at his jokes and watched out for him. He wasn't a tall kid, but he was tough, strengthened by years of early morning chores, paper routes, boxing (in the gym and on the street), running track, and riding his bicycle. He had grown into a positive, smiling, upbeat teenager, always looking for the bright side of a situation.

The carnival was the hardest job he'd ever encountered, seven days a week, seven shows a day. Sweat, dust, rain, mud. "Tired didn't define what I felt at the end of the day." Soon his bright cheer faced a severe challenge when the boss handed him his pay for a week -- $2.50. But he didn't give up, learning as he went, finishing out the carnival run and the nineteen-thirties in Florida. He wanted to get back home but didn't have rail fare. Instead, he joined Ida Cox and Her Dark Town Scandals.

Cox was a Georgia blues singer who started performing in the early twenties and had made it to Carnegie Hall on Christmas Eve of 1939 for a concert presented by the blues promoter John Hammond called "From Spirituals to Swing." This was the second of two powerful performances that became legendary as a showcase for African-American music played to a mixed audience. The event became legendary for carrying meaning beyond its stirring sound. For there, the black music community was exposed to the leaders of the American political left wing and given a glimpse of what was possible in an integrated environment. Rock 'n' roll and R&B were just around the corner.

But Cox's brush with the integrated musical future was brief. By the time Terry signed up for the troupe it was back on the Jim Crow roads of the South, a long way from the bright lights of New York. As the forties began, Cox, Terry and the Dark Town Scandals were on a rattling bus with no heat and no toilet riding through the hostile South, employing a white driver to fend off the police. Terry said Cox was demanding and bossy, a giant sized woman who "cussed like a sailor."

For six months, the show pushed on. Nobody in the band made money. The weather was too cold in the North, too hot in the South. Terry finally quit when he heard that Turk's carnival was nearby and he gladly rejoined the show. His former boss didn't last long, however. The show folded and a bunch from the carnival piled into the back of a flatbed truck headed back to St. Louis, 750 miles away. Four other carnival refugees and nine monkeys in cages composed the passenger list on the back of the truck. Turk and his girlfriend rode up front in the heated cab.

As usual, Terry made the best of it. He gave the monkeys names -- Twitchy, Chatty, No-Tail, Old Man Mose, etc. -- shared his food and found the monkeys didn't want to be bothered any more than the humans wanted to be bothered. "The trip wasn't too bad," he said, "other than the smell and the noise." But he was mighty happy to get out of that truck on Grand Avenue in St. Louis.

Terry spent the next year, his 20th, playing a small joint where his sister worked, struggling through a brief, difficult stint with Fate Marable's band and taking a couple more ill-fated road trips, one of which left him in the Flint, Mich., city jail for nine days on a phony charge of being a pimp. After being beaten up in his cell and called any number of racist names by the police, he was released and made it back to his sister's apartment in St. Louis in one piece.

But a new worry rattled his calm -- the Japanese bombed the U.S. base at Pearl Harbor in December 1941 and America entered a world war that had been raging for three years. Clark Terry, 21, was prime draft age. He spent a lot of his time rubbing his lucky rabbit's foot while back on his sister's living room couch, listening to jazz records. He had joined the musicians union during the run with Marable, however, and the membership paid off -- at the union hall soon after his time in the Flint jail he was tapped by the trombone payer Len Bowden for a brief gig that provided another sharp turn in Clark Terry's musical fortunes, a turn that would set up him for life.

By this time, early 1942, the riverboat scene had sharply declined but jazz flourished in St. Louis. Hundreds of swing dancers spilled across the shining hardwood floors of dozens of ballrooms around the city -- including the Chase, the Club Caprise at the Coronado, the Casa Loma, the Arcadia, the Castle, the Westminster, the Imperial -- and an even greater number of clubs kept the city's entertainment humming deep into the early morning.

Len Bowden's band wasn't as popular as the city's big three -- the George Hudson Orchestra, Eddie Randle's St. Louis Blue Devils and the Jeter-Pillars Orchestra -- but Bowden had a following that kept his group in steady work, an outfit that was solid and disciplined but that also could let go beyond the charted arrangements on occasion.

Bowden came from Alabama where he had organized a student group called the Bama State Collegians that traveled to New York in the late thirties, recording the hit "Tuxedo Junction." Bowden left the group after another musician edged him out of the leadership, heading to St. Louis to join George Hudson's outfit. Terry met him shortly after he came to town. Terry tried out for Bowden's next gig at the Castle.

Terry blew a confident horn at his Thursday audition and Friday night was decked out in the trumpet section of the Melody Makers, standing on stage at the Castle, a second floor ballroom in midtown, gazing at the reflecting lights sparkling off a revolving chandelier. Benches lined the walls but there were no tables, just an expanse of hardwood. The fancy dancers moved quickly to the center of the floor as "Franklin D. Roosevelt Jones" rang from Bowden's orchestra; a mixed crowd did the jitterbug, flipping and flying. Terry was paid $5 for the four-hour show, twice as much as he made in a week with the carnival.

Shortly thereafter, Bowden dropped a big surprise on Terry, who was still looking over his shoulder at the draft. The Navy was organizing musicians for big bands aimed at boosting morale across the country and Bowden's connections in New York and at the Tuskeegee Institute in Alabama had paid off. Made bandmaster for the program, he was in charge of recruiting musicians to volunteer to join the Navy and be part of a large program of military, concert and jazz bands.

Bowden was looking around St. Louis for players and Terry accepted. Others who joined up were trombone player and arranger Ernie Wilkins from Sumner High and Eddie Randle's band; Charles Pillars from the Jeter-Pillars band; Russell Boone, the drummer from the Tom Powell Bugle Corps, as well as players from the George Hudson and Fate Marable bands, many who went on to long careers as players and teachers.

After the war, for an example, Wilkins joined Hudson's band in St. Louis before heading to New York to become a stalwart in Count Basie's orchestra in the fifties. Wilkins' arrangement of "Every Day I Have the Blues" put Basie on the hit parade in 1954. Wilkins lived until 1999 and did jazz arrangements for such luminaries as Oscar Peterson, Sarah Vaughn and Ray Charles. Wilkins moved to Denmark in the late seventies and continued writing jazz compositions until his death.

Pillars had come out of a twenties band called the Alphonso Trent Orchestra, a popular southwest outfit that also included James Jeter. As the Jeter-Pillars Orchestra they played Cleveland until 1934 when they moved to St. Louis. George Hudson joined up as lead trumpet and the band began to play the Plantation Club, where it became a fixture. Jeter-Pillars played the Apollo in New York, toured the Pacific for the USO, played in New England for three months, then broke up after the war as the swing era died in the late forties.

Before its demise, however, the Jeter-Pillars Orchestra nurtured two of the most influential and innovative jazzmen to come through St. Louis -- Charlie Christian and Jimmy Blanton.

Christian came out of Oklahoma City, also influenced by the Trent orchestra before landing in St. Louis in the mid-thirties, still a teenager. He was one of the first jazzmen to play an electric guitar and is often given credit for inventing the style, but his work came a couple of years after the work of a St. Louis native named Floyd Smith, a pioneer of the instrument while in the Jeter-Pillars Band. Smith also played the Hawaiian steel, the acoustic guitar and the ukulele with such steamboat bandleaders as Creath and Dewey Jackson.

Smith played an electric solo on a recording called "Floyd Smith's Blues" in 1939, the same year Lonnie Johnson, working with Roosevelt Sykes, also recorded solo electric guitar. That same year, Christian left Jeter-Pillars to join Benny Goodman in Los Angeles. Christian created an immediate sensation with an electric solo in a Los Angeles restaurant. He wasn't able to enjoy his fame for long, however, dead from TB in 1942.

Blanton was another innovator who died young. Born in Chattanooga in 1918, he came to St. Louis in the mid-thirties and played the boats with Marable before joining Jeter-Pillars in 1937, a sensation from the start. He also played with the Randle band and Dewey Jackson. He got his first standup bass at the St. Louis Music Store. The veteran musician Singleton Palmer was there and remembered Blanton's play as "far ahead of bass players not only here but all over the country. Nobody had heard it before."

Duke Ellington, who was playing the Coronado, heard Blanton at a jam above Jesse Johnson's restaurant in 1939. The Duke hired the young bass man on the spot. Ellington carried two bass players for a few shows until his regular player quit, saying he could not compete with Blanton's skill. Like Christian, his style foreshadowed the end of swing and the coming of the bebop innovations of the forties that transformed jazz. But, also like Christian, Blanton did not live to see the change, another victim of tuberculosis, also in 1942.

Len Bowden gave the Navy's pitch to Clark Terry outside the union hall on a hot summer afternoon. Terry bit. Soon he was in Camp Robert Smalls, ready for what became known to musicians as the Great Lakes Experience. The base was 40 miles north of Chicago, 60 miles south of Milwaukee, on the shores of Lake Michigan. Fully segregated, all the musicians were black. The St. Louis contingent was joined by players from all over the country, 5,000 total during the course of the next three years.

Many came from New York, fresh from the Harlem Renaissance. Bowden and his men trained contingents of recruits, usually 25 each, forming them into swing bands that played out in the camps all over America and eventually the world, especially the South Pacific.

Off times from the training were spent jamming and doing concerts and benefits in Chicago, Milwaukee and Waukegan, Ill., the closest town to the base. One of the shows involved a fund-raising drive in 1944, a citywide "Forty Million in Forty Days" campaign to raise money to replace the cruiser *Chicago*, sunk by the Japanese. The show featured a crowd favorite -- Stump the Band -- where songs were called out and played by Bowden, Terry and his cohorts. This "A" orchestra also performed a series of Sunday shows on base that included all kinds of music, from classical to swing.

With this experience in his pocket it was no wonder that following his discharge in 1945 Terry was ready for the big time. Back in St. Louis, now staying at the apartment of Ethel Hut, the giant woman he had met on the carnival tour, he quickly landed a job in the George Hudson Orchestra, the top band in town. A confident, experienced young man, Terry decked himself out in a pawnshop zoot suit -- complete with a double-breasted jacket with wide shoulders, pants with big knees and skinny legs, and a pair extra long AAA Thom McAn shoes.

He met Hudson at the Castle. Hudson was even shorter than Terry, with a conked hair-do, medium brown skin and clothes that defined postwar hip. Hudson's regular gig was the Plantation Club, often backing traveling stars such as Lionel Hampton, Ella Fitzgerald, the Mills Brothers and King Cole. The routine put the Hudson group out front for two dance sets, then as backing for the rest of the night behind the headliner.

The club was run by organized crime figures, segregated and very plush. Terry took a larger and larger role in the organization of the band, doing arrangements, helping to make the Hudson band the hottest in town. Hudson came from Mississippi, born in 1910. He joined the Trent Band in 1930, went on to the Oklahoma Blues Devils and then the Jeter-Pillars Band in St. Louis in 1934. Hudson organized his first band under his own name in 1942, traveled in the late forties as the swing bands declined and by 1951 had settled into the moderate local scene.

Terry was tempted by several offers as the forties came to an end, working with such national greats as Charlie Barnet, Eddie "Cleanhead" Vinson and Charlie Ventura. Terry waited for the right offer, watching as the St. Louis jazz scene slowed in the post-war downturn. The right offer came in 1948 -- the Count Basie Orchestra, where he remained until 1951, when he moved into the pinnacle of his profession -- the Duke Ellington band.

Before he left St. Louis Terry met Miles Dewey Davis III. Like Terry, Davis played the trumpet.

Terry had a couple of encounters with Davis before the war, introduced to him in 1940 by Elwood Buchanan, the music teacher at Lincoln High in East St. Louis. Buchanan was a man who enjoyed sharing a beer with Terry at the union hall.

Terry attended "Buke's" music class where he watched as the stern teacher threatened to whack the 15-year-old Davis on the knuckles with a ruler. Terry remembered the student as a dark-skinned kid, timid and thin. "Stop shaking those notes and play straight," the teacher told his student. Later that year Terry saw Davis again during a roadhouse gig in Carbondale, Ill., the home of Southern Illinois University about 100 miles southeast of St. Louis.

Davis was in Carbondale to play with his high school band. Remembering his encounter in Buke's class he approached Terry and, as Davis recalls, "I asked him something about playing trumpet." The young Miles was in awe of Terry, who was six years older and a pro, on a paying gig, while Davis was in his high school band uniform, dreaming about his life as a player.

"Clark had on this hip coat and this bad, beautiful scarf around his neck. He was wearing hip butcher boy shoes and a bad hat cocked ace-deuce." Terry blew the youngster off, saying he didn't want to "talk about no trumpet with all them pretty girls bouncing around." Even though he was put off, Davis vowed that by the next time they met "I was going to be as hip, even hipper."

The next time they met was indeed different, a very different time, 1946. Terry had mustered out of the Navy; Davis had graduated from high school and landed a job with Eddie Randle's Blues Devils. The hottest after hours jam in those days was at the Elks Hall in an all-black club called the Rhumboogie, where the spillover from the shows at the Plantation, the Rivieria and other top jazz clubs landed for the late night action. Randle's band was playing that night and Terry had finished his gig with George Hudson, stopped off at a small joint for a couple of drinks out of a coffee cup, then dropped by the Rhumboogie for a nightcap. Terry remembered:

> As we made it up a long flight of stairs. I heard this fantastic trumpet playing. It was really wailing. I knew it was somebody I'd never heard around St. Louis before. I ran up the rest of the stairs, and there was this little timid-looking, dark-skinned cat up on stage, blowing some smoking notes!
>
> A few minutes later I walked up to him and I said "Man, that was mean!"
>
> He sneered at me and he said, "Yeah, motherfucker! You come here to hear me play now. But you fluffed me off when I met you in Carbondale! Remember?"
>
> I looked at him again and then I said, "Yeah, I remember. You're Buke's student, right? Dewey. Right?'

> He said, "Yeah, I'm Miles Dewey Davis, motherfucker!"
> I said, "Okay, Miles. It's cool."

Indeed, it was. Davis said Terry "became my idol on the instrument." Terry said not only was it the beginning of a lifelong friendship but also that night was the "beginning of my vow to never fluff anybody off again."

Terry and Davis grew up on opposite sides of the river and on opposite sides of the economic coin. When Terry was seven years old he was hauling ashes from the dingy alleyways of the tenements on the South Side of St. Louis. When Davis was seven he was riding a horse at his grandfather's farm in Arkansas.

Davis III was born May 26, 1926, in Alton, Ill., a small town just north of East St. Louis, made famous before the Civil War as a major stop on the underground railroad of slaves escaping from the South. On Nov. 7, 1837, Alton was scene of the murder of Elijah Lovejoy, an abolitionist printer who had been run out of St. Louis by pro-slavery mobs. After he set up a press on the east side of the river Lovejoy was attacked by a white mob, shot five times in the stomach and thrown in the water. His warehouse was burned and the press thrown in after him.

The first Miles Dewey Davis, the trumpet player's grandfather, was an educated black man who worked as a bookkeeper for a white plantation owner after the war, a remarkable man who made enough money to purchase 500 acres of land. During the period around the turn of the nineteenth century, however, he was run off his land by whites eager to claim the property and relocated in Alton, where Miles Henry Davis (sometimes referred to as Miles Dewey Davis II) was born in 1900.

Henry Davis was another man of education and achievement. He skipped high school and went to Arkansas Baptist College in Little Rock, a school that trained ministers, and graduated in 1919. From there he attended the nation's oldest degree-granting black college, Lincoln University in Pennsylvania, then transferred to Northwest University near Chicago and obtained a degree in dentistry with a specialty in dental surgery, all by time he was 24.

As a child, Davis III was told that "people in our family were special people -- artists, businessmen, professionals and musicians who played for the plantation owners back in the old days before slavery was over." His father's brother, Ferdinand Davis, attended Harvard, studied in Berlin, traveled the world and was the editor of *Color* magazine. His uncle was "stylish as a motherfucker" "a brilliant guy" who talked to his young nephew about Caesar and Hannibal. "He made me feel dumb." And so did his father. As a boy he looked at the wall of Doc Davis' dentist's office, saw his father's three college degrees and thought, "I hope he won't ask me to do that."

By 1962, when Miles Davis' music was bringing in money well into the six figures he said Doc Davis "was worth more than me." Doc was a high-priced dental surgeon, the first to care for blacks in East St. Louis, and also the breeder of expensive hogs on his farm north of the city. The family lived in a 13-room house in a white neighborhood. His mother, Cleota Henry, played violin and piano and decked herself out in mink coats and diamonds.

The family moved from Alton a few miles south to East St. Louis before Miles was 10 and Doc Davis set up his practice in the middle of the thriving city, in an area that had recovered from the race riot of 1917 economically. Still, there were no shortage of the reminders of segregation and racism. Soon after the family moved to the city, when Miles was still in elementary school, a white man came running down the street pointing at his house in the white neighborhood yelling "Nigger! Nigger!"

Doc Davis would have none of it. "My father went hunting him with a shotgun." He didn't catch the man but Doc said later that the incident left an impression. "I don't think Miles, a sensitive boy, ever forgot it."

Miles said later, "You're going to run into that Jim Crow thing regardless how wealthy you are. I can't get no freedom. Having money has helped me once in a while, but I'm not looking for help."

His mother wanted him to play the violin in the classical style. But St. Louis was a horn town, a trumpet town. As a child, Miles heard about dozens of famous trumpet players who had been on the boats, in the clubs, from Louis Armstrong to Duke Ellington to George Hudson. He listened to the radio late at night all through the thirties and into the forties, hearing Ellington, Lester Young, Coleman Hawkins, Billy Eckstine and Dizzy Gillespie. He heard the story of Charlie Christian. He met Clark Terry.

He got his first horn in 1936, age 10. He met Elwood Buchanan at the Attucks Grade School during sixth grade. The teacher came once a week to give lessons at the school and also taught at the Lincoln in East St. Louis, a public school where Davis went to both junior and senior high. Buchanan had his teeth fixed by Doc Davis; they shared a few beers now and then. Buke urged Doc to buy his son a trumpet and on Miles' 13th birthday, the year being 1939, Doc agreed.

The sound Davis learned during the next few years, the sound that made him -- with Armstrong -- the most famous horn player in American history was once known as the St. Louis sound. For Davis this sound came from Buchanan -- "no vibrato," the teacher would say, "fast and light -- no vibrato."

Davis also learned from Buchanan's teacher, Joseph Gustat, a classical trumpet player for the St. Louis Symphony who charged $2.50 for half an hour. Lessons from Gustat (also referred as Gustav or Gustaph) were far out of range for Terry. But Davis was on the other end of the scale and once in high school he made the trek on the streetcar to learn from a master.

Gustat insisted that Davis use a mouthpiece on his trumpet made by another German musician, Gustav Heim, who in 1904 and 1905 was the first chair with the St. Louis symphony and the inventor of the mouthpiece that determined the St. Louis sound. Heim's career was sterling and St. Louis played a big role. His name is lost in the vapor of history, but his effect on jazz in America through the playing of Miles Davis should not be forgotten.

Gustav Heim was born in Schleusingen, Germany, near Frankfurt on May 8, 1879. He studied trumpet under his father and at school and played cornet solo in the military band. In 1904 he immigrated to St. Louis in time for the World's Fair where his talent and distinctive sound landed him an immediate job in the prestigious Louisiana Purchase Exposition orchestra.

He went on to play in several other symphony orchestras, in Philadelphia, Boston, Detroit, and New York, where he was also a teacher before he died at 54 in 1933.

Heim trained Gustat. Gustat trained Buchanan, Davis' other teacher, so the progression of German influence on Miles Davis was clear. The Heim mouthpiece first used by Davis was made by the Frank Holton

Company, then in later years by Giardinelli. The Holton catalogue of 1920 noted that Heim "uses and assisted in perfecting the Holton trumpet" and says Heim was praised by "practically every noted (symphony) director who has visited America."

When Gustat first heard Davis he wasn't impressed. But the young Miles also wasn't distressed, he just practiced all the harder. His brother, Vernon, said he would hear him in the basement, practicing "long tones, slowly, looking for quality." At 13, his first gig was in Belleville, Ill., a white community near East St. Louis that was the local headquarters of the Ku Klux Klan. He made $6 playing for a white crowd accompanied by a sax player and a drummer from Lincoln High.

He would also play with friends at his house, welcoming as many as 18 players into his spacious basement. Still in high school he also played at Huff's Garden, a joint close to his house, and another place called the Moonlight Inn. He played Ned Love's, an East Side institution where performers from Lonnie Johnson to Tommy Bankhead performed over the years. Love's was located in another small town, Centerville, Ill., and had a big stage with a house rhythm section on hand.

There was a lot of blues played at these jams, as well as jazz. The blues reminded Miles of music he heard on his grandfather's farm in Arkansas, what he called "the rural sound." The sounds he started developing in these early years, the sound encouraged especially by Buke and Gustat were rounded sounds "with no attitude in it, a voice with not too much tremolo and not too much bass." This was the sound that could also be found in Bix Beiderbeck, rooted in the European brass bands. Within it, however, Davis was able to find the blues, an almost vocal quality that served him well in later years.

This combination of European brass and American blues once again demonstrated the St. Louis sound, the confluence of city and rural, the joining of different styles to make something new -- what Davis called "that St. Louis thing."

In 1942, he'd met a girl. Miles was now 16, still shy. The girl was a senior in high school; he was still a sophomore. She had a part-time job in St. Louis and she believed he would be famous someday if only he would step out of the world of his family and friends. He needed a push and Irene

Cawthon gave it to him. Buke had been pushing Miles to try out for Eddie Randle's band and Irene joined the effort.

Randle responded. Irene carried the trumpet with Miles to the Castle Ballroom and Miles stepped out in front of the crowd. He didn't impress the other players, but Randle saw something and hired him on the spot, saying the youngster "had the fundamentals." Just a few weeks later the band members played the Elks Club jam where Miles was on stage with two guys from out of town, Sonny Stitt and Howard McGee, players who brought with them the first sounds of bebop.

Randle said that night in 1943 Miles Davis began "growing out of this world. He was good and he didn't know it. He had a beautiful sound."

Things started happening fast.

He saw Charlie Parker, a jazz cat so fast on the sax he was called "Yardbird," then "The Bird." Davis then sat in with Kansas City sax man Lester Young at the Riviera, Jordan Chambers' club on Delmar, a gig that led to several offers.

A medium level player named Tiny Bradshaw asked Davis to join his touring band. Other offers came from Illinois Jacquet and McKinney's Cotton Pickers. But the Doc and Miles' mother wouldn't allow Miles to travel, but he wasn't too disappointed. He wasn't so bad off. He was just 17, playing Rhumboogie with Eddie Randle and the St. Louis Blue Devils, making $100 a week, driving his father's car to gigs. He already owned 10 suits.

Miles stuck with Randle, finishing high school, working his way up to musical director in the band. He learned his trade and wrote away to the Julliard School of Music in New York City for an application. He was accepted for the fall of 1944. He dreamed of playing with the bebop cats in New York City.

He got his dream sooner than expected, and it came in St. Louis. And it came with the help of an unusual ally, Jim Crow.

The Billy Eckstine Band, which included both Parker and trumpet all-star Dizzy Gillespie, came to play the Plantation in July 1944. The Bird and Diz weren't inclined to follow the rules of Jim Crow segregation. So when they and other band members walked into the club through the front door instead of the black entrance in back, a table of mobsters took note. The gig started, Sarah Vaughn was the singer, the mobsters settled down and all seemed well.

But during the break Dizzy came down off the bandstand and sat at a table with some white customers. This further perturbed the mob guys who started making noises about the band to the effect that it had to go.

Parker joined Diz at the table. One of the white men stared at Parker.

"What do you want? Am I bothering you?" Parker said. There was a brief standoff. That was rough enough for the club manager; the show was over. The next night the Eckstine band moved to the all-black Rivieria Club, Jordan Chambers' place on Delmar.

Davis heard about the move and started hanging around the Riviera listening to rehearsals, determined to meet Parker. One night, one of the trumpet players started coughing blood and had to be replaced. Gillespie remembered a kid with the trumpet hanging in the hallway and Miles got a tryout.

He made the grade and played with his heroes for two weeks to finish out the gig, but Eckstine wasn't impressed.

"I let him sit in so as to not hurt his feelings," Eckstine said later, "but he sounded terrible, he couldn't play at all." So when the band left St. Louis to continue the tour, Miles was left behind.

Nonetheless, the impact of those two weeks can't be underestimated. Davis had been depressed after Terry enlisted. The two players had been working together at Doc Davis' house. Miles, finished with high school, already was leaning toward New York. But playing with Eckstine's band "changed my life."

> I decided right then and there that I had to leave St. Louis and live in New York City where these bad musicians were.
>
> I've come close to matching the feeling of that night (at the Riviera) in 1944 in music, when I first heard Diz and Bird, but I've never quite got there. I've gotten close, but not all the way there. I'm always looking for it, listening and feeling for it, though, trying to always feel in it and through the music I play every day. Man, it was something.

In late September 1944, he boarded a train at Union Station for New York, passed his Julliard audition, started classes and began private lessons with William Vacchiano, the principle trumpet for the New York Philharmonic, blowing his horn through that Heim mouthpiece, diving into the clubs of Manhattan at night, listening to the birth of bebop, the fast tempo, the virtuoso style that imitated the scat singers of the thirties and was heard in the guitar playing of Lonnie Johnson and Charlie Christian and the bass of Jimmy Blanton.

The Second World War came to an end with Miles Davis in the front row for the beginning of modern jazz, led by Parker, Dizzy, Thelonious Monk, Art Tatum, Roy Eldridge and Lester Young -- the all-stars of the scene. The big swing bands began to diminish, the small groups began to rise. New chords were added, the sound came in angles instead of straight lines, the drummers abandoned the steady rhythm of the big band dance beats to jump up on the rims, stopping and starting. Trumpets clashed. Notes blared. The sounds the 18-year-old Miles Davis heard were new, swift and erratic. They came from the clubs in Harlem, especially Minton's Playhouse, his classroom jazz scene that fed a new music into the ears and minds of America.

Davis didn't last long in his real classroom, finding Julliard nothing when compared to the real thing a subway ride away.

At school:

> I remember one day being in a music history class and a white woman was the teacher. She was up front of the class saying that the reason black people played the blues was because they were poor and had to pick cotton. So they were sad and that's where the blues came from, their sadness.
>
> (He replied), "I'm from East St. Louis and my father is rich, he's a dentist, and I play the blues. My father didn't never pick no cotton and I didn't wake up this morning sad and start playing the blues." Well this bitch turned green and didn't say nothing after that. Man, she was teaching that shit out of a book written by someone who didn't know what the fuck he was talking about. That's the kind of shit that was happening at Julliard and after a while I got tired of it.

He kept looking for Charlie Parker. Davis attended shows at Minton's, the testing ground for bebop. He watched as a character from St. Louis, a supplier of Dexedrine who went by the name of Collar, tried his luck on stage playing the sax. Collar was ignored. A customer snatched another unfortunate player off the stage, dragged him outside and beat him up,

Davis finally caught up with Dizzy who led him to Bird. He introduced Miles to Monk, the uniquely angular pianoman, and for the next few years Minton's Monday night jam became legendary, with Bird, Dizzy, Monk and eventually Miles playing before 250-300 people jammed inside and another 500 trying to get in. The bebop scene spilled out of Harlem into the clubs downtown on 52nd Street where the white critics discovered the music and expanded its reach.

Miles made his first record, with Herbie Fields, a white Julliard student on sax, and Rubberlegs Williams, a friend of Bird, on vocals, in April of 1945. The Savoy disc was a blues record, but Davis gave it a bebop nudge. He stayed the summer, still in school, and then recorded with Bird and Dizzy in November. The war was over by then and New York was flooded with servicemen, Davis started landing gigs on 52nd Street and decided he had enough of Julliard.

He paid a surprise visit to his father in East St. Louis and gave him the news that he was quitting school. He said he had learned more in Eddie Randle's band then he had in New York. He said the St. Louis musicians were better than those in New York and that he was already moving away from bebop.

The dentist had some words of wisdom for his son:

> "Miles, you hear that bird outside the window?" Doc said. "He's a mockingbird. He don't have a sound of his own. He copies everybody's sound and you don't want to do that. You want to be your own man, have your own sound. That's what its really about. So don't be nobody else but yourself. You know what you got to do and I trust your judgment. And don't worry, I'll keep sending you money until you get on your feet."

The Esquire Jazz Book of 1947 named Davis a "New Star". He quickly became a fixture of the 52nd Street club scene. In 1949 and 1950 he recorded singles that became the album *Birth of the Cool*, an album that remained unreleased until 1954. A throwback to the jazz of the twenties and thirties, it served as a counterpoint to the bebop of the time. Its eight compositions saw the first time Miles was the leader. His partner on the disc was Gil Evans, who enjoyed a long association with Davis.

Meanwhile, as the fifties began he played with Parker and Gillespie. He dug the clubs large and small in Harlem and on 52nd Street, toured America and made a splash in Paris, jamming with The Bird and the exiled trumpet master Sidney Bechet. There, Davis met John-Paul Sartre, the existentialist philosopher, and Juliette Greco, an actress Miles said "was the first woman I loved as an equal human being." As they walked the streets of the City of Light the shy kid from East St. Louis was joyful.

Back in the United States, however, his personal life was falling apart. Before Davis had graduated from high school he and Irene conceived a child and they had had another baby as he rose in the music world. She and the two kids started the fifties in New York seeking a normal family life. They moved to Queens and bought a car. But by then Miles was a jazzman and, under the influence of Bird was hooked on heroin, working less and less and staggering through the postwar slump.

When Thanksgiving rolled around, Miles couldn't afford to buy a turkey. When Easter was celebrated all he did was draw on the eggs with a pencil. Doc and his mother had broken up and Miles was too embarrassed to ask for more money from home. He became depressed, withdrawn. The loan company wanted his car but he piled the family in and drove back to East St. Louis, where the car was repossessed and towed away from out front of Doc Davis' house.

Irene gave birth to Miles Davis IV at Miles' mother's house in Chicago in 1950 and they all made it back to New York where Billy Eckstine hired Miles for a gig in Los Angeles, a concert with the George Shearing Quartet Sept. 15, 1950. On the way from the show to the airport Davis and his drummer, Art Blakey, decided to pick up a little heroin for the flight home. They were busted by the Los Angeles cops. Miles tried to bribe a guard and was busted again.

After he was released, his father resumed the flow of money and through 1950, Miles shot up as much as the stipend would allow. *Ebony* ran a story headlined "Is Dope Killing Our Musicians?" with pictures of several prominent heroin users, including Billie Holliday, Dexter Gordon, Blakely and Miles Davis. His main gig was at Birdland on 52nd Street but the career trend was down.

He pawned everything. He wandered the streets.

He rallied enough to return to the recording studio Oct. 5, 1951. During production he woke to the challenge and made an exceptional album. Called *Dig*, it was the first disc to show where he was going with the new "cool."

The Bird watched from the engineering booth. Joining on the LP was Sonny Rollins, a young player destined to be a saxophone great who had been sharing the stage with Davis. On *Dig*, released by Prestige, Davis and Rollins were allowed to run songs longer than with the singles format, playing the song "Bluing" for seven minutes.

But outside, after the sessions, he went back to the same life, because "the same old bullshit was out there waiting for me."

While Davis was in the recording studio in New York, Clark Terry was about to take a big step in his career, ending a three-year run with the Count Basie band and taking a new gig, the Duke Ellington Orchestra. Terry thus launched his national career. As all the bands slumped at the start of the fifties, Basie had shorted Terry on a paycheck and knocked down his pay rate. These slights made it easy for Terry to accept an offer from Ellington, a job started Nov. 11, 1951, at the Kiel Auditorium, the entertainment palace in St. Louis (now the site of Scottrade Center.)

The gig was billed as the "Biggest Show of '51" with Nat "King" Cole and Sarah Vaughn as the vocalists, the most expensive vocal team in Ellington's career. The show also carried comedians Stump & Stumpy, the tap dancer Peg Leg Bates and several supporting musical acts. The tour started in Boston on Sept. 21, drew sell-outs of 5,600 people two nights at Carnegie Hall in New York and rolled into St. Louis living up to its billing. The response that the show got across the country showed there was still a big audience for swing in the fifties, especially when it came from the very best.

Joining the show while it was running full throttle on its second night in St. Louis, Terry was "as nervous as a rabbit running from an eagle." He'd had no rehearsal and was faced with a chart book of 500 songs. Added to this was the problem that the show was played with the band virtually in the dark -- the music sheets lit by tiny penlights clipped on the music stands -- and the fact that he faced a bandleader with a reputation for moving his players in and out without warning. For Terry, still just 30 years old, this was the crossroads of his career. "It was do or die," he writes about that night.

Terry managed; sweat dripping off his forehead. He got help from a friendly trombone player on what song Duke had called and met the challenge.

> The audience was spellbound, then standing and applauding or dancing in their seats while finger-popping, their heads moving while their eyes stayed glued on us like we were the fountain of life. The music was so powerful and electric, if I'd had a big plug I could have stuck it in the air and lit up the whole world.

Terry played with Ellington for eight years. He described Duke as having a "supernatural magic," a firm leader who lived behind a wall of privacy and a certain amount of superstition. The band was always 17 pieces with two vocals, one male, one female. The Duke had two valets. He didn't like the color yellow or the number 13. He didn't follow fashions, when cuffless trousers were the rage, the Duke's cuffs were three inches. He didn't like buttons. His shirts had hooks and zippers, just one button, hidden at the top under his starched collar.

He was constantly writing and recording. His live shows from the fifties dotted the shelves of record stores for years to come, concerts from Seattle in 1952, from Pasadena in 1953, from Los Angeles in 1954.

On July 7, 1956, Ellington was introduced to a new audience at the third Newport Jazz Festival, many drawn to jazz by the rise of bebop, a young crowd that slept in the park.

Terry was then the lead trumpet in the band, the equivalent of the first chair in a symphony orchestra, and was involved in the arrangements and stylistic nuances. Ellington, of course, was still the Duke, but Terry was given a measure of credit for the immense success of the performances, which ran counter to the small group trends of fifties jazz.

At the outdoor concert at Freebody Park amid the Gilded Age mansions of Newport, R.I., Ellington surprised the crowd during his last set by taking two overlooked songs from the thirties, "Diminuendo" and "Crescendo in Blue," and playing them together without pause. The performance, according to one writer, was the triumph of an old music made new -- "the good old rocking (R&B if you will) blues beat that has been too often missing in jazz in the last 15 years."

Well into the music a young woman in a black dress leaped from her expensive box seat and began to dance and soon large sections of the crowd of over 7,000 joined in, cheering and waving their arms to the beat of the band.

Time magazine rewarded Ellington with a cover piece on the performance and Columbia Records (which had just signed the Duke) put out a "recreated" album, *Ellington at Newport,* much of it rerecorded the next day because Ellington was dissatisfied with some of the playing. The record also included overdubbed crowd noise, facts not noted on the original sleeve. Nonetheless, it was the biggest selling LP of Ellington's career and locked him to a long and lucrative contract with Columbia. The original track was released again in 1999 on CD as *Ellington at Newport 1956 (Complete).*

Terry rode the Ellington express for the next few years, taking up the flugelhorn, spawning imitators, making records. But he was never a satisfied cat and knew that as long as he was with the Duke he would never run the band. And thus when Quincey Jones, who had learned the trumpet from Terry many years in the past, offered an assistant director job in his band with a big pay raise, Terry played a last show with Ellington in Paris then joined Jones in 1958.

He only lasted a year with "Q", however, mostly playing in the Harold Arlen blues opera *Free and Easy,* based on the 1946 Broadway musical *St. Louis Woman,* running at the World's Fair in Brussels. The English language show didn't go over in a French-speaking environment, however, and folded, leaving the troupe high and dry. Jones did a short tour with Terry and some of the other musicians, but Terry had gotten wind of a new opportunity and soon took it, becoming the first black to play in the NBC-TV network band.

He quickly joined another old friend, Doc Severinsen, in the house band for Johnny Carson's *Tonight Show* band. He stayed with Carson for the next 12 years, until the show relocated to California in 1972. In the Carson band it was Terry who brought the skit "Stump the Band" to millions of viewers, the skit he'd perfected during his Great Lakes Experience.

Terry died in 2015, age 93. He appeared on over 900 recordings, composed more than 200 songs, won a Grammy Lifetime Achievement Award (2010), and a Grammy President's Merit Award, was given three Grammy nominations, and two Grammy certificates. He was also author of numerous books and articles on jazz.

He obtained a Jazz Master rating by the National Education Association and held 16 honorary doctorate degrees. He organized the Harlem youth band and the Jazz Mobile in New York City. He was a tireless teacher at jazz camps around the world and at teaching seminars at various universities. During his last years, students came to take lessons at his home in Pine Bluff, Ark., from Australia, Israel, Austria, Canada, as well as all parts of the United States. He was a jazz ambassador for the State Department to Africa and the Middle East.

In St. Louis, he is a member of the Hall of Fame at Vashon High School, has a Walk of Fame Star on Delmar Boulevard and stands as a life-sized wax figure at the Griot Museum of African-American history. He was loaded up with keys to cities, trophies, plaques and other prestigious awards. The French and Austrians presented him with Arts and Letters Awards. His signature song was "Mumbles" a scat-style hit recorded with the pianist Oscar Peterson in 1964 that derived from the "Stump the Band" skit.

In 2014, Terry and one of students, Justin Kauflin, starred in an Award-winning documentary, *Keep on Keepin' On*. Filmed over a four-year period the movie, directed by Alan Hicks, shows the deep collaboration between the ill and immobile Terry and his 23-year-old blind student.

Terry's treatment of the young student is revealed as a last act of kindness and affirmation of his faith in such behavior. The film reminded jazz fans of another such act of kindness, one that probably saved the life of Terry's fellow musician, Miles Davis.

Davis reached his first major low point not long after recording *Dig* in 1951, then came back to East St. Louis for Christmas determined to clean up for his father's and his family's sake. He went to his father's farm and slopped the hogs, watched over by the Doc's maid. His mother searched his friends when they came to visit, looking for smack. But he hung around town too long, playing at the bars in St. Louis and getting involved with the daughter of a Brown Shoe executive.

He slipped off the farm into the streets of East St. Louis for small packets of heroin. When he ran out of money he went back to his father, who finally refused. When Miles began yelling, Doc Davis called the police and Miles spent two weeks in the Belleville, Ill., jail. When he got out, he talked his father into more money. He grabbed a train back to New York, and went back to the same life as before, hitting the road with a new group, fighting with other members of the tour, begging money.

In June 1953 he was back at Doc's farm, but the St. Louis junkies soon turned up and another dry period ended quickly. He was back on train again for New York.

Later that year Clark Terry was staying on 52nd Street, waiting to board a bus with the Ellington band. He was walking toward a restaurant called the Ham and Eggers, when he spotted "this bulk lying in the gutter on Broadway. I walked closer and looked and discovered that it was a person. I rolled him over with my foot and I couldn't believe my eyes. It was Miles Davis!"

What would have happened to Miles if his old friend from St. Louis hadn't been walking by at that moment? And what would have happened if Clark Terry wasn't the kind of man who was willing to find out who it was lying on a New York City street? How many others had walked by the apparent bum lying there?

And how did Miles, the drug addict, pay back his friend for this kindness?

The two trumpet players ate a good meal at Ham and Eggers then Terry took Miles back to Terry's hotel room a few blocks away. Terry put Davis to bed and left the room to kill some time before the Ellington bus left, getting a drink at the bar downstairs, telling Davis he'd be back in a couple of hours before he caught the bus. When he got back, Davis had cleaned out Terry's room, stealing his horn, his radio and all his clothes.

In November 1953, Miles was back on the Doc's farm, back with the hogs, more determined than ever to kick his habit. He stayed on the farm. This time he left the Doc better than when he arrived, thinking he was making progress. But he kept on using heroin during a six-month stint in Detroit, "dipping and dabbling." The quality of the dope in Detroit was inferior to that he could get in St. Louis or New York and he didn't have much money. He used less and less. He tried to slowly wean himself off the dope.

He recorded another well-regarded record while on a short trip from Detroit back to New York that spring, an album called *Walkin.'* This LP featured Davis' version of bebop, what was later called hard bop. He pushed forward his blues background again on the songs, recorded during two sessions in April of 1954. Unlike the rest of his life, his recording life was swift and certain, using the 12-bar blues format to dance off the mark, up the tempo and make another move into a new innovation. One critic said the recording allowed Davis to "rightfully reclaim his status as a primary architect of bop." *The New York Times* said the album "announced the arrival of hard bop."

Back in Detroit after the sessions, he returned to dabbling but by the end of the year had finally stopped using heroin. There would be plenty of cocaine in his future but from early 1955 on his career was defined by music rather than his personal failings.

The turn began that summer in Newport, the year before Ellington's equally stunning reversal. Here it was Miles on his own, battling his reputation as the unreliable drug addict. He wasn't booked for the show. But organizer George Wein, who had heard of his changed lifestyle, added him at the last minute to appear during a short slot scheduled to fill time for stage changes to get ready for Dave Brubeck, the star of the night. Piano innovator Thelonious Monk, sax master Gerry Mulligan, the rhythm section for the Modern Jazz Quartet and a couple of others were listed for the break. Now10 years removed from his star-is-born opportunity in St. Louis with the Eckstine band, Davis was the last-minute addition on the break set.

He rushed the stage in a white sport coat and black tie, pushed the horn against the mike and dominated Monk's composition "Hackensack" then went into ""'Round Midnight," Monk's 1944 song that Davis had recorded in 1953. The rendition of the jazz classic was flawless, his style immaculate, hardly the junkie Clark Terry found on Broadway two years before. Off stage stood George Avakian, Louis Armstrong's producer at

Columbia Records and a man who had resisted signing Davis since he first met him in 1946. This was a different Miles at Newport, Avakian quickly realized, and he signed Davis after the show.

The resulting album, *Round About Midnight*, recorded in three sessions during 1955 and 1956 and released by Columbia in 1957, became another in the growing list of Miles Davis classics, a record that grew in popularity as the years went by. The initial LP contained six long cuts performed by Miles and his new band, his most famed quintet -- John Coltrane, sax; Red Garland, piano; Paul Chambers, bass, and Philly Joe Jones, drums. In 2001, a CD of the master takes from the sessions were released on Columbia/Legacy label, then released again in 2005 when the music was published on a Sony Legacy Edition that included the live Newport performance of "'Round Midnight" and additional live material from the 1956 Pacific Jazz Festival.

In 1955, the quintet made a quick road trip before returning to pack Cafe Bohemia in Greenwich Village where Davis found himself free of the drug hustlers and pimps of 52nd Street. The audience was a new crowd -- "poets, painters, actors, designers, filmmakers, dancers."

This shy small man, not yet 30 years old, now had supreme confidence. He stopped bantering. Instead, he played his trumpet his songs with barely a pause between one and another. He stopped announcing the names of the tunes, now playing to an audience that was rapt and quiet, entranced by the bop. The beat writer Jack Kerouac and his girlfriend Joyce Johnson were there one night when a car crash outside the club broke the spell and the crowd ran out into the street. Miles just kept playing. He finished the set and said to the nearly empty room, "Thank you for the applause" and walked off the stage.

On the road in 1955, playing together outside New York for the first time, the third gig the famed quintet played was at Peacock Alley, a tiny club in St. Louis. The night was special for Davis. The Doc and his mother were in the audience and they were proud of his deal with Columbia, a big name company with real money. Paid a $4,000 advance, he signed for $300,000 a year. He was clean and stable. His classmates from Lincoln High were there and "everything just went beautifully in St. Louis while I was there."

The Peacock was located in Mill Creek Valley on the same block where Clark Terry's sister lived when he ran away from home. Not far from Union Station at 2935 Lawton, it was also in the same area where Tom Turpin's Rosebud Bar had incubated ragtime a half-century earlier. The Peacock opened in 1944 as the Glass Bar in the basement of the Midtown Hotel, a favorite of musicians due to its proximity to the train station.

By the time it was remodeled and renamed Peacock Alley in 1955 it had a national reputation for jazz, having already hosted Stan Getz, Dizzy and The Bird, Lester Young and Bud Powell. The club alternated jazz and blues weekends and featured a band put together by Henry Townsend that included a piano player named Roosevelt Carmichael, a sax player and three women who sang.

The Peacock was also the venue for Saturday radio shows hosted by the DJ Jesse "Spider" Burks for the jazz station KSTL, an AM station that broadcast from a studio near the levee. Davis brought the quintet back to St. Louis for a return engagement in July of 1956 then returned again in February of 1957. The Davis Quintet was recorded during appearances then on two Saturday afternoons.

The local Soulard label, first on vinyl, then on a CD, issued the shows. They feature the quintet playing "Walkin'" and many of the other hard bop and blues tunes Davis was developing at the time of one his greatest creative periods. He was also nearing the end of the run of the quintet, at a time when Philly Joe Jones and John Coltrane were both hooked on smack and acting more and more erratic. Gigs in Chicago and Baltimore followed the St. Louis shows before a scheduled month at Club Bohemia in New York where Jones and Coltrane were fired and the band broke up.

The recording at the Peacock begins at four in the afternoon with Davis calling out "Ah-Leu-Cha'," The Bird's bebop spinoff of "Honeysuckle Rose." Burks interrupts to ask: "Is that a foreign language?" Davis replies: "Charlie Parker's language." Next is "A Foggy Day," the Gershwin standard, then Cole Porter's "All of You," and the Dizzy favorite "Woody 'n You." Then comes "Walkin'," more than seven minutes of Davis hard bop.

Burks is excited:

> Miles Davis and the combo, ladies and gentlemen, huh? Miles Davis' trumpet and quintet. On tenor sax, Mr. Coltrane blowing tenor, ladies and gentlemen. We have on drums, just behind Mr.

> Coltrane, Mr. Philadelphia Joe Jones. And way over yonder on bass fiddle, one of the swingin'est bassists in the business, Mr. Paul Chambers, ladies and gentlemen. And never ceasing to swing, and so many inventive ideas on his instrument, playing piano we have Red Garland, ladies and gentlemen.
>
> And last but not least, St Louie's own favorite son, the leader of this group, Mr. Miles Davis, ladies and gentlemen. Now even though we're going off the air in a couple of minutes, the matinee goes on until seven, then Miles is back on the stand with the group at nine until one-fifteen.

During the last three years of the fifties Davis became the mature musician, the man who commanded a kinglike status in jazz. He drifted further from his St. Louis roots, rarely coming home, remaining generally in New York, playing sessions, writing with Gil Evans, his major collaborator, running his band combinations with steady handed skill. His drugs were controlled, his career lucrative and organized.

In three years he recorded 19 sessions, put out four classic albums -- *Miles Ahead, Porgy and Bess, Milestones* and *Kind of Blue* -- and began recording a fifth, *Sketches of Spain*, released in early 1960. On these records, he became the consummate jazz stylist. He used his notes to sing his songs. Already advanced from bebop to cool to hard bop he now invented modal, shifting from the usual chords and harmony of blues to the open-ended voice that gave his music the opportunity for unlimited solo virtuosity, a concept of which he, more than anybody, took full advantage.

Kind of Blue was the climax of the decade, the result of his five years of clean thinking, of his serious contemplation of the jazz and blues he was playing on a daily, nightly basis. *The New York Times* critic Jon Pareles called the record "voluptuous and austere." As late as 1998, nearly 40 years after its release, *Kind of Blue* was the best selling jazz album of the year, the only jazz album to ever sell 2 million copies. There is an eternal sadness to it, melancholia, starkness and weightlessness. The album came just as the decade of the sixties -- the decade of rebellion -- was about to open.

The year 1959 saw Dave Brubeck's *Time Out,* Louis Armstrong joining Duke Ellington's revival, Charlie Mingus and Cannonball Adderly producing popular records, television -- *Peter Gunn, Sunset Strip* -- driven by jazz, and John Coltrane releasing his masterful *Giant Steps,* and

Ornette Coleman making *The Shape of Jazz to Come.* Revolution was in the air. Here came the civil rights movement, the anti-war movement, the philosophical rise of Sartre and New Left theorist Herbert Macuse, sit-ins, lie-ins, boycotts and assassinations. Billie Holliday died in 1959 and John Kennedy decided to run for president.

Miles Davis was a cocky man with deep black skin who would repeatedly mock his white crowds, refusing to partake in the required stage etiquette. In 1959 he was beaten up by a New York City police officer in front of Birdland on a hot August night for no apparent reason other than his skin was black and his attitude was rebellious. His beating, unlike so many others, was front-page news. His lifelong hatred of racism was unabating even as he became rich and famous.

As he made *Kind of Blue,* Miles remembered the days as a boy walking on his grandfather's farm, a cast of old gospel ghosts playing in his head. He remembered the insults of his white neighbors and the hangings of blacks from the lampposts of East St. Louis. *Kind of Blue* was an album made from music that wasn't written down, music that was recorded in one take. "I was trying to do one thing and ended up doing something else," he said.

Miles Davis finished the fifties at the top of his game, moving his art forward at breakneck speed, taking jazz where it had never gone in all the long time since Joplin wrote "Maple Leaf Rag," and W.C. Handy composed "The St. Louis Blues."

He lived on until 1991 when he died in Santa Monica, Calif., at age 65. By then he had recorded over 100 records, won endless awards including nine Grammies and received countless accolades. By the time he was through he was recognized as the most innovative player in the history of jazz, at the forefront of several major developments in the music -- bebop, cool jazz, hard bop, modal and jazz fusion. He was still getting awards in 2015, named as the best jazz musician of all time in a BBC listeners' poll.

And while Davis beautified his St. Louis roots in his fifties musical rocket ship, others were busy on both sides of the Mississippi. Next on the bandstand: Ike Turner, Tina Turner, Chuck Berry, and Albert King. Each was as much music royalty as Miles Davis, once more joining the confluence of voluptuousness and austerity, all a part of that St. Louis thing.

Chapter Twenty-Two

The Rhythm of the Fifties: Ike and Tina at the Club Imperial

Step in my Rocket and don't be late,
We're pullin' out about a half-past-eight.
Goin' on the corner and havin' some fun,
Takin' my Rocket on a long, hot run.
-- Ike Turner, "Rocket 88," 1951

First we get the band, the band does their thing, then the band goes into this boom-da-boom-da-boom-da-boom -- the beat like galloping -- then over to the left of the stage you see the Ikettes all standing in a line -- like this engine ready to go down the track -- and then -- bang -- they hit it and they come right on stage all dancing and prancing -- the strobe light goes on and you almost fall over -- you don't know what's happened -- and there's these incredibly beautiful, vivacious gals with these miniskirts on -- then here comes Tina, the queen of them all -- man it was just something -- and all the clocks stopped -- time just stopped -- and you were in a zone until they were done with us. It was quite fantastic.

-- Guitarist Tom Maloney,
describing the Club Imperial

The building that once housed the Club Imperial sits on the busy corner of Goodfellow Boulevard and West Florissant Avenue, at the very edge of St. Louis, right on the county line in the northwest corner of the city. The two-story building was put up in 1928 as Imperial Hall, built as a dance hall, bowling alley and restaurant complex in an all-white neighborhood that was filling with factory workers. The hall flourished in the thirties and forties, becoming one of the biggest pleasure palaces in the city.

In 1952, George Edick, a newcomer from Chicago, purchased the hall, and then brought in swing bands like Stan Kenton's orchestra, advertising the club as "a nice place for nice people." But "nice" was fading in the march of "hip" through the city. Rhythm & blues was exciting the young crowd with new bands popping up in East St. Louis.

In 1954, Edick heard of a band playing there at the Club Manhattan called Ike Turner and the Kings of Rhythm. "Jazz wasn't good for me," Edick said. "I had to have good swinging music for the dancers. Black groups were the best, so I started booking them. One of our jitterbug champions told me about Ike Turner." Edick booked them to try to grab the new stylish audience of white kids in sideburns and saddle shoes. It worked.

With Clayton Love as the lead singer, Ike turned on the juice and got the dancers dancing up on the second floor above West Florissant. Edick also booked Chuck Berry and Albert King, Little Milton, jazzman Joe Bozzi and Jimmie Forest, who had the hit "Night Train." As the scene grew, he brought in more and more local bands to get the bodies in motion.

But it was Ike Turner who was the Imperial's king. His invention was the R&B revue, combining elements of small groups and big bands, with a lead singer, a backup singing group, a horn section, a lead guitar, bass guitar, drums and a piano leader ala Ellington, off to the side of the stage. Ike was the true pro.

By the time he started playing the Imperial, Ike had already carved out his place in rock 'n' roll history. Before he moved to East St. Louis and met a 16-year-old Sumner High School student who changed his life, Ike was on the top of the game.

Ike and the Kings taught the kids the scene, taught them how to do the Lindy and how to jitterbug. The kids brought in a flask hidden in their pocket to go with the beer Edick sold in the club. They hid behind the back posts off the dance floor to get in a little smooch.

There were many other musicians in St. Louis in the mid-fifties, but none as big as Ike. Chuck Berry immediately comes to mind, right there in 1955 with "Maybellene" -- one of the several rock hits that invaded the charts. He played the Imperial often, with his sidekick and collaborator Johnnie Johnson rattling the piano. But Berry didn't have a revue. He was a rocker in the style of the new wave of Little Richard, Fats Domino, Bill Haley and Bo Diddley.

Ike had the horns; he had the women in their skin-tight dresses choreographed step by step by Ike himself, drilled in rehearsals. He was a showman with a big show. He hit the charts four years before Berry did and by 1958 his dominance of the St. Louis scene was complete.

Izear Luster Turner, born in Clarksdale, Miss., on Nov. 5, 1931, was the son of a Baptist preacher who was beaten nearly to death by a white mob when Ike was five years old. The battered father was not allowed treatment at the white local hospital and a tent was built in the family's backyard where the preacher tried to recover. He died two years later, in 1938.

Ike's mother was a seamstress who once smashed the windows of her house with her fist to save Ike from a fire. She made money sewing custom clothes for the Mississippi ladies whose husbands owned the cotton fields. Ike learned the value of a dollar at her knee. The family was Creole and African American by blood. Neither mother nor father was content to get along or go along. By the second grade Ike was earning money from a paper route. He parlayed his cash into crates of baby chickens he sold in the spring, making enough profit to buy more chicks. He kept making money all the way to the day he died.

Delivering his papers, the young Ike got all over town. Walking around one day he heard a piano playing in the house of a friend from school. He went in and heard the blues piano man Joseph William Perkins, known as Pinetop or Willie Joe. When Ike saw the skill and the energy emerging from that player and his piano, Ike said, this music "excited me more than anything in the world; it put a burn in my mind."

He begin hearing Pinetop playing the *King Biscuit Time* radio show on station KFFA, 11:30 a.m. every day. Ike would catch the show by ducking school and heading over to a nearby pool hall. He asked his mother for a piano and she promised him one if he passed third grade. He did and she stuck to her end of the deal, paying $300 from her sewing savings, putting Ike behind his own piano before he was a teenager.

Through *King Biscuit*, Ike was also exposed to Sonny Boy Williamson II (the Rice Miller version) and from the rival WROX he heard the singer/guitar player Robert Nighthawk. Perkins gave Turner lessons on boogie-style piano and he learned to play guitar from listening to the radio, playing mostly country music on the guitar and boogie-woogie blues on the piano.

In his teens, Turner formed the Tophatters, a swing band playing Tommy Dorsey and Harry James, a high school band that had as many as 36 members. Here he met the trombone player Clayton Love. The two decided it was time to give swing a pass and start something different. Blues and jazz were the choices, influenced by a visit to Clarksdale by the drawling Texas bluesman Charles Brown and Amos Milburn, an R&B performer also from Texas.

The band was too big for both styles of music and split during Turner's senior year in high school, forming up into the Dukes of Swing and the Kings of Rhythm, directly reflecting the split in American music in the late forties and early fifties. The swing big band was ending as the era of R&B and rock 'n' roll began. Ike began sneaking out the window after bedtime, playing with the Night Hawk. Before he was done with high school, Turner moved out of his house into the Riverside Hotel so he could be closer to the radio station.

He heard B.B. King, another local bluesman, playing on the radio. He introduced himself one night at a show, and King, who was 25 when Turner was 19, let the young player up on the bandstand. They had met years earlier, when, as a 14 year old, Ike had come around the theater where B.B. was rehearsing. "You guys need help," he said to B.B., who let him play that night and again at the club five years later.

That meeting led to a session in Memphis where Ike Turner put his name on the list of records that lit the fuse that blew the bomb that made rock 'n' roll happen in the fifties.

Before there were any round records at all there was rock 'n' roll. Under one widely used definition, rocking and rolling is what makes the world go round. That's how Trixie Smith sang it in 1922 on "My Baby Rocks Me With One Steady Roll." This was a blues song, of course, nothing but the blues, but it's the first time the words were mixed together in a song title.

The thirties kicked up a little dust on the rock 'n' roll front with the big band rhythms moving quicker and quicker and the dancers starting to fly with the introduction of the jitterbug on the newly integrated dance floors of the big cities. An example would be "One O'Clock Jump," swing meets R&B, by the Count Basie Orchestra, but it still with a traditional sentimental embrace.

Boogie-woogie, a piano element of the new style, was not far distant from the St. Louis barrelhouse of the twenties and strongly related to ragtime. Big Joe Turner and the pianist Pete Johnson started something of a boogie-woogie craze in 1938 when they appeared at the "Spirituals To Swing" concert in New York City.

At the end of the war, *Billboard* magazine began running charts for jukebox plays of music by African Americans, the Race Record charts, featuring the Harlem Hit Parade. "The Honeydripper" by blues pianist Joe Liggins was No. 1 for 18 weeks in 1945. Here was music that had the feel of rock 'n' roll, if not the complete package. That same year the Bihari brothers formed Modern Records in Los Angeles, and began to scout for talent in the Midwest, landing eventually at the Sun Studio of Sam Phillips in Memphis.

Then came another element to the stew -- the jump blues. "Choo Choo Ch'Boogie" by Louis Jordan & His Tympany Five was a hit in 1946, probably the biggest ever for a jump blues song. This is still not rock 'n' but it was close. The next year, the *Billboard* reporter and future music maven Jerry Wexler pushed the term "rhythm & blues" forward to replace "Race Records." By now, the young crowd was starting to go for the new R&B, sexy stuff, the sax in the lead, deep moans from baritones, raucous action on the dance floor.

Also in 1947, Wynonie Harris, a ribald blues singer from Omaha, Neb., put out a proto-rocker called "Hard Ridin' Mama." In 1948 the charts contained several contenders for the first rock song -- Harris' "Good Rockin' Tonight" topped the R&B charts and threw the word "rocking'" into the air. But with the benefit of hindsight, it's clear that this doesn't have the real rock chops, the beat is too slow and while the sax is sexy it still doesn't have the feel of the genre to come.

A sax honker from Detroit, Wild Bill Moore, released "We're Gonna Rock, We're Gonna Roll," in 1948, a song that inches closer to the real deal, almost adding up everything needed. But still it didn't have the punch; nor did "Cornbread" with Hal Singer on the sax or even Scatman Crothers' "I Want to Rock and Roll."

In 1949, Muddy Waters, John Lee Hooker and T-Bone Walker all put out blues records featuring the electric guitar, bringing the style of Lonnie Johnson closer to the fifties. Another rock ingredient had been added. Atlantic Records was running by now and Savoy and King were also primed for the rock 'n' roll era. That same year, the 14-year-old Jerry Lee Lewis surprised a crowd with a preview of things to come by blasting "Drinkin' Wine Spo-Dee-O-Dee" on a piano outside a Memphis car dealership.

And just as the forties ended, all of a sudden we can find some real rockers -- Louis Jordan's massive hit "Saturday Night Fish Fry" and Jimmy Preston's raucous "Rock the Joint" both stuck their noses over the horizon. The new music was now clearly in sight.

The fifties thus dawned with a lot of rocking and rolling, the ship on the sea, the congregation in the church, dancers on the hardwood, lovers in the bedroom. Mass popularity was coming down the pike and real rockers started hitting the R&B chart. Ike was there on the list of the pioneers with his "Rocket 88," the number two song of 1951.

> No. 2 for the year 1950 was Fats Domino's "The Fat Man."
>
> No. 2 of 1951 was "Rocket 88" by Jackie Brenston and His Delta Cats, written and produced by Ike Turner. (Bill Haley covered "Rocket 88" that year.)
>
> No. 4 of 1952 was "Lawdy Miss Clawdy," by Lloyd Price.
>
> No. 3 of 1953 was "Hound Dog" by Big Mama Thornton.
>
> No. 1 of 1954 was "Hoochie Coochie Man" by Muddy Waters. No. 5 was "Shake, Rattle and Roll" by Big Joe Turner.
>
> No. 1 of 1955 was "Tweedle Dee" by Lavern Baker. No. 3 was "I Got a Woman," by Ray Charles. No. 6 was "I'm a Man" by Bo Diddley. No. 10 record was "Baby, Let's Play House" by Elvis Presley.

Also in 1955, Bill Haley & His Comets' "Rock Around the Clock" broke through on the Top 40 pop chart reaching No. 1 for eight weeks and was No. 2 for the year. This breakthrough was recorded in April 1954 in New York City with the full out combination of rock elements -- the boogie piano rhythms played on guitar, the blaring sax, the backbeat drumming. For the first time a white singer hit the top of the chart with rock 'n' roll.

In 1955, Chuck Berry came flying out of St. Louis to throw his hat in the ring with the No. 5 hit "Maybellene," followed by "Roll Over Beethoven," No. 2 on the R&B chart in 1956 and "School Days" No. 3 on the Top 40 in 1957.

In 1956, Presley grabbed the crown away from Haley and Berry with "Hound Dog/Don't Be Cruel" and "Heartbreak Hotel." That year both records broke through as No. 1 on the Top 40 chart, the two-sided hit No. 1 for the year and the latter No. 4.

By 1957 five rockers made the top of the pop chart. *American Bandstand*, with dancers who swung like the kids at the Club Imperial, made its national television debut in the summer of that year and the rock revolution was fully engaged.

Sam Phillips opened his Memphis Recording Service on a propitious date -- Jan. 1, 1950. Phillips, once the conductor of his high school orchestra in Florence, Ala., intended to record "singers and musicians from Memphis and the locality who I felt had something that people should be able to hear. I'm talking here about blues, both the country style and the rhythm style, and also the spirituals or gospel music and about white country music."

B. B. King recommended Turner to Phillips and during the ride from Clarksdale for the session, Ike and his band concocted "Rocket 88," a song about a car made at a factory in Wentzville, Mo., a suburb of St. Louis, the same town where Chuck Berry later built his Xanadu. Ike's saxophonist, Jackie Brenston, one of his playing partners from Clarksdale, suggested the song, about the new Rocket 88 put on the streets by Oldsmobile just that year. Jackie sang the song, giving the sax over to a teenager named Raymond Hill. Ike pounded out the right rocking rhythm on the piano.

"Rocket 88" went beyond the Fats Domino hit of 1950. In "The Fat Man" the rhythm was of rock was clearly there, that rocking beat of the forties. Fats gives a brilliant performance, yelling out a high-pitch wa-wa and beating the piano high and low, round and round. The backup is an afterthought on the cut, however; this is all Fats.

"Rocket 88" on the other hand has it all. There's the boogie-woogie thump right off the bat, the sexy sax riffs, the driving beat of rock 'n' roll, the swinging dance undertow, a virtuoso piano by Ike and a smooth, congealing singing performance by Brentson. And here we are invited to the party -- the signature party so well built into rock music -- somebody yelling "go, go" in the background, "boozin' and cruising' along."

Hill was just 17, a Clarksdale native and member of Ike's band who grew up in his father's club watching players like Night Hawk and Sonny Boy II. His solo here sets a standard for the miles and miles of such tenor sax solos to come. Hill later moved to St. Louis with Ike and was the father of Tina Turner's first child. Hill later joined up with Albert King.

"Rocket 88" ran up to No. 1 on the R&B chart and stayed there for five weeks, selling half a million copies on the Chess label. Ike got $20. Brenston got $910, largely because Phillips gave him writing credit and the Chess people in Chicago messed up the name of the band, calling it Jackie Brenston and the Delta Cats. We don't know what Phillips or the Chess brothers got.

Bill Haley's version was recorded three months later but did not make the national lists, perhaps because there was no drum on the cut. Also, Haley, still recording with his band the Saddlemen, had not fully committed to rock 'n' roll and was basically a country swing bandleader.

In 1952, Haley tried another rocking song, "Rock The Joint," but again it didn't have much success on the charts, even though it made a No. 1 hit in the Chicago local market and stirred up his white hillbilly crowd every time he played it. But Haley didn't go over with black audiences and the whites were confused. One night in Chicago he followed Dizzy Gillespie and many people walked out.

Some music writers put "Rock the Joint" by the Philadelphia R&B singer Jimmy Preston at the head the class as the beginning of rock 'n' roll since it was first made in 1949. It certainly has the party atmosphere and is plenty raucous with a lot of background yelling and wild sax solos. But the beat is mostly swinging and still has the feel of a forties dance band. That original reached No. 6 on the R&B chart, better than the 1952 Haley version, which still used a player slapping a bass guitar instead of a drum and changed the lyrics to appeal to a hillbilly crowd.

Like Haley, Preston came out of Chester, Pa., but Preston never hit it big and didn't do much beyond his original record. He quit recording in 1950 and was out of the music business in 1952, just as Haley covered his song,

"Rocket 88" was the real thing. Phillips, who had a lot of reasons to love Ike's song, proclaimed it the first rock 'n' roll record and Ike wasn't about to argue. Little Richard chimed in on behalf of Ike's claim and the song is a sure thing on all the lists of rock pioneering tunes. Ike was 19 years old.

It wasn't until Haley's "Rock Around the Clock" crossed over to the white audience that a rock made No. 1 on the *Billboard* Top 40 pop chart. By then, May 14, 1955, the rock revolution was already happening established on the dance floors and in the jukeboxes. Along with Haley, here came Berry and Presley breaking out of the starting gate.

By then Ike Turner had done some aging and some learning. He played with the likes of Howlin' Wolf, Roscoe Gordon, Bobby "Blue" Bland, Johnny Ace, Otis Rush, as well as his frequent partner, B.B. King. Turner also worked as a talent scout for Phillips and the Bihari brothers and for a short time moved to Los Angeles, where Jules Bihari started Modern Records in 1945.

With one or the other of the brothers, Ike traveled the South, sometimes getting trouble from racists along the way who didn't like seeing a white and a black together in the same car. This way of life didn't entirely please Ike and he became increasingly interested in the idea of moving into a bigger music scene. St. Louis beckoned.

He heard good reports from his sister. He decided to take a shot at a one-off gig at an East Side club called Ned Love's in 1954. This appearance led to a four-night slot on the weekends. Within weeks Ike and the Kings were double and triple booked on both the East Side and in St. Louis. He kept rolling and rock music took hold. He made the permanent move north to the confluence.

By the end of 1957, rock 'n' roll was moving full steam. The next year, however, it almost sank. Presley went into the Army. Buddy Holly, a hit-making hillbilly rocker in the Haley mode, was killed in a plane crash. Chuck Berry went to jail. And Alan Freed, the Cleveland DJ who had coined the term rock 'n' roll and starred in the 1956 film *Rock, Rock, Rock*, was under investigation for payola.

Ike Turner weathered the storm. His act was fully afloat on both sides of the river in St. Louis. The Kings of Rhythm were established at the Club Imperial and he had built his own club, the Club Manhattan, which he and the band transformed from a brick house to a thriving music venue in East St. Louis.

Ike played guitar, arranged, choreographed, booked, hired and fired, advertised, politicized, stayed out all night, but he didn't sing. He played 14 shows a week.

Billy Gayles sang lead or sometimes it was Otis Rush, Art Lassiter, Betty Everett, Jimmy Thomas or Tommy Hodge. Ike was one of the leading session players at this time, racking up the titles week after week on labels called Federal, Joyce and Cobra, dancing from contract to contract, often traveling to Cincinnati and Memphis. In 1954 he recorded under the name Icky Renrut for a St. Louis label called Stevens, a tiny label run by a father-son team that released just seven 45s.

The Club Imperial gigs were the highlight.

"We tore them up 'cause St. Louis was a jazz town," Ike said. "Here come us from down there playing the blues, and we were just drawing a trillion people."

George Edick said, "he had something different . . . He had horns, he gave it a big-band sound."

Clayton Love added, "Ike's was the band. Ike had a showmanship that really captivated people, white and black. He just had them going."

Gabriel, a black DJ and musician who started on St. Louis radio in 1953 and was still on the air in 2015, remembered:

> Ike Turner just took over this area. He created a ripple effect with his energy and ambition, he sent word back to Mississippi and was followed here by Albert King and Little Milton, he was a premier blues pianist who later became a great guitarist. (Ike) was just very impressive, he wanted to take the blues somewhere else, he wanted

> to be a popular musician -- he didn't want to play straight blues. By the early sixties his sets only included one or two blues songs. He was playing R&B, adding rhythm to the blues.

Gayles fronted the band in 1956 and 1957, and along with the recently restored Jackie Brentson, held several blistering sessions in Cincinnati for Federal Records. Ike bought a 13-room house on Virginia Street in East St. Louis and moved the whole band and all the followers into its ramshackle grandeur. And then, just when Ike thought it couldn't get any better -- enter Tina.

Annie Mae Bullock was 16 in 1957 when she went with her sister, Alline, to the Club Manhattan to see Ike Turner and the Rhythm Kings. Alline was dating Ike's drummer, an observant guy named Eugene Washington, who noticed the little sister mouthing the words to all the songs.

Ike paid Little Annie no mind until one night he was fooling around on the organ between sets with the B.B. King song "You Know I Love You." Washington noticed Annie singing quietly on the side of the stage and brought over a microphone. The voice made Ike sit up. Little Annie was invited up to sing the next set and afterward, Ike offered her a job. He was attracted to many of the women in his band, but the short, stocky Annie didn't appeal to his type. Like Ike, she had Cherokee blood in her family tree and looked like many of her solid female counterparts from the Delta. But her voice was different, husky, sexy.

Little Annie convinced her mother that Ike was all right and in 1958, the year of hard times for rock 'n' roll, the greatest female rocker of them all began her climb to megastar status under her new name, Tina Turner.

George Edick, the owner of the Club Imperial, died in 2002. His son Greg Edick, a burly bass player who grew up in the club and took over the ownership, met the bluesman Larry Griffin and me outside the club on a windy afternoon in 2013.

Greg is enthusiastic about showing off the place.

"Remember the lines all the way up the street to see Tina Turner, this was even before "'Fool in Love,'" he says, referring to the 1960 hit that put the duo of Ike and Tina on the charts for the first time. We head up a wide stairway to the second floor.

Larry: "The stairway, I remember Virgil at the top -- looking mean."

Greg: "He was the doorman. He looked like Mr. Clean. He never carried a gun. You had to leave the guns out here. That desk right here -- pay your 75 cents, leave your gun, see Tina Turner."

Larry came here as a teenager and looks around as we come out of the hallway onto the dance floor.

"Beautiful," his smile beams. "I forgot how cool a place this is."

Indeed, on this day in 2013 the dance floor is solid, covered in black-and-white checkered linoleum. Railings surround the mid-sized floor. Tables sit behind the railing. In the dark shadows of the afternoon, the Club Imperial feels like any dance club in the afternoon, a certain staleness cut with an edge of expectation, the feeling the lights could come on any minute. The sense a bunch of kids in the front of the line could spill through the door and rush for the best tables.

Greg is proud.

> Just look at it, man. We could get Artie (Dwyer) and them guys (the Soulard Blues Band) in here. We could tear off this linoleum; the floor from the sixties is still under there. This is the original shape since the sixties.
>
> The only thing that has changed is that the stage had a runway out further for Tina, she'd come out into the crowd. Ike would put an 18-piece orchestra up there.

By 1958, the band was renamed the Ike and Tina Revue. "A Fool in Love" in 1960 was just the first of a string of hits for the pair, six singles on the R&B charts in three years (four in the top five). The first hit was made at the Technisonic Studios, just outside the St. Louis city line in Brentwood, Mo., with Tina a last minute fill-in for another of Ike's singers.

Technisonic in St. Louis had been there since 1929 and cut early Chuck Berry as well as the Ike and Tina songs. On "A Fool in Love," Ed Canter, former president of Technisonic, was the recording engineer: "Ike Turner had written that song for somebody else. Ike showed up with this girl. Her name was Annie Bullock, but Ike always billed his act down at the Club Imperial as 'Ike and Tina Turner.' Whoever the vocalist happened to be became 'Tina.'"

The backup on the song included the Artettes, after the singer Art Lassiter, who sat out the session over a pay dispute with Ike. The Artettes that day also included the singer Robbie Montgomery, who soon became an Ikette. The idea that day was that Tina would sing the slot left open by Lassiter and once the trouble with Ike was ironed out Art's voice would be dubbed back into the cut.

But a guy named Juggy Murray, a pre-Motown New York record promoter who put out black artists on the Sue label, heard Tina's voice on the cut and immediately went to St. Louis, where he gave her $25,000 to sign with Sue. He wanted more records soon. Murray was the first music industry mover to recognize the voice of Tina Turner, a unique sound at that time or any time. She was not just a blues singer, not just an R&B singer; there was something dark and deep in her sound that made it stand out. She could shout and shout and did her share of it on stage, but even on "A Fool in Love" there's a touch of mystery in the voice.

Tina was pregnant (with Ike's sax player Raymond Hill) by the time the record hit the streets and Ike launched a tour promoting the record. Ike loved his tours and Tina wasn't about to argue. Taking no chances, however, Ike was training a new Tina on the side, just in case. She gave birth on the road in Los Angeles and found out about the other Tina from an Ikette. Tina found the unfortunate substitute and made sure she was long gone from the revue.

Ike and Tina then settled into a decade of nearly constant touring and performing, always making sure there were bookings in St. Louis three or four times a year.

Greg:

> At the end of the run (at the Club Imperial) they had a big sound system but at first they just had to use the big round speakers. No monitors. No such thing as monitors when they started. Ike would have between two and five horns. We let in 18-year-olds and roped off the over 21s, had a little fence between the 18s and 21s. But it never made no difference, I'm sure somebody passed a beer or two over the fence. It was just like a regular picket fence. We had mostly young kids. Lots of them between 16 and 17. They were supposed to stay behind the fence.
>
> *Trouble?*

> Virgil would just throw them out. Guy pulled a pistol, Virgil just took it away. Throw the guy out. Out the fire escape. There wasn't a bunch of bouncers here, just Virgil.

Larry remembered Virgil: "People had respect. He kept the lid on the place."

Greg:

> Virgil never carried a gun. Nobody running the place ever carried a gun. You have to know how to talk to people.
>
> In '63 (at age 13) or so I was taking Tina her sodas in the back room. Tina babysitted me when I was a kid. I would be the bar back. I'd always work. I'd sit up there with Ike and play music. He'd teach me 12-bar blues.

Greg points out a picture on the wall, taken under the awning of the club, his dad prominent, others including the sax player Oliver Sain, the Ikettes Robbie Montgomery and Stacy Johnson. And in the picture is also a guy named Herb Sadler, a guitar player who took the place of the young Jimi Hendrix after Ike fired him from the band.

Hendrix had been hired as a second guitarist for the Revue, but he was a big showoff, and Ike let him go: Jimi wanted to play long solos that brought the dancers to a halt. He wouldn't listen to Ike and was fired. Hendrix met Miles Davis at the club and Davis said Jimi's guitar sounded like a "machine gun."

Greg also knew Jimmy Forrest, who hit the charts with "Night Train" in 1951 and played the club piano bar for years. This small bar sat in the back of the room, beyond the reach of the under 21 crowd, and was something of a hangout for celebrities who came through town in the sixties. Forrest played in Fate Marable's band and with Jay McShann, then Ellington and had jammed with Davis at the Barrel Club in St. Louis in 1952.

The Rolling Stones paid a rowdy visit to the Imperial piano bar in July 1966 and booked the Revue as an opening act for a tour of England. The success of the tour led to Tina's appearance on the cover of *Rolling Stone* magazine in 1967, the first woman to ever appear on America's premier rock publication.

Tina was used to the white crowds at the Imperial where the girls did most of the dancing. In a later interview Tina said:

> I didn't know who the Stones were. They were just these white boys and Mick was the one who was always standing in the wings watching us. He was a little shy of me, but finally we started having fun and I tried to teach him some dances, because he'd just stand still onstage with the tambourine. He'd try things like the pony or some hip movements backstage and we'd all just laugh.

Stacy Johnson, a well-regarded singer, a one-time Ikette, sits with me one afternoon in 2012 on his couch in Soulard, in a room dominated by a giant TV. He's 68, a little worse for wear. There's a Kings of Rhythm poster from one of the band's European tours on the wall, but not much else is apparent in the way of memorabilia.

Johnson was born in mid-town St. Louis in 1945, into an affluent family. His mother owned a tavern near the downtown in a white neighborhood. "We were the third black family on the street, very interesting, I got to mingle with both races."

He saw the doo-wop groups on TV in the second half of the fifties, and when he was 12 he formed a group of singers that included his boyhood friend Vernon Guy.

"Did that lead you into a band?" I ask.

"No, that led me into reform school," Stacy answers.

He got expelled from public school for fighting. "I was a hot tempered, hard-headed kid" who spent a year and a half in reform school.

When he got out he came back to St. Louis and formed a band called the Superiors.

> We played all the current R&B favorites. We wrote a few of our own songs. I went from that to the Arabians, then the money started coming in. Same type of thing, we were doing the nightclub circuit and it was a matter of how much money was thrown up on the stage. I danced a little bit. But I was a singer from the start.

Then, age 15, in 1960, Stacy met Benny Sharp, the closest thing Ike Turner had to a rival on the East St. Louis R&B stages.

"Benny played everything." Stacy said. "He dabbled in everything, mostly R&B, but he played everything, and by that time Motown was real big, we did Temptation things."

Ike and Tina moved their headquarters to Los Angeles in 1962, and Benny stepped right into the void, moving into several of the regular bookings that the hardworking Ike and Tina Revue had been playing madly for nearly five years. At first, Stacy took to the road with Ike.

Stacy:

> You not only had to learn the act, you had to learn how Ike Turner was. He was very, very moody all the time. It was always almost like he was bi-polar. One day he was just a wonderful person and the next day you couldn't speak to him. I don't know if it was because he'd met Tina. That's the way he was -- he ran a tight ship. But I learned so much from just being on the road with Ike, day to day. I leaned how to dress, a little of the business, as much as he would let me, and learned the recording business, you know, how it worked at that time.
>
> Me and Vernon rode with Ike and Tina in his '63 Cadillac Fleetwood. And we had to ride in that for a couple of weeks and once we became permanent members of the show then we got to ride on the bus. I look back on that with a lot of gratitude.

But Stacy returned to St. Louis, not thrilled with life on the bus nor Ike's treatment of Tina and his employees. He went back to Benny Sharp for the 1963 record "Do the 45," made in Oliver Sain's new recording studio on the North Side, with Oliver on sax. In 1965 Benny made "Tired of Being Lonely" with Stacy on lead vocal. The band settled into the role of senior R&B band in East St. Louis, a lofty status held until the late seventies.

The rest of the Ike and Tina story took place on a galaxy far away from St. Louis. From 1963 until they flew apart in 1976, they lived on platforms of rarified air, Ike with his millions to spend on cocaine, Tina battling for her life, living for the time she spent on stage. During these years Ike nearly killed himself with his drug habit, then nearly killed Tina with his brutality. But Ike landed square and so did Tina.

They managed to put out over 80 singles during the 13 years on the road, sometimes making $10,000 for a gig, sometimes $300. There were peak points like the Phil Spector-produced "River Deep/Mountain High" in 1966, and "Proud Mary" in 1970, but mostly it was the relentless road, the arguments over sex, drugs, and money, then another ride in the Cadillac, another town, another show.

Tina was being abused the whole way, beaten with fists, kicked with shoes, shoved, harassed and made generally miserable all through the decade after leaving St. Louis. By around 1971 the money was rolling in and Ike was in control of all of it. The Stones paid $10,000 a show. In 1970 Ike made a $150,000 deal with Liberty records, and he spent $90,000 on a recording studio in Los Angeles. He won hundreds of thousands in Vegas gambling rooms.

In 1975 Tina played a role in the film *Tommy* and made a stunning appearance on an Ann-Margaret TV special. Her singing was getting sharper and sharper and more and more people knew about the hurdles Ike made her leap over on a daily basis. He, on the other hand, was lost in the drug dazed all-night cocaine recording sessions that failed to produce much music.

In June 1975 the pair had their last hit together, "Baby Get It On," which barely made the Top 100, reaching No. 88, a very special number to Ike Turner. Tina grew increasingly afraid; the rules seemed to change.

"Ike got worse," she said. "You never knew what you were getting hit for." She stayed away for a couple of weeks but he found her and beat her up. She was quiet for a while, then on July 1, 1976, the bicentennial of her country, Tina declared her independence and ran away from her hotel room in Dallas, leaving Ike in the dust.

"When he fought, he used things and not just his hands," Tina explained. On that last night, they drove in from the airport:

> By the time we got to the hotel, the left side of my face was swollen like a monster's. I never cried, though. I laughed. I laughed because I knew I was leaving. No more of this. I massaged him and cooed, "Can I order you any food, dear?" Then he made the mistake of going to sleep.

Tina split. A friend bought her a plane ticket home. "I felt strong. I felt like Martin Luther King."

They divorced in 1978. Tina said didn't she fight over money even though she had never gotten her share of the take.

"My peace of mind was more important. Whatever was involved in our lives—property, masters, royalty rights—he got."

However, Tina eventually wound up getting the ultimate music franchise, parlaying her skill on stage with an uncanny sense for what to record. Her shows were packed, her albums sold in the tens of millions, her personal life settled into a long relationship with a German record executive and she stayed mostly in Switzerland.

She staged a final, massive tour of North America and Europe in 2008 and 2009 that she said was a last celebration of the 50th anniversary of her first days on the stage in St. Louis. The final tour lasted seven months and she made the most of it, selling out 90 shows and grossing nearly $150 million.

Ike was dead by then, having suffered greatly from the stories of his abusive treatment of Tina. Her autobiography *I, Tina,* detailed the abuse and was made into the 1993 movie *What's Love Got Do With It,* which sealed Ike's reputation as a wife beater, charges he glibly tried to refute in his own book in ways that sounded more like confessions than refutations.

His long cocaine habit landed him in jail in 1989 but after spending 17 months in prison he emerged with a clear head and made two award-winning records, including a Grammy for the blues album *Risin' With the Blues* in 2006.

On Dec. 12, 2007, Ike Turner died at his home near San Diego. Little Richard, Phil Spector and others from his musical past attended the funeral. "Rocket 88" was played. The medical examiner said he had died from a combination of emphysema and "cocaine toxicity." In 2010 he was honored in hometown of Clarksdale with a marker on the Mississippi Blues Trail.

An attempt to honor Turner in St. Louis failed in 2007 when Mayor Francis Slay refused a request from organizers of the Big Muddy Blues Festival, where Ike was scheduled to perform, to proclaim Sept. 2 "Ike Turner Day" in the city. After the rebuff from City Hall, Turner cancelled the performance.

In an interview with the *Post-Dispatch* he said he had nothing against the city for its actions, but that "my personal life was what it was" and that it wasn't the "world's business." He said he was sorry for his treatment of

Tina, and that he had apologized to her and was sorry he had embarrassed her with "all this crap I did." He never admitted beating or raping her, however.

He did have one honor in the city where he made his name, a star on the St. Louis Walk of Fame in the Delmar Loop entertainment district. But he said he didn't care about that honor. "I don't care about the Hall of Fame. I just care to make people in the audience happy."

Meanwhile, Tina Turner's unprecedented career played out before the millions who bought her records and attended her tours, making 10 solo albums after the breakup with Ike and touring through three decades. Her albums sold, sold and sold some more, her combination of blues, R&B and rock was irresistible to a whole new generation of fans. Her voice became better, husky and soulful. She was right there, spot on. Her freedom from Ike released a performance talent among the greatest in the history of music.

Private Dancer in 1984 sealed her place in the musical pantheon. By 2010 that album had sold over 20 million copies. *Break Every Rule,* in 1986, sold over 8 million; *Foreign Affair* tallied nearly 20 million in 1988; *Wildest Dreams* in 1996 netted over 6 million; and *Twenty Four Seven* in 1999 rang up nearly 9 million. A compilation album, *Simply the Best,* in 1991, sold 19 million. Another compilation, *All the Best,* brought 6 million sales. And the *What's Love Got To Do With It* movie soundtrack added another 5 million.

Private Dancer and *Break Every Rule* both sent a remarkable seven singles onto the charts. She had 57 different singles reach the charts.

She was named to the Rock and Roll Hall of Fame 2013, the same year she married the German record executive Erwin Bach after a partnership kindled in the late eighties. She became a Swiss citizen, and made a few non-performance appearances in Europe. In the summer of 2015 People magazine spotted her in Zurich and described her as "making a statement with her makeup, rocking a bold red lip and effortless glow."

Little Annie had taken a long journey from Sumner High.

The cast of lesser musical lights who helped engineer the R&B and rock 'n' roll takeover of the music scene in St. Louis in the fifties and sixties was large, diverse and skillful. They were the bedrock to building the excitement, the day-to-day players who performed at a level rare in any U.S. city.

A few stand out as examples, led by **Benny Sharp and the Sharpies.** Sharp was from Tupelo, Miss., born March 27, 1930. He began playing guitar as a young boy and moved to St. Louis to make a living playing music in 1947. Soon he was leading bands that played the Red Top and the Dyna-Flow and was a regular on the scene throughout the fifties, the next best band behind Ike.

Sharp, who played lead guitar but didn't sing, gathered an all-star cast in his bands, several of who also had played for Ike and others who went on to make a living solo. He started with Stacy Johnson who had sung with a group called the Arabians. Then came Stacy Johnson's boyhood friend and singer, Vernon Guy, from the Cool Sounds.

He also added singers Herbert Reeves and Horise O'Toole from the Originals. Mike Crowder was on bass, "Bell Boy" Carter on drums, "Butter Cup" on sax and Oliver Thomas on the keys. An early version of the band was called Benny Sharp and the Zorros of Rhythm, another name was the New Breed, which featured the singer Little Miss Jessie Smith, who had been an Ikette in the pre-Tina days, moving over to the Sharpies in 1961.

The band had a few hits, including "The St. Louis Sunset Twist" in 1961, "Do the 45" in 1963, with Johnson and Guy (and Oliver Sain on sax) leading the way, and "Tired of Being Lonely" in 1965, with the soulful Reeves carrying the vocal load. The group made records for One-derful, discs that became hot collectibles in the Internet era. But the group is mostly remembered for its stage shows, with its array of upfront singers, both male and female (especially Little Miss Jessie) and a hot horn section often led by the dexterous Eddie Silver.

The group was in high demand as the sixties rolled along and with Johnson, Guy and Benny himself the stalwarts. The Sharpies saw a continuing changing cast, surviving even the shooting death of Reeves in 1972.

"He was doing the street thing," Johnson recalled, "and one of his constituents, whatever you want to call him, shot and killed him. He had beaten the boy up and the boy shot him. Tragic. But we went on with the Sharpies. We'd replace members and move right along the road, based out of here. I was working, coming home and chasing women."

Sharp was slowed by illness in the late seventies and left the stage in 1980 at the age of 50, turning to religion. By 1990 he had become an elder in the Refuge Temple in East St. Louis and was still living on the East Side, age 83, in 2014.

Vernon Guy and Johnson, the two old boyhood chums, formed a new Sharpie group that played around St. Louis in the eighties in a band that included Guy's nephew Paul Grady. Johnson soldiered on into the twenty-first century, mostly playing solo with backup bands put together for specific shows.

In 2012 a stroke almost brought Stacy down but the next year he was standing tall at a benefit at BB's Jazz, Blues & Soups, a show put together to help him pay his doctor bills. At 67, he was resplendent in a fifties-style red jumpsuit, his trademark baldhead covered by a sharp black bluesman hat. His friends and colleagues filled up the place on a hot July Sunday afternoon, with a show that featured an all-star cast of St. Louisans led by the Soulard Blues Band, Soul Endeavour and the Ground Floor Band.

Looking a little weak, Stacy managed two numbers, "Look Out" and "Rainy Night in Georgia." There was nothing weak about his singing, however, the voice creamy, everything well spoken and clear as a bell. We felt the sadness of the rain, the mist of the tears from the Ray Charles/Brook Benton standard. "Hoverin' by my suitcase, tryin' to find a warm place to spend the night." Stacy'd been there, traveling that road with Ike Turner.

But this wasn't Ike on guitar that day, it was Tom Maloney, one of the great St. Louis sidemen whose credentials run as long as that rainy night down south. He remembered a time when he was just 16 -- a night in 1967 -- and starting to play in bands when he paid his dollar to get into the Club Imperial, a high school kid thrilled by the Ike and Tina Revue. Maloney's memory is as sharp as a Sharpie.

At the Imperial that night:

> It was really crowded and smoky and we all go down front, as close as we can get. I wanted to see the way Ike played his chords, so I could learn them, you know. This was pure show -- just street theatrics, no special equipment. What they did that night was just incredible.

> And I remember Ike had this left-handed guitar player up there with him. And I would have to say this was probably one of the most high energy, highly polished, most dramatic shows I have ever seen.

Maloney didn't know the name of the left-handed guitar player that night, but as most every rock fan knows, Jimi Hendrix played the guitar left-handed.

Clayton Love was four years older than Ike Turner, born on Nov. 15, 1927, in Mattson, Miss., then moved as a child to nearby Clarksdale, where he remembered playing piano cutting contests against Ike beginning in elementary school.

Love's father lost the family's money in the stock market crash of 1932.

> My mother told him to go up to the bank and draw out our savings, and there was a lock on the (bank) door. And the day before, it was open, you see. People were jumping off buildings, committing suicide, it was tragic.

As the family suffered, Love took refuge in a leftover from the good days -- the piano.

> I came by piano as an accident, and I had no other choice, because nobody else in our immediate society could play it . . . Now I'd played around with the piano for a while, see, this was back in the forties, then I went away into the Navy. I was at the USO, that was the only place I could go at that age anyway -- I was 16, but had said I was 17.
>
> One day a photographer came in from the *Oakland Inquirer* and he was taking scenes of servicemen down there. So there I sat at the piano, and all these girls came around, and he came over and took our picture. That was the beginning, and I had to stick with it.

After the end of the war, Love spent four years at Alcorn A&M, which had been a black college in Mississippi since just after the Civil War, located near Vicksburg and Jackson in southern Mississippi. He graduated in 1949 and in Jackson in 1951 made his first record.

From there, Love recorded with saxist Raymond Hill and his band for Aladdin records in 1952 then moved to St. Louis to join Ike in 1954, and by 1957, Love was on piano and singing with the full band -- now called Ike Turner and the Kings of Rhythm -- live in the clubs and recorded in the studio. He made "The Big Question," a local hit that year. In 1958, just after Tina came along, Love went over to Bobbin, the independent St. Louis label, and joined the bassist Roosevelt Marks for "Limited Love"/ "Unlimited Love."

Love had no resentment against Tina for taking over his spot at the front of the Kings of Rhythm. "She and I were very close," he remembered in an interview with the *St. Louis BluesLetter* in 1999.

> She became attached to my wife and used to come over and babysit for our kids. I was advising her that she should think twice about the entertainment business. I told her it was a rough life. But she wanted to sing. She would learn my tunes and watch me singing on stage, I used to give her little hints and tips about performing. And as soon as I quit, Little Annie fell right into place.

Love played for the Sharpies and on his own into the early seventies, enjoying a standing gig during the mid-sixties at Al's Steak House in West County. He died Feb. 28, 2010, at age 82, having built a new career after he stepped down from the bandstand. He went back to college and received a master's degree in 1972 from the University of Missouri-St. Louis, then taught elementary school in the St. Louis public school system and later became an administrator at Vashon High School.

But Love never lost interest in performing and continued to make appearances in the revived blues scene of the eighties and nineties. Tom "Papa" Ray, the DJ, record store owner and blues harmonica player, said Love "had a wonderful way at the piano, and his vocals were always convincing and heartfelt." John May, the former president of the St. Louis Blues Society, compared Love to Ray Charles and Jackie Wilson, and said his style was as suave as his name implied.

May and the Blues Society were at least partly responsible for Love's swan song, a European tour billed as the St. Louis Kings of Rhythm in 1987 that also included Ike alumni Stacy Johnson, Billy Gayles, Robbie Montgomery, Erskine Oglesby and Oliver Sain.

Billy Gayles was born in Clarksdale Oct. 19, 1931, the same year as Ike, and moved up with Turner into the clubs and recording studios, usually as a singer. He was on the stage with Tina Turner in the 1957-1960 period.

By the seventies Gayles had his own band, playing locally, and the 1987 European tour gave him a shot in the arm musically. He played into the early nineties, with a band called Billy and the Preachers that included Steve Martin on guitar, Jon Rosen on the keyboards, and Mike Prokopf on bass.

Gayles' main contribution is "I'm Tore Up," his 1956 hit with Ike Turner's Rhythm Rockers -- "one drink, two drinks, three or four; I'm tore up -- drunk as I can be." Turner's guitar is in fine form on the cut and the horn section blasts sufficiently for this to count as ripping R&B. An early days disc, the record was part of the field of 1956 hits that solidified the rock movement.

The song has been a favorite cover for blues bands beginning in the seventies and all the way up to and including a horn-driven version by Duke Robillard's Jumpin' Blues Revue in 2009. In the summer of 2012 at BB's in St. Louis, Eric McSpadden led the Rough Grooves band with a harmonica take off on the horn part of the song while Rich McDonough was true blue to Ike's original riff. But the highlight was Eric's blasts on the harp and his convincing delivery of the line "drunk as I can be" even while looking fit and sober, his baldhead shiny in the lights.

McSpadden did the song again a couple of weeks later at the Blues City Deli, playing this time with Mojo Syndrome. He had the lead harp again and took the Billy Gayles lyrics seriously. Larry Griffin, my companion on the North Side tours, grabbed the guitar part this time, perhaps remembering the days he saw Ike up there on the stage at the Club Imperial, dancing a step or two out of the Billy Gayles-Stacy Johnson book of fancy foot work. Gayles' recording of "I'm Tore Up" also showed up on KDHX DJ's Ron Edwards "Nothing But the Blues" 2012 tribute to St. Louis blues artists who have died, next on the play list after Clayton Love's "Chain of Love."

Another of Ike's singers was **Art Lassiter**, famed for being the guy who didn't show up in 1960 when Turner recruited his new singer, "Little

Annie" Bullock, to fill in on "A Fool in Love." A pay dispute with Ike was apparently the source of the no-show, there are other stories, but what mattered was that the singing voice of Little Annie made its way to Juggy Murray in New York.

Lassiter was a large-sized man with the rich, deep voice that Ike favored for his lead singers. He blended well with Robbie Montgomery, who was an original Artette, an Ikette and who later became the highly successful St. Louis restaurant owner of Sweetie Pie's, with her own television series. Lassiter's luck wasn't this good, even though he, too, owned a restaurant.

Lassiter was born on the very cold night of Jan. 27, 1928, during a snowstorm in a North Carolina cotton field, where his father saved his life by warming the baby with bales of cotton. He sang gospel as a youth then left home at 14 to join his mother in Newark, N.J., where she had moved looking for work and a way out of the sharecropper life. While in Jersey, Lassiter fell in with a gospel group called the Jubilaires.

He missed World War II but went into the service in time for the Korean War where he sang in USO shows in the Far East. Mustered out of the Army in 1953, Lassiter and some army buddies took off driving across country. The car broke down in St. Louis and Lassiter entered an amateur contest to earn some needed cash. There he met Douglas Martin and brothers George and Murray Green and joined their group, the Bel-Airs.

By October 1955 the Bel-Airs had been renamed the Trojans, then the Rockers, and caught the eye of Ike Turner. Lassiter joined the Rhythm Kings, recorded two sides for the Bihari's RPM Records, then recorded again in March 1956. By then Lassiter was a fixture in Ike's stage shows. After his ill-fated failure to record "A Fool in Love," he remained in the group, singing duets with Tina and parts in the Ikettes, but by 1961 was cut loose from the stage shows. He had his one modest hit that year, "It's All Right," still backed by Ike.

Lassiter had visions of stardom but never made it. He worked in California, New Zealand and Canada, and then settled in Seattle. He later owned a restaurant in Hawaii where he sang and cooked southern soul food and BBQ.

"He lived for the stage. That's where he was most alive. He was a master of four-part harmony . . . and picked really beautiful songs. He truly was a dreamer," one relative said after Lassiter died Aug. 4, 1994.

Andrew "Voice" Odum was another background St. Louis performer in the fifties, moving to the city in 1955 and known mostly for his recording of "Take Me Back to East St. Louis" in 1961. When playing at Lorraine's Tavern in 1957, the Chicago bluesman Earl Hooker heard Odum's vocal work and begin calling him "B. B. King Jr." During this time Odum was a mainstay of the late night East Side scene playing with Ike Turner, Little Milton, Billy Gayles and the rest of the Rhythm Kings crowd.

Hooker often stayed at Ike Turner's house on Virginia Street in East St. Louis. In 1960, Odum caught a bus for Chicago and got a job singing with Earl Hooker, appearing on numerous records, including a 1968 waxing of "Take Me Back to East St. Louis," also recorded as "Going to East St. Louis." The original version of "Take Me Back to East St. Louis" (which is a different song from W.C. Handy and Duke Ellington songs that also use East St. Louis in the title) was credited to a band called The Hound Dogs.

Odum was born on Dec. 15, 1936, in Denham Springs, La., and had worked his way up the river, landing in East St. Louis about the time of his 21st birthday in 1957. The song was recorded in Belleville, Ill., a cut featuring Willie Kizart, another of Ike Turner's guitar players, with Odom sitting in for "Screamin'" Joe O'Neal, who was sick at the time of session.

Another St. Louis musician, **"Little Aaron" Mosby,** got the vocal credit on the cut but it's Odum singing and bandleader Kizart on guitar. "Little Aaron" was born in Pine Bluff, Ark., April 15, 1930, and came to St. Louis in 1948. He was also part of the fifties scene and wound up playing with such luminaries as Albert King, Chuck Berry and Doc Terry.

The Ike Turner sphere of influence wasn't the only thing happening in St. Louis in those days, of course. The rest of the cast also had plenty to say.

Billy Davis, Jr., a gospel singer born in St. Louis who was an original member of the 5th Dimension, the pop group that had five No. 1 hits, emerged on the St. Louis scene in 1958 as part of a vocal group called the Emeralds.

Davis was born in Kinloch in north St. Louis County June 26, 1938, and by age 11 was singing professionally for the Emeralds. That group evolved into the religious oriented Saint Louis Gospel Singers, which traveled for five years during the summer months.

He then established The Versatiles, which included another St. Louisan, **Lamont McLemore**, and Davis' future wife, **Marilyn McCoo**. The Versatiles morphed into the 5th Dimension, which in 1967 had its first Top Ten hit with "Up, Up and Away" and went on to win six Grammys. McCoo and Davis also won a Grammy as a duo after they left the 5th Dimension in 1975.

In the nineties, 'Davis played road show versions of the Broadway musicals *Dreamgirls* and *Blues in the Night.* The couple was still performing in 2014 on their "How Sweet It Is" tour, celebrating 45 years of marriage.

Davis also had a brief tenure with another notable St. Louis vocal group, the doo-wop oriented **El Torros,** which added another layer of diversity of the fifties scene. Formed by singer Lloyd Lockett in 1951, the group signed to a record contract with the Cincinnati King-Federal record company in 1956. El Torros made several discs but had no hits and went through many changes. The band had many St. Louis appearances, often backing out of town soul singers like Dinah Washington.

Davis was the replacement for another singer named **Fred Green**, who had recorded on the St. Louis Bobbin label in the mid-fifties as a member of the Mellards. Green joined El Torro in 1956 just before it caught the eye of Bobby "Blue" Bland, a strong selling bluesman from Chicago. He pointed them toward a record contract with the Duke label from Houston that led to two sessions and a couple of now nearly impossible to find old records.

Green's record on Bobbin was called, "Don't Make a Fool of Me," a 45 that in 2013 brought over $100 at an e-Bay auction. With The El Torros, Green was also involved in the release of two discs for Duke between 1957 and 1960, neither of which charted very well. "You Look Good To Me," recorded at a session in St. Louis in 1958, is another of these valuable collector records, put out on a 78 as Duke 194. In 1959 he recorded "Wham Slam Bam," also for Duke, with Little Milton on guitar.

Johnny "The Twist" Williams was a guitarist whose popularity drew big crowds to the Peppermint Lounge in suburban Belleville, Ill,. He recorded five sides for a local DJ before quitting the St. Louis scene and heading north. He hooked up with Koko Taylor in Chicago and played the lead guitar on her hit "Wang Dang Doodle" in 1964, a side that also included Buddy Guy and Willie Dixon. While in St. Louis Williams worked with Albert King and Andrew Odum.

"Screamin'" Joe Neal was born in St. Louis, then moved to South Bend, Ind., then returned to the banks of the Mississippi in 1959, inspired by Little Richard to record speed-ball rockers, taking his crazed stage act into the clubs around the city, adding a somewhat demented element to the wild, all-night R&B parties.

His favorite trick was to crawl around on his knees in the crowd and sneak up behind a woman while his band was playing away and scream as loud as he could, giving the customer a good scare, a good laugh and a story to tell. He'd then climb back up on stage and without missing a beat dove back into whatever rocker he was delivering. One night he leaped from on top of the organ into the crowd and broke his ankle and was carried off on a stretcher. The next night he was back on the stage.

He ran through the circuit of clubs, enjoying a long run at the Peppermint Lounge in the Delmar Loop with the guitarist Bennie Smith. Neal recorded at a studio on the North Side for a St. Louis gospel label called St. Louis Shippings, but only cut two sides. One of them was "Rock and Roll Deacon," where he gave the piano a memorable pounding while growling and shouting on a punk-like song that never lets up from the very beginning downbeat, capturing the frenzy of 1959 about as well as any single.

Screamin' Joe recorded again in 1966 and took a trip to Chicago to promote his new record, but by the time he came back to St. Louis the Shippings record company was out of business. He kept on going and in 1971 joined a band that included the young Tom Maloney on guitar.

Maloney and his band of young players helped Neal make a record, "Don't Quit Me Baby" at Oliver Sain's Archways Studios. The record, a remake of a 1959 Neal original, is mostly Neal doing his screaming vocal but also includes Sain on sax and a couple of competent lead solos by Maloney, who remember:

> Screamin' Joe had fallen on hard times by then. But he agreed to sing with the band. He was great -- nobody could touch him on James Brown or Little Richard -- it was quite an experience.

> Oliver was doing Joe a favor. He knew this wasn't going to be a hit record. But this was one St. Louis musician showing the spirit of cooperation that permeated the scene thought the city's musical history. Just a warm and wonderful thing that Oliver did for Joe. We in the band were not good players. But Oliver was very patient. It didn't sound too awfully bad.

Shortly after making the record Screamin' Joe was hit by a truck and paralyzed. There is no definitive evidence when (or if) Neal died.

While rock and R&B was the headline story of music in fifties and sixties (especially for the white crowds and the mainstream media) in places like St. Louis, the blues didn't die. Mainstays like Henry Townsend, Walter Davis and Roosevelt Sykes were joined by a new batch of players, new arrivals and home grown players alike who kept the North Side clubs humming and provided the foundation for the blues revival that gave another shot of life to that St. Louis thing.

Little Milton Campbell, a leading example of the new infusion of blues players, landed in St. Louis in 1955, another of the musicians from Mississippi connected to Ike Turner. He was born in the Delta on Sept. 7, 1934, in Inverness, a small town near Greenville. Milton's father, a bluesman himself, was known as Big Milton, and even though Little Milton was anything but little as a grown man, that was the name that stuck.

He started playing guitar when he was 12 and formed his own band while in high school, then met Turner, who was scouting talent in the early fifties. He recorded his first sides in 1953, with Turner on piano, in the Memphis studios of Sun Records. He recorded several more sides for Sam Phillips at Sun, then left the South to join Turner in East St. Louis.

"I met Ike during the time that he and his group and Jackie Brenston made 'Rocket 88,'" Milton said in a *Living Blues* interview. "We got to be pretty good friends from there. He always wanted to get into a little more than just being an artist or musician. He was always coming up with deals and meeting people that none of the rest of us really got to know too much about. He was like the brain thing."

Milton moved to St. Louis in 1955. He cut sides in 1957 in Memphis for the Bihari brothers, who had the St. Louis saxophone great Oliver Sain in the house band. Those records didn't go anywhere and Milton helped a St. Louis DJ named Bob Lyons start Bobbin Records, perhaps the most important of all the St. Louis labels. Milton recruited Sain and several others for Bobbin, including Albert King, Fontella Bass and Art Lassiter.

Milton's recording "I'm A Lonely Man," sold 60,000 on Bobbin with a lineup that included locals Larry Prothero on trumpet, Sain on sax, and Bass playing piano. In all, Milton made seven singles for Bobbin, including two that were released after Leonard Chess bought out Lyons and signed Milton and the others to his Checker label.

The late fifties and early sixties were the glory period of independent record labels, as they popped up all the over the country. Bobbin was the St. Louis version, but unlike Sun, Chess, Imperial (New Orleans) and dozens of others, Bobbin didn't last long enough in St. Louis to build up a national following.

The Bobbin catalog of 44 records, however, is filled with gems, running from 1958 to 1963. Lyons is the mystery man of St. Louis music, known to have come to St. Louis from Rochester, N.Y., and rumored to have moved to Florida with a pocket full of Leonard Chess' cash, but whose name doesn't crop up in the music histories after he sold out. The best look at Bobbin available is *St. Louis Blues Revue: The Classic Bobbin Sessions*, a CD released by Ace in 1996.

After Bobbin folded, Sain began his Archway label and continued to record dozens of St. Louisans, but again, the city never grew a recording industry of major status to call its own, a factor many see as a big reason why so many St. Louis musicians remained outside the hit making factories like Chess in Chicago or Sun in Memphis.

Milton pressed on, getting his biggest hit in 1965 when he rode the coattails of the Civil Rights movement with a No. 1 R&B hit "We're Gonna Make It." He moved to Chicago in 1967 and toured year round through the sixties and seventies with the Miltonettes, hitting such spots as the Apollo in Harlem, the Regal in Chicago, the Montreaux Jazz Festival in Switzerland, the Kiel Auditorium in St. Louis and the Medgar Evers Festival in Jackson, Mississippi.

He was steadily making records for Chess until Leonard Chess died in 1969, when he signed with Stax in Memphis. He continued to play

St. Louis regularly, including a memorable appearance with Albert King during the first St. Louis Blues Festival in 1986.

He said his time in St. Louis in the sixties was the high point of his career, "there was lots of work, lots of clubs on both sides of the river. On the Illinois side, the late clubs stayed open all night. And in Missouri you had the clubs in the city and the white clubs in St. Louis County. There was more work than you could handle."

Milton's last single was "Age Ain't Nothing But a Number" in 1983 and he entered the Blues Hall of Fame in 1988. He died Aug. 4, 2005, after a career that saw a total of 16 albums in the R&B charts along with 28 singles, four of them in the Top Ten.

Erskine Ogelsby was a St. Louis native, born Jan. 20, 1937, in Mill Creek Valley. He was playing in a band with Chuck Berry by age 14 at the start of the fifties, learning to play at Vashon High. These were in the days before his neighborhood was demolished by the city and there were several thriving music joints near his home where he could put to use what he learned in school.

With Berry he played a boogie piano in the joints. "We were just a little corner band, a guy who played a big upright blond bass . . . a guy, he was blind, that played drums. I think his name was Tommy. That was a little four piece" before Berry met his playing partner, Johnnie Johnson, and headed for his first big hit.

Ogelsby left Berry and joined the Air Force at the end of the Korean War, then hooked up with Billy Gayles and his band when he got out of the service in 1958. "It seemed the music jobs came quicker than the so-called day jobs. So I just started in and got to enjoy it. I met a lot of the local musicians, and it became very interesting and entertaining."

He was never quite able to escape the day jobs, however, always coming a little short in the pay department. So he washed dishes and for a time worked as a street worker for the YMCA helping the unemployed find jobs.

He got a degree in social work and worked with poor kids, but "the music was always pulling me. It got so when I played music late at night, I couldn't get up in the morning for my day job, and so I had to make a choice." He chose the sax and in the nineties, when the blues revival created new opportunities, Oglesby was finally able to have full-time career.

Along the way, he added his sax skills to records by Little Milton, Albert King, Ike and Tina Turner, Benny Sharp, and a host of other people. He also played jazz with the quartet Tres' Bien and with Terry Williams and the Sound Merchants. And he took part in tours of Europe with other St. Louis musicians.

There he got a new view of blues music.

> I equated it with being down and out, suffering and all that. But when I saw so many people liking it, I thought maybe I need to take a different look at it. Let me sit down and rethink this, and listen real good. And I started liking the blues. When I sat down and evaluated myself, I realized that this is inborn. I can do this with ease. It's a feeling, an emotion, and it doesn't necessarily have to be a negative.

Another blues performer, also loosely connected to Ike Turner, was playing around town by the early fifties -- **Tommy Bankhead,** a master bluesman who became another foundation of the eighties and nineties "Golden Age of Blues" in St. Louis. Bankhead was a Mississippi native, born in Lake Cormorant Oct. 24, 1931. He moved to St. Louis to play Ned Love's club on the East Side in 1949.

Bankhead's influences in the Delta included Howlin' Wolf and Sonny Boy Williamson II (Rice Miller). While playing around Memphis he met a couple of St. Louis players, including Boyd Gilmore, one of Ike's guitarists. Gilmore urged Bankhead to come play the scene in St. Louis. Once in town, he enjoyed a long stint at Love's and was a mainstay of The El Morocco on the St. Louis side of the river.

Bankhead formed his Blues Eldorados and made a living in the clubs of the North Side during the sixties, as well as a joint on Chouteau called Miss B's and a South Side stand named the Pinto Lounge. He made only a scant stab at recording, including an electric bass backup on a Henry Townsend record in 1961. Bankhead was still a closely kept secret of blues fans when the sixties rolled in, but his day would come later in the white bars of Soulard and as a leader in the blues revival.

Big George Brock was another arrival in the fifties and by 2016, more than 60 years later, was the last man standing of the group of St.

Louis bluesmen who began in the post-war period. Like Bankhead he later emerged during the revival of the seventies and the golden age of the nineties and were still alive and playing in the twenty-first century. Indeed, Big George was a headliner of the 2014 Bluesweek Festival, 29 years after he played in the very first such event sponsored by the St. Louis Blues Society.

Born May 10, 1932, in Grenada, Miss., Brock's father picked cotton and sometimes played the harmonica. When George was 10, his father gave him and his two brothers harmonicas for Christmas. In 1949, George and the family moved to Mattson, a town near Clarksdale, and the teenager began playing parties. He watched Sonny Boy Williamson and B.B. King at local clubs, played the rub board behind Robert Nighthawk, worked as a set-up man for Howlin' Wolf.

In 1953 he moved to St. Louis, intending to use his huge size to advantage as a boxer. His career as a fighter didn't work out and in 1956 he began playing at the Early Bird Lounge in a band called Foster, a gig that lasted three years and led to a 10-year run into the late sixties. He faded from view as the scene collapsed around him, but Big George's days on the boards were far from over.

In the late eighties, **Bennie Smith** had become the dean of St. Louis electric guitar players, built on a second career founded on his long life in St. Louis. Like Ogelsby, Smith was a native of Mill Creek Valley -- growing up on the eastern edge of the black neighborhood that was torn down beginning in 1959.

A cousin who came back from World War II carrying a ukulele introduced Smith to music. Born Oct. 5, 1933, Bennie was the seventh son of 14 children. By the time he was 12 he had a guitar, a little mail order Stella given him by his brother. He began picking at the strings, playing along with Bobby "Blue" Bland, B.B. King and Junior Walker on his radio.

He started hanging around the clubs in Mill Creek, especially in the area where the Jefferson Street Bridge now goes over the railroad tracks. In these joints he heard Ace Wallace and the Memphis bluesman Matt "Guitar" Murphy, a frequent visitor who later joined the Blues Brothers in Chicago. But for Bennie, Wallace was the real teacher, the one who "showed me so much on the guitar, a whole lot of things, how to hold my fingers, how to play everything."

He and Wallace began to play around on weekends. He also met Gabriel, the trumpet player and DJ. Smith, Wallace and Gabriel got a weekend gig near Fort Leonard Wood. They played Dots Lounge in North City where he met Ike Turner, Chuck Berry and the bass player Roosevelt Marks (the first black musician to appear on local TV).

Smith helped Ike Turner learn his licks on the guitar just after Turner arrived in St. Louis in the mid-fifties. Ike "was a pretty darn good piano player, but he wanted to play guitar. So we got together and started playing. He learned that song ("Okie Dokie Stomp") a different way, 'cause he wanted to put a whole lot of different stuff in it. So I think he called it 'Prancin,'" Smith said.

By 1958, Smith's guitar was beginning to be heard on records, most famously on Tina Turner's first recording, a single called "Box Top" on Gabriel's Tune Town label, cut in Ike's house in East St. Louis. He also recorded with Clayton Love and began to play the electric guitar, putting together a group called Bennie Smith and the Sportsmen, at times playing behind "Screamin'" Joe Neal and with players with names like "Woofer" and "Gawk" and "Chops."

He was described as a player with great technical mastery who knew how to innovate. "When Bennie went on stage, a lot of guitarists wouldn't go on after him," Gabriel remembered. "They'd try to copy his licks, but he would certainly show them up."

By the sixties Smith and his band had a six night a week gig at the Peppermint Lounge, a big nightclub at the western edge of the city in the area now called the Delmar Loop. Smith remembers the place as the biggest nightclub in the city in the mid-sixties, a club said to be run by the St. Louis cousins of the mobsters who started the original Peppermint Lounge in New York City.

The club closed, however, and Bennie got fewer big gigs, playing jams and sessions with the litany of St. Louis players like Oliver Sain, Albert King, Little Milton and Billy Gayles and backed travelers such as B.B. King and Aretha Franklin. He played the North Side but as the city emptied and many clubs closed, Bennie faded as well, working as a television repairman. He suffered eye problems and had a bad back from years of factory work and soon stopped playing in public altogether.

But when the eighties revived the blues, Bennie Smith reemerged as well, standing in the Baton Record Store not far from the old Peppermint Lounge on the Delmar Loop, wearing a green jump suit and a pork-pie bluesman hat, asking a young repairman if he could get his electric guitar fixed.

Ace Wallace was another St. Louis native, born June 18, 1925, regarded as one of the city's unsung blues guitar heroes. His father was a steel worker who played guitar. One day when Ace was 11 a fight broke out at a party at their house on the North Side. Somebody broke a mandolin over another partygoers' head during the scuffle. Ace took the broken pieces and made an instrument out of it. He soon learned to play.

During the war he served in the South Pacific then used the G.I. bill to attend music school. He soon found he knew as much as his teachers and in 1950 joined a traveling player named Yank Rachell as a sideman. Wallace, however, developed an eye condition and by his late 20s was blind. The government paid for treatment and rehabilitation and he learned how to cope with his disability.

In the mid-fifties he formed Ace Wallace and the Trumps and started playing the North Side clubs and the joints in Mill Creek Valley or for tips on the corner of Jefferson and Chouteau.

He met Bennie Smith and taught him how to play, then joined Big George and the Houserockers, where he drove the rhythm behind George's harp in a band that played for a decade at George's club, the Early Bird. At the same time, he was also part of a band led by the trumpet player known as Gabriel and appears on several of the trumpet player's recordings, adding a sterling guitar backing.

Wallace was still active as the blues revival started up, making a memorable appearance in Fairgrounds Park with Big George in 1975 that helped put blues back on the map in St. Louis.

His blindness and other ailments kept him from enjoying the golden age of blues in St. Louis, however, spending his last years in a nursing home. He still managed to record a few compositions on a drum machine and give guitar lessons to young students. He died in Feb. 28, 1996, at age 70.

The music career of Mitchell Hearns, known as **Gabriel,** has stretched across seven decades in St. Louis. He was still doing his midnight to 3 a.m.

slot as a DJ on KDHX in 2015. He was also a trumpet player, a record store owner and a producer. He got his start on the East Side in the fifties where he sometimes recorded as Flock Rocker. His age is a well-kept secret, although he says he was born "when there were still dinosaurs on the streets of St. Louis."

Gabriel made at least a dozen records on the Planet, Norman, Tempora 500 and Royal American labels, all out of St. Louis/East St. Louis. Generally these sides were led by Gabriel and backed by Bennie Smith, Ace Wallace and various members of the Kings of Rhythm. They included "East St. Louis Blues" and "Political Prayer Blues," with backing by the super-hot Smith on guitar. He also issued other artists on his own Tune Town label, including Tina Turner's first record.

His career as a DJ is far more long lasting than that as a performer, beginning in 1952 at WOKZ in Alton, Ill., then moving on the KATZ and KDNA before joining KDHX in 1989, where he spins records from his own collection once a week.

Doc Terry was born in Sunflower, Miss., in 1921 as Terry Adail and came to St. Louis after the war to work in the Army Depot in Granite City, Ill. He began playing his harp in East St. Louis, especially at the Red Top, Ned Love's and Huff's Gardens. His harmonica playing was described as a dead ringer for the original Sonny Boy Williamson (John Lee) who Terry heard as a young man in Mississippi.

He was a distant relative of Muddy Waters and came from a musical family. He formed a band called Terry and the Pirates and played clubs on both sides of the river through the fifties and sixties. He retired from the Army in 1971 and had a run into the mid-seventies where he played numerous gigs and recorded two records at the Technisonic Studios, including "Rock with Doc." By the end of the decade he had faded from view but reemerged in 1986 at the first St. Louis Blues Club Festival, one of the events that revived blues in the city.

He landed a long-standing gig at the Broadway Oyster Bar during the eighties and nineties, sharing the leads with the singer Patti Thomas. He died Aug. 24, 2001, at age 79.

Big Bad Smitty (John H. Smith) came to St. Louis in the early sixties and was a mainstay in the Houserockers, Big George Brock's band that played the Club Caravan and the Early Bird in the Central West End and was also a member of a band called Little Weaver and the Dynamites. He was born in Schlater, Miss., Feb. 11, 1940, and was a school dropout who began driving a truck in Jackson when he was 16. He took his nickname from a brief stint as a boxer in the fifties.

His major work came in the eighties and nineties as part of the blues revival and he made a successful album called *Mean Disposition* in 1991. He played for two years at Spraggin's Hacienda on the North Side starting in 1987 with his band Big Bad Smitty and the Upsetters and was part of the Davis Brothers band throughout the nineties. He was a mainstay of the St. Louis scene and played several St. Blues and Heritage Festivals even as his health deteriorated.

The Davis connection led to several European tours and two more albums late in his life. He died April 3, 2002, from diabetes that led to a stroke and the amputation of both legs.

Of all the musicians who joined the St. Louis music scene in the immediate post-war period, three can be judged to have joined the tiny number of American performers called superstars, players who went far beyond the others in fame and fortune, in innovation and pure magic.

We have seen how one, Miles Davis, came to become perhaps the greatest American jazz player ever, dying in California at the age of 65.

We have also seen how another, Tina Turner, was living quietly in 2016 in her villa in Switzerland, content to be retired a long way from the Mississippi.

The third was quite close at hand in 2016, a man who, like Turner, attended Summer High on the North Side and sang songs for a living -- Chuck Berry.

Chapter Twenty-Three

The Chuck and Johnnie Show: Trying to B. Goode

Never in a million years would I have predicted I would become close friends with Chuck Berry. He's so private, not reclusive really, but guarded. Guarded, that's a good word. Little by little, we started doing things. He really respected that I was being honest with him and showed the respect he deserved. We grew to be comfortable and really trusted each other. His private life is separate from mine and mine from his and yet we're good friends.

-- Joe Edwards, owner of Blueberry Hill

Sumner High School was the first high school for African Americans west of the Mississippi when it opened in downtown St. Louis in 1875. The population of post-slavery blacks began to be educated and move away from the riverside communities through the years between the Civil War and World War I. Many of these people, upper income people like Annie Malone, at one time the richest black woman in America, settled in the North Side community called The Ville. In 1908, Sumner students moved into a new school, the imposing red brick building that stands today on

Annie Malone Dr. just south of St. Louis Avenue. After the first war, the school became the heart of a community of upper echelon black doctors, lawyers, union leaders, small business owners and others who had managed to escape the grinding poverty of the South.

By the start of the second war, The Ville was filled with families living in rows of stately brick houses, many built as Gilded Age suburban mansions, others as middle class homes during the twenties and thirties. Other African Americans moved into smaller shotgun style homes, cottages and duplexes for people who worked in the factories that located to the north and east. Family life, work and church membership were the keystones that held the community together.

When Chuck Berry walked up on the stage of Summer High in 1941, he embodied the history of the neighborhood. He was the 14-year-old son of a flour mill worker and his wife, a stay-home mother who kept the finances straight, played the family piano in the living room and made sure everybody made it to church on Sundays, dressed to her specifications. Both she and her husband sang in the choir at the nearby Baptist Church. The family home sat just across the street from Sumner High, a block from the elementary school and adjacent to Tandy Park, the recreation area.

All of the whites who had once lived in the neighborhood had moved out by the Depression years and the first people with white skins Chuck saw as a child were firefighters battling a blaze next door. A white nurse also visited him from a downtown hospital after he suffered from pneumonia. Berry, who was born Oct. 18, 1926, lived in that first house just four years before the family moved to a bigger space in the same neighborhood, an improved residence that had a bathroom inside the house.

When Berry was six the family moved again, this time to a still bigger place, still in the same neighborhood, a five-room brick house with a full basement about 1,000 square feet on the main floor. Unlike the first two houses, this one, at 4420 Cottage Avenue, was still standing in 2014, a lonely soldier on a virtually empty Ville block. Bars blocked the windows, weeds clogged the yard, but the house was apparently inhabited.

Other ghosts of the old neighborhood still stood. His old grade school, Simmons Elementary on St. Louis Avenue, looked big and solid if the visitor ignored a few broken windows. Where the front yard once was landscaped it held a "For Sale" sign: "offered by St. Louis Public Schools for Redevelopment Opportunity."

The Depression had started by the time the Berry family moved into the Cottage Avenue house and while it was an improvement over the previous dwelling it quickly filled up, soon containing not only the six members of the immediate Berry family but also a hard-pressed cousin and his son, making eight people in the place. Berry slept at the foot of a bed shared by his two sisters. This house was also filled with music -- from the piano, from choir practice from the church and from the big Philco radio that broadcast Fats Waller, Louis Armstrong, Gene Autry and Kitty Wells.

A new member of the family arrived in 1933 with Chuck's baby brother Paul. This forced yet another move, to a larger, eight-room affair on Labadie Street. Here in 2014 stood an empty lot next to the Teddy Bear Child Care center, a block from what would have been a busy business district during Chuck's childhood. The school was only a block away and, as always, Chuck could walk less than five minutes to get his education. Dad was by then working two jobs, the mill and a second job working for a German family that owned a realty company and used him as a handy man.

Berry's father worked for the company from 1935 to 1964 and received a necktie when he retired.

Berry entered Sumner High in 1940. "Opportunity," he wrote in his autobiography. "New ideas, ideals, and eye dolls were there to be had."

He already had had some experience with girls, getting into trouble from his father and feeling the taste of the old man's strap. He'd also met a neighbor named Tommy Stevens, who sometimes got paid to play guitar in nightclubs. Berry had made his own guitar out of plywood and tried to learn how to play without much success, but by the beginning of the forties he knew he could sing, often listening to the choir practice in his house and to the jukebox at a joint across the street, getting alternate doses of gospel and blues.

Near the end of the term in the spring of 1941 he and Stevens went up on the stage at Sumner during a variety show called "All Men's Review," a dress-up affair sponsored by the student body for the entertainment of the whole school, students and faculty. Before this Berry had found himself the center of attention singing at neighborhood parties and much enjoyed the feeling, but this was his first appearance before a big audience. His choice for a song put him very much at the center again, only this time he was standing on a stage before hundreds of people.

He made a bold move. Nobody else on the program was singing blues so his selection, "Confessin' the Blues," was indeed audacious. "This is my confession baby/And I'm thrilled by all your charms/It seems like I'm in heaven/When I hold you in my arms." Berry was confident as he sang the song and "when I began laying out the love lyrics the school auditorium exploded with applause." Some in the faculty wasn't applauding, however.

> I realized as I was performing that the audience will respond if you give them what they want to hear and that regardless of your ability (meaning texture of voice) to deliver a song, they will enjoy the feeling that you put into it. At the completion of the selection, I was complimented again by a tremendous ovation.

The road to show business was now the clear path he wanted to take. A friend gave him a real guitar to play and he learned quickly. When the United States entered World War II he had the chance to quit school and get a job, but instead stuck it out at Sumner, especially enjoying parties with his classmates.

He was no model student. He and some friends started stealing gas and hubcaps, breaking into parked cars, smoking marijuana, drinking whiskey and sneaking into downtown strip clubs. He stopped going to Sunday school, avoided church. He took up with a girl who "showed me the way to manhood." But he was caught in the act by his father in a garage behind the house and was again whipped, a beating that led him out of the house more and more, staying instead with his 20-year-old sister, who helped him buy a car.

Berry got a weekend job spinning records for the black USO troops at a radio repair shop near his house and found this was a way to attract girls. The backyard house parties continued and Berry made steady improvements as an entertainer and as a fledgling lady's man, learning guitar chords from a book and from a neighborhood barber, paying less attention to his schoolwork.

Berry no longer fit in with the sons and daughters of the professionals who populated The Ville. He didn't get along with the athletes and the rich kids, he was out of his parents range at his sister's house, he wanted to party and play with the girls, the music of the blues had permeated his lifestyle. His father was by now working full-time for the realty company, often at menial jobs for low pay.

Still just 17 in the fall of 1944, Chuck decided he'd had enough of school, deciding to hang with two friends, a pair of Sumner dropouts, one who was "loudmouthed and lazy," the other "ugly as death eating a dirty doughnut." They were "rebellious and lazy;" they were "my kind of guys."

The three friends decided to get out of The Ville and head for Hollywood, But \heir money only got them as far as Kansas City so they turned around and headed back east toward St. Louis. They pulled three armed robberies of small stores that netted some cash, but their car broke down. To replace it, they stole another vehicle. The owner made a quick call to police and Berry and his companions were nabbed by the state patrol.

Chuck Berry, 18, had fallen out of the middle class. He'd had some fun but now was sent to prison, facing a 10-year sentence. He was a high school dropout, a day laborer who could paint and hammer, but was otherwise unskilled except at the guitar, a teenager in jailed at the Intermediate Reformatory for Young Men, known as "The Hill," two rows of two-story brick buildings filled with cells, two miles south of the Missouri State Penitentiary in Jefferson City.

Berry was given a Lysol bath and dumped into "the hole for a 30-day orientation." Through the food slot, he was able to talk to other inmates and learned the hierarchy of the prison. He charmed the main ringleader, a man called "Slim" who decided Berry and his two jailed partners were the victims of a bum rap. The three sentences added up to 30 years for "nine minutes' use of a guy's car."

> There were three guards, called dormitory masters, per building. All the black inmates were governed by the three black men and the white dormitories by the white. There were black and white hours for the gym, black and white sides to the mess hall, black and white visiting rooms, and toilets all catered and tailored to custom. Black eyes watched white ones and white ones watched black but no one had any vision of change.

Soon enough, Berry got involved with the inmate church and formed a four-voice singing group to accompany the Sunday service. The group included a professional musician about 10 years older than Berry, a guy everybody called "Po' Sam," who sang lead and had played tenor sax and guitar in Kansas City. Shortly, fellow inmates were crowding the services, sitting through as many as three sermons just to hear the music.

The quartet began to play the white dormitories. Berry wrote his girlfriend (no phone calls allowed) who arranged a trip to St. Louis for a church appearance by the quartet. The trips soon became routine. He had dinner with his family while home and the prison bandmaster stayed in the Berry house on Labadie.

Berry had another outing away from the Hill as a result of his boxing abilities, landing a spot in the Golden Gloves finals at the St. Louis Arena. His opponent, "a monstrous black gladiator-built dude" named Slillum Gillum, punched the inexperienced Berry around the ring quite easily before Berry learned not to stand still. But his running strategy quickly wore thin and Gillum knocked the teenager down. Berry wrote that the fight was over when "I remembered not to get up."

The vocal quartet had more success. And, with the support of the white daughter of the assistant superintendent at the prison, a secular boogie band was added, a group that included Slim, the ringleader, who worked as a stagehand and manager. Slim was 31. Po' Sam was 28; the other members were GG and Steff from the original quartet, plus new members, John and Hillary. Chuck was youngest at 19.

On the last song of one of the performances, Berry made a mistake, dancing with the white daughter of the assistant superintendent. Thirty white inmates protested, blocking the door of the dormitory where the show was held. Berry was threatened. Insults were hurled. The daughter defended him, however, and the tension was defused by her father's arrival. Berry was confined to his cell to wait for the racial tensions to die down.

Nonetheless, his 10-year sentence was reduced for good behavior, and he was released on Oct. 20, 1947, two days after his 21st birthday.

Seven months later, Chuck Berry met Thematta Suggs at the 1948 May Day celebration in Tandy Park. They were married before the year was over and by 2016 had remained so the rest of their long lives. Working for his father and brother as a carpenter, Berry saved money and bought a car. He left the old neighborhood, moving into a rooming house on Delmar in the center of the city.

But Berry couldn't keep up the car payments on his 1941 Buick and took a factory job, working nights at the Fisher Body plant. He also started looking for jobs singing and playing the guitar. He picked up private party work at $4 a night, age 24. Then "Toddy," his wife, told him she was pregnant. The whole family was involved in a baby boom, as his sister and the wife of his younger brother were also expecting.

Chuck and Toddy were able to buy a house out of their savings. They found a one-story, brick ranch house on Whittier Street about a 10-minute walk from the Labadie house, back in The Ville. The house, with bath and a full basement was small, about 1,000 square feet, and cost $4,500. At the close, Chuck counted out "the sweaty down payment" -- $450 in cash.

In 2015, the house still stood. Indeed, it was listed on the National Register of Historic Places -- five rooms, three built as the original house in 1910. Chuck and Toddy arrived in the neighborhood just two years after the landmark housing desegregation case of *Shelley v. Kraemer* opened the neighborhood to African Americans. The Ville was turning into the Greater Ville, a wider black neighborhood that was moving north, away from the central part of the city.

On the Whittier block where this unmarked national landmark sat during a visit in 2014, the Chuck Berry House was one of the few houses in bad shape. The majority of the homes on the curving residential street are well kept, small but neat. The front of the Berry house was only 22 feet wide, but for a pair of newlyweds with a child on the way, one can imagine how they would be happy to move in, escaping the rooming house on Delmar, back to the old neighborhood.

In 1956, two rooms were tacked onto the rear of the house, an addition built with concrete blocks and no windows that looked like an air raid shelter. The addition became Berry's music room, where he worked up his hit lyrics. When the application for the Register was made in 2008, a metal awning with a faded letter "B," hung above the front door. That was gone in 2015. A peek in the window revealed the smashed glass and rubble typical of the empty houses that dotted the North Side of St. Louis in the twenty-first century.

One neighbor said she hated the Berry house being on her block. She said it had been empty for years and there was no sign of any attempt to clean it up. There was no marking on the house to show who once lived there, just a ragged front yard that needed mowing and a muddy empty lot next door.

But this was the house where Chuck Berry rejoined the middle class. He had a home, a car, a child (current band member Ingrid "Darlin'" Berry) and soon bought a TV, an electric guitar and a reel-to-reel wire recorder. Before he went to jail he had picked up some riffs from the local barber, Ira Harris, and now went back for more lessons, this time on the electric guitar, which he found much easier to use than the four-string tenor guitar he had been playing. His grip was very wide, his fingers extra long and facile.

His old friend, Tommy Stevens, who backed up his bold move at the school assembly, asked Berry to join his three-piece combo and the group landed a Huff's Garden gig that lasted every Saturday from June until Dec. 31, 1952, a fateful night that had a deep impact on American music history.

Johnnie Clyde Johnson was born July 8, 1924, in Fairmont, W. Va., a coal mining town 1,000 feet above sea level. Johnnie's mother died when he was six months old. His mother's sister and her husband, also a miner, raised him.

When he was five, his aunt bought an upright piano for the house, treating it more as a piece of furniture than an instrument. She thought it would look good in the living room. Little Johnnie, however, had other ideas and at age five climbed up and began banging on the keys. At six he knew how to play "Cow Cow Blues," much to the amusement of neighbors who began gathering in the house for the little Johnnie show.

Johnnie said, "I taught myself" from the record on the Victrola, an old wind-up variety. He was probably listening to Charles "Cow Cow" Davenport, one of the many who claim to have "invented" the boogie-woogie style, saying the beat came to him after hearing his mother play "Swanee River" on the piano.

Johnnie gobbled up the music he heard on a radio station from Pittsburgh, country and jazz. "The music I did with Chuck Berry," he told biographer Travis Fitzpatrick, "it's got a lot of that big-band jazz in it. It swings." These styles he picked up as a child -- the boogie shuffle, swing and blues -- lasted him a lifetime.

At 10 years old, Johnnie was playing house parties, school events and had appeared on the local radio station. For a short time he lived with his biological father, Buddy Johnson, but soon returned to his aunt's house. His uncle died from the same coal miner's lung disease -- "the black damper" -- that later killed his father as well.

After entering high school Jonnie joined a seven-piece swing band, the Blue Rhythm Swingsters, and played his piano as much as he could. He lost interest in school and dropped out in 1941 after his junior year, just as Chuck Berry did two years later. Johnnie went to Detroit and got a job in the Ford plant, now 17 and completely on his own.

He joined the Marines in 1942, shortly after Pearl Harbor, serving in the first black company in World War II, one of the first 1,500 black Marines. He went through much of the war constructing air strips then was transferred to a motor pool where an officer asked him what he'd really like to be doing -- his answer was that he'd like to play the piano, the perfect answer for a unit forming a band.

They called it the Barracudas and it included members of the big bands of Glen Miller, Tommy Dorsey and Count Basie. The group became the premier military band of the war, rated even higher than the Navy bands coming out of the Great Lakes Experience. Johnson played behind the Bob Hope and Betty Hutton USO shows across the Pacific and back. He did not read music and had to memorize the swing patterns for each new song, but Johnnie said that he held a song in his head, full blown, then guided his hands to let it out. He never needed the music sheets.

After the war, he lived three more years in Detroit before moving to Chicago in 1949, looking for more opportunity to make music. He met Little Milton Campbell, who began getting him gigs at small clubs, playing blues. Johnson did well for the next couple of years, but his wife left and it was a rare moment when Johnnie turned down a drink. His ambition faded and his gigs started to wane. His day jobs dried up because of the drinking and he couldn't make enough off the gigs.

> Pretty soon I couldn't make the rent anymore and I was out on the street. This was the wintertime and it was cold -- lots of snow. If you stayed outside you'd freeze to death, and I had to learn quick where to go to keep warm. Most nights I kept goin' back and forth between the bus station and the train station trying to catch some sleep. When one kicked me out I'd go to the other until they kicked me out and on and on until morning.

He called his older brother, Pless, who had a connection with the railroad in St. Louis. Johnnie Johnson arrived in St. Louis March 31, 1952, leaving Chicago behind. He lived in St. Louis the rest of his life.

The Cosmopolitan Club in East St. Louis was a plush and popular joint. To ring in the New Year 1953, club owner Joe Lewis shunned the potential out-of-town talent and stuck with his house band, Sir John's Trio, confident Johnnie Johnson's three-piece would provide a rousing evening of entertainment for the 300 customers who would crowd in for the biggest night of the year.

The Cosmo wasn't a wild R&B hall. Ike Turner was still in Clarksdale. A few whites, especially those who enjoyed the jitterbug, had joined the predominately black audience. Tensions between black and white had eased during the war.

East St. Louis had become more liberal and attracted a late night crowd from across the river, its all-night policy having come in with the war production. Sir John's Trio played mostly standards like "Stardust" and "Stormy Weather," but also featured a rousing dance number called "Johnnie's Boogie" that included a left-hand riff straight from "Cow Cow Boogie" he'd learned when he was six.

Within two weeks of arriving in St. Louis, with a job, a warm room out of the icy Chicago wind, Johnson started putting a band together, first meeting the drummer Ebby Hardy and then a sax player named Alvin Bennett. Within four months Sir John's Trio was playing the Cosmo Friday, Saturday and Sunday bringing in $36 (about $300 in 2015) a night plus tips, a high paying engagement.

On the day of the show bringing in the year 1953 Bennett called in sick. Johnnie hired Chuck Berry to fill in for the night. Berry had a country style that fit within the blues and jazz the combo played. He went over that New Year's Eve as a black hillbilly, a novelty. He wrote it was the night "my career took its first step. If I could have stored the drinks that were offered me that night, I think I could have set everybody up in the house twice."

The band was rehired for the next weekend and then for a long run. Berry had a gift for performance, a glib expressiveness that included lots of looks over to his sidekick. Chuck would shoot in a song every once in a while that would show off "my hilarious hilly and basic billy delivery." St. Louis had a large number of country fans, most who loved to dance.

White and black mingled. There was a confluence. Johnnie's drawling piano matched the clarity of Chuck's diction. Berry could sing Muddy Waters in the down-home dialect and could pick out the words from Bob Wills tunes with clarity. Each portion of the white and black crowd, he said, was given "different kinds of songs in their customary tongues."

For the next two years Sir John's Trio filled the Cosmopolitan every weekend. The band hummed, getting ever tighter. "Whenever I played a riff with any pause in it, he would answer it with the same melodic pattern," Berry said of his piano partner.

Johnson hadn't been too confident about hiring Berry that first night. He was upset about Bennett's illness, which was very serious. A veteran saxman, Bennett had suffered a stroke, was paralyzed and would never play again, "a great loss to the musical community."

Johnnie had made several calls and was about to give up on trying to find a replacement. He was near the bottom of his list when he remembered Berry, the guitar player at Huff's Garden. Berry was free and Johnnie was soon impressed.

Berry only knew 12 songs, but had a knack for connecting to the audience. Johnnie, the bandleader, said of Chuck Berry:

> Sometimes in music you just click with another musician just like you would a person you meet at a party. The conversation just fits.
>
> He was a go-getter. Real ambitious right from the start. He wanted to make that money any way he could. He was different from me. All I knew about was makin' music. Chuck wasn't satisfied with that, though, just makin' music. It wasn't enough for him. Never was.

Two years later Chuck bought a cherry-red Ford Esquire station wagon and in the spring of 1955 took a drive to Chicago, looking to expand his career. He found Muddy Waters coming off the stage and asked him whom to contact to make a record in Chicago.

Muddy's answer: "See Leonard Chess."

Berry rushed back to his house on Whittier Street and wrote the lyrics to four songs. He laid them on tape and drove back up to Chicago. Chess was pleased, especially with a song Berry called "Ida Red," a tune that borrowed phrasing from the Louis Jordan style of jump blues.

Berry took the tapes back to Chicago and Chess liked what he heard. A recording session was scheduled for May 21. Chuck rolled back down to St. Louis where he gave the band the good news. He, Johnnie and Ebby Hardy, the drummer, packed up and drove back up to Chicago. No. 1 on the Top 40 that week was Georgia Gibbs' "Dance With Me Henry."

Berry added country riffs he had heard around St. Louis to his lyrics on his guitar. But it was Johnnie's piano that transformed Berry's guitar into rock 'n' roll.

The band battled through 36 takes to turn "Ida Red" into "Maybellene," the title changed by Chess when he realized Bob Wills had used "Ida Red" in 1938. The fully transformed song was dubbed "Maybellene" by Leonard Chess, who saw the name on a box of mascara sitting in the studio.

Chess had an idea about the song and insisted on getting it right. Johnnie said, "We had no idea what to do." Apparently, Chess did.

Of course, Chess got some help from the musicians. Hardy was at the center of the whole thing, drumming like a veteran rocker, running the real rock 'n' roll beat, like something off "Rocket 88." Willie Dixon was on bass to solidify the rhythm and Chuck and Johnnie killed the leads. The piano is a little hard to hear on the cut, but it comes in dancing and carrying on at the end. Chuck's vocals and his six-string electric guitar -- played with a double-string approach echoes Lonnie Johnson -- the singer/songwriter on the rock stage.

Starting with the opening guitar run, Chuck prances across that record. "Oh, Maybellene, why can't you be true?" Could there be a deeper question for a boy or a girl getting ready for the rock era?

When the song was released on July 30, *Billboard* said it showed "ace showmanship" and a "solid driving beat."

Following the session Berry went into Leonard Chess' office by himself and signed the contracts for Arc Music in his name only. The band was still the Sir John Trio on the way to the session. But the song came out under the name of Chuck Berry and Chuck Berry was now in charge.

Johnnie said:

> I could see Chuck taking over, but that's his personality type. Chuck has to be in control. Besides, we was becoming one of the most popular bands in East St. Louis, and everybody, including the whites, were wanting to check us out. Chuck was no ordinary singer: He made up his own words, talked to the audience, made faces.

And he was playing rock 'n' roll.

"Maybellene" went to No. 1 on the R&B charts and reached No. 5 on the pop chart, the first in a string of hits Chuck and Johnnie rattled off during the next few years. They collaborated on some of the most influential songs in rock history -- "Sweet Little Sixteen," "Roll Over Beethoven," "School Days," "Back in the USA," "Rock and Roll Music" and "Johnny B. Goode."

Johnnie paid no attention to business during these days, enjoying the ride. This was an attitude that a decade later left him living in the YMCA while Chuck moved into an 11-room mansion and opened the 30-acre Berry Park in the far western suburbs of St. Louis. And Johnnie's unwillingness to pay attention to the money, combined with Chuck's constant attention to the finances led eventually to a court fight between the partners in 2000, a fight over song credits that drew in some of the biggest names in the industry.

After the first Chess session the band's name was changed to the Chuck Berry Trio, then just Chuck Berry. Chuck became the star, Johnnie the loyal sideman.

Ebby had no taste for travel and quit touring in 1956. Chuck and Johnnie went on together as the front part of the act, hiring locals to fill the band out. Johnnie was with Chuck as Berry played the Mad Hatter of rock 'n' roll on the Alan Freed circuit, "The Big Show of Stars R&B," and in the films *Rock Rock Rock* in 1956 and *Mister Rock and Roll*, 1957. They played at Newport in 1958, (*Jazz on a Summer's Day*) followed up by an appearance on *American Bandstand.*

But Johnnie stayed home more and more, finding work with the blues guitar giant Albert King. Berry would pick up his guitar and his suitcase, take a cab to the airport or get in his car, using different locals in each city, coming home with bags of cash. He would come back to St. Louis frequently and play with Johnnie or they would meet in Chicago for recording sessions.

Albert King had moved from Chicago to St. Louis in 1955, arriving at a time when Ike Turner was on top. Chuck was a close second, holding down the weekends at the Cosmo Club with Johnnie and Ebby. As soon as King saw Berry's show he wanted to hire Johnnie and paid only scant attention to the hillbilly guitar player. "I got to get that man in my band," King said of Johnnie Johnson. "That's the baddest piano player I ever heard."

In the studio in Chicago Chuck and Johnnie put on a dazzling show. Chuck was a hard worker and Johnnie could play the piano all day and all night and all the next day. From 1955 to 1974, a grand total of 235 Chuck Berry sides were recorded at the Chess Studios near the lake on Michigan Avenue. Johnnie said he played on everything before 1962, and Chuck says Johnnie was on over 175 sides.

The main engine of the Chuck and Johnnie show was the early fast start, with "Maybellene" the kicker, a teenage love song driven by a car chase, a "motorvatin'" adventure featuring a speeding Cadillac and the cagy double entendre of the male mind -- car and girl, they are both motorvatin'.

"Maybellene" was a country name and an oddball one at that. Our narrator, driving along in a V8 Ford, spots his two-timing Maybellene in a coup de ville and dives into a wild race -- "a hundred and ten gallopin' over that hill/ Offhill curve, a downhill stretch" -- that ends when the Cadillac dies and "I caught Maybellene at the top of the hill."

Here was a cowboy song with a rock beat and a blues piano, the sound was new and catchy, the rock rhythm fully on display. The song was another reminder of that St. Louis thing -- that confluence of elements adding up to more than the sum of the parts to produce a musical breakout of innovation.

During the stretch from 1955 to 1960, the heart of Berry's hit machine, this was the Chuck and Johnnie show, with Ebby on drums and Willie Dixon on bass. Chuck took the money from Chess and paid Johnnie and the others per session, the figure $100 a day has been bandied around. Johnnie said he thought his was a good payday but he kept a full-time job to complement the session work.

Still, the start wasn't easy. In 1956, the band made the Top 40 just once and there was consternation at Chess headquarters. Maybe, the brothers pondered, it was already time to limit Berry's output. After all, Elvis made his first million dollars by the end of 1956. The white rocker from downriver in Memphis rolled out the rhythm and blues and reached the top of the hill first, leaving Chuck in the dust.

But the next year, the Cadillac hit 104 for Chuck, Johnnie and Ebby when the three of them caught fire, (don't forget Ebby and his impeccable rock beat). They cut 15 sides in 1957 and five of the songs made the Top 40 (four that year and "Rockin' and Reelin'" a No. 27 in 1973)

"Roll Over Beethoven" had been the band's only hit in 1956, where the dancing partner "wiggles like a glow worm," in a world where "if you feel you like it, go get your lover, then reel and rock it. -- I got the rockin' pneumonia, I need a shot of rhythm and blues -- Roll over Beethoven and tell Tchaikovsky the news."

In 1957, the real news was "School Day," reaching No. 1 on the R&B chart and No. 3 on the pop chart, lasting 15 weeks. "School Day," recorded in January, shows where rock 'n' roll stood entering '57, a year still shadowed by the Red Menace, a year where the flight from the big cities, very much including St. Louis, was underway. There was more and more mingling of the races in the cities at social gatherings like music clubs and dances but the neighborhoods remained segregated even as the populations shifted from tenements and aging housing in the city to new houses in the suburbs or to new government housing projects in the inner city.

"School Day" opened with the riff from "Johnnie's Boogie," Johnson's old tune from the Cosmopolitan Club, reworked to include a run from "Honky Tonk Train Blues" by Lux Lewis, a song that included a piano intro that sounded like a train whistle. Bob Crosby picked up the song for a boogie pianist in his big band in the thirties and Johnnie had heard it someplace, probably on a 1938 Crosby hit record.

When "Chuck played it on the guitar," Johnnie remembered," it sounded like a school bell ringin' and that was perfect for "'School Day,'" a riff that rings through electric guitars on a daily basis over 50 years later.

Chuck's lyrics on the song were appropriate for the Ozzie and Harriet/ Eisenhower fifties -- "the teacher is teaching the Golden rule," but you, you American teenage rebel, you can't wait for the bell to ring so you can to go "right to the juke joint" -- "you got to hear something that is really hot" -- "round and round you go" -- and here in the last verse comes the killer chant, the anthem of many of the participating rebels in the just-around-the-corner sixties, fledgling radicals who were maybe only 10 or 11 years old when they heard a 30-year-old Chuck Berry chuckle out the credo: "Hail hail rock and roll/ Deliver me from the days of old/ Long live rock 'n' roll."

"School Day" has enjoyed a long history, given a large leg up by the 1987 movie biography of Chuck Berry, *Hail! Hail! Rock 'n' Roll.* From the ground around that movie grew the tangled court scrap between Chuck and Johnnie in 2000. Cover versions of "School Day" abound, rock stars love to yell "Hail, hail, rock and roll." There's a version by Elvis from 1976, a live Led Zeppelin from 1973, Buster Poindexter did a version for the *Simpson's Sing the Blues* album and there are also covers by AC/DC, Eddie Cochran, Jan and Dean, the Beach Boys and Neil Young.

So what was this rock 'n' roll we hail? That was still a question in 1957. Chuck, Johnnie and Ebby had the answer by the middle of the year. "Rock and Roll Music," recorded in May 1957 and released in November, jumped up to No. 8. The teenagers heard it on the radio and bought the record and played it in their bedrooms and danced to it at the hamburger joint and in the gym on Friday night.

The definition of rock 'n' roll? Chuck had the answer: "It's got a back beat, you can't lose it, Any old time you use it." Our rock 'n' roll fan had "no kick against modern jazz," that is until it "sounded like a symphony." That forced the fan to go across the tracks to hear a "rocking band" where the sax was "blowing like a hurricane."

"Sweet Little Sixteen" and "Johnny B. Goode" followed in the Top 40 starting out in 1958. "Johnny B. Goode" was "Cow Cow Boogie" redone on the guitar. Johnnie showed Chuck the way he did it when he was a kid and Chuck took it and rocked it out on the six string, his big hands gripping across wide expanses of frets, blowing out the energy. There were more hits, "Sweet Little Sixteen" and "Carol." A Johnnie piano run on "Sweet Little Sixteen" is worth the price of admission.

The band released 24 songs that year. The Chess brothers now saw Berry as a cash cow and upped the ante. But the results were disappointing in 1959, then worse in 1960 and 1961, years Berry was fighting to stay out of jail. "Leonard and I both knew the recording session was inferior to the past ones," he said.

Before that trouble started, however, Berry moved into a new house in July 1958 on one of the St. Louis "place" streets, Windemere Place off Union Boulevard, near the St. Louis University campus. With the pregnant Toddy and two children, the newly crowned rock 'n' roll star bought an 11-room house on a semi-private street, just three blocks from Delmar. The family was moving into the upper middle class, the big house being the ultimate showcase. Berry's family had now gone from three rooms to 11 rooms. Hail, hail, rock 'n' roll.

That wasn't all. He bought 30 acres of land in the far western suburbs near Wentzville, Mo., naming it Berry Park. He had the idea of building a fully integrated park, with swimming, music, a restaurant, the works. After a long stint of negotiating and remodeling, he opened the park to the public in June 1961, holding a Father's Day picnic featuring a band called Austin Wright and the Caravans.

He also started a nightclub downtown with the same goal in mind, a non-discriminatory music environment. Chuck Berry's Club Bandstand opened March 20, 1959, on Grand Avenue, in what had been an all-white zone. Berry was aiming at emulating the Dick Clark approach, squeaky clean rock 'n' roll, sharp dressing dancers, African American and white.

Club Bandstand was "a mixed racial club that was catered to by whites." Berry was following a trend that had resulted in three other black-run clubs in the neighborhood, each getting more white customers weekly. Even so, the Grand Avenue crowd did not accept him. Many saw him as an "instigator," someone moving in to stir up trouble and drive down the prices.

On May 16, 1959, Berry put together a lineup unique in the history of the city. The all-star show featured the George Hudson Band, the city's sharpest big band; the soul-soaked tones of Little Milton; Ike and Tina Turner, the town's hottest act; and the national star Jackie Wilson, between nights at the Riviera Club. The venue was not in a city club or a big theater, the venue was one very familiar to Berry, the auditorium of Sumner High

School, where he had shocked the faculty as a teenager. The occasion was a benefit to help buy bats and balls for the local Little League baseball program. The cost to enter was 90 cents.

Berry was riding high -- briefly. As was all too usual in his roller coaster life, the high was but a prelude to the descent. For Chuck Berry was soon occupied with more trouble. It began on Aug. 27, 1959, in Meridian, Miss.

That August night in white-ruled Mississippi, a premonition: Five days into a five-week southern tour, a white woman ran up to Chuck Berry after a show, threw her arms around him and gave him a kiss. By now Berry had learned not to argue, he just headed for a side door as soon as the mob started forming up. Things got a lot worse.

On Dec. 1, 1959, at a theater in El Paso, Texas, Berry met Janice Escalanti, whose age Berry was uncertain of, a dark Native American woman who could have been in her teens or twenties. She was from Yuma, Ariz., a runaway who gladly accepted Berry's suggestion she come to St. Louis and work in his club.

At first, once in St. Louis after a long car ride across the southwest, Janice was happy in her new job. She wasn't the disciplined sort, however. She wandered away from her hatcheck stand and was no good on the door either. There really wasn't much she could handle. So Berry fired her and gave her a bus ticket back to Yuma. Instead, she turned tricks for two nights then came back to Berry's club. When he refused to see her, she called the Yuma police, hoping maybe they could put her up somewhere if she went back.

Instead, the St. Louis police arrested her. Janice had told the police in Yuma that Chuck had taken her to St. Louis to have sex. The claim led to charges against Berry for violating the Mann Act -- transporting a woman across state lines for "immoral purposes." He was found guilty March 4, 1960, but the verdict was overruled on appeal due to the racist outbursts of the trial judge. But in a second trial in October 1961 Berry was convicted again and sentenced to three years in jail and a $10,000 fine.

Berry entered the federal prison in Terre Haute, Ind., on Feb. 19, 1962. He was released from the Federal Medical Center in Springfield, Mo., Oct. 18, 1963, his 37th birthday.

He heard his music in the air, but it wasn't him.

In England, back in 1961, one of the people who bought a Berry album called *One Dozen Berries* was an English student named Mick Jagger. Holding the record on a train platform in London, the record caught the eye of a gaunt man named Keith Richards. Jagger and Richards got talking music. And when The Rolling Stones released their first single in January 1964 the A-side was a cover of Berry's "Carol."

While he was in jail Brian Wilson and the Beach Boys put out a Pat Boone style cover of "Sweet Little Sixteen" renamed "Surfin' USA."

And while Berry was waiting out the final week of his sentence, a foursome of mop tops from England, the Beatles, landed in America, looking like strong contenders in the rock 'n' roll market. The Beatles loved playing Chuck Berry songs on the BBC and his name spread around England in the mid-sixties.

This gave Leonard Chess the idea of selling Chuck Berry to Europe. Chess sent his son across the Atlantic to make the deal. New Chuck and old Chuck both sold well.

On May 9, 1964, Berry opened in London. At first, he snubbed the Stones, finally allowing Stones bassist Bill Wyman into his dressing room, where Wyman found Chuck Berry heating a frozen dinner on a portable stove, uncommunicative.

During the last show of Berry's European jaunt, a tightly packed crowd of proto-punk Teddy Boys, whipped into a frenzy by Berry's guitar work, leaped up on the stage. Berry gave them a look and duckwalked to the side of the stage where the two promoters of the show stood. Berry had made a rare exception and gone on this show without getting his usual bag of cash up front. The money was to be delivered promptly afterward.

"Did you get the money yet?" Berry asked one promoter, the Teddy Boys chanting in the background.

The promoter, a former wrestler, six-foot-five, crossed his arms and shook his head "No."

Berry quickly pivoted and duckwalked back out on stage, prepared to incite a riot and let the Teddies tear down the hall.

He looked back and saw the stricken expression on the face of the other promoter. He duckwalked back and the second promoter nodded his head that they had the money. Berry duckwalked some more. He unplugged his guitar from his amp, then duckwalked out the door, down the stairs and into a limo, where the cash was shortly delivered.

After he left jail, the Chuck Berry comeback powered forward. From February 1964 to March 1965, Chess released six singles, four of which made the Top 40 -- "Nadine" (No. 23), "No Particular Place To Go" (No. 10), "You Never Can Tell' (No. 14), and "Promised Land" (No. 41). The lyrics, written in the Federal Medical Center as Berry was going out the door of the prison system, were in the best Chuck Berry tradition, but the last of these singles, the obscure "Dear Dad" (No. 95), was lame. Appropriately, it was to be Berry's last appearance on the Billboard charts for seven years.

Chuck was different by then, not as full of energy as he had once been. After spending over a year and a half in prison and having great initial success during his comeback, he headed down again. By January 1965 his contract with Chess was up and he made a big money deal to move over to Mercury Records. Music had changed, the Beatles and Stones had grabbed the rock 'n' roll steering wheel and Berry was relegated to non-charting singles and greatest hits albums.

After leaving Chess, Berry cut the Mercury sides in St. Louis at the Technisonic studios. But *Chuck's Golden Hits* and the four other albums released by his new company did little on the charts.

And the partnership with his piano player was no longer strong. Johnnie was worn out from his job at the steelworks in Granite City and would show up late for recording sessions. He was drinking. Johnnie also saw a new Chuck. "He was angry at how the law had treated him and thought that everyone wanted to cheat him. He calmed down a little over the next couple of years, but he was definitely a different person after he got out of prison."

Meanwhile, Berry Park started having something of the scene Chuck had hoped for. In the late sixties Billy Peek became the regular attraction, drawing 200 to 300 people to low-key summer Sunday afternoon shows. Berry, Peek said, "had the whole schmeer. Anything you needed he had out there. It was a fun place; it was a lot of fun out there."

Berry was also busy with a new love -- San Francisco. Bill Graham, the promoter of the Fillmore, Winterland and the psychedelic sound, flew to

Berry Park to sign Chuck for a show after Chuck refused to negotiate long distance. Graham was then snubbed, no one met him at the airport and Berry didn't finalize the deal until Graham was back on the West Coast. But once things were straight, Berry played 17 shows in San Francisco in 1967 and by 1971 had done another 32, all with local talent, often with the Steve Miller band as his backup.

In 1971, he went back to Chess. In 1972, "Ding-a-Ling" rang the cash resisters. He and Billy Peek got a regular gig at the Rainbow Room in North St. Louis County. In 1973, a bass player named Jim Marsala joined the band for shows in Vegas and San Francisco and the piano man named Johnnie Johnson officially checked out of the Chuck Berry band after 28 years.

Johnnie had married for a third time by then and "Chuck was off in his own world. That was perfectly okay with me. I had my own life." Johnnie held down his day job at the steel plant and played weekends in St. Louis.

"I left (Chuck) because I was tired of traveling, and I especially didn't like flying. Most of the gigs involved that. I told him I would cool it for a while. I joined up with him again, but then he had some problems and he stopped touring for a while." Johnnie played with the band variously called the Sounds of the City, the Magnificent Four, the Magnificent Five and the Magnificent Six. He also worked occasionally with Oliver Sain.

At Berry Park, Chuck relentlessly added events. The music shows grew from small Sunday afternoon affairs into music festivals, culminating with a big national show July 4, 1974. The program listed the Band, REO Speedwagon, Peter Frampton and Leon Russell as headliners on a card that also had several local bands. But the local promoter scrimped on security and didn't make a scheduled payment to a New York company hired to produce the stage. The New Yorkers walked out the morning of the show, leading to the cancellation of Russell and Frampton. A feeling of chaos descended.

Ticket takers allowed perhaps 10,000 people into the park (about half the crowd) without paying and the receipts didn't add up for the promoters. Security issues lingered during new festival shows and Berry began thinking about other options when disaster struck.

Two girls swimming with his daughters drowned in August in the park's guitar shaped swimming pool. There were no lifeguards or depth markers.

The local police, who didn't like the festivals or the park, used the drownings as a reason for a raid, on Aug. 24, 1974, during the weekly Saturday night dance. Nearly 25 people, a dozen under age, were arrested for smoking pot and illegal drinking. Two weeks later a judge, citing a shooting, three alleged rapes and numerous code violations, shut the park down. Berry was served with a $100,000 lawsuit from one of the drowned girls' parents.

Next came the IRS. Berry always insisted he be paid in cash, stuffing money into his briefcase before or just after the show, keeping only scattered records of his income. Various tax cases were filed and it was 1979 before they were cleared. He agreed in the end to pay a $110,000 fine and serve a 120-day jail sentence. The government agreed to allow him one last European tour before he checked into the Lompoc Correctional Institution for his third jail term.

During his three months in jail he was productive, beginning work on his *Autobiography*, which eventually hit the streets in October of 1987. By then, a decade of decline had shrunk his touring gigs to about 40 dates a year.

The ride wasn't over for Chuck Berry, however. He had a big turnaround in 1987, not only from the book. Berry was then 60 and a plan was hatched for a movie to celebrate the anniversary that evolved into the film *Hail! Hail! Rock and Roll*, where Berry rocked out with Eric Clapton, Keith Richards, Robert Cray, all with a revived and refreshed Johnnie Johnson back on the keys.

The film was hatched during a Waldorf Astoria dinner around a table that included a young film producer named Stephanie Bennett, head of Delilah Films, and Richards, her English countryman. The connection of Chuck to Richards was Steve Jordan, the drummer for the David Letterman Band in New York City. Jordan had played with Richards on the recent *Dirty Work* album as well as the film soundtrack for Aretha Franklin. Soon thereafter Jordan found himself playing at the 1986 inaugural induction ceremony of the Rock and Roll Hall of Fame.

And it so happened that it was Richards who did the intro that night for Chuck Berry who went into the Hall with Elvis Presley, Buddy Holly, Fats Domino, Ray Charles, and six others.

"It's very difficult for me to talk about Chuck Berry," Richards said at the induction, "'cause I've lifted every lick he ever played -- this is the gentleman who started it all!" After the speeches were done, the Letterman band and Richards and a litany of rock 'n' roll stars piled on the stage for an all-star jam. Richards, already thinking about a possible Berry movie, decided Jordan could be the star of a band for such a documentary. Richards wanted it filmed in St. Louis.

After the meeting at the Waldorf, four people spent the next few months planning: Bennett, head of Delilah Films; director Taylor Hackford, maker of *An Officer and a Gentleman*; Richards in the role of musical director; and Chuck Berry, hoping for a jolt to a stagnant career.

After the planning sessions, Richards and Hackford flew out to Lambert and rented a car to get over to Wentzville. Richards had been thinking about his band for the movie and part of that thinking concerned Johnnie Johnson. Ever since the sixties -- when Stones band mate Ian Stewart would talk about the great boogie-woogie piano player who worked in Chuck Berry's shadow -- Keith wondered what happened to Johnnie Johnson. And on the second day at Berry Farm Keith asked about Johnnie.

"With Johnnie Johnson," Keith wrote in his autobiography, Chuck "had the perfect unit. It was made in heaven, for Christ's sake. 'Oh no,' says Chuck, 'it's only me that counts. I can find another pianist, and anyway I can get them cheaper, too.' It's basically the cheapness he was concerned about."

Maybe Keith expected a hostile response to his idea of Johnnie playing in the movie, but Chuck was all for it, "Chuck rolled right in there, and it was a good decision, because he got a great movie out of it and a great band."

Since the early seventies, when the Chuck and Johnnie show ended, things had not gone as well for Johnnie as they had for Chuck. In fact, the period from when he quit Chuck until he met Tom Maloney about a dozen years later was the low point of the great pianoman's arc. Johnnie went to work in the American Steel Foundry in Granite City in 1957 even as the hits topped the charts. He'd already been paid for the sessions; no royalty checks were arriving at his door.

For Johnnie Johnson, the year 1960 began looking up, joining Albert King. Johnnie didn't like to fly, but was ready to play the many gigs King played within driving distance of his house in Brooklyn, Ill., where King lived.

Then, just as the band began to jell, Johnnie's second wife shot him in the chest during a visit to see his children. He had divorced the first and wasn't living with the second. A bullet lodged in a lung.

The shooting came in September. Johnnie said the argument was driven by jealousy, the shots fired without warning -- four in all. The first shot missed an inch from his head, but he was hit by all three of the next shots, the last which put him on the ground.

She stood over him, the gun in her hand.

"But," Johnnie remembered, "she just throws the gun down and starts cryin'.'" He recovered and moved into Albert King's strongest band, with a 17-year-old drumming prodigy named Kenny Rice, plus Harold White and Little Freddie Robinette on tenor and alto sax, Buttercup Thompson on trumpet and Lee Otis Wright on bass.

This band grew popular very quickly in St. Louis, regularly beating Ike Turner and Little Milton at the battle of the bands held at Ike's Manhattan Club. One night, the band played on the top deck of the riverboat *Admiral*, while Count Basie played below. Albert King and his band drew the bigger crowd. Johnnie's new specialty was "After Hours," a song White remembers as sending the crowd leaping up on tables.

King, however, started touring behind his Blues Power style during the late sixties, leaving Johnnie at home more and more. In 1973, Johnnie decided to make another run at full-time music and quit the foundry. Six uneasy years behind the piano followed. Perhaps he had been misled by a road trip to Vegas with Berry where he made $500. He misjudged how much he'd be making in St. Louis and within a few months was facing a rent crisis. Chuck gave him a job, overseeing some Delmar property, maintenance work much like Chuck's father did for many years.

Gigs were still not forthcoming. In 1977 Johnnie was dealt a blow. Billy Peek, who had been on the road with Rod Stewart and knew Johnnie from the Wentzville shows, mentioned Johnnie to Stewart and Stewart, remembering the old Berry hits, asked Peek if Johnnie was still alive. Pretty soon Johnnie was trembling away on a flight to L.A. He had rejoined his career, he thought.

But Stewart never made the meeting with Johnnie, leaving him waiting in the record company's reception area the day he arrived. No record was forthcoming.

Then, two years later, drinking heavily and living in the YMCA, Johnnie got a call from Chuck, the first he'd received in seven years. The Chuck and Johnnie show was on again, making a record in Chuck's home studio in Wentzville.

The record was *Rockit*, the last studio album by the great team and the last of all for Chuck Berry. The record sounds a little old, some hackneyed stuff, but you can finally hear Johnnie. At last, Chuck had turned up the volume on the piano part.

In the early eighties, a St. Louis band called Sounds of the City had spun off from the Soulard Blues Band. The blues revival was spreading. Bands were in demand. Larry Thurston, who had been singing for Soulard, brought along Tom Maloney on guitar and Jim Miller on drums to get Sounds of the City started. Not long after, Gus Thornton, Albert King's bass player, was added when King wasn't on the road.

The band landed a weekly gig at the newly opened Broadway Oyster Bar and was starting to happen. Maloney knew Johnnie well, from all the years the two had spent in the swampy waters of the St. Louis music scene. Maloney decided to hire him for Sounds of the City and gave him a starting date.

That first night, in early 1985, Johnnie was late for the gig, now 62 years old, slowed by his lifelong drinking habit and all those hours in the factory. But he finally showed, arriving at the venue the Broadway Oyster Bar, after Maloney and the others had started the set. The club had a side door that led from the street to the stage, where musicians unloaded gear. The band was playing away when the side opened and here came Johnnie, dragging his instrument, an old-fashioned standup wooden piano on wheels.

Tom remembered the band was doing music from the English band Chicken Shack, the cool blues of the city.

> I see the door open for a minute and say "who's that guy?" -- then Johnnie comes back and he's dragging this piano and we stopped the song -- and we open door up wide and help him get the piano on stage and get his amp and we get it all set up -- and I say "Johnnie what would you like to play?"
>
> And he says "Well, I liked what I heard when I got here, Chicken Shack" -- so we jumped back into it and I'm standing back and I'm hearing him play and I'm hearing all those licks I

> heard on the Chuck Berry records -- and there he was playing them. I was just floored.

Within a month Sounds of the City was playing five gigs a week, sometimes seven a week. Johnnie was back in the saddle, rolling that left hand with a rocking beat.

In 1986, the first movie crew for *Hail! Hail!* arrived with its sound gear at the Berry ranch in a truck driven by Mark Slocombe, a St. Louis music store owner and sound engineer. He pulled up the truck, loaded with equipment ordered by Delilah Films, and walked into the house. He found Chuck in his clubhouse, the music room where the rehearsals for the movie were supposed to be shot.

"He was carrying a mop," Slocum said. "There was a leak in the roof of the bathroom; you could see sunlight pouring in back there." Slocum shook Berry's hand. "His hands were all crippled up. As I was shaking his hand, I was thinking that his fingers just felt so old and arthritic, the skin on his hand was just so limp."

Slocum found banks of expensive electronic equipment fried by the leaking water from the ceiling. As he explored the grounds, he found a bar loaded with dead bugs and spider webs in the ill-fated guitar-shaped swimming pool where the two girls had drowned, the water clogged with "brown muck and dead frogs."

When Keith Richards arrived to take over his job as the movie's music director, he too was shocked. In the music room, he saw a big screen TV showing a continual video loop of naked women "throwing pies at each other and falling down."

But the show went on. Rehearsals were held, rehearsals soon taken over by Johnnie's piano, rolling rhythms that stunned Richards and Clapton and the other stars.

"By the time the movie rolls around," Maloney recalled, "Johnnie had had all this playing all the time. So, he's liquid on his piano, he just flows."

Robert Cray, a young man from Portland, Oregon, drenched himself in the music and learned to play as well as the original. Chuck mostly lounged around on a couch in front of the stage, watching as Richards recreated the Chuck Berry band, all the while experiencing a dawning realization of the importance of Johnnie's playing in the Chuck Berry hits.

Slocombe's crew cleaned out the Cosmopolitan Cub in East St. Louis and a nightclub scene was shot there, looking something like the real thing. The movie was rehearsed and shot in five days.

The heart of the movie was a big show at the Fox Theater; the ornate entertainment palace featuring Chuck Berry in the very theater he was once told he could not enter. The night of the show Berry was a wreck. He had alienated everyone involved and the moviemakers decided not to take too big a chance with Chuck. They had the main sound feed for the film wired to amplify Richards' guitar work, with Chuck's volume kept low.

The show started and Chuck muffed the songs. The crowd was yelling and cheering but Chuck couldn't get the familiar songs to work. He played odd keys on songs they had rehearsed for two days at the farm. The songs stopped and started. The soundman turned up Richards' guitar some more.

Maloney and the Sounds of the City played a gig that night without Johnnie Johnson, Afterwards, Tom and bass player Gus Thornton went down to the Fox, around 11, thinking maybe the Berry show was still on. They went to the stage entrance and found the door open. They walked into the lobby and ran into a couple of friends who were leaving and gave up their seats -- second row, center.

The show went into the early morning, Chuck came out of his crank and, as the film makes clear, blitzed off a real performance. The team of Johnson and Richards didn't do badly in the backing and filling department, especially with Richards' guitar tuned loud into the riffs he'd learned from these very songs. With Johnnie and Richards playing at the major league level, Chuck also rose to the occasion.

"School Day" was last. Chuck was wheeled onto the stage in a red Cadillac convertible, early in the morning at the Fox Theater, on Oct. 18, 1986, his 60th birthday.

Chuck came up sharp in the film; the music had all the old zing.

Afterward, there was talk about the show all around town, talk that still goes on into the twenty-first century. You'll meet somebody in a St. Louis bar who was there during the late night segment of the Chuck and Johnnie show, the Berry/Johnson team laying down rock 'n' roll music 'til the break of dawn.

Awesome, they'll say; really awesome.

Chapter Twenty-Four

Mill Creek Destroyed, Gaslight Square, LaClede Town

1959-1974

In Gaslight you could just walk down, yeah, you know, just walk down. On a Friday night, there were people sitting in the windows, watching the traffic. And once you were part of it, it was just this swirl. You were in this certain jurisdiction and you were part of it. You could wind up anywhere. Just walking up and down the street was worth it, it was a whole night's work.

-- Art Dwyer, Soulard Blues Band

On Feb. 16, 1959, the headache ball flew in Mill Creek Valley. This time the wrecking crews were after a 100-block, 465-acre site in the very heart of the city, the biggest clearance project in St. Louis history. Here a far larger chunk of real estate was eradicated than from the riverfront in 1939 or the liquidation of the North Side property that led to the Pruitt-Igoe housing project in 1952.

Instead of a single neighborhood or two, the Mill Creek Valley headache ball was after an entire district, an area that had housed its residents since the very beginnings of the city in the seventeen-sixties.

Pierre Laclede, the French fur trader who settled the city, made the first claim to the low-lying valley just west of the Mississippi. Seeing an immediate need for wheat, both as food and for trade with the Osage, Laclede apportioned land for a mill to Joseph Taillon, a Canadian who was part of the original 30 settlers who came ashore with Laclede to establish a trading post.

Taillon, a slave-holding miller who had been living across the river in Cahokia, built a dam at about the spot where Busch Stadium stands today, less than a mile from the river. The dam harnessed pure rushing water from a spring that bubbled up about four miles west of the Mississippi, carving out the valley on its way downhill. Laclede called it La Petite Riviere (Little Creek) but it was anything but petite in the rise of St. Louis from trading post to a major American metropolis.

The shape of the valley is still quite sharp as seen by a baseball fan looking west in 2016 from the third level of Busch Stadium. This view contains railroad tracks and pilings, mounds of coal and dirt, low industrial storage and factory buildings of all manner of brick and aluminum, all sitting randomly amid a tangle of roadways -- from the elevated interstate to the broken remnants of old residential streets. There is plenty of open space out there too, lots filled with weeds, broken railroad ties, gravel and garbage you can see from the stadium way west to the Grand Avenue Bridge, three miles away.

Off to the north lays the downtown, an amalgam of steel and brick, mortar and plastic, a hodgepodge of high-rise structures, office buildings and parking garages, a sight that makes one think of construction toys placed upright across the playground by an untidy, architecturally unimaginative modern Paul Bunyan.

Taillon prospered at his mill, which he soon sold to Laclede, who in turn, expanded the mill. He cornered the grain trade with the Osage, but Laclede didn't get rich. Instead, he loaned money to others, too much money. After Laclede's death, his common-law wife, Marie Chouteau, bought most of the Mill Creek area at a public auction used to pay Laclede's debts. Her son, August Chouteau, acquired the mill and the millpond that sat below the dam.

Chouteau made the pond into a 100-acre lake, the city's first recreational center and park -- Chouteau's Pond -- a "sylvan" area with "high grassy banks that sloped down to the water's edge . . . a place for lovers, for holiday sports." The gorge formed down Mill Creek was lined with giant sycamore trees, the water fresh and clear and filled with fish.

Chouteau built a mansion on the bank of the lake. Not far away on a rock called the Four Courts, his son, Henri Chouteau, built his home. By 1849, with the city crowded in around the lake, Chouteau's Pond become a dumping ground for butchers' waste and the garbage from the homes and industries that lined its north and east banks. A cholera epidemic was blamed on the hygiene of the lake. It was drained by 1852 as a hazard to health. The creek was also diverted, submerged and joined into the city sewage system, the mill long gone.

Thus, the district that contained the city's first industry was also the locale of its first park and its first neighborhood of residential grandeur. By the eighteen-seventies its lowest lying area became the railbed for the trains that formed the bloodstream of western expansion and set the economic template for the Gilded Age. Train lines multiplied. Union Depot at 12th and Market was replaced by the majestic Union Station, another six blocks west, its opening celebration attended by 20,000 people in 1894.

Brick tenement houses were built along the tracks as soon as the rails were laid. The Great Cyclone of 1896 cleared more land. During the First World War African Americans arrived from the South taking jobs far better than their sharecropper past. With the crowding of houses and industries, the remaining mansions were cut up into apartments as their owners moved to new housing further away from the city center.

By the twenties Mill Creek Valley was a thriving community of black businesses and housing, the Harlem of St. Louis.

Then, following the end of World War II, city planners began using the words "slum" and "blight." The real estate interests itched to get their hands on the area, hoping to keep the city from emptying. After a battle over its future, these interests, joined by the forces of Civic Progress, engineered a wholesale change in the district. The headache ball began to creep ever closer to what was then called Railway Valley.

In 1955, the valley was home to far more than railways. Some 20,000 residents (95 percent black) lived there. They didn't call it a slum, they didn't see it as "a menace to health and safety; a community liability." It was not for residents to say. These people were powerless to do much at all about the actions of the city government.

When the headache ball swung in the early part of 1959, it was aimed at a neighborhood defined by the city as 13 blocks long and eight blocks wide. The borders were the train tracks on the south, the Olive Street business district on the north, the Grand Avenue theater area on the west and Union Station on the east.

Within this neighborhood in 1955 were 839 businesses, churches and other institutions. There were 52 barber and beauty shops, 47 grocers, eight specialty grocery stores, 26 liquor stores, 46 restaurants, 18 taverns, three theaters, seven billiard halls, two bath houses, 43 confectioneries, 13 hotels and four offices of lawyers.

The neighborhood had three schools, (two elementary and one high school); 15 community clubs, centers and lodges; 16 doctors, dentists and nurses; eight drug stores, eight furniture stores and three pawnbrokers.

Interviews conducted in the late nineties found people looking back fondly on the old neighborhood:

> There were lots of children and we had fun.
>
> We used to sit on the front porch, walk up and down the sidewalk, go around the corner for a soda.
>
> What we didn't have we didn't worry about.
>
> There was no reason to dislike it, because we had never been in any other area.
>
> That was the area were grew up in, went to school in, went to church in, so there was nothing else to look forward to.

To get across town to the Central Library on Olive, a tunnel under Union Station made things easy. If you captured a foul ball outside Stars' Park, where the St. Louis Negro League team played, you could take it to the gate and get into the game for free. You could buy pretty much anything you wanted in the neighborhood. Visiting relatives could stay in small hotels.

You could get live chickens and turkeys on Market Street; you had the Lincoln Market, the Sunnyside Market, Jake Jick the tailor, Sam Light's Pawn Shop, Angelo's Barber Shop, and the Turf Grill.

But in St. Louis the development pattern was destroy, flatten, rebuild. That's how it went, beginning with the knockdown at the levee in 1939, extending through Deep Morgan into the near North Side in the late forties.

Now it was Mill Creek Valley in 1959. The old neighborhoods could not withstand the need for the real estate interests to build new houses. These interests saw no profit in rehabilitating the housing stock, they ignored those who wanted to rebuild St. Louis neighborhoods a block at a time, they paid very little attention to the people who lived in the targeted housing, or to what the true condition of the stock. Out with the old, in with the new.

Many of the old Mill Creek mansions were in fact crumbling. Most of the housing needed upgrading of the sanitation. The city needed to pick up the garbage and weed the alleys. The landlords needed to fix the broken windows and upgrade the plumbing. But rehabilitation was less profitable than building new and new won every land use battle in St. Louis until the sixties. None of the needs of the neighborhood were addressed.

Urban planning was in the hands of Harland Bartholemew, who after the war called for bulldozing the "blighted areas" to the ground and starting over. He was a pioneer American urban planner who invented the "comprehensive" plan and in 1947 drew the line around the first 100 acres of the area he said should be leveled and rebuilt.

Bartholomew arrived in St. Louis in 1916, age 27, a civil engineer from Newark, N.J., well familiar with the crowded tenements and urban ills of New York City. He bought a new house for himself and his family in what was then a suburb, out on the far north side near the county line. He issued his first report in 1917 and his last in 1947, all aimed at spreading out the city, widening streets, transforming the old parts of the urban area.

The city's last Republican mayor, Aloys Kauffman, put forward an urban renewal bond issue in 1948 seeking funds for what opponents called "Negro Clearance." The bond was soundly defeated by voters who saw no reason to demolish a large mixed-use district in the center of town, a loss that also foresaw the defeat of the Republicans at the polls in the next city election in 1949.

But Kauffman's approach didn't die with the end of his mayoralty. The winner was Democrat Joseph Darst, a former real estate broker who said he favored a low-rise approach to urban renewal. But after a visit to New York he changed his mind, seeing federal funding as a road to high-rise building. By 1953, Cochran Gardens, the first high-rise housing project in St. Louis was finished and Pruitt-Igoe was underway.

Darst in 1951 set up the mechanism for big projects -- the Land Clearance for Redevelopment Agency. In 1955, Darst's successor in City Hall, Raymond Tucker, the smog fighter from the thirties, pushed through $110 million in public improvement bonds, which included money for the seizure and clearance of Mill Creek Valley.

By then, the informal city board of directors, Civic Progress Inc., was up and running, established by Darst, its front row seats reserved in City Hall, representing the industrial-real estate interests, now all-in on the wrecking ball solution to the city's problems.

Residents in Mill Creek who saw the writing on the wall began to move, scattering into the area west of Grand and into the North Side to houses sold by people, a majority white, moving west to the suburbs. The population of the city had already started to slip in the fifties, showing a decrease of 100,000 people during the decade. After the destruction of Mill Creek another 130,000 left in the sixties. The seventies saw the steepest decline in history, a drop in population of 170,000 people.

Many of the people in Mill Creek Valley relocated just north of the houses they left. By 1960 some 1,343 people out of 6,409 displaced had moved into new homes within walking distance of their old dwelling. Others scattered around the city, but only 669 people took advantage of the new public housing projects -- Cochran Gardens, capacity 704 units; Darst-Webbe, 1,289 units; Pruitt-Igoe, 3,000 units; Vaughn, 657 units. These were added to pre-war projects that accounted for 1,315 apartments.

This all added up to a grand total of nearly 7,500 government-backed North Side housing units, mostly low income, by 1958. Services in the area had fallen off so far under Darst and Tucker that in 1959, when the wrecking ball hit the first house in Mill Creek Valley, 80 percent of the housing in the neighborhood had been deemed "dilapidated." By then 80 percent also had no indoor toilets and 50 percent had no running water. Less than half the 1955 population was still living in the district.

The city had stopped picking up the trash. The empty dwellings were swarmed over by scavengers picking for antiques. They were freely busting up fireplaces and pulling off banisters, prowling at night, taking the doors, looking for pieces to stock the antique stores in Greenwich Corners on Olive and Boyle Streets -- what came to be called Gaslight Square -- just a mile away.

In 1954, the Land Clearance board declared that the Mill Creek presented a "growing menace, injurious, inimical to public health and safety and to the morals and welfare of the residents of Missouri." The original 100-acre rebuilding plan was expanded to a 330-acre site that would include a new highway -- the Daniel Boone Expressway (now I-64) -- running next to the tracks, right through the middle of the valley.

The original plan provided that families who lived in the area would be relocated to temporary housing then returned to the neighborhood into new housing. That idea soon disappeared when the wrecking began. One city agency gushed in 1958 that where stood a "jungle of decrepit shacks and weed-covered fields" would rise more than 2,000 modern dwelling units -- in towering apartment buildings and in two- and three-story multiple-family homes -- "surrounded with gardens, walkways and well-planned recreational areas."

The idea was that the city would acquire the land with the bond money added to the two-thirds of the total cost provided by federal matching funds. The land would then be sold to a developer selected by the land board. By a Sept. 10, 1957, deadline, 20 parties requested information on purchasi9ng the property.

The leading candidate emerged in the next month as William Zeckendorf, president of Webb and Knapp, a major player in the New York real estate world from a family that at one time owned Rockefeller Center and the Chrysler Building. The cost to redevelop the area was estimated by then at $200 million.

In November the board received a last-minute bid from local St. Louis investors and made a surprise decision to shun Zeckendorf. Instead the contract went to another company, City and Suburban Homes, a New York organized firm directly tied to a Civic Progress-backed alliance of a dozen St. Louis companies, the St. Louis Group. The work was parceled out between the two entities with the St. Louisans in charge of the start-up demolition.

Zeckendorf had been certain he would win the bid. "We had been told consistently we offered the best plan," he said, reminding the city and the public that his company had the deepest pockets and that his appraisal of the property value was the highest of the bidders. The city planning staff had backed the Zeckendorf bid, but the vote of the land board was 3-2 against Zeckendorf. He was then offered a 400-unit consolation prize even though he had insisted he would only accept 100 percent of the pie. He refused any smaller prize and went back to New York City.

And thus, two days after Valentine's Day in February 1959, a 3,000-pound wrecking ball crashed into a house on Laclede Avenue. The demolition process had an initial timetable set for 275 dwellings in the first 90-day period. This first house to knocked down had been there since 1877, rather late in the neighborhood's early history, probably because it was built in an area near a cemetery. The likelihood of ghosts prowling the streets made people reluctant to build on the spot.

By the time the ball flew, many of the Mill Creek houses had already been cleared of the antique features of the Gilded Age, stocking a small collection of stores in a T-shaped intersection north and west of downtown known as Greenwich Corners, adding to items picked from the North Side.

The Musical Arts Building, an ornate, three-story 1904 brick building that included a theater space on the second floor, anchored Greenwich Corners. Here Tennessee Williams previewed plays; the opera singer Helen Trauble studied and performed and actress Betty Grable put her legs in motion during childhood dance lessons.

The building also housed a music school with numerous classrooms as well as artist studios used to train painters and sculptors, giving the neighborhood a progressive bent.

Around the Arts Building were several of the antique stores, outlets that drew customers ranging from the highest socialite to the lowliest artisan, all trading in the scavenged goods. There were a few neighborhood restaurants and bars along the street, but nothing particularly notable until 1958 when the antiques/theater entrepreneur Jay Landesman arrived with his Crystal Palace.

Landesman was the operator of Little Bohemia, the artist bar that had moved uptown after the headache ball arrived on the waterfront in 1939.

In 1948, he founded *Neurotica*, a literary magazine "by and for neurotics." The purpose of *Neurotica* was to explore the mind of the anxious man, the person "who has been forced to live underground, and yet lights an inner darkness with his music, poetry, painting and writing." Little Bohemia served as a distribution point for the first issue.

The magazine led Landesman to New York to be closer to the publishing scene. There he ran head on into the Beat Generation. He met John Clellon Holmes, Allan Ginsberg, Jack Kerouac, and other Beat founders, just the kind of people he had cultivated at Little Bohemia.

By the spring of 1951, with eight issues of the magazine under his belt, he tired of the project. In his autobiography *Rebel Without Applause,* Landesman wrote that by the early fifties he realized that "violence was going to be part of the everyday life of the country and there was nothing *Neurotica* could do about stemming the tide. I was completely disillusioned and wanted a way out."

He returned to his family's antique business in St. Louis, a store located in Greenwich Corners. He brought with him Fran, the daughter of a journalist he married in New York in 1950. He and his brother bought a seedy gay bar near Grand Avenue and Olive, gutted it, filled it with antiques and opened a bar they called the Crystal Palace "to give Fran something to do."

The Landesmans exposed the brick walls and installed the flotsam of the city -- crystal chandeliers, drug store chairs, marble-topped tables, and sundry reclaimed "junk." Pickers arrived with more and more gleanings and Fran filled up the place.

A bar was set up and drinks became available.

The St. Louis bohemian set, displaced from the levee, settled into the new bar most afternoons. They were joined by other riffraff including newspaper reporters, liberal doctors, socialites (especially women art lovers), new breed advertising men, and a scattering of literary types. Alan Ginsberg read his epic poem *Howl* there before it was published. James Jones (*From Here to Eternity*) enjoyed several libations. Landesman booked the rising radical comedian Lenny Bruce and the local comic and civil right activist Dick Gregory.

By 1955, Landesman had decided he needed steady nighttime action in the place and after a series of bizarre lectures ("Squaresville U.S.A.: A New

Look at Main Street") he convinced Ted Flicker, the director of the fledgling Compass Players, to stage a few plays. The idea was improvisational comedy of a style recently born in Hyde Park in Chicago featuring Elaine May, Mike Nichols and Shelly Berman. The Compass Company was looking for ways to spread its wings and used St. Louis as the launch.

Landesman remembered:

> No one in the audience for the first night of the Compass at the Palace was likely to forget its impact. The stage was dark. Two of the players were planted at a table in the audience. They started to argue, until the audience was hollering for them to shut up. As the couple made their way to the stage, Flicker, a small, volatile man with a Mephistopheles beard, dressed in a black leotard, hopped onto the stage and shouted 'Freeze!' The lights went up on the performers. 'What happens next?' he asked the audience. "You tell us.'"

The company brought a "sharp, biting satirical commentary on contemporary manner and morals that left no doubt something was happening in entertainment in America." Compass evolved into another troupe, Second City, which in the seventies provided the seed cast for the television hits *Saturday Night Live* and *SCTV.*

For Landesman, however, the small space made it hard to make enough money to keep the players. The brothers naturally thought that if they had more space they could do better. So, in 1958, they shuffled on west the seven blocks up to Greenwich Corners, taking over a big store space at 4240 Olive that became available when the owner died. Here was born the volcanic epicenter of Gaslight Square.

> (It) was a cross between a church and a movie palace, without the reverence. The walls and ceiling were painted fire engine red, casting an unearthly glow over the proceedings, while the air of decadence was completed by a 50-foot mural of church stained glass, lit from behind, and complete with 'in memoriam' notices. The especially designed huge crystal and brass chandeliers added the necessary touch of frivolity.

The theater opened with a series of non-commercial plays that were met with unsold tickets and yawns. *The Nervous Set* changed all that. Flicker wrote the play from Landesman's unpublished novel. Fran Landesman was inspired to write the lyrics and Tommy Wolf, the piano player at the bar, wrote the music. The play opened March 4, 1959, and was an immediate success.

The national entertainment paper *Variety* attracted immediate interest among Broadway producers with a rave review:

> *The Nervous Set* premiered at the Crystal Palace saloon theatre to ecstatic packed house enthusiasm. *The Nervous Set* deals with the beat generation, sometimes tenderly, sometimes spicily, sometimes hilariously, but always entertainingly . . . The show has some twenty tunes, tailored to the assorted beatniks, squares, and snobs who populate the three acts.

The Beat literary movement had been bubbling in America by the time the play hit the boards. Jack Kerouac's *On the Road* had started its climb into the ranks of America's most influential novels. The "Beat Generation" label had reached the mainstream in November 1952 coined by novelist John Clellon Holmes in an article for *The New York Times Magazine* called "This is the Beat Generation." Holmes had already met Landesman in New York when the term gained currency.

Kerouac said he and Ginsberg had been using the word since 1945 and that it came from a Times Square denizen named Herbert Huncke ("Hunkie the Junkie"). He said he had picked up the word from circus and carnival people describing their wearying, rootless, nomadic lives. In the drug world, beat meant robbed or cheated.

Kerouac and Ginsberg were close friends of two other St. Louisans besides Landesman -- William Burroughs and Lucien Carr. Carr knew Burroughs from back home and met Ginsberg at Columbia University where Carr was a student. Carr introduced Kerouac to Ginsburg in 1944 at the West End Bar and Grill. And voila -- the Big Four founding fathers of the generation was formed, two of them from St. Louis. Another key early link was yet another St. Louisan, David Kammerer, a teacher of English and physical education at Washington University.

Burroughs and Kammerer went to grade school together in St. Louis. Burroughs described Kammerer as "the veritable life of the party, and completely without any middle-class morality." The homosexual overtones were clear, but not to the young Lucien Carr, who met Kammerer as his teenage student, a meeting than began years of pursuit of Carr by Kammerer that ended in New York with a sensational killing on the banks of the Hudson River not far from Columbia.

Carr's version of the killing was that he acted in self-defense late that night during a walk in Riverside Park, stabbing Kammerer when the older man made an aggressive sexual advance. Carr's weapon was a Boy Scout knife from his days in the St. Louis youth group.

Carr's education had been determined by attempts to get away from Kammerer, who was 14 years older than Carr and obsessed with the younger man's striking good looks, his snide wit and careless attitude. Carr made several attempts to run from his former teacher, moving from St. Louis to the Phillips Academy in Andover, Mass., to Bowdoin College in Brunswick, Maine, to the University of Chicago, and from there to Columbia, followed each time by the persistent Kammerer. Carr, after consulting with Burroughs and Kerouac, confessed to the crime (the other two were arrested as material witnesses) and the case became a running story in the New York press, with the *Daily News* dubbing the stabbing "an honor slaying" and referring to Carr as a "young Adonis."

The killing -- and the character of Lucien Carr himself -- was a crucial fable in the Beat founding myths, an incident that linked Carr, Ginsberg, Kerouac and Burroughs for life, making them the recognized core of the early Beats by the time Landesman met them in the late forties, a key element of *The Nervous Set.* Kerouac used the killing of Kammerer in his first novel (*Town and Country*) and collaborated with Burroughs in 1945 on *And the Hippos Were Boiled in Their Tanks*, a book that was not published until 2008, three years after Carr's death, and was made into the 2013 film *Kill Your Darlings.*

Carr pled guilty to first-degree manslaughter in the death of David Kammerer and spent two years in prison. After his release Carr was hired by the United Press news agency in New York in 1946 as a copy boy and spent the next 47 years working for the agency as a reporter, desk editor and editor-in-chief. He kept in contact with his friends but never achieved literary prominence and rarely spoke of his night by the Hudson. His normal gallows humor was not sparked by the topic. He kept his head down and was virtually unknown in the literary world until after his death in 2005.

He was Kerouac's best man in 1950, and provided Kerouac with several rolls of teletype paper from the United Press (later United Press International) storeroom that Kerouac used to write two drafts of *On the Road,* the first pasted together from scraps of cut paper, the second rewritten on a continuous roll of the yellow paper while living in Carr's apartment. Kerouac died in 1969, but Burroughs *(Naked Lunch)* and Ginsberg (*Howl,* dedicated to Carr) lived long lives, both dying in 1997.

Howl (1956), *On the Road* (1957) and *Naked Lunch* (1962) have each remained in print -- selling millions of copies -- since they were first published. Throughout their lives, Ginsberg and Burroughs made numerous public appearances, often arranged by their old friend, Lou Carr. The wealth garnered from the sales of the books and the personal appearances are not public knowledge, but of significance is the $2.37 million paid for the original scroll of *On the Road,* which uses the real names of Kerouac's friends rather than the fictional names he later substituted.

The words of Lucien Carr, the last man standing of the Big Four, live on as well, in thousands of newspaper files all over the country, in papers containing the tightly edited UPI copy that made up his daily work, often appearing on the front pages of 50 or more major daily newspapers on any given day from the sixties to the nineties, a style of journalism that dominated the news copy of his era.

As much as anyone during the second half of the twentieth century, this St. Louis product shaped how information was disseminated in America.

None of the Big Four of the Beat generation made it to the second decade of the twentieth century. Carr died in 2005, Burroughs and Ginsberg in 1997, and Kerouac in 1969.

***The Nervous Set* remains the only Broadway play** ever directly concerned with the Beat Generation. Veteran Broadway producer Robert Lantz saw the show at the Crystal Palace, read the reviews and decided to bring it to New York immediately, allowing only 10 days between the end of the St. Louis run and its opening on the Great White Way. Even with such a short window for changes, he insisted on major revisions, including wholesale changes in the cast, dropping the most popular song and adding a new ending.

Director Ted Flicker worked day and night to keep up with all the changes Lantz demanded. The new actress playing the heroine couldn't deal with the four-piece jazz band sitting on the stage. She was three inches taller than the hero and was supposed play a vulnerable victim, not a tower of strength. Flicker was forced to rewrite the book so the two lead characters never appeared standing together at the same time.

Landesman saw an emerging Broadway flop a mile away. He began throwing up after breakfast and telling his friends, "Give me three sticks of wood, a can of sterno, and I'll hit the road for hobo heaven."

On opening night, Landesman spotted Joseph Pulitzer, the publisher of the *Post-Dispatch,* on the street outside the theater, one of dozens of St. Louisans who had made the trip for the premier. As Landesman chatted with Joe Jr. up rolled Kerouac, his hand wrapped around a brown paper bag carrying a bottle of whiskey.

"Who's this dude?" he asked, looking over at the staid Pulitzer. Kerouac offered the publisher the bag and Joe Jr. took a long swig, then passed it on to Landesman as Kerouac began circling the other men, staring at them with a crazed look, staggering drunkenly.

There was trouble getting Kerouac into the theater and once seated he fell directly to sleep, "the original beatnik" snuggling up to Landesman in the next seat.

Larry Hagman, who later starred as J.R. on the *Dallas* TV series, played Kerouac in the *Nervous Set,* portraying the French-Canadian writer with a southern accent. Kerouac woke up when he heard his name mentioned on stage, but after the intermission went for a drink at the bar across the street and disappeared into the night.

The reviews were mixed. The *Daily News* was most enthusiastic, calling the show "the most brilliant, sophisticated, witty and completely novel production of the past decade." The *World-Telegram & Sun* said it was "exclusively for the beat, bop, and beret brigade." Walter Kerr in the *Herald-Tribune* looked beyond the play altogether, saying "There is nothing here that Cole Porter couldn't have done twenty times better, while well dressed."

The play flopped at the box office, closing May 30 after 23 performances. Landesman stopped throwing up and went back to St. Louis.

Just three weeks before Landesman opened *The Nervous Set* at the Palace, a tornado had almost destroyed his plans for his new theater in Gaslight Square. But the twister missed the theater and several of the other establishments that had already taken a tentative foothold in the area. Many called the storm "the ill wind that blew for the good." Indeed, many merchants took quick advantage of insurance settlements to remodel and brighten their businesses. Also, the small DeBaliviere entertainment strip was nearly destroyed and several businesses there took their money and moved to Gaslight.

The storm killed at least 21 people with hundreds injured. The twister hit at 2 a.m. in the morning Feb. 10, 1959, jumping from suburban Eureka into the middle of downtown, taking down a TV tower near Forest Park. Heading north, the tornado slammed down a brick building near the edge of the park, tore across Delmar at DeBaliviere then took aim at Olive and Boyle, the Greenwich Corners intersection that was home for the infant Square.

Smokey Joe Cunningham was an outfielder for the Cardinals who lived in the Square year around in an apartment across the street from the Crystal Palace. The wind smashed out the skylight of his flat. Cunningham said:

> My next door neighbor was an architect. It went through his place, through his bedroom wall and pushed his bedroom walls on top of the cars below. I dove in the back room and my buddy went into the kitchen; he ducked under a table and got stuck. He got a nail in the foot, but that was all. I thought it was a sandstorm. I looked down the street . . . all the buildings on the other side of the street were defaced. A little building that had been a tavern was leveled.

The next morning the news outlets descended on the street, television cameras and reporters crawled about, talking to storm survivors. By noon, crowds of nearby residents were also crawling around looking at the rubble and wreckage. Insurance adjusters and the new entrepreneurs followed. Everybody arrived just in time for the sixties.

One entrepreneur was Jimmy Miller, a 24-year-old student of architecture who came up with the idea of using doors blown out and shutters blown off during the storm to help rebuild. He also took a close look at the houses in Mill Creek Valley and started buying doors there as well.

Soon enough he had a warehouse filled with hundreds of doors and 6,000 shutters. He hired workmen to soak off layers of paint and varnish and bring the material down to the bare wood. These sold quickly, first to rehabilitating homeowners then to the new bars and restaurants that started filling the storefronts.

Paul Matrux, one of the pioneers in the block who was established by the time of the storm at the Gaslight saloon, built a new restaurant nearby with a 25-foot wall made entirely of Miller's doors. Miller had also salvaged wrought iron railing from the Grand Avenue Bridge that once spanned Mill Creek, selling much of it to Matrux for his new venture, the Continental.

By 1960, another of the square's innovators, Jimmy "The Picker" Massucci, who already owned the Golden Eagle and Opera House, opened a two-floor drinks emporium called Vanity Fair that featured dozens of telephone booths skimmed off the emptying streets of the valley. The Picker discovered an old warehouse in the demolition zone that was filled with nine barrels of croquet balls there for the taking. But what do you do with 3,000 croquet balls?

Miller painted half the balls white and the other half red, drilled holes and strung them from a fake balcony in Massucci's Opera House. It became the home to continuous Dixieland music and one of the square's biggest draws, featuring several of the old jazz players from the steamboats, including the tuba master Singleton Palmer.

"My whole needle is to find something discarded, take it out and place it in fine homes and restaurants. What is happening at Olive and Boyle is the way to rebuild St. Louis," Massucci said.

Along the street next to Smokey Joe's apartment, another early business operator, Dick Draper, rebuilt a row of houses and called them the Avacado Arms. Next door he opened The Left Bank, a restaurant, bar and art gallery that featured modern art. "Bohemian in atmosphere" was his slogan. And from outside the wreckage, from Milan, Italy, came another crucial addition to the scene -- a $1,200 espresso machine purchased for Montileone's Espresso. The machine brought the Euro-coffee experience to St. Louis long before the national trend.

On Aug. 21, 1963, gas lamps arrived -- 101 of them lighted along Olive and Boyle. The old-fashioned lamps replaced harsh incandescent lights and gave the place a softer, more old-fashioned look. A crowd of several hundred watched as Sammy Gardener's Mound City Six played "Meet Me in St. Louis" followed by politicians hoping to latch on to the popularity of the street.

By the time the lamps went on the Square was at its peak. In just four years after the 1959 storm, the district had exploded.

Joints named Laughing Buddha, the Other Side, the Dark Side, Marty's, the Black Horse, O'Connell's, the Three Fountains, the Silver Dollar and the Carriage House lined the south side of Olive. Down the north side sat The Living Room, Two-Cents Plain, Smokey Joe's, Port St. Louis, Kotobuki, Jorgie's and the Beef House. And there were still at least a dozen antique stores, filled with more and more salvaged stuff.

Time magazine gave it the full treatment in May 1962, taking on the long-standing St. Louis image problem.

> In the gazetteer of U.S. night life, St. Louis has never placed very high. Like Atlanta, Cleveland, Buffalo or Pittsburgh, it has been traditionally an entertain-at-home sort of town, and with the exception of a night at the Symphony or Municipal Opera, most of St. Louis spent its evenings the way much of the rest of the U.S. did: watching television or drinking beer in somebody else's living room.
>
> But now all that is changed. St. Louis finally has a place to go at night, and the place is Gaslight Square.

Why did this neighborhood become so successful so fast? Jack Parker, the long-time bartender and eventual owner of O'Connell's, said the answer started with location.

> When you went north, you had a black neighborhood. But it was not a ghetto or what-have-you. There were nice, single-family homes. There was nothing negative involved in that situation. To the south and southwest, you had a lot of great old buildings. Some were boarding houses, but the Landesman family owned a lot of these buildings. It afforded inexpensive rental housing to, let's say, the habitues of the neighborhood, who wanted to live in a hip area.
>
> "You had what was built at the time of the World's Fair, a three-story mansion. Now it's a rooming house with six or eight

> little broken up apartments. A lot of these people worked in the neighborhood as bartenders or waitresses. These were the places where they would live and it worked out well.

Then came the entertainers. The Square was a launch pad for new entertainers just as much as it was a place to start a new business. The list of those who played the Square between 1959 and 1962 is impressive: Lenny Bruce, Phyllis Diller, Woody Allen, Alan Arkin, George Carlin, Dick Gregory, the Smothers Brothers and a teenage Barbra Streisand.

"She kept her music sheets inside her bra," said Gaslight Bar owner Frank Moskus of Streisand. She was just 18 when she hit the Square and "was desperate to play her music. She would walk up and down the block looking for piano players who would play it so she could sing."

Streisand's show was reviewed by the *Post-Dispatch* as "frothy and funny" and said she was a "chic singer with vocal prowess unusual for a girl of 18."

"It wasn't a good living," said Chris King, who lived on the block and scrambled to make it as an actor and singer, "But the Square was not predicated on how much money you made. It was how witty you were, how talented you were. It was a great, gentle place. There was a great camaraderie among those of us who lived and worked there -- bartenders, musicians, all of us."

"I loved going to work and I hated to close," said Marty Bronson, a musician who owned Marty's on the south side of Olive, where his waiters and waitresses sang as they served. "I could have stayed there the rest of my life."

One of Marty's waitresses, Cheri Ann Schear, remembered Pete Flanders, the piano player who played the keys with one hand and blew the trumpet with another. She remembered Phyllis Diller wearing a fur coat and little booties. She remembered singing to Edie Adams, who was performing *Calamity Jane* at the Crystal. She sang for the bandleader Bob Crosby and the ballplayer (and St. Louis native) Joe Garagiola.

The jazz singer Jeanne Trevor had regular shows at the Black Horse and the Vanity Fair. She remembered "big crowds. Every night." She remembered going down the stairs into the Vanity Fair, right into what looked like telephone booths. "Every room had its character and spirit." She said after the joints closed for the night "everyone went to East Side if they wanted to hear more music." These were the days of Ike and Tina, of the R&B revues across the river. Cars would caravan across the Eads Bridge to East Side clubs for dancing until dawn.

In the Square, the Dark Side stayed open late. There, Trevor said, (supplying the quote marks,) "they didn't serve liquor." Miles Davis popped up there without warning. Spider Burks, the DJ, ran another of the "dry" joints.

There were also folk singers like the Swagman Trio, looking very much like the Kingston Trio, complete with short-sleeve white shirts and ties, singing at the Jack's or Better Bar. And Carolyn Hester, who gave Bob Dylan an early recording job, appeared at the Everyman with "a vocal range wide enough to support a herd of steers."

One reporter who called himself Oliver Boyle wrote in 1963 that it was impossible to talk on the street without shouting. From open doors on a warm May evening came the "moony bleat of saxophones, drums thumping and tubas blasting, bag pipes squalling like stuck pigs, tin can batter of banjos, blues singers, babbling crowds of customers and the cabarets' own music of complacent cash registers clanging bells."

The artist Bill Christman said when he was in high school he and his friends, too young to go into the joints, would "walk up one side of the street and down the other. There were all kinds of people who did this promenade, like they do in small towns. I'd never seen anything like it. All these things were built by hand. A lot of this stuff came from the old Mill Creek Valley, a lot of Gaslight Square was built from rubble."

At Danza's, Screamin' Joe Neal held forth on Friday and Saturday in the early sixties. Art Dwyer, a North Side bass player and founder of the Soulard Blues Band, would go down and sneak in to see the wild blues belter who liked to jump off the piano into the crowd. "It looked like the whole building was shaking," Dwyer said. The Screamin' Joe shows were "packed with all of us high school kids."

But as the nation changed, Gaslight Square did too. The Beats faded away into a media cliche replaced with the hippies, the New Left anti-war protesters, the civil rights movement and increased racial tension that spilled out into riots across the country. The go-go era came in big during the mid-sixties and Gaslight business owners bought in, hoping for more bucks. Burlesque joints opened. Other gimmicks sprouted up, perhaps the most unique could be found in the Living Room.

Billy Peek, the Chuck Berry protege, played there in the mid-sixties.

> There was a phone on every table. There would be a scantily-clad, very good looking girl sitting in the window, the switchboard operator. They had a number hanging from the ceiling above every table. Say you're with a buddy, you're sitting at a table. You see two girls across the room and you'd call them, ask them to have a drink or to have a dance.
>
> Onstage, we had a phone with a big red light. It was so loud in there you couldn't hear it ring. So the red light would come on and you'd pick up and they'd request a song.

The Living Room changed over to go-go and became the Pussy Cat Go-Go with the same owners as the sixties wound down.

During these late days of the Square, people complained and decay was in the air. There was still plenty to enjoy, the decline was mixed and came in small spurts. Meanwhile, a new generation of teenagers was strolling the three blocks. The young now wore long hair and flowing clothing, sandals and cut off jeans.

Tom Maloney, the guitar player who had been playing in bands since 1964, was one of those young strollers. By his senior year of high school, 1970, he was playing in a rock band called Tree that landed a gig on the Square. Before that he played in a series of groups in the youth Teen Town clubs or the Catholic-sponsored dances, bands with names including the Chaparells, the Malibus, the Dynamic Soul Revue and Soul Tree.

> After our Teen Town gig, we would make a beeline for Gaslight Square and walk up and down the street and look in the windows. It was such fun. We couldn't get into any of these places, but we got to hear music, sometimes bands from out of town, older guys we could learn from.

He mentioned Billy Peek, rocking at the Living Room as well as other local rockers -- Larry Knight and the Upsetters and Jules Glatoner.

> They were in the little clubs, the shoebox type of things. The stage would be right in the front window, so the action was visible

> from the street. You could see the go-go girls and the band right through the window.
>
> One night, we walked by the Rooster Tail and I hear this band and they are fabulous. I can remember it clear as a bell -- they are singing 'He Don't Love You' by Jerry Butler and I'm going 'oh my god this is as good as the record.' So I ask the doorman 'Who is this band?' and he says, 'Almond Joy' and I'm thinking that these guys were significant, they stood out big time.

Indeed. The name was in fact (and the year was 1967) and the leaders were the Allman brothers, Duane and Gregg. The band had been touring constantly but settled into Gaslight Square for a few months. It was here that Bill McEuen, a Los Angeles agent who took them west, discovered them. In St. Louis the band picked up two Alabama players, drummer Johnny Sandlin and keyboardist Paul Hornsby, players who remained associated with the Allman Brothers band for decades.

There was another legacy to the Allman's stint in St. Louis -- Devon Allman, now a respected player in his own right. He is the son of Gregg Allman and Sally Jay Jefts and was born in 1972 in Corpus Christie, Texas. The parents divorced while he was still an infant and he never met his father until he was in his teens.

By then his mother had taken him to St. Louis, where they lived a suburban life. He formed Honeytribe in St. Louis in 1999 with George Potsos on bass and Gabriel Strange on drums. He then had a stint with Royal Southern Brotherhood, that included Mike Zito, another St. Louis product, and Cyril Neville of New Orleans was formed in 2010. The band's debut album hit the *Billboard* blues chart at No. 5.

In 2015, Allman went solo, settling into a Friday Night Blues series the Ameristar Casino in suburban St. Charles, Mo., between tours. Zito also went out on his own, forming a new group, Mike Zito and the Wheel, and put out a new record in 2015 called *Keep Coming Back.*

Christman left St. Louis to attend Columbia University from 1965 to 1969 and was surprised to find a much different Square by the end of the sixties. "There was a radical departure," he said. "A ghost town feel about it."

Crime was often portrayed as the reason for the change, marked by the Dec. 30, 1964, killing of a woman named Lillian Heller, a legal secretary and artist who lived near the Palace. She was shot and killed in the first floor hallway on her way up to her third floor apartment in an apparent robbery.

Around the same time, the owner of a souvenir shop reported "numerous" break-ins. People who parked cars in the nearby North Side neighborhood complained of break-ins, storeowners began installing bars on the windows. Police, however, said the crime rate on the street was lower than it was on the same street before the Square became popular and chose not to assign a beat patrolman. Still, with major coverage of the 1964 killing and reports of fear among the female antique shop owners, business in 1966 was down 25 percent.

Pete Rothschild, who became of one the city's most prominent real estate developers, moved into the Square when he was 18, in 1967, into what he describes as a "squalid little apartment" where he lived for just two days before all his possessions were stolen. But he stayed, got a job at a joint called The In-Crowd running the first psychedelic light show in St. Louis, mixing colors in a concave clock face that was connected to an overhead projector and sloshed around while the band played. Later, he started the city's first underground newspaper, *Xanadu*.

He said the crime wave was overplayed and that when he moved in "it was right on the cusp between the beatniks and the hippies."

> At that time, the way people felt was of peace and love and of brotherhood. It was all encompassing. People down there accepted black people. For me, that was part of how cool it was. People were like-minded, kinda cosmopolitan.

Ron Elz, the DJ known as Johnny Rabbit, detailed another important factor, one that was not reported by the daily papers or the television news.

This was the opposition by the city's downtown hotels that lost business in their bars, restaurants and lounges because of the Square. Tourists, instead of having dinner in the hotel restaurant, would go to the Square in a cab, have a meal, take in a show, listen to a band, have a late night drink, watch the people and take another cab ride back to the hotel.

At a hotel like the Chase Park Plaza, a mammoth, high-priced establishment at the northeast corner of Forest Park, the restaurant and music club suffered. The hotel owners, Elz maintains, "got together with the cab companies and told them if they were ever caught taking people to Gaslight Square or suggesting Gaslight or not fighting people on going to Gaslight, they'd lose their cabstand. In those days, you had a major cabstand at any hotel in St. Louis." So losing a cabstand would hurt the cab companies.

The hotels would keep track of who took customers to the Square by hiring students to hop in a cab and say "take me to Gaslight Square." If the cabbie agreed, the students would take down the number of the cab and give the information to the companies. Soon enough, the cabbies were telling fares that the Square was dangerous, "you'll get killed, you'll get robbed."

There was also a Civic Progress element to this. The owners of the big hotels were tight with Mayor Alfonso Cervantes, who had been a partner in the Chase. "The city frowned on Gaslight Square," Elz said. "You would have thought the city would be behind it. It was a great destination."

Another problem was a lack of unity among the businesses, each fighting for its slice of the pie. Urban riots by blacks broke out in Harlem in 1964, followed over the next five years by similar race riots in Philadelphia, Los Angeles (Watts), Cleveland, Newark, Detroit, Minneapolis, Chicago, Washington, Baltimore, and several other smaller cities.

There was only a glimmer of such riots in St. Louis, but a growing local civil rights/black power movement fed the fears of the new nervous set -- those who feared losing their power. With a large black neighborhood just to the north of the Square, business owners started to sell their establishments. And they sold for a lot of money, prices based on the volume they were doing. These were not big corporate operations, these were small businessmen who had started on $2,000 in 1958 and were now being offered $50,000 to sell.

New owners moving in took a different approach. The antique store, bohemian, beatnik, Dixieland days were over. This was the swinging sixties and the new places featured loud rock bands, nearly naked women swinging from ropes, barkers shouting into the street. Drink prices went up. Minimums were added on top of cover charges.

Things grew more and more seedy, more like a carnival than an entertainment district. Finally, came the invasion of the hippies mostly from the St. Louis suburbs, but who were alienated from their parents and had no money and nowhere to stay, panhandling the tourists, looking for freebies at the clubs. Speed replaced marijuana as the rug of choice on the street. Drunks were more frequent.

The weekday business declined first, there weren't so many regulars arguing with their favorite bartender. Then, in 1971, the Musical Arts Building, the original core of the Greenwich Corners district, burned to the ground.

Street artists were barred from selling on the streets. City Hall grew more leery -- it never come through with parking lots or security patrols, And, by then, Mill Creek Valley had been picked out, leaving the remaining antique stores with less to sell.

And so, by the early seventies, the talk of developers turned to Laclede's Landing as the next big thing, a downtown area seen as safer, cheaper to develop, with empty old buildings owned by big companies that could be rehabilitated and made profitable. The Mill Creek development was struggling, the real estate interests needed a new market. The dozers had been idle too long.

In 1972, the aldermen passed a bill taking away the name Gaslight Square from Olive and Boyle, swinging their support over to a "downtown Gaslight Square" on Laclede's Landing.

The downtown Gaslight Square never matched its uptown predecessor. Laclede's Landing developed into an entertainment district that had a short time in the sun, especially at the club Mississippi Nights, a 1,000-person capacity musical center of some repute, in the eighties a steadfast home for local and national groups.

Other clubs and restaurants moved into the area but the density never matched Gaslight, nor did the music scene. A few restaurants like Hennagan's drew tourists to the area and there were several years where foot traffic was steady.

Mississippi Nights lasted from 1979 and lasted until 2007, two years after the city, which held the lease to the property, negotiated a deal with Las Vegas-based Pinnacle Entertainment to open a casino on the site. The casino was preceded by a series of highway projects that cut the area off from downtown. Once the casino came in and the roadways were established the Landing became little more than a forgotten area.

A walk there in 2015 was uneventful, a ghost town of ancient cobble stone streets and beautiful, under-utilized buildings, a historic oversight.

On the other side of Gaslight, however, beginning in 1972, the next big thing took shape. There on the old Delmar Loop a local music fan and a collector of pop icons by the name of Joe Edwards opened a new bar just outside the city line called Blueberry Hill.

Even though Edwards made no claim to creating the "next big thing" that's how it eventually worked out. Edwards had a vision of recreating the street life of the Square and convinced an active group of people in the University City government and the closest city neighborhoods to get involved. The Loop straddled both sides of Skinker Avenue, the city line on the western edge. Edwards found allies who worked together.

The Loop developed slowly over the next 40 years; there was no great explosion. In 2015, an ever expanding strip over more than six blocks included nearly 50 food outlets, another 50 retail stores, four live music venues. The strip is anchored by the Tivoli Theater, built in 1924; the Pageant, a 3,000 capacity concert venue; the Center for Creative Arts, a school of performance and visual arts; the Walk of Fame honoring 137 famous St. Louisans; and the Moonrise Hotel, a boutique hotel of 125 rooms. A trolley project up and down the street neared competition. Two new developments, a 14-story apartment complex and another Joe Edwards music venue took shape in 2016.

Elsewhere in town, the Grove showed promise, keyed by music clubs and bars in a strip known as the "Gayborhood." These include dance clubs, drag queens, and public art and the soul food restaurant Sweetie Pie's, home to a long running reality TV show starring former Ikette Robbie Montgomery.

The demolition of Mill Creek Valley was quickly accomplished during the height of Gaslight Square's rise to popularity in the early sixties. In what the NAACP called "the Negro removal project" blacks relocated quickly and saw no way to protest. In fact, many felt their lives would improve with a move and for some that proved to be the case.

Real estate agents arrived in the decaying homes that were left in the valley in the late fifties with briefcases filled with a cash incentive, talked the owners into selling, then spun complicated webs of financing for other homes in other neighborhoods, getting residents to sign on the dotted line for short-term loans that included balloons at high interest rates. Mill Creek people bought in suburbs like University City, Wellston and Pine Lawn or in the city near Delmar or along Chouteau.

Once the people left, however, redevelopment work in the valley proved to be neither as quick nor comprehensive as its promoters promised. Perhaps the very awarding of the contracts to three different development entities guaranteed its uneven progress. There was a master plan, but in practice, the hodgepodge of residential, industrial and transportation projects grew in fits and starts along the rails and up Market Street.

The development had several stages, some private, most public, financed with federal, state, city and corporate funds. St. Louis University was in the mix as was the Teamsters Union and the Teachers' Union Pension Fund. Missouri had its fingers on the road building, the federal government on housing. Corporations backed the warehouses and industrial components. The pie was sliced in many pieces.

One of the developers, James Scheuer, a 38-old New Yorker and chairman of City and Suburban Homes, said his vision for the development was to create "sparkle, glamour and gaiety. Done properly," he told the Chamber of Commerce, "a large-scale housing project can trigger a revitalization of the entire downtown area." But while the development of the nearly 500-acre tract did spawn a run of downtown development, their wasn't much glamour to be seen in the finished projects.

In 1962, the only things finished were the infant first phase of the LaClede Town development near St. Louis University, the shells of seven new commercial buildings and the skeletons of two 12-story apartment towers along Grand Boulevard. Residents were by then calling Mill Creek Valley "Hiroshima Flats" and the flight to the suburbs was on. There was a strike by construction unions that slowed building in 1963 and the Boone Expressway (eventually I-64) that cut through the valley bogged down.

The city Board of Aldermen, however, pushed the developers and the state to accelerate the projects and by 1965 things were rolling. There were 800 housing units competed and another 375 on the way. By then almost all the district had been sold for development, with over $50 million put into construction contracts. The Teamsters had committed $5 million and St. Louis University was in for $10 million.

Throughout the sixties and the seventies, money flowed into the downtown, inside and outside Mill Creek, with the Gateway Arch finally completed in 1965, a new baseball stadium costing $50 million finished in 1966, and several new, giant-sized office buildings with a total price tag of $65 million erected by 1975.

The Gateway Arch was the crowning glory of the Jefferson National Memorial Park, begun during the Depression with a federal grant from the Historic Sites Act and by a $7.5 million bond issue passed by city voters in 1935. Demolition of the waterfront properties began in 1939 and was finished in 1942. The area devolved into an empty space of mud and gravel until 1950 when Harry Truman dedicated the ground for the new federal park and the city planted the 40-acre site with grass.

In 1954 another $5 million in federal money got things going again after the Korean War and still more federal cash, $12.25 million and $6 million, came bubbling forth from Congress in 1958 and 1965. The stainless steel giant, meanwhile, made slow progress.

The design for the Arch had been awarded to Eero Saarinen in 1948. The victory for the Finnish-born, Detroit-based architect came over 172 entrants in a contest opened two years before, giving his firm a cash award of $50,000. His original idea was for a 630-foot steel structure surrounded by a small forest not unlike the vegetation found by Pierre Laclede when he and his fur trading settlers arrived in 1764.

Excavation for the Arch, however, didn't begin until 1961, following a long delay caused by the problem of financing the relocation of the elevated train tracks that cut across the site. All the delays meant that Saarinen was dead at age 51 before the work on the Arch actually began.

Ironically, it was the McDonald Construction Co. that got the contact to build the Arch and began pouring cement for the foundations on June 27, 1962. Once it was finished the Arch has forever been connected in the public mind with the Golden Arches of the McDonald's fast-food chain.

There were more delays, this time as a result of financing of the train that runs inside the Arch up to the top, but these, too, were ironed out and the first steel was installed in the foundation early in 1963. Another halt came that summer when engineers detected strain in the rods on the south leg, causing a two-month halt in the process.

The construction got rolling again, but on July 14, 1964, militant civil rights activists Percy Green and Richard Daly interrupted the workers' lunch hour by scaling the Arch to 125 feet, as a protest against the exclusion of blacks from the better paying jobs on the publicly funded project, joining dozens of such protests at construction sites around the country over the previous two years.

They stayed up on the steel structure for four hours while supporters held a news conference to explain the protest and announce the formation of a new St. Louis civil rights organization, one devoted to more militancy than had been seen before in the city, the group calling itself Action Council to Improve Opportunities for Negroes (ACTION).

There were no more protests or serious delays as the work resumed and a year later the two steel legs reached 530 feet and began to curve. On Oct. 28, 1965, the Arch topped out as the final section of steel slipped between the two legs of the giant sculpture. Several thousand people were on hand to give a cheer, 30 years after the first financing for the idea was approved.

After another two years of work on the visitor center under the Arch, the center and park were finally opened to the public June 10, 1967. Two months later trains began curving up to the view windows at the top. And it wasn't until May 25, 1968, that Vice President Hubert Humphrey, campaigning for president, officially dedicated the moment during a ceremony shortened by a driving rainstorm. Two more years passed before the grounds were finally transformed from a wasteland of mud to a landscaped expanse of lawn.

The structure, officially the Gateway Arch, remains the world's tallest arch and the tallest monument in the United States. In 2014 dollars the Arch cost just short of $100 million to build. The structure is designed to be a symbol of the opening of the West to American settlement and the expansion of the United States following the 1803 Louisiana Purchase.

The Arch caused plenty of excitement, catching the nation's fancy as a great architectural achievement, called by some the most engaging of anything built in the sixties. Nearly 2 million visitors had ridden the train to the top by the end of the decade. Hopes were high that the excitement would translate into revitalization of the whole downtown area.

There was another achievement in St. Louis at the same time that wasn't missed by the nation either, due west from the waterfront a few miles away from the Arch in Mill Creek Valley -- LaClede Town. Like Gaslight Square, it was an experiment involving a diverse collection of outsiders.

LaClede Town officially stood for just over 30 years, 1964 to 1995, but in the eighties and nineties much of it was emptied out, boarded up and abandoned. Then the headache balls arrived and like Mill Creek Valley and Gaslight Square, it was gone.

In cold fact, LaClede Town could be considered nothing more than a 65-acre neighborhood of clustered apartments, shops and amenities that housed more than 4,000 people where old mansions once stood. But while it flourished, especially until the mid-seventies, LaClede Town existed as another world.

A Washington University professor of architecture said in 1968 that the development proved that "even in a stodgy, old Midwestern town, where everyone thought segregated, class-conscious suburbs and ghettos took over inexorably, a huge untapped market exists for living in an urbane human stew . . . policemen, writers, storekeepers, Ethiopian exchange students, symphony musicians, jazzmen, truck drivers, decorators, miniskirts in all colors, size, ages and persuasions."

Embedded there also were three quarters of what would become the World Saxophone Quartet, as well as Ike Willis, the guitarist and front man for Frank Zappa; the drummer Benet Schaeffer (St. Louis Social Club, Jeremiah Johnson Band, Anita Rosamond Band, Gumbohead, etc.); his brother Dominic, tenor sax (The Rhythm Method, Bob Reuter Band, Go, Dog, Go!, The Leroy Pierson Band, etc.) and the psychedelic Crystalline Silence Band, "avatars of the hippie musician cultural myth" which practiced its Beatles covers in the development's coffee house and parked its multi-swirl tour bus in the parking lot behind the LaClede Town bookstore.

The comedian Dick Gregory lived there, as did he Arch-climbing activist Percy Green and the poet and performance artist Shirley LaFlore. Mick Jagger and Eric Clapton stopped by to check things out and the radical lawyer William Kunstler played softball during breaks from defending black militants. David Sanborn, then a local sax man who turned into a cool jazz star, played to overflow crowds at the Circle.

In 1968 there were 20 applications for every open unit. The manager of the development, former DJ and Gaslight alum Jerry Berger, personally selected every renter. The selections were made to carefully mix the stew, racially, economically and socially. There were income, racial and family-size requirements, but above all there were personality requirements.

"We plug the people into where they live," he said. "If two people are applying and one is carrying a football and one is carrying a big chip on his shoulder, we'll take the one with the football."

"The zeitgeist of that era was one of wrenching social change, and Jerome Berger's sense of community building was at the crest of that change," said Dom Schaeffer, the sax man. "Bringing a diverse population to live together in LaClede Town — black, white and Hispanic; artists, musicians, poets; people from all walks of life — was his goal. And he achieved it, for a time."

In one portion, two-story apartments surrounded a courtyard filled with benches and a rectangular fountain in a park that held activities that brought the residents together -- bar-b-ques, softball games hosted by the LaClede Town Losers, music performances.

The Coach and Four Pub was the late night joint and the Circle Coffeehouse became the cultural heart of the town. There was also a barbershop, two laundromats, and the General Store where a kid could buy a Twinkie and a soda for 25 cents.

At a reunion held in 1997, Barb Riley, an illustrator who lived there with her interracial family from 1968 to 1974, said, "What I remember most was being able to sleep with doors and windows open and never having to worry about your kids. You knew that wherever they were, they were safe. It's so hard to get anyone to understand what this place meant."

"Some nights, after the pub closed," Adele Harris, one of Riley's neighbors, added, "people would pour out onto our patio and the party would continue. Sometimes we'd look up and it would be daybreak."

Bob Blackburn, one of the first residents and a retired director of government relations for Washington University, remembered, "People who didn't live here came around just to be part of the ambience, if you will. There simply wasn't anything else like it -- certainly not in St. Louis."

The demise didn't occur on Berger's watch, he left a decade before the headache balls arrived. But many blamed his sloppy bookkeeping, flexible rules and his propensity for attracting governmental scrutiny for the development's demise. He was a flamboyant leader, rode around the development in his 1923 red convertible Rolls Royce and was rarely without his hep cat sunglasses. Overall, Berger said, LaClede "had a beginning, a middle and an end. I only want to remember the good times, and there were a lot of those."

There was also a consensus that the development was shabbily built in the first place and was not maintained. There were 30 maintenance workers at the start, a staff eventually cut all the way down to two. Federal support dropped after Richard Nixon was elected in 1968 and private investors who helped prop up the place stopped coming around, looking to the suburban promised land instead.

Berger's hip pocket approach to bookkeeping didn't appeal to government auditors; where Berger saw fun, the accountants detected corruption. There was also an influx from Pruitt-Igoe after the nearby project closed in 1972, bring with them a new level of higher rents enforced by the government that caused established residents to leave. Then came were drugs, gangs and expanding vacancies, a social toll hard to combat by residents who were never particularly happy to see the police arrive.

An audit in 1977 was particularly damaging. By then Berger and his brother, Earl, were part of a group, LaClede Associates, that had taken up a major ownership stake in 1972. The St. Louis Housing and Urban Development director demanded improvements in both the physical situation and the record keeping. HUD said that over $750,000 in lost rents had resulted from empty apartments in a four-year period.

The IRS went after Berger in April 1979, demanding over $25,000 in back taxes for unreported income from LaClede Associates. By then, his wife had moved to suburban Clayton and Berger was living with this brother in Los Angeles.

There was a $6 million renovation that was finished in 1985 and occupancy rose to 80 percent. But HUD refused to provide any help and the work was done privately. The city refused to pick up garbage or provide police protection. And, as a former resident said, the arrival of Ronald Reagan as the nation's chief executive in 1981 didn't help.

Former alderman Bruce Sommer said that at first, "everyone there wanted to make it happen. It was ours -- a total community, everyone felt connected to everyone else. By the time the Reagan era hit -- the Me Generation -- it just changed."

Rumors swirled around Berger, reported to be living in New York City and Morocco. Ron Elz, the KSHE-FM DJ known as Johnny Rabbitt, said the last time he saw Berger was at a party for Eric Clapton at the Chase Plaza in 1978. "He said he was going to live on an island."

Reached by the *Post-Dispatch* in Los Angeles in 1979, Berger said he would not be returning to housing management and walked away with no money. He summarized the 15 years he ran the experiment this way:

> I think everything we did was done in the spirit of housing acts passed by Congress. The housing pendulum is swinging to the right. You are punished for doing things now you weren't punished for before. If what happened with LaClede Town was good, it happened because there was a commitment from the city and the federal government and the people who live in LaClede Town.
>
> If what happened wasn't good, it happened because agencies and institutions were not committed to a pluralistic, socially integrated society.

Chapter Twenty-Five
Civil Rights in the Sixties: CORE to the Black Liberators

Far from being a marginal kind of place actually, St. Louis became in my mind a very significant place. (It) opens up a window to understanding not only black community development, understanding social movements, understanding patterns of racism, understanding quest of economics -- but in a way, helps us understand these dynamics in the nation overall.

-- Clarence Lang, University of Illinois, 2010

Even as the demise of Mill Creek Valley became a given, the leading role of St. Louis in the civil rights movement again appeared in 1957 with a surge of African American power at the polls. Nationally, it wasn't until after the Voting Rights Act was passed in 1965 that it became reasonably easy for a black person to vote. Not so in St. Louis, where black voices had been heard in the voting booths since 1896.

The effects of that voting had been felt in small ways, but the black population was small in number and the charter that had been in place since 1914 stood guard over a weak mayor system of fragmented government. This system kept real power outside City Hall in the hands of ward heelers controlled by the moneyed interests. First, that real power went by the name Big Cinch, by the fifties it was called Civic Progress, Incorporated

By then, the Great Migration increased the black share of the city's population. Also, Supreme Court decisions on housing and school desegregation in 1948 and 1954 allowed African American leaders to see voting as an institutional way to change. Perhaps a stronger mayor could mitigate some of the entrenched hiring, housing and educational roadblocks.

In 1957, black voters helped propel a liberal slate onto a board of freeholders charged with writing a new charter. The victorious freeholders included both the civil rights attorney David Grant and Mayor Raymond Tucker, a white liberal who favored integration.

The freeholders came up with a plan that would strengthen the mayor by reducing the number of aldermen from 28 to 15, eight to be elected citywide and the others coming from seven new wards. There would also be increased pay for the mayor and a shuffle of city departments that would weaken entrenched bureaucrats. Grant went along with the idea, but many new black voters saw it immediately for what it was, another stealth tool to keep African Americans where they stood -- at the bottom.

These voters realized it was virtually impossible to elect a black at large because of the white majority. Thus, from then until a citywide black majority could be reached, whites would stay in control of City Hall. Those blacks who favored the charter urged patience.

Showing how unsure they were of victory, the freeholders set the charter election for the hot days of August, putting a premium on ward organizations strongest in the white districts. From his orange crate in front of his funeral parlor, Jordan Chambers wasn't fooled by the new aldermanic proposal. He noticed what wasn't in the new charter, namely, a civil rights provision. He saw the measure as another trick by the white establishment to maintain control. Joining Chambers in opposition were labor union members and small business owners who detected the hand of Civic Progress behind the language.

Tucker became the big horse pulling the wagon for charter approval, joined by the Chamber of Commerce, the Republican former mayor Aloys Kauffman and the League of Women Voters. The mayor had just been easily reelected in April but the voters saw the charter as a different animal.

Chambers prevailed over Grant in the black community. The initiative went down. Blacks and working-class whites voted against Civic Progress and Tucker to stop the plan by a tally of 108,618 to 72,160.

Then an alderman who would later become mayor, A.J. Cervantes, tried another ballot scenario that pit Civic Progress against blacks, unions and small business. His plan would create a unified metropolitan district, ending city and county divisions that had stood since 1876. Similar initiatives had failed in 1926 and 1930.

The 1959 initiative was pushed as a way to bring the city together with its suburbs, where the white population was growing faster than black. African Americans again went to the polls to block what they saw as another power grab by the establishment and, again with the help of the unions and small businesses, defeated the issue. In the 19th city Ward, the stronghold of Chambers, the vote was nearly 95 percent against. The issue failed on both sides of the city line.

Another unification plan was rolled out in 1962. The new scheme called for a borough system -- 22 entities, eight in the city, seven in the county, and seven more straddling the dividing line. The plan received virtually no support anywhere outside wealthily white communities and lost on a vote of nearly 80 percent against. This was the last time such consolidation was suggested to the voters.

Thus, while other cities such as Chicago, were putting more and more authority in the hands of the mayor, St. Louis wouldn't budge. The result by 2015 was the continued split in government, with a unified city juxtaposed against a much bigger county made up of 90 municipal governments and the resulting maze of police departments, courts, fire districts and school districts. Even a new initiative called Better Together, launched in 2013, distanced itself from a ballot unification scheme, saying it was just exploring options.

A study done by the group, released in December of 2015, showed that fragmentation resulted in a high cost. "Our citizens are paying a lot for bureaucracy," it declared. This cost, the study found, was at the heart of high sales taxes, speed traps, court warrants and other methods of raising money, areas often pointed to by civil rights leaders as hitting blacks hardest.

No suggestion of a new ballot initiative came from the study, however. Refusing unification had become part of that St. Louis thing.

Raymond Tucker was born in St. Louis, Dec. 4, 1896, and received degrees from both St. Louis University and Washington University. The voters saw him behind his spectacles and pinched mouth as far more the Washington University mechanical engineering professor he was for 15 years than the politician he became. He joined the Dickmann administration in 1934 and crafted the plan that sharply reduced smoke pollution in the city in 1941. After that success he left politics to run the engineering department at Wash U until 1951.

Elected mayor in 1953 and 1957, he faced his toughest mayoral campaign in 1961, his support among Democrats sinking as he went for a third term. He edged through by 1,000 votes then lost in 1965 in his bid for a fourth term. The victory in 1961 came with the support of Chambers, who brokered a promise from Tucker to push for the desegregation of public accommodations -- bars, theaters, restaurants and other public places.

There had been plenty of agitation already at lunch counters, swimming pools and other public facilities in St. Louis before Tucker took office in the fifties, but it was not until the third-term campaign in 1961 that he and his City Hall supporters endorsed a law giving blacks the right to eat where they pleased. The restaurant association began working for such a stand in 1960. Along with Tucker, the next year saw the election of six black aldermen, including a former bus driver and salesman who was raised in Mill Creek Valley, William Clay.

In 1955, Clay, a SLU grad and army veteran, organized the NAACP Youth Council and began agitating for equal rights for African Americans. He won election to the board of alderman in 1959. As such he helped bring the public accommodation law to a board vote in 1960, but lost, 17-11. After the next election the aldermen passed the law by a resounding 20-4.

The law was major victory against Jim Crow in St. Louis, barring racial and religious discrimination everywhere serving food, as well as in hotels, recreation facilities like swimming pools, and in places of amusements like baseball stadiums. There was also a stiff enforcement provision, establishing a mechanism for complaints to reach city prosecutors.

In 1962, now against the background of increasing civil rights activism in the South, the aldermen, again led by Clay, passed an even more crucial law, banning discrimination in jobs. Clay gave his active support to the militant Congress of Racial Equality (CORE). This was the organization that started the Freedom Rides, taking the black rights battle into the South.

On May 4, 1961, boarding Greyhound and Trailways buses in Washington, 13 CORE members (seven black, six white) began a trip to test the Supreme Court decision integrating travel on interstate buses and trains. The law no longer allowed segregated toilets or dining rooms. Trouble began in Rock Hill, S.C., where three riders were beaten by whites, and continued as the riders plunged into the South.

In Alabama and Mississippi, segregationists called the CORE activists Communists and on May 15, Klansmen numbering at least 100 attacked the Greyhound in Anniston, Ala., smashing windows, slashing tires and setting the bus on fire.

The mob held the door shut as the bus burned, but an undercover police officer trapped in the bus pulled a gun and forced the mob to open the door just before the Greyhound's gas tank exploded.

Publicity also exploded across the country, bringing the civil rights movement to the front page and sparking discussions everywhere, empowering organizers like Clay in places like St. Louis to push their reforms forward.

When the second bus, the Trailways, reached Anniston, the KKK-led mob boarded the bus swinging clubs and bats at the riders. These riders fought back. The bus roared off and soon reached Birmingham, where the local sheriff, Eugene "Bull" Connor, also reached the front pages. He urged another KKK mob to attack the riders, leaving them bloody and battered. One CORE rider required 53 stitches. No one was arrested.

The headlines and photos brought the newly installed Kennedy administration into the fray, but Attorney General Robert Kennedy called the riders "extremists" and urged a cooling off period.

The riders abandoned the crippled bus and flew to New Orleans where they were joined by other militants, including a St. Louis contingent, vowing to ignore any cooling off and continue their rides throughout the South. By the end of the summer freedom riders criss-crossed Mississippi and Alabama, leading to 60 arrests and numerous incidents of Klan violence.

Just prior to the freedom rides, the St. Louis movement had been increasingly active, focusing on jobs. The NAACP and CORE were both talking with bankers, getting promises. In 1960, the NAACP picketed the downtown Scruggs-Vandervoort-Barney department store, carrying signs saying, "Swinging a Mop No Longer Appeals to Us. We Want Clerical Jobs." Students led by Vashon High senior Arthur Shaw met with store officials, but no blacks were hired.

In March of 1961, the youth group organized a march on the state capitol in Jefferson City that drew over 1,000 marchers from all 15 state chapters of the NAACP. The march protested the state legislature's failure to pass a law barring discrimination in public accommodations. CORE held demonstrations against the St. Louis Board of Education and a lawsuit was filed against the school board targeting discriminatory practices.

The pace of the movement elsewhere increased another step forward in 1962, with the integration of the University of Mississippi by James Meredith. There were also desegregation protests at several Howard Johnson restaurants along the east coast, freedom rides in North Carolina, local challenges to the status quo in the North as well as the South, and small group demonstrations led by CORE and SNCC, the Student Non-Violent Coordinating Committee.

In Cairo, Ill., about 150 miles down the Mississippi from St. Louis, one such demonstration led by SNCC protested segregation at the city's only swimming pool. As the small group of blacks stood in the street singing, a blue pickup truck drove down the center of the street straight at them. All but one of the demonstrators moved, a still anonymous, defiant 13-year-old girl who stood her ground until run into by the truck.

Then, in the summer of 1963, Alabama Gov. George Wallace stood in the door of a University of Alabama building to prevent two blacks from enrolling in the university. He was ordered aside by federal authorities and President Kennedy took to the airwaves to discuss civil rights. For the first time, he dropped equivocations, condemning segregation and racial discrimination and announcing his intention to submit to Congress a new civil rights bill, saying, "the rights of every man are diminished when the rights of one man are threatened."

In East St. Louis, home of the devastating race riot of 1917, the NAACP youth group started a campaign against the banks -- holding protests at five financial institutions that summer. Led by the white activist James Peake, these demonstrators grew more militant, going inside banks to form human chains in front of the teller's windows.

Also that summer CORE in St. Louis stepped up its campaign for jobs for blacks, especially white-collar jobs, and especially jobs for blacks in banks with branches in black neighborhoods. There, most depositors were black and almost all employees were not. Led by the white civil rights attorney Charles Oldham, CORE's former national chairman, the group called on five banks to hire 31 black employees in two weeks.

Here was another leading-edge action by the St. Louis movement, striking at a crucial community issue -- money. Voting wasn't doing it for these people, court decisions weren't making it either. These young protesters saw action as the way forward.

"CORE is tired of empty statements of high purpose," Oldham said. "We plan to break the pattern of discrimination and quota system that has been imposed by the banking industry . . . for the last 130 years." A study of 11 St. Louis banks found just 83 blacks out of 1,341 bank employees, only six of them in white-collar positions.

Beginning Aug. 3, 1963, CORE threw up a picket line at a Mound City Trust bank on the North Side, asking customers to tell the bank to hire "one more Negro." Then, on Aug. 15, CORE gave Jefferson Bank two weeks to hire four blacks.

Mayor Tucker appointed a commission to study the issue. The banks said this group, the Equal Employment Opportunity Commission, was enough. Bank leaders also said any protest at its banks would "impede the progress which is being made."

The Jefferson Bank, one the city's biggest, had recently moved a North Side branch a few blocks closer to downtown, opening a new branch at Jefferson and Washington, just north of the Mill Creek demolition. Before the move, two of the tellers in the branch were black. But when the new branch opened these tellers were no longer at work and there were no blacks at all behind the counters.

By then, with the national movement on the march, new people began showing up at CORE meetings, younger, more militant; outraged by the attitudes of people like Bull Conner and George Wallace. One of these new members was a skilled worker at the McDonnell Aircraft Corp., a radio mechanic by the name of Percy Green.

Born on Compton Hill on the south side of Mill Creek Valley, Green was 27 when he attended his first CORE meeting that summer of 1963. He was a 1954 graduate of Vashon High and a member of a Compton Hill street gang before attending St. Louis University. He got a job as a messenger at Washington University. While there he took a correspondence course to learn electronics and was hired by McDonnell. He was drafted in 1958.

> The awakening point in my life was in the army, the way black folks were given all the worst, the dirtiest details. I realized that the black man wasn't at the bottom of society because of his own choosing. And if the black child was dirty or neglected, it was because his mother was working all kinds of hours in Miss Ann's kitchen and was worn out.

He came out of the army in 1960 and got his old job at McDonnell back, paid 10 cents more per hour than his father, who had worked as a meat packer for 38 years.

> One day a friend asked me if I wanted to go to a CORE meeting. They were talking about the white power structure. They decried it as this invisible wall that black men came up against. There was a wall there keeping us on the outside. There was a wall we had to break through.

Green joined the picket line at the Jefferson Bank that August in 1963 and, in essence, has been there in one way or another for the rest of his life, one of the most prominent civil rights figures in St. Louis history. Still active in 2014, Green was a featured speaker during Black History Month and one of the 250 people featured in the 250th city anniversary exhibit at the Missouri History Museum.

Through his long life of protest -- some by himself, at other times in large groups, arrested over 100 times, climbing the Gateway Arch, unveiling the Veiled Prophet, the plaintiff in a landmark Supreme Court case, the manager of LaClede Town, one of the FBI's 1,000 most dangerous American radicals -- he spread his wings and a made an impact, practicing a philosophy of nonviolence, using street theater, never losing his sense of humor whether lying down or standing up. Looking back he sees a steady growth of black rights and black employment. But he's never been satisfied.

"There's much more to be done," he said in a 2014 interview.

> The issue is not only more and better paying jobs for black males, but females were left out of the picture, disabled people were left out of the picture, the whole gay and lesbian question has become a concern. And so that motivation then developed in broadening my scope as to the need to further initiate the activities and be a part of these types of activities to bring about change in the best interests of humanity.

His object through all the relentless protests was to make people more important than money and sharing more valuable than greed, "to restore human values to a place superior to property values."

On Aug. 28, 1963, Martin Luther King rose before the Lincoln Memorial and told the nation and the world that he had a dream, "a dream deeply rooted in the American dream – one day this nation will rise up and live up to its creed, 'We hold these truths to be self evident: that all men are created equal.'"

He called the condition of blacks 100 years after the end of slavery "a shameful condition" and that there was no time to waste in making the changes that would end segregation and bring blacks out from under the conditions in which they lived. He faced the sweltering crowd of about 250,000 people, 75 percent of them black people, and said:

> This is no time to engage in the luxury of cooling off or to take the tranquilizing drug of gradualism. Now is the time to make real the promises of democracy. Now is the time to rise from the dark and desolate valley of segregation to the sunlit path of racial justice. Now is the time to lift our nation from the quicksands of racial injustice to the solid rock of brotherhood.

Also speaking that day was Josephine Baker, the sensational St. Louisan who watched the flames of the East St. Louis race riot from across the river in 1917 at age 11 and had become the first black to perform at

Keil Auditorium in 1952. At the Washington protest in 1963, she wore the uniform of the French Resistance, the World War II anti-Nazi fighters of which she was a part. By then she was a citizen of France, having only rarely returned to her native city, which she viewed as intolerably racist.

In France she was an erotic sensation in “La Revue Negre” opening in 1925. She went on to a career in the Follies Bergere, dancing in a skirt made of artificial bananas. Her partner in her later shows was a pet Cheetah, who wore a collar made of diamonds. In Washington in 1963 she said:

> I have walked into the palaces of kings and queens and into the houses of presidents. And much more. But I could not walk into a hotel in America and get a cup of coffee, and that made me mad. And when I get mad, you know that I open my big mouth. And then look out, ‘cause when Josephine opens her mouth, they hear it all over the world.”

The 300 civil rights activists from St. Louis who had taken a 24-hour bus ride to attend the march heard her words and those of King and many others. The protesters at the Jefferson Bank also heard the words.

The March on Washington took place on a Wednesday and on that Friday, with the activist contingent back home, 100 St. Louis protesters defied a court order and stormed the bank building, sat down in front of the tellers’ windows, clapping and singing. Tucker had been practicing a policy of not arresting demonstrators and no arrests were made that day. The protest inside the bank ended peacefully after two hours and the pickets left the bank at closing time.

But Tucker by then was not pleased by events at the bank. He felt a 10-point program of reforms issued earlier in the year went far enough. He said the CORE actions violated the spirit of the Martin Luther King and the March on Washington. He said St. Louis was determined to move forward through the use of the “legal machinery and new channels of communication.”

CORE responded by saying the organization had given the bank ample time to hire blacks, but this had not happened. Oldham said dozens of blacks had applied at the bank but the only recent hires had been four whites with the same qualifications as the blacks.

The next day, Aug. 31, nine people identified as leaders of the action were charged with violating the court order against entering the bank. Federal Judge Michael Scott, acting without a hearing, ordered the arrest of the nine. They were Clay, Oldham and 26th ward committeeman Norman Seay, as well as the chairman and vice chairman of the CORE chapter, two former chairmen, and a minister. All were swept up and jailed over the weekend.

The Jefferson Bank attorney, Wayne Millsap, was made special prosecutor. Millsap was married to the daughter of the bank president and was a member of the Missouri Athletic Club, an exclusive group of white businessmen tightly connected to Civic Progress. Another member of that club was the judge, Michael Scott, a relationship the activists saw as a blatant conflict of interest.

The nine Jefferson activists were held in contempt of court on Tuesday, Oct. 3, and on Wednesday, Oct. 4, police arrested seven more activists for their roles in other protests, including Taylor Jones, one of the young leaders of the East St. Louis actions. Another East St. Louis leader, the high school student James Peake, was arrested the next Saturday during a new campaign at the Jefferson Bank where CORE members made tiny transactions such as depositing pennies to tie up the bank.

On Oct. 11, pickets marched from the bank to police headquarters, and then on Oct. 12, police arrested another 32 people at the bank. Adopting the tactics of the freedom riders, the demonstrators went limp. Police hauled them out of the bank. Adopting the tactics of Bull Conner, Tucker sent undercover police into the CORE meetings. Soon thereafter, members began getting threatening phone calls and harassment on their jobs.

On Oct. 14, a cooling off period was sought by the mayor and agreed to by CORE, a day after the bank vice-president Joseph McDonnell called the activists animals and declared the bank would never negotiate with CORE. "We wonder what our society is coming to," he fumed.

Sentencing came on Oct. 24 for the first of the 19 who been arrested in the various protests, including the CORE leaders. The lines all across the country had hardened since the first arrests and St. Louis was no exception.

From his bench in federal court, Judge Scott denounced the demonstrators for arousing "juveniles and young persons in the formative stages of their lives to act in contempt of the law." Clay and former CORE chairman Richard Curtis were handed the stiffest terms -- 270 days in jail and fines of $1,000 each. The minister, Charles Perkins, along with Oldham and Seay, got 90 days apiece and the rest 60 days each.

Scott refused to set bond and ordered all the defendants jailed until an appeal could be heard.

The cooling off period had the opposite effect hoped for by Tucker and his allies, ending with a rally that drew 1,000 people to City Hall, demanding withdrawal of city deposits from the Jefferson Bank. Another rally was held that night asking the same from St. Louis University, which in 1944 had been the first city university to allow black enrollment.

The next day CORE demanded the land development money from Mill Creek Valley be withdrawn from the bank and rallied at the Housing Authority office. Over 200 people marched into the City Hall rotunda singing the new national protest anthem, "Which Side Are You On?" Tucker needed a plain-clothes police escort to leave his office, but demonstrators allowed his limousine to drive off without trouble.

The bank protest had become what CORE called a "general strike against racism."

Percy Green had been on the picket line since the bank protests started. He moved into the forefront of the demonstrations in November when he stayed behind after a sit-in by 25 activists in front of the City Treasurer's office. Reading a copy of a new book by the New York television journalist Louis Lomax called *The Negro Revolt,* Green refused to speak to police or move from the spot on the floor. Police put him on a stretcher and carried him away.

By then, Scott had released the "Jefferson 19" on bond and they remained free as the appeals crawled through the courts.

CORE had grown from 25 members in August to 300 in November. Militants like Clay were formulating strategy to push aside old-line Democrats during the next round of elections in 1964 and 1965, favoring Tucker's rival, A.J. Cervantes, for mayor, and Warren Hearnes for governor.

Economic boycotts were the strategy for the upcoming Christmas season and on Nov. 21 another 20 people were arrested for stuffing leaflets into merchandise at downtown stores. Twenty-five more were arrested for the same tactic on Dec. 4. There were 22 more arrests at City Hall on Dec. 31.

The legal battles rolled toward the new year and so did the name-calling. As 1963 came to a close, the *Globe-Democrat* ran an inflammatory 10-part series of articles "documenting" the influence of Communist groups inside CORE.

The stories said the group was "heavily infiltrated." Headlines blared "Rev. King worked with Red front," "CORE officials hold positions in Red-Front group," "former Red played active role in protest at bank," and concluded that CORE "may be used as an unwitting Communist tool."

But this kind of red-baiting had little effect. Cold War rhetoric was nothing new to the movement. Picketing continued daily at Jefferson Bank. Then in February 1964, as city fathers began a celebration of the city's 200th anniversary, CORE threw up a 40-person picket line at the Chase Park Plaza Hotel complaining about the lack of black jobs at the Gateway Arch, still under construction at the federal park on the waterfront.

They called the Arch a gateway of "Manifest Destiny" and a celebration of the extermination of the native tribes. This viewpoint threw cold water on the Civic Progress optimism over the gleaming steel structure and the urban development projects in Mill Creek and the North Side. CORE continued to battle against what it saw as a laggard attitude by the city's white leaders on integrating housing and jobs.

When Lyndon Johnson, the new president, came to the city in February to meet with Civic Progress, Tucker and other boosters at the Chase, CORE organized another protest. A group of more than 100 people gathered at Forest Park near the hotel. Police had assured them that they would not be harassed as they pressed Johnson for quick passage of a new civil rights law that was before the Congress.

But just as Johnson arrived and the group began a four-block march from the park to the hotel, police swooped in and arrested 86 people.

Police said they arrested the marchers before they could start a "major disturbance." Those arrested were taken to police headquarters downtown and held for several hours until word reached the officers that LBJ had left the Chase for the airport. None of the activists were charged.

Waiting for the demonstrators to be either charged or released, black lawyer and state representative from the North Side, Hugh J. White, told a reporter he was furious at the lack of progress in the city and that he had been lied to by the police.

"I'm getting sick and tired of this non-violent business. The next time we are going to give the police a good excuse for arresting us. If they are going to treat me like a mule, I'm going to act like a mule," White said.

Nationally, civil rights stayed on the front page as a bombing in Birmingham, Ala., killed three children. Rioting killed two more blacks there in August. Nothing from St. Louis made the network news. Indeed, by then the Jefferson Bank had backed down, ending the protest.

On March 31, CORE chairman Lucien Richards, stood outside the bank to announce hiring of the four black tellers activists had asked for seven months earlier. He also said 15 other banks had hired 80 blacks during the long fight and that no more demonstrations were necessary.

The bank's president, Dillon Ross, told a different story, saying, "it is ridiculous beyond any description to state that this bank has met anyone's demands relative to employment" and said the bank's policies remained just the same as they were in 1950. He called the activists "law violators" and said the demonstrations were nothing more than "petty annoyances."

There was, however, no doubting that the black tellers were in fact working at the bank on April 1 where they hadn't been on March 31. Other companies around the city endorsed Tucker's 10-point desegregation plan. Other businesses hired blacks to avoid being picketed. In July the mayor provided a count that showed that retail outlets and department stores in the city had hired 400 new black workers in sales, service and craft sectors, a 32 percent increase in a year's time. His commission said 15 banks, including Jefferson, had hired 86 blacks in the clerical sector in the last year.

More remarkably, a black owned bank called Gateway Bank was established in 1965 on the North Side, the first of its kind in Missouri. Co-founder Clifton Gates, a member of the Board of Police Commissioners, committed to providing banking services and loans to the community of North St. Louis. The loans were somewhat scant as the bank was undercapitalized and afraid to take risks, but the opening was seen as progress for the black community.

In Washington, the Twenty-Fourth Amendment was adopted to abolish the poll tax, dousing an ember left glowing in the South after the Civil War that kept poor blacks from voting. CORE, SNCC and other rights groups opened a registration drive to bring more blacks into the voting booths in time for the 1964 election and sent delegates to the Democratic National Convention to try to unseat an all-white Mississippi slate.

Then, on July 2, 1964, Johnson, a Texan, signed a sweeping Civil Rights Act he had finessed past the white, Southern representatives in Congress. The act made Jim Crow illegal, barring discrimination based on race, color, religion, or national origin.

The nation took a breath and many, especially white liberals, thought that perhaps there was a solution in sight.

But another shock found the front pages in August -- the bodies of three missing civil-rights workers, two of them white, the other black, had been discovered buried in Mississippi. The young men, part of the campaign to register black voters, had been arrested on a speeding charge, released into the hands of the KKK and killed. The oldest was 24.

The arrests, the legal battles, the time spent in jail, the time spent on the picket lines, all these factors took a toll on CORE in St. Louis and elsewhere. And just as the local Democratic Party had split into two factions, the civil rights organization split between those who wanted to obey the law and win elections and those who wanted more direct action. These lines had generational and economic components, the action-faction younger and less well off, the other side older and more settled in their homes and jobs.

In the summer of 1964, Percy Green was neither as young as the youngest activists, nor was he as poor as the poorest, but he was ready for action. Indeed, he and others in CORE left the establishment of the civil rights movement to form a new group. He and the new members decided take a stroll up the incomplete Arch to a height of about 125 feet.

The climbing of the Arch on July 14, 1964, remains the singular St. Louis event remembered from the sixties civil rights movement. And the name Percy Green remains the name people remember when the St. Louis civil rights movement reaches the dining room table in the twenty-first century.

The idea for the climb and for the founding of Action Council to Improve Opportunities for Negroes (ACTION) came from Green, He said by the time the seven-month-long protest at Jefferson Bank was over "many members were battle fatigued or afraid of arrest. Half of the organization wanted to go into community service, which was safe and did not cause confrontation. The other half wanted to keep active."

The issue remained jobs. Both Green and the favorite of the old-line faction, Charles Oldham, wanted to see more blacks hired in more jobs. The question was how to get the companies to change decades of discrimination. Oldham said Green was "very bright, very dedicated to the movement, always on the picket line. But I felt (his) approach was not the best since I was convinced that the process of moderation and reconciliation and the use of nonviolence was the best method."

Green and white fellow CORE member Richard Daly climbed up the Arch on a stainless steel surface ladder used by the workers, who were eating lunch. Workers ascended the structure on an elevator that ran up the leg beside the ladder and asked Green and Daly what they were doing. The protesters said they were fighting for job equality and refused to leave.

When a construction supervisor, M.J. Hillman, rode up to ask Green to leave, he responded that he would stay up on the Arch until "I starve to death." Workers then continued up to the top and began work again after erecting a barrier that kept the climbers and workers separated. About 20 pickets marched around the bottom of the leg until the two came down after about four hours. They were arrested when they reached the bottom.

Green carried a pair of binoculars to gaze at the surrounding scenery and keep his eye on police and pickets on the ground. When he came down he fell off the ladder to the ground and forced police to carry him away. Daly also went limp. Both were released on bond and Green was on time for his midnight shift at his job as a radio mechanic at McDonnell Aircraft.

The charges stemming from the incident were dropped a few months later when CORE agreed to stay away from the Arch while the Park Service reviewed hiring practices. But the ramifications of the incident didn't end for Green, who was later laid off from McDonnell and staged two protests at the company.

"McDonnell had many skeletons in its own closet," he said, "and the fact that I was protesting racism in other large corporations and agencies, they felt uncomfortable, not knowing when I would expose them."

He reapplied for his old job in 1965 and when he didn't get it, hired a lawyer and sued under the provisions of the new Civil Rights Act. It was the court case resulting from his firing, not the more sensational climb up the Arch itself, that is what Green's legacy in St. Louis and the nation rests upon.

James S. McDonnell, a pioneer aviation engineer born in Denver, founded the McDonnell Co. at Lambert Field in 1939. It later became McDonnell Douglas and merged with Boeing in 1997. He learned to fly in the twenties and graduated as an engineer from MIT in 1925. During World War II the company received major defense contracts and jumped from 15 to 5,000 employers by the time the Japanese surrendered. The company had a slump after the war but by 1948 developed the Phantom jet and became a major supplier of fighters during the Korean War in the early fifties.

In 1954, McDonnell got its first contract to make what became the next generation of fighters, which were introduced into service in 1960, in time for the Vietnam War. The company soon became the leading U.S. producer of jet fighter planes.

McDonnell also pioneered guided missiles and was well positioned to share in the spoils of the space race, which began in the mid-fifties as a Cold War competition between the United States and the Soviet Union. On July 1, 1961, the Russians put the first man into orbit, just three weeks ahead of the Americans.

Next came the race to put a man on the moon, which McDonnell played a leading role, gaining a substantial share of the defense contracts for the Mercury and Gemini projects. President John Kennedy spoke to workers at the McDonnell plant at Lambert Field on Sept. 12, 1962, telling them that their efforts were essential to America and to dozens of other countries. These countries, he said, "would not be free if it were not for the power and determination of the United States."

In his speech, Kennedy said putting a man on the moon before the Soviet Union was crucial:

> I can imagine no action, no adventure, which is more essential and more exciting than to be involved in the most important and significant adventure that any man has been able to participate in the history of the world.

Green was part of that effort, until 1964. In the mid-sixties McDonnell was the largest employer in Missouri, but had no room for Percy Green. After his Arch climb he did not get his job back.

But *McDonnell Douglas Corp. v. Green,* decided in 1973, became one of the key decisions of the civil rights movement, doing for jobs what *Brown v. Board of Education* did for schools and *Shelley v. Kraemer* did for housing. The decision in *McDonnell* by the high court was 9-0.

By the time of the decision McDonnell had merged with the Douglas Corporation, the largest employer in California. The merger made the combined companies, McDonnell Douglas, the largest aerospace company in North America, with 30,000 employees.

The Green case was filed in July 1965, a year after the Arch protest and close after two other ACTION actions near the company plant Green and several others staged to protest his long layoff and the defense giant's general hiring practices, saying they were racially motivated.

The first new protest was a "stall-in" where five roads were blocked near the plant during the morning rush hour by cars that stopped and turned off their engines until police arrived. The other, held on the second anniversary of the civil rights act, July 2, 1965, was a "lock-in" where Green put a chain and padlock on the front door of a building that stopped workers from leaving the plant.

Three weeks later, McDonnell advertised a job that fit Green's work qualifications. When he applied, the company turned him down, basing its rejection on Green's actions in the "stall-in" and "lock-in." The case claiming discrimination was filed soon thereafter but wasn't decided until eight years later in favor of Green. Until the decision there was no substance in case law to the Civil Rights Act provision against job loss for actual civil rights actions.

Green's lawyer, Louis Gilden, said the effect of Green's victory before the court was "incredible." It set the standard for establishing the facts of proving that discrimination existed, and could be applied not only to blacks but also to "women, to people over 40 who couldn't get a job because of age, to members of certain religious groups."

Gilden added that the decision allowed minorities and women to get their foot in the courthouse door. The standards were straightforward: you had to prove five things: "that there was a job opening, that you applied for the job, that you were qualified, that you did not get it and that you were black (or a woman or over 40 or a member of a religious group)."

Green had had some practice on the highways before the actions at McDonnell. He and his ACTION cohorts got started in March 1965 by tying up rush hour traffic on three major roads. He and Ivory Perry, another ACTION activist, lay down on the new Daniel Boone Expressway, the superhighway that ran through Mill Creek Valley. Police were finally forced to haul away the protesters off the exit ramp.

Perry was born in Arkansas and came to St. Louis in 1954 after being awarded two Purple Hearts for being wounded in Korea. He was a regular picket at the Jefferson Bank and had spearheaded a campaign against use of lead-based paint in housing projects.

The traffic actions were initially designed to express solidarity with blacks who marched supporting voting legislation that became the Voting Rights Act five months later. Johnson had defeated the right-wing Republican candidate Barry Goldwater in the 1964 election in a historic landslide, giving his civil rights agenda a ringing endorsement. He carried all but six states -- five in the South and Arizona -- in collecting over 61 percent in the popular tally.

The U.S. electoral map changed in the election, with Democrats routed in what had been the "solid South" because of Kennedy's pro-civil rights stands. Johnson, the southerner, carried everything outside the South.

The election pushed those opposed to civil rights into the minority. Even so, they were a determined minority. Green's traffic tie-up coincided with events in Selma, Ala., where on March 7, 1965, the "bloody Sunday" attack on marchers left 50 activists hospitalized after police used tear gas, whips, and clubs against them.

The Selma incident gave a major boost to Johnson's proposed voting reform legislation, further isolating southern members of Congress. Passed in the Senate by a 77-19 vote, it languished for a month because of stalling tactics in the House before being approved 333-85. Martin Luther King and other civil rights leaders surrounded Johnson as he signed the bill into law on July 9. The act outlawed many practices that prevented blacks from voting.

Just like Ferguson would become nearly 50 years later, Selma became a rallying cry for the civil rights movement.

The St. Louis city election in April 1965 put a new mayor in office. This was Alfonso Cervantes, the candidate of the "young Turks" led by William Clay and Hugh White. Cervantes thwarted Tucker's run for a fourth term as the incumbent's support of the Mill Creek clearance and his handling of the Jefferson Bank protest proved fatal. He was seen as an old line Democrat no longer attuned to changing times and carried just 40 percent of the black Democrats in the party primary.

Cervantes was no Martin Luther King, no one was, but he knew where his support came from. Four months into his term he assembled a group to study how to improve black employment opportunity. He was a small businessman, having run a cab company, and was not as cozy with Civic Progress as Tucker. He also recognized there was a problem looming for St. Louis -- the growing division between the black neighborhoods in the city and the white suburbs to the West.

Cervantes was also no young Turk, even though Clay and White supported him. Born in St. Louis on Aug. 27, 1920, he was a product of St. Louis University and served in the Merchant Marine in World War II. He was first elected alderman in 1949.

As the rights movement entered a new, more divisive phase in the second half of the sixties, the mayor's main interest lay in defusing civil rights militancy while maintaining the status quo, something anything but attractive to activists black and white. In August of 1965, Cervantes called a meeting of black leaders to try to come up with a program on black employment. Clay was put in charge. Green was not invited.

"Little will be gained by demonstrations and nuisance marches," Cervantes declared. "The time is now at hand for problem-solving and they will be much easier to solve if we direct our energies to the harder work of negotiation, persuasion and motivation."

Clay called for blacks to return to politics. Green pointed out that many of the Jefferson Bank 19 never returned to the picket lines and were never arrested again. Several had lost jobs and incomes from involvement. The case against the Jefferson Bank defendants finally played out in

August 1967 when the Supreme Court refused to hear an appeal and eight defendants returned to jail.

But Civic Progress and Cervantes was in no mood to reopen the civil rights disputes for the previous few years and talked Judge Scott into granting parole provided they publicly apologize. Most of the activists rejected such an apology and remained in jail until the end of their terms. Clay, who had served 105 days already, was preparing for a run for Congress and in 1968 was elected.

Green wasn't pleased by the moderation. "The majority of people who say demonstrations are no longer appropriate are either tired or contented or they have given up the fight." He foresaw no change through the moderate approach and he was proven correct, at least on the question of jobs.

The city Equal Opportunity Employment Commission reported in 1966 that nearly 70 percent of area firms employed no blacks at all in high-salaried fields. Worse, it said 60,000 blacks were "sub-employed," either out of work altogether or working below their skill level. And, despite the downtown and Mill Creek construction boom, 12.7 percent, 150,000 blacks, were unemployed in St. Louis in 1968.

Ivory Perry, then a 24-year-old resident of the North Side, talked to a reporter in 1968 about his life, reflecting on race riots that had torn across the country following the April assassination of Martin Luther King, killed in Memphis, just 300 miles downriver.

There was plenty of cause to riot in St. Louis, he said, and while the city's official history says there was no rioting in the city, Perry tells a different tale. The causes for discontent were many, even with the success of the Jefferson Bank protests: "People living eight in a room, eating beans and fatback and molasses. Only place they want to let you move is the places they've torn up. Landlords patch up the front and let the plumbing go to hell. And rats."

By then the Supreme Court had issued an addition to *Shelley v. Kraemer* saying it was legal for the federal government to regulate housing practices in order to reverse discrimination. In St. Louis, a federal employee trying to implement the decision found that "low income families and decent housing just don't match up" and implementation proved all but impossible. The real estate interests were as tough to crack as ever.

Just across the river from downtown, SNCC organizer H. Rap Brown appeared in 1967 in East St. Louis and 200 people raced through the East Side city, destroying white-owned businesses, throwing firebombs and looting, demonstrating in the pattern of rioting that, on a far larger scale, had hit several northern cities like Newark and Detroit. In East St. Louis police moved in to quell the action and a 19-year-old black man was shot and killed.

Scattered looting sparked up the next day, but was squelched by 100 state and city police.

And after the King assassination, Perry, quoted in Gerald Early's *Ain't But a Place: An Anthology of African American Writings About St. Louis,* says: "There were riots in St. Louis but the news media made an agreement with the police department that if they didn't have it under control within a half hour, they weren't going to televise it."

Perry added there was a "big one" near Pruitt-Igoe on the North Side. "They tore up three or four police cars, killed some dogs. I was down and involved in it because I was driving a cab at the time so I stopped to see what was happening and the police came and started throwing tear gas and it was terrible."

He also said there were other riots, "some downtown," others near the Club Imperial on the North Side on the April night when King was shot.

> Had a few buildings burning, but they squashed it.
>
> I was out there. I was one of them out there saying that it didn't make sense to burn out where you live at. I was one of them out there all night long. I asked a lot of businesses to close -- they tried to have me arrested, saying I was threatening them, but I was trying to keep down trouble, you know. But anyway they agreed to close and nothing happened. But if they had stayed open, you never know what would have happened.

Still, it is safe to say that all the committees, all the talk, along with the scattering of the black communities by all the land developments, had its effect in keeping the peace in St. Louis during the sixties. City Hall, police and their allies in the business community, as well as the moderate black leadership and black ward Democrats acted quickly after the King assassination to urge patience.

Neither northern nor southern, St. Louis may have fit the statistical profile of a city ripe for a major riot, but apparently the psychology wasn't there. Perhaps, despite all the poverty and unemployment, the level of desperation wasn't there.

The lasting image is one of moderation. Instead of firebombs, demonstrators, organized by churches and moderate blacks, held candles as they marched following King's death. Some 30,000 people walked peacefully downtown on Palm Sunday, two days after the shooting. The mood was one of sadness, not anger.

The reaction was far different nearly 50 years later when a white policeman shot a black teenager on a street near a low-income housing project in Ferguson, Mo., just across the city line in North St. Louis County.

As an aside to the events of the sixties, the man convicted of the assassination of King, James Earl Ray, was a native of the St. Louis metro area, born in Alton, Ill., in 1928. He dropped out of school when he was 15 and served in the Army at the end of World War II. He was a career criminal, first arrested for a burglary in California in 1949. He returned to St. Louis in the early fifties and in 1952 robbed a taxi driver and served two more years in Missouri.

In 1955, he was convicted of mail fraud for stealing money orders in Hannibal, Mo., north of St. Louis, and did more time, three years at the federal prison in Leavenworth, Kan. He held up a Kroger department store in St. Louis in 1959 and was sentenced to 20 years, a stern sentence because of his repeat offenses.

By the spring of 1968, Ray had been released from prison. Following the April 4 shooting of King in Memphis, Ray managed to elude police for over two months, finally captured in London. He was the only man convicted of the King killing but conspiracy theories surrounded him until his death in prison in 1998. One of the theories held that Ray and two other men hatched the plot to kill King in a St. Louis saloon, but was never proven.

Another factor in defusing the more militant side of the civil rights movement around the country and in St. Louis was the Johnson administration's War on Poverty programs, including a job placement center in St. Louis run by an agency called the Human Development Program. Well-funded by federal dollars it hired 700 employees, including Percy Green, Ivory Perry and Norman Seay.

Other programs -- Medicare, Medicaid, Head Start, Model Cities, and various work-training programs -- were passed by Congress and federally funded. These programs drew many civil right activists into their ranks. Militants criticized these efforts as more of the same, highly publicized, well-funded, but aimed at pacification rather than change.

At the same time, the Black Power movement rose in opposition to the moderate approach, expressed nationally by the Black Panther Party and by the Black Liberator group in St. Louis. The latter group was founded following the King assassination and established an office in North St. Louis in the summer of 1968. Seen as a direct threat to the government, the group was quickly infiltrated by the FBI and was short-lived.

Files recovered years later by researchers under the Freedom of Information laws found clear evidence of a "systematic and coordinated attack" against civil rights groups by the FBI under Director J. Edgar Hoover's counterintelligence program (COINTELPRO) which directed slanderous letters about sexual relations to fellow members, planted spies in meetings, provoked illegal actions and publicized (especially through the *Globe-Democrat)* alleged communist infiltration.

One letter found in the files, for example, was signed "A Soul Sister" and was sent by the St. Louis FBI office "to the black husband of a white woman" who was working in ACTION. The letter said the man's wife was "having sexual relations with other men." The St. Louis agent later reported that the couple had broken up and that the FBI's efforts "certainly contributed very strongly"' to the separation.

In reality, neither ACTION nor the Black Liberators were nearly the threat the Hoover FBI made them out to be. Like the Panthers, the Liberators sponsored youth activities, a free breakfast program and made alliances with white anti-Vietnam War activists. The organization donned the black berets and paramilitary garb of the Black Panthers and pushed an ideology of black nationalism and self-determination for ghetto youth. It also made an issue of the tension that resulted from the predominance of white police from the suburbs in the black North Side.

On Aug. 17, 1968, Rep. Adam Clayton Powell, a militant New York activist in St. Louis for a speech, was given protection by the Liberators, who said he needed the guards because of a "general threat upon the lives of black leaders." Powell made an appeal to black businessmen to use economic power to "forge their way into the nation's mainstream."

Following the speech, police arrested two Black Liberators as they walked to their cars and charged them with carrying weapons. This incident touched off a conflict between the Liberators, police, and government officials that included shootings, bombings, and beatings.

That year armed nationalists fought with police in Cleveland, leaving eight black demonstrators and three white police officers dead; Black Panther membership rose to 5,000 in a dozen states; demands were made by students for black study courses in numerous universities; and over 125 riots took place following the King assassination.

On Sept. 5, 1968, following the arrest of Liberator leader Charles Koen after the Powell speech, bullets were fired into the 9th Precinct's North Side headquarters on Lucas Street as well as the window of a police lieutenant's home. A firebomb was later thrown into the real estate office of a black member of the police board.

The next day, Liberator headquarters was destroyed. Residents reported they had seen plainclothes policemen break in and destroy the offices. Police blamed the Zulu 1200s, a smaller black nationalist organization, for the damage.

On Sept. 13, Koen and fellow Liberator Leon Dent were stopped by four white police officers for a defective brake light. Koen and Dent were arrested for alleged weapons possession and assault and taken to the 9th precinct. According to the Liberators' lawyer, Dent and Koen were then hustled to the basement of the station house and beaten, their heads bloodied and bruised and their fingers broken by clubs. Police said Koen and Dent attacked the officers inside the police station and the beatings were in self-defense.

The police action roused a wave of support for the Liberators.

Support from CORE and ACTION was not a surprise, but the moderates, including Clay, by now a Congressman, also denounced the station house beatings. The NAACP, United Methodist Church, the

St. Louis Archdiocese, ACLU and the anti-war groups Students for a Democratic Society (SDS) and the Committee for War Resistance also expressed solidarity.

On Sept. 15, demonstrators marched to Mayor Cervantes' home. About 200 protesters surrounded City Hall the next day and Ivory Perry threw himself in front of a car in an intersection, clogging traffic. A leader of the Urban League, the most conservative of the civil rights groups, said a review of police brutality in the city must start immediately, as "disregard for human life must be halted before the city has to contend with an ugly civil disturbance."

On Sept. 30 activists marched from the Old Cathedral to Busch Stadium, arriving in time for the opening game of the 1968 World Series between the Cardinals and Detroit Tigers. On Oct. 10, the ACLU filed suit to end police harassment of rights groups, but the judge refused the injunction, saying the suit was an effort "to rock the boat" and in three days of testimony he heard "no evidence to show that police were engaged in any pattern of harassment."

But the police campaign was effective. By the end of 1969, because of the costs of defending themselves against a series of arrests, the destruction of the headquarters, and police and FBI undercover work inside the organization, the Liberators had become ineffective.

The last straw was when a St. Louis police agent appeared before Congress to claim that Koen was recruiting black street gangs in a criminal conspiracy. Fearing more prosecution, Koen had had enough of St. Louis. He left the city and returned to his native Cairo, Ill. He didn't return to St. Louis until 1971 when he was sentenced to six months in jail on his conviction for the attack on the police in 1968.

After the Liberators faded, ACTION and Percy Green became the focus of police and FBI scrutiny. Neighbors of the group's headquarters in the Central West End were harassed and Green was kept under watch, one of 15,000 activists that the Nixon White House wanted immediately arrested in case of a declaration of martial law caused by a national emergency.

By the end of 1969, the focus of the protest movement had shifted to the larger and more vocal anti-war movement. On June 7, 1970, anti-war demonstrators held a march near Washington University that drew 45,000 people to protest the American bombing in Vietnam and the shooting of students at Kent State in Ohio by the National Guard.

For the time being, the civil rights movement had had its day in the sun. Richard Nixon, the law and order candidate elected president in 1968, was no LBJ.

Chapter Twenty-Six

Jazz Remade: The Black Artists' Group

1968-1972

(The Quartette Tres Bien was booked in 1963 to play the Apollo in New York, opening for Dizzy Gillespie): They wanted us to open the show with the curtain closed, playing the song ""I May Be Wrong, But I Think You're Wonderful." And we started playing the song and I heard this funny sound in the back and it was Dizzy Gillespie behind the other curtain playing with us. Dizzy said he liked to play with musicians who swing and I guess we fit that category. We had a different sound and we were quite explosive at the time and that created a lot of excitement.

-- Jeter Thompson, 1986

Away from the civil rights battles, urban development and the shift of a large percentage of the population, St. Louis in the fifties and sixties was, as usual, alive with music.

Welcome to one home, for an example, the home of Marsha Evans. Destined to become a big part of the blues scene, Evans grew up on the North Side during this period in an environment that ran counter to the stereotype of blight in the black neighborhoods. Her family took full advantage of the deep waters of the St. Louis musical opportunities.

Evans' father was Leonard Bolar, lead trumpet for the George Hudson Band, the city's most popular swing outfit. Her mother, Justine Bolar, was a member of another popular group, the Legend Singers, and often joined the Hudson gigs. She also sang in the chorus of *Showboat* at the Muny summer theater in Forest Park.

Justine's sister, Marie, was another musician. During the fifties she played piano in St. Louis Recreation Center programs and was responsible for Marsha's first gig, a duet with another sister, Cheryl, on the stage of the Kiel Auditorium -- an all-star revue of kids picked from rec center programs around town. The appearance on the big stage came before Marsha was ten.

"My dad was a wonderful musician and we had so many musicians pass through our house," she said during a 2014 conversation.

> It was nothing for Lou Rawls to come to our house -- along with many other jazz musicians. Not many houses had a piano back then. But we did, so our home was always full of music, and these were people who not only could play music, but who were knowledgeable about music.

She sang from early childhood, from before she can remember. She was in a dance troupe from the nearby Mildred Franklin School of Dance as well. "We were performing when I was five, we were getting paid then to perform, sometimes far away. I remember getting stuck in Illinois. We were the only blacks."

She took ballet and tap, she played the Kiel rec center revues until she was too old for the youth programs. "I don't want to sound conceited, but, my sister and I, well, we were good. We sang the 'Five Pennies,' 'Side by Side,' 'Mountain Greenery.' We did a little jazz version of that" -- she snaps her fingers and gets the beat -- "totally unexpected."

Evans lived on the North Side during the last days before it was changed by the destruction of Mill Creek Valley, before the recession of the early seventies emptied the nearby factories.

She walked every day to school at Sumner High until she graduated in 1969: "It was one of the best neighborhoods around. In the fifties, the moms and dads were in the homes, and these were well-manicured, beautiful homes, a real all-American neighborhood."

From across the room, her husband, the bassist Jimmy Hinds, chimes in.

> This town was a pear tree town, there were fruit trees in every yard. Cherry trees, peaches, apples. And everybody had those grape vines dripping over the garages in the alleys.
>
> *Marsha:* It was like a *Leave It To Beaver* neighborhood. When the streetlights came on every kid was home, playing in the front yard. A totally different world.
>
> *Jimmy:* You had to leave the neighborhood to get into some mischief.

By age 16, Marsha joined her father in the George Hudson Band, as one of the singing Georgettes. "I would do my homework between sets." In the band she met a sax player who told her about the Young Disciples, a city program in East St. Louis.

Here she crossed paths with the civil rights movement in its late-sixties black power phase. Allan Merry, who grew up on the East Side and had worked with Ray Charles and Ike Turner, organized the Disciples band out of a collective of men and women. He also had a short-lived record label called Gateway, which recorded the band under the name The Young Disciples & Co.

Evans met Merry through a member of Hudson's band and began singing with the group while in her last two years of high school. Here she ran into the Black Artists' Group (BAG) and met some of the most innovative and controversial artists the city ever produced. Here were more of the people who made up that St. Louis thing.

The Black Artists' Group emerged against the national backdrop of growing militancy in the civil rights movement. Here came Black Power leaders like Stokely Carmichael of the Student Non-Violent Coordinating Committee (SNCC) and Huey Newton of the Black Panther Party as well as the militant black nationalist Islam movement and the believers of the philosophy of Malcolm X.

The St. Louis artists' group was born in 1968, the year of the King assassination. That year a group of actors staged *The Blacks,* an avant-garde play by the French expressionist writer Jean Genet, a one-time homosexual prostitute, originally performed in Paris in 1958. The large-scale, stylized drama was aimed at shocking its white audience through exposure to white hypocrisy and its complicity in the subjugation of the black culture.

The play was performed on July 31 and Aug. 1, 1968, at a theater on a college campus in Webster Groves, a white suburb not accustomed to being confronted with issues of race and poverty. The show was intended to go on the road but the initial response of shock and embarrassment didn't convert to box office receipts and the play closed.

But a byproduct organization, the Black Artists' Group, was created. Thirteen actors and seven musicians formed a political collective to express and promote music, dance, theater, the visual arts and creative writing. The musician who had written the music for the play, Julius Hemphill, became the president of the group. One of the musicians he had recruited, Oliver Lake, became treasurer.

The musicians put together another event to celebrate the launch of BAG, a performance at the St. Louis Art Museum in Forest Park. A sell-out crowd about two-thirds white crammed into the folding chairs of the museum auditorium for opening night. The musical line-up included most of the jazz all-stars that emerged from BAG: Hemphill, Lake, Hamiet Bluiett, Floyd LeFlore, J.D. Parren, Bobo Shaw and Scrooge Harris. During the next few years Lester Bowie, Baikida Carroll and Marty Erlich would join them.

But the initial response from the liberal crowd was dismay. This was new music. People had never heard such squawking and squeaking.

The experimental sound was just part of a multi-media performance of an original work called *The Third World.* Players wandered the stage while horns blared. The players then picked up items from a table to use as instruments, joining the other musicians by making sounds having little or nothing to do with the horn sections -- whistles, bells, car horns and sundry other metal and wooden devises.

The crowd began to leave. But as they did, others took their seats in the small auditorium and soon the place was full again. This time the audience stayed on course and gave the musicians, dancers and poets a standing ovation at the end of the show. BAG was on the air.

Julius Hemphill eventually became best known for founding and leading the World Saxophone Quartet. The group was formed in 1976 and became a decades-long commercial success without abandoning its avant-guard origins. Hemphill's leadership experience, developed in St. Louis, came from the Black Power ideology that "all black art is political."

Hemphill held the figurative baton in the BAG rehearsal room and on stage. His "Hard Blues," a 20-minute piece of experimental sound that appeared on the seminal *Dogon A.D.* in 1972, is a masterpiece of progressive free jazz, an expression of the black experience, jangling, soothing, harsh and tender, "almost as if he were playing a horn made out of a steel pipe with a sax mouthpiece attached."

Born in Fort Worth, Texas, in 1940, he learned the clarinet first, then moved on to the tenor sax, inspired by Gerry Mulligan and instructed by jazz clarinetist John Carter. He came out of the army in 1966 and joined up with Ike Turner, moving to St. Louis as an R&B sax player. By 1970, Hemphill had formed Mbari, his own record company, and released the *Dogon A.D.* and *Blue Boyé.*

This was a period when Hemphill taught and influenced numerous players in St. Louis, including David Sanborn, who launched his own career in 1975. Sanborn's sax styles were recorded on dozens of albums, solo and backup, over the next 40 years. He became the leading pop sax player in America and won six Grammys by 2015.

Hemphill directed BAG's signature multi-media piece, *Poems for a Revolutionary Night* in 1969, performed in Gaslight Square and on the North Side to enthusiastic and diverse audiences of black working class and professional people, establishment white liberals and students, audiences typically about two-thirds black and one-third white, a mix very unusual in St. Louis. The shows were often performed in LaClede Town, as well as the Loretto-Hilton Theater in Webster Groves, at the Gateway in Gaslight Square and the Berea Presbyterian Church, the only one of 43 Mill Creek Valley churches to escape the headache ball.

Hemphill, however, soon tired of fighting forces from outside and within BAG. There was squabbling over federal money between paid and non-paid staff, there were charges of sexism -- the jazz bands were male, the dancers female -- and some problems between the mixed races. The St. Louis newspapers obsessed over supposed drug use and off-color language.

Then in 1970, the conservative hammer of the Nixon administration cut off funding.

BAG lasted until 1972 in its vibrant form and was still officially alive until 1974 when the federally funded Model Cities program was killed. By then BAG wasn't able to survive commercially. With federal support removed by the Nixon administration, the old money philanthropy dried up, liberals pulled out their support. BAG vanished.

But the musicians lived on, spreading their St. Louis roots around the world in a series of remarkably successful careers.

Hemphill moved to New York and in 1976 formed the World Saxophone Quartet with fellow BAG members Oliver Lake and Hamiet Bluiett. The fourth member of the all-sax unit was David Murray, a California product who had the ability to play difficult, long phrases.

Under Hemphill's direction the WSQ featured a free funk progressive style and a wealth of African influenced innovation, the group made nine records before Hemphill left the group because of illness in 1989.

He also had several side projects during what became known as the New York Loft Movement, where musicians took over empty factory lofts in the Soho section of Manhattan. These dwellings became high-priced years later but in the early Hemphill era were a cheap-housing hotbed of black art, music and theaters, a BAG-like environment that was a fertile ground for innovation and black cultural progress.

In the mid-eighties, Hemphill formed the Julius Hemphill Sextet and a big band configuration that contained echoes of Miles Davis and included the St. Louis players David Hines and J.D. Parran. An album from the group was released in 1988, just before Hemphill left the WSQ.

In 1988, he made the *Julius Hemphill Big Band* album and the sextet produced the memorable *Fat Man* and *Hard Blues* in 1992, the latter named to *Downbeat*'s Top Ten CD list that year. He also wrote *Long Tongues: A Saxophone Opera*, presented at the Apollo Theater in 1990.

By then Hemphill was weakened by chronic diabetes and he died at age 57 in 1995, hailed as "one of free jazz's most visionary composers" and "among the most important musicians of his generation."

Hamiet Bluiett had been the first of the BAG members to leave St. Louis. He paved the way in New York for the Loft Movement, arriving in lower Manhattan in 1969. The loft scene was summarized in 1976 by a 5-disc set called *Wildflowers* filled with music from 28 different ensembles, 11 of them from St. Louis.

These groups broke away from the high price jazz clubs of mid-town Manhattan to such an extent that Robert Palmer of *The New York Times* wrote that the "Midwesterners have rendered New York jazz all but obsolete." The paper was also exuberant over the World Saxophone Quartet -- "the most exciting new jazz band of the 1980s" -- of which Bluiett was a founder and was still involved with in 2014. Over his long career he had by then made over 40 albums.

At a Missouri Botanical Garden concert in July 2012, the 72-year old Bluiett turned something of a homecoming show into a delight under the Midwestern sky, performing in his quartet -- joined by D.D. Jackson, piano; William Parker, bass; Amid Drake, drums -- before a crowd relieved to sit outside on a 100-degree night. Hamiet wore a long white shirt and white pants, looking like a patron saint from some mythic time.

Between sets he wandered in the crowd, hugging several old friends, carrying his giant baritone sax slung on his back. He did a progressive rendition of "The St. Louis Blues," he did "Ode to Life," and bounced around the stage, playing off his world-class rhythm section, sending everybody home smiling and chatting, just another free St. Louis concert with another master.

His style didn't have the intensity of the original days of the free jazz movement that night. Over the years he became more blues oriented, with a smoother infusion of sound. The baritone in Bluiett's hands seemed somehow smaller than it should be, hitting higher notes, swinging, filled with romance. His tone was accessible, it didn't squawk like in the BAG days. But there's no confusing it with the smooth jazz like that of Sanborn, the kind of jazz music that dominates the twenty-first century market. Bluiett, on a tune like "The St. Louis Blues," for instance, takes us out of the mainstream, into a place somewhere between the moon and the stars.

Bluiett was born Sept. 16, 1940, in Lovejoy, Ill., just north of East St. Louis. His first teacher was his aunt, an East Side choral director. At age nine he took up the clarinet and when he went to Southern Illinois University in 1959 he started playing the flute and the baritone sax.

"I wanted to play baritone; that was my favorite," Bluiett said in a 2014 interview. "But I had to wait until I was big and strong enough to play it." He became the world's leading player of the instrument, a horn that is bigger than the tenor but not as big as the bass.

Bluiett joined the Navy band in 1961 and stayed in the military until 1966 when he met Hemphill in St. Louis and started the process that led to BAG, taking the leadership role in the group's big band. He was drawn to New York before the trouble started in BAG and avoided the downhill slide, instead laying the ground for others to join him in Soho.

His career flourished and *The New York Times* called him the "Babe Ruth of baritone." Before helping Hemphill get the sax quartet off the ground Bluiett was part of the Charles Mingus Quintet and Sam Rivers' large ensemble. He has also been a teacher throughout the United States and a design consultant to saxophone manufacturers.

> The saxophone is a support instrument, but I have been fortunate enough to be recognized as someone who has stood out front in that supporting role. In terms of the instrument I chose, I may have settled at the bottom of the totem pole, but I like to think of myself as being at the very top of that bottom. Now I've had my share of bad performances, but I don't let disaster go to my heart the same way I don't let praises go to my head.

Like Bluiett himself, the World Saxophone Quartet's early bleating, incoherent style evolved into something more diverse, the harmonic combination of the styles Miles Davis pioneered. In the many WSQ records can be found many styles, even Dixieland. There is also be-bop, Ellington, world, all held together by the underling power of Bluiett's baritone sax.

The early twenty-first century was not particularly kind to Bluiett. In 2002 a fire in Harlem destroyed his home and many of his possessions. After the fire he moved back to the East Side of St. Louis, where he was helped by his many friends and, partially supported by the Jazz Foundation of America, got back on his feet.

He returned to New York City in 2012. There he suffered two strokes but continued to appear in various shows, including a benefit for the Jazz

Foundation in 2014 and at the Vision Festival in the summer of 2015, age 75, leading his new group, the Telepathic Orchestra.

Oliver Lake, the third original member of the World Saxophone Quartet, was born in Marianna, Ark., on Sept. 14, 1942, and moved to St. Louis in 1944. He joined a drum and bugle corps at age 13 and began playing cymbals and the bass drum. At 17, he started taking an interest in jazz and by the mid-sixties, after graduating from Sumner High and attending Lincoln University, he was playing the sax. He formed the Lake Art Quartet, which debuted at the Circle Coffee House in LaClede Town in 1967.

Lake had met Hemphill earlier; both attended Lincoln University, the black college in Jefferson City, Mo. They started discussing how to organize a black arts cooperative in St. Louis along the lines of a similar group that had formed in Chicago.

Hemphill thought the Chicago group was too narrow and suggested to Lake that a wider view should be taken, an organization Lake recalled, "which included all the artists we had been associated with -- poets, visual artists, dancers and actors." While future BAG musicians developed plans for a collective, impetus was also underway to form a black theater company in St. Louis.

Actor and director Manlike Elliott and an English teacher from the private Country Day School named Russell Durbin had been talking about forming such a company. This idea led to the staging of Jean Genet's *The Blacks.* This in turn put musicians on the stage and Lake and Hemphill were two of them.

As BAG declined, Lake journeyed to Paris in 1972 with other members of the collective, where they stayed together playing as an ensemble for a year. Lake played on his own in Europe for another year then relocated to New York City, moving to the loft scene until the founding of the WSQ in 1976.

From then on, he has done it all: solo sax concerts, theater pieces including poetry; the creation of the reggae-based group Jump-Up; performances in Russia, Africa and Japan; commissions from the Brooklyn Philharmonic Orchestra, the Amherst Sax Quartet and the San Francisco Contemporary Players.

Lake also developed a second career as an arranger, working with pop singer Bjork, rocker Lou Reed and the rap group A Tribe Called Quest.

He has collaborated with a variety of choreographers, and with the Native American vocalist Mary Redhouse, the Korean kumongo player Jin Hi Kim, the Chinese bamboo flute player Shuni Tsou. He performed with Mos Def and Me'shell Ndegeocello.

On his website, Lake says he views the spectrum of his performance as all parts of the same whole, be it "Dixieland, be-bop, soul, rhythm & blues, cool school, swing, avant-garde jazz, free jazz, rock, jazz rock."

In 2014, Lake continued a schedule of performances, including things like the Freedom of Sound festival in Montclair, N.J., where his show headlined a suitably eclectic musical bill that also included a drum duet between Andrew Cyrille and Pheeroan akLaff; a set by the multi-reedist Henry Threadgill with the pianist David Virelles; the Dolphy Bass Clarinet Quartet and an academic symposium.

Lake was joined in Montclair by the jazz sextet Tarbaby, a group that he has been performing with regularly, doing everything from up-to-the-minute originals to takes on Fats Waller and John Coltrane. In April he performed in Middletown, Conn., at the Wesleyan University Center for the Arts, fronting his Oliver Lake Big Band.

The last months of 2015 found Lake, 73, on tour in a jazz trio in Switzerland. His most recent U.S. tour drew rave reviews, including one, from the *Seattle Times* that said the reedman "showed clearly that he has figured out how to play the saxophone and speak in the same place, with the felicity of a blues man and the relevance of a contemporary poet."

Lester Bowie was another of the Sumner High group of musicians who joined BAG in 1968 and came under the spell of Hemphill's influence. Bowie traveled to Europe in 1969, returning from a summer in Sweden to St. Louis in 1971 to catch the last wave of BAG.

Bowie was born in Frederick, Md., on Oct. 11, 1941. He moved to St. Louis in 1953 with his family. His father became a music teacher at Hadley Technical High in North County, but the family lived in the city, which put Bowie right into the blend in the Sumner High Band's trumpet section. After he graduated he met and married the St. Louis singer Fontella Bass, who was recording at Oliver Sain's Archway Studio (with Marsha Evans on backup vocals).

Bass had her "Rescue Me" hit record in 1965, just after she moved to Chicago to work for Chess Records. Bowie went along and joined the Chicago version of BAG, the Association for the Advancement of Creative Musicians, then founded a band of his own in 1968 called the Art Ensemble. He began recording for Delmark Records, the transplanted St. Louis label originally called Delmar, which had a studio near the DeBaliviere strip before moving north. Bowie recruited a few St. Louis players like David Hines to play with him in Chicago before he left for New York.

One writer described Bowie's trumpet style as having an "exceptionally large stock of effects, including half-valving, bent notes and a wide vibrato," all part of the St. Louis style of trumpet playing that had been employed through the years by musicians like Miles Davis and Clark Terry, dating all the way back to Charlie Creath and the riverboats.

Bowie's father not only taught music, he played in brass bands, as did his uncles and his grandfather. Like Marsha Evans, Bowie's house was filled with music. Before he met Bass, Bowie did a stint in the Air Force playing in a military band, he traveled with a tent show called Leon Claxton's Harlem Revue, and rode the road with Albert King, Little Milton, Aretha Franklin and the Temptations. Once with Bass, he played in her road show as well.

By 1974 he was divorced and living in New York, joining Hemphill on the album *Fast Last,* a record that showed off a flamboyance he developed as he perfected his act, a combination of dancing and mugging for the crowd, dressed in a long white smock accented by a pointy beatnik beard.

He said that when he was in high school on the North Side, "I was what they called a gifted child. The teachers' were very angry with me 'cause I didn't want to be like they wanted me to be. I wanted to relax, have fun." His gift was a high IQ and a talent for the trumpet.

But it was a talent often overlooked in his St. Louis days, where the innovative jazz scene was often underground because "to be a musician was not considered an honorable profession. A great saxophonist had to become a house painter to stay in St. Louis. The community didn't think that jazz was important enough to support."

Once in New York in the seventies, Bowie started making well-received albums -- especially *The Fifth Power* in 1978 and *From Roots to the*

Source in 1980, a record where Fontella Bass joined him on gospel-tinged cuts. This record previewed Bowie's inclination toward R&B. He played a twisted, innovative turn away from the old Ike Turner style, a form that magnified the shouts and moans, now played on horns in the jumpy Bowie fashion.

He went on to form an nine-piece group called Lester Bowie's Brass Fantasy that made five records between 1985 and 1995, each receiving good reviews and stronger sales than usually seen for what were classified as jazz novelty records. This group included four trumpets, two trombones, a tuba, a French horn and a drum, a New Orleans brass band set up but without so much of the funk.

He also started an organ ensemble, kept a steady stream of R&B covers, played a tribute to Ellington, dove into the organ music of Jimmy Smith and managed to hold together the old Chicago group, the Art Ensemble, playing a heavy slate of gigs.

During the last part of the twentieth century, Bowie's album count passed 60. He recorded through the years as a solo and a sideman with David Bowie, Jack DeJonnette, David Murray (from WSQ), Bobo Shaw (from BAG), Fontella Bass and Sun Ra. He even appeared on a comedy record with Bill Cosby.

Bowie died at 57 in 1999 at his home in Brooklyn, N.Y.

Baikida Carroll, was born Jan. 15, 1947, in St. Louis and grew up on the North Side, further downtown than Marsha Evans, in the Soldan High area. His mother was a Miles Davis fan and pulled him out of school for matinees at Rhumboogie. His father played sax and piano. Carroll, who took up the trumpet, met Lester Bowie during the summer following his sophomore year when he was playing local backup in gigs with Albert King, Ike Turner, Little Milton and Oliver Sain.

At Soldan, Carroll became concerned he would be drafted into the Vietnam War where several of his friends had been killed. He opted to instead follow the Clark Terry example and enlisted before being drafted, hoping he could pay music while staying out of Southeast Asia. This is precisely what happened.

He wound up in Virginia Beach, Va., at the school once called the Navy School of Music, then called the Armed Forces School of Music. He attended classes and was sent to Germany, where he spent the next three years studying music composition, leading and arranging a 21-piece jazz band and playing in late night big band jams.

When he got back to St. Louis in 1968, BAG was on the launch pad. He threw himself forth, jumping at the chance to play with Hemphill, et. al., displaying his skills in the BAG Orchestra and working as an actor and teacher of composition and trumpet. During his four-year run with BAG, he took a jazz master class from a St. Louis jazz master, Oliver Nelson, offered at Washington University.

But there were never enough gigs and never enough money for the cooperative to function. The traditional clubs didn't like free jazz and various combinations of players would meet in empty North Side garages or in tiny apartments. Carroll and Hemphill often met at Forest Park, blowing their horns into the open fairways of the golf course. One of the garages even had a name, the Hairy Hut.

By 1972, Carroll was tired of fighting in the War on Poverty and joined the group from BAG who set off for Paris -- a group composed of Oliver Lake, Floyd LeFlore, Bob Shaw and Lester Bowie's brother, Joseph Bowie. Before he left St. Louis he played on the sessions that produced the record *NTU: From Which Creation Begins* with Lake and a band of BAG members, his last hurrah in his hometown. Carroll lived in Paris until 1975, when he moved to New York.

Carroll became a sideman and educator. Most of the efforts are in the free jazz movement, the music of tone, texture, blank spaces, shocks and let downs. Played in the grown BAG style, it also showed harmony, reminders of music from the past and that abstract quality of trying to find what isn't there, looking for a future.

Carroll provided these musical remarks playing with Lake and Bluiett, and with Murray and DeJohnette. Carroll also headed up his own group in the eighties and made a solo album along the way. His productivity slowed over the years, but the reviews were good for a CD called *Marionettes on a High Wire* released in 2001.

He was also a successful teacher, heading up programs in the New York area, including a stint at Queens College. In 2015, Carroll toured the world, wrote music for Broadway and collected grants. His live gigs became scarce but in 2014 he appeared with his old BAG colleague Oliver Lake at the Stone in New York City's East Village.

Floyd LeFlore, another native of St. Louis, was in the same classes at Sumner as Lake and Bowie, as well as with the pianist John Hicks, drummers Philip Wilson and Scrooge Harris, trumpeter David Hines and several other BAG players.

"We had some really hip musicians," LeFlore remembered of his high school years. "Hicks was cool even then -- he had a hip little trio, he had a suit and tie, he had that look. Phillip was cool, too. Philip was an organ trio-type dude."

LeFlore, like Carroll and Bowie, played trumpet, and was also part of the Paris exodus.

The Paris group debuted in 1972 at the Grand Palais on the Champs-Elysees, playing free jazz for the Parisian audience at a citywide festival of the arts. The reaction was all positive, the French loved the American jazz and the Americans found a group of expatriate dancers, writers and plenty of other musicians in a seventies community of the kind they had left back home. One show after another followed.

The reception in France was a relief for the group after the sour end in St. Louis. LeFlore remembered: "Things were going great. And then, you know, all good things in St. Louis must come to an end, and it seemed like we didn't get the audience support. Sometimes we were playing to an empty room."

Following the return to America, LeFlore was one of the few members who came back to St. Louis, playing local gigs throughout the eighties and nineties.

He married the poet, Shirley Bradley, and their daughter, Lyah Beth LeFlore, took up the artistic mantle, becoming the NAACP Image Award winner in 2012 in the Best Literary Work: Debut Author category for *The Strawberry Letter: Real Talk, Real Advice, Because Bitterness Isn't Sexy.*

LeFlore died in his hometown in 2014.

The woodwind expert **J.D. Parran** joined LeFlore in St. Louis during the BAG experience and then left in 1977 for a recording career based in New York. He's played on over 50 records, jazz, pop and classical, adding Shirley LeFlore to his group Spirit Stage for recordings in 1995 and 2005.

The BAG drummer **Bobo Shaw** returned to St. Louis from Paris in 1971 and joined the Arts Ensemble in Chicago during the seventies with Hemphill and Lake. Shaw recorded in the eighties with Billy Bang, a New York free jazz violinist, and also for the Moers and Black Saint labels in the nineties. Shaw stayed in St. Louis and recently (2010 and 2011) hooked up with Scrooge Harris for the Drum Line, a presentation of the Nu-Art Series at a downtown art gallery.

Another BAG member, trumpeter **David Hines**, was killed in a motorcycle accident in 1991, not long after he toured with Lester Bowie's Brass Fantasy. Hines was a St. Louis native who learned how to play the piano in Eddie Randle's funeral parlor as a child.

Another of the Sumner High grads, Hines worked in Gaslight Square, toured with Albert King and Little Milton and in 1968, was a mainstay of the Ike and Tina horn section. He was a friend of LeFlore but played only infrequently with BAG and did not make the trip to Paris.

Instead, Hines joined the Woody Herman Big Band after his time with Ike and Tina and in 1970 took the lead trumpet job in Ray Charles' touring band. He also taught in St. Louis and in the eighties was the director of the University City High School jazz band.

Another peripheral BAG player was **Marty Ehrlich,** a multi-instrumentalist who moved from Minnesota to St. Louis with his social worker parents when he was 10. The family lived in University City, the socially conscious western suburb just outside the city limits where Ehrlich started his musician career through the alternative poetry scene.

At readings he met Lake, Shaw and Hines and his love of jazz began to overtake his classical training. He attended the New England Conservatory of Music, graduated in 1978 and went to New York City, where he caught up with Hemphill and enjoyed a long music career, including stints in the Human Arts Ensemble with Shaw.

He eventually wound up in the East Village of New York, connected to the Knitting Factory, where he accompanied dance classes, taught private lessons, and did weddings and parties. Ehrlich hooked back up with Hemphill in 1990 in the saxophone sextet and continued his performances into the twenty-first century with over 100 recordings under his belt.

Another sixties jazz musician was the piano player **John Hicks.** Born in Atlanta, he came to St. Louis when he was 14, in time to get in on the Sumner High scene. He went on to Lincoln University and Berklee School of Music in Boston before moving to New York in 1963, where he hooked up with the blues star Big Maybelle.

Another St. Louisan who made a long career elsewhere, Hicks played in Art Blakey's Jazz Messengers, worked with Betty Carter and Woody Herman and was a regular member in the Mingus Dynasty Band. He died May 10, 2006, three days after he played at Harlem's St. Mark's United Methodist Church, where his father was once minister. Hicks was 64 years old.

As the free jazz innovators wailed away in the BAG milieu in the sixties, one player stood far above the others on the traditional side -- Singleton Palmer, perhaps the most popular jazzman to stay in the city.

His reputation in St. Louis was not only because he played a tuba, not the usual jazz instrument. Nor did it rest on his records. Palmer's reputation came from the eight years he delighted thousands of people who made Gaslight Square a required destination, be they tourists or locals. On the Square, Singleton staged the rebirth of Dixieland.

Born in St. Louis Nov. 13, 1912, he was blowing the trumpet by age 11. By 14, he was playing in a band. His father bought him a standup bass violin and his teenage band got some downtown gigs. "My daddy used to come down and bring me home after I got through playing. I think that he was enjoying the music more than I was."

Soon enough, age 16, he was in a touring band, the Eddie Johnson Band, playing the "Duck's Yas Yas" in places like Cincinnati. He knew the tuba by then and soon landed a job on a riverboat, dropping out of Sumner High. The tuba was his ticket, nobody else played it, and because of his trumpet training Palmer had the dexterity to make things happen. He had twice the speed of other tuba players.

"I never was as good a bass violin player as I am a tuba player; I'm better as a tuba player," he said in an interview with the Missouri History Museum. "The people like it."

Three years later, 1933, he was playing on a Streckfus steamer with Dewey Jackson, making the run up the Ohio to Pittsburgh. Jackson remained a musical colleague throughout Palmer's long life and Palmer was able to help Jackson make a comeback in the early sixties. During the thirties, Jackson worked with both Charlie Creath and Fate Marable before striking off on his own.

Both Clark Terry and Jimmy Blanton were part of the revived riverboat scene in the late thirties but the steamboats were gone soon after the war broke out in 1941. Jackson, by then one of the best trumpet players in a town of trumpet players, quit music to manage a hotel.

Palmer got a job at Scullin Steel. The company had a 45-piece big band that played for the employees in the cafeteria every day during lunch. He played Sousa and light symphonic overtures, "all in our overalls."

As the war ended, Palmer hooked up with George Hudson, playing the ballrooms, did a record with Clark Terry, provided some back up for Jimmy Forrest, the "Night Train" man who would later hung out at the Club Imperial's small bar. Then in 1947, with a good word from Terry, the tuba player landed a big fish -- a job in Count Basie's 18-piece jazz band, traditional and swing. He toured for three years.

But he quit Basie in 1950, thinking there was more money in St. Louis. The swing bands were shrinking and the DeBaliviere Strip on the West Side of town was bubbling.

After he quit Basie, the first thing Palmer did was form the Singleton Palmer Dixieland Six and started leading Dixieland jam sessions every Sunday at the Universal Dance Hall on the newest entertainment street in town. He played DeBaliviere for eight months at the hall, but because the group was integrated, it had trouble getting other bookings. He put together two versions of the band, one all black and one mixed.

The entertainment strip had developed after the war and was popular in the early fifties, with everything from dance clubs to a giant skating rink in a building that was put up during the World's Fair.

The DeBaliviere Strip, however, only proved to be the prelude to Gaslight. After the tornado in 1959, many merchants took their insurance money and moved across town to join the fun in the Square. Left behind on DeBaliviere was a place that gave a different meaning to the word strip.

This time it meant the slow taking off of clothing -- featuring people like Blaze Starr, "The Hottest Blaze in Burlesque;" Candy Barr, who served time for shooting her second husband and dated Jack Ruby; and "Evelyn West and her $50,000 Chest." The Terrance Lounge, which featured live jazz acts before and after the competition from Gaslight Square, also stayed around on the strip until it burned down in 1970.

Palmer said he "had a ball" playing DeBaliviere, but when the Opera House in Gaslight came beckoning, he packed up his tuba and took residence on the Square, where "every night was like New Year's Eve." His Dixieland Six there featured Robert Carter, who had played trombone for Ellington, and Lige Shaw, a drummer who could "play, tip his hat, take his sticks and hit them on the floor and they would go up in the air and he would catch them coming down."

A *New York Times* music writer ran across a Singleton Palmer record one day in 1963 and discovered a group that loved to play the old music with a fresh twist, a "vitality" "a verve;" "vivacious," "buoyant. The tunes are some of the war horses of the idiom ('Beale St. Blues,' 'Dixieland One Step,' 'Wolverine Blues,' and so forth) but Mr. Palmer and his men freshen them with their own personalities and his men freshen them with their ideas."

The album in question was *Singleton Palmer at the Opera House*, one of six records he made while at Gaslight.

He was 80 years old when he died in 1993, having stopped playing for only his last few years. By then, too, he had retired from his night porter job, work he did for 25 years, including the whole Gaslight period. Palmer seemed always to be smiling, even while playing the tuba. He favored bow ties and suspenders and was quite bald.

An interviewer, University of Missouri professor Irene Cortinovis, was surprised to hear that in 1971 the popular Palmer was still working a "day" job:

> *Palmer:* I work as a porter at Fact, Incorporated, at 1706 Washington. This month I'll have been with them 19 years.
>
> *Cortinovis*: Well, and you've been able to work steadily all that time -- well, that must have been after you stopped traveling then?
>
> *Palmer*: Oh, yes.
>
> *Cortinovis*: You mean, all during the Gaslight days and everything you stayed with them.

Palmer: What I would do is to leave Gaslight and go right down there.

Cortinovis: Good heavens, when did you sleep?

Palmer: I'd get off from Gaslight at one o'clock and get down there by one-thirty and I'd work until nine.

Cortinovis: My gosh!

Palmer: I did that for eight years.

Cortinovis: Are you still doing it?

Palmer: Yeah. It's kind of difficult now, because I always like to carry my instrument home when we get through playing on a single engagement.

Palmer's songs are scattered through compilations of the city's trad jazz and the Chicago Dixieland Stompers did a tribute, *Blues for Singleton Palmer*, for Delmark label in the fifties.

> They called our band a Dixieland band, but to me it isn't. It's just a swing band. Our type of jazz is different than what they play in New Orleans, they play their tunes slower. We have a tendency to play ours a little up; same way with the Chicago jazz — they play theirs faster than we do here. The fellows here got quite a bit of the New Orleans jazz from going down on the riverboats. We still have St. Louis jazz; I have to hold up for St. Louis.

Palmer's music was a St. Louis thing and in a way, so, too, was the music of **David Sanborn**. The biggest difference was that Sanborn, like Miles Davis and Clark Terry, didn't spend much time in St. Louis once he found his sound.

Sanborn was born July 30, 1945, in Tampa and came to St. Louis as a teenager. By 14, he was playing his sax with Albert King and Little Milton and all along has maintained that his style wasn't really jazz,

> Most of the contexts I've played in have been either blues based or R&B or straight out rock and roll.
>
> I used to go to Gaslight Square and walk down the street and hear cabaret acts, jazz acts, blues, folk singers, all this stuff and that's what got ingrained in me, the idea that great music is great music. I took that sensibility out into the world.

The sensibility was that of a confluence, a combination of elements that added up to more than the sum of the parts.

Sanborn's introduction to the saxophone came at age three as part of the treatment he received after he contracted polio.

His exposure as a teenager came directly from the Blue Note Club in East St. Louis, where that blend of R&B, blues and jazz was played from the late fifties up to 1967. The music kicked off at 11 and Sanborn was often there as a teenager, first taken across the river by BAG drummer Phillip Wilson.

Sanborn sat in with Hamiet Bluiett and the drummer Kenny Rice, both fixtures at the club. He also played with Julius Hemphill in LaClede Town before leaving for California in 1967. He played Woodstock with the Paul Butterfield Blues Band and then toured with Stevie Wonder and The Rolling Stones, eventually landing in New York where he came under the influence of Gil Evans.

His first album, appropriately titled *Taking Off,* was released in 1975 and his first hit came with *Hideaway* in 1979. A song from the disc *Seduction* was featured in the film *American Gigolo* and Sanborn rolled on in the eighties and nineties with a series of best-selling records that combined his R&B base with the jazz he heard as a teenager. He won his first Grammy in 1981.

Sanborn rarely appeared in St. Louis once his career took off, but he was part of the first Webster Groves Jazz Festival in 2001. He has been a supporter of the city's new jazz center, playing during its opening season in 2014 as well as in 2015. He also booked another four-night stand for 2016.

The new club at the center, Jazz at the Bistro, brought back a tradition of live jazz to the city every weekend.

There were several other jazz players from the fifties and sixties not to be overlooked:

Tenor sax **Bob Graf** had a short glimpse of the big boys after launching his career in St. Louis from Peacock Alley and another place called the Show Bar, a jazz club that drew crowds in the fifties in the Central West End. Graf had runs with Basie, Chet Baker, and Woody Herman. But by the mid-sixties he was repairing instruments in St. Louis, playing the occasional gigs until his death at the 54 in 1981.

Graf spent time in St. Louis with guitarist **Grant Green,** born in 1935, a child prodigy who fell under the spell of Charlie Christman. Green played all over as a teenager in the fifties, working strip clubs while underage. He started recording in 1956, playing with Dean and Forrest. In 1960 he left for New York after a run at the Holy Barbarian on DeBaliviere.

Once out of town, however, Green fell into the drug scene after landing a well-paid gig as the house guitarist for Blue Note Records in New York. He appeared on 80 albums during the sixties but became unreliable. He died from heart problems at age 43, in 1979.

Sammy Gardner, a clarinet player who was born in St. Louis in 1925, was almost as well known on the Square as Singelton Palmer. He held down the show at the Tiger's Den during much of the sixties and was a tireless teacher of traditional jazz. After the end of Gaslight Square, he moved to Pensacola, Fla., for a long run as a traditional jazz player at the nation's first Rosie O'Grady's. He lasted until 1995, age 70.

Chris Woods was a musician in St. Louis whose music didn't quite carry the load. Although popular during the fifties with a diverse mastery of reed instruments, Woods kept working as a bus driver. Before the war he had played with the Jeters-Pillar outfit and hooked up with Tommy Dean in the early fifties.

Dean was from Louisiana and was determined to make a splash. He had been Eddie Randle's piano player and took out on his own in 1949, continuing to look for that hit in the early fifties, with both jazz and R&B sides, but never made the big time and died in 1965.

Woods left for New York just as Gaslight took off, hooking up with Clark Terry and eventually joining the Basie band in 1983. Unfortunately it was too late for Woods, he died two years later from cancer. Terry said Woods was one of the most underrated of the St. Louis players, "I'm happier with him playing by my side than almost anybody I know in the business," Terry said.

Gaslight Square also saw several female vocalists, some singing nightly in the Dixieland clubs, other recycling the oldies, torch or blues, using just a microphone and some fancy clothes, with often just a piano to lean on.

The mainstay on the Square was **Clea Bradford**. Born near Clarksdale, Miss., her family moved soon after her birth to rural Charleston, Mo., down in the southern boot heel of the state, not far from Sikeston, where the last lynching in the state's history took place. Her mother was of Choctaw, Ethiopian, and Creole descent, and her father was a Cherokee, roots she took pride in throughout her long career, often dressing in traditional Native American clothing. She was nearly six-feet tall, with high cheekbones and a demanding stage presence.

Her father was a Baptist preacher, her mother involved in the church choir. She was pushed forward to sing "I Come to the Garden Alone" in church at age 3. Her grandfather taught her voice, harmony, and sight note reading and by 13 she was running her church choir.

Her mother separated from the preacher as the war broke out and when Clea was seven. In 1942 she found herself in St. Louis, moving into a house down the street from Jimmy Forrest. The sax man was just off a spell with Jay McShann and was about to join forces with Andy Kirk's big band. His big hit with "Night Train" hadn't yet happened and wouldn't until 1952.

By then Clea had grown up with a front row seat at her friendly neighbor's house where Forrest rehearsed and held jam sessions with locals like Oliver Nelson, who had worked his way into the Hudson swing contingent at age 15. A tenor sax, Nelson in 1950 joined the Louis Jordan big band.

Also around the house was Clark Terry, then in the Hudson band, and the very young Miles Davis, who didn't leave home for Julliard until 1945. Terry was just back from the Great Lakes Experience, and encouraged Bradford to sing.

Later, she said she owed her intricate vocal style to the intricate trumpet passages of Clark Terry. At 15, she began sneaking off to the Red Rooster on the East Side to sit in with the players she'd met in Forrest's living room.

In 1952, at 17, Clea Bradford landed a 32-week gig at Fausts, another East Side joint. But she had trouble managing to live on $10 a night and when she heard of green pastures in Detroit, she began a ramble around the country that lasted until 1962 when she moved back to St. Louis for her run on Gaslight Square.

She got an apartment in LaClede Town and appeared nightly at the Tres Bien, backed by the Quartette Tres Bien -- with Jeter Thompson on piano. "Some Day My Prince Will Come," jazzed along by the pianoman, popped out as a regional favorite, getting airplay, but it was made in St. Louis on such a small label (Norman), the national exposure didn't happen.

Then along came St. Louisan Dick Gregory, who signed Bradford up for his Kool Jazz Festival tour of 1964, appearing at the Apollo in Harlem -- a long way from Charleston, Mo.-- with Dizzy Gillespie. And it was Gregory who probably introduced her to a friend of his, Hugh Hefner.

Hefner signed her up to tour his Playboy Clubs where sharky customers drank drinks and listened to music amid the bunny-clad waitresses. Bradford soon was running a regional office from St. Louis for Playboy as well as performing on tour and in Gaslight. Hefner built her a "space age" building on Lindell for a regional headquarters -- a building that stood out amid the brick for his all-black facade and circle design. The neglected building was still standing in 2014, the etched Playboy bunny logo found on a concrete patio out front.

In 1966, Bradford did a Soviet Union trip with pianist Earl "Fatha" Hines, 35 shows with an unrehearsed band. The next year it was Mexico, with the well-rehearsed Woody Hermann band and the St. Louis BAG man John Hicks on piano. By then, however, Gaslight was starting to seem different.

She moved to Los Angeles in 1970 to a new job at the Playboy headquarters. The move had been suggested by Oliver Nelson whom she had met as a girl in Jimmy Forrest's living room. He had been on the West Coast since 1967 and offered sessions and jobs writing scores for movies and television.

From L.A. she toured for the next 20 years, saying at the end of it she was not a big star but was a "huge twinkle." She died in 2008 in Silver Springs, Md., after a second career as a voice coach in Washington, D.C.

Her sister is Janie Bradford, a songwriter for Motown Records.

Jeanne Trevor was born and raised in Harlem and moved to St. Louis in the late fifties to join the scene on Gaslight Square. Her performances continued into the second decade of the twenty-first century, all along presenting a straight ahead, mainstream style that had little to do with originality and everything to do with knowing and pleasing her audience. She channeled Ella Fitzgerald, Billie Holiday and Sarah Vaughn through a voice trained for opera.

Her category for her singing style is not jazz, but "modern America," tackling blues, gospel and Latin in her shows. On the Square she worked the Dark Horse, Vanity Fair and Le Jazz Hot and made an album in the early sixties with Quartette Tres Bien.

Trevor's first solo album didn't appear until 1998. In the meantime she had toured the world, played the Muny accompanied by the St. Louis Symphony, won a Grammy for her work on commercials and was honored on Jeanne Trevor Day -- Sept. 24, 2010 -- called "the first lady of St. Louis jazz." She celebrated the day by kicking off the University City Jazz Festival.

On her *Love You Madly* CD she uses scat and sings in Spanish and French. A highlight is an R&B transformation of the bop anthem "Work Song." She also does some old tent work on "Give Me Jesus." Support on the record comes from St. Louisans Willie Akins on the sax and Simon Rowe on piano.

Trevor maintained that she was not the first lady of St. Louis jazz, giving that honor to Clea Bradford. But she accepted the crown after Bradford left the city in the late sixties and kept a firm grip on the title for over 40 years.

There was also **Ceil Clayton,** who had studied at the New England Conservatory and came to St. Louis after the war, landing a regular gig at Mr. D's Steak House. She sang her way through the Gaslight period, cutting two albums on the Norman label, both mixtures of standards and contemporary tunes.

She left the city in the late seventies after selling pianos and sheet music to get by. She moved to Scandinavia and didn't return to St. Louis. One of her albums recently sold for $225 on eBay.

Jean Kittrell had a long run as a vocalist in St. Louis, taking advantage of the revival of the waterfront in the late sixties, working numerous gigs, often fronting the St. Louis Ragtimers. She had grown up in Alabama, studied music in Mississippi and Chicago and worked in Virginia before landing in St. Louis in 1967.

Kittrell played the Old Levee House on Laclede's Landing, the waterfront River Queen Restaurant and on the revived *Goldenrod*

Showboat. She kept up her studies during her career and received a PhD from Southern Illinois in 1973. She was chair of the English Department from 1987 to 1990, playing jazz piano and singing on the weekends aboard the *Lt. Robert E. Lee* steamboat in St. Louis. She retired in 2008.

And, also not to be overlooked in this rich period of St. Louis music:

Jeter Thompson was a native who started playing piano at five years old and made his first professional appearance in 1946 as a 16 year old at a downtown strip club called the Coconut Grove. Thompson was senior class president of Sumner High in 1948, went into the army, then worked music joints until the opening shots of Gaslight Square where he did his most popular work in the **Quartette Tres Bien.**

In 1963 Thompson went into business on the Square as a partner in Tres Bien Club, a small place that sat next door to the Gaslight Bar and featured traditional jazz. The group made 12 albums, most of them in the sixties, including steady sellers *Boss Tres Bien* and *St. Louis Blues.*

The original group broke up in 1973 with the fading of the Square and the closing of the club. There was yoeman roadwork during the last years of the group, appearing at the Apollo in Harlem, with Sarah Vaughn at Powell Hall in St. Louis and the It Club in Los Angeles.

Following the demise of the group, Thompson joined up with his twin brothers Harold and Howard in the Trio Tres Bien, a group that still performs in St. Louis, often adding Thompson's niece, Danita Mumphard.

The jazz scene in the sixties also saw the revival of ragtime, led by the **St. Louis Ragtimers**, opening at the Natchez Queen, a mock riverboat on Gaslight Square, not long after the band was founded in the summer of 1961. The group moved over to the much larger Buttons and Bows in 1964 and grew increasingly popular; doing for ragtime what Singleton Palmer had done in reviving Dixieland.

On May 22, 1965, the restored *Goldenrod Showboat* on the Mississippi River was reopened with a Ragtimers show. Later that summer **Trebor Tichenor** and the group organized the first St. Louis Riverfront Ragtime Festival, three days of jazz, Dixieland and ragtime on the Goldenrod. Players from Chicago, Tampa, Cincinnati, and Denver joined the Ragtimers during the festival.

The group carried on with minor changes for 52 more years. In 2013 that ended after a final performance at Sheldon Hall, where old-timers caught a morning show. The originals -- Tichenor, Bill Mason, Don Franz and Al Stricker -- played a lively set that included all the favorites, from "Maple Leaf Rag" to "The St. Louis Blues."

Tichenor died at age 74, in 2014 not long after the show. He was remembered as one of the foremost experts in the genre, which he had been studying, playing and teaching most of his life. Tichenor built a collection of 10,000 piano rolls and sheets of ragtime music.

His life on the piano began at five when a music teacher arrived at his house in Webster Groves for his first lesson. Trebor ran out of the house and hid in the bushes. "I was a 5-year-old and afraid," he later wrote. His mother was adamant: "You start piano lessons today." By 13, he discovered ragtime. His grandmother took him to antique stores where he began to build his collection.

Tichenor was the piano player in the group and the only full-time Ragtimer. Stricker, the singer and banjo player, taught school; Franz played the tuba and was a businessman; Mason was on trumpet when he wasn't driving truck.

Tichenor co-founded the magazine *Ragtime Review* in 1961. He hosted a weekly radio program *Ragophile* and was the co-author of *Rags and Ragtime: A Musical History*. His odd first name came from his father, Robert, a suburban doctor who took his name and spelled it backward to form his son's name.

Chapter Twenty-Seven
The Sixties: Albert King and the Integration of Music

1955-1968

Silence fell over the room and all eyes and ears turned to me. I have never felt younger, whiter, shorter, or more insignificant. Albert leaned forward and extended his long arm directly over my shoulder to get at some popcorn. Leaning close, he smiled, flashing two gold front teeth, and told me to commence my questioning.

-- **Alan Paul**, ***Guitar World***

Albert King was born into the tradition of the Mississippi Delta. He could barely read or write. He slapped the mule behind the plow before he was 10. He chopped wood and picked cotton. His father died when he was young. He shunned school, drawn instead to the guitar. His mother took him to church where he sang the Christian gospel.

He was the kind of man who could have fit tidily into the mythical foundations of the blues.

But that wasn't Albert King. No, he was a big, round man who didn't fit a small square of stereotype. Certainly, the music that made him a guitar hero to a huge audience in the sixties and beyond contained a shadow of the Delta, but the essence and originality of his sound, the things that grabbed a generation, didn't come from the Delta at all, nor did they come from Chicago. No, like so many American musicians, Albert King's music is part of that St. Louis thing.

Born April 25, 1923, on a plantation near Indianola, Miss., his real name was Albert Nelson, but he changed it for a marketing ruse, claiming to be the half brother of B.B. King. Albert's father played guitar but died when Albert was eight. About that time, the family -- there were 13 children -- moved 150 miles north into Arkansas.

King learned guitar on a homemade "diddley bow" -- a contraption made of a single string of bailing wire run between nails on a board, sometimes held taut over a glass bottle. King was left handed and even when he got a professional instrument (in the early forties) rather than restringing it for the left hand, he played it upside down, creating a unique sound.

Once in Arkansas, during the Depression, he sang with the Harmony Kings Gospel Quartet. Then, still in his teens, he played his first professional gig as part of In the Groove Boys, a blues outfit from Osceola, Ark. He made his first appearances in St. Louis on the road with this band but was still working day jobs in Osceola to make his rent. His climb onto the stage was slow.

He moved to Little Rock, gigging and driving a bulldozer, watching his "half-brother" B.B. King and other Delta singers rise into the charts. In 1952, by now 29, he landed in Gary, Ind., and had a brief stint with Jimmy Reed as a drummer, playing in South Bend, then in Chicago, where he made a record in 1953.

The record went nowhere and King moved back to Osceola. He caught up with In the Groove Boys for more local gigs. He spent his days back in the cab of the bulldozer. A mere mortal might have given up on professional music. But in 1956, the relentless King, by then 33 years old, moved to St. Louis, where he settled on the East Side.

There he developed a blues style all his own, the urban, psychedelic combination that left his Delta roots in the distance, a wisp of fog over the morning cotton fields. His new music instead grew in the hot afternoon of the urban mash at the confluence of the Mississippi and Missouri rivers, where he was surrounded by people like Ike Turner and Chuck Berry, by Benny Sharp and Oliver Sain, by Johnnie Johnson and Henry Townsend.

And there, too, he ran smack into the tradition of a man he had heard about when he younger, a man named Lonnie Johnson, the New Orleans transplant who in St. Louis in the twenties began playing the guitar note-by-note with a pick.

King wasn't the only player who fell under Johnson's influence. It was Lonnie who laid the ground for all the electric players who followed him. Henry Townsend said it was Lonnie Johnson who inspired him to pick up the guitar after he heard him play at the Booker T. Washington Theater. B.B. King put Lonnie ahead of Robert Johnson in influence. The singer and record producer Victoria Spivey, a close friend of Johnson's in St. Louis, said that by the sixties, "Everywhere I turn I hear Lonnie."

And Albert King said it was Lonnie Johnson's playing who got him to give up his gospel singing and start playing guitar in the first place. It was this Johnson he was trying to copy when he picked on his diddley bow as a child. Johnson had taken the guitar from the back of the stage to the front. Along with him, he also took Albert and B.B. and Jimi Hendrix and Eric Clapton, Stevie Ray Vaughn and Duane Allman.

King settled near the Mississippi River in Brooklyn, Ill., about three miles north of the Eads Bridge. He started meeting all the established St. Louis players. He took part in the early morning cutting contests that were part of the traditions of the city all the way back to the ragtime piano players, honing his style as he went, competing with Townsend, then primarily a guitar player. He played with people like Roosevelt Sykes and the second Sonny Boy Williamson. He met Ike Turner and Little Milton. He heard Chuck Berry, who said that in the mid-fifties King, "began climbing into the Ike and Chuck level."

In 1959 Milton arranged for King to record for Bobbin Records, the local label Milton ran with Bob Lyons. By then, just at the brink of the sixties, King had purchased a new Flying V electric guitar, first offered by Gibson in 1958. This was billed as a "space age" model, appearing not long after the Russian Sputnik space flights.

Played upside down and left-handed, he began to make this guitar cry, bending the strings to gain a powerful effect on his raucous blues. This was something along the lines of what Lonnie Johnson did when he mimicked the violin on his guitar. King also started to add the St. Louis horn sounds of the R&B revues, styles that dated back to the riverboat era and the Deep Morgan saloon jams.

"Let's Have A Natural Ball" brought some of King's personal confluences together. It was recorded as a Bobbin single in 1956 but not released on an album until 1962 on an LP called *The Big Blues.* The song previewed what became known as the surfer guitar style ("This Morning") and the album also included "I Walked All Night Long" that directly affected the Texas guitar champion Stevie Ray Vaughn.

King in those days also developed a ferocious style on stage and off. He was the original Big Albert, his muscles honed from the bulldozer. He developed a reputation for a fast temper.

"A person needed to pay attention when Albert was mad," said Stacey Johnson, the male Ikette, who played with King in the mid-fifties.

Bobbin Records lasted in St. Louis only until 1962 and King was its most productive artist, cutting 18 sides in four years. Oliver Sain, who personified the St. Louis horn sound in the sixties, was another regular on the label, often providing backing. Drum prodigy Kenny Rice, who had learned his chops from Lige Shaw growing up in the all-black North County suburb of Kinloch, also found a mighty groove with King.

A Bobbin tune called "Don't Throw Your Love On Me So Strong," released in 1961, was Albert's first hit, reaching No. 14 on the *Billboard* R&B chart. By the time of that recording, he had put together the Original Albert King Band, a group that for the first time on a King record included Chuck Berry's piano player and composing partner Johnnie Johnson.

Five years earlier, when King saw Johnnie playing with Berry at the Cosmopolitan Club, Albert turned to his companion and said, "I gotta get that man in my band. That's the baddest piano player I ever heard." Johnson was loyal to Berry but King wouldn't give up trying to hire the piano player.

When Berry went to jail in 1960, Johnson threw his hat in with King. By then the piano man was tired of the Chuck Berry rock 'n' roll machine, and it was a relief to return to his blues roots. He'd played "Maybellene" enough.

There was a marked improvement once Johnnie was on board in the King band. Johnnie "played what we call 'a full piano,' meaning he just filled it up," said the band's tenor sax, Harold White, who was Jimmy "Night Train" Forrest's brother-in-law and a respected East Side player. Johnson "wasn't choppy like a lot of pianists," White added. "He filled in the gaps and there was no empty intervals. He had what we call soul in his playing."

Rice, the band's 17-year-old drummer, said he would sneak in and "watch all those big bands like Albert, Ike Turner, and Chuck (Berry) so it was a big honor to be playing with one of my heroes at such a young age." Buttercup Thompson on trumpet, Freddie Robinette on baritone sax and Lee Otis Wright on bass filled out the band.

Here was the band where King iced the cake of his sixties urban style that separated him from all the other blues guitar players to ever take the stage.

With White leading the horn section and Johnson in control of rhythm, the band played a far bigger sound than the sum of its parts. Albert was soaring; beginning to demonstrate what critic Dave Marsh says was "the most amazing string bending known to humankind." His blues never lapped into the danger zone of technical doodling, he remained a tender spirit and told his story through his honey-smooth, one-of-a-kind voice. He used the St. Louis style of leaving plenty of space between the notes. He was never in a hurry to show off his own brilliance, leaving his musicians to play.

To say he was a big man was an understatement. He stood at least 6-feet-5-inches, weighed in the 250-pound range. His hands were as big as Chuck Berry's. He was sometimes called the "Velvet Bulldozer." He liked big hats. He had plenty of hair, kept close cropped and neat, no Afros for Albert. His face often gleamed with sweat as he played through and around the notes, sometimes looking up, other times keeping close track of the right hand on the frets. He sometimes wore a little mustache under his nose. He sometimes clenched a corncob pipe during long solos. He favored tailored-suits on stage, ala Lonnie Johnson.

The music was there, but in the fifties the recognition lagged behind. He switched to King Records in Cincinnati, where Lonnie Johnson had his forties hit "Tomorrow Night," a song that impressed B.B. King because of "a dreamy quality to his singing and a lyrical way with the guitar," attributes that could easily be ascribed to the style Albert King developed in the sixties.

The Bobbin and King sides (later collected in the Modern Record CD *Let's Have a Natural Ball*) did well in the Midwest but King felt he was not getting enough money. He jumped King for another St. Louis label, Coun-Tree, where he recorded four sides not far from his home in Brooklyn. Again, he felt he wasn't getting the money he deserved. He loathed the idea of going back to the bulldozer.

So, he took to the road. And here he found his new audience. Here was the birth of Blues Power.

The sixties were upon the youth of America and the blues got new life behind covers by The Rolling Stones and the Eric Clapton bands. The British blues had landed on American shores.

To this point in segregated America, the blues had not crossed over in any major way from the black to white audiences. B.B. King didn't hit the *Billboard* Top 40 until 1964 and even on the R&B charts traditional blues had been fading.

As the civil rights and Black Power movements grew, many African Americans came to associate blues with the slavery days and the cotton pickers of the South. Rising middle and upper class blacks felt blues came from the other side of the tracks. The churches frowned on blues -- it was still the devil's music. White adults saw it connected to the nasty, gut-bucket areas of the urban scene.

But in the white youth culture something very different was happening.

One of these young whites was Tom Maloney, born in 1952 and raised in suburban South County during the era of the Catholic Youth Club's entertainment nights and the Teen Town dances sponsored by the city. There Maloney saw people like Bob Kuban, Marcel Strong and Johnny Kaye, bands that put mixed race groups up on the stage, playing music that appealed to white teenagers.

Maloney talked about the days of yore from his comfortable bungalow in South St. Louis County, in a town called Mehville, an inner-ring suburb not far from the Mississippi River, just a mile and half from the house where he grew up.

At the Teen Town dances in the early sixties, Maloney remembered:

> There would be a black person singing or maybe playing a horn, so this was white kids kind of thumbing their noses at the tidy, white racism of the day.
>
> When I grew up if a black guy walked down the street he could get his ass kicked real quick. About when I was a junior in high school I was in a band called the Malibus which had some black singers. We rehearsed in my house with the black singers. My parents were cool with it, but I'm sure the neighbors were on their porches going, "what are those guys doing here?"
>
> My biggest musical influence as a kid was my parents. They both played piano in the living room. I'd hear them play "Maple Leaf Rag." They'd nail that happy, joyous sound. As a little kid that sound of the piano sent me into joy and ecstasy. I used to run in a circle and just dive into the pillows.
>
> There was something in me -- in 1963 I got my first transistor radio that I could hold under my pillow late at night. Each song was like a half-hour TV show in my mind. Where I lived down by the Jefferson Barracks Bridge close to the river late at night on a foggy night you could pick up Little Rock, Arkansas. I would hear what we would call the crying string -- I didn't know it was Albert King.
>
> The crying string is the same as the bent string. It probably comes from all the way back to Django Reinhardt, from pulling the string to get the vocal quality out of the note. Albert took that whole thing to another level. He was a perfect example of someone who didn't have a musical education but had it in him and did something with it.

Maloney played all through high school, putting together bands for the Teen Town shows, playing different styles of guitar in different groups -- the Nightmares, King James and the Royals, the Chaparells, the Malibus, the Dynamic Soul Revue, Soul Tree, up into the late sixties, still not out of high school.

On some of the gigs his bands opened for Bob Kuban, the star of the Teen Town shows, a big man in the rising music culture of youth in St. Louis.

Kuban was white, born in 1940 in North County, near the river just over the city line. His introduction to music was through the junior high public school class on music the young Chuck Berry appeared at an assembly. When Berry asked for somebody from the class to come up and play the drums, Kuban put up his hand. This took a good deal of courage.

Berry was impressed as Kuban winged it through several songs, managing the rhythm as Berry played "Maybellene" and a few other hits. Berry finished the set. Kuban never forgot:

> He turned around to me and said, "Hey, you're a pretty good drummer. How long you been playin'?"
>
> "About ten minutes."
>
> "Whadda' ya' mean?"
>
> "I've never played before in my life."
>
> "You kiddin'!'
>
> "Naw."
>
> "'Well, you did one heck of a job!" Chuck said.

The exchange changed his life forever. In 2016 Bob Kuban was still making a living playing the drums.

At 18, in 1958, Kuban began sitting in with Ike and Tina at the Club Imperial. He started his own band that year after graduating from Riverview Gardens High School, Bob Kuban and the Rhythm Masters. His popularity grew, he played dozens of Teen Town gigs then graduated to the clubs and parks, forming Bob Kuban and the In-Men in 1963, with a lead singer named Wally Scott, a soul-style white singer who appealed to the black crowd and added a new dimension to the Kuban band. One fan remembered the group playing at a Rec Center in Jackson Park, next door to the near North Side projects.

There were 200 people inside the field house at the park and 2,000 more people outside. Kuban and the band pulled up to the tennis courts on brand new BSA motorcycles, blue and orange. They were bad boys, Brando style.

Kuban, Scott and the In-Men played Gaslight Square virtually every night in 1963 and 1964. In 1966, the band hit the charts with its one and only hit, "(Look Out For) The Cheater," reaching No. 12 on the *Billboard* Top 40 and No. 7 on the *Cashbox* survey. Kuban was suddenly on *American Bandstand*, playing Whiskey A Go Go in Los Angeles and the Cow Palace in San Francisco.

Kuban and his band opened the new Busch Stadium downtown in 1966 after being the last to play at the old Sportsman's Park (which by then had also been called Busch Stadium) on the North Side. The band was lifted by helicopter and flown from one ballpark to the other.

"A stage was erected in center field," Kuban said. "The gates opened and hundreds, probably thousands, of screaming teenagers ran out on the field to dance to our music."

Scott, the singer, started seeing dollar signs and quit the band to go solo. The band was never the same, even with a brief reunion. Scott toured with a cover band but his later career never got off the ground. The former singer disappeared in 1983 and his body was found four years later, the victim of an apparent plot by Kuban's former girlfriend and her lover, James Williams, who was convicted of killing Scott and his own former wife.

Kuban held the act together, however, playing into the twenty-first century at dances at ballrooms like the Casa Loma, doing fully retro soul-oriented shows to mostly white audiences of still-dancing baby boomers, doing most of the singing himself from a perch behind his drum set at the front of the stage.

Maloney had seen a lot of Kuban by 1970, even performing his own versions of the soul sounds of the sixties. One night, at the Prince Nights Palace in suburban Belleville, Ill., on the East Side, Maloney's style was forever changed. That night he stopped in to see Albert King, by then riding his *Live Wire Blues Power* album that had been recorded at the Fillmore Auditorium in San Francisco.

> This was after the soul thing happened and died out, then the hippies embraced the blues. The hippies were bringing Albert King into their little psychedelic dungeons. When I saw Albert King in 1970 it changed me. I'd never heard anybody like that and I dearly love Albert King to this day.

King had changed by 1970, too. When he went out on the road during the mid-sixties, a scout for the Memphis-based Stax Records spotted King. In 1966 he recorded "Crosscut Saw," a blues tune first made in 1941, but redone completely with the power of the Flying V and an Afro-Cuban rhythm. He stayed with the Memphis label until the mid-seventies when Stax started falling apart.

His second year with Stax was the breakout -- the album *Born Under a Bad Sign*, an LP Marsh calls "a blues monument." King told his audiences, sweetly, "If it hadn't been for bad luck I'd have no luck at all." On the recording he wasn't backed by his St. Louis band but instead used the Stax house group, the Memphis Horns and Booker T. Washington.

But he was able to put in play all the experience gained in St. Louis and now, a full-grown 44 years old. King was on his way to San Francisco where his urban style of tenderized blues struck gold with the psychedelically infused, recently longhaired white crowd of young music lovers. Here were the teens and college students who didn't buy into Pat Boone. Here King would finalize his urban, psychedelic blues -- reaching about as far from the Delta as a man could wander.

The San Francisco connection in the person of rock promoter Bill Graham walked into Ike Turner's Club Manhattan in East St. Louis in 1967. He watched a set and offered King $1,600 to play three nights at the Fillmore Auditorium, which had just launched with acts like the Grateful Dead, Jefferson Airplane and the Allmann Brothers.

"In '66 and '67 the average 17-year-old kid did not know who Chuck Berry or B.B. King or Albert King were," Graham said. At the time audiences were still divided in most of the big cities along racial lines. Keith Richards said "it was a brave move" by Graham to throw mixed acts on the stage in front of a white crowd.

But that's exactly what Graham did. He booked the young Jimi Hendrix and the English bluesbreaker John Mayall with Albert King for a performance on Feb. 1, 1968, and used the same mixed race approach when he opened Fillmore East in New York later that year. King was thrilled. Color didn't matter to Graham. King said:

> I hadn't made $1,600 for three days in my life. He said, "How much deposit do you want?" he asked. I said, "$500" and I got it.
>
> We started out at the old Fillmore but it was too small, so we had to move to (the larger) Winterland. He kept us for three more weeks. People had been waiting to hear me play for a long time before I even showed my face out there.

These shows not only changed the way guitars were played around the world, but also made King one of the few singers to attract white fans while maintaining his black audiences in places like East St. Louis and on the R&B circuit. The San Francisco gigs have become so famous they generated one of the most valuable posters of the rock era, a flying eyeball drawn by the artist Rick Griffin that sold for over $7,000 on eBay in 2012.

Opening night at the Fillmore East in New York City. March 8, 1968, had Albert at the top of the bill. The undercard included the folk singer-songwriter Tim Buckley and a new group called Janis Joplin and Big Brother and the Holding Company, who were in the midst of making their landmark *Cheap Thrills* album. King thus joined a list of the biggest names in rock, as shown by the bookings Graham laid on the New York City club in the next two months: The Doors, The Who, Traffic, Jefferson Airplane, Hendrix, Sly and the Family Stone and The Byrds.

These venues -- the two Fillmores and Winterland -- were far smaller than the bands became accustomed to soon thereafter, the Fillmore in San Francisco held just 900, Winterland about 2,000 and the Fillmore East a bigger 3,600. Not long after, in the early seventies, the rock acts started filling stadiums with crowds of 15,000 and up, pushing Graham out of business. He closed both Fillmores in 1971.

A bitter Graham said:

> The rock scene in this country created by a need felt by the people, expressed by the musicians, and, I hope, aided to some degree by the efforts of the Fillmores turned into the music industry of festivals, 20,000 seat halls, miserable production quality, and second-rate promoters.

King continued to play anywhere he could. He appeared in small clubs as well as the bigger venues, adopting his Blues Power theme as a compliment to Black Power, drawing a white audience like no other black performer. In October 1968 at a midtown New York club called Steve Paul's The Scene, King stood before a buzzing amp and declared: "If you don't dig the blues, you got a hole in your soul. This is what they call blues power" and blasted off into the night.

The New York Times reviewer noted: "For most white audiences at least, the blues has always been a musical nicety to be observed and applauded at a respectable distance. But Mr. King, one of today's blues heroes, takes his idiom and lays it in the audience's lap, right there with the cigarette ash and ketchup stains."

He appeared on *American Bandstand* that same year then took a tour of England before an appearance back in New York at Carnegie Hall. On Feb. 22, 1969, King played a joint performance with the St. Louis Symphony at Powell Hall, a remarkable jump from places like the Club Manhattan and the Cosmo Club.

Also in 1969, he was back in Europe with the American Folk Blues Festival and played other festivals at Ann Arbor and Newport. He opened his own club in Oseola, Ark., in 1970 and appeared on a national television commercial for Miller Beer. He kept up the schedule as best he could, running all through the seventies, still based at his house in Brooklyn, Ill.

In 1971, he told *Newsweek* magazine that finding the white audience meant, "my days of paying dues are over. Now it's my turn to do the collecting."

In the late seventies, he and his touring band appeared frequently at J.B. Hutto's, a new club in the western St. Louis suburbs, a new joint that drew the white crowd to black blues bands like Albert King's. The house band there was led by Larry Davis, a black singer from the East Side, and attracted a white crowd of blues lovers who would make the drive to see local St. Louis acts mixed with national shows.

Another club that attracted a white audience to see black performers, Mississippi Nights, had opened downtown at Laclede's Landing by then, but it mainly featured national acts.

Hutto's was an "important part of the St. Louis story," said Ron Edwards, who was Henry Townsend's playing partner during the last decades of his life. Edwards remembers a B.B. King show on the North Side in 1968 where he was one of only four or five white people out of a crowd of 300.

The same was often true on the East Side in the sixties and seventies, but Hutto's was different, with mostly white crowds watching people like King, John Lee Hooker and Lightnin' Hopkins play the relatively small venue.

For Albert King, the shows at Hutto's were just another in the continuing growth of his white audiences across the country, even playing Radio City Music Hall in New York.

Perhaps Albert King's most enduring performance came in 1983 on a Canadian TV show that became the CD/DVD *In Session*, a celebration of a 10-year friendship between the black man who started out on a homemade diddley bow in Mississippi and Stevie Ray Vaughn, a white guitar player from Austin, Texas, whose abusive alcoholic father worked in an asbestos factory.

Stevie Ray, born in 1954, got his first guitar when he was seven, a toy model from Sears. Living outside Dallas, he learned to play by ear, listening to the Albert King, B.B. King and Otis Rush on records. He dropped out of school at 16, got a job at a hamburger joint, playing in a band at night. By 1983, he had made his first album and was on the brink of becoming one of the greatest of America guitar slingers.

Vaughn first met King on the stage of Antone's, the Austin club that introduced University of Texas students to the blues. Antone's was similar to Hutto's in that it brought the black blues players to the attention of a white college oriented audience.

King agreed to let Vaughn sit in that first night in 1973 for one song, but after hearing the young Texan, Albert kept him on stage the rest of the night. Vaughn then made a habit of sitting in whenever King was in Austin. The *In Session* performance was filmed Dec. 6, 1983, capping the year Stevie Ray broke out.

Earlier that year, in May, SRV's King-inspired licks helped propel David Bowie's "Let's Dance," to No. 1. The following month Vaughn's *Texas Flood* was released, led by his first hit single "Pride and Joy." The album reached No. 38 on the *Billboard* chart, an impressive showing for a blues album.

The televised session included many of King's core concert material with only one SRV tune, "Pride and Joy." The music washed along with the hipness and ease of two pros doing what they do. King was obviously in charge, remembering "little Stevie," the "skinny kid" who sat in at Antone's. Throughout, King coolly reminded his protege who was the boss. King says he heard "Let's Dance" and comments, "Yeah, I heard you doing all my shit on there. I'm gonna go up there and do some of you'rn."

The two guitar players were flanked by the solid rhythm section of Tony Llorens on organ and piano, his brother Michael on drums, and the East St. Louis bassist Gus Thornton — the same outfit that accompanied

King on his two post-Stax Fantasy albums — *San Francisco '83* and *I'm in a Phone Booth Baby*, the last two records of his career.

The band is totally oiled.

Both lead players show a magic restraint as they play together, sometimes with King on rhythm, at other times with the roles reversed; but neither noodles, neither leaps forward to show how good they are; neither loses the tender tone of the King repertoire. They are easy with one another, the tough-guy Albert King reputation replaced with one of a dad teasing a son. And while producing two hours of exceptional music the work also documents the change in America 20 years after the civil rights movement began; the young white Texan showing his utter respect and admiration for the big urban black man.

Vaughn later remarked:

> During the lunch break, Albert went around to everybody looking for an emery board. I didn't think anything of it. We were jamming on the last song and come to the solo and he goes "Get it, Stevie!" I started off and I look over and he's pulling out this damn emery board, filing his nails, sort of giving me this sidelong glance. I loved it! Lookin' at me like "Uh-uh, I got you swinging by your toes." He's a heavy cat.

Gus Thornton, the bassist based in East St. Louis, had by then become a fixture in King's band. Sitting in his home along tree-dappled East St. Louis neighborhood in 2013, Thornton's memory of the days with Albert was bright.

Thornton was a product of the Young Disciples, the Black Artists' Group-inspired program for young musicians in East St. Louis. He joined when he was 17, in 1968, and first met Albert King in 1970.

> The Young Disciples were opening for Howlin' Wolf and this guy comes around. He was joking. He really put us down, calling us a Sears and Roebuck band, so I asked the bandleader who was this guy talking about us like that. He says "Albert King." I had seen him on TV but never in person. We talked a little bit. And that was the last time I saw him until some years later.
>
> By 1977, I was working with Jerry Walker, Jerry and the Soulful Five. We were playing up there in Brooklyn (Ill.), the

> 2 a.m. and 7 a.m. shows. We'd come outside when the sun was already up. Albert used to come in there and he'd sit at the bar and he and Jerry would trade shots with each other. Albert lived up there. Strip clubs surrounded his house.
>
> Walker was also from Brooklyn. He was in the police up there. Albert, too, he was some type of cop but not a real cop. An unofficial cop up there. He had a badge. Honorary. When I was 15-16 I used to listen to his records and me and the Disciples we used to try to play him.
>
> I started working with Albert in '77, just days before Thanksgiving. The snow was this deep that winter and he had been after me to join his band. He wanted to replace the bass player, but he was a guy I knew and I was reluctant to replace him. But Albert's manager, he had been the trumpet player in my band. He said Albert wanted the bass player out anyway so I decided it was okay. I'd never been to California.
>
> We loaded up the bus at the Holiday Inn down there in East St. Louis went to Palo Alto, Calif. We did San Francisco and just worked our way back.

Thornton was full time in the band for two years, then came off the road to play locally in St. Louis for various groups as one of the most in-demand bass players in the city. His style is so smooth he blends in with just about any blues group. King would see him occasionally and "about once a month" would call Thornton.

> We would talk and he would try to get me back into the band. I really didn't want to go back in. I was working with people like Ralph Butler and Kenny Rice, a whole lot of local gigs, really hip gigs, right around here. I didn't need to travel. I was meeting a whole lot of people and things were working out pretty good around here.
>
> But he asked me (in 1983) to come back in and as a favor I said I'd go back out there for a little while. So I went out there and I just ended up staying. We did the *San Francisco '83* album; we did the *Phone Booth* album. Now, usually guys use the studio cats for their albums, but Albert he wanted to use us. People talk about how hard Albert was on people. He can be but if he really likes you, he likes you. I got back in the band just in time to do that *San Francisco '83* album -- same people as the *In Session* album.
>
> We were driving back from California and he told us to be ready in a few weeks because Stevie Ray was going to produce an

> album with us. Something went wrong and it never happened. But we did the other thing with him, *In Sessions*. Didn't rehearse it at all.
>
> The record company brought it all together. The night before we had a meeting about what we were going to do and the next day we did it. *In Session* took one day. Started early in the morning. Had lunch and went back in and by the end of the day we were done. When we did that I took it for granted. I knew it was a really cool thing to cut something with Stevie because he was my friend and we all liked each other and liked the way we all played.
>
> I had heard Stevie on the David Bowie album when I was listening to the radio one day. On that song 'Let's Dance' it sounded like Albert playing a solo. You know nobody could really play just like Albert but this sounded like Albert. I found later that was Stevie Ray Vaughn.
>
> That day when we had the Session thing I asked Stevie about that and he said when he had that solo he couldn't think of nothing else to do so he just started playing some Albert King licks. Real cool.

King continued to record and tour until he was 69 years old. He was in Memphis following a show in Los Angeles when he died from a heart attack Dec. 21, 1992. He was planning to tour Europe with B.B. King and Bobby "Blue" Bland at the time of his death. He still maintained his home in Brooklyn, the house that was surrounded by strip clubs where there was easy access to an early morning shot of whiskey.

Stevie Ray Vaughan wasn't so lucky. He died before King, killed in a helicopter crash in Wisconsin at the height of his career, Aug. 27, 1990. He was 35.

Another exceptional player who got started in the sixties in St. Louis was the horn master, Oliver Sain. Arriving in 1959, Sain stayed and stayed, played and played, a nationally known sax player whose weekly gig at an intimate downtown blues club delighted music lovers all the way up to his death at age 71 in 2003.

Sain's music was a big part of that St. Louis thing during six decades -- a mixture of style and presence, his straight blues, the big horn sound, the crowded stage of musicians, the R&B, the soul, the Motown, the tender gentleness of musical finesse, of talent and of learned skill. He ran a recording studio and taught school kids, he mentored, he cajoled, he promoted St. Louis whenever and however he could.

All the while Sain remained true to his school -- musical excellence. In 1977 he said:

> In America everything has to be defined and put in a little cubbyhole. This is this, this is that. This is R&B. This is urban contemporary. To me it's all just music. I've only heard two kinds of songs in my life -- one that I like and one that I don't like. If I don't like it you can name it anything you want to and I still won't like it.
>
> People in the studio will ask, 'Do you have this gadget, or that computer?' I say, if you don't have a song you don't have anything. It's the song that counts. If you don't have that you don't have anything.

Sain's wake, held at Eddie Randle's Funeral Home on the North Side was a standing room only music festival, featuring an open casket and marked by a host of faces smiling and happy, each shedding a tear or two for a man clearly loved all around the city. The bassist Jimmy Hinds ran the show, telling the players to just line up and get up when he called their name.

Those names included Little Milton, the man who invited Sain to come to St. Louis in the first place; Marsha Evans, who started recording with Sain in the sixties; Robbie Montgomery and Herb Sadler, regular players for Sain's boyhood friend, Ike Turner; Erma Whitesides, the soul singer; the harp player Papa Ray ever "The Soul Selector;" and keeping the beat, the drummer Kenny Rice.

Also present was Johnnie Johnson, whose first comeback album was produced by Sain. Johnson had jumped into the national eye through the 1987 film *Hail! Hail! Rock 'n' Roll* and was playing with Tom Maloney in the Sounds of the City in 1992 when Sain approached him to do a solo album. Johnson had turned down Chess for such a record, but Sain was a friend, someone he felt close to as part of the St. Louis community, someone he had jammed with and sat-in with.

And, the ever-humble Johnson said, "I figured that I probably wouldn't get the chance again if I turned it down this time. So I told Oliver I would do it."

Sain recruited an all-star St. Louis lineup for the sessions -- including Stadler, who had been Turner's guitar player; singers Stacey Johnson, another Ike alum; and the former Chess singer Barbara Carr. St. Louis stalwart Steve Waldmann added another guitar and Keith Robinson handled the drums. Sain himself, of course, provided the sax.

The result was *Blue Hand Johnnie*, which includes a memorable version of "O.J. Blues," a Fats Washington song that highlights the rapport between Johnnie and Oliver. The record includes two more Washington tunes plus two originals -- "Slow Train" and "Way South" -- by Sain. The record also includes "Johnnie's Boogie" the pianoman's theme song he played live for many years but never recorded. Sain's direction gave Johnnie, who was still doing a lot of drinking, the chance he needed to step into the national record stream.

"I was real intimidated by the whole thing," Johnnie said later. "I just let Oliver do what he thought was best."

Sain said: "Johnnie was tired of fooling around with musicians. I think that was one of the things that drove him away from Chuck Berry and that whole rock 'n' roll scene. As long as I was running things he was happy because he knew I was reliable and that I would take care of things for him."

Johnson earned best keyboardist in the *Rolling Stone* critics' poll for the album, getting some long-overdue recognition. Had their been a category for best favor to a deserving friend in need, it would have gone hands down to Oliver Sain.

At Oliver's wake, one of the most emotional performers was Marsha Evans, who met Sain in the sixties when she was a teenager singing with the Young Disciples. He heard her and asked her to come to the studio where she sang backup for one of his new singers, Fontella Bass, who recorded the 1965 hit "Rescue Me."

Evans remembers the days:

> I started going to the studio and started hanging around, that's what you did, if you were serious about making it in this business that's what you did, you wound up in Oliver's studio.
>
> He would call me. Background. I'd do all three parts. One day, he said Fontella Bass wants to record an album. My heart

> skipped a beat. This was after the time of "Rescue Me." We recorded her album *Free* -- that album is one of the best she has ever done.
>
> Offbeat. Avant-garde. She wrote songs for it. Sain wrote for it. She and I did all the background. I was really good at making up the background, I have to admit that. Harmony was my thing. I would just make it up and we'd do it.

Free was released in 1972, a commercial flop. Bass was married to Lester Bowie, the BAG trumpet player and jazz innovator, and the record is Bass' homage to the style and taste of the BAG period. But recognition came over the years and *All-Music* calls *Free* a "lost classic that deserves space in any record collection . . . a deeply spiritual and moving examination of post-civil rights America."

Evans and Sain became lifelong friends. He put her on stage many times, especially at the Wednesday shows every week at BB's Jazz Blues & Soups in the nineties.

She visited Sain's bedside the day before he died and sang "Let's Stay Together." Sain moved his fingers along with her as she sang as if he was still playing his sax. "We'll always be together," she told him.

Oliver Sain was born in Dundee, Miss., on March 1, 1932, and moved often with his mother as a child, spending a short time during the forties in St. Louis, but mostly living in Memphis. Sain was the grandson of Dane Sain, the guitarist in the Beale Street Sheiks.

In Memphis, he attended high school and learned to play the bugle and the trumpet. He went to Mississippi Valley State in Bena, but soon quit and returned to Memphis to join a band led by his mother's husband, Willie Love, a piano player who backed Rice Miller (Sonny Boy Williamson II) and appeared on the *King Biscuit* radio show.

In 1949 Sain moved to Greenwood, Miss., where he met the talent scout Ike Turner. He was drafted in 1951 during the Korean War and came out in 1953, relocating in Greenville, Miss., where Love and his mother were then living. There he met Little Milton Campbell and learned to play the tenor sax.

Campbell subsequently moved to St. Louis and Sain went to Chicago to reunite with Howlin' Wolf, whose band he had been in West Memphis in 1950. In the Chicago days in the late fifties Sain also played with Elmore James and met the Chess brothers.

He appeared ready to join the Chicago blues full time until he got a call in 1959 from Milton, who was playing in Turner's Club Manhattan and needed a sax player for a night. Sain lived in St. Louis from that night on.

"There was so much musical activity in St. Louis," Sain said. "Between Ike Turner, who also had moved here, and Little Milton, Clayton Love and others it had the people in a trance. People in the area, if they like you, they embrace you."

He formed his own band with Little Milton as the singer and cut 16 sides with Milton and on his own for Bobbin Records before 1962 when his old friends from Chicago, the Chess brothers, swallowed it up. Milton followed the label to Chicago but Sain stayed in St. Louis, building the Archway Sound Lab on the North Side. There he became a double threat -- musician and producer.

"He was a perfectionist," Bass said. "And he always talked as he worked, talked to the other musicians to inspire us. We inspired each other. He had a lot of humor about everything, from politics to the junkie on the corner. Oliver was a character."

His version of "Harlem Nocturn" from Bobbin in 1962 and his *St. Louis Breakdown*, a greatest hits collection issued in 1996, are must-have Sain records, encompassing a career that touched the St. Louis music scene directly in the heart. As Little Milton put it, "I don't think you can mention anything musically about St. Louis without mentioning Oliver Sain."

Fontella Bass was a woman who wouldn't toe the record company line even after a million selling hit. Like Sain, she was given an emotional St. Louis sendoff after her death, which came late in 2012 at age 72. At her memorial she was praised as a woman who lived life "straight up -- no chaser," and as someone who added a "great deal to the rich landscape of St. Louis music."

Her best known performance was certainly the 1965 hit, "Rescue Me," but it was only a brief moment in a musical career that spanned seven decades, from the time she first started to sing at the Pleasant Green

Baptist Church in North St. Louis until her stunning appearances at the Big Muddy Blues Festivals in the early days of the twenty-first century.

Her family was drenched in church music. Born in St. Louis on July 3, 1940, by age five she was playing the piano with her grandmother, Nevada Carter, at the Buddy Walton Funeral Home. Her mother, Martha Bass, was a gospel singer who took the 9-year-old Fontella on the road with her in the Clara Ward Singers. In a 1989 interview, Fontella remembered the tour:

> Everybody would sing their song and ask the church to pray for them. I sang "How About You," and pretty soon people would come to church just to hear me sing that song. But when I had it real good, the other kids started to sing that song, so I had to learn another one.
>
> We would sing from town to town. One night we'd go 50 miles, the next time another 50, the next night we'd get to New Mexico, and on like that clean over till we'd get to California. When we'd get tired of singing, we'd just fold up and come home.

At 16 years old she met Willie Mae Ford Smith, a St. Louis performer who was one of the most important gospel singers of the twentieth century -- and now a fellow member of the St. Louis Walk of Fame on Delmar Boulevard.

Fontella wanted to join Smith's group on the spot. Her mother wouldn't allow it. Instead, Bass got a piano job at the Showboat Club, which was anchored in the Mississippi near Chain of Rocks. Bass' singing always reflected these early gospel influences, especially once they blended with her other experiences while growing up -- the rock 'n' roll she was hearing on the radio, and in the blues and jazz at clubs in East St. Louis.

In high school she started playing piano with J.C. Story & His All-Stars. The band won a talent contest preceding a Ray Charles concert. The *Argus* ran her photo and she was on her way. She graduated from Soldan High School in 1958, singing teen hits like "Tutti Frutti."

She auditioned as a singer for a show passing through St. Louis and for two weeks sang with the Claxton carnival, making an enormous $175 a week. She was preparing to go on to the next town when, "my mother literally dragged me off the train."

But she lasted long enough with the carnival to catch the eye of Little Milton at about the time he and Sain were running Bobbin records. Bass' first appearance on a record came in 1962 on Little Milton's Bobbin cut "So Mean To Me." Her first solo was "I Don't Hurt Anymore," a bluesy vamp on a song made a hit by Diana Washington.

Also in 1962 she appeared (on Bobbin) on a fine example of the work being done by the Oliver Sain Orchestra on "Honey Bee." In 1963 she recorded "I Love a Man" with Ike Turner and the Ikettes and did a duet with Tina Turner on "Poor Little Fool," a song written by Sain and released on the Dallas label Vesuvius in 1964.

But Bass had a dispute over a New Year's Eve booking in 1965 and quit Sain. By then Bobbin had closed and along with Little Milton she decided to move to Chicago. She married Lester Bowie, who had also quit Sain. They decided to try a new city.

Milton, now working for the Chess, had a No. 1 R&B hit in March 1965 and Bass signed with the label. There she teamed with Bobby McClure, who was also from St. Louis and had sung with the Sain revue. They had a hit "Don't Mess With a Good Thing,"

Ironically, the song was written by Sain -- he'd penned it on a car ride while driving from St. Louis to Chicago for the session. Producer Billy Davis added a dance beat called the Uncle Willie and Fontella went onto the *Billboard* charts for the first time, lasting for 15 weeks and reaching into the Top Five.

Davis then brought in Phil Wright, an arranger, and began putting together the song that would become "Rescue Me." Davis recorded Fontella's vocals during a long session at the Chess studios and also got the bass line and the drum. The writing credit went to Carl Smith and Raynard Miner, who had written the Little Milton hit.

Bass always disputed the writing credit on "Rescue Me," saying she "was tricked out of the publishing" rights.

> Anybody can do rhythm takes. You have to put the melody over the top of them. When we were recording that, I forgot some of the words. Back then, you didn't stop while the tape was running, and I remembered from the church what to do if you forget the words. I sang, 'Ummm, ummm, ummm,' and it worked out just fine.

She was paid $11,000 for the artist royalties, but felt that was too low. All the others concerned said she had nothing to do with writing the song, except Pete Cosey, the guitar player who thought she had "embellished quite a bit, especially the ending."

Davis estimated the record sold somewhere between 700,000 and 1 million copies. But the Chess royalty rate was lower than other companies and to be certified as a million seller the company had to open its books to the Record Industry Association of America. Leonard Chess refused to open his books to anyone.

Either way, the song was one of the label's biggest hits. It reached No. 1 on the R&B charts and No. 4 on the pop charts and lasted 19 weeks. *Cashbox* named Bass the No. 1 female R&B for 1965 and No. 4 in the general female vocalist category behind Petula Clark, Shirley Ellis and Marianne Faithful.

"Rescue Me" made her name and stuck with her the rest of her life, hitting at a time of the increasing popularity of soul music. Some dubbed it the "biggest hit Aretha Franklin never had." It's timing and title helped make a big favorite of the troops in Vietnam, sung along in the jungle with a whiskey bottle in hand.

Fontella didn't get rich. "Rescue Me" led to increased arguing with Chess over the royalties. An LP followed the hit but it didn't sell well, nor did her follow-up single, "Recovery." She decided to go to Paris with Bowie where the couple, talking radical politics and sporting sky-high Afros, joined several members from the St. Louis Black Artists' Group to play and promote black nationalism and avant-garde jazz.

She recorded *Les Stances A Sophie* and *Art Ensemble of Chicago With Fontella Bass* with Bowie, records that had no chance commercially but that are now well-known jazz LPs sought by collectors. In 1972 she returned to the United States and did the *Free* for Paula Records, a company out of Shreveport, La., made with Martha Evans at Sain's studio.

Free includes the powerful cuts like "To Be Free," "Talking About Freedom," and "My God, My Freedom, My Home."

When this didn't sell either, Bass retreated to St. Louis and aside from a single, "As Soon As I Touched Him," in 1977 for Epic, she stopped recording until she found new energy from the church. Her first gospel album, *Promises: A Family Portrait of Faith,* was released in 1991 with her mother and brother.

She was struggling to make a living until she caught a break when American Express used "Rescue Me" in a commercial without her permission. She obtained a settlement that finally gave her the pay-off she was due from her hit. In 1995, she made another gospel LP, *No Ways Tired,* and began singing at the Mt. Beulah Missionary Baptist Church in University City, giving St. Louisans in the know a chance to hear her voice every Sunday morning.

She also parlayed her earlier experiences in Paris to pull off successful tours of Europe and played occasionally around St. Louis. In 2001, she had a memorable appearance at the Big Muddy Festival when she showed off her European touring band, including the St. Louis multi-instrumentalists, the Bosman Twins.

"I wish more people in St. Louis knew about her," longtime friend Dwight Bosman said after her death. "She was known and well-loved all over the world, in Germany, Switzerland, Italy and France, doing international festivals where they would chant 'Fontella, Fontella.'"

She was certainly well-loved by the crowd at the Jan. 4, 2013, memorial, where Dwayne and Dwight Bosman led the horn section for a rousing finish at the Shalom Church City of Peace in Florissant. Evans, who had opened for her in Europe, lived up to her mentor's reputation on "Every Day I Have the Blues" and on the finale where everyone joined in on "Rescue Me," the words and sentiment never more powerful, the voices of the black women throughout the crowded church ringing in perfect harmony.

Outside the Sain sphere of influence, the sixties also saw a number of successful St. Louis rock bands develop, mostly connected to the psychedelic music called acid rock. Unlike so much St. Louis music, however, none were particularly innovative. Still, they had their following:

Mike and the Majestics, which was notable for launching the career of the singer Michael McDonald, who left town in 1970 at age 18, later sang backup with Steely Dan and became a full time member of the Doobie Brothers in the mid-seventies.

He grew up in suburban Ferguson and said, "In St. Louis growing up, music was always very important. You were defined by the music you listened to and that was something you shared with your friends." He had won five Grammies by 2014.

McDonald appeared at a Christmas show at the Fox Theater in 2015, evoking the police shooting of the unarmed black teenager in Ferguson and asking the audience to pray for peace. The show also included the Doobie's protest anthem from 1976, "Takin' It To the Streets." Always an eclectic singer, McDonald moved through the show with something for everybody from Christmas carols to R&B.

The Aardvarks were a major club draw in the sixties who grew long hair and covered Beatles songs like "Paperback Writer," opening for arena shows for Janis Joplin, Iron Butterfly and Traffic.

Mike Newman was the lead singer and guitar player, joined by Jean Burman, on rhythm, keys and flute. The band played at the 1970 St. Louis Pop Festival at Keil Auditorium on a bill that also included Country Joe & the Fish, the Amboy Dukes, Blues Magoos, and the Stooges.

The Acid-Sette was led by Jan Marks and Joe Marshall and covered songs off the radio. They were notable for their slogan: "Take a trip with the Acid-Sette; price of admission . . . your mind."

Other sixties bands included: **Hour Glass (the Allman brothers), Spur, Truth, The Touch, Good Feelin', The Del Rays, Purple Martin and the Belaeraphon Expedition.**

There were two more notable musical adventures in the St. Louis sixties scene: One, the founding of a nationally trend setting radio station, KSHE, and second, the beginning of the Mississippi River Festival, a unique outdoor concert series that hosted a sterling list of folk, rock and folk-rock bands over an 11-year period. Both of these innovative institutions added to the diversity of the St. Louis scene.

FM radio rock -- music that extended outside three-minute Top 40 songs into the psychedelic era of longer, even 12-minute album cuts -- was born in the sixties. Bob Dylan's "Like a Rolling Stone" paved the way for the new radio format, a song fully six minutes long released in the summer of 1965, at first cancelled by its parent Columbia Records.

The song was saved when Shaun Considine, release coordinator for Columbia, took a discarded copy to a newly opened New York disco popular with celebrities and media people. The demo was played and the next day a DJ for a top 400 station who had heard the song called Columbia and demanded a copy.

The song was recorded on both sides of a 45 record and flipped over by the disc jockey. Naturally, other bands and record companies saw the commercial possibilities and in the spring of 1967 the first of the new format stations started on FM in San Francisco. St. Louis joined the trend immediately, opening its own FM rock format outlet within six months.

The station was KSHE, "The Pig" and was the last vestige of that era still broadcasting 2016, still playing the format as "Real Rock Radio."

The KSHE ad proclaimed in November 1967:

> Hear the voice of the raconteur.
>
> Thrill to the sound of music precisely programmed for the avant-garde.
>
> Make way for the newest . . . most fascinating concept in broadcasting in this century . . . a veritable kaleidoscope in worthwhile listening.
>
> You'll hear radio in depth with all the excitement of Gaslight Square, the sophistication of the New Yorker, the charm of a first kiss, the worldliness of the Wall Street Journal. Don't miss this new adventure in sound. KSHE 94.7 megacycles.

The station had been on the air since 1960, started in the most humble fashion by Ed Ceries, a ham radio enthusiast in suburban Crestwood, as a "beautiful music" station for suburban housewives. He built a studio in his basement and began broadcasting as K-SHE, the Lady of FM, working a shoestring budget. He sold the station four years later for $50,496 (including his $40,000 antenna) to Century Broadcasting of Chicago.

The station was moved out of the basement into the city, to an old office building on the west side of town where it remained for 22 years, hiring such DJs as Ron "Johnny Rabbit" Elz and gradually adopting the full-on rock format -- "200,000 watts of flower power."

Meanwhile, around town, at Washington University, in Forest Park and at Keil Auditorium, the big cats arrived. The Beatles played at the new Busch baseball stadium in 1966. The Yardbirds appeared at Wash U, outdoors in the central quad, the Jefferson Airplane flew in July of '68, followed by Quicksilver Messenger Service at the World's Fair Pavilion in Forest Park. Eric Clapton and Cream previewed its unreleased the *Wheels of Fire* album at Kiel in April of 1968, paid $3,500, plus 60 percent of the gross and a case of St. Louis brewed Falstaff beer.

A crowd of 3,500 attended, the first big rock show promoted by KSHE, a show memorable to many as the night drummer Ginger Bakers threw up on his drum kit during "Toad." For the first time the smell of marijuana smoke wafted through the city's most venerable auditorium.

Clapton didn't last long with Cream and in 1970 formed Derek and the Dominoes with St. Louisans Bonnie Bramlette and her husband Jim Delany, who had been playing as **Delany & Bonnie**. Bramlette was born in Alton, Ill., and began on Gaslight Square with the Allman Brothers. She joined Albert King at age 14 and the Ike and Tina Turner Revue at 15. She was the first white Ikette, playing for the first three days "in a black wig and Man Tan skin darkener."

She also sang back up for Little Milton and Fontella Bass, working at Archway Studios. She left for Los Angeles in 1967, and formed Delany & Bonnie & Friends, opening for Clapton, Leon Russell, George Harrison, Dave Mason, Rita Coolidge, Gram Parsons and John Lennon before joining the Derek and the Dominoes. With Russell she co-wrote the anthem "Give Peace a Chance."

She and Delany broke up in 1972, but her career rolled along over the years, acting, song writing and recording as a solo act, making 11 albums and appearing on TV on the Rosanne show and *Fame.* She also made occasional appearances in St. Louis, usually in small venues with little publicity.

The sixties St. Louis rock scene also included the Castaway Club where KSHE broadcast live shows three days a week. According to the code for the club, located in the North County suburbs, 400 was the capacity, but 1,000 people packed the place. Light shows started there in 1968 with Chuck Berry performing with Michael McDonald in his backup band. But in 1969, a local paper carried a story saying drugs were being sold openly and the club closed shortly thereafter.

The Rainy Daze Club in Chesterfield was bought by a member of the Belaeraphon Expedition, a high school student named Todd Kromer, who ran it as a rock club beginning in April 1967. The club featured locals as well as out of town bands and also featured a full-scale psychedelic light shows.

Free shows at Forest Park evolved into larger and larger crowds with bands like Kiss, Rush, and the Charlie Daniels Band. This was the stage for annual KSHE birthday parties that have continued into the present.

Across the river on July 1, 1969, Janis Joplin and Big Brother and the Holding Company opened the Mississippi River Festival, an outdoor concert series like nothing else in the country. Here was a continuing outdoor weekly showcase of folk, rock and blues that saw performances ranging from Arlo Guthrie to the Paul Butterfield Blues Band every weekend all summer for 12 seasons. The series, sponsored by Southern Illinois University in Edwardsville, was an easy drive from St. Louis.

Sold as "Woodstock without the mud," the first season drew a total of 90,000 people, most on blankets and in lawn chairs, under the stars on warm summer nights.

The third show of that first series, July 21, 1969, a show headlined by The Band, may have been the most intriguing, known for a surprise appearance by a singer billed as Elmer Johnson but who was really Bob Dylan. This was his first appearance on the road since a show in New York held as a tribute to Woody Guthrie over a year earlier.

A blogger named Guam was there:

> The Band concert was (at) an outdoor venue with the crowd on a slope down to the stage. Mostly, the crowd was stunned to see Dylan come onstage with The Band. He had been in seclusion for years. His singing fit in nicely with The Band in a basement tapes sort of way.

In 1971, The Guess Who drew 32,000, a record crowd for the run of the festival. In 1975, the full season drew 250,000, the high water mark of the festival's history. These outdoor shows, always including the odor of marijuana, had been controversial and usually short-lived around the country. To be sponsored by a university and not a rock promoter made the Mississippi fest unique and was responsible for its longevity.

There had been a backlash from conservative elements of the community throughout its history but the festival held together until 1980. By then one of its major defenders at the university died. The locals complained about traffic and the noise. The word was spread that drugs (marijuana) were being sold at the venue. There were break-ins of parked cars. Also, the quality of the music drifted lower, with bands like The Captain and Tenille appearing. By then, Ronald Reagan was president; the sixties and the seventies were over.

After the 1980 season, the university pulled the plug. Over 1 million tickets were sold in 12 summers.

The Grateful Dead never appeared at the Mississippi River Festival but the band played St. Louis early and often. The San Francisco psychedelic heroes worked their way through numerous St. Louis venues in the late sixties, reaching the Fox for a defining monument in Dead history and a magic moment in St. Louis music history -- the night a ham radio buff from a small town on the East Side saved the show for the Grateful Dead.

The night was Feb. 2, 1968. The hero of the story, Bob Heil, started playing the pipe organ in the giant Fox Theater when he was 14. He was 28 when he got a frantic call from Jerry Garcia desperately seeking a sound system for that night's show. The Dead's soundman -- the LSD maker Stanley Owsley -- had been arrested and both Owsley and the sound gear went to jail.

Garcia called the right guy. Heil was as familiar with the giant speakers in the theater as anybody. He had been experimenting with bigger and bigger systems, ones that he brought from home and proved capable that night of filling a 20,000-seat theater with rolling-free Dead sound, live and in person.

> I was experimenting with amps. At first it was like a passionate hobby, like the radio, but I soon saw these guys coming in with these little columns under the impression that they were going to fill up a 20,000-seat hall. In 1968 there was nobody else doing

> what I was doing, so I felt that I had to build some kind of monster sound system for them.

The show was a musical watershed. The sound that Heil produced made it possible for the big stadium era that began early in the seventies and gave rise to the big guitar bands like The Who, Foghat and Iron Butterfly. A reporter for the trade magazine *Performing Musician* met Heil years later.

> He still shakes his head at the thought of what went on that night. The culmination of the music industry dropping the innocent trappings of the hippie era and now calculatedly targeting a mass mainstream audience, as personified by the once musically meandering Grateful Dead on the cusp of releasing the tighter, radio-ready songs of the seminal *Workingman's Dead* and *American Beauty* albums.
>
> And Bob Heil, who turned a lifelong fascination with ham radios and music into what would become the template for the modern concert touring sound system that was ready to roll the moment the moment arrived.

That night at the Fox was nothing but another part of that St. Louis thing -- the man, the band and the speakers coming together in 1968.

Chapter Twenty-Eight
Baseball: Browns, Blacks and Birds

1927-1968

It requires some courage to predict that colored baseball is to supersede the white brand, but someone has to think ahead . . . We therefore wish to go on record that it will. If the Browns and Cardinals admit the St. Louis (black) Giants to a three-cornered series for the local championship this fall, it will begin in St. Louis right away.

-- St. Louis *Post-Dispatch,* 1912

On Sunday, Sept. 28, 1953, the St. Louis Browns played their last game, watched by 3,174 fans in Sportsman's Park. Some of the customers swung an effigy of outgoing owner Bill Veeck from a rope in the right field stands then flung the dummy into the field.

When the 12-inning loss to the Chicago White Sox finally came to an end, the stadium band played "Auld Lang Syne." The teams filed off the field to no great ovation, the Browns' misery completed by their 100th defeat of the year. The Sox finished in third place in the American League, 11 1/2 games behind the pennant-winning Yankees, who took their fifth straight AL title. The Browns were buried in the cellar by a 46 1/2 games.

The St. Louis team was so hard up as the season wound down it had been rationing baseballs for weeks. No batting practice was allowed the last two days for fear of losing precious hardballs. On the final day, with the game going on and on, no new game balls were available to put in play and the umpires began recycling used balls that earlier in the game had been tossed aside. The *Globe-Democrat* reporter said the last ball "had a gash on it from seam to seam."

Browns manager Marty Marion remembered his last season in St. Louis as "a disastrous year."

> You weren't winning. You had no support. Hell, it was just horrible. And there was nothing you could do about it.
>
> All I can remember, after the (last) game all the kids came around the clubhouse, and everybody was throwing uniforms away, giving them to all the kids. We threw them from the clubhouse window. All the kids were outside. I wish I had kept mine.

Veeck purchased the Browns in 1951, giving long-suffering fans reason for hope. He used a series of gimmicks to raise attendance from 295,000 to 520,000. He sent a 3-foot-7-inch batter to the plate. He gave fans the final say on managerial moves. His first baseman juggled hardballs between innings. He hired former players who had performed for the rival Cardinals, including the great Rogers Hornsby. Marion himself was a former Cardinal star. But Veeck could never find a way to win games.

"I would have run the Cardinals out of St. Louis, I'm sure of it," Veeck said.

He was looking good in his second season with the Browns when the owner of the Cardinals, Fred Saigh, ran into tax problem. Saigh, also owner of the Railway Exchange Building and other downtown landmarks, bought the Cardinals in 1947 from an ailing Sam Breadon, the Pierce-Arrow car dealer who had been a part of the Cardinal ownership since 1917.

Veeck salivated as out-of-town interests swarmed toward the Redbirds. He dreamed of having the city's baseball fans all to himself. But the Cards were saved for St. Louis when Gussie Busch, the Budweiser beer baron, flexed his monetary muscle. He bought the Cardinals and Sportsman's Park for the Anhauser-Busch Brewing Co., a move that sent Veeck looking for a way out of town.

Thus, 1953 became a lame duck year for the Browns, lots of rumors but no action. He moved the team to Baltimore in 1954.

The Browns had never had much success on the field, with several owners and a loyal following, but always in the shadow of the Cardinals, which became the second best team in baseball behind the powerful New York Yankees.

Only once did the Browns reach the World Series and there, in 1944, they ran into none other than the hated Cardinals. It was the last World Series where all the games were played in the same ballpark.

The futility of the Browns stretched over 52 seasons, from the time in 1902 when the original Milwaukee Brewers were transplanted to St. Louis and joined the newly formed American League. There had been plenty of baseball in the city before that, dating back to play as a child's game in the first half of the nineteenth century. With the Civil War still very much active and people traveling the country by rail more than ever, professional baseball in St. Louis started in 1864.

That year, a contractor named Jere Frain, who also played second base, formed the St. Louis Empire Club and started play at Lafayette Square. Other clubs, many with players who were veterans of the game from the Army camps during the war, formed up, the Unions and the Reds being two of them. An old-timer remembered Frain's arrival: "A great tall boy came among us. He was a stranger who had come from somewhere in the East, and on our field (Lafayette Park) he laid out a diamond and showed us how to play the modern game of baseball."

Baseball in the city spread from there. By the end of the nineteenth century professional baseball settled down into two leagues, National and American, comprised of eight teams each. A World Series was first played in 1903 between the winners of the leagues. By then St. Louis had its two teams -- the Cardinals in the National League and the Browns in the American.

From 1902 to 1953 the Browns came in first once, second twice, third five times and fourth five times -- a total of 13 first division. The club finished in second division (fifth through eighth) exactly triple its first division finishes -- 39 times, including 12 seventh place finishes and nine last place finishes.

The Browns lost 100 or more games 10 times and 90 to 100 games 19 times. The team finished a remote 64 1/2 games out of first in 1939, a year when they lost 111 games. This was not a fluke. There were five other years when the team was over 50 games behind.

When Veeck packed the circus truck and took the show to Baltimore, the Browns had just come off their eighth straight losing season. The stretch, from the end of the war to the end of the Browns, included three last place finishes, four seventh place finishes and once in sixth, a mere 37 games behind.

A millionaire named Phil Ball had been running the Browns for six seasons in 1926, the year the Cardinals battled the Yankees for the championship. Since 1875, there had been a ballpark on Grand Avenue where Sportsman's Park was built in 1882. The Brown Stockings played there until 1891. The park sat empty until 1902 when the Browns were formed.

The cozy park on the North Side was pleasant for the fans, who could almost reach out and touch the players, but not for the Brownie players or for the owner. Ball was nearly broke by 1920. He made a deal with the Redbirds, allowing the Cardinals to use the park for $35,000 a year rent plus half the maintenance.

Ball expanded the stadium to 33,000 seats in 1925, just in time for the Cardinals to cash in on Branch Rickey and the great teams of the twenties, thirties and forties. While the Browns were losing, losing, losing, the Cardinals brought the World Series to Sportsmen's Park nine times between 1926 and 1946, winning six championships.

Even with the rent from Breadon coming in Ball couldn't produce a winner. There were no Stan Musials on the Browns. Ball, an argumentative sort who didn't know the game very well, died in 1933. He didn't get to view his team's upcoming horror show.

The war years were the only time the Browns played well for any extended period, with first division finishes in three out of four years and a berth in World Series in 1944. The appointment of Luke Sewell as manager mid-way through a dismal 1941 season paid dividends in 1942 when Sewell turned his shortstop, Vern Stephens, into a power hitter.

The Browns by then had Bill DeWitt, a protege of Rickey's, who in 1936, was instrumental in rounding up a group of men led by the Kansas gas baron Donald Barnes to buy the Browns.

Once Barnes and DeWitt took over, the carnage of the thirties was forgotten, especially in 1944. The Browns finished third in 1942, still 19 1/2 games away from the top. In 1943, the club slipped to sixth but was only eight games under the .500 win percentage mark. Then in 1944 the team began to win, taking a solid lead in the early part of the season, before falling behind by September.

With five games left, the Browns and Tigers were deadlocked on top of the American League standings. That's the way it still stood on the last day of the season, Browns against New York at Sportsman's and Detroit playing Washington in DC. The Tigers were beaten by Dutch Leonard's knuckleball. The Browns sold out the park in their game against the Yankees, needing a win to take the pennant.

Sewell went with Sig Jackucki, a right-hander with a 12-9 record and a drinking problem. Appearing nervous before the big game, a teammate gave him a shot of whiskey before he warmed up and the fortified Jakuki pitched well, giving up just two runs. Chet Labbs, a lightly used outfielder, hit a pair of two-run homers, Stephens added another long ball and the Browns won 5-2.

Meanwhile, the Cardinals had managed to keep Stan Musial, Marty Marion, Mort Cooper and other first-run players out of the military draft. The Birds rolled to their third straight National League crown, running away from second-place Pittsburgh by 14 1/2 games. Musial, the youngest rookie of the year in history, hit .347 at age 22. Fellow-outfielder Johnny Hopp batted .336 and Cooper was 22-7.

Stephens, who batted .299 and led the league in RBIs with 109, led the Browns. Behind him, however, was a dimly lit lineup of players like singles-hitter Mike Keevich. The Cardinals had averaged .275 for the year, 20 points higher than the Browns, and the bookies weren't taking many bets on the Brownies in the Series.

Still, baseball will be baseball and the Browns quietly snatched the opener before 33,242 fans. Cooper lost the game even though he gave up just two hits, one was a two-run homer to George McQuinn, a wiry Virginian with sneaky power who surprised Cooper. The Browns held fast behind Denny Galehouse (9-10), who was pressed into the start because of the tight pennant race and got the 2-1 victory with a seven-hit complete game played in just four minutes over two hours.

The Browns fell behind in the second game 2-0 in the fourth but tied the score with two of their own in the seventh. The game went into the 11th, where the American Leaguers had a chance after McQuinn belted a lead-off double.

Then third baseman Mark Christman, a local product who batted .271 during the year, tried to bunt McQuinn to third, but the Cardinals pitcher, Blix Donnelly, took a chance and made a blind throw ahead of the runner, a throw that went into his third basemen's glove perfectly on the bag.

McQuinn was out, the threat squelched and the game ended in the bottom of the frame when the Cardinals' Whitey Kurowski laid down a good bunt and Ken O'Dea, who made a career as a pinch hitter in five World Series, slapped home the winning run. The Browns were by no means finished, however, and took the third contest 6-2, scoring four runs after two were out in the third on five singles and a wild pitch. The Cardinals roared back with a 12-hit attack the next day, beating Jackucki to even things at two games each.

The Series thus came down to best two out of three.

Mort Cooper, the Cardinals' ace, was ready for this fifth game and stopped the Browns on a seven-hit, complete game shutout that turned the Series to the favored Redbirds. The National Leaguers finished the job quickly with a 3-1 victory in a sixth game that took only two hours, six minutes. The finale was keyed by a Stephens throwing error on a rushed double play and a 3 2/3- inning shutout relief stint by Cardinal righty Teddy Wilkes, a diminutive New Yorker who had been the best Redbird hurler that season after Cooper.

He came in with two Browns in scoring position, one out and Christman again in a crucial spot. He tapped a roller to third, however, and the lead Brown runner was out at the plate. Then Red Hayworth, the Browns light-hitting catcher (2 for 17 in the Series), came up with two out. Wilkes got him to fly to center then finished off the Browns with nine straight outs in the final three innings to secure the Series.

Even in defeat, management was good to the Browns after the game, throwing a party at the Chase Plaza. Jackucki wasn't there; he got a head start on his drinking and kept it up for two more days, found in Illinois broke and dirty, lying in an East Side gutter. But an unknown Samaritan recognized the Brownie pitcher and did the right thing. As Jackucki teammate Don Gutterridge put it, they "cleaned him and sent him home."

The party only lasted two more years for the Browns. In 1945, the team had another winning year at 81-75, six games behind in third place. The '45 team is best known for its one-armed outfielder Pete Grey, the only such player to make the majors. He played 61 games, hitting .218 in his only major league season.

In 1946, the team finished in the first division for the last time, placing third behind Detroit and Washington. Stephens led the league with 24 homers and Nels Potter, a right-handed pitcher who won 19 games in 1944, had his last good year with a 15-10 record, 21 complete games and a 2.47 ERA. But Potter, like the rest of the team, was on shaky ground, pitching only three more years with just 13 more victories.

In 1946, the club sunk back to its lowly status in the second division, finishing 38 games behind in seventh place, even as the Cardinals won their sixth championship after a fourth straight National League title. That was, however, the last NL crown for St. Louis until 1964.

The Browns got nowhere near the top of the AL again. In 1947, the club found the cellar and for the rest of the team's life finished either seventh or eighth every year, losing 101 games in 1949, 102 in 1951 and 100 in the final season, 1953.

By then, even with increased attendance spurred by Bill Veeck's antics, the team was heading out the door. Not that Veeck didn't give it a mighty go in his three seasons in St. Louis. Veeck had won the 1948 AL pennant in Cleveland and on July 5, 1951, bought the Browns from the DeWitt brothers. Veeck was the son of a man who had been the Cubs' general manager and had spent his life in baseball, sometimes successfully, always controversially.

Buying the Browns, however, was Veeck's greatest cliff diving act. "Many critics," one writer said, "were surprised to know the Browns could be bought because they didn't know the Browns were owned." Immediately after arriving in town Veeck began attacking the Cardinals' announcer, Harry Carey, and barred Fred Saigh from his usual special box seat at the stadium. He installed a gallery of pictures of Browns' players in the shared stadium and held a gala celebration of the fiftieth anniversary of the American League.

Falstaff beer, brewed in St. Louis by the Lemp family, sponsored the celebration and Veeck promised plenty of beer as well as a "special surprise" for the event, to be held Aug. 19, 1951, a day that lives in baseball history.

As the fans entered the park that Sunday, a doubleheader against the Tigers, they were given a slice of cake, a box of ice cream and a mysterious, tiny can of Falstaff. The Browns lost the opener of the twin-bill and the party started between games.

A band made up of ballplayers played at third base, the first baseman did juggling tricks around the bag and a trampolinist leaped up and down at second. Then a wagon carrying a giant birthday cake emerged and was hauled to the mound, and the PA announced the arrival of a "brand-new Brownie."

Out of the cake, much to the puzzlement of the 18,000 fans, popped Eddie Gaedel, 3-feet-7-inches tall, weighing 65 pounds. Veeck had outfitted Gaedel, who had been hired through a Cleveland theatrical booker, in the uniform that had been made for former team owner Bill DeWitt's son, Bill DeWitt, Jr. The number on the back of the shirt was changed from 6 (the son's age when he got the uniform) to 1/8. Eddie was told he would bat leadoff in the bottom of the first.

Gaedel was no baseball player and once he realized he was being sent up to face a major league pitcher with a hardball in his hand, he tried to escape from the clubhouse. A Veeck assistant told Gaedel there was a sharpshooter on the stadium roof who would stop him from leaving the stadium if he tried to run away.

The smallest hitter in major league history thus went up to bat. The umpire was aghast, but the Browns manager was carrying Gaedel's signed one-day, $100 contract in his pocket and the little man, overcoming his fear, stepped into the box. The pitcher, a lefty named Sugar Cain, thought about throwing underhand to the plate, but instead tried to pitch the ball into the tiny strike zone. He failed in four tries and Gaedel trotted down to first where he was replaced with a pinch runner. The crowd cheered and laughed in delighted.

The uniform was given back to the 9-year-old DeWitt Jr., who by 1995 had become principal owner of the Cardinals. When Veeck was inducted into the Baseball Hall of Fame in 1991, DeWitt still had the uniform and it went to Cooperstown complete with the "1/8" on its back. One of the most popular items on display in Cooperstown, the uniform returned to

St. Louis in 2014 and was installed in the new Cardinal Hall of Fame at Ballpark Village next door to Busch Stadium.

Gaedel died 10 years after the stunt after a mugging in Chicago. He was 36. Cain was the only ballplayer to attend the funeral.

Later, Gaedel's bat -- a scale model made for DeWitt -- was stolen from Eddie's mother by a man posing as a representative of the Cooperstown Hall of Fame. But the bat was eventually returned to Gaedel's family and was auctioned for $44,000 in 2013. A photo of Gaedel in his uniform (but not at bat) was also sold that year, going for nearly $7,000.

A different picture, this one showing Eddie standing at the plate, his little bat cocked in hitting position, is the most lasting memory of that day. Jack January of the *Post-Dispatch* took the photo from the on-deck circle, hoping Gaedel wouldn't swing at the ball. January's shot captured the catcher on his knees with the ball in his glove, Eddie looking almost fierce, ready to swing even though the pitch had already safely passed him by.

That same summer Veeck obtained a tall right-hander for the Browns' pitching staff, 45 years old, well experienced but with only two seasons in Major League Baseball. His name was Satchel Paige, an African American who was perhaps the greatest pitcher of all time.

Paige had to wait nearly all his life before blacks were allowed to play in the league, the color line finally broken in 1947 by Jackie Robinson of the Dodgers. Paige was the seventh African American to play in the majors, hired by Veeck in Cleveland in 1948 in time to help (6-1, 2.48) the Indians win the AL championship and the World Series. Veeck brought Paige with him to St. Louis in 1951.

Organized African-American professional baseball didn't begin until 1920, but blacks had been playing ball much longer than that. In 1887 there was the League of Colored Base Ball Clubs, in 1906 the International League of Independent Professional Baseball Clubs and in 1919, the Negro Texas League.

The first game of the National Negro Baseball League was played in Indianapolis with the local team, Taylor's ABC's, losing to the Chicago Giants on May 2, 1920, by a score of 4-2. The St. Louis Giants, which had existed for decades in one informal way or another, were one of the eight initial Negro League teams, finishing third that season with a record of 33-23.

The St. Louis team played its first official Negro National League game against the Kansas City Monarchs in a Mill Creek Valley ballpark later called Stars Park. The opening day crowd filled up the stands and many were contained behind ropes in the outfield. Play was stopped in the ninth when the crowd stormed the playing area after a Giants' batter was hit by a pitch. Order was restored but the Giants lost to the Kansas City 2-1.

The American Giants of Chicago took the first black pennant and won the NNL flag again in 1921, followed closely by St. Louis and Kansas City. In 1922, a remodeled Stars Park opened for the Mound City team, revamped and renamed the St. Louis Stars. The stadium was a comfortable ballpark located about where Harris-Stowe University is today. The Stars played there for 11 seasons and were one of the top three teams in the NNL during that period.

The Stars led the half-season standings (the pennant races were divided in half with the two half-season champs holding a playoff for the league title), in 1925 and 1928. In 1930 the Stars won the first half title and defeated Detroit in a playoff for the league title. In 1931, as the league started to suffer from the Depression, the Stars won both first and second half titles in the six-team circuit. But after the two championship seasons the club folded.

Paige never pitched for the Stars but he had appeared frequently in St. Louis before joining the Browns, first as a fire-balling strikeout pitcher then as a rubber-armed junkball specialist. As that, he managed to get major league batters out as late as 1965 at age 59 when he appeared for one game as the starter for Kansas City, throwing three shut-out innings, giving up just one hit in his fifth decade of pro baseball.

The seventh son of a gardener, he was born LeRoy Paige in Mobile, Ala., July 7, 1906. At age seven he took a job at the train station where he rigged up a pole to carry bags and earned the nickname that followed him the rest of his life. Satchel wasn't much for school and found himself running with Mobile's street gangs. He was arrested when he was 12 and sent to reform school. There life improved over his days on the streets and there he began to play baseball.

Paige joined a Mobile semipro team when he was 18, in 1924. He was nearly 6-feet-4 and weighed just 140 pounds. But Paige had already developed the whipping motion that gave him the stamina to pitch nearly every day and the ability to fire a fastball that only rarely could be hit. By 1926, he was making $200 a month pitching for the Chattanooga Black Lookouts in the Negro Southern League.

From there, Satchel followed the money, playing for black pro teams in Birmingham, Baltimore and Nashville before joining the Pittsburgh Crawfords. The club featured several of the best black players in America but did not belong to the league. The Crawfords rolled up a record of 99-36 in 1932, playing against teams both black and white, led by Paige's 23-7 record. The next season his record was 31-4 and he was paid $250 a month ($3,600 a month in 2014 dollars), the highest pay of any black player.

Even in the depth of the Depression, Satchel saw the fans crowding the stands every time he pitched. He demanded more money for the 1935 season. His contract requirements came not long after he beat the Cardinals' top pitcher, Dizzy Dean, and a squad of white players 1-0 in a 13-inning exhibition game in 1934, a game played at Wrigley Field in Hollywood, Calif., a replica of its Chicago's Wrigley Field.

Dean, the stalwart leader of the Cardinals during the thirties and star of the 1934 World Series, said he had seen most of the great pitchers of the era, and "I know who's the best pitcher I ever seen and it's old Satchel Paige, that big lanky colored boy."

One the fans at the game in Hollywood that day was Bill Veeck, a 20-year-old college dropout.

> The greatest pitchers' battle I have ever seen. Even in those early days Satch had all kinds of different deliveries. He'd hesitate before he'd throw. He'd wiggle the fingers of his glove. He'd wind up three times. He'd get the hitters overanxious, then he'd get them mad, and by the time the ball was there at the plate to be swung at, he'd have them way off balance.

After failing to reach a deal with Pittsburgh, Paige pitched for a mostly white team in 1935 that barnstormed from a base in Bismarck, N.D., and then went back to the Crawfords in 1936. The next spring agents of Domincan Republic dictator Raphael Trujillo followed Paige to New Orleans and convinced Satch to jump to Santo Domingo.

Trujillo also got other players, including former St. Louis Stars outfielder Cool Papa Bell, to join up. Not surprisingly, Trujillo's team, with Paige on the mound, won the local tournament for the dictator. Paige and the other players were kept under armed guard at a private villa. Despite high pay and plenty of perks, Paige and the others rushed out of the country after the tournament.

The appearance by Paige and the other black stars in the Domincan Republic helped turn the country into a major source for pro players in the United States. In 2016, there were 83 major leaguers from Dominica out of the total of 800 players in Major League Baseball.

Another dispute with the Crawfords led Paige to another country with strong baseball ties – Mexico. Pitching almost every day in the Mexican League, his great right arm gave out in the 1938 season. His explanation for his sore arm didn't have anything to do with the amount of games he was throwing. Satchel blamed the spicy Mexican diet, which he said upset his delicate stomach. Still, he could not raise his arm above his shoulder and one doctor said he was finished as a pitcher.

Not quite. He developed a curve and some junk, including a trick pitch he called the hesitation ball. With his arm rested, he went back to the Kansas City Monarchs, and led the team to four Negro American League titles beginning in 1939. In 1942, he won three of the four Monarch victories in the first Negro World Series since 1927.

Paige settled down in Kansas City during the forties, pitching for the Monarchs as a kind of roving star, playing in both league games and exhibition games, awaiting the integration of the major leagues. The call came from Bill Veeck in 1948.

Like so many things in America, black baseball existed in a parallel universe before integration, separate and unequal, developing at about the same rate as its white counterpart.

The first pro game between African Americans is considered to be a contest between club teams from Jamaica, Queens, and the Weeksville Unknowns from Brooklyn that took place in 1859 in New York City. After the Civil War, black leagues sputtered in and out of existence, none sticking around long.

In 1884, a 27-year-old catcher named Fleet Walker was the first acknowledged black to play in the white major leagues, appearing on the roster of the Toledo team of the major league American Association, playing 42 games and batting .263. Another black player, however, may have been first, the more obscure Bud Fowler, who jumped from major league team-to-team beginning in 1878.

Both Walker and Fowler played during the 1887 season when seven black players were found on rosters in the International League, a Triple-A league just below the majors. Altogether that year, 33 black players were performing professionally in various minor leagues and Jim Crow didn't hide their presence.

But the influx of black pros into the minor leagues stopped there. A reaction from the racist community that ran white baseball was led by the Cubs' manager Cap Anson, who one writer described as holding "repugnant feelings, shown at every opportunity, toward colored ball players." Anson engineered the imposition of a self-regulating, informal agreement among the owners to bar blacks from the majors that took effect in 1888 and lasted until 1947.

The pressure to integrate built with the success of the Negro League in the twenties and thirties. Crowds of 8,000 to 10,000 regularly attended games to watch players like Paige, Cool Papa Bell, Josh Gibson, Hooks Dandridge, Home Run Brown, Mule Suttles, Leon Day and Hilton Smith.

Bell was the best player to perform for the St. Louis Stars. He was born in Mississippi and came to St. Louis in 1917. His playing days began on the semipro Compton Hill Cubs. He went on to another semipro team in East St. Louis where he worked in a packing plant before joining the Stars in 1922. He was considered the fastest player in the Negro League, routinely ripping his way from first to third on a sacrifice bunt.

Bell was an outfielder and a leading hitter on the Stars' title-winning teams of the late twenties, routinely batting above .350. In 1974 he became the fifth Negro League player to be inducted into the Baseball Hall of Fame (Paige was the first). He retired from playing in 1946 and became a scout for the Browns in 1949. He lived in St. Louis the rest of his life, a familiar figure at City Hall where he held a job as a security guard. Bell died at 88 years old in 1991.

His bronze statue sits outside Busch Stadium along with other Hall of Famers. He has a star on the Walk of Fame, a street named after him and was ranked No. 66 on *The Sporting News* list of the game's greatest players.

Mule Suttles was another Star, playing on the team from 1926 to 1931. With 129 home runs, he is considered one of the best long-ball hitters in the Negro League. He once hit a ball over the 60-foot centerfield fence in Havana, Cuba, a ball that sailed into the sea. In five Negro League all-star games he compiled an .883 slugging percentage and won the 1935 game with an 11th inning homer.

As the Negro League players remained in their segregated status, other sports renounced Jim Crow.

In 1936, "The Brown Bomber," Joe Louis, won the heavyweight boxing championship; Jesse Owens won four gold medals at the 1936 Olympics and in 1940 the Harlem Globetrotters, then a serious pro team, won the world basketball tournament. Civil rights legislation began in 1936 when FDR established the Office of Minority Affairs. And soon thereafter the nation saw its first black congressman, first black general and the first voting rights act. But no black baseball players.

In 1938, the owner of the Washington Senators, Clark Griffith, said, "There are few baseball magnates who are not aware of the fact that the time is not far off when colored players will take their places beside other races in the major leagues."

On July 4, 1941, the first black baseball game since 1921 was held in Sportsman's Park, a contest featuring the Chicago American Giants and the Kansas City Monarchs. KC won 11-2 behind the pitching of Satchel Paige before a crowd of 19,178.

Later that year, on Oct. 5, another St. Louis crowd of over 10,000 paid to see Paige pitch against Bob Feller, the Cleveland fire-baller who had won over 20 games three straight seasons. Feller and his white big league team won 4-1 over Paige and his black barnstormers.

The owners held fast to the color line during World War II, but in 1946 a group of three players, including a young Negro League rookie, Jackie Robinson, appeared at Fenway Park in Boston for an early season tryout put together by the black newspaper writer Wendell Smith.

Robinson had not played much baseball since graduating from UCLA four years previous to the workout, but was deemed "pretty good" by a Red Sox coach who never contacted any of the players again.

Branch Rickey left the Cardinals in 1942 after 25 years to become general manager of the Brooklyn Dodgers. His purpose was to engineer integration. He scouted for two years before he settled on Robinson to mix the drink. One potential prospect was scratched from the list after he was asked what he would do if he was taunted by a fan about his race. "I would kill him," said the potential Dodger.

Robinson was a different sort. He had grown up in a poor family in Pasadena, Calif., attended UCLA but didn't graduate. He played professional football in 1941 then went into the Army. After the war he tried out for the Kansas City Monarchs and won the shortstop job, hitting .387 and attracting the eyes of several scouts.

Rickey had the quiet ability to work behind the scenes and made sure he had support among the owners before he signed Robinson to the Dodgers' farm club in Montreal in 1945. There were two major arguments against blacks entering the big leagues -- that they were inherently not good enough to play with whites and that white fans would boycott the games. Rickey thought both reasons were pure bunk and would melt away as soon the African-American players took the field.

Robinson proved Rickey's point in his first minor league game. He hit a three-run homer in his second at-bat, then bunted for a single, stole second, moved over to third on an out and was balked home after breaking the pitcher's calm by bluffing a steal of the plate. He got two more hits, stole another base and scored twice, again balked home by another jittery pitcher.

By July 1946 he was hitting .354 and had scored 57 runs in 59 games.

This wasn't good enough, however, for the lords of baseball. That same July a group of owners led by the Yankees issued a report on race that was approved by a 15-1 vote (only the Dodgers' dissenting). The report was the last stand against integration of the game. The study purported to show the poor quality of black players and blamed "the problem" on a lack of training. The owners urged a waiting period of undetermined duration.

The wait proved to be of short duration. Robinson saw to that, batting a torrid .625 during a 1947 spring training series with the parent Dodgers. There was no stopping his addition to the Major League roster to open the 1947 season.

He won Rookie of the Year, putting up a .297 batting average, leading the league in stolen bases and sacrifice hits, finishing second in runs scored with 125. His ability had nothing to do with the color of his skin. As he slid safely into home again and again, he was clearly good enough to compete.

The second argument against integration melted away just as Rickey had predicted. Attendance in fact soared, starting with the Dodgers' first series at the Polo Grounds in the Bronx against the New York Giants, where 52,000 saw his first Saturday game.

And, probably more important than RBI or stolen bases numbers was Robinson's ability to turn his cheek to a steady barrage of racist insults from the baseball fans and players. He was isolated on road trips. He was spiked and hit by pitches. Players threatened to walk off. He received numerous death threats. Robinson persevered.

The Browns also broke the color line in 1947, signing two black players, Hank Thompson and Willard Brown. Veeck, with the Indians, had jumped in to promote the second black, outfielder Larry Doby. That made the two Browns the third and fourth black players in the modern era. The Browns hoped the fans would come out to see the new players but the team remained near the bottom of the standings and nothing management could do worked to get the seats filled until Veeck took over in St. Louis in 1951.

Thompson and Brown both joined the Browns in July 1947. Both had been better-than-average good players in the Negro Leagues, both with the Kansas City Monarchs. The Browns, with their usual ineptness, had nobody to bring along the players like Rickey did in Brooklyn with Jackie Robinson. They were brought to the majors cold turkey, with no minor league experience, no spring training. Neither Thompson nor Brown did well in St. Louis, both returning to KC after a month.

On July 20, they appeared in the same game, a contest against the Red Sox at Sportsman's Park. It was the first time two African Americans were written onto the same lineup card in modern baseball history -- Thompson at second base and Brown in center field.

Thompson did not make the kind of splash seen in Brooklyn. He hit a respectable .256 in 27 games in his first month with St. Louis, but decided to rejoin the Monarchs in the Negro Leagues where he felt more comfortable.

He was a solid ball player, however, working his way back to the majors in 1949, playing for the New York Giants until 1956, hitting a lifetime .256 with 129 homers and 482 RBI. He was a part of the Giants 1951 National

League champions and was a key member of the 1954 Giants team that won the World Series, hitting .364 and scoring a team high (better than teammate Willie Mays) six runs as the Giants swept Cleveland.

Willard Brown was a total flop, hitting just .179 in 21 games in the majors. He came to the Browns after a sterling career in the Negro League, so good he was inducted into the Baseball Hall of Fame in 2006. He earned the nickname "Home Run" Brown in Kansas City, leading the Monarchs to five pennants between 1937 and 1942. He then went into the Army, landing in France on D-Day. But he was never the same player after the war.

While in Cleveland in 1948, Veeck, in addition to Larry Doby, added Satchel Paige, the seventh player to break the color line. When Veeck bought the Browns in 1951, he brought Paige with him. During his three-season run in St. Louis, the aging pitcher appeared in 126 games, almost all in relief. His ERA was under 4.00 two of the three years, winning 18 games and saving another 26.

His impact on the team went beyond the statistics. He arrived eight days after his 45th birthday. He put a rocking chair in the bullpen. He did as he pleased, coming and going, warming up or not, always protected by Veeck.

His manager, Marty Marion, said Paige "ran the club. Not me. Everything Satchel wanted, Veeck would do. Veeck loved Satchel." When Paige pitched 12 innings in a 1-0 victory over the Tigers, Veeck bought him a $100 suit. When Marion fined him $5,000 for skipping an exhibition game, Veeck's assistant said, "Hell, Veeck ain't gonna take his money."

Paige estimated he threw in over 2,500 games in his career, pitching winter and summer for 30 years, sometimes pitching in 150 games a year. He estimated he had thrown 100 no-hitters and played for 250 different teams over the years, most of them on a one-day, one-game basis, many semipro or all-star teams during his many barnstorming tours.

Officially, he won over 600 professional games in the Negro Leagues, the majors and the Caribbean. Cy Young, the major league standard, won 511 (46 in St. Louis) out of 908 appearances over 22 years.

When Paige reached the majors in Cleveland in 1948 he was greeted with open arms by the Indian fans, drawing 201,829 in his first three starts. His showmanship never faded, even if the fastball did. Sometimes he would wave his outfielders off the field, seeing no need for their defensive presence.

He lived by his own rules of conduct:

> Avoid fried meats, which angry up the blood;
> If your stomach disputes you, lie down and pacify it with cool thoughts;
> Keep the juices flowing by jangling gently as you move;
> Go very light on the vices, such as carrying on in society -- the society ramble ain't restful;
> Avoid running at all times;
> And don't look back. Something might be gaining on you.

The world of the St. Louis Cardinals franchise, especially in the years from 1926 to 1968, was a very different place in the baseball universe than that of the St. Louis Browns or of life in the Negro League. The Cardinals, after all, had Branch Rickey much of that time and they also had two pitchers, one white and one black, Dizzy Dean and Bob Gibson, who provided the exceptional blend of skill and character needed for a high-class team.

This 42-year stretch, beginning with Grover Cleveland Alexander's defeat of the New York Yankees in the '26 Series and continuing through Gibson's surprising seventh game loss to Detroit in '68, saw the club win eight championships and 12 National League titles. Only the mighty Yankees did better, with 18 championships and 25 American League titles.

The Yanks and the Cards -- the dominating teams in baseball history -- met five times in the World Series during this period, with St. Louis taking three Series and New York two. While the Cards and Yanks were winning 26 World Series, all the other 18 teams combined totaled 16 championships, the most (four) coming from the combined Brooklyn/Los Angeles Dodgers. Only Detroit with three and the Philadelphia Athletics with two managed multiple Series wins, hardly enough to hang a dynastic hat on.

Once the Cards climbed to the top of the National League in 1926, a climb that took 44 years to achieve, they stayed a while, winning the pennant again in 1928, 1930 and 1931, taking the Series in '31 with a four games to three victory over the Athletics.

The 1931 victory avenged a loss to the same Philadelphia club in 1930, when pitchers George Earnshaw and Lefty Grove each won two games, stopping a Cardinal attack that during the regular season had produced 12 players who hit over .300. The end of the dead ball era and the outlawing of the spitter made everyone in the league hit better, but the Cards were the best, until the Series, when only one batter crossed the .300 line.

The next year was a different story as a stocky outfielder who had risen through Rickey's farm system, the 5-foot-8 Pepper Martin, took charge of the Series, lighting up the national spotlight by hitting .500, stealing five bases and scoring five runs in the seven games.

In Game Two Martin stretched a single into a double in the second inning, then stole third and came home on a sacrifice fly; in the seventh, he singled, stole second, raced to third on an infield out and came home in a cloud of dust on a squeeze bunt. In Game Five the Cards took control of the Series, led by Pepper again, three-for-four with a homer, two singles (one a bunt) and four RBIs in the Cards 5-1 win.

By then, Martin ("The Wild Horse of the Osage") was a cool 12-for-18 in the Series. When spitball pitcher Burleigh Grimes got the best of Earnshaw 4-2 in the seventh and deciding game, the Cardinals had their second world championship.

But a big change had also occurred in '32 in Birdland with the arrival of Jay Hanna Jerome Herman Dean, also known as Dizzy. Winning 18 games his rookie year, Dean led the league in innings pitched and strikeouts. He also made an immediate impression on everyone he met, a boisterous country rube spotted by a Cardinal bird dog at an Army camp near San Antonio.

He was the son of a sharecropper, born Jan. 16, 1910, in Lucas, Ark. His mother died when he was seven and his father moved Dean and his two brothers (Paul and Elmer) often, getting whatever schooling he could for his sons, but generally leaving them uneducated.

Dean picked cotton and played baseball. The games sometimes were played just among the family. His father had remarried and Dean had three stepbrothers, enough to compose makeshift teams, using the handle of a hoe for a bat and a baseball made of tape wrapped around a rock or an apple core. Sometimes the brothers gambled on the games against other sharecropper teams, winning or losing a dollar a game. With Jerome pitching the Deans usually won.

Two of the stepbrothers enlisted in the Army and in 1926, Jerome, 16, lied about his age and joined, too. His father vouched for age 18 and made up the town of Holdenville, Okla., as Dean's birthplace to make sure the authorities didn't find out his son's real age. He pitched for the 3rd Wagon Division team then for the 12th Field Artillery, winning a game 4-0 under the eyes of a Cardinal scout, one of the many sets of eyes Rickey had sent into the countryside to drum up talent for his ball club.

Dean's commander told the scout his pitcher could throw hard and had a good curve. He also said Dean was the "dizziest kid I ever had in my outfit." And so it was, Dizzy Dean.

Dean signed with the Cardinals' in 1929 and won 17 games at Class A St. Joseph, Mo., playing under an initial contract that paid $100 a month.

After seeing Dean pitch a few times, Rickey brought him up to Class AAA Houston in August of 1930. Dean by now had a reputation for "borrowing" cars and driving them down one-way streets the wrong way. He was one very brash young man. When first meeting Rickey, he called him "Branch" and said, "I'm Dizzy, the fella who's gonna win you a lot of ballgames. I can win you a flag."

In his first game in AAA Houston he struck out 14 and won 12-1, then won five straight games before the end of the season, striking out 16 in the season finale. With the Cardinals battling for the '30 NL pennant, Dean was called up, meeting the team in New York City, carrying two suitcases that contained only several dozen Wild West novels.

On the last day of the season, after the Cards had clinched the pennant, Dizzy made his major league debut in Sportsman's Park against the Pirates, pitching a complete game, 3-1 victory, throwing a three hitter off a major league mound at age 20. The St. Louis *Star-Times* declared that Dean was "destined for stardom. The youngster showed burning speed, a wide, sweeping curve, a clever change, and best of all, unusual control for a rookie. You should know this young man."

Years later the Pirates said most of their lineup was drunk that day at the game in the aftermath of a night in the bars of East St. Louis. Much of the time was spent in a club owned by Pirate pitcher and St. Louis native Heine Meine.

But no matter the condition of the opposition, a win was a win and during the off-season Dean began a series of bargaining sessions over pay that stretched through his career. The initial reaction from Rickey after the first such session foreshadowed all the rest: "Judas Priest!" Rickey said, upon emerging from the talks, "if there was another player like Dean in baseball, as God is my judge, I would most certainly get out of the game."

Dean signed for $3,000 but before spring training of 1931 started, he ran up a tab of $2,700 against the pay, spending on hotels, sodas, cigarettes and comic books. When Rickey complained, Dean said, "That's okay. You'll think of something."

Rickey then put Dean on a strict budget; he was to only receive $1 a day (pay all too similar to that of a sharecropper). Rickey cut off all of the rookie's credit in the spring training town of Bradenton, Fla. Then Dean missed a practice and manager Gabby Street blew up in front of the team. Dean turned in his uniform and said he was going to play for a semipro team in San Antonio.

But Rickey intercepted his rookie before he could get on the train to Texas. They talked in the owners' limo and Dean emerged brandishing a $5 bill and was back on the roster. He went fishing the next day and Street suspended him again. Again he went to Rickey. Again Dean was back on the roster.

But Street got his revenge when the season started. Dean sat in the dugout for over a week with no playing time, then was sent back to Houston where he proceeded to spend the full season, going 26-10 with 303 strikeouts. That year he got married and his spending on soda and candy dropped sharply. "I handle the money," Pat Dean said. "What I say goes. I'm his banker, bookkeeper, manager and girlfriend."

Dean made the major league club easily in the spring of 1932, dubbing himself the "Great Dean." He mocked batters from the front of the mound. When a hitter dug in his back foot in the batter's box, Dean would stride down off the mound and yell, "keep on diggin', cause that's where they're going to bury you." His record was 18-15, appearing both as a starter and a relief pitcher, sometimes pitching in back to back games.

The team's hope for a third straight NL pennant was all but gone by June. The Cardinals were under .500. Dean staged a brief walkout, but came back after a meeting with Rickey. Street took the fall for the team's failures and Frankie Frisch, the team's second baseman, took over as manager midway through the season. Things didn't get much better for the Cardinals in 1933, but they did wind up over .500 at 82-71 in fifth place, 9 1/2 games behind.

Dizzy went 20-18 in 1933, set the record for most strikeouts in a game with 17 against Chicago, led the league in strikeouts for a second year and produced a 3.03 ERA. With his brother, Paul, signed up for the 1934 campaign, Dizzy predicted an easy flag for the Cardinals. "Paul's going to be a sensation," he said. "He'll win 18 or 20 games. I'll count 20 or 25 myself. How are they going to stop us?"

Still, the Cardinals were on no one's radar to win the pennant, picked fourth best in a poll of 97 journalists, 40 of whom picked the New York Giants to take the crown for a second consecutive year. Indeed, Dizzy and Paul walked out twice during the season over low pay, players fought each other in the dugout and on Sept. 5, the Giants held a seven-game lead.

That day the *Post-Dispatch* ran a story under the headline. "Seven Game Lead Too Big to Overcome, Redbirds Now Concede." Frisch called a meeting and the club began to win. But so did the Giants and 10 days later the Cards had made up just two games. On Sept. 15, however, the Dean brothers each won a game of a twin-bill between the contenders before a crowd of 62,000 at the Polo Grounds in New York.

Frisch by then was going with what amounted to a two-man rotation, pitching Dizzy and Paul, Dizzy and Paul, during a stirring drive for the pennant that included 20 wins in their last 25 games. On Sept. 21, the brother act put on their greatest show to date during a double-header against Brooklyn.

Dizzy didn't give up a hit until the eighth and won 1-0. Paul did him one better, throwing a no-hitter to win the nightcap 3-0. "If I'd knowed Paul was gonna throw a no-hitter, well I'd a throwed one, too," Dizzy said.

On the season's final weekend, the Cards were one game behind as the Giants imploded, losing to the seventh-place Phillies and the sixth-place Dodgers while Dizzy shut out Cincinnati 4-0 on Friday and Paul took the Reds 6-1 Saturday. On Sunday, coming back on one day's rest, Dizzy pitched another shutout for his 30th win of the season, and the Giants lost their fifth straight, defeated again by their cross-town rivals, the Brooklyn Dodgers.

Dizzy Dean's fame soared into the national stratosphere. He had done what he said he and his brother would do. Between them they won 49 of the club's 95 victories. Dizzy's ERA was an NL second-best 2.66, Paul's was 3.43. Dizzy saved seven games, Paul two, giving them a part in 58 wins, more than the last-place Reds or the seventh-place Phillies managed as an entire team. Dizzy led the league in wins, winning percentage, complete games, strikeouts and shutouts.

One reporter wrote:

> Dizzy Dean is a strange looking fellow. He has high Slavic cheekbones and a large big-lipped mouth, which is never quite closed. He never seems to change his expression. He chews no gum or tobacco. He spits often. When he walks to the dugout after an inning is over no one speaks to him on the way. He speaks to no one, but trudges with his eyes on the ground and his mouth open.
>
> (Another wrote:) Dizzy Dean is the game's greatest showman since Babe Ruth. He's never too busy to chat with hotel lobby fans and will give autographs anywhere at any time. The only people he insults are those who make gyp sales to ballplayers. If Jerome Herman had had an education, he'd have made good at anything. He's generous to a fault. If a small boy wants an autograph and has no paper, Dizz will tear off a cuff.

Naturally, the Series went to the Cards, defeating Detroit in seven games with Dizzy winning two and Paul winning two. There was a lot more to the St. Louis team in 1934 then the Deans, however. This was a team that pulled its identity from the Depression itself. Here was the Gashouse Gang.

This was a team from an industrial city in the Midwest. The players had no manners. They were gruff and they were hard. They dove into bases and flew after loose balls. Dizzy not only mocked the batters verbally, he fired inside fastballs to hitters known to hit inside fastballs and he dropped low curves to low-curve specialists. He had no respect for the rich and nothing but love for the poor.

The team gained grudging support from fans hard-pressed to pay admission in the worst year of the Depression. Only 7,500 people showed up for opening day, but there were 36,000 on hand for the opener of the World Series. A city responded to what *The New York Times* called "one of the most spectacular uphill drives in baseball history," from "an alien cast that ruthlessly wrenched a pennant from the grasp of the Giants."

Dean was the star, as goofy a hick from the sticks as you could invent in a Hollywood screenplay, complete with a silent brother and a happy wife. Frisch, the manager and second baseman, was the leader both on the field and in the dugout, plying the experience he gained in winning successive NL titles with the Giants in the twenties.

Batting cleanup was Joe Medwick, a New Jersey native who worked in a copper factory before he finished school, all muscle, a man who held a high opinion of himself. He didn't get along with the Deans but he loved Frisch almost as much as he liked knocking the cover off a baseball. He batted in 106 runs in '34 and led the team in batting during the Series with a .379 mark.

The shortstop was Leo Durocher, a Boston-bred malcontent whose years as one of baseball's leading lips were only just beginning. He gambled, hustled pool, wore pricey suits, and was Babe Ruth's roommate for two years with the Yanks. In his playing days he often financed his lifestyle with bad checks and was beaten up by Ruth when caught lifting cash.

On the field he took no prisoners, his gleaming spikes slashing sliding runners. On the bench he had the meanest language in the league. He and Frisch were masters of the double play. And Durocher was dead clutch. In eight World Series he batted .294, had 58 hits in 50 games, hit 10 doubles and stole nine bases.

Pepper Martin, the third baseman and the hero of the '31 Series, was back in form. He had a penchant for midget car racing and sliding headfirst, described by one Depression sportswriter as an "unshaven hobo who ran the bases like a berserk locomotive." During the Series of '34, like Medwick and first baseman Rip Collins, Martin rattled Tiger pitching. "The Wild Horse of the Osage" had 11 hits in the Series, scored eight times and batted .355.

The Cardinals won the opener behind the great Diz 8-3, helped along by five Tiger errors on the Detroit home field. The AL champs bounced back to win 3-2 the next day against Wild Bill Hallahan, who Frisch sent to the mound to give the Deans some rest. Back in St. Louis for the third game, Paul won 4-1, but with no Dean pitching the next day the Cards took a 10-4 drubbing, knotting up the Series two games each.

After that loss, except for one meaningless inning, Frisch put no one not named Dean on the mound again. Dizzy was stunned, however, in the fifth game by a pair of late-inning homers that gave Detroit a very good looking 3-2 advantage with the Series heading back to the Motor City. There the Tigers needed just one more win.

But the Deans prevailed. Paul drove in the winning run and pitched a complete game victory in the sixth game then Dizzy breezed in a lopsided, anti-climatic finale 11-0, helping his own cause by getting two hits in a decisive, seven-run explosion in the third inning. The Detroit fans didn't take the drubbing in good cheer and the game was almost called off when bleacher fans pelted Medwick with all manner of fruit, beer bottles and cigar butts in the sixth.

Medwick's crime was a hard slide into third the previous frame that resulted in a brief fight with the Detroit fielder. The fans demanded Medwick's removal from the game. But the big outfielder had only contempt for the Tiger faithful and began playing catch with a stray apple, tossing it back and fourth with his centerfield teammate.

The Times called the outburst "one of the most disorderly scenes ever witnessed at a World Series game." The incident took a bizarre turn as the Commissioner of Baseball, Judge Kenesaw Mountain Landis, rose from his seat behind third and summoned the disputing players to a kangaroo court along the baseline. Medwick wouldn't apologize to the Tiger third baseman, police spilled onto the field and took Medwick away "for his own safety."

All this mattered not at all to Dizzy Dean. When the game restarted he continued to fire bullets across various parts of home plate, at times throwing the ball and turning his back to laugh as another Tiger went down on strikes. His obvious enjoyment continued into the locker room where he raced around wearing the pith helmet of an African explorer, mugging for the cameras with a rubber Tiger doll, draped over his shoulders, holding it in his teeth by the tail and squeezing it in a headlock. Things had never been this much fun before.

Here was the Gashouse Gang in its glory – the image of Dizzy Dean with the tiger by the tail.

The club's nickname wasn't used much until the next season when a Chicago writer mocked his hometown Cubs after a particularly tough loss to the Cardinals. The writer noted the Cubs had gone to bed early on a train ride to New York, teasing the players to watch out "or the Gashouse Gang will get you."

The New York writers picked up the phrase and it has lasted in baseball history. There was no gashouse district in St. Louis, however, and the term probably derived from Lower East Side New York street slang for a tough district run by dirty urchins who flaunted authority, responded to a raw deal with a renewed attack and eventually proved quicker, faster and smarter than their opponent. These were traits much valued by the baseball public in the Depression, a time when just about everyone was getting a raw deal.

This Gashouse Gang baseball team was an impossible bunch of underdogs who slashed and slid, stole and slammed, doing anything necessary to win.

Cardinal baseball was thus firmly embedded in the culture of the city by these wild men of Grand Avenue and has never faded from public affection. The city sometimes sees itself as a place of "blues, baseball and beer," each part of the three-legged stool upon which the happiness of the city rests. Each is part and parcel of that St. Louis thing and whether or not the city is appreciated by the rest of the country, its denizens, much like the beloved Gashouse Gang, could care less.

The Cardinals remained near the top of the standings for the next 20 years, moving away from the Ruthian power model by using its ever growing farm system, building on its pitching, producing scrappy, fast, well-defensed teams built on the Gashouse model. The club finished above .500 in all but one season between 1934 and 1953. In those two decades the Birds won five NL titles and four more World Series championships. The Cardinals also had seven second place finishes and another four times finished third.

But by the mid-fifties, after the Browns left town and the Stars folded and the National Leaguers had the city to themselves, a troublesome downward trend developed, mostly the result of the team's failure to put African Americans in the lineup. The Dodgers, Indians and Giants built winning formulas based on the new infusion of black players, but the Cardinals lagged behind.

These integrated teams rose by beating St. Louis at its own game, using the Gashouse model of pitching and speed to rise to the top for battles against the still powerful Yankees in several classic Series.

The Birds, despite playing in a city with a thriving black culture, waited until 1954 to integrate. The Yankees of 1953 were the last all-white team to win the World Series.

In 1949, Robinson led the league in hitting at .349 and Don Newcombe went 17-9 pitching to Roy Campanella and the Dodgers won the NL pennant, edging the Cards by a single game. In 1951, Willie Mays and Monte Irvin led the Giants to the NL crown, winning a playoff over the Dodgers. The Dodgers won again in 1952 and 1953 and Mays batted .345 to lead the Giants to the crown in '54.

All these were black examples of game changing players entering the league. The Dodgers (with Branch Rickey wheeling and dealing) in 1954 had five blacks in the starting lineup -- in 1955, a Dodger team known as the Bums finally beat the Yankee machine in the Series.

With Gussie Busch in charge of the Cardinals beginning in 1953, change came slowly in St. Louis. By 1959, the team had finally collected some excellent black players, obtaining pitcher Bob Gibson, outfielder Curt Flood and first baseman Bill White.

But the manager, Solly Hemus, a hard-nose infielder whose racism couldn't be hidden, was unable to meld the players into a winner. Even the team's greatest player, Stan Musial, who stood with the black players against Hemus, was shunted to the sidelines. Hemus said Gibson would never make it in the big leagues and kept Flood on the bench, leading the team to a seventh-place finish as the fifties ended.

Hemus was replaced in 1961 with the placid Johnny Keane, a lifetime Cardinal who had been managing in the minor leagues since 1938. His first move was to restore Musial and Flood to the lineup. The team moved up to third in 1960 and was second in 1963, the racial tension dissipated and the club started acting like a team.

In 2014, Stan Musial's statue stands bold and massive in front of the latest edition of Busch Stadium. A mile or so to the north, the new

Stan Musial-Veterans Bridge (the Stan Span) soars across the Mississippi River. In 2011, Musial was awarded the Presidential Medal of Freedom by the nation's first black president, Barack Obama, who called Musial "an icon untarnished, a beloved pillar of the community, a gentleman you'd want your kids to emulate."

Teammate Tim McCarver, summed him up:

> The impact of a man like Musial on a bunch of ballplayers can't ever be exaggerated. Year in and year out it was more than his seven batting titles that made an impression on his teammates. Those who spent time around him recognized that he was a person of good character and decency. He tried to lead by example. He wasn't much of a talker, a special pleader or a clubhouse lawyer. He was just a good man.

Musial joined the Cardinals in 1941 and was a mainstay in the 1942 championship season that ended in a five-game victory over the Yankees in the World Series. He won his first batting title the next year, hitting a rousing .357, and was part of a losing effort in the Series, again against the Yanks.

In 1944 and 1946, he hit .347 and .365 in leading the Cards to NL titles and Series victories over the Browns (4-2) and the Red Sox (4-3). But after appearing in four Series in his first five years on the team (he was in the service in 1945) that was it for Stan the Man's World Series career. The Cardinals after 1946 didn't see the Fall Classic again until 1964, the year after Musial retired. He finished with a .331 lifetime average, hitting above baseball's gold-standard of .300 in 17 seasons.

Once a dead-armed Class D pitcher, he became one of the game's greatest all-around players, named to Major League Baseball's All-Century team in 1999. His numbers were stunning -- 3,630 hits, 475 home runs and 1,951 RBI. He was one of only three players to amass over 6,000 total bases (the other two are Hank Aaron and Willie Mays) and in 2014 still stood second on the all-time list. And, during his entire playing career, including 3,026 regular-season, 23 World Series and 24 All-Star games, Musial was never once ejected from a game.

No player got more hits with a single franchise than Musial and they were equally divided, 1,815 at home and 1,815 on the road, including two hits in his first game and two hits in his last. He was elected to the Hall Fame on his first try, in 1969.

Stanisław Franciszek Musial was born Nov. 21, 1920, in the coal mining town of Donora, Penn., the fifth of Lukasz and Mary Musial's six children. He began playing semi-pro baseball by the time he was 15 and was a top high school basketball player.

The University of Pittsburgh offered him a basketball scholarship at the same time as the Cardinals offered a pro baseball contract. Musial's father wanted his son to attend college, but Musial's mother and the school librarian talked the father into agreeing to baseball. Musial signed as a pitcher in 1938.

He was paid $65 a month and began his climb toward the major leagues. In 1940, with Class D Daytona Beach in Florida, he played the outfield between pitching starts and hit .311 with an 18–5 pitching record. A shoulder injury suffered in the outfield in August 1940 ended his pitching career and shaped a swing unique in baseball.

A left-handed hitter, Musial stood in a crouch with his back nearly square to the pitcher, his eyes nearly hidden behind his shoulder. The stance gave the appearance of a coiled rattlesnake, ready to rip the bat through the strike zone. He rarely struck out and hit both with precision and with power.

In 1941 he walked into a fierce pennant race, a 20-year-old playing in the majors for the first time, showing immediately the calm, clear demeanor and cool play in the clutch as the Cards battled the Dodgers. In 12 games he collected 20 hits in 47 at bats for a .426 batting average. The Cardinals finished second that year and Musial won a permanent spot on the team.

As the Cardinals became a second division team in the fifties, Musial was switched from the outfield to first base and continued his steady hitting year in and year out.

Off the field he played a role in the integration of the game during those years. He had been on teams with black players in his teenage years, including Buddy Griffey, the grandfather of Ken Griffey, Jr., the great home run hitter who retired in 2010. Musial was openly supportive when Jackie Robinson broke the color line in 1947. Musial stood up for pitcher

Joe Black and was praised by fellow Hall of Famer Willie Mays for joining a group of black players in a card game before the All-Star game in the late fifties.

After retirement in 1963, Musial held court at his St. Louis restaurant, on hand to meet and greet the customers, signing countless autographs and talking baseball. He would play "Take Me Out to the Ballgame" on his always handy harmonica, even playing at his Hall of Fame induction and on an episode of the television show *Hee Haw.*

Surprisingly, the enduring nickname did not come from the home fans. Rather, in a testament to his widespread admiration, the nickname came in the 1946 season during a June 23 game in Brooklyn when Dodger fans chanted "Here comes the man!" whenever Musial came to bat. The story went into the St. Louis *Post-Dispatch* and Musial was thereafter known as Stan "The Man."

He invented the "fist bump," convinced that shaking hands with another player led to catching a cold.

One-time Cardinal catcher and St. Louis native Joe Garagiola said, "He could have hit .300 with a fountain pen."

Opposing pitcher Preacher Roe of the Brooklyn Dodgers, when asked how to pitch Musial said, "I throw him four wide ones and try to pick him off first base."

Another Dodger pitcher, Carl Erskine, said, "I've had pretty good success with Stan by throwing him my best pitch and backing up third."

A 19-year-old Musial married his hometown sweetheart, Lillian "Lil" Labash, in 1940 and they remained together throughout their long lives. They had four children and lived in a modest home in suburban St. Louis. He signed autographs for anybody who showed up on his front porch.

Musial died Jan. 19, 2013, at age 92.

Teammate, restaurant owner and broadcaster Mike Shannon said, "Everybody in St. Louis, every kid in St. Louis, wanted to be Stan Musial. He was the best."

Upon his retirement Musial explained his good nature:

> Maybe one reason I'm so cheerful is that for more than 20 years I've had an unbeatable combination going for me — getting paid, often a lot, to do the thing I love the most. The love is important, but let's not pretend, so is the money. My old Cardinals coach,

> Mike Gonzales, used to say to me, 'Musial, if I could hit like you, I'd play for nothing.' Not me. But I wouldn't play for the money without the fun."

Musial made just $1.26 million his whole career, far short of the average yearly pay of $4 million for a player in 2016.

After he quit playing Musial went into the Cardinals front office as a vice-president but didn't have much to say about the running of the club, now in the hands of general manager Bing Devine, field manager Johnny Keane and Gussie Busch in the owners' box. The second place finish in '63 gave the brain trust a lot of optimism for '64, but even after the acquisition of Lou Brock filling a hole in the outfield, the team couldn't seem to get going.

At the All-Star break in July, the Cards trailed the Phillies by 10 games and were one notch below .500, but two important things happened in the first week after the break. Keane held a team meeting that rattled through the club, exposing shortstop Dick Groat as a "whispering Smith" undermining the manager. Groat apologized and everyone felt better.

The second thing involved first baseman Bill White, one of the team leaders, a power hitter who wasn't hitting for power, with just 30 RBIs at the break, half what he had driven in by then the previous year. His power was flagging due to an injury to his shoulder that nagged him since spring training. The team doctor hadn't done much about it but a friend told him about a specialist in New York City who had treated President Kennedy. The doctor gave White a shot in just the right place in his shoulder and he responded with six hits in a doubleheader that completed a series sweep of the Pirates. Things were looking up.

But no sooner had White began hitting, the pitching gave out. The team was still 10 games back. A sweep of the NL-leading Phillies helped but the rally died again. Then Devine brought in a coach who noticed a glitch in the pitching motion of Bob Gibson, the team's most important pitcher. Gradually, during August, Gibson came to life and the team started to creep up the ladder.

About this time an 81-year-old ghost named Branch Rickey reappeared in the Cardinal landscape. He had been hired the previous year as a special consultant in charge of watching over Bing Devine's handling of the players. Devine was fired in August 1964, but Rickey didn't want the general manager job. Busch hired Bob Howsam whose first job was to fire Rickey. Gussie was, in effect, now running the team.

During all this turmoil in the executive suite, the players began to play. Gibson led the way. Mike Shannon, brought up from the minors, completed a powerful lineup. White was knocking balls around the yard. The Cards went 31-13 beginning on July 24 and by Sept. 9 had trimmed the lead from 11 games to six.

But no one predicted what would happen in those final weeks of the '64 season. No one could have.

The Phillies had long been a doormat of the NL. But with Jim Bunning and Chris Short leading a solid pitching staff and Richie Allen and Johnny Callison providing the muscle, the Phils seemed in the driver's seat all year.

On Sept. 21, the Phils led by 6 1/2 games, in first place every day since the middle of July. But a daring steal of home by Cincinnati catcher Chico Ruiz began an impossible 10-game losing streak by the Phillies, a streak that featured Bunning pitching on three or even two days rest, Short was pressed into the same killer schedule. Bats fell silent up and down the lineup.

First Cincinnati, then St. Louis charged at the Phils, the Redbirds accomplishing a remarkable sweep of five games in Pittsburg along the way. The season came down to a three-game series between St. Louis and Philadelphia beginning on a Monday at Sportsman's Park, the last week of the season. The Cards needed a sweep to take over the league lead.

The Cardinals had found the formula. Gibson pitched, White hit, Groat fielded, the newcomer Barney Schultz brought in a knuckleball from the bullpen. And then there was Bob Uecker, a clowning reserve catcher, who was one of Bing Devine's last pickups before he was fired.

Uecker loosened up the Birds with his standup routines at his locker and with a running card game called Ugly. Uecker collected mug shots from a friend who was a Philly cop and made a deck of 52 of the ugliest crooks. He also pitched batting practice every day with teams of five pitchers on each side. Gibson batted .500 and hit over 20 homers in the Uecker League.

Gibson stopped the Phils in the opener 5-1 for the Cards' sixth straight win. The next day, the sore arm of Phillie Dennis Bennet was no match for the charging Cards and they won their seventh straight 4-2 as the Phils went 1 for 9 with runners in scoring position and left eight on base.

The third game saw Bunning on the mound on two days rest, pitching against a red-hot and well-rested Curt Simmons, who had won five in a row. McCarver homered in the second to give the Cards a 2-0 lead and it was nothing but more pain for the Phillies, completing their Philly Phold, losing their 10th straight, 8-5.

On the last day of the season, the Cards needed to win one more and did just that in resounding fashion, coming from behind with an 11-4 win over the Mets, finishing the year a game ahead of both the Phils and the Reds. Simmons, Gibson and Schultz all pitched in that final victory, with the knuckleballer getting the last two outs with two men on base.

The seventh game of the 1964 World Series was the last time the two best teams in baseball history -- the Cards and Yanks -- met head to head in the championship game.

Most significantly for baseball and for the nation itself was the fact that the starting lineup for the Cardinals included four black players -- a final destruction of the myth that a black ballplayer couldn't handle pressure, and wasn't as good as a white player. That myth had held sway for over 80 years in the national pastime of America, a myth that the white ownership of the sport had fought long and hard to maintain.

Indeed, when the players ran to their positions before a sold out crowd, here came four African Americans -- Bill White to first base, Lou Brock to left, Curt Flood to center and strolling to the mound the great Gibson, Bob, right handed pitcher, 6-feet-1, 189 pounds, 19-12 during the season and recent winner of a Series-saving fifth game in Yankee Stadium.

He was pitching on short rest and had gone 10 stressful innings in the fifth game victory, striking out 13, walking just two and surviving a shocking, game-tying homer by Tom Tresh in the last of the ninth to prevail 5-2. That win gave the Cards enough of an edge to be able to suffer through a sixth game loss to the powerful Yanks, who thrashed St. Louis on the Cards home field 8-3.

Now the teams were even. Both had their ace on the mound, Gibson had filled that role for the Cards all season long, even as he struggled in the first half. Mel Stottlemeyer, a rookie who had dashed into Yankee Stadium in mid-year and won nine games in 12 starts, was on the mound for the Yanks, who had seen their usual ace, Whitey Ford, beaten in the opener, his arm dead, his record setting World Series career over.

But Stottlemeyer had stepped into Ford's shoes to beat Gibson in Game Two, had given up just two runs in a no decision in Game Five and was up for the third time in the Series, facing Gibson in Game Seven, with both hurlers going on short rest of three days.

Gibson felt good early, striking out Mickey Mantle, the star Yankee cleanup hitter, his first time up. Mantle was playing his last Series and was symbolic of the aging Yankee juggernaut. The Series was his 12th in a career that began in 1951 and included seven Series victories, 18 homers, 42 runs scored, 40 RBI in 65 games.

During the '64 Classic, Gibson faced Mantle 12 times and struck him out on five of those at bats. The best the Mick could muster against Gibson was a harmless walk in Game Two until hit a three-run homer as the Yankees rallied in the final contest. The hitting star for the Yanks in the Series was Bobby Richardson, the pesky second baseman who had 13 hits.

And it was Richardson who was at bat in the top of the ninth, two out, nobody on, Cards leading 7-5. Clete Boyer and Phil Linz had homered in the inning off a tiring Gibby and the tying run was in the on-deck circle in the person of Roger Maris, the slugger who in 1961 had broken Babe Ruth's long-standing home run record.

Richardson just wanted to reach base to give Maris a chance. McCarver, the Cards catcher, went out to the mound and said to Gibson, "He's been hitting the ball away pretty good. Let's try something new." Scouting reports showing that Richardson could hit the inside pitch had been wrong and Richardson had been feasting on the outside pitch all Series.

"I threw him a fastball in tight," Gibson said. Instead of waiting to work his way on base, Richardson swung at that first pitch. He hit it off his fists and popped it up meekly on the right side of the infield. Shortstop Dick Groat yelled to the second baseman Dal Maxville, "Don't let it hit you in the coconut."

Maxville made the routine catch and St. Louis was World Champion once again.

Sportsman's Park had been renamed Busch Stadium in 1953 and the Cardinals played there until 1965 when a new stadium, called Busch Memorial Stadium, was finished downtown. That stadium, like the old one, was privately financed, a $20 million project with $5 million from the brewery, $2.5 million from May Company and the rest from other supporters of a downtown revival.

Sportsman's Park had been remodeled by the Busch ownership and, with its compact 30,000 seats and numerous nooks and crannies, was a comfortable place to watch a game. Open and breezy, it handled the summer heat and had the feeling of a well-worn baseball glove. But the neighborhood around it was in flux from the movement of population in the fifties as established North Side blacks began moving into the suburbs, replaced by refugees from Mill Creek Valley.

Gussie Busch and his fellow members of Civic Progress came to support a plan for 31 acres of downtown development that included the stadium, a side project to the Mill Creek Valley demolition. The stadium project sent the wrecking ball through the city's Chinatown section near the riverfront. Next door to the stadium the city installed the Spanish Pavilion from the 1965 World's Fair in New York.

The Cardinals opened the 1966 season in the old park on the North Side, playing their last game on "Grand North Grand" May 8, almost 90 years to the day when pro baseball was first played there at the Grand Avenue Grounds.

While it had a few architectural features such as a ring of 96 arches around the top that mimicked the nearby Gateway Arch, the new stadium was part of the fifties penchant for cookie-cutter multi-purpose facilities popping up around the country, The new stadium was also the home of the football Cardinals, who began tearing up the grass in the fall of 1966. The Gridbirds played there for 28 futile seasons, never reaching the National Football League playoffs. The team moved to Arizona in 1987.

The grass turf lasted until 1970 when it was replaced with an artificial surface. The heat in the stadium was notorious. Summers were hot enough in St. Louis, but things at Busch Memorial were made hotter by a sunken field design, limited irrigation and new Astro-turf. Players and fans alike often could not see the baseball in flight due to the reflection off the field.

The heat, too, was a problem, sometimes 10 degrees hotter on the field than in nearby neighborhoods.

The problem wasn't solved until yet another new stadium was built in St. Louis, opening in 2006 with a grass field and plenty of ventilation.

The baseball team was initially very successful in the 1966 facility, winning the pennant and World Series in 1967 and coming back to take the NL crown again the next year, losing to Detroit in the 1968 championships. These were storied teams led by Gibson, Brock, Flood and McCarver, but that also included new successful hitters like first baseman Orlando Cepeda and Roger Maris, who came over from the Yankees.

The Boston Red Sox of 1967 was the "impossible dream" team that went from a ninth place finish in 1966 to the AL flag in just one season as the hated Yankees dropped all the way to ninth that same year. The pitching star for Boston was Jim Lonborg who went 22-9 during the regular year and won his first two Series starts.

Gibson sat out two months of the regular year with a broken leg, but was more than healthy during the Series, also winning his first two starts. The match up everyone had been waiting for came in Game Seven when Lonborg took the mound for the Sox, opposed by Gibson for the Cards.

Played in Fenway Park in Boston, the finale was no contest. Lonborg was pitching on just two days rest and Gibson was unstoppable, throwing a three-hitter in a 7-2 Cardinals rout. Flood dashed home on a wild pitch in the third, Gibson hit a solo homer in the fifth, and second baseman Julian Javier iced the victory with a three-run homer that followed a Boston error.

The next season was all Gibson during the regular season. His pitching performance that 1968 year was so overwhelming the major leagues lowered the mound the next year, making it easier on the hitters. But for those who saw Gibby throwing in 1968 there was nothing like it in the history of baseball.

Gibson pitched to a 1.12 ERA, went 22-9, threw 13 shutouts, had 28 complete games out of 34 starts and walked just 65 in 308 innings pitched. By July the Cardinals raced far ahead of the league, standing at 49-15 with a 14 1/2 game lead. During one streak Gibson allowed just two earned runs over 96 innings, an eight-week stretch when his ERA almost disappeared entirely to 0.19.

McCarver was behind the plate as the balls came whizzing in and later explained how good Gibson was:

> He could put a ball in a space about four inches on the outside part of the plate with his fastball or slider, and he could throw a riding fastball anytime you wanted. It sailed, almost like a slider. It was his best pitch. It stayed on the inside of the plate to left-handers and the outside part of the plate to right-handers. Plus, he was so consistent with that pitch the umpires started giving him pitches just off the plate. They were almost unreachable by right-handed hitters.

In the '68 World Series opener he completely shut down the Tigers, striking out 17, walking one and giving up just five hits, four singles and a double. Only one Detroit runner reached third and Gibson struck out the side in the ninth to complete the victory. Mike Shannon watched it all from this position at third base. "It was like pitching against Little Leaguers."

The Cards quickly surged into a three games to one Series lead, with the Cards taking Game Three 7-3 behind homers by McCarver and Cepeda, and then romping 10-1 in the fourth game. All that was left was one more win. When the Redbirds took a quick 3-0 lead in the fifth game, it looked like the talented Birds were going to win a second straight championship.

But baseball is sport marked with cliches, two of which hold ever true -- the only sure thing is that there is no sure thing and the game isn't over until the last man is out. That last man went out three days later and it was Tim McCarver, retired on a pop up to end the seventh and deciding game with the Tigers a 4-1 winner in the game and a four games to three victory in the Series.

The Detroit nine had rallied in the seventh inning of that crucial fifth game to take a 5-3 win, then trounced the Cardinals 12-1 in Game Six behind Jim Northrup's grand slam to knot the Series at three games apiece.

Gibson then reached the end of his greatest season by losing the seventh game. He allowed three runs in a decisive seventh inning where the Tigers capped their remarkable comeback. The big play was a two-out triple by Northrup that scored two runs and broke a scoreless tie.

The triple was a drive to center that Flood initially misjudged. He started in, then realized the ball was going over his head and couldn't make the catch as the ball landed just short of the outfield wall and hopped off the fence.

After the game a dejected Flood went to Gibson, "It's all my fault."

Gibson, ever the philosopher, replied, "It's nobody's fault."

Chapter Twenty-Nine
Quid Pro Quo: Missed Opportunities

1965-1993

(City officials) just let us walk away. Today, they'd give away the store for those jobs.

-- Eldon Renaud, United Auto Workers, 2011

By the sixties, while the great black athletes such as Gibson, Brock and Flood were cheered by thousands of baseball fans -- white and black alike -- and the great black musicians like Albert King and Oliver Sain entertained increasing numbers of mixed audiences, St. Louis as a whole still saw a wide racial divide.

A civil rights movement led by African Americans who were accommodating, reasonable and almost entirely non-violent had emerged, willing to bargain. Barely a hint of the kind of rage and blood that flooded other American ghettos was openly expressed at the confluence. And even with failing housing projects, relentless poverty, reshuffled neighborhoods and a stark decline in the North Side, the black population continued to hold hope for a brighter future, working for equal opportunity through elections, education and peaceful protest rather than bombs and flame-throwing rhetoric.

In Detroit, Harlem, Philadelphia and Los Angeles swaths of urban landscape in black neighborhoods were destroyed by firebombs and looting.

In St. Louis the destruction came from wrecking balls and bulldozers hired by developers and authorized by the city. Official destruction of African-American homes and businesses tore open the central core of the city -- the riverfront smashed, the near North Side and Mill Creek Valley leveled.

Looking at Mill Creek Valley or Pruitt-Igoe in 1965 just about anybody could see this was a mistake. Mud flats and broken cement stood in once thriving neighborhoods. Needle-strewn playgrounds replaced parks. The idea that uprooted residents would soon return to nice, new homes was beginning to be understood as a pipe dream.

The condition of the city became uncomfortable even in segments of the elite, and a new, revised vision emerged beginning in the mid-sixties, a vision that emphasized building over destroying. Equality between the races, some in the top echelons of power said, was maybe, just maybe, a desirable goal.

To the fore came a reformer, a liberal replacement for the wrecking-ball swingers who had occupied the mayor's chair since the Depression. Here was a small businessman who was not a real estate broker -- a man called "Al," a white man who could sit in the same room with blacks and go beyond stereotypes. Here came A.J. Cervantes, a convincer, a talker of great stamina and charm.

Here was an opportunity for change. Here came a chance for St. Louis to cast away its discriminatory ways and bring the power of diversity that so enhanced its music into City Hall. Here in the mid-sixties came a chance for the white citizenry to step across the line and share some of its privilege --education, jobs, housing -- with black Americans. It had taken 100 years since the end of slavery, but the moment seemed at hand.

Raymond Tucker had been mayor for three terms, from 1953 to 1965. He had approved and overseen the Bartholomew-inspired destruction of the inner city. Tucker the technocrat, the expert, agreed with the goals of Civic Progress and the real estate interests. Urban removal was good for business.

Tucker barely squeezed into office when first elected, but urban liquidation kept him there, with ever more support from the business elite. That support reached its high-water mark as the wrecking balls flew in Mill Creek.

Plans were still being made to keep on moving through the city, aiming the headache ball next at racially integrated areas -- Soulard, Lafayette Park and the Central West End. But aldermen both white and black allied to stop new havoc. They became increasingly vocal when they saw the bulldozers heading their way.

The rumbling from below had almost nailed Tucker in the 1961 Democratic Party primary. The central corridor from Grand Avenue out to Washington University turned on the technocrat for the first time, giving him only a slight majority where he had previously had strong support. Tucker won that primary by just 1,272 votes. Republican opposition in mayoral elections had by then become token and Tucker won his third term in the general election.

But four years later the voters threw the technocrat out.

The opposition rallied around Al Cervantes, the former head of the Board of Aldermen. He promised a new look. He carried a briefcase full of anti-Tucker credentials. He smiled and slapped backs; he had a flamboyance unseen in city politics in decades. Tucker turned negative in the election campaign, labeling Cervantes the candidate of a "motley crew of ambitious ward politicians." Sounding far more like a politician than an expert, Tucker said the Cervantes crowd was "unwilling to put the broad interests of this city ahead of the narrow interests of the ward."

Cervantes spoke out for the neighborhoods. He championed the poor, landing majorities in wards populated by blacks whose voting strength was now over 35 percent and who became activated by the civil rights movement. In 1965 Cervantes also carried South Side wards populated by poor and working class whites, taking the victory over Tucker by 14,442 votes.

Cervantes was astute as well as flamboyant. He understood the weak-mayor system of St. Louis government and ran against its quiet current by making noise. He was a salesman and a promoter and as such was one of the most colorful characters to hold the mayor's gavel in the long history of the city.

As he took office in 1965, the national waters around him had turned mighty turbulent. The first U.S. combat troops were in Vietnam, Martin Luther King's supporters were attacked by snarling dogs in Selma, Malcolm X was assassinated, the Watts ghetto of Los Angeles blew up in a race riot that left 34 dead and 1,000 injured.

By then, too, long, determined protests by blacks in St. Louis became a movement, at Jefferson Bank, at the Gateway Arch, at an appearance by Lyndon Johnson at the Chase Plaza. The time was ripe for this movement in this year in history.

Cervantes was no Martin or Malcolm. He sought to diffuse the movement with study groups and development of the city's central corridor. He waited to bring the black leadership into the system. But his spoken goals to the public emphasized racial and economic injustices. He was not looking for new neighborhoods to destroy.

Cervantes arrived as mayor having played the political game throughout the previous 15 years, the postwar period of urban decay and official optimism. The city, he said in his 1965 inaugural speech, faced an "unprecedented fiscal crisis" that could only be solved by economic development. He said it was time to build, "the wrecking job is over." He emphasized that equal opportunity and the end to segregation was imperative.

He dove into the water with a rhetorical splash, but it wasn't one that impressed those who wanted real change. There was skepticism even from supporters who looked at his first day in office without amusement. Unfortunately for the city that day was a portent for the future.

On April 6, 1965, "Al" held two inaugural events, one in City Hall and one at the Chase Plaza. The partying in the Rotunda of City Hall was a first for the 67-year-old landmark, a truly historic occasion. For the swearing-in, the hall was adorned with dark green hanging garlands and shields bearing the coat of arms of the French king, Louis IX, the crusader and namesake of the city whose statute stands in front of the Art Museum in Forest Park.

Prior to the ceremony, musicians strolled among women wearing ball gowns and cocktail dresses, with Carmen Cervantes joining her husband on a grand entrance down the marble staircase to the tune of "The Coronation March."

A vice president of Monsanto announced the mayor and 50 other dignitaries including the aldermen, the honorary colonels in the state militia and a number of business, labor and educational leaders. Civil rights leaders remained outside the halls of power.

The party moved on after the inaugural address to the Chase Plaza where the guests ate, drank and danced, saluting the smiling mayor at every opportunity. He couldn't help lap up his moment as Sun King of St. Louis. Still, given his background, his rise to prominence, and his liberal talk, many whites believed that if anyone could breach the racial and economic divide that plagued St. Louis; it would be this salesman from the South Side.

Alfonso Juan Cervantes was born in St. Louis Aug. 27, 1920. His family, which eventually included three boys and three girls, lived in a two-story brick brownstone two blocks south of Tower Grove Park. His father sold insurance, his mother tended to the house and the children.

In the thirties, A.J. began running a magazine route to make a little money, then set up a miniature golf course in the back yard, charging Depression putt-putt golfers a dime a round. The last hole featured a final putt that went through a hole in the basement wall, so A.J. could make sure nobody played for free.

All wasn't roses for the family, however. The father was sometimes missing. A.J., age 16, took off, heading to Los Angeles. There he worked menial jobs and took classes at Hollywood High and Los Angeles Junior College. He also launched his career as a promoter, convincing the owners of the sprawling El Rancho Grande nightclub to hold rumba contests. Cash prizes and good bands brought in the crowds.

These teenage years gave the young St. Louisan a taste of the high life. Later, Cervantes the public figure, said:

> I don't talk a lot about my time in California. Not that I try to hide it. I consider my family. You could ask me if I want my children to do the same thing -- go out on their own at a very early age -- and my answer would be no.
>
> Also among conservative people in St. Louis, such things as show business, nightclubs and dancing might have some stigma attached. I understand this.

On Dec. 7, 1941, Cervantes was still in Los Angeles running his rumba business as a 21 year old when the Japanese attacked Pearl Harbor. He enlisted in the Merchant Marines and learned to operate a radio. After the war he came home to visit his mother, intending to return to L.A., but was convinced to stay in St. Louis, live at home and work with his father to learn the insurance business.

A clever young man, he promptly hatched a plan to sell insurance to truckers who had recently left the service. The G.I. Bill gave 100 percent financing to veterans who wanted to buy trucks. A.J. went to the truck stops to nail down the insurance on the newly purchased trucks, pocketing the commissions. He was just as successful there as he had been at the rhumba contests and the miniature golf. He was on the road to financial success.

Twenty years later, when Cervantes became mayor, his list of assets included real estate in St. Louis and at the Lake of the Ozarks resort in rural Missouri, part ownership of the Laclede Cab Company, a directorship of the Lindell Trust banking and financial service firm, his own insurance agency, a substantial share of a 23-story office building downtown, a liquor-store bonding business and ownership of wholesale cigarette companies in Missouri and Illinois.

Trim, 5-feet-11 inches tall, tan, weighing in at 185 pounds, 44 years old when he became mayor, he had been "first bitten by the political bug" in 1949, when he was 29. He joined his 15th ward Democratic organization after a meeting with a friend who had attended the inauguration of Harry Truman. After the meeting the friend suggested to Cervantes that he run for a seat on the Board of Aldermen. Republicans had held his ward for several terms. Maybe it was time for a change.

He enlisted his wife in his campaign. "It was just to have been a hobby," he said, "an outside interest we could share." He and his wife hit the streets, hoping to erase his status as a political unknown. "Carmen took one side of the street and I took the other."

He addressed his first crowd of ward workers at Colombo's Tavern on the Hill (now O'Connell's Pub.) Cervantes met Joseph Darst, then running for mayor, and asked for his support in the race against the aldermanic incumbent, the Republican Louis Lange.

Darst won. Cervantes won. The election swung power to the Democrats, 15-14, on the Board of Aldermen. The Cervantes victory, won by a margin of 48 votes, was the crucial seat that gave the majority to the

Democrats, giving Darst a good chance to push through his programs. The excitement of the victory led to more excitement during the first seating of the new 1949 board in City Hall. The clerk, reading the roll of new members, intentionally skipped over Cervantes and another Democrat, giving the majority at 14-13 to the Republicans.

Pandemonium ensued as the Republican parliamentarian ruled the Republican clerk was within his rights in leaving off the two Democrats from the roll because of unspecified "irregularities" in the ballot. TV cameras, a new element in the democratic process, rushed forward as the sheriff, a Democrat named Tom Callahan, landed a solid punch on the aging parliamentarian.

"Fists and flowers flew as the zoom lenses focused now on the president's dais, now on an individual slugging match," Cervantes remembered. "Screaming profanity reached astonished viewers with no network censors to intervene."

Cervantes did not join the fight. His wife was sitting next to him and she was pregnant. He and Carmen skedaddled across the hall to the city registrar's office where a cooperative Republican clerk checked the election results and registered Cervantes as a legitimate winner in the 15th ward. The majority was saved for the Democrats and two weeks later when the legalities were ironed out Cervantes was finally seated.

His wife gave birth to a baby boy, A.J. Jr., a few months later without problem. (A.J. Jr. grew up to become a record producer in Los Angeles and in 2006 released a documentary film about his father.)

Cervantes cut his political teeth on the Board of Aldermen -- his hobby -- during the next 10 years. He instituted regular "beef" sessions in 1952, providing a night of open talk for citizens to air complaints. He got himself elected head of the aldermanic Traffic Committee and toured the city looking for useless stop signs. He made allies in the neighborhoods. The St. Louis Junior Chamber of Commerce named him Outstanding Young Man of the Year. He established recreation programs for the elderly.

In 1955, he tried for the aldermanic presidency but lost. He tried again in 1959, the year the headache ball flew in Mill Creek Valley. This time he won, establishing himself as one of the three top officials in the city. In

1961, he pushed through a new building code that helped stimulate new neighborhood construction.

In 1963, however, a Tucker ally pushed him off the board, a setback that gave Cervantes time to solidify his support for the upcoming mayoral race. For campaign manager he hired Anthony Sansone, was a man from his neighborhood with many political ties around the city. Sansone was effective in the 1965 race, but his connections later tarnished Cervantes and were a factor in his downfall.

Once the dancing at the Chase Plaza was over on inauguration night, Cervantes settled into a 14-to-16-hour a day routine as mayor, changing the sometimes part-time ethic of the city's chief executive with non-stop meetings, speeches, ribbon-cuttings and flights of idea-brainstorming. He installed red carpeting and colorful furniture in his office "to show the new spirit of St. Louis, a forward looking city, not a stodgy place."

He took a trickle-down strategy on civil rights, thinking that if the city prospered so would the poor. He launched a national sales campaign aimed at changing the city's image. At the same time, he appointed committees to work on ending job discrimination, hoping more equality and more jobs would bring erase the racial divide.

Soon a headline in the *Globe-Democrat* read "Has St. Louis Kicked Off Its High-Button Shoes?" In a speech to reporters at the roof garden of the Hotel Pierre across the street from Central Park in New York City, Cervantes said the city had not only disposed of the high-button shoes but also "hiked her skirts and is racing -- most undowager-like -- to the head of the pack in the exciting American urban renewal race."

Cervantes swung his own wrecking ball over a smaller area than his predecessors. In less then a year, however, construction was underway downtown on the new Busch Stadium, on the Mansion House apartment project that cleared four blocks along North 4th Street, on new highways and on secondary projects near the just-finished Gateway Arch which opened in October 1965.

Work was also afoot on projects that stemmed from the $6 million bond issue passed of 1962; projects generally run by the Civic Center Redevelopment Corporation, a downtown business group. Civic Center raised another $20 million and the city borrowed $30 million more to develop the city's core.

But it wasn't the old ways of redevelopment that got Cervantes' juices flowing in those early days of his administration. He had bigger, more original ideas that focused on the image of the city. These ideas, while interesting, had nothing to do with the divisions that prevented the city from making real improvements.

While the ballpark and the other downtown building projects were left over from the Tucker years, Cervantes' two dearest pets, and biggest mistakes, were all his own -- the Spanish Pavilion and the *Santa Maria* sailing ship.

The Spanish Pavilion was built for the 1964-65 New York World's Fair in Flushing Meadows, a sleek, white, modern structure used for splashy art exhibits. *Life* magazine called it the "jewel of the fair." The ceilings were Pyrenees pine, the gallery included Picasso; there were traditional Spanish iron gates -- a blend of Moorish and sixties.

Cervantes bought the building with $2 million in privately raised funds and cited a Chamber of Commerce estimate that predicted a $6 million return and a draw of 2 million visitors a year. The Pavilion would emphasize a new St. Louis industry -- tourism -- an industry "that doesn't smoke or pollute the river."

The Pavilion would be a third leg of a "tourist triangle" in the heart of the city -- the Arch, the new ballpark and the Pavilion. Instead, the Pavilion became "Cervantes' Folly."

The building was dismantled in New York, shipped by rail and reassembled at Market and Broadway at the very heart of the downtown, near the end of the old Osage trail used by eighteenth century whites as the first road west from the Mississippi River. When Cervantes took office, the southwest corner of the intersection of Market and Broadway had been empty for two years, an eyesore at the very heart of the city.

For over a hundred years the spot housed a series of theaters, starting in 1852 with the Varieties Theaters, an oval-shaped affair patterned after a theater in Paris. The opulent facility had a floor that could be raised to slope downward during plays and leveled for Grand Balls for high society. One of the largest variety houses in the West, thousands came to see elaborately staged productions of the works like the prototype of the musical comedy, "The Black Crook."

The Varieties eventually proved too expensive for its own good and went broke. After a change in ownership, it opened again as the first-class

Grand Theater in 1881, only to be destroyed by a fire in 1884. An entirely new facility was built, opening as the Grand Opera House Sept. 14, 1885, that stood until 1963.

The venerable Opera House had featured a Moorish style of elaborate decoration and architecture. The seating capacity was 2,300, featuring two levels of curtained boxes where the rich could sit in privacy along the sides of the stage in lushly appointed spaces on velvet-covered chairs and couches -- the luxury boxes of the day. Buffalo Bill played there, as did Edwin Booth, the greatest actor of the time and father of Lincoln's killer.

By the sixties burlesque shows and strippers replaced the actors and opera singers. In 1963, it was nothing but a parking lot and Cervantes thought something had to be done.

The Spanish Pavilion opened with a parade and music on May 25, 1969. Just as in the nineteenth century, crowds from the city and thereabouts flocked to the facility where they sipped sangrias in the Casa Cervantes Bar or laughed at the antics of Jerry Lewis in the second floor theater.

But the crowds quickly abated, attracting less than half of the expected totals. The mayor wasn't able to overcome the growing fear of the downtown. Thousands of whites had by then fled the city with no great desire to return. Also, prices in the restaurants were too high for the St. Louis taste. The opulent carved ceilings, tiled floors and modern art were an attraction for one visit, but repeat business was scant.

The scheme didn't last long. A bankruptcy petition for the Spanish International Pavilion Foundation, representing 18,000 donors, was filed June 15, 1970, barely a year after the Pavilion opened, showing costs of $2 million above original estimates. The operators didn't have cash flow to make payments on a $2.5 million loan.

Howard Baer, the department store mogul, said that Civic Progress had gone along with Cervantes "in spite of the almost unanimous feeling that the project was ridiculous. Actually they were a little afraid of him." The tuxedo set stopped sipping sangria at Casa Cervantes.

And once they saw the Pavilion failing, the bankers pulled the plug, ready to pounce on the failure of the man they saw as an opponent, putting personal vendetta ahead of the city's success. A proposed dinner theater met with no fund-raising success and the mayor had bigger issues with which to deal. The building sat empty during Cervantes' second term, a constant reminder, in the heart of the city, of his flopped production. This was no Hollywood rhumba contest.

The Pavilion "was not my most brilliant coup," Cervantes said.

Along the riverfront in the summer of 1970 sat Al's other pet -- the *Santa Maria,* a reproduction of the craft in which the Spanish explorer Christopher Columbus sailed across the Atlantic in 1492.

The replica was built in Spain and was another World's Fair leftover. An 80-foot long vessel, its planks cut from the forests of the Pyrenees, it contained all the fifteenth-century gadgets Columbus would have used -- navigation instruments, cannons, water barrels. Cervantes thought that mooring it on the Mississippi levee just below the Arch would bring 500,000 tourists a year to St. Louis.

After the fair the boat went to Washington DC, for an unsuccessful run as a tourist attraction before going up for auction. Cervantes outbid Laurence Rockefeller for the boat, paying $375,000. The ship was taken apart and towed by two tugs down the Atlantic, into the Gulf to New Orleans, then up the river to St. Louis. Fourteen tons of internal gear was trucked across the country. Everything was reassembled in St. Louis and the ship was moored next to the old steamboat *Becky Thatcher* on the levee, opened to the public on April 25, 1969. The opening was modest, about 450 people a day, far lower than expected.

But Cervantes was optimistic, saying the ship "lived up to everyone's expectations."

He was enjoying dinner in the Toledo Room of the Spanish Pavilion on a Sunday night two months later, watching a summer storm blow up over the river. He was called away from his table to the phone where an anonymous voice said he had just seen the *Santa Maria* floating down the river.

First the mayor laughed, thinking the call was a joke. "My flagship was not scheduled to maneuver." But this was no joke. The wind had whipped the river into a gale-force frenzy and broken the *Santa Maria* and the *Becky Thatcher* from their moorings. Still tied together, "the ghost of Columbus' ship and the namesake of Tom Sawyer's girlfriend were engaged in a dance of death."

Over 100 people were eating dinner on the *Thatcher*; the *Santa Maria* was closed and empty. Cervantes reported the incident: "As the two craft careened drunkenly together in the turbulent stream, the shriek of the wind was matched by the screams of the diners on the *Becky Thatcher*."

The *Santa Maria* hit the shore first, crashing into the Monsanto pipeline pilings, cushioning the blow for the *Thatcher*. "There were no serious causalities -- except my boat," Cervantes said.

The *Santa Maria* was salvaged and in 1970 lodged safely on top of two barges in site of the shoreline, a looming hulk that the *Post-Dispatch* called "a 110-ton barb in the side of the Mayor." For three years there it sat, all during Cervantes second term, until it was sold to a Florida promoter and shipped to Cape Canaveral. There it had its third try as a tourist attraction, but burned to the water line and was destroyed in June 1974.

The *Thatcher* left the riverfront in 1975 and became a dinner theater in Pittsburgh. The old riverboat had far better luck than the relic of Columbus' flagship, enjoying a long life until it sank in the Ohio River in 2010 during a snowstorm.

Just as St. Louis contains virtually no trace of the 40-year Spanish ownership of the city during the late eighteenth century, there was also little left in 2015 from the Spanish Pavilion. At first, the building sat empty. A plan for a city aquarium was met skeptically. High weeds grew up around it. Boy Scouts were recruited to cut the grass.

Local hotel developer Donald Breckenridge took control of the building in February 1973. Cervantes left office shortly after, his mayoral goals washed up on the shoals of his missed opportunity, losing the primary to John Poelker, the Civic Progress candidate.

Breckenridge built a tower above the Pavilion building and opened the Breckenridge Pavilion Hotel in June 1976. The hotel flourished next to Busch Stadium during the seventies and eighties until another slump in the downtown. Breckenridge sold out to Marriott in 1996.

The hotel in 2015 was the Ballpark Hilton, an impressive facility with 676 guest rooms in two towers over 20 stories high. The hotel was named best in the city for 2009 by *the Riverfront Times*, citing its plush feel, its indoor swimming pool and mid-week bargains. The lobby areas also held an outstanding collection of Cardinal baseball photographs, including a collection devoted to Dizzy Dean. One of the photos captures the Diz cavorting after the 1934 World Series, a tiger's tail in his mouth.

Marriott took out the last public reminder of the Pavilion in 1997, the 350,000 blocks of Flemish pine that formed the centerpiece ceiling of the first floor restaurant and bar. Soon after the Marriott bought the place in 1996, it was discovered that the underside of the ceiling was lined with asbestos and the toxic fire proofing material made it impossible to remodel the area or salvage the wood.

But a close look found that not all was gone after all. In the kitchen of what was once Casa Cervantes remained a floor of orange quarry tiles from Spain, very thick and very durable.

The Cervantes administration took another deep blow in 1970 when *Life* magazine -- a venerable American institution that had started in 1883 but was only two years short of its demise -- ran a seven-page spread alleging that Cervantes was tied to the St. Louis "underworld." The specter of campaign manager Tony Sansone had come back to haunt the mayor. A St. Louis reporter named Denny Walsh, a one-time writer for the *Globe-Democrat,* sold the story to *Life* after it was rejected locally.

Tying Cervantes to the Mob came just a year after his election to a second term. Ironically, he had just made crime the major issue of the second term in his inauguration speech, saying it was the new No. 1 problem in the city. His civil rights commission had amounted to very little by then, fear had chased away many residents both black and white, and the North Side continued to deteriorate. With Richard Nixon now president, "law and order" was in the air.

Cervantes said he planned to use "all the power of my office" to reduce armed robbery, theft and vandalism through a new action program. He asked the citizenry to fight criminals and support "morality by our personal examples and by making it clear that crime simply will not be condoned in any segment of our community."

Cervantes, who had dropped out of school and left home at 16, had developed a particular dislike to the young protesters who were marching in St. Louis and across the country in the late sixties. In 1967 he had called draft card burning demonstrators "dirt" and said anti-Vietnam demonstrators were "seeking some way to avoid their responsibilities."

In 1968, while a delegate at the Democratic nominating convention, he stood with Mayor Richard Daley of Chicago, backing the Chicago police force during the protests outside the convention by thousands of young anti-war demonstrators, actions later decried by a federal investigation as a "police riot." Cervantes, speaking on Chicago television, said, "We need law and order in America. When these hippies, Yippies, or dirty kids or whoever they are, try to take over a city, you have to keep it under control."

As he started the second term he set up a new crime commission and named a long-time ally, the attorney Morris Shenker, as its head. The *Life* article made much of this appointment since Shenker had represented Mob figures during federal hearings in the fifties and later was the lawyer for Jimmy Hoffa, the Teamster president who was alleged to have had tight ties with organized crime.

The article also said that Cervantes was directly linked to St. Louis crime families through Sansone, his campaign manager and close friend who *Life* called "the mayor's liaison" with the Mob. Cervantes denied the story, calling it a "fairytale" and "an outright falsehood." He sued *Life* for libel, seeking $12 million in damages, but the court threw out the action, saying Cervantes had "wholly failed to demonstrate" that the story showed a reckless disregard for the truth.

The expose in *Life* was a big part of Cervantes' downfall, but it was a mere blip in the St. Louis story of organized crime.

First had been an Irish gang, Egan's Rats, who operated beginning near the turn of the twentieth century. Lasting until the twenties it profited from bootlegging, armed robbery and voter fraud. The Rats battled and defeated one rival Irish gang called the Hogan Gang and another called the Bottoms Gang.

Italian crime mobs had also been present in the city from the turn of the century. From the twenties through the sixties the Italian mob was in the hands of the Vitale family until the death of Johnny Vitale in 1961. The godfather Tony Giordano, Vitale's successor, died of natural causes in 1980. A power struggle ensued, leading to the death of Jimmy Michaels, the husband of Sansone's daughter. Michaels was head of a Syrian mob centered on the South Side and was killed in a spectacular car bombing on I-55.

In April 1983, federal authorities indicted Paul Leisure, said to be the chief enforcer for the Italians and Giordano's bodyguard, for the bombing. Leisure's brother, a cousin and others were also indicted in connection with three murders. Leisure, a business agent for Laborers' Local 42, had been the target of a car bombing in 1981, losing his leg but surviving.

He and four others were subsequently convicted in the Michaels killing. Authorities said Michaels had been a longtime ally of the Italians and was protected by Giandano. Leisure, however, didn't feel the same, probably because the Italians had allegedly killed his older brother in 1964. Leisure died in prison in 2000.

Shenker, Cervantes' crime commissioner, died in 1989 at age 82. He was investigated several times but never indicted until the last year of his life when a grand jury accused him of conspiring to conceal hundreds of thousands of dollars from the IRS at the time he was working for the city of St. Louis.

Shenker arrived in St. Louis in 1922, a 15-year-old Russian immigrant. He worked his way through Washington University law school, beginning practice in 1932. As well as a defender of Hoffa and other mob figures he was also a founder of Dismas House in St. Louis, a rehabilitation center for ex-convicts.

He was a part owner of the Dunes Hotel and Casino in Las Vegas, a hotel reputedly purchased with money from the Teamsters pension fund, the retirement goldmine controlled by Hoffa. There were also reports that Hoffa was in contact with Shenker in 1975 on the last day the Teamster president was known to be alive.

The Pavilion, the *Santa Maria* and the Mob allegations were distractions from the main stem of St. Louis life. Another was a proposed airport for the East Side that never got off the ground and was another nail in Cervantes' political coffin. But Al Cervantes was a complicated man and his tenure a complicated story.

He provided 1,000 new public service jobs by obtaining $5.2 million in federal money. He arranged financing for 150 new single-family homes. And, most importantly for the future of the city, he helped bring the strategy of rebuilding houses instead of destroying them into the public mind. In some of the neighborhoods, particularly on the South Side and the central corridor, this approach worked, in other places, especially the North Side, it didn't.

Indeed, his was an approach, at least indirectly, that led to the saving of Soulard, the Central West End, Kingsbury, Shaw, and other neighborhoods from the fate suffered by the North Side.

Soulard was his biggest success.

The city's oldest and most historic neighborhood, founded by families that arrived with Laclede, was in dire straights by 1970. The population of the South Side neighborhood had gone off the cliff from 1960 to 1970, dropping from 12,875 to 6,024. Barely 10 percent of its housing stock was considered in good shape, with 40 percent in need of immediate repair, another 40 percent needing extensive restoration and the other 10 percent needing complete structural overhaul.

City planners called Soulard obsolete and as early as 1947 gave it the description "blighted," the death sentence description of the urban removal movement. The Third Street Expressway, the precursor of the Eisenhower Interstates, hacked off a corner of the area in the fifties, cutting off views of the river from the hill above downtown. Dead-end streets that once led downtown gathered dust in the concrete corners. Absentee owners began cutting up grand houses that were built before 1875. Real estate speculators began salivating.

The density of the 268-acre area dropped by half between 1960 and 1970, 40 percent of the dwellings had been demolished over the 10 years, large numbers of houses were boarded up, and the area had been virtually cut off by more highway projects designed to fill suburbs further south and west.

But in 1972, just before Cervantes left office, the rhetoric, if not yet the reality, had changed regarding the fate of Soulard

Vietnam veterans, young sixties radicals and social reformers, young couples with children, government employees, poverty workers in the Model Cities programs and outsiders of all sorts had stumbled upon the neighborhood as a low-cost, quality neighborhood with great potential, the Haight-Ashbury of the Heartland. These newcomers were mostly white and as such they met only sporadic opposition from the real estate developers.

A 24-year-old Harvard graduate who wore a beard and who kept his sense of humor, Bob Brandhorst, was just one of many urban pioneers who drifted into the area. He helped start a program called Youth, Education and Health in Soulard that aimed at securing low-income housing. The Soulard Neighborhood Improvement Association formed in 1969. The neighborhood gained status on the National Register of Historic Places in 1972.

A breakfast program for kids started. The neighborhood began promoting urban homesteading and conducted tours of houses available for restoration. Banks began erasing the red lines that had been drawn around the neighborhood.

By the early eighties the neighborhood was on the road to recovery. An entertainment district built around blues clubs that featured lineups of black players from across town popped up as the musicians found gigs and a new audience of white fans.

The same phenomena (without the clubs) occurred in the nearby Lafayette Park and the Shaw neighborhoods, again with urban homesteaders from the sixties saving the still standing brick houses. Small businesses followed the homesteaders; new attitudes toward old houses arose.

In the far western part of the city Kingsbury, soon renamed Skinker-DeBaliviere after its boundary streets, an even more promising development was seen with the establishment of a local bank to outflank redlining. There a strong organization grew up around St. Roch's Catholic Church. Washington University, the fast growing college just outside the neighborhood, began feeding students into the renewed housing stock. Skinker-DeBaliviere was the most integrated of the homesteading neighbors and by 2015 remained one of the nation's few 50-50 white-black neighborhoods, its community council still strong.

In 1972, a *Post-Dispatch* article said that for Soulard and other neighborhoods around town, "The big question is whether enough home-loving gamblers can be attracted to the neighborhood in time to save it." In places like Soulard and Skinker-DeBaliviere the answer became clear as the housing stock was rehabilitated and the vans pulled up with new residents.

The North Side of Delmar, however, was a very different story. Services were scant and the city's major banks kept no-loan redlining in place. The approach was similar to what it had been along the levee in the thirties and in Mill Creek Valley in the fifties. The black-owned Gateway Bank, which was formed after the Jefferson Bank protests, struggled, never capitalized by the old money of the elite. The institution finally failed in 2009 and was sold to the Central Bank of Kansas City.

Cervantes did not benefit politically from the restoration of the central neighborhoods. His encouragement of community groups came too late for results to be seen. His enforcement of housing codes, street cleaning and tree trimming programs were likewise slow in development but paid dividends later.

He watched as the dynamite blew down Pruitt-Igoe on the near North Side. The Pavilion and the *Santa Maria* kept pushing themselves into the newspapers even as community groups were quietly meeting.

By 1972, opponents smelled weakness in the Cervantes camp. He talked about running for governor. A group of youthful Democratic aldermen led by Richard Gephardt, a conservative from the South Side, formed a coalition called the "young Turks" and began to attack the mayor, especially over the *Life* magazine article.

"A lot of these charges may be untrue and unfounded," Gephardt said, "but the vast number of people halfway believe these disclosures, and this erodes the confidence and credibility in government." Citing the Pavilion and the *Santa Maria*, "you have projects that make the business community look askance at the way the city is run."

Gephardt and four other aldermen refused to attend a Cervantes fund-raising dinner and threw their support behind Comptroller John Poelker. So did Civic Progress, never a Cervantes supporter. Cervantes had throughout all three runs for mayor the support of Bill Clay, the civil rights leader from the North Side who had taken over Jordan Chambers' role as the city's leading black politician after the Jefferson Bank fight.

Clay's support played into the hands of the Gephardt faction. It labeled Cervantes a "machine politician." Clay delivered the black vote for his ally again in the 1973 primary, but it wasn't enough. Poelker carried the white vote on the South Side for a close victory of 48,941 to Cervantes' 43,340.

Poelker had been an FBI agent from 1942 to 1953 and while Cervantes' alleged connection to organized crime was the silent gorilla in the room in the campaign. Another obstacle was a belated promise to help develop the North Side.

Poelker's neighborhood development emphasis was on the Central West End where black families were evicted. Cervantes ran again in 1977 but was again defeated, this time by the low-key James F. Conway, a candidate backed full out by Civic Progress stalwarts like beer baron Gussie Busch, aircraft maker James McDonnell and Boatman's Bank mogul Clarence Barksdale.

This time the election was a runaway, but, like Poelker, Conway only lasted one term, his closing of Homer G. Phillips Hospital on the North Side costing him the election in 1981, losing virtually everywhere in the city to Vince Schoemehl, an alderman from Skinker-DeBaliviere, who had been a steady critic of the closure and of Conway's redevelopment policies.

Gephardt, meanwhile, became one of the city's most successful politicians, promptly moving to West County where he found conservative Democrats. Gephardt, solidly supported by white suburbanites, was elected to the U. S. House in 1977, remaining in office until 2005. He was House Majority Leader from 1989 to 1995 in the Clinton administration and Minority Leader from 1995 to 2003. He made two runs at the presidential nomination, 1988 and 2004. He was elected 14 times from the 3rd District of Missouri. He left Congress after his second presidential failure and became a leading Washington lobbyist with clients including health care and drug companies as well as Boeing and Goldman Sachs.

Cervantes never ran for office again after his second defeat in the mayoral polls. He taught at St. Louis University and attended to his many business interests. He died quietly in 1983 at age 82.

Several new plans emerged as Cervantes went out the door, plans that went back to the days before the civil rights movement. In essence, the plans called for a triage approach to the city's depopulation problems -- save those alive and let the crippled die.

One was at first called "New Town in the City," a quality environment with the luxury of suburban living and vitality of the city living. The new town would be located in the midtown area west of the Central Business District from Lafayette Park on the south to Delmar on the north, a total of 1,250 acres, 18,500 units of housing, 40,000 to 50,000 people of various socio-economic backgrounds. The North Side was ignored.

Gephardt and the Young Turks to the Board of Aldermen introduced bills in 1973. They were followed by a 1975 comprehensive plan submitted to the city Plan Commission, drafted by an urban planning company called

Team Four, the first comprehensive plan in the city since the Bartholomew Plan of 1947.

This plan and the Gephardt bills were based largely on research conducted by the RAND Corporation, the conservative think tank that was developed after World War II by military and business planners. RAND thinkers included men like Henry Kissinger, the architect of the American bombing campaign of Cambodia during the Vietnam War, and Herman Kahn, an advocate of the theory of the winnable nuclear war. The company in the sixties and seventies added other areas of study to its analysis of war: urban planning, criminal justice, infrastructure and social welfare.

The thinkers looked closely at the racial division of St. Louis into north and south. The Gephardt legislation never became law but represented the change in rhetoric following Cervantes' defeat, calling North St. Louis "an insignificant residential area not worthy of special maintenance effort." The bills called for the preservation of 74,000 buildings in South St. Louis and the demolition of 70,100 buildings on the North Side where "rehabilitation would be uneconomical."

The Team Four plan was never officially adopted but people like Bernie Hayes, a longtime radio commentator and writer, watched how its ideas and assumptions effected the changes in the city over a 40-year period. He and many others became convinced that City Hall and Civic Progress in effect adopted the RAND outlook and the Team Four design. The result was a North Side that in the twenty-first century is decidedly separate and very unequal.

Hayes came to the city too late to enjoy Mill Creek Valley. The Harlem of St. Louis was gone, all gone, fully leveled by the time he arrived from San Francisco in 1965. Rebuilding had not yet begun in earnest. The displaced had resettled elsewhere, some on the North Side, others further out in North County in places like Kinloch, Ferguson, Dellwood and Florissant. Meanwhile, the Pruitt-Igoe, Darst-Webbe, and Carr Square projects were emptying inside the city. The black population was on the move.

Hayes, coming from the West Coast, remembers his first impression upon arrival in St. Louis in a word: "strange."

> I couldn't believe it.
>
> St. Louis was lagging behind in everything, especially the social movements, the civil rights movement, the political movements, it was just a strange city. And it was a cliquish city. Coming from out of town if you aren't a St. Louisan you are ostracized. Even the people from East St. Louis -- they were treated as outsiders. Except the musicians -- the music world was the only thing that was totally integrated.
>
> (In the seventies) new areas opened to African Americans and other minorities. Blacks started moving out of the city and that killed the North Side. Plus gentrification, there was that too. Then came the Team Four Plan.
>
> Let the weak die to save the strong -- let the North Side die -- no essential services -- the central corridor, the Central West End and so forth, most of the services would go to the South Side. The Chrysler plant closed, Chevrolet plant closed. This is also when they closed Homer G. Phillips Hospital.
>
> This was devastating to black people, there is now (2012) not a single hospital bed north of Delmar, not one bed. And that was part of the plan. And there hasn't been one bed now for 30 years. The clubs went. People had no jobs, no money. They couldn't go to clubs. The area started to be empty by '79 or '80. Mill Creek was an earlier version, same idea.
>
> Team Four was a stealth plan. Those who fought against it had no power. The black aldermen had no voice. In the eighties there was a recession. In the black community that recession was a depression.

One gauge of St. Louis health, its population, continued to roll downhill all during the sixties. By 1970 the population was 622,236, down 17 percent from 1960, reaching all the way down to the level of the World's Fair year of 1904.

The decline wasn't a big surprise, the other rusty cities in the Heartland were going down in population as well: Cleveland (14.2 percent), Pittsburgh (14), Detroit (9.3). In 1976, census estimates in St. Louis showed another 17 percent drop, to 519,345, making what was once the No. 4 city in the nation No. 24. Dallas, Houston, Atlanta, Miami and Phoenix were the big winners. St. Louis was well on its way to becoming what the Brookings Institute called the nation's "most distressed" large city. Nearby, East St. Louis was deemed the worst similarly distressed small city.

In 1970, with Cervantes in his second term, the central city counted for just 26.4 percent of the larger population district, that area covering St. Louis County, three smaller Missouri counties, plus East St. Louis and environs on the Illinois side of the river. The overall metropolitan area was ranked 11th in the country in 1970 and in 1980 was 12th.

In 1980, the city's standing was down two more notches to No. 26 and still falling. At the end of the seventies the population stood at 452,801, the lowest since the last decade of the nineteenth century, the decade when Stagger Lee shot Billy. The seventies saw the biggest free fall in any decade for the city, losing 27 percent, 170,000 people. This made the drop from the fifties through the seventies almost 400,000, a stunning 46 percent. At the same time (from 1940 to 1990) the percentage of African Americans in St. Louis soared from 13 percent to 47 percent. St. Louis had truly become two cities, divided and unequal.

The population in St. Louis County nearly passed the city in 1960 with the two entities having virtually the same share of the count -- 750,026 for the city versus 703,532 for the county. But by 1970 the county roared ahead, reaching 951,353 compared to the city's 622,236. The 1980 comparison showed a far wider distance with 973,896 in St. Louis County compared to 453,085 in the city. By 1990 the population difference continued to widen: 993,529 to 396,685.

As the county grew, meanwhile, a hodgepodge of independent municipalities developed. Many had their own police force, their own courts, their own city government, some all-black, others all-white. A separate St. Louis County government, also with its own police kept the peace in the areas left over, the unincorporated area. Some of the new cities became mixed, with large numbers of blacks in cities run entirely by whites, a division had implications in the events of the twenty-first century.

By the end of the eighties the population drop in the city was slowing with "only" a 12 percent decrease to 396,685 in the 1990 count. By then, Mayor Victor Schoemehl was beginning his third term, overseeing what some observers called an "urban renaissance" -- an $80 billion downtown investment of demolition and reconstruction.

Also, by then the nation had passed through what was called the Reagan Recession, officially dated July 1981 to November 1982, caused by a dramatic drop in interest rates in the spring of 1980 and an equally sharp rise in those rates in the fall, just prior to the election of former actor Ronald Reagan to the White House. Unemployment was high (over 10 percent by the end of the period) and the prime interest rate soared to 21.5 percent in June 1982.

Embedded in this distressing context, St. Louis continued to struggle with its decline in population and its dirty, weed-infested streets. Over a two-decade period by the start of the sixties, St. Louis County saw five times as many government housing loans then in the city. By the time civil rights leaders realized the extent of bank redlining it was too late.

The 1973 RAND study said, "St. Louis does appear to have the opportunity to reduce the rate of its decline, but even this reduction requires new sources of revenue outside its own jurisdiction." This new source had to be federal dollars. Washington realized this after the urban rioting in cities around the country in the sixties, but even by 1976 there was still twice as much loan money sent into St. Louis County as reached city neighborhoods.

These neighborhoods, the victims of "urban abandonment," were "like an elderly couple no longer sure of their purpose in life after their children have moved away." The bland approach exhibited by the two mayors after Cervantes -- Poelker and Conway -- left the status quo. City Hall sat by, looking the other way as the moving vans headed along the new, elevated highways heading for the county.

Dissatisfaction built in those who decided to stay. And here came an answer for disgruntled voters. It was a 34-year-old former member of the New Left Students for a Democratic Society, Vincent Schoemehl. He was a resident of the Skinker-DeBaliviere neighborhood who had been a fierce critic of Mayor Conway while a member of the Board of Aldermen. Like Cervantes he had been a salesman and a promoter.

He was elected alderman in 1975 as a white ally of the unions, the civil rights activists and a champion of the neighborhoods, especially those in the racially mixed central corridor. He was one of 11 children and a year before the 1981 mayoral contest began using his siblings and neighborhood friends as grassroots organizers who pounded the sidewalks of the city, ringing doorbells and shaking hands.

At first, the newspapers and the city's ward leaders gave him no chance. But he quickly won over Bill Clay with a promise to reopen Homer G. Phillips Hospital.

Schoemehl also took advantage of a report that Conway favored cutting the 2,000-member police force by 500 officers and produced a clever television ad that showed a police car driving out of the city. Conway denied the claim, but couldn't change the perception of a penny-pinching administrator.

Conway had been considered a cinch to return for a second term. On the eve of the Democratic primary one alderman predicted a four-to-one victory for the incumbent but city Democrats rose up at the polls to demand change. Schoemehl was the smashing winner -- 70,507, about 67 percent, to Conway's 32,683, or about 31 percent, the biggest upset victory in the history of St. Louis politics.

Schoemehl swept the North Side. Clay, who had been serving in the U.S. House since 1968, called him "a silver-tongued, gold-throat orator who said all the right things and even used the right tonal inflections when comparing his own history of hardship to the plight of many of our race." Some of the black wards voted six-to-one for Schoemehl. Another opportunity for change was on the doorstep at the confluence.

Homer G. Phillips Hospital was an imposing state-of-the-art facility that sat near Sumner High School in the heart of The Ville. Opened in 1937, it was the result of a finally kept promise to the black community 14 years previously, in the bond issue of 1923.

Phillips was an attorney and political activist who was the son of a former slave. On June 18, 1931, age 51, he was reading a newspaper waiting for a streetcar on Delmar Avenue. Two men, identified by a witness as black youths, slowly approached him at the stop. One slammed Phillips in the face with his fist, then shot him point blank several times.

Phillips, who arrived in St. Louis before the 1904 Fair, was an activist, the founder of the Citizens' Liberty League, which fought for African American rights after voters approved the 1916 ordinance legalizing housing segregation. Two teenagers were arrested in the killing, suspected of taking revenge in an insurance case, but neither was convicted. There were several other theories. Phillips had many enemies due to his law practice, both black and white.

The case was never solved.

But the hospital that bore his name was built, opening during the Depression as a segregated hospital for blacks, celebrated by 5,000 people at the dedication ceremony. The facility, which still stands and is used as a retirement home for the elderly, is richly textured architecturally, its four wings and Deco design making a striking landmark on the North Side.

As well as treating black patients in their own neighborhood, the hospital was originally a training facility. By 1948, one-third of the graduates of black medical schools in the country were trained at Phillips. By then the hospital staff had a national reputation for treatment of the acutely injured, credited with pioneering the techniques and technology for intravenous feeding and for the treatment of gunshot wounds, burns and bleeding ulcers, saving many lives in its emergency rooms.

The hospital was integrated in the fifties but continued to see mainly blacks patients. In 1964, reports began to surface about City Hall intentions to save money by combining Phillips with City Hospital on the South Side, the other city-run hospital. African Americans from Mill Creek Valley used that hospital before the destruction of the neighborhood, but by the mid-sixties were moving further and further north, closer to Phillips.

For 15 years, the battle over the hospital was fought, even as the North Side slowly drained its population and the budget shrunk at Phillips. Conway deemed the South Side facility better equipped and closed Phillips in 1979, much to the dismay of the black community. One writer said the move reflected the status of "blacks in St. Louis and also indicative of the political maneuvering on the part of area businesses, universities and elected officials who decide on civic issues outside the influence of the electorate." Others saw Team Four at work. Let the weak die.

The 200,000 blacks living on the North Side suddenly had no hospital.

Then, in 1981, came the white knight, the young Schoemehl, promising to save the hospital. Clay was delighted, feeling it was about time for "those who flagrantly trample on their constituents' right to adequate health care to be taught a political lesson." Clay's assessment of the political realities in the North Side concluded that "a black candidate for mayor was not a viable option," and decided to give Schoemehl a chance.

But Schoemehl couldn't deliver the hospital to the black community. He conceded he had made the promise "without looking closely at the issue."

When Conway closed the hospital he failed to switch operating authority to the state and federal government. To be reopened the hospital would have to be treated as a new facility and meet all kinds of new regulations. Conway also gave away the former power of the mayor to reopen the hospital by executive order, something Schoemehl thought he could do when he made the campaign promise.

Unable to change the city charter to reopen the facility under the old conditions, in 1982 Schoemehl tried to pass a $64 million bond issue to bring the hospital up to code. This vote failed as a divided black vote couldn't overcome the South Side's white bloc. Schoemehl needed a 60 percent majority to pass the bond and could only muster 53 percent. Every North Side ward saw a slippage in support for the mayor. His relations with the black community were never the same.

Schoemehl turned his attention to other issues. His desktop slogan was "Ready, Fire, Aim." He pushed a Cervantes-like barrage of programs, most of them promoting downtown and the central corridor neighborhoods. These programs won him election twice more, in 1985 and 1989, giving him 12 years in office.

The downtown was transformed. Sixty-five new projects rose during his tenure. He cleaned up neighborhoods with tree trimming and increased trash pickup. He launched Operation Brightside, under which 12 million daffodil bulbs were planted in public places. He promoted Operation Safestreet, providing low-cost locks and security systems to residences and businesses.

He helped attract the Blues hockey team and the Rams football team. He oversaw the building of a domed stadium for football and helped launch an entertainment district along the water at Laclede's Landing. He promoted what became known as the Gateway Mall that opened space in front of the Old Courthouse.

In October of 1982 the Cardinals were back in the World Series for the first time since the days of Gibson, Brock and McCarver. Schoemehl took full advantage to sell the city, glowing in an interview with *The New York Times,* "I couldn't be happier, I've got a billion dollars in construction going on; we just received a $10-million federal grant for redevelopment and the Cardinals are in the World Series."

The article went on to give the city a recession-busting boost in a few priceless paragraphs saying:

> Local restaurateurs, hotel and motel operators and other service business owners say the Series has been a tremendous boon to their local economy, adding millions of badly needed dollars. The Cardinals symbolize all that is good about St. Louis in the view of many residents.
>
> "The Cardinals are hot, they really are," said Elizabeth D. Cook, a housing consultant who has lived in St. Louis six years. "It ties it all together, what I have been saying about the city. The city is in the midst of a boom, just like the Cardinals. The Cardinals were lousy for years and now things have turned around, just like they have for the city."

The story contrasted a Bureau of the Census report that St. Louis "had the dubious distinction of losing more of its population during the 1970s than any other city," adding the ominous statistic that "if the rate of exodus continued the city would be a ghost town by the year 2015."

The Times contrasted this forecast with the way things were going under Schoemehl, quoting St, Louis booster James A. Van Sant, the president of Lukens General Industries: ''We have the Missouri Botanical Gardens, which is outstanding, a dozen or so major corporations based here, an important new opera company, the well-known St. Louis Symphony, the St. Louis Art Museum and a healthy university community."

In 1985, Schoemehl and the city hit the peak of its recovery. On Aug. 8, 1985, the nation's largest enclosed urban mall, the St. Louis Centre, opened at Washington Avenue and Seventh Street between two longtime downtown department stores, Dillard's on the north and Famous Barr on the south. Just 11 days later Union Station, the venerable rail center, was reborn as another downtown shopping mall.

Some 30,000 people attended the opening of the Centre, a day marked by bright skies, bright balloons and Bob Hope. The design of the mall was quite different from the cookie cutter suburban malls that were dotting the country by then, pulling shoppers away from downtowns everywhere.

The Centre -- 350,000 square feet for $176.5 million -- featured a large glass barrel ceiling that illuminated an arcade that filled four blocks between the renovated Dillard's and Famous Barr and gave shoppers stiff necks gazing straight up at skyscrapers above. Escalators crawled between floors. All white interior and exterior finishes made it look like an ocean liner. The circle on the top was a reminder of a Mississippi paddleboat wheel.

A dramatic photo of the Centre was put on the cover of the architecture book *Interior Pedestrian Places,* which featured prominent public interior spaces throughout the world, and was subject of a glowing feature in *Fortune* magazine, which said, "There is plenty to see and do near downtown's new office towers and hotels. St. Louis is becoming a city to which you might want to take along a spouse on a business trip. This outcome is amazing for a city that has been losing ground for generations."

Union Station, which had been closed in the early seventies, was renovated into a "festival market" and hotel by the Rouse Corporation and opened to more downtown hoopla Aug. 19, 1985. The station, which had been a signature landmark in the city since 1894, had been devoid of train traffic since 1978, just two years after it was declared a national landmark.

But the station was saved by a thunderstorm that closed Lambert Field the next year. One of the delayed passengers was the president of Oppenheimer Properties of New York, James Levi, who decided to take a tour of the city while he waited for the airport to reopen. When he saw the station from his car window he pulled over and had an epiphany, thrilled by the medieval castle tower, the expanse of the Grand Hall and the soaring arches of the train shed.

Shortly thereafter Oppenheimer bought the station for $5 million. Levi tried to obtain local financing for a shopping mall in the station but had to turn to Rouse, a Baltimore firm that had developed the forward-looking Harborplace there as well the award-winning Faneuil Hall in Boston. Levi stated the obvious when asked why he and Rouse took the leap when no one else would, calling Union Station "a truly grand piece of property," and also stated the contrary -- "in my view St. Louis was a sleeping giant."

By the time it opened six years after Levi was delayed at the airport, 6,000 people paid $35 each for a preview of the new station, now complete with a 550-room Omni Hotel and a train shed filled with everything from hot dog stands to gourmet restaurants, "a city within a city." The press was ecstatic, the crowds poured in day after day; enjoying what *Fortune* said was a "truly sumptuous piece of elegance."

There was also the renovation of the even more sumptuous Fox Theater in midtown, the 42-story Metropolitan Tower on Broadway, the 910-room Adam's Mark Hotel on Chestnut and Fourth Street, the new headquarters of Southwest Bell, a total of 23 new and renovated buildings completed in 1986 alone.

Naturally, not everyone was happy. As Schoemehl said later, "I'm a risk taker. Always have been; always will be. Sometimes they work out, sometimes they don't."

At the opening of the Adam's Mark, organizers for the community group ACORN (Association for Community Organizations for Reform Now) raised questions about employment of blacks and the poor and also questioned the heavy taxpayer involvement in all these projects. St. Louis was setting records in federal financing in the "blighted" downtown. ACORN called the financing "welfare for the rich," and said the new structures were intended to "drive the poor out of St. Louis."

Echoes of the old civil rights movement began to be heard again.

One black alderman, Freeman Bosley, Jr., opposed the development, saying that while the city got a "beautiful skyline" what its residents, especially the half who were black, really needed were "jobs, a piece of the action." The developers were almost all white, the crowds flocking to the new centers were almost all white, the division of the city into two sides, white and black, was even more pronounced as one side (white) recovered and the other (black) remained in decline.

The closure of the Chevrolet plant on the North Side in 1981 had lost the equivalent of all the jobs created downtown. ACORN pointed out that the lost jobs on the North Side were skilled union jobs, the majority held by African American workers. Many of the jobs downtown went to minority workers, but these were mostly low paying, low skill clerk and janitorial work.

Unemployment on the North Side in the mid-eighties remained in double digits and was 25 percent and higher among black youth. Homelessness began to grow, a by-product of all the knocked down housing and the high unemployment of the Reagan Recession. For the first time, the city set up an agency, the Homeless Services Network, that coordinated a series of charity efforts to provide temporary and permanent housing for those who couldn't afford the rents.

But even with the rent-free Hope House and a series of charitable efforts, by 1989 only half of the city's homeless people had a bed to sleep in at night. By then the city was spending $785,000 on homeless services.

Meanwhile, City Hospital on the South Side had become a shambles. Newspapers reported nursing shortages, a 30 percent absentee rate by the staff and a lack of drugs and other supplies. In 1985, the city began moving patients out of City Hospital, taking them to the city's dividing line, Delmar Boulevard, where a newer, recently vacated private hospital sat empty.

That facility became Regional Medical Center and the county's poor patients landed there as well when St. Louis County Hospital was also closed. The move resulted in 1,200 layoffs and put the operation of the hospital in private hands. The cost of running it was about the same as that of City Hospital but by 1993, the American Medical Association said it was running smoothly and gave an award to the mayor for his actions.

By then Schoemehl was well into his third term having defeated Bosley in 1985 and Alderman Michael Roberts in 1989. His support, however, had slipped -- from 69 percent to 60 percent. The racial mix had also changed, dropping from over 50 percent black support in 1985 to 30 percent in several black wards in 1989.

That never-ending St. Louis thing -- racism -- reached up and grabbed the mayor. He left City Hall in 1993, shunning a try at a fourth term for an unsuccessful run for governor, never to return to public office.

Clay, his former black ally, said Schoemehl had become "a tool of Civic Progress." Clay changed that while once a champion of blacks, Schoemehl's "legacy is one of showing preference and bias in disbursing government resources to a limited number of people in downtown St. Louis and the West End and showing gross neglect of the city's North Side and near South Side."

A black alderman added, "Basic services in this town have taken second place to hype."

Another elected black, Comptroller Virus Jones, said, "Vince is a salesman -- but when he closes a deal, he empties out the pockets of the city of St. Louis."

Homeless advocate Larry Rice said, "Vince Schoemehl has been a very fine mayor for the upper-income folks, but he is not a friend of poor people."

The head of the Chamber of Commerce agreed, "He has been a good friend to business." U.S. Sen. John Danforth, the heir to the Ralston-Purina fortune and worth an estimated $40 million in 1994, praised Schoemehl as a "forceful advocate for the city of St. Louis." Dick Gephardt, by 1993 the majority leader of the House of Representatives, said, "The construction boom in downtown has really made St. Louis 'Comeback City.'"

But for all the dust and flurry of the Schoemehl years (1981-1993), violent crime in St. Louis rose 20 percent, the population of the city dropped 12 percent, jobs declined by nearly 70,000, and residents in poverty increased by 3 percent to a staggering 24.6 percent.

On the other side of the final ledger, the city's earnings increased by 50 percent, the building boom attracted $3 billion in private money and $80 million in federal funds, and 16,000 new or rehabilitated dwelling units were added.

"Everybody has a way of seeing things," Schoemehl said as he left office. "No matter who you are some people fall outside your scope. Over a period of time, those people who fall outside your scope end up being deeply frustrated. They deserve a chance to be included. I think it's good you aerate government now and again."

Bernie Hayes pondered the Schoemehl years in the strange city from the long distance of the twenty-first century:

> After 1979 that's when the city itself became more progressive and started talking. But it's a racially divided town. We're still talking. And it's the same issues. It's economic.
>
> People who have money will buy a politician. Black or white. They'll support their campaign and those favors have to be paid back. There's reciprocity. Quid pro quo.

Chapter Thirty

Nights on the Mississippi: the Clubs and the Performers

1970-2007

(At the Red Top on the East Side) you'd see cars out front, but no lights on the outside of the building to speak of. But you'd go inside and it would be just as lively as it could be, wasn't that big of a place. I remember the dirt floor; it was the only club I ever went in that had a dirt floor. They would dance like crazy.
-- **Joe Edwards, owner of Blueberry Hill**

As the Grateful Dead tried its new sound system at the Fox and the Mississippi River Festival got its legs on the East Side, Bernie Hayes was finding his legs in his new town, that "strange" new place -- St. Louis. He was 30 years old when he arrived in 1965, an experienced radio voice who had been around music his whole life.

Hayes' mother had a beautiful alto singing voice and was a stay-home housewife until her death in 1954. His father died in 1942. Both parents were raised in Alabama, met in Florida and got married in 1930 in Jacksonville. They moved briefly to Chicago then back to Florida, where Bernie was born Sept. 16, 1935. Shortly after his birth the family moved again, to the South Side of Chicago not far from one of the centers of American music -- the Regal Theater.

Hayes graduated from Phillips High School, captain of the football and track teams. He enlisted in the Air Force and by 1953 was on the air from his base in Alaska. He came out of the service a trained radioman, having avoided Korean War action. From there, Hayes joined another war -- the battle for black respect on the airwaves.

As he explained in his book, *The Death of Black Radio,* his fight was against "racial bias and discrimination," that "long and established way of life in America," a war for "dignitary and nobility." The fight began in 1956 in Alexandria, La., on KDBS-1410 AM, soul and gospel, and has continued unabated into the second decade of the twenty-first century, where he could be found in St. Louis, 80 years old, working on WGNU radio and KNLC-TV.

In 1962, he was in Chicago, a DJ on the first black-owned radio station in the Midwest, a station run by the Chess Brothers. In 1964, Bernie moved to the soul staff of KSOL in San Francisco, but shortly returned to the Heartland, getting a job on KATZ in St. Louis, beginning his half -decade run on the confluence airwaves.

Hayes quickly found a home by the river, especially at an East Side club called the Blue Note, one of the last of the venues that supported the original blues and soul revues. He was lucky to arrive when he did, when the clubs were still hopping on both sides of the river, especially on the North Side of St. Louis. Most of these clubs would disappear over the next 20 years as the black artists headed for Soulard and lower Broadway and the soul revues grew rusty and out of style.

But from 1965 to 1970, the Blue Note and its house band, Leo's Five, provided local music fans -- white and black alike -- with a rare moment at a rare time, original jazz that absorbed the R&B of the past into the kind of innovative jazz being played by that East St. Louis native, Miles Davis. Hayes quickly became the No. 1 afternoon show in St. Louis and soon added a midnight Saturday broadcast renown for its innovation.

Hayes recalled:

> The Blue Note was the most attractive club to whites on the East Side. They would come over -- and blacks from St. Louis, too, -- they would come over after hours. Leo's Five -- the scene -- the

> camaraderie, you didn't notice color, it was beautiful, just to drink after hours.
>
> Lots of tables. Very efficient operation, the waiters, the waitresses, the cooks, everybody was there. Chezie Mae was the cook -- "Cooking with Chezie Mae" -- that was a Leo's Five song. The place reminded you of the Village -- that kind of atmosphere; but not hippie or like that -- but as for people enjoying each other -- the camaraderie.
>
> Leo's Five was the best jazz group in the area.

The group was based around Fred Prothro, trumpet; Don James, organ; Charles "Little Man" Wright and Hamiet Bluiett, sax; Kenny Rice, drums; Leo Gooden, vocals. Many others sat in -- Albert King, Al Valentine, Grant Green, Eddie Fisher, Yuseff Lateef, Lou Donaldson, and Shirley Scott -- a musical collective.

> They played every night, they would play with Benny Sharp and the Sharpies, they would play R&B and jazz. They could go either way, Leo's Five would do the R&B just as much as jazz.

Leo Gooden, who played in the band and ran the club, was born in East St. Louis on Sept. 8, 1927. His mother worked for Buster Wortman, the rackets king of the East Side, a one-time client of Morris Shenker, the former St. Louis police commissioner and Jimmy Hoffa's attorney.

Gooden was obese and as a youngster suffered such vicious teasing he stayed away from school.

> When he would skip school he would always hang around older people -- the old politicians and guys who were much wiser in knowledge. He came up from a very early age under those older guys' wings.
>
> He had what you'd call street knowledge and that's how he got his schooling. He had no formal education. He got into politics at a very early age and became a member of the Democratic organization, which was run by all the top black politicians in East St. Louis. Leo was like their son, they did anything in the world for him. He had all types of influence."

Gooden opened the Blue Note on Aug. 25, 1961. He took an old union hall and added a bar, restaurant, bandstand, dance floor, the works.

There were bedrooms for the bands and an adjacent building for the record company. Oliver Sain, Little Milton and Fontella Bass highlighted a lineup Gooden brought into the club. Out-of-towners like Lockjaw Davis and Albino Red Chapman joined the house band for the initial shows, but by 1965, jazz and Leo's Five had taken hold.

Gooden developed a tiny empire of labels and put out several singles and two albums before he died from a stroke in 1966. These records from the LG Family labels are backed in one way or another by Leo's Five. A compilation of 21 sides from the Leo Five sessions includes four Albert King songs, a rousing vamp on "Johnny Comes Marching Home," and originals like "Hold It," "Cookin' With Chezie Mae" and "Frederick's Dream."

Rice's vibrant drums and the power of Don James on the B-3 are what make Leo's Five happen. These two were infused into the St. Louis sound, James having played the Sportsman's on Finney in the North Side and Tony's Lounge, Union and Easton; in several spots on Gaslight Square and alongside Evelyn West and her "$50,000 Chest" at the Stardust on DeBaliviere. Rice had been drumming through the clubs on the East Side -- El Patio, the Red Top, the Manhattan, the Mellow Cellar on Pendelton, the Moonlight Lounge.

The music produced in Leo Gooden's Blue Note is what in the twenty-first century is called funk-soul, a style in today's music so pervasive as to be almost invisible. But when Don James hit the keys, Kenny Rice shot the downbeat and Hamiet Bluiett blew his alto sax, there was more than style, there was music history in the making. The movement toward free jazz also lingered just at the edge of Leo's Five, waiting to break out.

The club didn't last long enough to see Lake and Bluiett and the St. Louis jazz contingent take Manhattan. The death of Leo Gooden was too much to overcome for the Blue Note, which closed in 1970. Leo's partner, Otis Blue, ran the club until his brother was shot and killed in an incident outside the place, adding to the growing unease about crime in East St. Louis.

Once the Blue Note was gone and KATZ no longer had the live broadcasts, Bernie Hayes rounded up investors and helped launch KWK. He started with just himself and a program manager. After only two weeks on the air, three more DJs came aboard and broadened the "Soul of the City" format. The station increased its power and could be heard in Memphis and Detroit.

KWK captured a large portion of the African-American audience and most of the white R&B fans. Celebrities started dropping by the station: James Brown, Stevie Wonder, The Temptations. But in 1972, the company's ownership, seeing a bigger market, moved to Detroit and the new management demoted Hayes from managing director to advertising salesman. Hayes and seven other DJs promptly walked off the job, leaving the station off the air for a week.

By the end of the seventies, after sporadic radio and television gigs, Hayes left his DJ days and began what turned out to be the landmark of his career, the radio talk show.

In 1979, his was the first black radio talk show in the St. Louis area, back on his old home of KATZ. Hayes also started the first black talk show on radio station WGNU in 1985. He went on to a career that led to induction in the St. Louis Radio Hall of Fame, The Greater St. Louis Association of Black Journalists Hall of Fame and the Black Hall of Fame.

He also made a documentary radio broadcast "The History of Black Radio in St. Louis" as a companion to *Death of Black Radio.* In the second decade of the twenty-first century, Hayes teaches at Webster University, is a regular columnist for the *St. Louis American*, and sends steady blog messages on his Internet outlet *Bernie Hayes Understands.*

The Blue Note wasn't the only club to die in the seventies, just one of the first. The seventies and eighties saw the end of the reign of the North Side clubs, as well as the death of many on the East Side. Many of these clubs remain obscure, alive only on the memories of the many people who played, stayed, and then left for higher ground in the suburbs.

While the Club Imperial and the Riviera drew the big names, the heart of the North Side live music business from the sixties until the nineties was in small clubs that drew regular crowds. Take Gino's Lounge for example, a joint that opened in 1973 and lasted all the way into the twenty-first century, sitting just over the city line in Pine Lawn, one of the small jurisdictions in North St. Louis County.

Gino's was killed in 2002 by a road-widening project that helped cars get from Natural Bridge to the I-70 freeway five minutes faster. The powers that were (and are) decided that widening a road was more important than allowing a small businessman to run a neighborhood meeting place that for 29 years provided a social environment. As a symbol, the fate of Gino's couldn't be better -- cars in St. Louis seem to have supernatural importance, four-wheeled gods that get first choice over all the best places; the riverfront, Mill Creek Valley, the edge of Forest Park, etc., etc.

Gino's was owned and operated by Gene Norman, born in 1938 in Mounds, Ill., just north of Cairo. He came to St. Louis when he was 15. He got a job with Bernie Hayes at KATZ in 1969 then opened his club in a low-slung storefront not far from the Club Imperial. The place held about 75 people.

Norman started with DJs and bands: Little Milton, Oliver Sain, Benny Latimore, David Dee, Artie Blues Boy White. Norman said:

> Gino's was a low down bar, but we got plenty of politicians, the prosecuting attorney, like that. The food was always free. We'd have Blue Mondays where my wife, Yvonne, would fix up apple-pear cobbler and BBQ and we'd get Little Milton or somebody like that to come in and play.
>
> Only thing we had was a pool table when we opened up. Had a stage, but most bands played on the front side of the building. They brought their own equipment. Little Milton would get $800 to $1,000 a night. But mostly I would have my own bands, house bands, low scale artists. They'd get $250 - 300.
>
> I charged $5 on the door and that took care of the bands. We had David Dee a lot -- good quality. Also Willie Al Green, Skeet Rogers, Little Eddie (Butler) and the All-Stars.

Norman was also a record producer and made the first version of Dee's 1982 hit "Goin' Fishing." But, Norman said:

> I got screwed out of the money because I didn't know anything about the business. I didn't know. I found out later. Sony picked it up and it became a hit overseas.
>
> We had a good crowd every night, Monday through Saturday. We had a legendary DJ when we didn't have bands, Jules Carlos, he was part of the limbo craze in the seventies.
>
> People talk a lot about crime, but I didn't have crime. I worked with the police. I was an alderman.

And, my crowd, you see, was controlled by the music. The people in my place were like family. My philosophy -- you come to my place the first time, I'd introduce you to somebody else, you come back and you look for me and I'm not there, say, you'll find the guy I introduced you to. You'll feel welcome that way.

They were like a family in my place.

Then came the construction on Jennings Station Road and it took three years -- that put me out of business. They did a year, then for a whole year they didn't do anything -- left everything all tore up and people can't come to the place.

Other North Side clubs included:

-- **Helen Herd's Moonlight Lounge** in The Ville at Goode and Easton (now MLK Drive). It held 125 people and featured name acts including Albert King, Billy Gayles, Howlin' Wolf and Big George Brock.

-- **Sam Hamer's Silver Dollar** on Natural Bridge and Goodfellow -- a big place, up scale, up the street from the Goody Goody restaurant, near the Club Imperial.

-- **Clinty's Western Inn** -- Page and Ferguson, blues, Big George, David Dee.

-- **Finney's** was on Dr. King Drive, a club that had an adjunct club out in the suburbs for summer concerts that drew 3,000 to 4,000 people and offered cabins to stay overnight.

-- S**praggin's Hacienda Lounge** - MLK close to Goodfellow. Big Bad Smitty was playing there into the nineties with his band the Upsetters.

-- **Witt's Lounge** -- Cora and MLK, a few doors down from Finney's, in a basement; formerly called the Lush Inn Lounge.

The Santa Fe Lounge at Academy and MLK -- Norman:

If you only served what was called 3/2 beer (3.2 percent alcohol) -- now what is usually thought of as "light" beer -- you could bend the rules on age limits. That's how the Santa Fe got started, a small place along the main commercial district.

James DeShay, born in Mississippi in 1919, ran the Santa Fe. He was a guitar player who landed in St. Louis in the forties and hooked up with Little Walter Jacobs, the Hall of Fame harp innovator. In the fifties, DeShay played with Robert Nighthawk and Big Joe Williams.

At the Santa Fe he brought in Tommy Bankhead and a piano player named Roosevelt Carmichael, a player approved of by Henry Townsend, who liked Carmichael's originals.

Other joints from around the city:

-- **The West End Waiters Club** -- at 911 North Vandevanter, started during the war as a place for after hours restaurant industry types, but died in the early sixties.

-- **Caravan Club** -- Big George Brock's club in the Central West End.

-- **The Dot Club** -- A DJ lounge -- platters from the fifties, sixties and seventies music, with Dave Dixon, who ran a talent show. Out of towners sometimes popped up here, including Elmore James.

-- **Peppermint Lounge** at Delmar and Skinker, a Twist club with DJ's spinning platters into the seventies. Mobsters with New York connections reputedly opened this place.

-- **Edward's** in Kinlock -- Fontella Bass made her start on the stage on this North County joint.

-- **The Chesterfield** -- 18th and Franklin -- The St. Louis home for Memphis Slim.

-- **Dynaflow** -- Cass and Jefferson -- Albert King headquarters.

-- **Harlem Club** -- still there in 2015 at MLK and Whittier -- DJ, band sometimes, a neighborhood bar, 60 years old.

-- **Glass Bar,** in the Midtown Hotel, opened in 1944, Henry Townsend with his band played there in the mid-fifties, as did Miles Davis when the place was called the Peacock Bar, a victim of the Mill Creek clearance.

-- **Joe's Corner** -- Fourteenth and Cass -- Roosevelt Sykes and Joe Willie Wilkins held forth there in early sixties.

-- **Sadie's** -- On Delmar in the sixties and seventies, a speakeasy of sorts, a favorite of the Delta pianoman Pinetop Perkins, also called the Hole in the Ground.

-- **James Jump Place,** 16th and Franklin. Ace Wallace played there with Doc Terry. Wallace also had the food concession at Big George's Early Bird club and appeared with Gabriel regularly at another joint called Nora's, an early place on South Broadway.

> Wallace's last appearance was with Big George at an outdoor concert at Fairgrounds Park in 1975.

Back on the North Side, Marsha Evans and Jimmy Hinds remember the **Club Misty** from the seventies and eighties. It was on MLK and Sarah, featured Albert King, plus Sherilyn Brown, a big venue that was once a Woolworth's in the heart of The Ville.

> *Jimmy:* If you wanted to drink liquor you bought a set-up. Ice bucket and the glasses. Maybe soda. You bought the liquor from them, a half-pint. You know, a bottle, a pint or a half-pint.
>
> *Marsha*: It was a one-stop shop. You could sometimes bring your own on a BYOB night. That would be a special night. They'd advertise.
>
> You may have had a tablecloth that was usually plastic. On a card table or a wooden table. Pretty naked tables. Waitresses would come around with the food, set ups, the ice, you know. Ashtrays, cigarettes, all kinds of things on the table.
>
> *Jimmy:* A lot of the bars had rotisseries on them, big polish sausages.
>
> *Marsha:* The women -- You'd dress with a nice jersey, a skirt. Men -- a dressy sweater -- vanlon -- suede strips on it. Very expensive. And slacks. Nice shoes, you know like Ike would wear.
>
> Misty, yeah, that old dime store could seat 500 people. Not much of a dance floor. Then we would go over to the London House for after hours. Misty was R&B and variety. The Corvettes. Or we'd go to the Rivieria; they had the big dance floor.

Club Riviera was Jordan Chamber's place on Delmar, probably the best known spot in St. Louis during the fifties and sixties, taking over from the Booker T. Washington Theater. The Riviera was gone by 1969, burned to the ground in a fire. This is the place Miles Davis first heard Charlie Parker play live. Its last years were nothing like its prime after Chambers died in 1962.

Chambers' first job for the city of St. Louis was driving a team of workhorses in the early days of the twentieth century. By 1944, when the Riviera Night Club opened its doors, Chambers philosophy of "take all you can and give up only what you must" worked in the Depression and he and allies like the attorney David Grant fought the fight against the white elite, slowly gaining ground.

One commentator said of Chambers, "There is no Uncle Tom in Jordan Chambers. Unlike some black leaders, Chambers' power was not granted by whites, but built from the grass roots."

The Riviera was his office and headquarters in the latter third of his life, the time when Chambers controlled enough jobs and was owed enough favors he couldn't live long enough for all the payback. By the early sixties, when the players who would define the next 20 years were stepping up, Chambers had the Riviera. At first, he rotated the best big bands in town, including the Jeters-Pillars Band, then the George Hudson Band.

In the slump after the war, Chambers closed the Riviera for a short period. That created the opportunity for jazzmen Lloyd Smith and David Hines to open up the Musicians Club, half a block east of the Riviera on Delmar. The after-hours joint featured classy jazz and attracted the big names rolling through St. Louis -- Frank Sinatra, Ava Gardner, Count Basie, Duke Ellington, Louis Jordan.

Chambers reopened and soldiered on, running a reduced schedule and less elaborate shows. But in the mid-fifties he ran up against the shuffle of population. Where a couple who had lived nearby in Mill Creek Valley could get a cross-town bus to the Riviera, the same couple in Kinlock had to drive 35 minutes. Black flight took its toll.

Then in the summer of 1958, an off-duty policeman working as a bouncer for Chambers tried to arrest a 19-year-old as customers left the club at 2:30 a.m. The customer broke away from the officer and three other youths, these brandishing switchblade knives, attacked the Deputy Constable, Rubin Peppers. The constable pulled a black jack from his belt and began hitting his attackers.

About 20 other policemen responded to the call for help and the crowd was quickly controlled. Two people were hurt, four arrested. The headlines rang out. "Unruly Crowd at Club," "Fight at Club Riviera." By the time Chambers died from heart disease in August 1962, the club was not what it once was.

In 1964 it was sold to a group led by another black politician, Jet Banks, who had taken Chambers' seat as 19th ward committeeman. Banks ran into trouble with the city and lost his liquor license for selling afterhours liquor in 1967. By 1969 Banks was in foreclosure and the Rivera was no more.

The building burned to the ground in 1970.

Gene Norman said the regulars in his bar started dying off or moving by the beginning of the eighties.

> And the music changed. The young people didn't like the blues. They wanted hip-hop. The black musicians went to the South Side where the kids listened to the blues. They liked the blues over there, so these bands went over there.
>
> Hey, I was intending this bar to be my retirement. Let another guy have it and he didn't last a year. All around 2000, a lot of people died off. The hip-hop crowd was never dedicated to one bar. They would take off to the next bar. These bars would open and close, fast. The blues fans they would stay loyal. Not these hip-hop guys.

Tom "Papa" Ray, the harp player and record store owner, arrived back in town in 1980 after a hiatus of nine years. I asked how he first reacted to the North Side blues scene. He leaned over on his stool in an upper floor of Vintage Vinyl, his record store on the Delmar Loop. He frowned, then flashed a grin.

> Dire . . . and interesting.
>
> I found the blues scene was pretty minuscule -- you could see Silvercloud playing in the Central West End on a Wednesday night. You could check out Tommy Bankhead from time to time, but beyond that the local blues scene was pretty dead. Bennie Smith and Johnnie Johnson weren't playing. Henry Townsend wasn't playing much. Other than that you had your national touring packages at places like Kiel.
>
> There were a few places like Sadie's Personality where Bankhead played. A congenial dive. It probably wasn't that safe, but you could go down there.

Ron Edwards, the guitar player who became a DJ on KDHX when it started, was one of the first from the white South Side to go to **Sadie's Personality Bar,** a dive located at Union and Wabada, not far from Sportsman's Park. Edwards had been jamming with a harp player named Steve Kauffman, who knew about Tommy Bankhead and his Wednesday gigs at Sadie's. Edwards:

> Sadie's Personality Bar was typical -- a little bar, family owned, I met Henry Townsend there. Bankhead got very little money there, it was a neighborhood gig and a lot of friends would come

> by. Steve had just met Silvercloud who had just come back out and was playing music at a place called Reflections in the Central West End. Leroy Pierson was there in Cloud's band.

Silvercloud (real name Rudy Coleman) was an important player in the blues revival. He had been out of music for 20 years when he started playing again in the mid-seventies. Born in March 1933 in St. Louis County as Rudolph Valentine Coleman, his mother and uncles all played. "There was lots of wax in the house."

He started sneaking into clubs when very young, saw Memphis Slim at the Riviera in 1947 and was impressed. He also saw Slim at the Glass Bar, the Chesterfield Bar and the Harlem Night Club on the East Side where Slim alternated with T-Bone Walker during the early fifties. Slim's hit "Every Day I Have the Blues" was a cover of the Sparks Brothers/Henry Townsend song first heard in St. Louis in the thirties.

Memphis Slim, born John Len Chatman in 1915, spent three years in St. Louis, playing Casey's Blue Room in Kinloch, the black suburb just east of Lambert airport in North County. Cloud, meanwhile, took up piano and studied at the Downbeat Music School for two and a half years before he started Rudy Coleman and the Rhythm Rockers in 1954. He billed himself as the "Little Boy with the Memphis Slim voice." He was 21.

He found an audience at the Arrow Inn in West County and began making a living in the suburbs. "The country clubs paid good money and we played the exact kind of blues we did across the river. The only difference was the audience's reaction. People in the white clubs would whistle and clap while in the black clubs they would scream and holler," he said.

Silvercloud sat in with Slim several times, the last time at a spot called the Mambo Key Club in East St. Louis in 1960. That last night, Cloud remembers, Slim spent the whole last set dancing, leaving the young Cloud to play all his songs.

That year, Memphis Slim went to Europe. He settled in Paris in 1962, where he lived until his death in 1988. He had toured Europe with Willie Dixon in 1960, in the first American Folk Festival. Slim and Dixon released several albums together on Folkways Records, the first a live set with Pete Seeger at the Village Gate in New York City.

Slim made numerous appearances in Europe during the next 25 years, appearing on television, acting in French films and performing regularly in Paris and on return visits to the United States.

Silvercloud, meanwhile, worked a day job at the General Motors plant on the North Side until he was laid off in 1975. He got back into music because he had little other choice.

> I'd been out of work from the plant and had been looking around for a place to earn something performing again. One day I found myself walking down Euclid in the West End. I was disgusted and so frustrated. In my mind I kept thinking over and over, my life is mighty cloudy, so very cloudy.
>
> Then the old saying came to mind, "In every cloud is a silver lining." I smiled and with a bit of humor said, "Well, hell, as cloudy as my life is I must be Silvercloud."
>
> I walked into a place called Reflections. It was empty and the bar was up for sale. I told the bartender if he'd put a piano in the bar I would drum up some business. The next day I came back and there was a piano there for an audition.
>
> The house filled up within an hour and when the owner dropped by he couldn't believe it. Soon I was working Friday and Saturday nights.

By 1980, Cloud had put together a new band and was playing at the Caleco, also in the Central West End, with Keith Doder, Steve Kaufman and Doc Terry. Bluesman Leroy Pierson played Monday nights. Cloud also hired a drummer called Earthquake and the piano player Elijah Shaw. Other names Cloud remembers from those years are Little Amos, Mark Kimes, Jim Burns (an eventual television star), and Bobby Betts.

In the late seventies Ron Edwards had become a regular at Sadie's Personality Bar.

> Small, I'd say the bar held about 60 -- not a big crowd. That went on for a while. Eventually students from Washington University started coming down. They didn't understand the concept of respect for the local bar. This wasn't some club where you come down and start moving the tables and start dancing -- this wasn't

> that kind of place, and wait a minute, you don't do that -- you come here and you don't do that.
>
> Meanwhile, James DeShay had this other club, the Santa Fe, this bigger club. DeShay would be behind the bar and he had a flying V Gibson and he played two styles -- he played the old Charley Patton style and the Robert Johnson vintage country electrified stuff.
>
> The club put on several acts and sometimes it wouldn't be until midnight when DeShay would come out from behind the bar and put on his whole show, three revues he did. Steve (Kauffman) would play, he had a guy who would sing like Howlin' Wolf, he got a sax up front and he had a whole show thing going on there. The Santa Fe was a better, sizable blues club. It held 150 crowded, two storefronts.
>
> Tommy Bankhead then met Keith Doder, then in his teens, who became the protege. Doder had been a clarinet player but he picked up the harmonica and Tommy would let him get up at Sadie's. Keith just loved the blues and he'd get up there and he didn't know what key it was. Doder really developed into a great player.

Keith Doder had a direct link to the St. Louis harp tradition of John Lee Williamson (the first Sonny Boy) through the playing of Little Walter Jacobs, who had been blowing harp at the Santa Fe on a regular basis. Little Walter discovered that putting a small mike right next to the harp produced a sound that could compete with the guitars in the newly electrified bands of the late thirties and forties. He produced an impressive, distinctive sound that Doder adopted and made his own.

That progress is heard on *By Invitation Only,* a record put out in 1989 by the Blue City Band, a living reminder of the late seventies, early eighties sound that was coming out of the North Side. The band consisted of Jeff "Dog" Breihan on guitar; Harry Crawford, bass; Charles "Skeet" Rogers, vocals; and David Tims, drums. The album cover lists a host of others who played on the disc, including Charles Taylor, Bob Lohr, Tommy Bankhead, Ron Edwards, Larry Thurston and Jim Rosse.

Briehan plays lead guitar and is especially effective on "Blues Is My Religion," a song Doder wrote. Briehan is the author of another classic on the album, "Blue City Bounce." He later played for the George Jackson Blues Band, Dogebo, and was with the rock band, The Heaters, at the time of his death in 2012.

Skeet has carried his career along since then without a break, billed in 2015 as Charles "Skeet" Rodgers, The LovelyMs. HY-C & The Inner City Blues Band, a seven-piece outfit that plays Beale's on Broadway often, Hammerstone's in Soulard frequently, and the Old Timers on Halls Ferry Road on the North Side every Sunday. Skeet also has experienced several Albert King road trips, played bass in the *Hail! Hail! Rock 'n' Roll* movie and toured 10 years with David Dee.

"Cap" Tims remained a mainstay in St. Louis as well, winding up drumming with the Ground Floor Band that also is a regular at The Beale. On *By Invitation Only*, Tims nudges over into a little rapping on "Devil's Music" and sings the lead vocal on "Blues Is My Religion."

Of the others, Bob Lohr in 2015 was Chuck Berry's piano player; Edwards is on the air for KDHX and Rosse played trumpet in the Jeremiah Johnson Band.

The Blue City Band was formed of black and white musicians and stood out as another transition from the North Side to the South Side, landing gigs as the new clubs opened from 1978 on -- the Broadway Oyster Bar, BB's Jazz Blues and Soups, Mike and Mim's.

In 1997, Doder was recruited by Chicago bluesman Jimmy Rogers and traveled throughout the United States, Canada, and Europe as a featured harpist. Doder filled the shoes of a long line of blues harpists who had backed Rogers, who said Keith reminded him of Little Walter.

In 2002, Doder was involved in another sometimes overlooked album from St. Louis, *School for Fools,* recorded in the new Benton Park Studios. Levon Helm, the aging drummer of The Band, flew in for the sessions, Feb. 26 and 27, and was joined by Johnnie Johnson on piano, Tom Maloney on rhythm guitar, Rich McDonough on lead guitar, Gus Thornton on bass, Larry Thurston on vocals and Doder on harp, an all-star lineup of the young St. Louis players who had stepped into the limelight as the South Side took over the live music scene.

School For Fools went through two more East Coast sessions before release; 12 original blues songs that provide a sparkling, modern take and reflect that continuing St. Louis thing of combining and melding numerous styles -- from the booming vocals of Thurston to Helm's rapid fire drumming. All told, 18 musicians had a hand, but the core group was solid St. Louis.

Thurston, known as "Larry T" got his start just about the time the blues was reviving and the venues were reshuffling south. He was an early member of the Soulard Blues Band, which formed in the late seventies and has remained foursquare on the scene ever since. He spun off into the Sounds of the City in the mid-eighties with Johnson, Thornton and Maloney then began playing on the road with Matt Murphy and James Cotton, a pair of players based in Chicago.

Murphy, a guitar player who had performed with Memphis Slim, formed his own band in the mid-eighties, a group that morphed into the second Blues Brothers band. Dan Ackroyd and John Belushi, the original blues brothers, invented the group as a skit on *Saturday Night Live* and had a hit movie in 1978, a film that helped revive blues all over the country.

Belushi died from a drug overdose in 1982 and Thurston took over the lead singer slot in Murphy's new Blues Brothers band that formed in 1988. This band toured the world for five years. Thurston eventually tired of the travel and retired in 1994, taking a day job in St. Louis. By then he had two Blues Brothers albums, *Live in Montreax* and *Red, White & Blues*, under his belt.

He became the pastor at the New Covenant Christian Church on the North Side and formed Thurston Ministries in 2012, but didn't give up playing the occasional gig with the city's best players, who always had room for his soulful voice. In fact, *School For Fools* came from just such a side appearance when the Brooklyn, N.Y.-based songwriter Jeff Alexander happened to catch a Johnnie Johnson set at Off Broadway, another of the new clubs on the South Side.

School For Fools was Thurston's first and only lead album, grabbing critical acclaim in blues circles worldwide. One such review came from the writer Chris Puyear in the magazine *Moblues*, saying the record has "an old familiar sound, good old style blues. You would think you were listening to an older band that had been together a long time, even the lyrics seem to be seasoned, but at the same time it is all new -- new lyrics, new music.

"You don't have to listen to it a dozen times to get the feel, this CD hits you right the first time out."

Thurston also sang on the last Johnnie Johnson album, *Johnnie Be Eighty and Still Bad*, released after Johnson's death in 2005, a record that also included McDonough on guitar and Thornton on bass.

Doder didn't retire, playing a hectic schedule of gigs through the eighties, nineties and into the middle of the two-thousands, finally slowing down from illness around 2006. He played all the big clubs, plus smaller joints like Riddle's on Delmar, the Corner Bar and Graham's Grill & Bayou Bar, and appeared at the Big Muddy Blues Festival on Laclede's Landing in 2005. He also was a big part of the launch of the Harp Attack shows in mid-decade. Doder died on July 19, 2010.

Even as the music died in Gaslight Square and the North Side in the seventies and eighties, there was no stopping that St. Louis thing, The music played on, especially just across the very dividing line that separates the city. There, a unique joint sprung up on the Delmar Loop, that confluence of geography, race and economics that straddles the city/county line north of Forest Park.

There, Joe Edwards and his wife Linda bought an old pool hall just outside the St. Louis city limit in 1972. The street then was derelict, half its storefronts empty. Politicians on both sides of the line were doing nothing to save the area, but Edwards had a big collection of stuff he needed to store and the big, old building seemed as good a place as any. He wasn't rolling in money, but Edwards was an optimist, a guy who favored flowered shirts and long hair, Elvis records and psychedelic posters.

Where others saw blowing dust and broken glass, Edwards saw opportunity and in the second decade of the twenty-first century, he can drive his vintage convertible down Delmar and see a row of success stories, for him, his neighborhood and his city.

The old pool hall is the street's biggest success, slowly developed into Blueberry Hill, a 10,000-square foot emporium of food and entertainment. Here, Edwards displays thousands of pop-fun items from many things Elvis to all things Howdy Doody. There's the Pac-Man Room, a retro-game room with all the best in old video games; there's a dart room; and there's a music venue downstairs, the Duck Room, which has seen hundreds of shows, including two decades of regular performances by the greatest vintage item in all of St. Louis -- Chuck Berry.

The rest of the street heading east toward downtown has slowly followed Blueberry Hill's success, giving St. Louis a district that can be called thriving.

Post-Dispatch columnist Bill McClellan, something of a vintage item himself, summed up Edwards as "an unusual combination -- a hippie-visionary-business type." Edwards' vision was of a restored neighborhood, a place that was fun, safe and reasonably priced. When he opened, Gaslight Square was in steep decline, the downtown had yet to see its "urban renaissance" and the city's music history was mentioned only when the subject was ragtime. The North Side was starting its slide, the Soulard scene was just starting and the blues revival was still five years away.

During high school, in the mid- and late sixties, Edwards had become an aficionado of the East Side music scene, traveling across the Eads Bridge late at night to places like the Red Top and the Cosmo Club, developing an appreciation for blues, rock and R&B, becoming a hardcore music fan.

Sitting years later near a classic grand piano on an early afternoon at Blueberry Hill, Edwards remembered the high school days of a half-century previous.

> They were not real strict about IDs over on the East Side. We looked pretty young and we were young. We went there a lot more than the North Side clubs. Over there it was late night, we could stay up to 3 or 4 or even 5 in the morning, even while in high school.
>
> But as the sixties went on, things changed. A friend of my brother got knifed to death over there outside one of the clubs. Some people started to feel it was a little too dangerous to go to the East Side. So there was a hiatus from the early seventies into the late seventies when the clubs on the North Side were still going but not many white people or people from the South Side went to the North Side.

Edwards saw there were people out there looking for a new place, a music venue on the Delmar Divide that could attract both white and black customers. He slipped into the breach slowly. His street wasn't built in a day.

Like the city itself, the location of Blueberry Hill was its destiny. Edwards was officially in University City, not far from the old streetcar loop that gave the street its name -- the Delmar Loop.

The streetcar ran from downtown out to what in the thirties was just beginning to develop as one of the nation's first suburbs. Blueberry Hill, growing slowly during the seventies, found itself in the center of a city/suburban hub, a place where the North and South Side could mix. The Loop had been an entertainment area since before the World's Fair and had developed into one of the most progressive areas of St. Louis County, starting with the city's first mayor -- E.G. Lewis.

By the seventies, University City was a diverse neighborhood, half black, half white, that had developed quickly in the previous two decades as an adjunct to Washington University, an industry that did not leave St. Louis in the out flux and did not pollute the air as it grew into an Ivy League-level institution.

U City today is still anchored by its 135-foot, domed City Hall, a 1903 building constructed in time for the nearby World's Fair in Forest Park. Edward Gardener Lewis, a newly minted magazine publisher, built the domed monument.

Lewis arrived in St. Louis from Connecticut, landing in the late eighteen-nineties when the area contained farms and small farming communities like Mount Olive and Sutter Valley. Delmar Boulevard, sometimes called Bonhomme during its first entertainment district days, started as a dirt road that ran from the west to meet the city line at Skinker then headed west downtown toward the river and turned into Morgan Street (as in Deep Morgan) after it crossed Grand.

The landmark All Saints Church opened in 1901 north of Delmar and west of Skinker, not far from what became the Loop. Delmar Race Track near Lewis' new buildings served the World's Fair and beyond. The Delmar Garden Amusement Park was on the western end of Delmar Boulevard.

Lewis made his first money selling patent medicine and a popular insect repellant. Then he saw a new market, a magazine for women. He bought an existing St. Louis publication called *Winner,* renamed it *Woman's Magazine* and quickly turned it into the nation's largest circulation periodical.

A yearly subscription cost 10 cents. Free delivery in the rural areas of America and penny-per-pound postage in the cities gave him easy distribution. In 1902 he bought an 85-acre tract in what is now University

City. In 1903 he began the construction of the Lewis Publishing Company headquarters and Press Annex on the site.

Between 1903 and 1915, he bought more and more land and built more subdivisions. He also built what became the domed City Hall -- the Woman's Magazine Building, an octagon made of brick and limestone. For the World's Fair, Lewis installed the world's largest searchlight on top of the dome, an eight-ton electric light 135 feet above the street that beamed out over of the city.

He also built an adjacent building known as the Egyptian Temple next door to the dome, where he founded an Art Academy, the American Woman's League, the People's University, the American Woman's Republic. Lewis started two daily newspapers and opened two banks, including the U.S. People's Bank, a mail-order operation that intended to sell postal money orders in direct competition with the Post Office.

In 1906, University City was incorporated and Lewis was elected mayor three times. Beginning in 1905, he was the target of postal authorities, charged that the magazine's information on self-sufficiency and independence for women was fraudulent and could therefore not be sent through the mail. He was taken into court in 1912 and while he was not convicted he was tangled in continual litigation the rest of his life.

In 1915, Lewis had had enough of the attacks from the government, now in hands of the reactionaries in the Wilson administration. He packed up his operations and left University City for California where he established a utopian community on the Pacific Ocean -- the American Women's Republic. He went bankrupt in 1924 and died in 1950.

Lewis was acquitted of all charges from the government but Postmaster General George B. Cortelyou was successful in shutting down his publishing empire.

Joe Edwards grew up in the neighborhood. He went to college at Duke University and returned to St. Louis in the early seventies. His family was colorful, reasonably well off, but not made of the stuff that gave them a seat on the board of Civic Progress. One of his grandfathers invented storm windows; another devised the mechanical pitching machine. The young Joe opened Blueberry Hill Sept. 8, 1972, standing behind a bar that had been hauled across town from Cherokee Street.

The *Globe-Democrat* reported that Edwards and his wife had borrowed $10,500 to open the place. The article characterized the building as a former "dank warehouse" with a leaky roof and "the musty aroma of an unfinished basement." The neighborhood, it added, was part of a "down-and-out" area that contained various "characters that roam the street" who appeared "as rough-looking as the storefronts."

But Edwards became the biggest thing on Delmar since the Celebrity Club and the antics of the comic Davey "Nose" Bold were all the rage at the corner of Skinker and Delmar in the fifties. Bold made a live album produced by Gene Norman there that drew a good review from *Billboard* for an act that included hot jazz on the piano, funny hats, and plenty of mirth.

The first draw of Blueberry Hill was its stock of "near beer," the 3.2 percent Depression invention that Edwards sold for 35 cents a can to an increasing thirsty group of students and locals. He was forced into the plan when the University City council turned down his application for a liquor license. He featured two varieties of the beer, Schlitz light and Schlitz dark.

The bar also soon featured that most low overhead of sports -- darts, spawned shortly after the place opened by the suggestions of the customers.

Today's Blueberry Hill hosts a variety of dart leagues and the oldest pub tournament in North America. The 42nd annual was held on Mother's Day weekend 2014, with 14 events held across 21 dartboards with $10,000 in prize money.

The physical bar in the place was made in the eighteen-forties, the mirror behind it even earlier. The booths came from Gaslight Square and the Baden Hotel on the North Side. The wooden telephone booth is from Union Station. In 40 years the beer list grew from two in the can to 18 on tap and 62 bottled. There are also cans of Schlitz on hand, but it is no longer 3.2 percent.

The club didn't include live music until 1985 when Be Vision, a psychedelic rock band, played what Joe called the Elvis Room, a downstairs venue that held about 200 people when packed and was lined with cases of Elvis stuff from the Edwards Childhood Collection. Before the Elvis Room, however, a club named Blueberry Hill couldn't fail to provide music. Edwards had been collecting records all his life and now was his chance to play them.

At first, he said:

> We just had the jukebox. That was before CDs or the Internet or anything so we just had records. I had a big record collection. At the time I had 30,000 45s. I had everything that made the Top 10 on both the pop chart and the R&B chart from 1950 until they stopped making the 45s.
>
> I like the music, but I'm also a collector, so I decided to fill in all the gaps. Some of it never came out on CDs, more than half was not Top 10, a lot of the best music never made the Top 10.

The jukebox grew to 150,000 selections before the drive that ran the player gave out in 2014. A new digital replacement wasn't quite the same.

Edwards had spent the first mornings of his ownership out in front of the place, sweeping up glass and getting to know the cast of characters that inhabited the street. Instead of seeing shadows, he saw light. He had a realization that was quite different from that often seen in the bulldozer mania that struck the city in the forties, fifties and sixties. Like the Vietnam vets in Soulard, Edwards thought it would be best to restore, not destroy. "Within a week of opening Blueberry Hill, I realized that I wouldn't make it if the neighborhood didn't make it. I talked to other residents, to City Hall, to police."

He helped form the Loop Business District to work together to save the street. He watched over everything, served on all the committees, went to all the meetings. "Joe guarded (The Loop) like a mother hen," said McClellan.

Where there had been broken glass and that dank basement smell, by the end of the eighties there stood a popular club with a thriving music venue. Edwards soon also owned the building across the street, which he rented to Cicero's, which also featured live music, especially Johnnie Johnson. The Elvis Room was in essence competing with itself, but Edwards knew he had to build up the feeling of street life on Delmar.

> People would say why do you rent to the competition? He's playing music too. But it was good for both of us. People went back and forth. They'd pay a small cover charge at Cicero's then at break time, they'd come over here and pay a small cover charge at the Elvis Room. Wonderful bouncing back and forth.

About this time, he met Johnson, who was just emerging from retirement but still driving the bus at the senior center.

> I tried to book him as often as I could. I loaned him money so he could get a phone installed so I could call him to book him. That was so heart breaking. This was before *Hail! Hail! Rock 'n' Roll.* I knew him separately from Chuck Berry. I knew them not together, but separately as well. I really liked both guys.

This attitude of cooperation with his neighbors, both on the South and North Sides has produced the most vibrant street in the city, where black and white mingle, where black-owned small businesses compete with white owners. By 2015, The Loop had become one of America's great streets, a confluence of music, food, and small businesses.

BB's Jazz, Blues and Soups was the next big club story in St. Louis music, opening in 1976 on South Broadway, not far from Busch Stadium. The bottom part of the building dates to Frenchtown in 1848. A three-story addition was added to the top of the building around the turn of the nineteenth century and the building was used as a hotel until 1969.

The hotel had 37 rooms on its second and third floors when it was called Phil's Hotel. Before that it had also been a boarding house and reception hall, a retail outlet and a house of prostitution. BB's was started by St. Louis bar veterans Bob Burkhardt and Mark O'Shaughnessy and initially stayed open for just a year and half, running on a shoestring. Crossover North Side musicians played amid a collection of funky antiques, a wood burning stove and a variety of art posters.

"Bob Burkhardt and I started hanging out at Phil's Hotel Number 2," O'Shaughnessy explained. "We both liked the cheap beers and cheap drinks." Burkhardt was experienced in the business from a pair of bars, Muddy Water and Rusty Springs, but the initial BB's lasted only about a year and half.

The club made the most of the time, bringing in Oliver Sain and his supporting cast from across the Delmar Divide, prompting complaints from the segregation crowd. O'Shaughnessy said:

> At that time, people were really kind of uptight in St. Louis. They didn't like places where black people and white people mixed. We

> got a lot of threatening phone calls from people who didn't like us dancing together, listening to the same kind of music.

Henry Townsend soon joined Sain on the BB's card and the word was out that blues could be played away from the North Side. But the building sucked up money and the doors closed in 1977.

Burkhardt then opened the Broadway Oyster Bar down the street, which in the early years of the twentieth century grew into another stellar St. Louis club. Under the ownership of John and Vicki Johnson it expanded from a tiny joint into a full-out music venue, heavy on the flavor of New Orleans both in its food and its music.

O'Shaughnessy held onto 700 S. Broadway, doing a lot of remodeling, reopening again in 1980 and then closing again after a year. He leased it for three years, but then left it empty again until 1996, when BB's began its run as one of the top blues clubs in the city and in the United States.

O'Shaughnessy had a new partner by then, John May, a bass player from Colorado. May's experience in the club wars came from another of the joints that ran upstream to bring the blues into the forefront of St. Louis music -- a place in West County they called J.B. Hutto's.

Ron Edwards, the bottleneck guitar player and KDHX DJ, was also at Hutto's at the start.

> It was in a mall-like area -- it was way out -- it was a real piece to get out there. A good-sized place -- bigger than the Santa Fe Lounge by a third. There was a raised area where we sat up and played, he made a stage out of that. Back section was elevated. Long bar, tables. A lot of national acts -- Larry Davis (brother of Boo Boo) was his house guitar player for a whole summer -- we opened for Lightnin' Hopkins there, the only time in my lifetime that Hopkins was in St. Louis, one of the lost thrilling moments I can remember.
>
> We got blues lovers from all over town. It would have never survived as long as it did with just people from out there. But if it was the Central West End or somewhere downtown it would have survived a lot longer. There were locals but at the same time people would make the trip out there to see specific artists.
>
> Hutto's was primarily blues and all the St. Louis musicians came out there and played. Hutto's is very important for the

> story of St. Louis music because of what came out of this place. J.B. (Hutto) would come and Henry (Townsend) and Sunnyland Slim -- they would walk around and stand on the bar, pulling the long chords.
>
> It was also a venue where the blues players could play, where people could be exposed to them without going to a real small bar on the North Side. That would be uncomfortable.

What eventually became the St. Louis Blues Society was organized at a restaurant next to Hutto's out of discussions between (Hutto partner) Frank Babcock and John May and Sam Valenti and Edwards.

> We needed an organization to promote blues because it was difficult to get anything in the newspaper and it was difficult to get anything on the radio anywhere and these artists were suffering from a terrible lack of exposure. People in the community don't know what they have here. People from Europe came here and go crazy but people from here don't know its happening. So we put together a group of maybe 10 or 11 people.

The society was formally begun in 1984 and in 1986 it put on the city's first big blues festival. The Blues Fest was held at the fourth big club of the period to open -- Mississippi Nights, a sprawling venue on Laclede's Landing that opened in 1979.

Jay Farrar, who with Jeff Tweedy, formed Uncle Tupelo on the East Side in the late seventies played frequently there. Tupelo, a combination of country and punk rock, was the club's signature outfit. Tweedy and Farrar later split and formed two new bands, Wilco and Son Volt. Ferrar remembered Mississippi Nights:

> Love it or hate it for many reasons, but Mississippi Nights was a venerable institution that consistently served up live music in St. Louis that no other venue could match.
>
> Maybe the stage was too high or the ceiling too low or the bouncers too surly. Sure, the sound system couldn't overpower the people drinking and talking near the bar — but Mississippi Nights, with its abundance of old brick and wood, had character.
>
> Mississippi Nights was like a portal to a musical world that existed outside the Midwest. Some shows I'll never forget: The Replacements opening for X, Wall of Voodoo, Sonic Youth, the

> Ramones, the True Believers, Husker Du, with Chuck Berry and Joe Edwards together in the audience.

The club started small, then expanded to a 1,000 capacity venue in 1987, becoming the top nightclub in the city. It captured the national punk trends, the college rock explosion and still had room for blues players and country rocker Merle Haggard during a time of great change in the music business. Nirvana played there, as did Lucinda Williams, Police, Joe Cocker and Blues Traveler.

"I remember seeing Nirvana and thinking, 'Wow, this is going to change everything,'" said Richard Fortus, a member of Guns N' Roses who started in the St. Louis rock band Pale Divine. "It was one of the best shows I've ever seen."

All this came during the period when big venues with big-ticket prices became the rule across the country. To be sure, St. Louis reflected this trend, but it also kept the independent spirit alive at Mississippi Nights, BB's, the Oyster Bar, Hutto's and the new places in Soulard.

In the mid-nineties rumors began to circulate and planners began looking to redevelop Laclede's Landing, which had faded following an initial burst as the "downtown Gaslight" in the sixties. But once again the city started eyeing big money, the fatal lure that destroyed something to get something bigger and better.

Trying to increase its profits and keep the business going, Mississippi Nights switched emphasis to the "emo" (emotional punk) and jam band (Grateful Dead spinoffs) styles that had emerged on the coasts. Country was also not forgotten with shows by Willie Nelson and Dwight Yokum pushing the hayseed envelope.

The club got national attention when George Thorogood and the Destroyers used part of a 1995 show on a live album. Another national group, They Might Be Giants, put an original song about the club on its *Venue Songs* album, released in 2004 using the new "online" format prior to its release on CD.

The club then ran into the familiar roadblock to progress in the city -- City Hall's power to sponsor mistaken redevelopment schemes. Mississippi Nights was soon shuttered, its music silenced by the Lumiere

Casino. Money won out over art. The city held the lease to the land and when the casino came calling, the city opened its palm wide. Once again, a thriving area was turned to a ghost town by development. The Landing in 2015 was but a flickering ember of memory dominated by the sounds of slot machines.

The last jam at Mississippi Nights came on Jan. 19, 2007. The last band standing was The Urge, a local group that had played dozens of sellout shows at the club. Led by the singer Steve Ewing, The Urge built its following during the late eighties and nineties with a horn and guitar driven hash of rock and blues, another of the confluence bands that bubbled from the Mississippi mud.

The group officially broke up in 2001 but has played numerous reunion shows since, including that final Mississippi Nights jam. The Urge officially reunited in 2011 and released a new record in 2013. The Urge encompassed many of the styles Mississippi Nights saw over its 27 years of existence -- alt country, hardcore, ska, heavy metal, R&B and blues. The Urge's appearance at the club's finale induced a *Riverfront Times* reviewer to call the crowd "bonkers."

After the sale to Pinnacle Entertainment, a Las Vegas-based casino operator, one of the Mississippi Nights' owners, Rich Frame, said he was looking into the idea of a new club in midtown, near St. Louis University. But the new club never happened.

Meanwhile, Joe Edwards opened two new venues -- the Duck Room, the rugged, small venue in the basement of Blueberry Hill in 1997, followed in 2000 by the sumptuous Pageant Concert NightClub, a 2,000 capacity theater that was named after a movie palace that sat three blocks away and had been demolished. These two venues took over the bands that had played Mississippi Nights, adding to the revived music scene.

The Pageant was the scene of four packed shows by The Urge when it got back together in 2011, shows that resulted in the live album *All the Way Live*. Another album, *Galvanized*, was released in 2013.

By then Hutto's was also gone. But BB's, the Broadway Oyster and Bar and Beale's on Broadway were all successful on South Broadway, as were dozens of other music venues, a shifting sea of openings and closings providing fresh water for the bands and the audience.

Chapter Thirty-One

The First Annual Blues Festival: Just Call the Song

1986-2015

That first festival saw north, south, East St. Louis all getting together. The festival was kind of a watermark. It was an indication of the good things to come and the St. Louis audience proved that afternoon that they embraced the blues and that they could take all that we could give them.

-- Art Dwyer, Soulard Blues Band

At the 1st Annual St. Louis Blues Festival, held at Mississippi Nights on March 22, 1986, the revived blues arrived fully developed at the confluence. Ron Edwards called the marathon show "the Woodstock of St. Louis." Aimed at publicizing the growth of blues in the city, it was not the very first such festival, there had been previous attempts in the sixties. But this was the show that stuck, that started a long stretch of yearly fests that brought the various styles of blues to the front of the music stage in St. Louis.

Edwards, Mark O'Shaunghnessy and John May ran the show, the St. Louis Blues Club (aka St. Louis Blues Society) was the sponsor. Robbie Montgomery, Ikette turned restaurant queen, emceed along with Lou "Fatha" Times, the enduring radio voice who died in 2014.

The opening act, James Crutchfield, came on at 11:30 in the morning. The Fest ran for over 14 hours, until the club closed at 2 a.m.

Edwards called the lineup "a wonderful list." Looking back after 30 years that list contains a who's who and what's what of the blues revival that carried on in St. Louis through the eighties, the nineties and into the twenty-first century.

11:30 a.m. -- James Crutchfield -- A veteran pianoman most closely associated with the Venice Cafe where he performed regularly for 12 years. The Venice opened in 1988 and Crutchfield began playing there almost immediately, performing every Wednesday night up until his death in 2001. His wooden leg remains displayed in a glass case at the back to the bar that serves as a tribute to a beloved performer.

Crutchfield was born in Baton Rouge on May 25, 1912, and started playing piano in his teens. He loved trains and would jump on one frequently, riding the rails all over the country during the forties, eventually winding up in St. Louis in 1948.

> I heard that train whistle blow. I just had to go. Couldn't stay still to save my life. So I ended up here, got here about two in the morning. There were so many people here I couldn't find a place to sleep. Women were laying out asleep with their babies in their arms.

He wound up in Gaslight Square working for 10 years at Rosalee Lovett's Left Bank bar. In the late fifties, Crutchfield played regularly with a drummer named Bat the Hummingbird at the last bar located at 2220 Market Street, the spot where Tom Turpin built his Rosebud Café at the turn of the twentieth century. The venue was destroyed during the Mill Creek Valley clearance.

Crutchfield's style of play wasn't far removed from the ragtime strains of those days. He adopted the barrelhouse roll of St. Louis piano soon after his arrival in town and played it for the rest of his life.

Charlie O'Brien, the policeman who searched for obscure musicians, got him a record date with Speckled Red, a session that eventually saw light as *Biddle Street Barrelhousin',* a record that captured several blues piano players including Stump Johnson and Henry Brown and was released on CD in 2003.

Crutchfield traveled with Henry Townsend to the Netherlands in 1983 on a tour of Europe where he made a CD called *St. Louis Blues Piano,* released in 2001.

That Crutchfield was first up at the 1st Blues Festival was no accident. O'Shaughnessy was Crutchfield's guiding promoter, getting him gigs in the new Soulard clubs -- the Broadway Oyster Bar (opened 1984), Mike and Mim's (1979), the 1860 Saloon (1982) and eventually at the Venice, where his band included Bennie Smith and Sharon Foehner. By then Crutchfield was living in Soulard and his annual birthday party at Molly's (opened in 1991) was a highlight of the year.

Crutchfield favored a yellow leisure suit and talked in a rapid, clipped fashion. He was 89 when he died, playing right up to the end with his same rapid, barrelhouse style. His had been a tough life but he lasted.

Venice club co-owner Paul Cuba, who died not long after Crutchfield, said:

> He wanted to be straight-up. I remember he had a stroke on a Sunday and showed up for work on Wednesday in pajamas and a sport coat, wearing his hospital wristband. I said, "James, what're you doing here?" "I gotta play. I need the money." So I paid him to go home and take a break.

A connection with Bennie Smith led to new bookings for Crutchfield in the nineties as a member of Bennie Smith and the Urban Express, a rock band led by another St. Louisan who came out of retirement because of the blues revival.

Crutchfield's death in 2001 prompted a spontaneous Second Line parade through the streets of the neighborhood. The owners of the Venice found his wooden leg at the funeral home and got permission from his family to prop it up in the club as part of a memorial to the pianoman.

12 noon -- Tom Hall -- A native St. Louisan who got his start as a player at 22 when he took bluegrass banjo lessons, joining a band called the Franklin County Donkey Club. At a gig in central Missouri he heard a Mississippi John Hurt record -- "I'd never heard anything like that. I was floored!"

Hall loved Hurt's finger picking style. He bought the record -- *The Best of Mississippi John Hurt* -- and went into his bedroom and taught himself how to play. "I could hear the bass goin' like this, and I could hear the finger picking, and I knew it was one guitar and I just had to figure it out."

For the next three years:

> I'd get me a six-pack of tall boys, sit myself in that room and slow everything down to 16 and figure it out.
>
> I was trying to flat-pick at the time; couldn't hold a pick, though. I heard Hurt, and that was it. Let it roll, play it back, let it roll, play it back. Figured out the chords, asked people how to do it.

By the time of the '86 festival Hall had helped form a popular Soulard band, the Geyer Street Sheiks, but the group broke up in a haze of alcohol and "artistic differences." Still, his job as a bartender dissolved in the music.

> My hobby evolved into my job. I can't afford to quit. I can pay my bills, and I don't know what else I'd do, though I've thought about quitting a million times.
>
> (Before the guitar life was) nothing -- tending bar, painting houses, whatever, getting drunk, hanging out in the street. I had no direction. It gave me an identity. I kinda had a weird childhood. Playing guitar saved my life. Sometimes I think it's gonna kill me.

At a show at Joe's Cafe on the city's west side in 2012, Hall sat below an open coffin attached to the club's wall.

He toyed with a National Steel guitar, a six-string monster treated with gentle care and precision. The confluence arrived in his hands, through his fingers on those tough strings. He did tunes by Hurt, by Robert Johnson, then looked up from the instrument to tell the crowd, "This one's from here in St. Louis" and launched into "Frankie and Johnny."

Hall plays often with the singer Alice Spencer, a former Sheik, in a duo they call T&A. He also has been part of the Bozo's Hometown Skiffle Band, River City Rhythm, The Fighting Molly McGuires. His BBQ Band with Tom Maloney and Dave Black evolved into The Illusions. He's played on street corners and bars, in fancy theaters and toured Ireland and Europe. He's dabbled with music from Madagascar and Argentina.

He's been heard on NPR, shared bills with Albert King, Lightnin' Hopkins and Guy Clark. Hall is the youngest musician listed by the

Missouri Historical Society on its list of the best of Missouri's blues performers. He's had his guitar stolen; he's suffered a broken shoulder that left him unable to play or pay his bills.

One Sheik reunion was in 2013 after the accidental fall that broke his shoulder. He was depressed. He'd lost his desire to perform. The reunion gave him a new life, 40 years after he started playing.

> Not playing guitar for two and a half months gave me a lot of time to think. And then the support I got . . . These people, I need to pay them back. Not just individuals. A whole crowd of people. I'm giving it my best shot. And I'm enjoying it.

He and Spencer appeared as T&A at the 2014 Bluesweek Festival, almost 30 years after that appearance at Mississippi Nights in the first such fest. And in 2014, T&A released a CD called *Untitled aka The Kitchen Record* and won a trip to Memphis by winning the St. Louis Blues Challenge.

The future? "Make a better living is what I want to do. Enjoy myself. Make good music. What else can you ask for?"

12:30 p.m. -- George and Ethel McCoy -- The niece and nephew of Memphis Minnie, a brother and sister act raised in East St. Louis who appeared infrequently. The pair recorded in the sixties -- including a session in East St. Louis by a field team from Adelphi Records, a session that also featured Henry Townsend and Henry Brown.

The pair was part of a famous family that included their father, Joe McCoy, who worked with Minnie, a blues belter from the Delta. Minnie played guitar and sang from the twenties to the fifties. George and Ethel's father Joe was also known as Kansas Joe and also played with his brother, Charley McCoy, as Big Joe and the Mississippi Mudders.

The large family of Mississippi musicians was also loosely related to the Mississippi Sheiks, and included Robert Nighthawk (Robert Lee McCoy), one of Townsend's main playing partners in the thirties. The McCoy's daughter, Bonnie McCoy, grew up in East St. Louis and became a singer in her own right, releasing a record, *Child of the Blues,* in 1979 that included songs by both her father and her aunt.

The 1969 Adelphi recording includes Ethel's memorable "Penitentiary," wherein a woman chooses to serve time for murder rather than suffer the abuse of her lover. Also prior to the fest, in 1982, the duo pressed *At Home with the Blues*, a disc that includes Lonnie Johnson's "St. Louis Cyclone."

1 p.m. -- Big George and the House Rockers -- When Henry Townsend died in 2006, George Brock became the patriarch of the blues in St. Louis, the oldest of the original Mississippi Delta players who came north in the Great Migration. During seven decades in the city Big George resisted the effects of the confluence. He never changed his style from the roots of the Clarksdale music he heard as he grew up, an area where, Brock says, "The blues grew like grass out of the ground."

In the twenty-tens, he still gave St. Louis music fans a direct pipeline to Delta styles dating back into the twenties. George sits on the stage, a century of history dressed in red.

In 2015, he lived near where Sportsman's Park once stood on the North Side. He wore a giant hat, a flowing velvet cape, tailored suits of colors that can only be described as garish, clothing right out of the super-fly era. His hands were giant; his harmonica disappeared into them when he brought the harp up to his mouth for a lung full of solo blues.

> The blues ain't nothing but the truth.
>
> I have lived the blues, I have sung the blues, I know all about the blues. Anytime that you see the things that I've seen, been the places I've been, you know the truth. The songs ain't nothing but the truth. I was raised up with the Delta sound and I don't change that sound.

He was born May 10, 1932, in Grenada, Miss., along Highway 51, about 70 miles south from Clarksdale. His father picked cotton and so did little George. At 10, his father gave Brock and his two brothers harmonicas for Christmas. George carried his to school, impressing his classmates.

After the war the family moved closer to Clarksdale along Highway 49. He heard Sonny Boy (the original) and B.B. King on the radio and played a rub board behind the Night Hawk, house parties with Memphis Minnie and the McCoys and set up the stage for Howlin' Wolf. In 1953 he moved on up Highway 61 to St. Louis -- "There gotta be something better somewhere" -- and sat in at the Early Bird Lounge on the North Side.

He formed up a house band there called the House Rockers. He played the Hideaway, the Moonlight Lounge, the Riviera, the Western Inn and the Red Top. He became manager of the Early Bird and in 1956 hired a guitar player named Albert King. In 1968 he took over ownership of the Early Bird, changed its name to Club Caravan and brought in Little Milton, Jimmy Reed and Muddy Waters.

His career flew by until 1970, when tragedy struck the big man. Working the door at his club, Brock threw a rowdy customer out of the bar but the man came back at closing time, packing a gun. Drunk and out of control, the disgruntled customer began firing shots. One of the bullets blew through the club's kitchen wall directly into his wife's temple. He found her dead in the kitchen.

He closed the club and went into a 15-year funk before returning to win a battle of blues bands contest that netted him the giant gold belt he still proudly wraps around his waist for performances.

Big George received a rousing reception at the 1st Blues Fest. He went back into business, opening the New Caravan Club at Taylor and Delmar in the Central West End, playing there himself every weekend for three years.

In 2005 he finally recorded his first album, *Club Caravan,* and had reached the age when he became a respected elder of the blues. Later that year he took part in Mississippi Public Broadcasting's Native Sons concert series. That October, he blew his harp on *Mojo Priest,* an all-star blues album put together by the actor Steven Seagal. He was named winner of the Blues Foundation's Comeback of the Year. The next year he put together another record, *Round Two.*

He returned frequently to Clarksdale, where his extended family includes James "Super Chikan" Johnson. He appeared there at festivals and at Ground Zero, Morgan Freeman's popular "juke joint." In 2015, he remained a frequent visitor to St. Louis stages, appearing most often at BB's.

Brock missed national fame by a decision made in the early sixties. Muddy Waters, a Delta playing mate, set him up with an audition in front of the Chess Brothers in Chicago. They wanted to sign him, but he refused to buy into the label's payment policies. He wanted royalties, a deal killer for Leonard Chess.

But Big George soldiered on, eventually shaking off the death of his wife and building his mostly local following, a treasure for St. Louis and Clarksdale. He claims to have fathered 42 children; he says he knocked out Sonny Liston during a sparring session at a St. Louis gym in the fifties. He says he once wrestled a bear; he says he took on a "huge Mongolian fighter" brought in for bouts in Mississippi.

His take on the blues ignores the urban influences of the early Lonnie Johnson years or the impact of hearing the urban radio stations. He talks about where his music comes from:

> Way back in the slavery days, way back, way back. You just out there by yourself. They come to you, you'd start in singing them, making time, beating on the log, keeping time, hitting on a tree. Just any way to keep time.
>
> I can write a blues right on the bandstand. You'd think it has been out for years, but it's the first time I thought of it. I made up many of my songs going down the highway, going to play or coming home from playing. I have had many people come to me and say I don't know what I'd do if I just sit at home. You made me feel so much better I can go back home now and be with my problem now.
>
> Some of it is uplifting and some of it is sad music. But the blues is telling you something that happened to somebody. Somewhere in the world it done happened to them.
>
> St. Louis has the best blues talent that there is -- but you never can get nowhere here -- you get to the top of the line here but that's as far as you gonna get.

2 p.m. -- Piano Slim Blues Band -- Robert T. Smith, Slim stands on the pathway of the St. Louis piano players, a Texan whose keyboard mastery owed itself to a gunshot to the back.

Smith was born Aug. 1, 1928, in La Grange, Texas, and was a saxophone player in the clubs in and around Houston and San Antonio in the late forties. But the shooting made it hard to hold the sax, so he switched first to drums, then piano. He worked the keys for a while in Odessa and then moved to Houston where he met up with bluesmen Henry Hayes, Gatemouth Brown and Little Willie Littlefield.

In the late fifties, Don Robey, a Texas music promoter who managed Brown, heard Slim play and recommended him to Bob Lyons of Bobbin Records in St. Louis. Slim recorded only one record for Bobbin, but once in St. Louis, he stayed, playing the North Side.

His Bobbin side was the popular local hit "Workin' Again" in 1959, performing both piano and vocals. Once the city's blues revival picked up steam he was tapped by the Swingmaster label for two albums, *Mean Woman Blues* in 1981 and *Gateway to the Blues* in 1983.

These records, plus his appearance at the 1986 festival, led to six European tours as well as local and national appearances with Tommy Bankhead. In 1991, Slim appeared with Bankhead, Oliver Sain, Doc Terry and Johnnie Johnson on a Wolf label collection called *St. Louis Blues Today.* Slim also started a band he called Blues Inquisition, with whom he made another record, *Minnie Skirt*, in 1993. Another Slim record was *St. Louis Blues,* shared with Henry Townsend in 1980 and released in 1985, also on Wolf.

Until the end of his life on Dec. 30, 2011, Slim played occasional clubs, made another record for Swingmaster, *Sneaky People* (2003), and drove a cab to help make ends meet. His funeral notice said he had outlasted all of his 17 brothers and sisters and three of his children. He left behind three daughters, three stepchildren, 13 grandchildren, five great-grandchildren, and a long legacy of boogie-woogie, blues and R&B.

Ron Edwards, Henry Townsend's sideman in the eighties, nineties and twenty-aughts, said Slim played the deep blues, "not as complicated as Johnnie Johnson, but he's a guy who shouldn't be forgotten."

3 p.m. -- Leroy Jody Pierson -- By the time Pierson reached the stage at the first blues fest, he had done what he once considered impossible -- a white kid who grew up in the suburbs who could play the blues. It was, he said, "the total opposite of everything I was trained for. I was trained to be a stockbroker or something like that."

Born in 1947, he grew up just over the city line in the middle class suburb of Ferguson, Mo. His father was a businessman who played western swing as a hobby and owned lots of records.

Family outings included trips to clubs to see John Coltrane, Muddy Waters and Albert King. Leroy's father also worked hard to make the money to send his son to what was considered the best of private schools -- the

Country Day School, an all-male school with roots all the way back to the pre-Civil War era when it was founded by the father of T.S. Eliot.

Many St. Louis notables attended the school, including Morton May of the May Department store; Bill DeWitt, owner of the Cardinals baseball team; U.S. Senators John Danforth, Thomas Eagleton and Pete Wilson, who was also governor of California; and William McChesney Martin, longtime chairman of the Federal Reserve Bank and partner in the St. Louis-based A.G. Edwards brokerage firm.

Pierson was expelled before he graduated and finished high school at McCleur in Florissant, a public high school in an integrated area of North County that included Ferguson. Pierson says he was kicked out of Country Day "for not fitting in." As he puts it, "I went from being the poor kid in the rich boy's school to being thought of as the rich kid, although we were always pretty much middle class."

> Country Day was all boys and all white.
>
> Country Day, like the great majority of the schools at the time, was a racist institution to the core. We had many teachers at Country Day who had been active CIA. Revolution in Guatemala -- half the school would empty out, the teachers were all gone. Right wing -- I've kept some textbooks just to prove to people how crazy it was.
>
> One of my textbooks was called *The Protracted Conflict*, which was published by the John Birch Society, about the evils of communism. I had teachers telling me in class that there were 60,000 Chinese communist troops training in Mexico to take over Texas. And here this was supposed to be the greatest center of learning in St. Louis.

Like many middle class contemporaries in the sixties, Pierson's mind began to reel. Vietnam and the civil rights movement hit at the same time. Pierson got in trouble when at 15 he danced with a black singer at an event at the Old Warson Country Club, a staid West County institution. He watched the rich boys toe the line and decided he wasn't interested.

> I decided I was not interested in wealth, and I was not interested in people that controlled wealth. I didn't want to be around them. I didn't respect them. What I did respect was people that had

> nothing who made something of themselves. Especially Henry Townsend.
>
> Henry didn't even have any schooling. Henry didn't have anything. You can't imagine how I identified with Henry Townsend, how I wanted to be like Henry Townsend. Henry can take a car apart and put it back together, and he can take a computer apart and put it together.

Pierson started learning guitar, listening to Gabriel's show on the radio and buying blues records. He attended the liberal Beloit University in Wisconsin, a school that prides itself on "cooperative rather than competitive learning." Arriving there in 1966, he began organizing and promoting music shows featuring his favorite bluesmen, starting with a lineup that featured Son House, Fred McDowell, Arthur Crudup and Junior Wells, all deep blues pioneers from the Delta. Four years later his shows had 18 acts and he was among the players as well as being the promoter.

> I didn't really start playing until I got to college. The promoting was really the key to all the personal experiences. It's one thing to get next to an artist and say 'hey, I love your stuff.' It's another thing to get next to an artist when you've got a thousand dollars in your back pocket for him. You get their attention a lot quicker like that. So I would bring all my favorite people up to Beloit and then the ones I really liked, I would get close to them and start visiting them at home.

He began traveling through the South looking for blues performers and old records, the lost 78s of another era. He found plenty, paying 50 cents a disc, building an impressive collection.

> It was like I had a calling. I literally could not force myself to think of anything else. I just couldn't . . . I couldn't stop thinking about this music. I couldn't stop thinking about these people. I couldn't stop thinking about the guitars. I couldn't stop thinking about the records.

Back in St. Louis, in the early seventies, he began playing with his idol, Henry Townsend. He wrote liner notes and articles for the several magazines that were spawned by the blues revival. He put together a collection of his own records and released it on his own label -- Boogie Disease Records -- called *Take a Little Walk With Me,* which focused on Chicago players from 1948 to 1957, issued in 1976. He then founded Nighthawk Records, issuing regional collections.

In 1974 he took to the airwaves, starting a radio show on KWMU called the "Missouri Tradition," a show that brought the St. Louis players into the forefront to help show the effects of the confluence on the blues. That show became "The Baby Face Leroy Blues Hour" then -- following a new infatuation with reggae -- he began the first National Public Radio show on the genre-- "Beat Down Babylon."

He found many similarities between blues and reggae and in 1985 the Leroy Pierson Band did a one-month tour of Jamaica with Rockin' Dopsie and the Twisters, a zydeco band from New Orleans. There, Pierson played the Jamaican Jam-Fest and the World Music Festival, sharing the stage with Yellowman, Lionel Hampton, and the Mighty Diamonds. In 1987 he toured Africa and the Middle East, performing shows in Iraq, Yemen, United Arab Emerites, Sudan, and Quatar.

In 1988, two years after his set at the first blues fest, he put out his own record, *Rusty Nails*, and was a mainstay on the solidified St. Louis scene, playing a regular gig at the Broadway Oyster Bar.

That show later morphed into the twenty-tens as a regular Friday appearance at BB's where every week Leroy transports the modern audience into the juke joints of yore. He's a somewhat rumpled, slighting balding man in his 60s, wearing a yellow shirt and suspenders, some loose tan pants and a pair of black hard-toed shoes. He plays an electrified guitar in the finger picking style. He sings with his eyes closed, inviting the listener inside the music just like he is, still suffering from the boogie disease.

"You boogie for the doctor, you boogie for the nurse, you keep on boogieing till they put you in the hearse."

3:30 p.m. -- Clayton Love -- Love was the Ike Turner sidekick who remained in St. Louis after Ike joined up with Tina and fled to Los Angeles. His 1986 appearance was one of his last. By then he was working as an administrator at Sumner High and came out of retirement for the performance.

The Fest led to Love's swan song, a European tour billed as the St. Louis Kings of Rhythm in 1987 that also included Ike alumni Stacy Johnson, Billy Gayles, Robbie Montgomery, Erskine Oglesby, Oliver Sain and Jimmy Hinds.

The tour led to a double LP released on the Dutch label Timeless that led off with five tunes from Love. In 1991, he also made an album for Modern Blues Recordings with fellow ivory ace Johnnie Johnson called *Rockin' Eighty-Eights,* a nod to the original Ike Turner hit.

He died Feb. 28, 2010, at age 82.

4 p.m. -- Blue City Band -- Keith Doder's vehicle that was just getting rolling, bringing the Little Walter style to the South Side. The band, Doder's first, also included Rich McDonough, another rising player, but one who lasted far longer that Doder, right into the twenty-tens.

5 p.m. -- Soulard Blues Band -- By 1986 this was a veteran blues outfit, decked out in yellow wedding blazers with black piping and tuxedo shirts, dancing across the stage, swinging the crowd into the night set. "They came out rehearsed and they came dressed," said Ron Edwards.

The Soulard band had emerged from Sadie's Personality Bar on the North Side, the bar where Tommy Bankhead played regularly, a small box of a room where people jammed up forward for the blues. Dwyer began going to see Henry Townsend and Doc Terry and the Night Hawk at the club and met Doder, then Edwards, other seekers of the true St. Louis blues. They had come to the right place.

By then it was 1977 and Dwyer was living in Soulard, working as a teacher's aid in the projects, teaching 65 to 70 children per classroom. He got a job as a union organizer, working for a boss named Trotsky, organizing health workers for Local 13, a job that led to routine arrests.

Dwyer was the son of a St. Louis PD homicide detective, 8th District, on the far North Side out by Calvery Cemetery and Walnut Park. Dwyer's childhood street was in Harney Heights, just north of I-70, just south of Walnut Park, a tough neighborhood that eventually became a center of drive-by gang shootings. Dwyer was long gone from the neighborhood by then. He had worked as a cop in his early twenties but was drawn to music. Dwyer remembers:

> I've got four sisters. Three are older sisters, and they had the dance bug real bad. I was a teen in the fifties, my sisters brought home Rufus, the Dells, everyone that you know, James Brown, The Drifters, and Marvin Gaye. There'd be a dance, and all these good-looking' little gals would be running around, but nobody would dance with them. So me and my buddies, we'd go shopping down on Kingshighway, at Joe's Clothes. We'd get our hi-fashion, hi-collar, white-on-white shirts, with a pair of Sanzibelts, banister half moons, man! And we could dance!
>
> We got mobile. We operated from the North Side, we'd go all around. I was affected by St. Louis stuff as much as anything. Winston Rose, Alvin Williams, they had their little band; they were bad! The Rockin' Riondos, they were bad. I heard them in some of the nicest places and some of the regular joints, you know. Every Tuesday night, up at the Club Imperial for fifty cents, you know who -- Ike and Tina Turner and the Ikettes. St. Louis musicians were just tearing me up.
>
> (After leaving the police force he worked the river) -- tugboat deckhand, it was a great job. I worked a while with a carnival, now them boys are fast! Carnivals are a scuffling business. I picked up "carny" language from them. It's a variation on pig Latin. I worked at a couple of boilermaker plants, but in my neighborhood you were a success if you got over at the Chevy plant and got a job. But I never got that damn job! I tried for a while there. Maybe I was lucky, I don't know.

In the mid-seventies, Dwyer hooked up with the players at Sadie's, Big Al (a North Side harmonica player/singer), plus the veterans, Bankhead, Townsend and Terry. Dwyer says:

> These were guys we all learned from, continually. You wonder if you are gonna have the moves -- first of all, you wonder if you're gonna live that long, and then have the moves and the brain power to pull them off, and these guys have got it all, man!
>
> Anyway, we'd work at Sadie's, making seven bucks a night, but I didn't give a shit, because there was some gal up there (whistles), she reminded me of one of the Ikettes, you know. All

> she had to do to me was smile, you know. I couldn't talk, couldn't even pronounce my last name.
>
> Then I started a new band, and we were sitting around one time, thinking, "what do we call it?" Bill McKenna, he came up with the name, Soulard Blues Band. They didn't call Soulard "Soulard" back then, they had the market down here, but they didn't call Soulard "Soulard" at the time. Well, Billy said, "let's just call it the Soulard Blues Band" and the rest is history.

McKenna was the original drummer, Steve Albert was the guitar player and vocalist and Dwyer was on bass. Larry Thurston joined soon thereafter, answering an ad Dwyer put in the *Post-Dispatch* for a singer. Then came harp player Jim McClaren:

> Jim can play the styles of the masters all night long, You know - Sonny Boy, Little Walter, Slim Harpo. That's quite an accomplishment in a lifetime. But he's unique, because he's got his own style. You can identify it. Man, he comes up with some unbelievable riffs and stays on the attack.

So did the band, quickly digging into the new Soulard scene. By the time of the '86 Fest, Rondo Leewright had come and gone as the front man and formed his own band. Kirk Grice joined as the steady drummer, part of a 13-year stretch. Thurston was the singer, Rich Cotton was on sax, and Buzzy Morton was the guitar.

Rondo was the lead on the band's first album, *Soulard Blues Band* in 1981, with the lineup then including John Maltanry on drums, Bob Horridge on the B-3 organ along with the core group of Dwyer, McClaren, Cotton and Thurston.

In 1984, another record was made, *Nothing to Lose*, with Thurston, Cotton, McClaren, Dwyer along with Grice on drums, and a new guitar player, Tom "Hard Luck" Maloney.

By 1986, Dwyer was driving a Cadillac on the streets of Soulard, seen wearing a black leather jacket, heard listening to an East Side station blaring R&B from the radio. The Caddy wasn't new, of early seventies vintage, the rust spots accenting the white paint job.

In its first eight years the band had included 20 players, with Dwyer the mainstay. "Nobody in our band postures. We pull together. Maybe it's because we are all city boys. We've been through all this hard times growing up."

In a 1988 interview, Dwyer sang the praises of his Soulard neighborhood:

> We're around people who like music. Everybody knows each other and everybody appreciates what other people are doing. It's good and healthy. The blues allows for more of that feeling to commune through. It's a minor cult here.

The band played afternoon concerts at the University of Missouri-St. Louis, it played the Veiled Prophet Fair, blues cruises, benefits and at regular club gigs, including the Monday night jam at the Broadway Oyster Bar beginning in 1978, which in 2016 was the longest standing blues jam in America.

> It's a school for some guys. We sometimes have a guy who is playing for the first time on stage. We try to take care of him -- guide him through the experience. As soon as a guy plays -- and whether he likes the experience or not -- we make him on honorary Blueshawker.

The club numbered above 100 by the second decade of the twenty-first century.

Larry Griffin was a member, having joined the band in 1987. He played on *Long Gone*, Soulard's third album and stayed until 1994. His son, Aaron Griffin, played in the band in 2014.

Larry:

> We worked. Gig after gig after gig, two a day, three a day. A lot of corporate things. Art had lots of contacts around town. I lived in Ferguson, out by UMSL. It was an inner suburb. Downtown in 10 minutes. Paid $188 a month rent. Went to work to become the best singer and guitar player I could be.
>
> They all sang. All of them -- McLaren, Rich Cotton, Kirk, Art -- I wasn't a front man then who could get up and say follow me, we all sang. After a while you get on your game and you know what to do. We had some great times. Rich left and Brian

> Casserly came in. We made him a singer. I was there the night he was hired. Maloney was before me, Buzzy came in, then I came in, then when I left, Maloney came back.

Casserly was another player who went from the jam to the full-time band. He remembers:

> Artie Dwyer approached me and said, "We are going to make a change in our band, would you like to be in it?" -- so I came into it -- I remember the first show, he said, "When you sing, just sing naturally, don't try to be a persona, just sing naturally."
>
> The first time I had a rehearsal with Soulard he asked me to do "The St. Louie Blues" and I kind of did it ala Armstrong and Art stopped the band and said, "No, man, don't do that, just sing with your natural voice, just sing it" -- and I remember looking around at the rest of the band -- so I started singing natural and pretty soon I became the lead singer for that band.
>
> Art was very adamant about the horn section -- about how you are there to support the singer -- I learned how to do that -- how to educate the horn players how to back up an artist -- how a band backs up the person who is doing the singing -- that's one of the things that I know I have a talent for -- being in a band and developing that flow -- it's easy for me to go from sideman to front man because basically the thing is that I'm amongst a bunch of musicians.
>
> At the time in the nineties, who got more enjoyment backing up a solo then playing a solo? All the players were fabulous musicians and to do that on the fly in the moment, to be able to back up something that isn't written out, that is worked out immediately on the stage -- its an addictive thing -- because it becomes powerful -- more than a sum of its parts thing -- and during that time it was great to be a sideman but also it's great to be a front man in front of that because when it's happening it's the best feeling -- the best of what music is -- the moment that makes live music what it is.

6 p.m. -- Silvercloud and the St. Louis Blues Band -- Rudy Coleman was born in 1933 and grew up in St. Louis County, in a house filled with his parents' records.

Rudy Coleman and the Rhythm Rockers got rolling in 1954, billed as the "Little Boy with the Memphis Slim voice." In the mid-eighties he put bands together with Doder, Kaufman and Doc Terry. Leroy Pierson played with him Monday nights. He brought in horns, Junior Walker, Roy Akers, Erskine Ogelsby.

He continued playing into his eighties.

7 p.m. -- Tommy Bankhead and the Blues Eldoradoes -- Larry Griffin, determined to play music, quit his job as a teacher in Texas and returned to St. Louis in the mid-eighties. Tommy Bankhead was by then playing in Soulard. Griffin, speaking of the years '85, '86 and '87:

> Tommy was the only Mississippi electric blues band playing outside the North Side, There were still other guys playing on the North Side but they weren't out playing in the circle where white people heard them. Boo Boo Davis was playing on the East Side, there were guys playing at the Red Room over there, but Bankhead was the first guy playing on both sides of the river and both sides of town.
>
> Bennie Smith was back playing by then but not with a band. Henry Townsend was around but just did special occasions, birthdays at the Allen Avenue Restaurant, but he didn't play out anywhere very much.

Bankhead, born on Oct. 24, 1931, was a Mississippi native who landed in St. Louis in 1949, age 17. He'd heard of the St. Louis music scene from one of Ike's guitarists. In short order, Bankhead caught on.

Bankhead made a living in the clubs on the North Side during the sixties and seventies, and then became the pioneering bluesman in Soulard. He first played at the edge of Mill Creek Valley at Miss B's on Chouteau. He formed the Landrockers then the Blues Eldorados. Keith Doder was on harp.

Bankhead played electric bass backup on a Townsend record in 1961, but it wasn't until 1983 that he made his own album, *Bankhead*. Doder's harp is a highlight of that record, but it doesn't outshine Bankhead's guitar work and uplifting singing.

Once he got rolling on the South Side, there was no stopping him. He played 17 years at Mike and Min's, a smallish club that held down the corner of Tenth and Geyer. Bankhead rotated with many more in its corner setup. He played the blues while the neighborhood came to life. The new residents drank in the bars and dug live music.

Mike and Min's had opened just after the repeal of Prohibition. It survived in its dive bar status, greeting the blues revival with open arms. One week in 1981, the lineup included Ron Edwards, Keith Doder and Bob Case on Thursday, Silvercloud on Friday and Soulard Blues Band Saturday.

Over at Hilary's that night Marsha Evans and the Coalition and at Carnegie's on Lafayette were Steve Marino & the River City Revue.

Other clubs followed in rapid succession along the streets of Soulard. By 1994 they included the Allen Avenue Restaurant, the 1860's Saloon, Great Grizzly Bear, Johnny's, Molly's, Melanie's, the Heartbreak Hotel and the Venice Cafe. By then the citywide list in the *BluesLetter* included 46 clubs.

Bankhead played a steady schedule on the South Side all through the eighties and nineties. He also was a regular headliner at the city's annual blues festival and appeared on an iconic poster for the 1995 event under the heading "Happiness is highly overrated."

His health began to fail in 1997. A benefit concert brought all the big names to BB's to help with the medical bills, including Oliver Sain, Johnnie Johnson, Bennie Smith, Henry Townsend and the Soulard Blues Band.

Bankhead recorded two albums late in his life: *Message to St. Louis*, released in 2000 and *Please Accept My Love*, recorded three months before his death on Dec. 16, 2000. The record was released in 2002.

The albums provide a tidy summation of Tommy Bankhead, easy blues with a sweet voice and a gentle, old school guitar. Both are backed by the band Cryin' Shame, with appearances by Oliver Sain and Bob Lohr.

Bankhead was true to that St. Louis thing. He made few forays out of town. Instead, he helped build the blues revival. John May, the BB's owner and bass player for Cryin' Shame, said Bankhead was a "true gentleman, always ready with a smile and a laugh. Tommy has played the blues. He had earned the right to call himself a 'bluesman.'"

8 p.m. -- Billy Peek Band -- Twenty-six years after he appeared at the first Fest, this blues guitar singer was still on the festival lineup in the twenty-first century. He ripped open his set at the 2012 Bluesweek with a run through of blues and rock standards -- "Everyday I Have the Blues," "Roll Over, Beethoven," "It Hurts Me Too," "Down Home Blues," "Sweet Little Sixteen," "Reap What You Sew," and "Hoochie Coochie Man."

He paused, took a breath. He pulled the mike closer. Here came his story. He's told the story many times. Now he stood on a stage not far from where Stagger Lee shot Billy, only a few blocks from where W.C. Handy heard a blues picker on the Eads Bridge and just across the street from when Frankie shot Johnny.

Billy talked:

> I was born and raised here in St. Louis and I grew up on a street not far from here, Tower Grove Avenue, and on the street there was this pool hall called Slimey's, and as a kid I used to hang out there all the time and on the juke they had the "Big Lip Blues."
>
> In St. Louie you got to have the big lips to say it like Bluuuuse, like that, yeah, that's what I'm talking about. So when I first heard that sound I had to learn how to play it. Where can I learn to pay the blues? And everybody said, you go to East St. Louis in the wee hours and you can learn how to play the blues.
>
> So one day I got up the nerve and went up to a guy over there and asked, "Where can I learn how to play the blues?"
>
> And he said, "I got bad news, son, a white boy can't play the blues."
>
> "But . . . but . . ."

Billy looked stricken, then courageous, then excited. Then he jumped his guitar, slamming a triumphant riff, and shouted, "But I'm a Tower Grove boy … and I stole everything he put down." And with a firm nod to his band, Billy lays down his one-hit wonder, "Can a White Boy Play the Blues?"

His lessons came direct from Ike Turner every Tuesday night in the front row of the Club Imperial. He first saw him in high school in 1955. "Up until that time, I never seen a guitar played like that. I stood there in front of Ike watching his fingers."

Soon enough Ike began letting him sit in with the show. "He'd give me his guitar and I'd get up, play a song and give it back to him. I was thrilled to death."

At 15, Billy heard "Maybellene" and his life changed. He decided to devote himself to rock 'n' roll. In 1958, Peek joined the Chuck Tillman band, a sax-driven rock outfit that led to an appearance on St. Louis Hop, the local *American Bandstand* knockoff. He soon landed a slot opening for his idol, Chuck Berry, at the Casa Loma Ballroom on the South Side. That led to gigs with Al Lassiter and the Ardettes and the ABC Revue. A black DJ called Peek "a blue-eyed soul brother." He also played in Gaslight Square with Bonnie Bramlette.

He made an ill-fated dive into the waters of the Los Angeles scene in the mid-sixties but came back to St. Louis by the end of the decade. He could play originals, covers and all the Chuck Berry songs. He anchored an all-star backing band at the Mississippi River Fest in 1970, playing behind Berry, Bo Diddley, Jerry Lee Lewis, and Garry U.S. Bonds.

Peek joined Berry's show in Vegas and had a regular gig at Berry's estate in Wentzville, where he played the Berry hits at weekly outdoor shows on Sunday afternoons.

Then, in 1975, he filled in for Berry on *Don Kirshner's Rock Concert,* a show that happened to be seen by English rock stalwarts Ronnie Wood and Rod Stewart. Stewart hired Peek to play Berry riffs with Stewart's touring band and Peek was gainfully employed for nearly six years, doing four albums and three European tours with Stewart.

Following the Stewart years, Peek settled into an active schedule all over the St. Louis region, telling his story, asking his question and playing his song. He has made three solo albums.

He played a continued residency at the Backstreet Jazz & Blues Bar at the Westport Plaza, the same St. Louis mall where J.B. Hutto's once stood. By 2016, Peek played a steady schedule of suburban shows and summer afternoon winery gigs in the surrounding counties.

9 p.m. -- Henry and Vernell Townsend with Ron Edwards -- Townsend had a band in the early fifties but slowed down playing music and got a job collecting debts as the sixties began. He did a studio album in St. Louis with Tommy Bankhead called *Henry Townsend: Tired Of Bein' Mistreated* in 1961 and held a session here and a session there with the guitar player Mike Stewart and the pianoman Henry Brown, but not making many appearances, unless it was to collect money for Independent Merchants, where he went to work in 1959.

One of those collections resulted in good fortune for Townsend. The company sold jewelry, furniture, appliances and other goods on credit. It was Henry's job to collect from a woman named Vernell and "it just went into an affair. What I'm saying is I took her and her debt."

They were together until Vernell died in 1995, "we hit it off pretty good," Henry said. "It was more harmony than it was anything else. We had some pleasant moments together, and sometimes she wished I was in the kitchen and I wished she was downstairs somewhere."

In 1980, after turning down numerous invitations, Townsend played Europe and made two LPs in Austria on the Wolf label, one solo and one with Vernell, the first time they had recorded together.

She recorded again in 1984 and the joint appearance at the First Blues Fest was part of a mid-eighties run of activity for the couple. "Vernell," Edwards remembered, "had that wonderful stage presence and put a whole period touch on it."

When he, Vernell and Ron Edwards took the stage in 1986 at the 1st Fest, Henry was 75 years old and presumed to be retired, at least according to one press account. He had recently been the subject of a career-capping documentary, *That's the Way I Do It,* a documentary that was important, Edwards says, "because it established somebody as having this long term relationship with the city."

Townsend also brought St. Louis to national attention when he won a Heritage Fellowship as a "master of the arts." It was time to rest and relax, putter in the garage, maybe fix a clock.

Not Henry. He was instead about to launch a new career, that of the "patriarch of the blues" in St. Louis. For the next 20 years he played this role, holding famous birthday parties, recording albums, headlining festivals, playing at BB's, at Allen Avenue, at the 1860 bar, traveling, staying at home, fixing a few television sets.

In 1988, opening night of the the third St. Louis Blues Festival to Townsend. He played a solo set, then jammed into the late night with Robert Lockwood Jr., a Chicago bluesman who came from the same era as Townsend. The day had been proclaimed Henry Townsend Day in St. Louis. Other St. Louisans at the festival, held at the St. Louis Arena, were Albert King, Fontella Bass, Johnnie Johnson and Oliver Sain.

In 1997, an album considered by some to be Townsend's best, the record called *Mule*, was rereleased on a CD. It had been made in 1980, called "powerful, wonderful singing, moving, impressive, inspiring" but was only available on vinyl until 1997.

In 1998 Henry resumed his long recording career, which began in 1929. In his eighth decade of session work, just short of his 90th birthday, he made *88 Blues* on Joe Edwards' Blueberry Hill label. With Ron Edwards on the bottleneck, Henry is sometimes on guitar himself, but mostly on piano. The record is about as close to a club night with Henry as one can experience electronically. It was recorded live in one take at the Sheldon Hall and features the kind of music Henry made for years, writing the songs live on stage.

In 1999, Henry celebrated his 90th birthday and received another proclamation from another mayor. He released *A Blues Life*, the book that best captures St. Louis music in the twenties and thirties.

In 2000, Swingmaster released more of the material he had recorded solo in St. Louis in 1981 and 1983 as well as cuts from Amsterdam, captured during his 1987 tour. The CD was called *Henry Townsend: Blues Ace;* it includes 15 original Townsend takes.

Catfish put out another of the many Townsend compilations of old 45s in 2000, then in 2001 came another original record, *Henry Townsend: My Story,* recorded with Edwards in Salina, Kan., late in 1999. Here was more of the classic Townsend style and turned out to be his last full album.

In September 2006 he traveled back to Grafton, Wis., for a ceremony and concert honoring him as the last surviving musician to record for Paramount Records, one of the leading labels of the twenties and thirties. He died there Sept. 24, not long after he became the first person honored at the Grafton Paramount Walk of Fame.

"He wasn't in it for the money. He believed in the music. It told a very honest story," said Mark O'Shaughnessy.

10 p.m. -- Rondo Blues Deluxe -- Rondo Leewright had been rolling on his second career since 1979 when he hit the stage at the first blues fest in 1986. He was 40 years old, the leader of his own band, a veteran of the St. Louis blues revival, a standard bearer for the level of music that resounded in the city by the mid-eighties.

His day job repairing copy machines was over by then. Rondo was full go as a bluesman, another of those unsung masters of St. Louis, virtually unknown outside the River City. Rondo spread the music built from a combination of styles, a confluence that gave forth a revived sound, a blues that mixed rock and funk. He was a leader in a new generation of the revue Ike Turner perfected thirty years before. Rondo put Howlin' Wolf and Joe Cocker on the same stage with his trademark -- "Somebody say yeah!"

When Rondo joined the Soulard Blues Band in 1979, the city was starting to bounce away from the recession. The disco craze had run its course. In 1985, Vince Schoemehl and the city hit the peak of the "urban renaissance."

People had an appetite for the urban shopping centers and for urban music. Soulard Blues Band and Rondo's Blues Deluxe rose as the top two bands, with Soulard at Hutto's, then the Grizzly Bear and Mike & Min's. Rondo became the star of Blueberry Hill, jamming the Elvis Room week after week.

Rondo's guitar player, Steve Waldman, said:

> His idea of doing a show was basically just showing people his heart. Rondo operated purely on emotion. There was never anything that was calculated about it. He was a great front man, but he was a natural front man — never scripted.

Joe Edwards opened the Elvis Room in Blueberry Hill in 1985, booking Rondo in a weekly rotation.

"We became great friends. I was a great sponsor of his and a great supporter of his," Edwards said. Rondo's three albums all came under the Edwards' wing, including his debut with *Rondo's Blues Deluxe Live at Blueberry Hill*, which best captured the excitement of the band and the venue. Just as quickly as he bloomed, however, Rondo faded.

"He was just a great showman, had a great voice and a great sense of how to entertain a crowd and play to a crowd. He really worked a crowd," Edwards said.

But he didn't last long.

> He was just starting to go. I had him lined up for a tour and some blues festivals. I don't know what it was -- I've often wondered if

> it was the fear of success syndrome or not. Or if it was just that crack -- crack-cocaine -- came into his life at the time. Early nineties. It was just amazing -- he was ready to hit the big blues festivals, in California, all around. But then you couldn't depend on him to show up. And it all just fell apart. The band was just great. Really talented.

Rondo arrived in St. Louis as an adopted child. A mix of African American and Spanish, he was taken in by a white Catholic family in Robertson, Mo. His birth name was Ronnie Norris, his mother Anna Norris (DeCost) and father Clyde Jones, a member of the Jones Brothers band that played throughout the northeast.

Ronnie Norris was born Dec. 18, 1945, in Broxton, Mass. He was six when Esther and Louis Leewright of Robertson, an African-American suburb that butted up against Lambert Airport, adopted him. The town got its name from the company that built the glider that carried Mayor Becker to his death in 1943.

Ronnie's mother was Spanish and his father was black. The family lived in Selma, Ala., until 1951 when Ronnie's stepfather arraigned a deal to have him adopted.

Off he went to Robertson, which was settled by the French at the time St. Louis was a trading post, 10 miles away from the downtown. In the nineteenth century it was known as Fairmont, then Algum. In 1918, Robertson Aircraft was founded on a field north of the airport in an unincorporated area of St. Louis County.

Charles Lindbergh was the company's most famous employee, hauling mail to Chicago and points in between.

Rondo graduated from Berkeley High in 1962, and formed his first band, El Rondo and the Jades, a name made up to sound Latin and give an explanation for Rondo's dark complexion. The club didn't hire blacks. Segregation in Missouri wasn't, after all, much different from that in Alabama.

The stage name stuck and so did the act, filling the El Rancho with El Rondo week in and week out. The Jades made a record, "Crying in My Heart," at Oliver Sain's Archway Studio in 1966. Rondo and the Jades lasted until the end of the sixties when his gigs faded and he began repairing copy machines.

But he couldn't get the music out of his system and when the blues began to revive in the seventies, Rondo was ready to join in, building his reputation week after week in the sweaty confines of the Elvis Room. That is until the cocaine craze of the eighties and nineties claimed him. He used it to fuel a frantic stage style. Edwards and Rondo's band mates saw the fall coming and tried to get him to stop, but Rondo couldn't, wouldn't, and didn't.

His gig list grew smaller after 1997, when he was pulled down by the first of a series of strokes. By 2006 he had to use a motorized chair. Still, he got around, doing the occasional vocal gig with old friends. He died in 2011, survived by his wife, four daughters, four sons, 18 grandchildren, eight great-grandchildren and numerous Jones and Norris relatives.

Edwards:

> He didn't perform the same after the crack. He'd show up late. He wouldn't show up at all. The band was really getting messed over.
>
> He had the signature thing -- "Somebody Say Yeah" -- almost like you were in church, it wasn't corny with him -- he made it work. He talked in the songs, "Somebody Say Yeah" -- and the crowd would go along with it. I would go see him week after week. There was a period of time -- for about a year and a half -- I saw him every week. That's how exciting it was. I was there as a fan -- a very vocal -- "yoo-hoo" type of fan. Sometimes I was probably too loud. But I enjoyed it that much.
>
> I spent a lot of time and money to try to break a St. Louis act out big in the blues scene. And this was the one band that could have done it. It's a sad tale.

11 p.m. -- Oliver Sain with special guests James DeShay and Barbara Carr -- Three mainstays of the blues, funk and soul scene.

In 1986, Sain had another decade and a half of music to play.

Even after a cancer diagnosis in 1994 he continued on, running Archway Studios and playing gigs around town, settling into a weekly Thursday night date with the singer Marsha Evans at BB's all the way up until his death, Oct. 28, 2003.

There has been talk since his death of a Sain Museum at the old Archway Studios building on Natural Bridge in the North Side, but it hadn't happened by 2016. The building stood, an empty lot next door, a beauty salon in front of the big brick building that once housed the liveliest recording studio in the city, as usual, unmarked by the city.

Shortly before he died, Sain said he felt the blues music in St. Louis was strong.

> People want to hear this music, but we need to promote the great talent in this city more. The city fathers don't value blues like they do in Memphis and New Orleans. Those cities sell their music as part of their product and St. Louis needs to do the same. But here it's not like that. They don't care! They're strictly politicians.

12 midnight -- David Dee and the Hot Tracks Band -- Twenty-six years after the show at Mississippi Nights at the 1st St. Louis Blues Festival, David Dee and the Hot Tracks -- the last surviving R&B revue from East St. Louis remained on a steady schedule. On an afternoon in 2012, the group lined up on stage at the Webster Groves Jazz Festival. Dee was grizzled, but dressed well. He wore blue, from the shoes to the hat. He also wore a flying V around his neck.

He started in the East St. Louis of 1963 when places like the Cosmopolitan Club were supporting five or six full-scale revues, complete with Supremes-type female singers, full horn sections and deep-throated blues stars. Dee had a hit, "Goin' Fishing,' a 1980 R&B platter that got Dee out of East St. Louis just as it started to fade. He also played with the Oliver Sain Revue and has played through the years, sometimes on tour, sometimes at BB's.

He showed plenty of ginger at Webster Groves. The band started the warm up with the "Theme from Shaft," followed by the appearance of three female singers -- anchored by Leslie Dee and Gina Dee, David's two daughters, and rounded out by Watisha Hill. Leslie poured out "I Will Always Love You" to conclude the diva portion of the show and we got the big intro for David, greeted by a big hand by the crowd of about 300 people.

He did "Goin' Fishing," his "tribute to St. Louis women," and his other hit, "Working Blues Man," then went into several more rowdy dirty blues of the type that made Ike & Tina Turner stars. Dee finished with "Two of Us" with his daughter, a 20-year veteran of the show. Smiles were seen all around at the close.

In 2016, Dee gave a repeat performance of his show at the opening of the National Blues Museum, playing the same set-list with virtually the same line-up, drawing the same cheers from the same type of fans, keeping the music alive.

The idea of the first festival was to get publicity for blues music in St. Louis.

What the bands accomplished over the next 30 years of shows is the big payday for St. Louisans. Many dozens of other performers emerged around this time who didn't appear at the Fest, the most notable being **Bennie Smith,** the guitar man who in the mid-eighties had just come out of a long hiatus.

In the early sixties Smith, a native of Mill Creek Valley who was playing guitar by the time he was 12, had a six-night-a-week gig at the Peppermint Lounge on Delmar, then the biggest nightclub in the city. Run by the St. Louis cousins of the mobsters who started the original Peppermint Lounge in New York City, it faded when the twist craze came to an end.

Bennie then played the North Side, but as the city emptied and many clubs closed, Bennie faded as well, instead twisting wires and replacing tubes in televisions through the late sixties and seventies.

But he couldn't stay away forever and began to take notice of the revival. One day in 1983, he brushed off his repairman jump suit, planted his pork-pie hat on his head and took his guitar into the Baton Record Store on the Delmar Loop.

The repairman Bennie Smith met there was Michael King, a 22-year-old former motorcycle repairman from University City who had learned to fix instruments.

> I had no clue who Bennie was, nobody knew who he was. Bennie was an unknown at the time. He played in the fifties, played in a bunch of St. Louis bands, he played with Ike and Tina Turner, all those bands, but he had retired a long time ago and he never made no money.
>
> He was just a somebody, just a nobody somebody. He would come in all the time -- come in during the middle of the day with this green jumpsuit on. A string here and a string there -- in that

> sense I knew who he was, he was this old guy who needed to fix his guitar. He'd come in and he'd say, "I need a little E, a little E, gimme a little E."
>
> One day the guitar just didn't work, so he brought it in and I finally got to see what he'd been putting that 'Little E' (string) on. He'd been putting them on this Harmony Silhouette, that's what it was called, a funky little guitar that was very similar to a scaled down Fender Jaguar, it had a very surf look to it. He brought this thing in one day and this was a guy who is supposed be a TV repairman and all that, he said he couldn't get any sound out of it.
>
> He left it and I found the problem with it. It was that when you put the plug in the jack, every once in a while that nut loosens up and it spins and it yanked one of the wires off the terminal. I just soldered it back, no big deal, boom -- it had sound.
>
> So the next thing I did was take it out on the floor where I always tested guitars. I got to see if this guitar makes a sound. So I plugged into one of those Fender Reverbs.
>
> And oh, my God, what a sound!
>
> I heard a bunch of guitars in that store, but I wasn't a player then. I could just diddle around, but you immediately knew if you had a guitar or not. This one had a tone you could not touch. Now those pickups on that guitar… if you Google it -- Google "Golden Tone Harmony pickups." You'll see, they are coveted now.
>
> I fell in love with this guitar. The size of it, too, it was just this little dinky guitar. At that point I said I want to learn how to play guitar. So, you know, I asked Ben, 'you want to sell this, trade it for another?' He says, "Noooo." He says, 'No way."

Bennie's longtime playing partner and manager, Sharon Foehner, the daughter-in-law of the great ragtime player "Gaslight" Gale Foehner, arrived in St. Louis in 1987. Not long afterward she was playing her bass at the newly opened Venice Cafe near the A-B Brewery in west Soulard. She had grown up in segregated Rochester, N.Y.

> I played a little around Rochester in the eighties, jammed around, playing at parties and different places. There was a rock 'n' roll revival going on then on a grass roots level. I got to play a lot of Stones, Deep Purple, house parties, playing bass. It was fun. I had a lot of fun.

Her future husband Doug Foehner came to St. Louis in 1985 and raved about the music scene. "'Sharon,' he says, 'there's all kinds of blues here, you got to come. You got to come live here.'

> So I says, "Oh, snap"' I decided I'd go ahead and get on. I decided to get away from the techno-pop that was going on in upstate New York -- the only way you could make money there was to play Billy Joel. The last time I read the sheet music for "Feelings" I said I can't do this shit no more. Are you serious? I can't go that way. I walked out before the gig ended and said this is not for me. So I came to St. Louis in April of 1987.
>
> *So how did you find it?*
>
> I found it segregated.
>
> *More so than upstate New York?*
>
> No, about neck and neck. There, I lived in the suburbs. My mother worked her butt off to get us into the suburbs. As a result we lived in a nice neighborhood. But a nice neighborhood surrounded by Caucasians. That was a little bit of a drag at times. But I came here and I found the same attitude.
>
> I used to work at Steak 'n' Shake, (a fast food joint) right off Hampton and I was walking home from work one morning near the park there and some mother-fucker tried to hit me with a car. I had to dive into some bushes to get away. Just minding my own business, just walking along with my stupid Steak 'n' Shake shit on. Yeah, right. I learned you don't mess around with St. Louis. Especially the wrong spots. 2012 you still don't do that.
>
> *Did you play the North Side then?*
>
> No. I was on the South Side. My husband worked over here. Bennie showed me some of those clubs, but there weren't many then. And I wanted to play Soulard, Dogtown. When I first got here I noticed there wasn't too much intermingling of musicians unless you were playing just straight up raw blues. Guitar Frank played with James Crutchfield, but it took a special cat.
>
> Frank was one of the most truly color blind guys in town. He was putting me with black dudes when it wasn't popular to do that. I met up with James and Frank when they were doing the Soulard house tour in 1989. I thought, wow how cool is this and they said we play the Venice on Wednesday and I thought, cool, let me bring my stuff down. So I brought my stuff down and played a little music. How cool was that?

So I brought my stuff down every Wednesday night for about three months, starting around November, just sitting in. What the hey, this is kind of cool. March or April they offered me a job. I said hey, I'll do this, this is fun. I couldn't believe it. So every Wednesday night for 11 years I played with James. I met a lot of musicians through that job.

That job at the Venice led me to a cat named Joel Slotnikoff and that led me to Bennie Smith. Without Joel there would have been no Bennie for me. Bennie was Big Bad Smitty's rhythm guitarist. Slotnikov was like a headhunter type. He wanted to get something authentic going on when he saw a lot of inauthentic things going on. At one time he was the president of the Blues Society.

So I met Bennie through Joel and when Durious Montgomery did not get hired to go on the 1993 tour to Europe with Big Bad Smitty they decided to let me stand in for him. I didn't have a practice, a rehearsal one with these people. When I got on the plane to go to Europe was the first time I actually met Bennie. At the airport in St. Louis.

We were supposed to have rehearsals but stuff always happened. So I go, 'Hey, what's up?' The first time I played with them on stage was in Holland, in Utrect, the first time I played with them in all my life.

Big Bad had a big head. He made a little money and it went right to his head. He started treating people real poopy and everything. He started tasting that money for the first time and he didn't know how to act behind it. Idiot. He was obnoxious, but I loved playing with Bennie.

What was the Venice like then?

It was a great place to play because they encouraged an artist attitude. There was always some artistic endeavor going on. More art started accumulating but it was sparse back in those days. They did Tuesday to Saturday -- never advertised. People would come there because it was cool and artsy and eclectic. People would hear music there that was a culture shock. Not many people were listening to barrelhouse blues in their 20s.

So it was something they hadn't encountered and it was in their own backyard. Young people, people trying to sneak into bars underage, musicians who wanted to see how the hell are you keeping up with that nut. I had a secret weapon. When I was younger I'd played in the chamber orchestra and you play in the chamber orchestra you had to have ear training.

So every day when we practiced they'd tell you sit down in front of the piano and they'd tell you close your eyes and they'd play and they say 'What is that?' So I had to learn that. That was a little training I'd had in school and that was the only way I got through playing with Crutchfield. A little theory and a little common sense and you can play with anybody.

Foehner played with Smith at the Venice and elsewhere from 1993 until 2003, becoming manager of the band.

Bennie's style?

It was so eclectic; he could play the rawest blues or get very sophisticated and play something like 'Faraway Places' with James on piano. He had a lot of musical interests. He'd play jazz with the cats on Sunday's at Hammerstones. He was intrigued with jazz and wanted to learn a lot more about it.

A set?

He might start with "Green Onions," with some cool jazz. We played "Take Five," right off the top of his head. It's not something we'd sit around and practice. "Caravan." He liked the light jazz. Then he'd go to Muddy Waters, Sonny Boy. Whatever he felt like playing. No set list. When I was first playing with Bennie he was drinking heavily, he'd drink a lot. As the years went by he slowed up and started treating himself better. He would play what he wanted. He told me if I wanted to learn how to play the music we were going to have to work.

He wasn't going to sit around the house and teach me, the point was that I was going to have to learn it on stage with him. While we was getting paid, I thought, I can do that. We played four or five nights a week -- that took place for two or three years -- shoot, we did private gigs, at the Log Cabin in LaDue, we toured for the Missouri Arts Council, playing at junior colleges, with Tom (Maloney) and Bennie. It was fun! Traveling with Tom was fun.

Tom and Bennie were two cats who know how to play counter rhythms -- one cat would do one rhythm and that other guy he wouldn't play the same rhythm, he'd play counter. It was beautiful. I couldn't ask for more. I heard Tom playing at one spot then I'd go down with Bennie. I could hear Tom playing.

I had approached Tom at the Oyster Bar and I told him how much I'd love it if he was playing with Bennie. Tom was going

> overseas and when he came back he didn't know if he was going to be working. I was like, dude, if you got a minute, come on down, please. From then after that, in '97, crazy. It was banging back then.
>
> It was a good time to play music in St. Louis back then. It was still pretty segregated. There were some bands that played on the North Side that never came into St. Louis. Some from the East Side that never played here. It was surprising. In a strange way I felt like I bridged some of the gaps. I brought Bennie and Tom together and they were great together, great musicians. I remember a New Years with Tom and Bennie and Johnnie Johnson. You remember something like that.
>
> God dang, that was something else.

Smith never left St. Louis, getting all the work he could handle, fighting his aching back and playing his gigs, dapper in his cap, often in a suit and tie, playing the songs he knew so well, fronting what he called the Urban Express, with mainstays Foehner and Maloney along with many sit-ins, playing songs like "Drown in My Own Tears" and "Sweet Home Chicago" to "Back at the Chicken Shack" and "Johnny B. Goode."

Smith was also a fixture of a Blues Society sponsored Guitar Master Series, held for over a decade at BB's, the true guitar master whose style was passed on to Ike Turner in the fifties. Maloney said, "He was the root of the St. Louis guitar sound, amazing. Bennie was unique."

He received numerous honors in his last few years. On Oct. 5, 2003, there was a proclamation from mayor Francis Slay declaring Bennie Smith Day. The Board of Aldermen also named him "Dean of St. Louis Electric Guitarists." He played all the festivals, and during the 2006 Big Muddy event Slay again honored Smith, declaring another Bennie Smith Day. And he was winner of the *Riverfront Times* reader's award for Best Blues Artist during each of the last years of his life.

Bennie died Sept. 9, 2006, just a week after the Big Muddy, from a heart attack. He was 72.

Two more pylons in the foundation of the St. Louis music scene -- a record store and a radio station -- were built during the blues revival of the eighties, buttresses that stood strong in 2016, remarkable survivors of the Great Recession at the end of the twenty-aughts.

The record store, opened in 1980 and expanded in 1983, was eventually called Vintage Vinyl, the name it carries into the twenty-tens, its store still stuffed with those floppy old school records first developed by Columbia in 1948, made of a goop called polyvinyl chloride, pressed into a flat disc, grooved and spun on a player at 33 1/3 revolutions per minute. The disc was contained in a cardboard sleeve produced with often elaborate artwork and detailed information about the music and its makers. The thing was once called an LP (long playing) or a record or nowadays, vinyl.

The store opened in May of 1980 on Delmar, a few storefronts down from its present location just inside University City next door to Blueberry Hill. The two music aficionados who got it running, Tom Ray and Lew Prince, were in 2015 the very two who run it on a day to day basis from a loft packed with records, posters, old Chinese food containers and stacks of magazines and newspapers.

To get it started, Lew says, "We put together about 300 bucks."

Tom, who went to school at Webster University, then went East to play harmonica and get involved in the music business, adds:

> I was in Manhattan and Lew and I decided we wanted to open a store here. By that point I'd cultivated a relationship with a number of music reviewers who had a lot of records. I ran a jazz club in New York called Axis in Soho that had major contemporary jazz artists -- all the people from BAG (the St. Louis Black Artists' Group) plus Sun Ra. I'd met Oliver (Lake) in '74.
>
> I was running the club, booking so-called loft jazz. We did well. I'd always loved blues but at that point I was more interested in jazz.
>
> At that point (1980) the record industry was coming off a considerable high point and was entering a depression, as was the whole country. Lew and I felt it was a good time to open a used record shop because we knew they did well in a depression. Besides, nobody was doing it the way we wanted to do it.

For seven months before the store opened, Tom and Lew hauled used records to the Soulard market every Saturday. They started drawing long lines and began looking for a real store. They found it on Delmar and by 1984 had eight employees. In 1990 they moved up the street to their present location and by 1999 had 36 workers.

Then came CDs. Then the digital revolution arrived, spinning faster than 33 /1/3 rpms. The store hung in there, however, while many used record stores failed and predictions of the demise of vinyl were rampant in the land. The Great Recession of 2008 helped business. The hip-hop samplers and scratching DJs in the clubs also has not hurt.

The store celebrated its 33 1/3 year anniversary in 2013. *USA Today* named it one of the nation's Top Ten record stores in 2014. Vinyl lives.

Tom and Lew were not only business owners, they were directly connected to the revival of the St. Louis music scene as it evolved south.

The three of us (me, Tom and Lew) establish beachheads amid the loft clutter, awaiting reinforcements of fried rice and sweet-and-sour shrimp one afternoon in 2012, yacking about St. Louis, its music and the division of the races. Naturally, the conversation fell on the North and South divide.

> *Lew:* Everything has to do with the town being legally segregated until 1950. Black people, especially older black people, felt much more comfortable on the North Side. And not having to deal with the bullshit it took to go into the South Side. If you were black in 1980 and you went far enough south of Delmar you were going to get stopped on your way home. You just were.
>
> We lived in Webster Groves and my kids -- who were born in '89 and '91 -- one of them said to me one day driving home from school, "Daddy, how come the police only stop black people?" My kids noticed and that was in the nineties.
>
> *Tom:* But there was more fluidity among the musicians. Way more.
>
> *Lew:* Yeah, black musicians were incredibly accepting of the young white players. The first time I talked to Henry Townsend, I just looked him up in the phone book. I was a freshman at Webster College, living in the dorm.
>
> I called and he answered and I said, "Is this Henry Townsend the blues man" and he said "uh-huh" and we talked for about 35 seconds before he said, "You one of those white boy guitar players?" I said "Yeah" and he said, "Come on over." I did and hung out there maybe three or four times.
>
> Months later I get a phone call. Late. On the dorm phone. It's Henry and he says, "you ought to come over right now." Like

that. I had a VW microbus and I cruise on over and Roosevelt Sykes is there. They were playing and reminiscing. That was '72.

Tom: The reason St. Louis never has had a national reputation is there was never anybody in St. Louis to record the artists. Muddy, Sonny Boy Williamson, Jimmy Rogers, you name them, all those guys came here before they went to Chicago. And if there would have been some smart white guy in the late forties to record, the concept of the Chicago blues as it exists now would not exist.

Lew: Take a look at the people who made it. It's people who left. Ike, Milton, Albert, they left. Chuck. The guys who stayed here didn't make it big. Look at Tommy Bankhead; he stayed because he had a good job in the sheriff's department. I wanted to promote him. Do some colleges. He said. "No way, my job comes with a pension man. Blues don't come with no pension."

Tom: But, personally, in St. Louis, I think the domestic blues scene is better than anywhere. Better than Memphis. There is no Marquis Knox in Memphis.

The radio station, KDHX, had roots in Gaslight Square but didn't get going in its free form, listener-supported FM format until 1987. KDHX is successor to KDNA, one of the nation's first counterculture stations, a station that went on the air Feb. 8, 1969, its artists and audience spun out of the Gaslight scene.

Two partners put up the money for the fledgling experiment in radio in St. Louis, partners who had already started a station in Seattle: Lorenzo Milam, who started the alt-radio KRAB in Seattle and Jeremy Lansman, who dropped out of Clayton High to go to radio school. He was in Hawaii building a radio station when he answered an ad Milam had placed in *Broadcasting Magazine* seeking an engineer to join the Seattle effort "who was willing to suffer nobly for a cause."

Milam remembers the start of the station in St. Louis:

> After one of our weekly differences of opinion on the programming of KRAB which caused Lansman to get my attention by breaking out most of the windows in my houseboat, I banished him to St Louis to build KDNA. I had some doubts as to his ability to get anything done without me hectoring him, but he got the station up and running in no time at all.
>
> It was, however, less the BBC for the Middle West (which was my ideal) and more like the voice of Catalan Spain from the

> thirties. I was concerned that his Anarcho-Syndicalist gang there in the dying Gaslight Square area of the city could make a go of it, but, to my surprise, it survived, and heartily so.
>
> In fact, its noisy programming irritated the city fathers so much that they invited Richard Nixon's COINTELPRO operatives to come to town to see what they could do to put it out of business (we found all this out later from documents obtained from the FBI under the Freedom of Information Act).
>
> Not only did KDNA survive the ministrations of COINTELPRO, it succeeded in inspiring a bevy of similar stations in such unlikely places as Atlanta, Dallas, Cincinnati, Miami, Indianapolis, Pittsburgh and Madison, Wisconsin.

Milam's style was free form with the DJs playing whatever they wanted. There were no commercials; support came from Milam himself in start-up money, then from listener donations. The station lasted until 1974, the object of police drug raids (charges were dropped) and in the face of relentless assaults from evangelist Bill Beeny, who sought to have KDNA's license assigned to himself.

But money was the ultimate downfall. There wasn't enough to operate as Gaslight died around them. The station sold, however, for $1.4 million and after KDNA's debts were paid Lansman used the remainder to form the Double Helix Corporation, dedicated to a new station, KDHX.

Ron Edwards was one of the original disc jockeys when the new station finally started in October 1987, a powerful community radio outlet of 43,000 watts with a transmitter that covered a 90-mile radius around St. Louis.

For the first year and a half it was broadcast out of a shack below the transmitter tower in a farmer's field in South County near Arnold, from a six by eight room with a portajohn outside. Edwards remembered:

> When you drove there, you had to know exactly how to get there -- there was no fence around the place, nothing -- the land had been rented -- there was a wooden structure under a 500-foot tower sitting on one of the highest spots -- that's why there is such a great signal, it's 500 feet straight up and its right on top of you -- (sigh) if there had been a tornado . . .
>
> The first time I went out there I thought I was on at seven but I was really on at eight -- the training consisted of me watching

> the guy in front of me turn the dials -- there was no training -- playing records and cassettes -- we had a transistor radio as the monitor -- you turn it off when you're talking -- there would be bugs flying in and you hope they didn't hit the needle of the record player -- honest to god this was in this guy's driveway/ You make a left in the opening in the weeds -- suddenly you come into an opening in the clearing -- you could see the tower but you couldn't figure out how to get there.
>
> You'd go in the room and lock the door and if you had to take a leak you'd run to the portajohn outside. The second week I was there I took my National (steel guitar) and played the station's first live blues.
>
> In May '88, during our second pledge drive, I arranged with Tom Ray to come out and do a couple of songs with me and what I did -- I had access to a mixer and mikes -- I took a wooden chair and sat in the gravel driveway with a microphone with my guitar, no amp, with my little mixer. Tom was late and he comes roaring up -- it was dark -- he almost ran over the man and his wife who owned the land -- you couldn't see anything. We did 'It Hurt Me Too" -- right out in this country shack.

Edwards is a classic radio voice, a big part of that St, Louis thing, a man with a philosophy:

> I'm not a DJ -- I'm not interested in spinning tunes. DJ to me means spinning records in a club. I think of myself as a programmer front to back -- the rest comes in sequence for a story and a connection -- I never had a show that didn't have a list --I've done 1,200 shows -- I'm not coming there to play cuts, we've got people who can do that, the station is full of them -- others understand.
>
> This is a commitment for me. I spend between 10 and 14 hours a week and that includes going there and coming back, doing the show, doing the research.
>
> I do this for myself. I want to educate people on the older artists that should not be forgotten but at the same time it forces me to pull the CDs out and listen to them because I realized in life I was so busy. I realized I'm not listening to music. I didn't have a CD player in the car for a long time and that deadline is so relentless it gets your mind going. It is mental stimulation. It's the putting it together and listening to the music and understanding why this music moves me so much. It's what I love.

Chapter Thirty-Two
Johnson v. Berry: Why Can't You Be True

2000-2015

I asked Johnnie what prompted him taking legal action and he told me, "It was George (Turek)."
George asked him, "How much royalties did you get?"
Johnnie said, "None. (George) couldn't believe that, and he got things going. I figured I got paid at the time, and he (Chuck) said he took chances, so (Chuck) got the royalties."
Johnnie is basically a trusting fellow. He says he just figures other people are the same as him.
As Johnnie puts it, " I wouldn't do that to somebody, so I figure they wouldn't do that to me."

-- Dr. Claude S. Mundy, court deposition, Jan. 14, 2002

Case No. 4:00CV-01891 ***Johnson v. Berry***, a civil action in the U.S. District Court for the Eastern District of Missouri, was filed Nov. 29, 2000. The suit was settled in favor of Charles E. Berry, Isalee Music Company, on Oct. 21, 2002, having never reached trial. Instead, the substance of one of the most publicized royalty cases in music history was never ruled on, being decided when a judge threw out the suit "on statute of limitations grounds." No matter who was right, it was filed too late.

But the case went much further than an issue of timing. The suit redefined the history of the relationship between Johnnie and Chuck and thus threw a new story into the invention of rock 'n' roll. That revisited relationship sent Berry/Johnson into the same rarified atmosphere as other song-writing teams such as Lennon/McCartney and Jagger/Richards. Jonnie Johnson was given a seat at the table of those who invented rock 'n' roll.

Even so, the royalties -- estimated as well over $6 million -- remained 100 percent in Berry's briefcase.

The songs in question included the mother lode of rock 'n' roll -- "Maybellene" (1955), "Roll Over Beethoven" (1956), "Brown Eyed Handsome Man" (1956), "School Days" (1957), "Rock and Roll Music" (1957), "Sweet Little Sixteen" (1959), "Little Queenie" (1959) and dozens more, all with Johnnie Johnson on piano, Ebby Hardy on drums and Chuck Berry on guitar and vocals, all with only the name Chuck Berry on the Chess Record label and on the copyrights.

Johnnie's publicist at the time of the suit said the songs were a partnership: Berry lyrics, Johnson music.

> Johnnie would compose the music in his head and not realize that he composed the songs. And Chuck would take advantage of this and register the copyright in his name. For many years (Johnson) was a serious alcoholic and it's taken him a long time to realize that these contributions still constitute songwriting.

The suit came in the wake of *Hail! Hail!* *Rock 'n' Roll,* the movie that revived both Berry's and Johnson's career, a filmed concert at the Fox Theater in St. Louis in 1987. The movie brought Rolling Stone guitarist Keith Richards in contact with Johnnie. Richards became the most powerful several musicians to point out to Johnson that he deserved half credit for the hits.

Another of those players was Tom Maloney, the St. Louis sideman who brought Johnnie into his band in 1985. Soon after they started playing together a light went on in Maloney's mind.

> I got a request to do "Johnny B. Goode" and caught myself mid-count off. I said to myself, "Let Johnnie start it off, it's his song."

> It goes OK -- Johnnie plays it but it doesn't sound like what's on the record. I realized that that's the way Johnnie played it and Chuck heard that and he took that -- Johnnie was swinging it and Chuck was really pounding it.
>
> Chuck joined Johnnie and that rubbed off on him. To say Johnnie invented that swinging rhythm, no, that goes all the way back to the boogie woogie and who knows how far back. But that's what Johnnie is doing. Chuck stood next to Johnnie and the imprint is indelible. I don't think Chuck has ever done anything to deny that or hide that.

"Tom was one of the main ones that asked me about the royalties," Johnnie said in his deposition for the lawsuit. Tom asked: "'How come you're not getting your royalties?'" But Johnnie did nothing, he was content to play his piano and have a few drinks.

In his book, *Life*, and on film in *Hail! Hail!* Richards says much the same thing. Referring to a moment during rehearsals for the movie, he says, "I asked Johnnie Johnson: 'How did "Sweet Little Sixteen" and "Little Queenie" get written?"

> And he said, 'Well, Chuck would have all these words, and we'd sort of play a blues format and I would lay out the sequence."
>
> I said, "Johnnie, that's called songwriting. And you should have had at least fifty percent. I mean, you could have cut a deal and taken forty, but you wrote those songs with him."
>
> He said, "I never thought about it that way, I just sort of did what I knew.'

Richards says he looked closer at the technicalities of the Berry songs.

> I realized everything Chuck wrote was in E-flat or C-sharp -- piano keys! Not guitar keys. That was a dead giveaway. These are not great keys for guitar. Obviously, most of the songs started off on piano and Chuck joined in, playing with his huge hand stretching across the strings. I got the sense that he followed Johnny's left hand!
>
> Chuck Berry's playing had such an effortless swing. None of this sweating and grinding away and grimacing, just pure effortless swing, like a lion.

During *Hail! Hail! Rock 'n' Roll,* Johnnie was in good form. He'd been playing steadily for two years in Sounds of the City, gigging almost every night. Chuck, on the other hand, had been playing less often out on the road, using pickup bands in each town to save money. Richards:

> Chuck had to come up to Johnnie's mark. To be a musician playing below your mark is soul destroying, and Chuck had been doing that for ages, to the point where he was completely cynical about the music. It was weird and funny to watch Chuck catching up to Johnnie.
>
> Chuck Berry was a big disappointment.

After the movie was released, along came George Turek, a former Navy pilot and Houston millionaire who stumbled across Johnnie in 1992 as the result of a last-minute cancellation. Turek was in Memphis on a pilgrimage to Elvis Presley's Graceland when he dropped into a Beale Street club and saw a guitar player named Jimmy Johnson, a Chicago bluesman in the midst of a comeback. Turek and his fiance danced the night away and decided to book Jimmy and his band for their upcoming wedding, a huge affair for an airplane hangar in Michigan the next year.

A few months before the wedding, Jimmy Johnson told Turek he couldn't make the wedding, he had booked a European tour. Turek then remembered a CD he had heard that he at first thought was Jimmy Johnson but was really Johnnie Johnson. He decided to swap out the guitar Johnson for the piano Johnson and booked Johnnie for the wedding, still a few months away.

In the meantime, Turek and his bride-to-be were driving through St. Louis on their way to Texas and on a whim he called Johnnie's number to see if he was in town. Coincidences tend to pile up at the confluence and Turek's next Interstate exit happened to be the very turnoff to Blueberry Hill where Johnson was playing that very night. He had just returned from a tour the day before and was lined up at the Elvis Room. Turek was much impressed.

The show at the wedding in 1993 was a smashing success, and in 1995, Johnnie invited Turek to come see him play with Chuck at the New Orleans Jazz and Heritage Festival. Johnnie was by then putting out his own solid CDs, touring steadily and playing solo, but had not been playing much with Berry.

Turek, who had still not seen the movie, accepted the invite and watched Chuck and Johnnie at the Jazz Fest on April 30, 1995, playing Sunday afternoon under the hot southern sun before thousands of people. The day's bill also included Allen Toussaint, Ray Charles, Earl King, Snooks Eaglin, Magic Slim and many of the best New Orleans bands.

Berry had the third highest billing of the day, but it was Johnnie who took charge of the show. Most of the people watching weren't sure who that burly man was up there -- that big guy rolling out the big piano rhythms. Johnson held the crowd, bringing out the piano sounds that had been lost on the Chess records the fans had heard. Now, they heard a new sound from the old hits, the sound of piano-driven rock and blues; a new dimension to music that was 40 years old. Word spread through the dancing crowd as to the identity of the piano player. Even Chuck seemed bemused as he watched the skill of his old partner. Oh, Maybellene, why can't you be true?

Turek had not heard Chuck and Johnnie together live before that day at the Fest.

"Imagine my surprise," Turek said, "when Johnnie starts playing this amazing rock 'n' roll piano. I realized it was Johnnie I had been hearing on those records."

Later that year Turek saw *Hail! Hail!* He listened carefully to Richards' explanation of the obvious collaboration between Berry and Johnson. Turek had the money for the lawyers and the publicists and was determined to make a difference in Johnnie's life. Turek formed a group he called Team Johnnie and began a march toward two goals -- Johnnie's induction into the Rock and Roll Hall of Fame and the capture of the lost song writing royalties.

Another musician who took notice was Greg Martin of the country rock band Kentucky Headhunters who worked with Johnnie in 1997 on an album called *That Will Work*. During the sessions, Martin casually said to Johnnie, "I know you are getting royalties for the work you and Chuck did together." Johnnie said, "No, I'm not getting any." And that, Johnnie added later, "raised some eyebrows."

Another conversation was with Little Richard, a strong advocate of musicians' right to royalties from the early days of rock 'n' roll.

From Johnnie's deposition:

> *JJ:* Little Richard said, "I know you are a rich man, getting all those royalties from Chuck Berry music."
>
> *Attorney:* And you corrected his view on that?
>
> *JJ:* Naturally.
>
> *Pressed on why he didn't pursue the issue, Johnnie said, "I threw it out of my mind."*
>
> *Attorney:* What did you tell Keith Richards?
>
> *JJ:* Well my role was actually putting music to the lyrics (Chuck) had written and I knew nothing about supposed to be getting royalties from it; so the only question -- the only answer I could give him was that I wasn't aware of this.

Others, including bluesman Bo Diddley and the New York guitarist Jimmy Vivano, also raised the royalty question. Johnson didn't join ASCAP, the organization that protects musicians' royalty payments until after *Hail! Hail!* In 1996 he got new management, making a deal with TCI of New York, the group that handled Bo Diddley, Wilson Pickett and the Yardbirds. He finally moved into the ranks of the modern musicians, getting full value for his skills on the keyboard.

But Johnnie, all during the eighties and nineties, did not raise the old copyright questions, even as he emerged from obscurity, gave up his bus driver job and became more and more recognized as one of the founders of rock 'n' roll.

Claude Mundy, the psychiatrist who examined Johnson for the case, concluded that "it was only when someone took him by the hand and essentially forced the issue that he was able to appreciate his entitlement and pursue a legal course of action."

And that someone, the doctor said, was George Turek. For Johnnie, however, the lawsuit was a double-edged sword, an action he did not welcome.

Maloney:

> The thing to remember is that before Chuck Berry ever had a gig there was Johnnie Johnson. He hired Chuck -- Chuck wrote the great lyrics -- Chuck had a vision and was very eager to succeed -- it was the vision that he wanted to be big in country, blues and pop music.

> Once the idea of a lawsuit got going there were people close to Johnnie who thought it would be a good idea. There was big money involved and Johnnie did not have the heart to tell them not to do it. He couldn't say no, don't do it. People close to him had invested money and time into the project, but I never believed Johnnie's heart was in it.
>
> Johnnie said, "Tom, I wish this whole thing had never happened."
>
> And there it is. I can't tell you how many phone calls I got (after the suit was filed.). So many people were aghast that Johnnie would do this -- people here in town -- they thought what could this be. They looked at it like there was a war. I had worked pretty hard for quite a few years to build an image for Johnnie -- the fact that he did not need Chuck or Albert King -- he was Johnnie Johnson!
>
> He had his own greatness. Just let him play the piano and you'll see why and everyone did.
>
> And so to have his track record besmirched (by Berry's lawyers during the lawsuit) and made to look greedy, well, that was wrong. (*Rolling Stone* critic) Dave Marsh listed Johnnie as the fourth most important piano player in rock history -- Little Richard, Fats Domino, Jerry Lee Lewis, Johnnie Johnson.
>
> Johnnie is the quintessential sideman, how do you make him the front man? You have to have the personality -- you have to be bent toward being the front man. I'm the same way as Johnnie. As a child I'd watch *Ozzie and Harriet* and I wanted to be the guy behind Rickie -- that's what I do. Made it hard to present him to the public because of this.
>
> Johnnie was so stressed by the lawsuit he wanted to be out of St. Louis. They went into things like him not being competent. I lay that at the feet of George Turek.

In 2000, Berry's attorney was approached two weeks before the suit was filed. He threatened to conduct "an extensive media campaign" against Berry unless the matter was "promptly settled."

Berry refused to discuss a settlement and his attorney said, "Chuck has had enough bad publicity during the last few years." This was a reference to Berry's latest legal battle -- a 1990 suit brought by several women who claimed he spied on them with a camera in the ladies' bathroom of his Southern Air restaurant near Berry farm in Wentzville. His guilt in the case was never proven but he made a million dollar settlement with the 59 women who sued him. Berry claimed that he had the camera installed to catch a worker suspected of stealing from the restaurant.

The Johnson suit was badly timed for Chuck. The court papers were filed just three days before Berry received the Kennedy Center Honors for his "contribution to American culture." No mention was made of the Johnson lawsuit at the awards show and the praise was all for Chuck Berry, the first performer to receive such an honor who had served in prison. He sat beaming in the presidential box as Little Richard, the Black Crowes and the B-52s performed "Sweet Little Sixteen," "Johnny B. Goode" and other hits.

The original complaint listed 56 songs that Johnson alleged were collaborations between he and Berry. Johnson's attorney, Mitchell Margo, alleged that Berry received royalties "far in excess of $6.2 million" for the songs and said the singer had a net worth of over $10 million.

Berry could not provide records of the total amount of royalties but said Johnson was usually paid $125 a session during the fifties run of hits.

The arguments in the case were clear. Margo said the "music written by Mr. Johnson and Mr. Berry is inseparable and, combined with poems written by Mr. Berry are interdependent parts of a unitary whole." Berry's lawyer, Martin Green, argued that Johnson had "no evidence to support his claim aside from his own testimony and the music itself." He said the "absence of evidence is appalling" and that neither of the parties in the suit can "recall in details the events of 40 years ago." He added that even without the statute of limitations, the case held no merit since "Mr. Berry was the sole author of each of the songs as to both the lyrics and the music."

Johnson's legal argument against the statue of limitations was to say he was incapable (due to alcohol abuse and a poor education) of understanding his right to the royalties.

In his deposition, Berry's attorney pushed hard on this question.

> *Attorney:* Have you always been able to manage your own finances?
>
> *JJ:* Yes
>
> *Attorney:* Have you ever been found by any court to be incompetent in any way?
>
> *JJ:* No.

> *Attorney:* Have you ever been diagnosed by any doctor as having any type of mental problems?
>
> *JJ:* No.
>
> *Johnson said he had started drinking after serving in World War II and became "addicted to it" in 1949. "I just had to have it."*
>
> *Attorney:* Did your drinking affect your music playing?
>
> *JJ:* I can't recall that it did, I don't remember ever not being able to play.
>
> *Attorney:* Did Mr. Berry ever encourage you to drink?
>
> *JJ:* No; no, no way.

This exchange eliminated the "incapability" argument regarding the statue of limitations. The case was dismissed.

Green said Berry had no hard feelings.

"He likes Johnnie very much, considers him a friend and expects to play with him in the future," Green said. "He doesn't blame Johnnie for the lawsuit. He blames some of Johnnie's advisers."

An appeal was filed Jan. 16, 2003, and dismissed March 28 of the same year.

The closest person to Johnnie during all this was his wife, Frances. She was born Frances Miller in St. Louis in the late thirties. Both parents were also born in St. Louis. Her father's family was from Mississippi and her mother's from Kentucky. She grew up downtown, in the Biddle Street district, east of 12th Street, in the heart of the city's entertainment area, not far from the bar where Stagger Lee shot Billy Lyons.

She said the neighborhood when she was a child was "beautiful."

> One block would be Italian, then black. A poverty thing. The races were united by that factor. There were the little grocery stores where you could go in get candy and stuff. We didn't really mix, but we'd have a block and they'd have a block, you know, that way.

Her father was a photographer and worked in a pecan plant. He later divorced her mother.

At the time I met Frances, in 2012, she lived in the house she shared with Johnnie, in the North County suburb of Florissant, the house where

Johnnie Johnson died in April 2005 at age 80 -- a tidy middle-class home on a curving street of brick, ranch style houses.

Her living room was crowded that day with piles of Christmas presents and a decorated tree that barely fit in the corner. Photos on the walls showed her and Johnnie with Eric Clapton, Keith Richards, Bonnie Raitt and Buddy Guy as well as with her many children and stepchildren. She wore a sweatshirt and casual slacks as well as a diamond pinkie ring and a large diamond bracelet.

Her speaking style included sharp flourishes of emphasis. She talked slowly at times then rattled off the tale in a rapid-fire manner. She conveyed a sense of power and authority. At times she was emotional and teared up when talking about her husband's death. She said she was in her mid-70s but wouldn't give a birthdate.

> ***Let's talk about the conflict with Chuck Berry***. Hail! Hail! Rock 'n' Roll *was '87. Did you go to the shows?*
>
> We were together, but not married yet. I went to the rehearsal at the Fox the day before the taping. It was nice. They were beautiful, Eric (Clapton), Julian Lennon, Keith (Richards). It was beautiful. There was a party during the rehearsal. We were all back stage. They were doing whatever they were doing.
>
> *How was the music?*
>
> It was okay. For what they wanted, it went better at the rehearsal than during the actual show from what I heard. I didn't go."
>
> *What was Chuck doing at the rehearsal?*
>
> I don't even remember seeing him. It was a fun time. I love Keith, he is a true friend. He's beautiful. I couldn't really understand him though, his accent, you know. Johnnie could, he got along good with him. I met some beautiful people. Those people and the one I met the years after.
>
> *What happened after* Hail! Hail! Rock 'n' Roll?"
>
> Things started changing right away. Eric sent for him. The 24 Nights (an annual show Eric Clapton began in 1987 at the Royal Albert Hall in London). That's where Johnnie met Buddy Guy and Albert Collins.
>
> I love Buddy Guy -- he got the Kennedy Center honors -- he's a great person. I love most of them that I've gotten to know personally; they are receptive, warm.

> Johnnie was a genius, but lazy. I was his worst critic, the times I would really hear him play -- I mean really play -- was after an argument, a disagreement and he'd start playing the piano.
>
> *In the house?*
>
> Oh, yeah. And he would play stuff that made me say, "See you just act stupid." I would tell him about it sometimes and he say, "Frances, I play what they want to hear."

After the 24 Days shows Richards hired him for the album *Talk Is Cheap* with Richards' band, Expensive Winos. Then Bob Weir, the charter Grateful Dead member, hired Johnson for his touring band, Rat Dog.

Johnson toured in 1996 and 1997 with Weir for a year, Hawaii, Portugal, Sweden and Australia, playing 67 shows.

Frances said Johnnie had slowed down his drinking by then as his new career blossomed. Frances said he was a happy man the final 15 years of his life.

> As long he could play he was a happy man. Johnnie just loved to play, even the times before the lawsuit, when he and Chuck would play together at Blueberry Hill. Joe (Edwards) called and asked if they could play together. It was some of his happiest times when him and Chuck played. They were a team.
>
> *Even at the end?*
>
> They got along all the time. They had one fight. And I was there. It came up at a dinner at Joe Edwards' home. They had that one fight -- I ain't going into that. But they had one fight and they never did that again. No more of that.
>
> *Then how did the lawsuit come about?*
>
> We were approached. And we were approached because we were ignorant, that's why we were approached. We did not know.
>
> *You were approached by who?*
>
> Friends. Friends who were interested in Johnnie being compensated for what he'd done.
>
> *And you trusted these people?*
>
> Oh, god, it come up listening to Keith and the rest of it -- it all kind of fell in. Doing the pretrial stuff, whatever, I heard Chuck admit it. I was more pissed than Johnnie was. Cause you screwed my man and that's my job. That was my attitude.
>
> *How did Chuck treat you?*
>
> With respect.

He didn't see you as an instigator?

I don't think, no, I don't think so. I was gung-ho Johnnie. One time, I don't know where we were, probably Blueberry Hill, it must have been during the time when they were playing. Chuck says to me, "I love the way you watch Johnnie when he's playing." I says, "Well, he pays me to do that. I don't want to see you." He laughed.

Do you ever go see Chuck anymore?

I want to. I don't drive at night and then when he's up on the boat I don't. I want to.

Well, you know Joe Edwards would send a car out here anytime you wanted to see Chuck.

Oh, I know. Joe, Joe. You know that was one of things that bothered me the morning Johnnie died. I wanted to call Joe. He should have been one of the first to know. And I felt bad about that afterward.

How'd he find out?

On the 11 o'clock news.

Johnnie died without being sick very long?

He had some little petty ailments but he died from natural causes and he died at the right time at the right place and he died with the prettiest smile. That helped me so much.

He didn't suffer?

Not with that smile. I called my pastor. Him and his wife, they got here quickly.

In this house?

Yeah. I said to my pastor, '"Look at that smile. It was one of two things -- either God came and got this man or it was a good-looking woman. Two choices."

It really made it easy for me because he didn't suffer. With that smile I knew his transition had to have been beautiful, because Johnnie wasn't noted for smiling a lot. He looked 20 years younger. When I realized he was gone and I called 911 -- all I could say was "Baby, rest in peace." I mean it helped me.

There was an outpouring when he died, what did you think then?

I was ... *(she pauses, regains her composure)* that's when I realized what I really had been married to. That was when reality set in. My God, the respect, the phone calls, there's a friend in Australia who said if anything happens to this big lug let me know. When I contacted him -- he was here.

Bobby Weir was on tour, he chartered a plane to get here, Buddy Guy was going somewhere to do a recording. Bo Diddley was leaving the country. All these people called to say what do you want. Different record companies, it was just beautiful. The flowers were from everybody. Eric, he sent flowers. I wish I had of had somebody to take pictures of each flower arrangement, but you don't get but one chance at that.

I asked Johnnie about Chuck once, about when they met. He said Chuck knew maybe 12 songs. That's why Chuck transitioned to piano keys. That made sense to me then. That's how it happened.

Johnnie was good. Just lazy. And the alcohol. And about the lawsuit -- if I had of had any idea I would have initiated it myself. We were talking about some big money. I'd of looked pretty good. OK.

But Johnnie made a statement that he knew he did not write the songs. He was proud and he would say some stupid things from time to time. I didn't even know to get his music registered.

Richard Young, (of the Kentucky Headhunters) called me and said Frances, call this person. Johnnie had two or three albums out by then. If Johnnie had known this when him and Chuck were recording he would have said no, the music is mine.

I saw in the movie that he was asked if he wrote the music and he said no, but what he meant was that Chuck wrote the lyrics. That's it. That's it. He put the music behind it. But he didn't know nothing about that. I say, give Johnnie 50 cents, something to drink and a piano and he'd stay there all night.

I've met some great people and I have so many fond memories. I can remember everything -- I know -- I was there. Everybody liked Johnnie. I was the lucky one. He was ours not mine.

Somebody brought it up about the people that asked Johnnie to record with them. Dozens, hundreds, who knows. But you ask how many people has Chuck recorded with? Nobody. None.

We never lived like he was Johnnie Johnson. We lived as husband and wife. He played the piano, he'd go out of town, he'd come back. We'd go to church. He's ours.

Part of George Turek's strategy to get Johnnie into the Rock and Roll Hall Fame was to enlist the support of Chuck Berry. Turek had met Berry at the Jazz Fest in New Orleans when Berry and Johnson played together and then ran into him in 1996 at the Slammy music show in St. Louis, where Johnnie was awarded a lifetime achievement award.

Frances said that later, at a dinner at Joe Edwards' house, Turek met Berry again. By then the Texas millionaire knew Johnson better and had grown resentful of Berry, living in a mansion while Johnnie lived in a small house on the North Side. "I could barely stand to look at the guy," Turek said, but he needed Chuck's alliance to get Johnnie into the Rock Hall. The lawsuit was still a few years away.

Frances said that at the dinner Berry was in good form telling stories about the early days on the road. One story mentioned how he and Johnnie got into some kind of argument and Johnson, a much bigger man than Berry, pushed Berry up against a wall. Berry laughed about giving in to the powerful pianoman. He said he couldn't remember what the fight was about, but Johnnie did.

"I remember," he said to Chuck, "you took all the money for yourself and weren't gonna split it up with me and Ebby."

Turek went back home and thought about getting Berry's name on a letter endorsing Johnson for the Hall, figuring it would be difficult. "The way he (Berry) seemed at the dinner with all the lying and narcissism, I figured there wasn't much of a chance."

But Berry didn't see it that way. Edwards said the letter would not be a problem and when Johnnie called him to ask, Berry said, "I'd do anything for you, Johnnie." Johnson also said that Berry "was real nice about the whole thing and said he hoped I got in, 'cause I deserved it as much as him."

The Hall was not easy to crack, however, since Johnson's name didn't appear on any of the Berry records and he never received any writing credit for the songs. But a new category covering such cases as Johnson was created at the Hall for sidemen and Johnnie was in, inducted March 21, 2001, in a class that also included Michael Jackson, Paul Simon and Aerosmith.

Richards, who had inducted Berry into the initial class of Hall of Famers in 1986, also did the honors for Johnnie, lavishing praise of the man who provided "the foundation of Chuck Berry's seminal rock 'n' roll."

By then the old collaborators were lined up against each other in a battle of court papers.

Neither side really lost the case, however, unless it was considered strictly about the money.

By then Johnson, the legal loser in the case, had put out three albums, had been recognized as one of the best blues artists in St. Louis by the *Riverfront Times*, had a star on the Walk of Fame on Delmar, had been the subject of Johnnie Johnson Week in St. Louis and had been seen by thousands of people in clubs in the city during uncounted shows.

The first album of his career, in 1987, was *Blue Hand Johnnie,* featuring vocals by Barbara Carr and Stacy Johnson. It was followed by *Rockin' Eighty-Eights*, perhaps his best effort on CD, which came in 1990. The record included Clayton Love and (the St. Louis) Jimmy Vaughn and leads off with a tribute to his wife, the song "Frances."

Then came *Johnnie B. Bad* in 1992. Joined by Richards, Clapton and many others the album was what *The New York Times* called "a long-overdue tribute to one of rock-and-roll's most talented unsung heroes." In 1996 and 1997 he did the Rat Dog tour for nearly a year and a half.

After the 2002 verdict he put out two more albums, including the final effort, at age 80, called J*ohnnie Be Eighty and Still Bad*, featuring St. Louis musicians Gus Thornton, Larry Thurston, Rich McDonough and Joe Pastor, a record that was cut live less than a year before Johnnie's death.

His last performance came just a week before his death, playing a special blues concert on Laclede's Landing on April 3, 2005.

BB's co-owner John May noted that after Johnson's death Henry Townsend became the last man standing of the performers who formed the core of the blues revival that started in the late seventies. May reflected:

> All the old guys are from a completely different school. They play until the day they die. I've seen it with Oliver Sain, and Tommy Bankhead, and Henry Townsend is still out playing. All the old-school guys are tough. They grew up with hard lives and played music all their lives.

Reports of Johnson's 2005 show at the Landing noted his usual skill and verve. Berry, told the news of Johnnie's death, said he wanted to host a tribute to Johnnie at the Edward Jones Dome, the city's biggest stadium. "I'll try my best to fill that sucker." Instead. a less ambitious tribute was held at the Pageant Theater April 29, less than two weeks after Johnson's death.

The show, put together by May and the St. Louis Blues Society, brought together 16 acts. Emceed by DJ Bernie Hayes and Tom Ray, with Frances

Johnson and Henry Townsend (age 94) in the front row. The artist list included Silvercloud, Ron Edwards, Larry Thurston and the Soulard Blues Band, the Rich McDonough Band, Billy Peek, Erma Whiteside, Kim Massie, Marsha Evans, Bennie Smith, Stacey Johnson and Chuck Berry.

A new tribute to Johnson was planned in 2016 for a revived Big Muddy festival at the Landing to feature an all-St. Louis docket of players. His memory was still fresh 10 years after his death.

Berry's life after *Hail! Hail! Rock 'n' Roll* saw a recharged entertainer. His main gig was a monthly show at Blueberry Hill started on Nov. 26, 1996. By 2014 he had logged 209 performances without missing a month until he cancelled the November gig. Edwards helped celebrate Berry's 89th birthday in 2015 by bring some of Blueberry Hill's famous chicken noodle soup to the Berry birthday party.

"No other superstar rock and roller has played that many shows in one single venue," Joe Edwards said.

In 2014 Berry was unable to travel to Sweden to accept a $170,000 check as winner of the Polar Music Prize. Dave Edmunds, the British rocker, accepted the prize for Berry.

In 2013, Berry made the trip to Cleveland where he attended a weeklong celebration of his career in a new exhibit at the Rock and Roll Hall of Fame. "I'm 86 years old," he said after playing what *Rolling Stone* called a "short, raw set," at Cleveland's State Theatre. "And I'm happy to be anywhere!"

He also sat through tributes from country singer Merle Haggard, rapper Darryl "DMC" McDaniels, guitarist Joe Bonamassa and New York Doll David Johansen. DMC turned the rebellious "School Days" into a pro-education hip-hop anthem and Haggard made "Memphis" into a country twang. Hip-hop guitarist Malina Moye played Berry's "Stop and Listen," full of wah-wah and feedback. *Rolling Stone* said the song "didn't sound anything like Berry, but it made an impression."

Berry himself made a stab at "Johnny B. Goode" but lost the tempo until saved by his daughter Ingrid who sang the lyrics.

In 2011, Berry was spry and smiling across from Blueberry Hill where his eight-foot, duck-walking likeness made of bronze was unveiled before a cheering crowd of about 500 people. The statue was erected despite opponents who objected to the monument, citing Berry's legal troubles during his long career.

"I won't keep you long," Berry, wearing his trademark boating cap, told a crowd that gathered for its unveiling despite heat surpassing 90 degrees. "I don't know how to speak, I just sing a little bit. I'm going to say thank you again, and I love you all."

Among those sending greetings to Berry was Elvis Costello, who said he was glad to see a Berry statue "in St. Louis where it belongs," and fellow rock pioneer Little Richard, who called Berry "the greatest entertainer in the world."

In 2010, Berry had collapsed during a New Year's show in Chicago (61 years after he filled a hole in the Johnnie Johnson Trio in East St. Louis). He recovered in time to play his next show in St. Louis and showed no signs of ill effects at the dedication ceremony.

Berry generally refused interviews over the years, but did speak to reporters during his 2012 visit to the Rock Hall. Seated next to Edwards, this lifelong opponent of segregation commented on Barack Obama's election as president:

> I never thought that a man with the qualities, features, and all that he has (could) be our President. My dad said, "You may not live to see that day," and I believed him. I thank God that I have.
>
> I am hearing very little. I'm wondering about my future. My singing days have passed. My voice is gone. My throat is worn. And my lungs are going fast.
>
> *(He apologized to the people who saw his show every month.)*
>
> They're having a great time from memory. And I hope that I can continue to enhance their memory because it looks very dim, like I said, you know.

Previously, in comments before a show at the Duck Room in 1998, he had mentioned to a *Post-Dispatch* photographer "the thrill is gone." Nevertheless he said he would keep on playing the shows because "of the warm relations between Joe and myself. I didn't ask to be accepted here, but that acceptance means a lot."

That year he also gave an interview with the *Post-Dispatch*, where he gave a rare comment about his home town, saying:

> Fame didn't take me away (from St. Louis) because my family is here. One thing I found out is every place is pretty much the same. The language may be different, and there may be a difference in architecture, and the relations between people may be a little freer, like New York. But in St. Louis you just have to know where to go to find different things.
>
> *His advice to young musicians:*
>
> Work on a flat guarantee and always get paid in advance. You can make more working on a percentage, but if you do, you have to have somebody watch the box office. Then you have to have a couple of people watch them. And before you know it, you've' got an entourage coming out from the back stage to the front office.

In *Hail! Hail! Rock 'n' Roll* he strolled through the lobby of the Fox Theater, the grand, ornate movie palace where as an 11-year-old African American he couldn't buy a ticket to see *A Tale of Two Cities* in segregated St. Louis. Chuck Berry remembered thinking:

> I'll be back.
>
> What inspired me to play here is what this represents, not what it is. It could be a corner bar. It's what it represents. Elegance. Decency. A strive for a better manner of life. In the theater where I saw *A Tale of Two Cities* we didn't have such elegance. I don't mean the decor. I mean the clientele. There was hollering from the balcony; when a scene came on you expressed your feelings. Here, you get polite applause and that's enough.

Chapter Thirty-Three

Baseball: Five Decades with the Cardinals

1969-2015

La Russa is being honored for guiding teams he managed to 2,728 wins — a total that ranks third in baseball history. But here's the rub — about 43 percent of all of those wins were recorded when La Russa was managing Mark McGwire and winning because of his prodigious power. That's the same Mark McGwire who has been denied inclusion in the Hall because voters believe that prodigious power owed a great deal to steroids.
Which to me begs the question: By what logic can the guardians of the Hall vilify McGwire for his pharmaceutically assisted feats — yet glorify La Russa, who benefited most from those same feats — and who, by the way, conveniently played dumb while his slugger morphed into the Incredible Hulk?

-- Bryant Gumbel, HBO sports, 2014

The Cardinals were the kings of baseball in 1969, even after the loss to the Tigers in the distressing '68 Series. The St. Louis nine won two of the previous five World Series and three of five National League pennants.

The Redbirds had the game's greatest pitcher, Bob Gibson (MVP and Cy Young winner), had four players of the top seven in the 1968 MVP voting, and a farm system that showed no sign of wearing out. No one predicted the long dry spell that laid ahead -- a span of 36 years produced just one world championship.

The king of beer, August Anheuser Busch Jr., ruled the Cardinals during most of this period, a man who once supposedly said, "No matter how rich you are, you can only drink 30 or 40 beers a day." The brewery had bought the club in 1953 and it became the life work of this man, called Gussie by the public, Gus by the insiders and Mr. Busch to the underlings, including the ballplayers, who worked for him.

He was an heir to the founders of a company started in 1869, bringing a light lager from Germany to America, a beer branded Budweiser, a beer the founding Adolphus Busch called "that slop." The beer suited American tastes and was compatible with Louis Pasteur's methods that made it possible to kill micro-organisms in liquid through rapid heating and cooling, making it safe in bottles for mass consumption.

Adolphus deployed his pasteurized beer in refrigerated rail cars from the central hub in St. Louis, able to ship his product long distances without fear that the suds would spoil. By the time the old German brewer died in 1913, he was worth $60 million.

Gussie, grandson of Adolphus, was born March 28, 1899. By the time he was 25, he was superintendent of brewing and took over the beer division after his father died in 1934. He became A-B president after the death of his older brother, Adolphus Busch III, in 1946.

By then Gussie had amply demonstrated his ability as a promoter. In 1933 he pulled a stunt that left the word Budweiser forever on the sudsy lips of post-Prohibition America. To celebrate the end of the dry days, he marched a team of eight Clydesdale horses hauling a wagon with the first case of Budweiser down Pennsylvania Avenue to the White House.

When his company bought the Cardinals in 1953 he declared, "My ambition is, whether hell or high water, to get a championship baseball team for St. Louis before I die." He had to wait until 1964 for that first championship but by the end of the decade he was riding high, full of confidence and ready to show a group of equally confident players who was the real boss of St. Louis baseball.

The late sixties were the times that were a-changing all across the country. And 1969 was the year of Woodstock, Vietnam, Weathermen, Black Panthers, Stonewall, Manson, the Gap, Abbey Road, Monty Python, Sesame Street, the moon, Altamont, and the first strain of the AIDS virus to reach America. In St. Louis, the Spanish Pavilion opened downtown, the leader of the Black Liberators fled the city, a rent strike began in Pruitt-Igoe, and the Veiled Prophet Parade, for fear of crime, moved to daylight hours for the first time.

Baseball did not escape the turmoil and the Cardinals were at ground zero of a revolt that changed the game forever.

The history of the game had seen many attempts by the players to form unions, to fight control by owners and escape what was known from 1876 as the reserve clause -- a phrase added to contracts in the new National League requiring that the five best performers on each club play for their current team "in perpetuity" unless released by the club, a lifetime guarantee put in the hands of the owners.

Players who objected to the language were promptly fired and blacklisted from the league. Few objected at first, thinking the clause could guarantee them jobs and seeing a danger in becoming "free agents" looking for teams.

But it soon became clear that the clause was an instrument of slavery for any up-and-coming star, a way for the owners to pay less for more years. In 1885, however, Monte West, a Columbia law school grad who played shortstop for the New York Giants and was married to a Broadway actress, defied the owners. He organized baseball's first union, the Brotherhood of Professional Base Ball Players.

He and other players issued a manifesto that declared, "Players had been bought, sold, and traded as though they were sheep instead of American citizens. Like a fugitive slave law, the reserve clause denies him a harbor and a livelihood, and carries him back, bound and shackled, to the club from which he attempted to escape." The owners responded by imposing a salary ceiling and demanding the players pay rent for their uniforms.

In response, many of the National League players jumped to a new circuit formed by Ward in 1890 called the Players League. One of the NL organizers, the former star pitcher Al Spalding, declared war on the Players

League and began alternately threatening to blacklist players or offering them higher salaries to rejoin the National League.

There were already two leagues and three leagues proved one too many. The Player's League didn't have the money to advertise and draw fans. It folded in a year. The National League, feeling the power, swallowed up the other remaining league, the American Association, and continued to impose the reserve clause. It also banned black players.

Another major league, the American League, with much the same rules as the older National League, emerged in 1901. The AL posed a severe challenge to the senior circuit in its earliest years, paying more and drawing more fans.

In 1912, the American League star Ty Cobb, the game's greatest player, threw a tantrum that led to the first player's strike. The scene was New York City, the Washington Heights neighborhood, Hilltop Park, home of the New York Highlanders.

Playing for Detroit, Cobb decided he had enough of a particular fan, a ward politician working for the local machine, Tammany Hall, a noxious character who heckled Cobb with unrelenting. The boisterous heckler had lost all but two of his fingers in a printing press accident, so was not much of threat to Cobb. Nonetheless, the Tiger star leaped into the stands between innings, attacking the fingerless fellow with his own fully maintained fists, as well as his spiked shoes, kicking the man while he was down.

Police finally helped an umpire pull the enraged Cobb off the man. Cobb was suspended and his teammates refused to play on the next home stand, starting the first player's strike May 18, 1912. A team made up mostly of college players was recruited at $25 each to take the field for Detroit to play the defending world champion Philadelphia A's.

Deacon McGuire, a Tiger coach who had 25 years in the league, was the catcher, age 48. Joe Sugden, another coach, played first base at 41. The manager, Hughie Jennings, 43, pinch-hit. The A's led 14-0 after five innings when the game ended. One wag called it "the most farcical lineup the majors ever had known." Cobb was shortly reinstated and the game returned to its regular practices, the reserve clause all but unmentioned, embedded into what became accepted practice in the major leagues through what was known as the "player's agreement."

As the sixties came rolling to an end, the law was still in effect, upheld by the Supreme Court in 1922, challenged in 1946 (by Cardinal pitcher Max Lanier), then again in 1953, when a suit reached the Supreme Court again and again lost. That ruling said that baseball did not constitute interstate commerce, thus player contracts drawn in the separate states were bulletproof against U.S. intervention, i.e. the High Court was helpless against the owners' inside curve.

Sixteen years later, 1969 arrived. Four new teams were formed and a new division structure was established, opening a new round of playoff games, the division series, three-of-five between the three division winners and a wild card in each league. A league championship followed, then the World Series. Major League Baseball now had 24 teams and an immediate $500,000 from the national TV networks.

The players wanted a share of this revenue and they finally had a union man ready to get it. His name was Marvin Miller, a veteran of the steelworker's union, named the first executive director of the Players' Association. He began immediately to negotiate a new contract with the owners, who were still working with Spalding's "national agreement" that long before had crushed the Player's League.

The owners saw trouble and let a small glimmer of light into the talks. Miller negotiated the first Basic Agreement in 1968, a contract that gave the players the right to a grievance system and a minimum pay of $10,000 a year. There was support for a study of the dreaded reserve clause. The players also wanted part of the television money for health care, life insurance and pension benefits. The owners balked, refusing to cede any more money. Tension built as the temperatures warmed in Florida.

The calendar turned over and early in 1969, Cardinal ace Bob Gibson appeared on television's *Tonight Show.* He later said he decided to go on the show because he was concerned the public didn't have much sympathy for "greedy" ball players asking for more money.

"It was curious to me and the other players," Gibson said, "that there didn't seem to be much parallel sentiment concerning the greed of the owners, despite the fact they had just signed a new television contract."

Gibson's season for the ages in 1968 was fresh in the minds of viewers. Baseball didn't like his 1.12 ERA and changed the rules in the off-season, lowering the pitcher's mound and tightening the strike zone.

During his appearance on the show on Feb. 4, just as spring training was about to start, Gibson threw a hot coal in a cold bucket and suggested the players were considering a strike.

By March, nine Cardinals, most of the core players, had already refused to sign contracts for 1969 (not including Gibson, who inked a $125,000 deal without much fuss). The Cardinals of the sixties had become a fully integrated team led by its great black players. The victories of '64, '67 and '68 had made the ownership very happy. But Gussie Busch was in no mood in 1969 to give in to the pay demands of the newly empowered players. As spring training rolled around Gussie Busch was fuming. He was a man used to getting his own way.

Curt Flood, the seven-time Gold Glove center fielder, was one of the holdouts. On March 1, he met with Busch and received a profanity-laced tongue-lashing.

"Labor annoyances were not what he (Gussie) had envisioned when he took up baseball," Flood said. "They could not be classified as a wholesome sport. They were no fun at all. They boded ill for the future of the game. What would become of the fans? The fans? Mr. Busch decided to attack us on behalf of the fans."

Busch called the players together on March 22 and launched an assault. He brought with him his corporate leaders of beer and baseball and members of the press. He said that player pay demands would drive the fans away from the parks, that the average worker in the seats was sick of players "getting fat" and "thinking only of money."

Busch had his speech printed and distributed to company stockholders and employees in a fancy pamphlet. "It doesn't take a crystal ball, gentlemen," he said, "to realize that with so many fans so aware of the big payrolls in baseball, they will become even more critical of all of us."

"He accused us of manhandling our devoted fans," Flood said. "He deplored methods of our Association. He warned that failure to mend our ways would ruin St. Louis baseball. He depicted us as a rabble of ingrates headed for a fall. Having humiliated us to the best of his ability, he exhorted us to go forth and win another pennant."

The speech came in the very heart of the glory days of the Budweiser brand when it was the unquestioned No. 1 beer in America and the world. In the fifties, Anheuser-Busch had strengthened its national image by sponsoring shows featuring Jackie Gleason, Milton Berle, and Frank Sinatra. The Busch name was emblazoned on a new stadium in downtown St. Louis. Branch breweries were opening across the county. In 1967, the team had drawn over 2 million fans for the first time in 1967 and matched the total in 1968, nearly doubling the league average both years.

But Gussie's tirade dramatically weakened his baseball team. By 1972, three years after the speech, Busch's prediction had come true. Attendance had dropped to 1.1 million, 10,000 fewer per game than in 1969 and below the league average.

But the reason was not player pay; it was because of the team's play on the field. For 13 years after the speech, the Cardinals failed to win even a division crown.

People in his corporate world who disagreed with him found themselves gone, and so did players who wanted an extra glass from the brimming Budweiser barrel. In 1969, first baseman Orlando Cepeda, a renegade, was traded. Flood went after the 1969 season, a season where the Cards finished fourth, 13 games behind the Mets. In 1970 the team was fourth again, 10 games below .500. Tim McCarver, gone. Roger Maris, gone. In 1972, the club finished fourth again with only two starters from the '68 World Series team still aboard the sinking ship.

All but Flood accepted their fate and went quietly to other teams.

McCarver, the team leader, cool behind the plate:

> I'll always think the trade (of Flood) contributed largely to the disintegration of the Cards in the seventies, but that's baseball. We all wished we could have stayed with the Cards. We thought we could win. But it wasn't to be.
>
> If you go around in life looking for fairness and trying to analyze whether people are getting what they deserve, you are wasting your time. Fairness, to be blunt about it, doesn't exist in this world, and I don't say this with any residual bitterness.

These players shrugged -- it is what it is.

Flood wasn't exactly itching for a fight. He'd been with the Cards for 12 seasons, coming to the team after just two years in the minors as a 20-year-old.

Just 5-foot-9-inches, Flood was all muscle and grit, a player who covered centerfield with ease and had a rifle for a throwing arm. His career numbers (all but 21 games with the Cards) show a .293 batting average, with six seasons over .300, 636 RBI and a 226-game errorless streak that included an entire season (1966) when he handled 400 chances without a error.

Union boss Marvin Miller was also ready. Flood declared war, refusing to report to the Phillies. He was determined he would not be traded without his consent. Baseball had found its Abraham Lincoln.

The union hired Arthur Goldberg, a former Supreme Court Justice and U.S. Ambassador to the United Nations, for the courtroom. The trial opened May 19, 1970, in district court in lower Manhattan. On the stand, when Flood was asked what team he wanted to play for, he said, "the team that makes me the best offer."

The trial took 10 weeks, produced 2,000 pages of transcript and presented 56 exhibits. At the end Flood lost, but the judge suggested "reasonable men" could find a solution outside court. "We are convinced that the reserve clause can be fashioned so as to find acceptance by player and club," the decision maintained. The lower court had moved from "no" to "maybe."

Flood, having faced the wrath of Gussie Busch up close and very personally, wasn't convinced the owners were reasonable enough to negotiate a deal. But after sitting out the 1970 season he signed a demeaning offer with the lowly Washington Senators. He played only 13 games, hit just .200 and quit baseball.

The case was appealed to the Supreme Court, but the justices upheld the lower court in a 5-3 ruling. Still, Flood, as he so often did from his leadoff spot, had set the table for winning the game. The death of the reserve clause came a few years later, in 1976, when grievances filed by a pair of pitchers, Andy Messersmith of the Dodgers and Dave McNally of the Orioles, were upheld by an arbitrator citing the Flood case, saying it was time for the owners to get rid of the hated clause.

Flood's rebellion was accepted by then by the public, the press and the fans in the stands. The owners caved, aware that the fans wanted to read box scores not legal briefs. By 2003, the mean salary of a ballplayer in the majors had reached $1 million a season.

Flood, never inducted into the Baseball Hall of Fame, lived in Europe for several years after his baseball career and died in 1997, losing to pneumonia after a battle with throat cancer from chewing tobacco.

Gussie Busch, a man not much taller than Flood at 5-feet-10-inches but who sometimes roared like a lion, died before Flood, lasting until 1988 at age 90, time enough to see his team revived and reach edge back into the upper echelons of baseball once again, playing (and losing) three World Series in five years beginning in 1982. Busch left the active management of the company in 1975, just a year before the final demise of the reserve clause.

Until then Busch also kept busy with his various non-baseball interests, especially Grant's Farm, one of the St. Louis area's biggest tourist attractions. The estate was first purchased by the Busch family in 1903 and gradually grew to the 281-acre property, located on the edge of St. Louis. Gussie opened it to the public in 1954.

The farm included a 34-room French Renaissance chateau built for Gussie's father in 1914 (not open to the public) and a private zoo (known as the family menagerie) where Gussie enjoyed training his own chimpanzees and elephants before donating them to the St. Louis Zoo.

The estate got its name from U. S. Grant, the Civil War hero and two-term president. Grant met his wife when he was stationed at Jefferson Barracks in St. Louis prior to the Mexican War. Julia Dent Grant grew up just across from the current entrance to the property. There Grant built a log cabin that was later dismantled and moved over to the Busch property.

Julia Dent's family home, White Haven, is part of the National Historic Site. She and Grant lived in the cabin during the quiet period in his career between the Mexican and Civil wars after their marriage in 1848.

In addition to the mansion, barely visible to the public, the farm is composed of gentle rolling countryside, quiet deer parks and horse stables that proved to be a hit with tourists. No Disneyworld this, just an old-fashioned park, with a central beer garden where two free glasses of fresh Budweiser are given out to every adult. Admission is free but there is a parking fee for the closest lots.

In 2013, over 600,000 people visited Grant's Farm, making a total of nearly 25 million visitors since 1954.

The farm is home to the Clydesdales, the giant work horses that once pulled beer wagons in Germany and are a regular feature of Opening Day and postseason games at Busch Stadium. Gussie once rode horses in rodeos and often chased the fox across fields near St. Louis. The stables also hold several other breeds, including hackneys, hunters and jumpers, all standing in close view of the patrons. Sometimes they get close enough to pet and are groomed to within an inch of their lives.

In 2015, a feud broke out between the Busch heirs over the future of the farm. One side wanted to keep it the way it was, the other wanted to turn the farm over to the St. Louis Zoo. The dispute was still ongoing in mid-2016.

When Gussie Busch died he was worth over $1.5 billion just in stock, with millions more in land and personal holdings. In 2014 Forbes magazine ranked the Busch family the No. 17 richest in the country and the No. 1 richest in St. Louis at $13 billion, ahead of the Pulitzer family by about $2 billion.

St. Louis also has a distant connection to the U.S. most-rich Walton family ($152 billion) through Paige Laurie, the granddaughter of the late Bud Walton, who founded Wal-Mart in 1962 with his brother Sam. Laurie grew up in Columbia, Mo., socialized in St. Louis and had a sports arena in her name at the University of Missouri until her college roommate admitted doing Laurie's homework.

The settlement of the reserve clause did not alleviate player resentment against owners like Gussie Busch. Indeed, the biggest labor dispute in the history of American sports up that time brought the baseball season of 1981 to a complete halt for a 52-day midseason strike. The walkout led to a distorted split season that left the Cardinals in second place for both halves (pre-strike and post-strike) and kept them out of the playoffs even though they had best winning percentage overall in the National League Eastern Division.

The dispute came over the corollary to the reserve clause -- free agency. Owners wanted money back for the loss of newly freed players who signed with other teams. Or, short of that, they wanted a player in return, what amounted to a trade, something that would keep player pay down, a de facto reserve clause.

Play stopped in June for 50 days, 712 games, and an estimated $146 million was lost in players' salaries, ticket sales and broadcast and merchandise revenue. By the end of July the owners had had enough and a compromise was reached.

The result harkened back to Al Spalding, who wanted protection of his top five players against encroachment by other teams. Another strike, the biggest ever, in 1994, ended the season Aug. 11 and washed out the whole postseason.

This time owners gave in to a slightly restricted system the players could live with. Indeed, it was under this post-strike system that player salaries soared. The big homer chase in 1998 was a jolt the game needed, bringing attendance back to 70 million (after a drop to 50 million in 1995).

Another deal in 2011 guaranteed more astronomical salaries for baseball players. St. Louis continued through the years to resist the top rungs of the salary ladder, placing only one player, pitcher Adam Wainwright, on the list of the Top 100 single season payoffs. That salary, $19.5 million for 2014 (when Wainwright won 20 games but faltered in the postseason) barely squeezed onto the list at No. 96. The Cardinals rated No. 13 on the overall big league payroll list.

And yet, since 2000, St. Louis had placed 12 clubs in the post season over 15 seasons. Only the Yanks (13) had more. The Cards had the most wins in the playoffs, edging out New York 65-62 after the 2015 tournament. And yet, looking at that list of 100 top salaries, there are 33 slots that contain names of Yankees, including seven out of the top 10.

And now back to the play-by-play: Whiteyball.

Following the downtrodden seventies, the team ended a 13-year streak without a playoff appearance in 1982, having found the "White Rat" across the state in Kansas City. Tired of battling an owner just as unforgiving as Busch, he wanted a change and took over the Cardinals in 1980.

Dorrel Norman Elvert "Whitey" Herzog was born Nov. 9, 1931, in New Athens, Ill., a small town near the Peabody coal pits about 35 miles southeast of St. Louis. There he was known as Relly, a kid with a first baseman's mitt dangling from the handlebars of his bike, always ready for three games a day on the sandlots.

"We had it better growing up," Herzog said at his induction to the Baseball Hall of Fame in 2010, reflecting on that small-town childhood.

"For kids today, everything is organized. I don't see kids having as much fun as we used to have."

His high school class of 1949 numbered 34. The town of 1,500 had 16 taverns, a place where the locals drank the brew bottled at the local Mound City Brewery where Herzog's father worked. His mother had a job in a shoe factory.

He liked to skip school and hitchhike up to Belleville, Ill., where he could catch a bus into St. Louis and Sportsman's Park. He'd plunk down $1.25 for a glimpse of Stan Musial or Enos Slaughter or Vern Stephens, money he earned by delivering newspapers before school and digging graves after class. On his day at Sportsman's, he'd get there early to collect batting practice balls to supply the sandlot games.

"The principal would never tell my mother," Herzog said. "He'd call me up to the office and we'd end up talking about the ballgame. I wanted to be a ballplayer." The high school baseball field is now Whitey Herzog Field.

Just 5-feet-8-inches and 130 pounds, Herzog led his Yellow Jacket school team to the state baseball finals in his junior year, playing centerfield and pitching. New Athens lost the title game to Granite City, when Herzog, playing his first game at night, lost a fly ball in the lights.

In 1949, he signed with the mighty Yankees and reported to the Sooner State League in McAlester, Okla., and in his second year there batted .351. The young center fielder looked like he might make it as a big leaguer. But the Yanks had another center fielder in the minors that year. He was also fresh out of high school, a strapping kid by the name of Mickey Mantle.

Still, Herzog reached the big leagues in 1956, by then tagged "Whitey" by an Oklahoma sportscaster because of his sun-bleached blonde hair and then "White Rat" due to his resemblance to pitcher Bob "White Rat" Kuzava, who threw for New York in the early fifties and also featured a flat-topped haircut.

In spring training that rookie season, the Yanks were getting ready for an exhibition game against the Dodgers at the Yankee camp in St. Petersburg, Fla., when the Yankee manager, Casey Stengel, told Herzog that Mantle was sick and put Whitey into center field. As things work out in baseball, the rookie got a chance to win the game with the bases loaded.

But this was no boy's book. Instead of a game-winning homer, Herzog's liner found the glove of a leaping second baseman for a double play. Mantle was soon back in the lineup, on his way to the Hall of Fame.

During that spring Whitey became fascinated by Stengel, the "Old Perfesser" who once told his catcher, Yogi Berra, "If we're going to win the pennant, we've got to start thinking we're not as smart as we think we are." In a 25-year managing career Stengel won 10 pennants and seven World Series, including five in a row, and was ranked the third greatest manager of all-time by the *Sporting News*.

Herzog was not around Stengel long, but the Yankee manager was a big influence, leaving Whitey's mind full of "little ideas on fielding, hitting, approaches to baseball, every one of 'em essential to understanding it right and clean as a well-hit ball.

> Like the best teachers, he gave you the big picture in little doses, and he was flashing them to you all the time, like a good catcher with his signs. If you were smart and gave it enough thought, you learned them all and eventually saw how they all fit together.

His playing career was mediocre. He never played a major league game in a Yankee uniform. He appeared in just over 600 games, hitting a lifetime .257 in an eight-year run that ended in 1963 after a dismal season with the Tigers where he batted .151 as a pinch hitter. He suffered from dizzy spells caused by an infected inner ear and never played again.

He found ways to stay in the game he loved, however, climbing from scout to coach to manager, beginning in Kansas City, working for another of the game's great personalities, Charlie Finely, who paraded a live mule around the outfield at Kansas City Athletics games.

He later went to the expansion New York Mets as a third base coach, then to the fledging California Angels and wound up back with the Kansas City Royals in 1975. Like the Mets, the Royals were a new team formed in the expansion of 1969. Herzog began to demonstrate his knack for managing, winning the AL West in 1976, 1977 and 1978. But he lost the league championship series each year, each time to the Yankees. In 1979 he finished second in the division and left Kansas City after battling the team ownership.

Hired by Gussie Busch during the 1980 season, Herzog was the last of four managers piloting the club during a chaotic fourth-place finish. He told Busch, "I'm shocked at what I see on the field. If I had known it was this bad, maybe I wouldn't have come." The club hadn't won a Series since 1967 or a pennant since 1968 and had only been close to a divisional crown in 1974.

"I've never seen such a bunch of misfits," said Whitey. "Nobody would run out a ball. Nobody in the bullpen wanted the ball. We had guys on drugs -- and another who sneaked off into the tunnel between innings so he could get a hit of vodka."

He also found the fabled farm system lacking. He studied the prospects and found few interesting. He looked at the spacious home park and decided he needed speedy fielders, base-stealing hitters and exceptional relief pitchers. But his first priority was a catcher. At the winter meetings prior to the 1981 season, Herzog engineered four trades involving 22 players.

One of the players he obtained was Darrell Porter, a powerful catcher overlooked because of a reputation as a cocaine user. Herzog was familiar with Porter from his days in Kansas City and told him he had faith in him, faith that he could kick his addiction. He told Porter he thought the Cards could win a championship.

Getting the catcher he wanted allowed Herzog to make other moves, putting his subpar defensive catcher Ted Simmons at first and moving hard-hitting first baseman Keith Hernandez to the outfield. He was shaking the bottle hard and had nothing to lose.

Simmons didn't want to play first and Herzog traded him, sending a notice to the rest of the squad that the White Rat meant business. In June of 1981 he took another chance on a player with a bad reputation, getting pitcher Joaquin Andujar in a trade. He had control problems both around the plate and in the clubhouse. He behaved bizarrely, often showering in his uniform.

Then Whitey had more trouble -- star shortstop Gary Templeton began complaining he was too tired to play day games after night games. This led Herzog to make the trade that changed everything for the Cardinals in the eighties, swapping Templeton, who had batted over .300 four times in six seasons and had stolen 91 bases in 1979, for a light-hitting but acrobatic shortstop, Ozzie Smith.

The Wizard of Oz became a Hall of Famer and one of the greatest Cardinals of all time and, along with another speed merchant, Vince Coleman, was the heart of the Runnin' Redbirds of the eighties. Coleman had played two years in the Cardinals system, stealing over 100 bases each season. Upon reaching the majors in 1985, he made over 100 steals for three straight seasons and led the NL in burglaries the first six years of his career.

With his flurry of moves Herzog had also assembled a group that could get on base, a trait that Stengel had perfected in New York. In 1982, 1985 and 1987, St. Louis finished second, first and first in walks in the NL, and were first in on-base percentage each year. Not coincidentally, these teams all won National League championships and the White Rat was manager of the year in '85.

From 1982 to 1987 the Cardinals also had a group of exceptional fielders, especially those up the middle of the field who could cover ground, led by Smith at short, second baseman Tom Herr and center fielder Willie McGee. The rest of the lineup followed suit. For a couple of years, Ken Oberkfell, who had also played a lot of middle infield, played third base. Then Terry Pendleton took over, and he proved to be Gold Glove-caliber on the hot corner.

The team didn't hit home runs and wasn't encumbered by slow moving outfielders. Coleman, Andy Van Slyke, Lonnie Smith and McGee cut off liners and corralled the long fly balls in the big field at Busch Stadium throughout the decade, giving a solid staff of pitchers, including Hall of Fame reliever Bruce Sutter, the courage to let the opposition hit the ball, keeping runners off the bases from walks.

Sutter was a prize catch for Herzog in time for the '81 season, and the righty closer led the league three of the next four years, posting 45 saves in 1984, smashing the single season record of 38 which had stood for 11 years.

The Cardinals sent more team to the World Series than any other franchise in baseball during a 10-year period of parity among the clubs. Still, no team dominated and the Cardinals lost two of the three years they made the finals. That one Series victory under Herzog was memorable, however.

The 1982 Series victory came over the Milwaukee Brewers in what was known as the Six Pack Series or the Suds Series, a championship battle that extended the full seven games and one that the Cards pulled out by winning the last two games at home.

The Brewers that year had taken the Eastern Division title from the Baltimore Orioles on the last day of the season, then won the AL pennant from the California Angels on the final day of the three-of-five-game playoff series after having lost the first two games.

These Brewers were dubbed Harvey's Wallbangers, a club that belted homers at a stirring rate, managed by Harvey Kuenn and led by MVP Robin Yount, Cy Young winner Pete Vukovich and home run leader Gorman Thomas. They started the series by stunning the Cards, taking the opener on the Cardinals' home ground 10-0 but lost 5-4 when the Redbirds rallied in the eighth on a bases-loaded walk in the second game.

The Brewers took control of the Series by winning two out of three in Milwaukee, including a 6-4 squeaker in Game 5, led by Yount's second four-hit game of the Series. The Cardinals came back home needing two victories to win the title.

Game 6 was a tour de force for the rookie St. Louis pitcher John Stuper, who stopped the leading offensive team in baseball on four hits in a 13-1 rout that included a six-run sixth inning. The game was interrupted twice by rain, played under a tornado watch with temperatures in the forties, the wind whipping. Delays shattered Milwaukee pitching. Stuper was undaunted by the long delays, finishing what he started, not allowing a run until the meaningless ninth.

A riotous six-run sixth turned the contest, an inning of perfect Whiteyball, even after it was stopped by a downpour. The frame began with a leadoff double by Dane Iorg, then singles by McGee, Herr, Hernandez and George Hendrick, a walk, two wild pitches and an error. The Redbirds were constantly in motion, scratching, dashing and sliding everywhere as the Brewers melted.

The victory set up a Game 7 match between Vukovich and Andujar, each team's best hurler. It was much smoother, better played, and far more exciting than the previous night's rout, decided by another sixth inning Cardinal rally.

The contest, again played in blustery 40-degree weather, was the 28th time a Series went the limit, a match won by Andujar, who lasted seven strong innings just five days after he had been struck on the right knee by a one-hop liner to the mound. "The knee bothered me from the very first inning," he said. "But I told my teammates that tonight nothing was going to beat me."

With the score tied at 1-1 in the top of the sixth and the crowd of nearly 55,000 people on the edge of their seats, the Brewers got to Andujar for two runs. Jim Gantner doubled. Molitor bunted. Andujar fielded the ball and fired wildly to first. Gantner scored, Molitor to second and Milwaukee had a 2-1 lead. Yount chopped a single to the right side, Molitor to third. Then the power hitting first baseman Cecil Cooper hit a long sacrifice fly. Molitor came home and Brewers led, 3-1.

But in the bottom of the inning, still facing the Cy Young-winning Vukovich with one out, Ozzie singled and Lonnie Smith doubled to put men on second and third. Kuenn brought in the lefty reliever Bob McClure. Herzog brought in Gene Tenace who walked to fill the sacks, still with one out.

Hernandez strolled to the plate, the crowd roaring in the cold night. Herzog went against the book, Stenglesque, letting his lefty hit for himself against the lefty specialist McClure. The White Rat had a feeling, an instinct.

And Hernandez, batting on his 29th birthday in the critical moment of the Series and the season, laced a two-run single on a 3-and-1 pitch to right center that tied the game, 3-3. Hendrick, with runners on first and third, then nubbed an opposite-field roller through a drawn-in Brewer infield to drive in the winning run, a hit that would have never made it through a Herzog-created defense.

The Cards added two insurance runs in the eighth and Sutter was spotless for the close. St. Louis had its ninth World Series.

Fireworks exploded over the western bank of the Mississippi River. Police on horseback and others deploying attack dogs tried to hold back the surging crowd, but thousands overwhelmed the force and stormed the field. The fans were determined to take a part of the game home, clawing up hunks of the artificial surface before they were finally spent after 40 minutes and left the stadium to continue their sudsy party in the downtown streets.

Looking back over the record book from the start of official pro ball in 1876 through the twentieth century and into the present, we see regular surges of success that have made the St. Louis Cardinal franchise (including early years as the Browns and the Perfectos) the second most successful team in baseball history (behind only the Yanks in playoff appearances and World Series titles).

Success has come in waves -- 1883-91, 1925-31, 1934-49, 1963-68, 1982-87 and 1996 to the present (2015.) In each period there were steady first division finishes, league pennants and World Series titles (11 total, or 12 if you count the Browns 1886 victory over the Chicago White Stockings, now known as the Cubs). Overall, counting from 1882 to 2015, the team won 10,571 and lost 9,763.

In the twenty-first century the team has won MLB crowns in 2006 and 2011. The Cards also picked up three more league championships in the first 13 years of the new century, bringing the total to 19 pennants over all (23 if you count the 1880s American Association flags.)

But before the thrills of the twenty-aughts and twenty-tens came the late-eighties and nineties. Here the Cardinals were again central in the history of the sport.

Not for greatness, however -- not for Old Pete, Stan the Man, the Wizard of Oz or Bruce Sutter's lockdown closings. Instead, St. Louis played a central role in a cheating scandal that began to unravel publicly in a locker room in Busch Stadium in 1998.

Indeed, this locker room is as historical a spot as Sportsman's Park or Cooperstown, for it was there that a muscular Cardinal hero by the name of Mark McGwire hung his clothes. And it was also there that a wandering scribe saw a mysterious brown bottle labeled with a word he didn't recognize.

That word was androstenedione.

Bill DeWitt, Jr., who had grown up in St. Louis in a family drenched in baseball, owned the Cardinals by then. His father, Bill DeWitt, Sr., had been a protege of Branch Rickey and was team secretary of the Cardinals by age 17, then vice-president of the Browns, later taking over ownership and overseeing their only AL title, then selling out to Bill Veeck in 1951.

Bill Junior was a batboy for the Browns, his was the uniform the tiny Eddie Gaedel wore to amuse the St. Louis fans in 1951. Bill remained close to baseball as his father moved to Detroit to take over the Tigers then to Cincinnati, where his Reds won the pennant in 1961. In 1965 Junior graduated from Harvard Business School, spent a short time with his father in Cincinnati until the elder DeWitt sold out in 1967.

By 1979, DeWitt, Jr., had founded Reynolds, DeWitt & Co., with Merce Reynolds, an oil investor who later became partner with George W. Bush and was an influential money raiser in Bush's presidential campaigns. Meanwhile, DeWitt's firm built Arby's thin-sliced roast beef sandwich into a multi-million dollar chain.

In 1988, DeWitt and Bush headed up the group that bought the Texas Rangers. The team was mediocre, consistently under .500 and never made the playoffs until after both Bush and DeWitt were gone. Instead, DeWitt went back home to St. Louis and pulled together another group, this time buying the Cardinals from Anhauser-Busch in the spring of 1996.

The group included a crowd of high school classmates who had made it big. This list included the great-grandson of a longtime Cardinal owner in the twenties and thirties, Bush's future ambassador to Belgium, a breeder of Kentucky race horses, a director of Rawlings Sporting Goods, a Pulitzer and a Taft -- Dudley Taft, a co-owner of the cartoon company that created Fred and Velma Flintstone and Huckleberry Hound.

The 17 known owners in this original partnership tallied up $4 billion in assets in 2001. By then they had seen the great home run derby of 1998 and were about to see a full-scale scandal that emanated from that little brown bottle in Mark McGwire's locker.

McGwire's rookie card from 1987 shows normal biceps, normal forearms, a normal man. The *Sports Illustrated* cover from Oct. 5, 1998, shows a man with monster biceps, Popeye forearms and thighs ready to pop from his uniform pants. He hit 70 homers that year, breaking the paltry 61 home run record of Roger Maris (hit in 1961) with an outlandish display of power, much of it put on display in the spacious confines of Busch Stadium, a playing field built for speed and defense, its power deep and wide. Maris, like Babe Ruth (60 homers in 1927) before him, had a short porch of 295 feet in his power zone. McGwire had to send his long balls into what became known as Big Mac land, 330 feet from home.

Baseball had suffered through the strike in 1994 as the players continued to stack up piles of money and the owners had visions of red ink.

McGwire and his homering rival Sammy Sosa turned the red ink to black. *New York Times* sports writer George Vecsey gushed about an upcoming Cardinals game: “Tonight, in the shadow of the Gateway Arch, the big man will flex muscles broad as the river that flows past. Baseball lives.”

They were massive muscles, indeed, drawing big crowds and big smiles all the ‘98 season. In Miami on Sept. 1 and Sept. 2 he hit two homers each game, bringing his total to 59. Sosa, a Latin outfielder playing for the Cubs, hit No. 57 on Sept. 4, and belted No. 58 on Sept. 5.

Maris had died in 1985. But the Cardinals flew in his wife and four sons for a three-game set with the Cubs and Sosa in early September. Maris had finished his baseball days in St. Louis, playing his final two seasons as a Cardinal, 1967-68, years when he was never right physically. But he was a useful player on two pennant-winning teams, even though his homer total was way down due to a bad hand.

Maris died age 51 in 1985 from Hodgkin’s lymphoma.

Maris did not enjoy his 1961 run at Babe Ruth’s record of 60 home runs. Too many fans and writers felt Maris’ record would be tainted because Maris played in more games. The league had expanded from 16 teams to 18 in 1961 and switched from 154 games to 162. Also, the far more popular Mickey Mantle, who wound up with 54 homers, chased Maris in his run for the record.

This time both McGwire and Sosa enjoyed the chase. McGwire hit his 61st homer Sept. 7, a 430-foot blast. Greeted at home plate by his 10-year old son, he tossed the boy in the air and waved to his father, who was celebrating his 61st birthday behind home plate; he waved to the Maris family and blew a kiss to heaven, to Roger Maris. The stadium burst with affection for the slugger.

There was little suspense the next night. The first pitch to McGwire, a right-handed batter, was a slider away, slipping across the corner, low in the strike zone. McGwire was so strong, able to get his bat around so fast, he was somehow able to pull that low-and-away ball. Most hitters trying to pull such a pitch would bounce out to short or third, a hard hit ball might be a single to left. But most hitters would go the other way with such a pitch, slapping it out toward right field. This hitter’s swing, the McGwire swing, however, was not the swing of most hitters. McGwire was able to drill the pitch to the left field corner where it cleared the fence, traveling 341 feet, his seventh homer in seven games, his 15th in 21.

Cardinal radio announcer Mike Shannon, who had played in the 1964 World Series, burst out:

> I haven't seen anyone like him, and you're never going to see anything like him. In Mark McGwire, what you're talking about is John Wayne, Paul Bunyan and Superman rolled into one. You're never going to see a show like this.

McGwire was born Oct. 1, 1963, in Southern California, in Los Angeles County, in a town, Pomona, once devoted to growing oranges, now 150,000 population, then already 80,000 and swarmed over by the suburban sprawl. McGwire was one four brothers, all athletes, all over six feet and more than 200 pounds. Mark was a jock in high school, playing baseball, basketball and golf for Damien High, an all-male Catholic school.

His father was a dentist who coached the Little League team and watched his son hit a homer in his first at bat. McGwire was also the best pitcher on the team and by the time he reached high school he could throw a 90-mph fastball.

He pitched a little at USC after he chose college over pro baseball.

He got a slow start his first two years but hit well enough (31 homers in 237 at bats) in his junior year to make a 1984 U. S. Olympic team that lost the gold to Japan 6-3 in Dodger Stadium. McGwire had a less than Bunyanesque Olympics with no homers in 21 at bats, four singles and none driven in.

Still, all but two of the players off the team became first round draft picks and McGwire was snared by Oakland 10th overall. He became a full-time major leaguer in 1987.

At Oakland he was unanimous Rookie of the Year, hitting 49 homers to set the rookie record. He played 12 seasons with the A's, four that netted division titles, with three straight AL pennants (1988-1990) and one World Series, a four-game sweep in 1989 of the archrival San Francisco Giants. Big Mac and his Bash Brother, José Canseco, led the club that year and through the championship, the Series that was delayed by an earthquake.

McGwire's 363 home runs with the club broke the storied Philadelphia/Oakland franchise home run record. His biggest big fly was probably the game winning solo shot in the bottom of the ninth of Game 3 of the 1988 Series against the Dodgers, the only game the A's won in the finals.

McGwire's numbers were steady through the next few seasons but in 1991, age just 28, he hit a deep snag, slumping all year to a .201 average with just 22 homers. He recovered in 1992 with 42 long balls, saying he dedicated his off-season to weightlifting instead of golf. But nagging foot injuries the next two seasons threatened his career. He could only play a total of 74 games for the two seasons.

He played just 104 games in 1995, but seemed much improved, stronger and larger, especially in the biceps and the thighs. He stepped to the plate with confidence and belted 39 home runs in 317 at-bats. In 1996, McGwire led the league in homers with 52 homers in 423 at-bats. His .312 was a career best and he led the AL in slugging and on-base percentage. Big Mac was back.

His manager and mentor, Tony La Russa, however, was gone, by then running the Cardinals, taking over the dugout seat in St. Louis from Joe Torre. In the 1995 season, the A's finished 67–77. The Haas family, with whom La Russa had a close personal relationship, sold the team after the death of Walter Haas, Jr. In 1997, the A's traded away McGwire to join La Russa with the Cardinals for three pitchers for the future: T.J. Matthews, Blake Stein, and Eric Ludwick.

Ludwick pitched six games with the A's, Stein was 5-9 career with a 6.60 ERA, and T.J. Matthews was 24-15 with a 4.78 ERA. McGwire hit 70 homers and 147 RBI in '98 for St. Louis, then followed it with 65 homers and again 147 RBI in '99. In 2000, the nagging injuries recurred. This time, however, they meant the end of his playing career, appearing in under 100 games in 2000 and 2001.

McGwire was 38. Given his 583 home runs and that blown kiss to Roger Maris' wife, Big Mac should have been able to ride off into a nearby coaching box and enjoy life. Instead, there was the matter of the little brown bottle.

Eventually he would admit to using bodybuilding steroids, the stuff that made it possible for him to belt those homers. Fans in the stands knew he was bulking up just by looking at the various bodies who came up to bat, comparing those bodies to the players batting in the sixties and seventies. Something had turned normal human beings into Paul Bunyans. But the powers that were kept a policy of deny, deny, deny.

"Everybody I know in the game of baseball uses the same stuff I use," McGwire eventually said.

McGwire and Canseco were the two most obvious specimens, working under La Russa, slamming their giant forearms together in celebration after the big homer. Looking at them you hear the clanking of weights, the grunt of the Olympian lift.

The outside slider became reachable. The inside pitches could be quickly fought off. The World Anti-Doping Agency, the National Football League and the Olympics banned the drugs. But it wasn't until 2004 the fearful lords of baseball banned that andro.

Then in 2005, much to McGwire's dismay, came the release of Canseco's book *Juice: Wild Times, Rampant 'Roids, Smash Hits & How Baseball Got Big.* Canseco made a case for the positive effects of steroids even as he outed his fellow users in the locker rooms. In what may be the most influential single book in the history of the game, Canseco said he and his teammate on the A's had injected the drugs together, starting the year McGwire broke the rookie record, 1988.

Following the Canseco revaluations, Congress got on its horse and summoned the Bash Brothers and 11 players and owners to hearings on steroids. Sosa flatly denied he used drugs, others gave variations on the "everybody did it" theme.

At the hearing, McGwire gave a nervous, tearful, statement:

> Asking me or any other player to answer questions about who took steroids in front of television cameras will not solve the problem. If a player answers "No," he simply will not be believed; if he answers "Yes," he risks public scorn and endless government investigations.
>
> My lawyers have advised me that I cannot answer these questions without jeopardizing my friends, my family or myself.

Soon after came a question from Rep. Elijah E. Cummings, D-Md.:

> Are you taking the Fifth?
>
> *McG:* I'm not here to discuss the past. I'm here to be positive about this subject."

> *Rep. William Lacy Clay, D-Mo:* Mr. McGwire, we are both fathers of young children. Both my son and daughter love sports and they look up to stars like you.
>
> Can we look at those children with a straight face and tell them that great players like you play the game with honesty and integrity?
>
> *McG:* Like I said earlier, I'm not going to go into the past and talk about my past.

A *New York Times* columnist said McGwire had become "a sodden hunk of aged and post-verbal sadness." In Hall of Fame balloting in 2007, McGwire was denied approval. Just after the home run record a portion of I-70 near the St. Louis ballpark was named "Mark McGwire Highway" but in May 2010 a bill was passed in the Missouri legislature changing the name to "Mark Twain Highway."

Five months previous to the name change, McGwire had finally fessed up, admitting to a decade-long use of the drugs.

"I wish I had never touched steroids," he said. "It was foolish and it was a mistake. I truly apologize. Looking back, I wish I had never played during the steroid era."

He said the heaviest use was in the 1989-90 offseason and after he was injured in 1993. He said he had used the drugs during the home run record season of 1998, but only to help recover from injuries. The admission was apparently a condition of his return to the Cardinals under La Russa as hitting coach that same year, 2010.

La Russa retired in 2011 and McGwire went off to the Dodgers as hitting coach in 2013. In 2014, the Cardinals played the Dodgers in the division series, beating McGwire and the league-leading payroll three games to one. He became bench coach for the San Diego Padres in 2016, still unable to crack the Hall of Fame.

La Russa, however, was inducted into the Hall of Fame in 2014, the third winningest manager in baseball history. He won the World Series as the skipper of teams in both the American (Oakland) and National Leagues (St. Louis), and accumulated six pennants and 12 division titles in his 33 seasons.

La Russa changed the way managers manipulated their bullpens, one guy pitching the seventh, another the eighth, then finally the well-defined closer, the pitcher who could save a season or a World Series.

La Russa also had a front row at the birth of the steroid era with his Bash Brothers in Oakland. He said at the induction in Cooperstown that he tried to head off the scandal, going to A's general manager Sandy Alderson with concerns about the drug use, but got nowhere.

"We had our suspicions," La Russa added, there were "guys hitting stronger but not working out. I went to Sandy and ownership about this. And they told me flat off, 'Right of privacy. It's a collective bargaining issue.'" He also vehemently defended McGwire, "For a lot of reasons, a ton of reasons, I believe in Mark. Period. End of conversation."

La Russa was born Oct. 4, 1944, and raised in Tampa, Fla. His parents, of Italian and Spanish background, encouraged an early interest in baseball. As a second grader, he argued with his mother, who insisted he wear a white shirt and dress pants for a graduation ceremony. Instead, Tony wore his gray flannel baseball uniform and cap.

His parents worked at the Perfecto-Garcia cigar factory near downtown Tampa and lived in an apartment not far from a baseball diamond, where he played all day, mostly with older boys. "The dominant sport to the point of being a religion was baseball," he said. "Baseball was by far the sport that we were exposed to the most. I had a special opportunity to play baseball, get to love it early."

The night of his high school graduation in 1962, La Russa signed with the Kansas City A's, getting $100,000, a white Pontiac Bonneville (with black leather seats) and the promise of college tuition.

Soon thereafter, however, he injured his arm in a hometown softball game and was only good enough to scratch out a living over 15 seasons, mostly spent in the minors, getting into 132 major league games during six different seasons, hitting .199. All the while, though, he was going to school, getting a business degree from South Florida then spending five years getting a law degree from Florida State in 1978.

Choosing baseball over lawyering, La Russa took a minor league manager job offer from the White Sox. He quickly advanced to AAA. But when "I got there," he said, "I felt totally unprepared. I was a lousy player and I only managed a little bit. I was hanging on by my fingernails and had no expectation that I would have a long career."

He moved up to the majors quickly, however, and ran the Sox from 1979 to 1986, then Oakland from 1986 to 1995. He joined the Cardinals in 1996 where he managed until 2011, getting 1,408 wins in his 16 seasons in St. Louis, seven times over 90 wins, a .544 winning percentage overall. Along the way he collected two World Series titles, three pennants and four Manager of the Year awards.

Taking over from Gussie Busch in 1996, La Russa and new managing partner Bill DeWitt broke a run of eight years without a title by winning the regular season division and the division playoff before losing the NL pennant to Atlanta in a seven-game set. They lost 15-0 in Game 7 to Tom Glavine, who pitched shutout ball and hit a crucial, bases-clearing triple.

After that loss came the big years of Big Mac, but the home run derby didn't result in pennants. In 1997 through 1999 the club finished fourth, third and fourth. In 2000-01, McGwire's last two years, both cut short by injury, he only played in half the games, hit 32 and 29 homers and batted .187 that final year.

But starting in 2000, La Russa's clubs put the name St. Louis atop the Central Division day in and day out for three summers, winning more than 90 games each year. In the first year of the new century, behind Jim Edmonds and Mike Matheny, St. Louis won the Central Division by 10 games. The Redbirds swept the Braves in the division series but lost to the Mets in five games in the league championship, by now a La Russa trend -- four playoff berths with no Series appearance.

But in the middle of the aught-zero decade, La Russa was a master. His teams made the postseason six out of seven seasons during 2000-06. He ran relief pitchers in and out, inventing the match-up specialists, defining the role of the closers and showing how important the quick switch was in the finals.

For La Russa, the big regular seasons didn't translate into World Series. The next two years, 2001-02, resulted in more sorrow in the lower rounds of the playoffs, losing the division series to Arizona in 2001 and the Giants in the league series in 2002, four games to one both years.

But the manager saw things in the long term. He took up a "trust your gut" mantra, referring to himself as a "relentless grinder." DeWitt stuck with him.

The team finally broke into the World Series in 2004 but ran into the history-minded Boston Red Sox, a team that had performed the miracle comeback in the league championship to beat the Yanks after losing the first three games. The Sox, guided by general manager Theo Epstein, were on their way to their first Series victory in 89 years. There was no stopping Boston as the club swept the Cards and their 105 regular season wins out the door.

Two years later, La Russa won a World Series trophy in St. Louis, the first Cardinal championship in 24 years. Having failed with the big winners, over 100 games twice and 90 games three times, La Russa turned to a lowly bunch who backed into a pennant with a 12-17 September and just 83 wins, a mere five games over .500, the lowest winning percentage by a Series winner in a non-strike season.

"There were few times during the year we could put it together," La Russa said. Indeed, the team was at its best only twice all season, in the first two months and at the very end, when a rookie closer got a hot hand and a wiry shortstop provided the clutch.

The club opened 2006 in a new stadium with an old look, a third straight 100-game season. Chris Carpenter took the Cy Young and Albert Pujols won an MVP in 2005. Hurt eight weeks into the 2006 season, Pujols already had 25 homers and 65 RBI. He came back three weeks later and added 24 and 72 more during the rest of the season.

The Cards were 34-19 at the end of May, but injuries that brought down center fielder Jim Edmonds and rotation pitcher Mark Mulder sent the club reeling in a midseason 14-23 swoon. The recovery came just in time, a seven-game September winning streak that left the Cardinals ahead of Cincinnati by 7 games and Houston by 8½ with 13 to play.

But the Redbirds then lost seven in a row; "mugging the lead," La Russa called it. And the edge fell to a half-game after the Astros won their ninth in a row and the Cardinals lost again.

Pujols drove a three-run winner against Milwaukee. The Cards beat the Brewers again the next night and the magic number for St. Louis was one. Fans began chanting the Braves' tomahawk chop in the stands, hoping Atlanta would beat Houston. Houston lost and the race was over, the Cards didn't need to win their last game.

St. Louis beat San Diego three games to one in the division series and moved on to the Big Show with an excruciating NL championship series, victorious four games to three over the Mets. The seven games came down to one at bat in Game 7: Adam Wainwright, the rookie reliever, vs. Carlos Beltran, the Mets slugger.

The score was 3-1, St. Louis. The Mets loaded the bases loaded, two out, last of the ninth. Quickly, Wainwright put Beltran in an 0-2 hole. Beltran waited for the fastball, looking outside the zone. But Waino spun a surprise curve, a beauty, a big breaker, tumbling down over the outside edge. The umps don't like to pull a called third strikes on 0-2 in the regular year, but in the playoffs they have different eyes.

Called strike three. Beltran was out. Game and series over.

The next act for the Birds was the World Series against heavily favored Detroit. The Cards had won 83 games compared to 95 for Detroit in the regular year; the Tigers had beaten the Yankees in the divisional round and Oakland in the league playoffs. The Tigers had a lineup of stars: hitters Ivan Rodriguez, Carlos Gullen, Magglio Ordonez, plus moundsmen Kenny Rogers and Jason Verlander.

La Russa's opening move of the Series was to place a rookie right-hander, Anthony Reyes, on the mound. La Russa couldn't pitch his ace, Chris Carpenter, until the third game. Reyes had had a hot streak late in the season, but bombed the last week. La Russa's gamble worked. Reyes pitched effectively for the win.

Game 2 went to Rogers and the Tigers, but Carp was all set for the crucial 1-1 tiebreaker. Edmonds gave him a 1-0 lead in the fourth and Carpenter went eight innings, no walks, six strikeouts, three hits, giving St. Louis the edge. Game 4 was one for the trademark team resilience, the propensity to win close contests -- the score was 3-0 for the Tigers, then 4-3 St. Louis, then 4-4, then finally, 5-4 Cards on a David Eckstein RBI double, giving them a three games to one lead in the Series.

The Redbirds didn't want to see a sixth game. They had led three games to one in the 1968 World Series against the Tigers, but lost in seven. They lost again after the same big lead in the 1985 Series against Kansas City, and again lost the same advantage in 1996 NL playoff against the Braves.

The Cards took Game 5 and the Series behind Eckstein's' bat, the pitching of Jeff Weaver and some bungled fielding by the Tigers, in a tense 4-2 game at the new stadium. In the ninth, La Russa went with his hot closer, the rookie Wainwright.

He got into trouble when Sean Casey doubled with one down, then walked the tying run to first base with two out. Brandon Inge, however, was an easy out for the rookie, falling behind 0-2 then swinging at another crucial Waino curve to end the Series.

"We had some really good teams and we just never made it," center fielder Jim Edmonds, a Cardinal since 2000, said after the game. "We just kept plugging along and hoped we got another shot. We got a shot and we played good ball at the right time."

The 2009 team won the Central Division and Pujols won his third MVP. But the Dodgers swept the division series. The next year saw second place, 10 games over .500, not good enough for the playoffs.

The 2011 season wasn't exactly rocking for the Redbirds in August. Tony La Russa's shingles were the talk of the lobby bar at the Chase Hotel where the manager lived during the season. Third baseman David Freese was out with a broken hand. Then Pujols was hurt in a collision and was out for six weeks. The team stalled in July, hovering near the division lead but not much above .500.

A new swoon soon left them reeling south, down by 10 games on Aug. 25, just six weeks before the end of the regular year. "That's as bad as it can get," the manager said after a sweep at home by the Dodgers. "We're going to have to reverse that."

Reverse it they did, beating Milwaukee five out of six and sweeping the Braves to climb to within four games of the wild card spot with 16 games to play. La Russa's hot closer had emerged in Jason Motte, a flamer who solved a problem that nagged the team all year. The rotation was as strong as ever. At the plate Lance Berkman had come to town, a ghost of the Astros, only this time there to help his former foes.

On Sept. 21, a healed and healthy David Freese belted a homer that gave the Birds 12 of 14. They trailed by a game. The season came down to the final day, tied with Atlanta for the wild card spot.

Carpenter made short work of the Astros 8-0 clinching at least a tie depending on the outcome of the Braves and Phillies who battled into the 13th before Hunter Pence drove in the winning run for the Phils and sent the Cards into the playoffs. The run from 10 1/2 games back with a month left was the biggest comeback after 130 games in baseball history.

"We had nothing to lose," said Carpenter. "We were already out of it. People we telling us we were done."

From a season ripe with drama came a postseason positively Shakespearean. The drama started in Game 4 of the division series before the second-largest crowd in Busch Stadium III history, 47,071, where the Cardinals, facing elimination in the five game set, came from behind to win behind Freese's two-run sixth inning homer.

Phillies slugger Ryan Howard, a St. Louis native, stood at the plate in the eighth as the tying run, but the lefty match-up specialist Marc Rzepczynski struck out Howard. Motte got the save as center fielder John Jay made a sliding grab of a liner to end the game.

The tied series went back to Philadelphia, where the home nine was favored to win the deciding game. After all, the Phils had set a team record of 102 victories during the regular season and had Ray Halladay, the Cy Young ace, on the mound for the Game 5 clincher. St. Louis had Chris Carpenter.

According to the cliche, a game between pitching aces is as often a slugfest as one that produces a basket of goose eggs. Not this game, one of the classic pitching duels in postseason history. Card Rafael Furcal led off the game with a triple and Skip Schumaker drove him in with a double. That was it for the scoring. The eggs piled up the rest of the way. Carp gave up three hits, Halladay six. The final was 1-0, St. Louis.

"Chris was unbelievable, he really was," Halladay said. "Everything was down, everything was moving."

Neither starter issued an unintentional walk.

Milwaukee beat St. Louis 9-6 in the opener of the National League championship, Prince Fielder hitting a go-ahead two-run homer. The Cards rattled the boards for 17 hits in the second game and won 12-3. In Game 3, St. Louis held a 4-3 lead from the fourth inning to the end. Milwaukee then tied the Series back up again with a 4-2 victory behind Randy Wolf.

Back home, the Cardinals nailed another NL pennant, knocking Milwaukee pitching around to win the final two games to take the NL pennant. Freese was hot, hot, hot. He hit .545 in the six game series, powered three homers and drove in nine runs. He had 12 hits and scored seven runs. Redbird outfielder Matt Holliday also got in on the fun with a .435 Series. The bullpen was also there, closing with Motte, setting up with Lance Lynn and Arthur Rhodes, pitchers who posted a combined ERA of 0.00.

Entering the ninth inning of Game 6 of the 2011 World Series, the Texas Rangers had a 7-5 lead and a three to two edge in games. The franchise founded in the expansion of 1961 as the new Washington Senators, moved to Texas in 1972 and never won a Series title either place, the third longest drought (behind the Cubs and Cleveland) in baseball.

But here they stood, three outs away from ending a 52-year wait. As the game headed into the bottom of the ninth, Ranger officials gathered in a Busch Stadium party room near the clubhouse, eyeing cases of chilled champagne. Tony La Russa called his bullpen and told them not to just run away if they lost, but to remember to take part in a tribute to the fans after the last out.

Neftalí Feliz had the ball, rookie of the year in the American League in 2010, a hard throwing righty with 32 saves in 2011.

LaRussa:

> I thought when you're down two runs to their closer in the ninth -- this guy (Feliz) is a legitimate 1-2-3 and they're shaking hands. You try to get something started. You don't try to hit three home runs. Once you get something started the other club worries.

Feliz got the first hitter but Pujols broke an 0-for-10 with a ringing double. Albert clapped his hands, clad in the gladiator hitting gloves out there on second base. Then came another out. Just three more strikes for the first ever Texas championship.

But Berkman walked and Freese stepped up. Two on, two out.

Freese flashed that high school smile, he dug in, righty vs. righty. He swung, behind on the Feliz fastball. But he made solid contact and the ball zipped into right field. For a moment it looked like outfielder Nelson Cruz was going to catch it, but no, he staggered around a little and it got by him. Triple for Freese and the game was tied. Freese's grin went enormous as he pounded around in celebration over there at third. It was 7-7. The bubbly remained on ice in the Texas party room.

On to the top of the 10th where up came Ranger Josh Hamilton, the MVP in 2010, an All-Star in 2011, batting .298 with 25 homers in the regular year. And boom, Hamilton blasted one out of the park off a Motte fastball and it was 9-7 Rangers.

But St. Louis didn't quit. In the last of the 10th, here came the Runnin' Redbirds reincarnate. Descalso singled, Jay singled, Lohse sacrificed, Pujols was passed; bases loaded, one out. Theriot 's run-scoring groundout made it 9-8.

Then Berkman stood in, the veteran Astro outfielder who had delivered the milk and eggs for the Cardinals all season.

> I figured I was in a no-lose situation. If you don't come through right there it's only one at bat and it's over with, and they might talk about it for a couple of days. It's not that big a deal. If you come through it's the greatest.

Berkman flipped a golf shot off his bat into the outfield for his third run batted in the game. It was now 9-9.

David Freese was born April 28, 1983, grew up in Wildwood, Mo., in St. Louis County and went to Lafayette High where in his senior year he hit .533. He was considered the best prep infielder in Missouri.

After graduation, however, he surprised his coaches, relatives and friends by turning down a baseball scholarship at the University of Missouri, saying he was bored and burned out on playing a boy's game. But the itch didn't go away. Freese still wanted to play.

Working for the Rockwood schools, he laid tiles, fixed cabinets and spent the summer enjoying life. At Mizzou he joined the fraternity, pledged Sigma Alpha Epsilon and began to party -- an 18-year-old out of the box. "My GPA was just brutal, and I was headed down the wrong road."

He started asking himself, "What am I doing?' He decided he was ready to play ball again. The year off, he said, "kind of brought me back to the game and helped me realize how much I missed it. I called my mom and said, 'Let's go.'"

He enrolled in Meramec Community College and moved home. There he promptly had the first of a series of incidents involving drunken driving, getting a DUI in 2002. But he bounced along, getting in his work at the batting cage as well as at the parties. He became an all-American college player in 2004.

For his junior and senior years he transferred to the University of South Alabama, playing two seasons there. He was named the Sun Belt Conference's best player in 2006 and was drafted by the San Diego Padres.

The Cardinals got Freese in 2008 in a trade of an aging Jim Edmonds. Freese played AAA in Memphis in 2009, hitting .306 with 26 home runs and 91 RBI, playing slick defense, a performance that sent him to the big club projected as the full-time third baseman for 2010.

But another offseason DUI got in the way. Still, he battled through the bad publicity and did what the team wanted him to do, landing the full-time job in 2011. His late season tear wasn't as much unexpected as it was phenomenal, beyond anything Freese had shown before.

And here he was, leading off the 11th inning of Game 6 of the World Series. The score was 9-9 as he stepped in against relief pitcher Mark Lowe at almost 1 a.m. on a cold night near the Mississippi River. The Cardinals had twice been down to their last strike and twice had staved off elimination.

Freese was guessing change from Lowe, who once could fire the ball 100 mph, but was now a middle reliever pressed into service due to the demise of Feliz.

Lowe was the eighth pitcher of the night for Texas. Freese clawed some dirt with his cleats, put on his hitting face and worked his helmet down tight on his head. He was the hottest guy in the lineup. He had the attention of the crowd in the park and at all the bars in the city, well after midnight, a roaring, consuming baseball game. Last of the 11th. Score tied. One run wins it. Batter and pitcher played cat-mouse, cat-mouse, battling to a full count.

Then came the change-up. Here was the train Freese was waiting to catch. He put the bat on it and away it flew, a hit clean and crisp, straight out to the batters' eye over the centerfield wall. Hamilton stood helpless. He took a look and made a step or two toward it. No use, the ball was gone. The game was over. 10-9.

Cardinals win! Cardinals win!

Game 7 became a true anticlimax. Carpenter was in control and the offense tacked up a 6-2 winner for the Cardinals 11th World Series title, four games to three.

Freese's postseason hadn't gone well at first, hitting just one-for-nine in the first three games against the Phillies. Then in Game 4 after his first time up against Roy Oswalt, he realized he wasn't planting his front foot quickly enough. "From that moment, everything took off."

For the whole 2011 postseason the stat line is as impressive as it gets: .397 with five home runs, 21 RBI, 50 total bases and 25 hits, all playoff records. He was MVP of the Series and the NLCS.

After the Game 6 winning homer, Freese said:

> I was worried about getting on base, leading off an inning, taking a walk, breaking a bat, single, whatever. The full count came, and I knew he had a good change-up. So I kind of had that in the back of my head.
>
> For so many reasons, I shouldn't have been there. I shouldn't even be in this game. We kept coming back. We've been doing that for a long time.

La Russa retired after the Series, the only manager of a World Series winner to take such a step.

Freese was on the club two more years -- the 2012 season, where he hit a solid .297 with 20 homers and 79 RBI as the team again went as far as the NL championship series, losing in seven games to the Giants; and in 2013, where he wasn't as a good a hitter but the club made the World Series again (the fourth time in 10 years), losing to the Red Sox in seven games. There were no heroics for Freese this time, he batted under .200 in each Series, going just 3-for-19 with seven strikeouts.

His average in 2014 was average, .262, but his new club, the Los Angeles Angels, had the best record in baseball, a fine year until they were swept out the division championship by the underdog Kansas City Royals.

Even without La Russa, the Redbirds kept winning, making another dash toward the Series in 2012 before losing the league championship to the Giants; once again squandering a three games to one lead, dropping three straight at the end by a combined score of 20-1, one of the worst collapses in baseball history. In Game 6 the Cards couldn't solve Ryan Volgelsong and in the last stand lost 9-0.

The finale turned on a bizarre double hit by Giants outfielder Hunter Pence, a ball that hit Pence's flying broken bat three times before dropping in past the reach of Cards' shortstop Pete Kozma. Two runs scored easily and a third crossed when center fielder John Jay fumbled the ball. The rout was on and the Series was over, the Giants winning their second title in San Francisco and seventh overall.

The Cardinals, in the second year under former catcher Mike Matheny, were back in the Series in 2013 after a 97-win regular year and victories over Pittsburgh in the division series in five and over the Dodgers in the NL championship in six.

The Red Sox prevailed in the World Series, however, winning in Fenway Park in the sixth game, the first time since 1918 Boston could celebrate a World Series-clinching victory in their ancient ball yard. The key hit in Game 6 came in the third, when Shane Victorino rattled a two-out, bases-loaded double that killed Cards rookie Michael Wacha, whose mortality had been in doubt after giving up just three runs in 29 postseason innings.

Instead, he handed the Sox six runs in Game 7 and left in the fourth, his face twisted in failure. The Series was the third winner for the once downtrodden Sox in 10 years, their eighth overall.

Wacha was back in 2014, this time on the mound as the Cardinals season came to a stumbling close. The Red Sox wouldn't be there, going from the best in 2013 to a last-place AL East finish, 25 games out of first and 20 games under .500. St Louis, on the other hand, scrambled to their 12th division title, playing what for them was a ragged year, never coming together until September, when they knocked off the Brewers, holders of the league lead for 150 days.

The Birds clinched on the last regular day, then, powered by an unlikely 10-9 victory, laced the Dodgers in four games in the division series. St. Louis had reached a fourth consecutive show in the NL championship.

For those 12 divisional titles since 1969, the Cards had taken the Series just the three times -- 1982, 2006 and 2011. Not a bad record. Not a record to be overly upset by, but not a great record either, not one the fans wanted and/or accepted. And indeed, the city's 250th anniversary provided another disappointment at the ballpark, with San Francisco winning the NL title over the Cards four games to one.

The team's performance in 2014 was once again at the center of baseball, having watched the steroid era die and building a team around the small ball concepts of Herzog and La Russa, defense and pitching, a good thing to do as the homers stopped sailing over the fence and batting averages fell to the lowest since 1972, not that low since the end of the Gibson-era. The Cards were last in the league in home runs with 105, not far ahead of the number McGwire hit by himself in 1998, a season when the Cards led the NL with 223 homers.

But that was a year when everything was different on the field, 15 teams in baseball hit over one homer a game. In 2014 just four clubs accomplished that average.

Steroids were all but gone in the game, with only the return of the tainted Yankee named Alex Rodriguez ruffling the sports pages. The Cards had Jhonny Peralta on the team in 2014, a year after he was banned for 50 games. But he didn't look anything like the Incredible Hulk.

The Birds scraped out wins, with just 16 more runs all year than its opponents.

The low-scoring nature of 2014 put a big price on pitching, something of which the Cards had plenty. They went 32-23 in those slippery one-run games and of the 90 wins in the regular year over half were by either one or two runs.

The veteran utility player, infielder Daniel Descalso, rubbed his chin in contemplation and said, "It was a strange year. We had to battle and fight and claw to just stay in this race."

More to the point, the Cards were dependent on pitching. They tried to find a veteran to go along with ace Adam Wainwright but were left to fend with the youngsters -- especially Trevor Rosenthal, the 24-year-old fireballer who was second best in the NL with 45 saves. Rosenthal, however, lost six games and blew six others, the 10th worst of all the NL's regular finishers.

Pitching, naturally, decided the postseason for the Birds.

The first problem there had to do with the team's best hurler, the 20-game winner Adam Wainwright. He slumped in August with what he called a "tennis elbow" then revived in September to propel the club to the division title. But by the time he reached the Game 5 showdown in NLCS, the big right-hander had thrown over 200 pitches in two starts in the playoffs, not making it out of the fourth inning in either of his games against the Dodgers or Giants.

He came back strong in Game 5, only to be betrayed by the bullpen, which had been scattered and tattered by poor performances all the way through the league series.

In Game 2, the Cards lost their all-star catcher, Yadier Molina. He, his bat, his bullet-arm and his handling of the pitchers -- none of that was around for the last three games.

In Game 3, lefty specialist Randy Choate found himself atop the mound in the 10th with the game knotted 4-4, but gave it away in a snap, walking the leadoff man, giving up a single, then flinging the ball wildly away on a play to first on a sac bunt, allowing the winning run to score.

The Cards lost Game 4 when one of the young studs, Shelby Miller, couldn't hold a 4-1 lead. In Game 5, getting a good performance from Wainwright, St. Louis held a 3-2 edge entering the eighth. Rosenthal was rested in the pen, but had been inconsistent and Matheny apparently had lost confidence.

He had lefties coming up on the Giants. Marco Gonzalez had been used too much, but there were also Choate and Maness. Game 5 -- down three games to one, this was it -- Matheny called in Michael Wacha.

Doctors uncovered a stress fracture in his pitching shoulder in late summer and he was out for two months plus. The injury was still mending when Matheny found him throwing in the bullpen in Game 5 of the World Series. Wacha, a 23-year-old from Texas A&M, came in to start the bottom of the ninth. 3-3.

First, Wacha was wild. A walk, a single. You could see it coming. Wacha, desperate to throw a strike, any kind of strike, came down the middle on Giants outfielder Travis Ishikawa, a journeyman from Seattle, who batted .274 in 47 regular year and had hit but.385 in the Series with seven driven in. He knew how to hit a fading fastball down the middle just above the knees. Game and series. The Giants headed on to win the World Series for the third time in five years.

Pitching was even more important for the Cards in 2015, the tenth year of the second Busch Stadium.

With all the gears clicking, the team took off to a 22-7 start, their best opening run since 1887. Holliday set a record by reaching base in his first 45 games of the season. Six players were selected for the All-star game. By the halfway point of the season, the team's top four pitchers had a combined ERA of 2.84, the best for the club since 1968. The staff finished under 3.00.

By the end of the year, the team had won 100 games for the first time since 2005, but the Birds were wheezing and wounded, racked by injuries to Wainwright and Holliday. Young pitchers were overworked; Molina was again ailing. Rookies had taken up the slack but were fading. The record for the last month of the year was 15-13, no longer the team of April.

In the division series the Cards slumbered through a three games to one loss to the excited Chicago Cubs, looking for their first World Series victory since 1905. John Lackey faced Jon Lester, a pair of teammates on the Red Sox, in the first game, the only one the Cardinals managed to win.

Trying to get the big two game edge in the best-of-five series, Matheny sent out Jaime Garcia, the oft-injured lefty who had come through down the stretch. Garcia, however, was ill. He said later he hadn't been able to sleep for two nights. He was feverish and chilled. He seemed confused on the mound, unable to make a play on a bunt. He gave up five unearned runs in two innings and the Cards couldn't rally.

In Chicago, the Cubs drove their starving fans crazy by hitting six homers to win 8-4 in Game 3. The Cards could not pull themselves off the mat in Game 4, losing the contest and the series.

Theo Epstein, the new president of the Cubs, had been in charge of the Red Sox during its historic 2004 season, beating the Cardinals in the World Series to cap the first Red Sox championship since 1918. After beating the Cards, fans of the downtrodden Cubbies hoped for more magic. There was nothing of the sort, however, as Chicago lost to the Mets in the league championship, keeping the Cubs' World Series drought alive at 107 years.

Entering 2016, St. Louis hadn't won a Series in four years.

Indeed, there had been 13 divisional titles since 1969 and the Cards had taken the Series three times -- 1982, 2006 and 2011. Not a bad record.

A new philosophy had emerged, a corollary to the running, pitching, farm club tenants of the past eighty years.

GM John Mozeliak:

> Realistically the most important thing you've got to do is get into the playoffs. That's a very simple way of thinking about it. You have to win your division. You have a higher probability of having October success. That's really how we think about it. Or, at least, how I think about setting goals for this club going forward.
>
> Once you get in, things happen. If you don't get in, nothing can happen.

Chapter Thirty-Four
A Musical Safari on the St. Louis Scene

2012-2015

Even if other cities tried, they could never reproduce St. Louis's musical heritage. Hometown pride is powerful, and St. Louis can find it in the blues.
-- **Andrew Scavotto**, ***Hidden Assets***

When my wife Marilyn and I reached the start of the Oregon Trail in 2011, we stashed our stuff in our very own house made of St. Louis brick and commenced to nose around the music scene. We'd heard, from the players who reached Oregon during the decade-long run of our music club, that there was much entertainment to be had at the confluence. But we also had that lingering image people get from outside the city -- drab, dangerous, difficult.

The truth about cities can only be discovered first hand. As a veteran of the journalism wars in the Northwest, in New York City and in Washington DC I was naturally cynical of what I had heard. The wife and I became explorers in the contemporary River City, looking for answers to questions about the St. Louis music scene.

At first we were confused, the swirl was kaleidoscopic, the lights spinning. I quickly realized that I could never catch up to everything going on, to all the combinations of style and nuance available on any given St. Louis night. I found that listings were generally useless, even in the age of the Internet. The city's only surviving daily newspaper, the *Post-Dispatch*, in print or online, barely touched the city's offerings, concentrating mostly on visiting stars. The "alternative weekly" *Riverfront Times* did better, but still leaned heavily toward a narrow crowd. Other online listings were acceptable within the small scope of their own niches, but even the listings by the clubs themselves were often inaccurate or incomplete.

I was a man on safari, thrown ashore from a sailing ship without a map. A few months later, after some hacking through the brush, I saw some light. I found the oldest of all the information was best -- word of mouth. Like-minded explorers told me where to find the guitars and the horns, the drums and the voices. I found these Middle West folk friendly, helpful, rarely coy or competitive. They weren't interested in guarding their territory or conniving a buck from a stranger. This was no Vegas, no New Orleans. Nobody asked me where I got my shoes.

Here was a tribe interested in having a good time -- the more the merrier. One local told me there was a core of about 2,000 people out listening to music every night. I started seeing the same people at the same venues. Finding the music in St. Louis took a little doing, but with a little patience and the willingness to listen, the rewards were great.

What I found was quality. From outside the city it is impossible to see the mountain-high level of this quality. The music revolution in St. Louis is not televised. It can't be experienced on Facebook or at home on the couch. Diversity, history and affordability all run ahead of Chicago or Nashville, or Austin or Athens, Ga. St. Louis is no one-trick pony.

We started with the blues, but also found rock and jazz and country. The blues peaked in the nineteen-nineties but by no means did they disappear, even after the many early twenty-first century marches to the cemetery: Bankhead (2000), Crutchfield (2001), Sain (2003), Johnnie Johnson (2005), Townsend (2006), Bennie Smith (2006), Ike Turner (2007), Clayton Love (2010), Rondo (2011).

These players were still fresh in the culture of the underground when we arrived in town. They had been directly seen and experienced by the current players and fans. These performers were also teachers. They shared their knowledge. Their music lived on after they died.

They had become a part of that St. Louis thing, just as all the others did before them, adding to a fabric begun in Babe Conner's music factory and in the syncopated rags of Tom Turpin, stitched together with so many others over 13 decades. Blues rubbed against the walls of discrimination in jobs and education. And while the city was doused in plenty of apathy and historical amnesia, an underground flourished.

Indeed, I found myself tipping my pith helmet and raising a glass. The city, to the consternation of only a few, was still more or less unscathed by the kind of takeover of the music by corporate interests that has reduced other scenes (see Austin, New York, Nashville) to tourist venues featuring the $12 burger or the $8 draft beer. No, the St. Louis we found was not like that.

There, you can quaff a refreshing cold can of Stag at the Venice Cafe for $2 or an excellent microbrew made fresh just around the corner for $4. The rule is no cover, low cover, rarely a ticket over $10.

While the city retained its Southern roots and its racial chasm, the music fans and the players dropped any pretension of superiority and had a good time.

So, please accept our invitation to join our safari, starting on a cold Thursday night in January 2012. Come along as we step into the neon glow of Joe's Cafe.

Joe's is a modern juke joint. Filled with a cascade of found objects from the rubble of the city, it includes a big portrait of "Evelyn West and her $50,000 chest" and the original sign that once introduced the multitudes to Gaslight Square.

Joe's is billed as "The Poor Person's Country Club -- Music Club & Miniature Golf Course." Its items, hundreds in number, are arranged just so with the eye of the artist Bill Christman, a sign maker, co-founder of the City Museum and creator of this pseudo-private club for his neighborhood and his friends.

The joint started Oct. 23, 2003. Here Christman tells us how it began, talking about a "tribe" called the Soulard Blues Band:

> One balmy August night in 2003, three of the "tribe," (Art) Dwyer, (Bob) Kamoske & (John) Mondin waxed lyrical at the

> Excelsior Club north of Forest Park on Union Boulevard for an audience of 12 patrons. I told Art Dwyer we could probably assemble 30 or more audience members at my art studio and sculpture garden, Thus was born Joe's Cafe; we charged $5 for the Band and the patrons supplied their own booze.
>
> Over the next few years, Joe's Cafe was shut down by the city of St. Louis not once, but twice; each re-opening featured the fabulous Soulard Blues Band. Our destinies somehow entwined through thick and thin. Whoda thunk?

The place is still BYOB, bottles of whiskey and coolers of beer encouraged. A balcony hangs around the back and sides, a raised area under a neon sign reading "RADIO" adds to the depth of the place. Old tables of various sizes and shapes are surrounded by an equally diverse collection of old chairs. The colors are muted, red and gold. A crusty guy sells popcorn baskets ($1) from behind a bar. Outside is a garden filled with more stuff, Bob's Big Boy, a full sized plastic buffalo, a pond with two levels of splashing water. You better get there early for a seat.

There we see Tom Hall, the veteran country blues player, appearing on that January night. After his first four songs, he looks at his smart phone, stops a minute, looks up at the crowd, quizzically. "This one's from here in St. Louis," he says. "The text? No, the next tune, 'Frankie and Johnny.'" He plays it quickly, making the story clear. He does "Come On In My Kitchen," the Robert Johnson standard. A couple of young women giggle -- "sssh," others admonish.

That summer it's a 52nd birthday party at Joe's for Brian Casserly, the "Big B," often seen with the Soulard Blues Band, but on this occasion has a trio, with a veteran, Curt Landes, on piano and a youngster, Paul Niehaus IV, on standup bass.

Christman starts the night by passing out black derby hats. Casserly is rotund and round. The derby is his trademark. He walks through the crowd before the show saying hello to friends. Some munch cheese and crackers, others connect with a bottle of Jack Daniels.

Before starting the set, Casserly beams around the room and starts talking: "This is what my aunts and uncles talked about when they described the clubs in New York and San Francisco they went to when I was a kid." He doffs his derby in the direction of the owner,

"My hat is off to Bill Christman. He's a man who lives the unapologetic life. And this is the hippest, coolest thing I do."

He starts with a rendition of "The St. Louis Blues" done in the Armstrong style, which is as good as it gets. The crowd springs to its feet in ovation. Next, Casserly launches into "Bye, Bye Blackbird," the 1926 hit often associated with a couple of other St. Louisans, Josephine Baker and Miles Davis. Casserly says his family "would sing it in four-part harmony sitting round the living room, my mom picking on her banjo."

On "Smokestack Lightnin,'" Landes, a St. Louisan living in New Orleans, rolls a heavy left hand, St. Louis style, and Niehaus beats down the rhythm on his big tall bass, the top of which sometimes get tangled up in the box fans hanging from the ceiling. Bill and his helpers bring out two giant sized birthday cakes as the band wails through a NOLA-seeped "When the Saints Go Marchin' In," a reminder of the departed Bankhead, Crutchfield, Sain, et al.

A couple of friends join the band -- drummer Dan Conner and harpist Sandy Wellman on Albert Collins' "Black Cat Bone." Casserly finishes the night with "What a Wonderful World," Armstrong's 1967 tune once used to brighten a nation locked in division over the Vietnam War. Casserly finds similar spirit sending his crowd, weary of the political deadlock of the Great Recession, out into the warm summer night, smiling just like old Satchmo.

In a chat after the show we find that Casserly's St. Louis experiences began early after his father left Long Island for a job at McDonnell Aircraft in the mid-sixties. The family settled in the suburbs near the plant, in St. Charles, where Brian says he was "surrounded by cows and tornadoes."

> I wanted to be a sax player -- my father wanted me to play oboe -- the neighbor behind us said if you play trumpet I'll give you a trumpet. So I joined a singing group and played trumpet for them -- played trumpet and trombone for them. Been playing trumpet for 40 years.

He played jazz combos in high school then moved to California for a short time but came back to St. Louis.

> I sold my trumpet to get back to St. Louis. When I got back, I got into a new rock 'n' roll band -- in '82 -- the Serapis -- needed a horn section -- reunion rock 'n' roll with jazz horns -- Zappa, Chicago, Steely Dan, ska, reggae -- down on the Landing, mid-eighties -- Kennedy's, Hennigan's, Uncle Sam's Plank house, Lucious Bloomer underground. That was a wild club, people would fall into mikes so we had to hang mikes from the ceiling -- crazy -- nothing but people -- it was the place to go until three in the morning.

He played the riverboats, played with Charlie Creath's grandson, played with a TV sportscaster in a Dixieland Band.

Then, one Monday, Casserly took his horn and his round hat and went down to the Broadway Oyster Bar for the jam. Soon he was the lead singer and horn specialist in the Soulard Blues Band.

Another style entirely was also heard on another trip to Joe's, a hot summer night with the usual good crowd rearranging the chairs and tables for some St. Louis style Country Western swing ala Bob Wills. **The Palominos.** In 1935, Wills and the Texas Playboys had a big hit with "The St. Louis Blues," and the Palominos don't disappoint the Joe's crowd with a jazzy, upbeat treatment. These are a bunch of veteran players, all with swinging nicknames, led by Gary "Big Joe" Hunt on guitar; Johnny "Alamo" Jump, vocals, guitar; Bob "El Guapo" Briendenbach, steel; Justin "Kid Shelleen" Branum, violin; Vince "Bunk House" Corkery on violin.

They all wear the proper hats, but they aren't fooling anybody about rural roots. This is city country right from the get go.

That start is stirring, the two fiddles in the lead on Woody Guthrie's "Union Maid," followed by "Deep Water," a 1947 Bob Wills song, then three fiddle tunes starting with "Stoney Point." The show hits all the gears, the band is as tight as they come, all the harmonies spot crisp.

Before we venture onto another spot, we stay at Joe's for a star-is-born saga from the little juke joint, the story of Nikki and Matt Hill.

Joe's was just half full this night. Matt Hill is unfamiliar to the neighborhood people who frequent the place. This couple, just in their twenties, had only recently left their North Carolina roots, looking to use St. Louis as a launching pad to a career in music. Matt:

> The blues scene there was non-existent. There's no clubs there. The only thing you could find were like 17 blues jams a week. There was no money in any of them. Nobody was hiring any bands. No real gigs. The same 10 jammers came out and played the same four songs they've been playing for 10 years.

Looking for fresh water, Matt met a drummer in St. Louis named Joe Meyer who introduced him to former Fabulous Thunderbird Preston Hubbard, a bass player based at the confluence. Meyer hounded them to move. Nikki:

> It's very attractive here. It's right in the middle of the country. It's cheap. There's tons of clubs. People are great. We came to St. Louis one weekend. And when we drove back and got home, we had decided. Why don't we just move?

That night at Joe's Cafe was just after the move and Nikki had yet to step up with Matt and the band. She sat quietly by herself in a back booth as Matt, Meyer and Niehaus carried on, playing a number of Matt's originals. He put on a show, flinging himself on the stage, howling and chirping, surprising the crowd at every turn.

On the tenth song of the second set, he gestured to Nikki, a strong looking black woman wearing a colorful headscarf. She had no interest in playing the stage wife and when she grabbed the mike, there was no doubt she was something special, jumping right into "Rip It Up," the 1956 killer rockabilly tune first record by Little Richard and covered by Bill Haley and the Comets in the earliest days of rock 'n' roil.

She followed up with another Little Richard song, "Send Me Some Lovin'" off the same early rock page. Matt beamed, the staid crowd danced and he shouted, "This is one of the coolest gigs on the planet."

Cut to two years later and the band is called the Nikki Hill Band. The couple, with Joe Meyer still on drums, has recorded an album and played all around the world, opening for Jimmie Vaughn in Texas, killing audiences in Chicago,

On her Facebook page, Oct. 16, 2014, Nikki posted:

> I have flown 39 times this year, with seven flights to go (not counting the other various forms of public transportation), in 11 different countries, and at least 36 states. I work hard, and I play harder. Turn off your fucking TV.

By the last month of 2015, the pair was still on the roll. A first full-length album, *Heavy Hearts, Hard Fists,* well reviewed, a record that "adds some sultry R&B and Stones-style riff rock to her '50s-rooted rock ' n' roll."

Another place we find is the Blues City Deli, a tiny sandwich shop near the Busch headquarter brewery. The cover at the Deli is zero dollars, even when a performer like Nikki Hill plays. She doesn't forget that the Deli helped get the band its start.

The Deli opened in a remodeled brick building in 2004 after a neighbor told former drummer Vinnie Valenza about an empty building perfect for his budding sandwich business. He'd started in a food truck in the Soulard Market selling hot dogs after giving up 10 years on the stage. He filled the walls with classy posters, paintings and folk art tributes, mostly focused on St. Louis blues greats, but also including out-of-towners like Howlin' Wolf and Muddy Waters.

By 2014, during his 10th year in business, Vinnie, a constant, smiling presence behind the register, finds his place jammed six days a week for lunch and for his twice-weekly live music shows. Vinnie:

> We get a crowd of music lovers, the regulars on Thursday and Saturday, But we also get a lot of younger people, many who are people who come for lunch during the days we don't have music. These are neighborhood people, blue collar, white collar, all kinds, and they, the ones who eat here every day, they are the ones that allow me to do this.
>
> The whole idea in the first place was to bring people together no matter who they are and that's what's happened.

On a summer Saturday, a typical show at the Deli rattled the big window behind the band during a homecoming appearance by a national touring player with deep St. Louis roots, a one-time refugee from Hurricane Katrina known as Rockin' Jake.

Jake and his band were on a three-day, five-gig ramble through the center of a 100-degree plus dome of Midwest air. Awaiting him -- a rousing crew of blues fans out for some music despite the triple-digit temperatures.

He fires off some traditional blues -- "HooDoo Man" and "Do What You Got To Do," then salutes the crowd and the city -- "So great to be back -- what a great blues town -- all the names -- Big George, Rich McDonough, Country Bill -- shout 'em out." Names fly from the crowd, "Oliver Sain, Henry Townsend," he waves his white porkpie hat and launches into "Just Can't Lose the Blues," an original from his days in New Orleans.

He came to St. Louis after he was chased from his home by the winds of Hurricane Katrina in 2005, on tour in New England when the storm hit.

"I watched it on TV from Maine. Just shocked. At first I thought we had dodged the bullet, then the levees broke," he said.

Instead of going back home, he joined his wife who had evacuated to Fort Worth, Texas.

> Then I get a call from my landlord saying you better get down here right away -- stuff is all over the walls, mold all over everything. You better fix this place up, he says. I had a day and half to get everything out and when I got back the city was a bizarre place. People walking around like zombies.

He was saved by St. Louis, however, getting a free apartment for six months through a storm relocation program funded by the Lipton Group, a property management company. "We got to St. Louis and to a person everything was generosity and an outpouring of support. Fans of the bands donated money and I just grew into the music scene."

He continued touring but played the city several times a year, becoming a mainstay at the Deli and a frequent headliner at BB's. As he did he built his reputation as one of the best blues harp players in the country. He put four albums under his belt and plays 200 gigs a year. He left St. Louis in 2012 to join his 90-year-plus mother (Rockin' Mom) in Florida.

At the end of the show that hot summer day at the Deli a bouncing woman dancing a foot from the front of the stage downed an entire bottle of Jake's trademark Badmouth hot sauce and yelled, "We love you, Jake."

Other bands found at the Deli show off the confluence. They include:

-- **Funky Butt Brass Band,** appearing the same day as the Voodoo Fest in New Orleans, putting on a performance of NOLA funk that saved us a 10-hour drive and a $90 ticket. This St. Louis contingent featured Adam Hucke, trumpet; Ben Reece, sax; Aaron Chandler, trombone, vocals; Matt Brinkmann, sousaphone: Tim Halpin, guitar, vocals; Ron Sikes, drums.

It's surprising how well the large horn sound works in the tiny Deli space. St. Louis has been a place for horns for a century. In-your-face brass might be a rugged brew, even at $2 a beer. But Vinnie is a master of the soundboard and manages to make the music easy on the tenderest ear.

This show includes a gentle tribute to Rob, a Deli regular (the quiet guy who always stood over by the door) but is no more on this earth. FBBB plays him out with a dirge, working into some second-line magic in a horn romp that elicits white-hanky waves and a few tears. The set also provides a tribute to Oliver Sain as the band brings many shouts and few more tears with his classic "St. Louis Breakdown."

--Miss Jubilee and the Humdingers: The war is on, soldiers pour through Union Station. Here is a swing band that also dives into R&B, blues and ska. The band lineup can change for its many gigs but is always centered on the forties vocals of Valerie "Miss Jubilee" Kirchoff and the drumming of Dan Conner. Horns abound, hitting that clear note of the St. Louis sound. Kirchoff may be the best-dressed singer in the city, her thrift store outfits never failing to bring a compliment from her steady and devoted crowd.

The young group was formed in 2007 aiming to revive the swinging sounds of forties hot jazz to bring out the dancers. She and Conner created a high-energy jump blues band, a style they've mastered over the years. The group rehearsed for six months before its first show, fittingly held at the Casa Loma Ballroom, a venue virtually unchanged since it opened in 1927. The ballroom centers on its 5,000 square foot hardwood dance floor. Fifties R&B and early rock was added later to Miss Jubilee's set list, one as varied as any in town.

Miss Jubilee has been known to play three gigs in a single day, pushing far beyond the confines of the Deli and Casa Loma, ranging to regular appearances at BB's Jazz Blues and Soups, Beale's on Broadway, the Shafley Bottleworks, the jazz brunch at Evangeline's, the Missouri Botanical Garden, the Thaxton Speakeasy, the Cherokee Street Jazz Crawl, house parties and just about every festival in town.

--Aaron Griffin and Mojo Syndrome -- Aaron put out his first record before he graduated from high school and has played in a variety of groups, including the Soulard Blues Band. His style is built on the tradition of modern blues that carries all the elements of St. Louis blended into the Chicago riffs of the fifties, sixties and seventies. His CD was released at the Deli in 2012 before a cheering crowd that included his mother down front and his father, Larry Griffin, playing guitar in a band that also included the veteran St. Louis harp player and singer, Eric McSpadden.

Griffin and McSpadden have played together longer than Aaron has been alive.

Aaron remembers while growing up going to his father's shows and listening to blues tapes at his house. He was given an acoustic guitar when he was eight and took lessons from sideman Tom Maloney, moving on to an electric guitar when he was 11 then started to go the blues jams in Webster Groves. Naturally, Aaron is soaked in the tradition of Bankhead, Boo Boo Davis and Big George Brock.

Griffin is a graduate of the Baby Blues Showcase, an annual event for young players organized by Jeremy Segel-Moss and held at BB's the Sunday after Thanksgiving.

A third juke joint in town is the most unlikely, perhaps the most obscure club in town. Called **Kinda Blue**, it is located down a dead end street on the South Side, not far from the roaring Interstate. Its owner has taken a duplex house and made half of it into a tiny bar, drinks are BYOB; the bar sits almost on top of the zone (not really a stage) where the band plays.

Records are pasted on the ceiling and posters line the walls. Cookies and munchies are provided for the 20 or so people who pack the room. Jazz is the main entertainment with players like Dave Black, Brian Vaccaro and Joe Mancuso appearing. These are all quality musicians who appear around the city.

Black was winner of the *Riverfront Times* artist of the year for jazz in 2011 and the founder of Brilliant Corners in 1997. He also works with Javier Mendoza, a Latin-pop singer/songwriter and Asako Juboki, a violinist for the St. Louis symphony and teaches music at Webster University.

Vaccaro is another teacher. He released an album with his trio in 2011. Mancuso is a singer of jazz standards who won the *RFT* best jazz vocalist award in 2012. He appears at a variety of venues around town, including the Sheldon Theater.

Another regular group that appears there is **Western Satellites,** anchored by veteran St. Louis singer Margaret Bianchetta and the ace lap steel player Bob Briendenbach, with John Furber on guitar, and Vince Corkery on bass. They call their style Americana Blue Swing. The sound in the tiny joint was excellent, the quality surprising for such a place. It's a house party.

Bianchetta is well known around St. Louis both for her singing and flute playing. She performed nationally in the band Spatz in the mid-eighties and made a record with her next groups, Hot Club Canary. She then held forth as the leader of the Mighty Big Band, an R&B outfit that also featured Ike Turner alum Billy Gayles.

She is also the organizer of a bizarre annual Christmas show, Noelathon, held at BB's for over 20 years, featuring local bands singing Christmas tunes with wacky lyrics.

BB's Jazz, Blues & Soups is the best-known club in town. Its history dates back into the years when blues was making its revival and has flourished into the twenty-first century. Not only jazz and blues can be found there, but also soul, funk, rock and country. It holds benefits and raffles, contains a museum of posters and photographs, stages the annual Baby Blues Showcase and celebrates birthdays and anniversaries.

Looking at its calendar for just the third week in November 2014, we find listings for 14 different acts, including Mancuso and Black together on a Monday, a benefit on a Sunday. Local blues bands, out of town blues bands, solos, duos. Some the players, like Leroy Pierson and Tom Hall, are at the heart of the scene, others, like Aaron Griffin and Marquis Knox, are up and coming.

Two groups of regulars were of particular note that week -- **The St. Louis Social Club** and **Rough Grooves**, both of whom feature a big man with a big reputation, Rich McDonough, a hard guy for the explorer of the music scene to miss, a man whose story is the story of that St. Louis thing.

He is in his early fifties, a high school dropout from South County who quit school when he was 16. His father was a pipefitter. His first full-time job was in a department store warehouse. There was little music growing up, "we weren't the Jackson family" Rich cracks wise as we talk outside the club one night.

At 17, he saw an ad for a B.B. King album on TV and decided that was the way to play a guitar. The year was 1980, classic rock was the style, hip-hop and MTV were about to be born. This music didn't interest him, however, but records by Albert King, ZZ Top and the Allman Brothers did.

In 1983, McDonough met Keith Doder and started going to the North Side. He started playing with Doder at Witt's Lounge on Martin Luther King Boulevard.

He played in jams with Tommy Bankhead at Sadie's. He played with Sain and Johnnie Johnson. At the time, the mid-eighties, Larry Griffin was playing with Bankhead and had to leave town for a couple of weeks, so McDonough filled in.

> Tommy was always really cool to us young guys, That's why everybody really loved him. A lot of the big guys were really cool. Very little did you run into somebody who would run you off.

Then he heard Rondo Leewright.

> That's what I really wanted. I followed him around with my guitar. He'd let me sit in at the end of the night. When I found out he needed a guitar I called him on the phone and he said "Do you play slide?" I said "yeah."
>
> I didn't play it. I had only the most basic idea of slide. It was baptism by fire in his band. In the first two or three months people got a chance to hear the worst slide you ever heard. But the band was very patient and I started developing my sound.

McDonough started with Rondo when he was 24 and played with him for five years. They played Blueberry Hill every Friday night, played BB's, played on the East Side, playing five, six nights a week. He went to Europe with Rondo in 1990.

Once the demons of addiction laid Leewright low, McDonough played with the remnants of Rondo's band until he was asked by Art Dwyer in 1997 to join up with Soulard. In addition to that group he played with Larry Griffin and Eric McSpadden. He was now a real bluesman, in demand.

Rough Grooves evolved out of that time. McSpadden was the harp player. Sharon Foehner joined up in 2003 to play bass. McDonough went on the road with Rockin' Jake for a few long trips (including one to the Oregon Coast) but the band kept going.

When he tired of the road, he came back home and settled into the regular Rough Grooves gigs at BB's, also playing with the St. Louis Social Club. He is a festival mainstay. In 2012 the Blues Society named him Artist of the Year.

"I just keep on keeping on," he says, pushing back his chair and heading back up on the stage to play another heartfelt, sometimes daring set of blues, sitting in his chair on the side of the stage, his electric guitar a toy in his big hands, an expression alternating from peace to pain.

Rough Grooves scattered in 2015, each member branching out into new duos, jams and regular appearances: McSpadden playing with Griffin; Foehner as Sharon Bear with Doug Foehner; and McDonough in the Rhythm Renegades, a band that also includes John May, and in the new Green McDonough Band with singer Laura Green and bass Jonathan Schumacher.

Its members remained, however, as charter members of **The St. Louis Social Club**, an all-star group that only plays together during gigs at BB's. The lineup varies at times but usually includes McDonough, guitar; McSpadden, vocals and harp; Foehner, bass; along with Benet Schaeffer on drums; Casserly on trumpet; Maloney, guitar and various keyboard and sax players. Formed in 2002, the band doesn't record or tour.

Also on the list for BB's that November week was **Joe Pastor and the Legacy Jazz Band**, led by Pastor, a percussionist, vibraphone player who's played with Rough Grooves, the Soulard Blues Band, Boo Boo Davis, and drummed alongside Johnnie Johnson. His jazz compositions range from classic to avant-garde.

Another is **"Bumblebee" Bob Kamoske** whose guitar does indeed float like a bumblebee. He's also played with Soulard and others around town, but by 2015 generally performed solo. His steel guitar has something in common with the Joplin rags and with hillbilly country blues.

Marsha Evans and the Coalition is often on the bill at BB's as the stirring blues singer, a onetime backup for Fontella Bass and lead singer for OIiver Sain, continues her illustrious career. Her voice is as fresh as ever, stirring and cocky, filled with emotion. Recently she's headlined both the Big Muddy and BluesWeek festivals, made memorable New Year's Eve appearances, and stopping in Soulard and at various house parties, weddings and other private events.

Blind Willie and the Broadway Collective is also often on the bill at BB's. Willie is Willie Dineen and he's not blind. He plays jazz in the cool style and the free style, listening to his audience and deftly rattling the sax at several depths. He moved to St. Louis as a teenager and began playing the saxophone in college. In 2011, he released a record of all original material called *Born to Horn.*

Down the street from BB's we found another of the foundation clubs of St. Louis, the Broadway Oyster Bar, home of the longest running blues jam in America. The building was built in 1843, a stop along the dusty wagon road in and out of the city. Its been added on to and subtracted from until it's stage is a kind of outdoor indoor venue, a patio heated in winter and warm in summer bands playing every night with a music schedule of at least 10 shows a week.

In 2015, owners John and Vicki Johnson made their most recent expansion, adding new room to the restaurant, this one filled with collected items from New Orleans.

BOB is connected at the hip with the Crescent City down the river, its Cajun food voted best in St. Louis year after year, imports from NOLA appearing regularly on the bandstand. Funky Butt plays here often as does **Aaron Kamm and the One Drops.**

Kamm's style is a blend he calls roots reggae and Mississippi River blues. Add a little dub, soul and jazz and you have a confluence gumbo -- whatever Kamm feels like throwing into the pot. The band has made three records and has recently been doing some Middle West tours.

The N'Orleans connection took root in BOB when Johnson, a former painting contractor, took over the joint nearly 15 years ago. He makes frequent scouting trips to the Big Easy, looking for bands and recipes, making contacts with crawfish suppliers and picking up an occasional voodoo doll.

To call this a dive bar was once probably accurate. But under the Johnson guidance the food got better, the kitchen got bigger and the bands grew in stature and quality. The club has lost its sleaze. To prove the point, when you visit one of the newly remodeled rest rooms, take a look around at the extravagant tile work on the walls. To say the Oyster Bar is a mainstay of underground St. Louis is to state the obvious. At the bar we found out-of-towners and people who swear they are there every night.

The Monday jam at BOB is special, conducted under the watchful eye of Art Dwyer, leader of the Soulard Blues Band for over 35 years. There's nothing like this jam anywhere this explorer has been, not in New Orleans or New York, not Chicago nor Austin. Let's drop in one night for a peek; an initial sighting not long after our safari began in 2012.

The heat on this July night has slightly abated and the unconditioned tropical air is soft on the outdoor patio of the Oyster Bar. Tonight's special is $5 for Tchoupitoulas Tea, a deceptively sweet concoction suitable as long as the drinker can pronounce its name.

Dwyer, his Rasta pony-tail gleaming in the stage lights, his shirt and slacks cool and perfectly pressed, waves a hand from behind his standup bass and, with the ease of an Ellington, hits the downbeat. With him are Marty Abdullah on vocals; Dr. Drum (Kirk Grice), drums; and Tom Maloney, guitar. Maloney dominates the first set doing a particularly lively run on "Down Home Blues" and taking flight on "The Thrill Is Gone." His is a touch not felt in the Chicago-style blues players, a subtle softness that leaves room to get down to the heart of the matter.

Abdullah, billed as the welterweight champion of the rhythm and blues, sings out a soulful style that connects directly with the crowd. His voice is filled with silk and smoke, and his impish look draws in everybody from all four corners of the room. Just the latest in a series of exceptional lead singers of the Soulard bunch, Marty never skips a beat.

As the band does its thing, jammers start flowing in, stacking instruments, looking around, talking to friends, slurping down a beer, taking a quick shot from a small glass. First up is sax player Art Pollard, who steps in on "All Night Long," with a smoothness we expect in this town. He's from across the river and his most regular gig is Sunday morning at the Community Mission Baptist Church in East St. Louis.

Artie steps aside for the second set to let Paul Jackson, who sang in Oliver Sain's band, stand out, playing his electric bass as he shows off his years of experience and his smoky voice on "You Send Me."

Others up and going include Chuck Loeb on harp; Catfish on drums; Maliki Grice, the 12-year-old Son of Drum, on electric bass; Larry Griffith on guitar, Mike from Indiana on guitar, Slim from Memphis on bass and Dan Connor from Miss Jubilee, the night's third drummer.

Eventually Dwyer comes back up to complete the circle, the night cooler still, the drinks warm and cozy, the crowd easy and settled. He can still say Tchoupitoulas.

In 2015 the jam still prospered. On a late night in November, your intrepid explorer finds a new player in town up on stage, a Texas transplant named John McVey, playing lead with the Soulard contingent. McVey was leader of the popular Houston band The Stumble before relocating in Austin. He didn't find the scene there what he was looking for but is excited to now be in St. Louis. In late 2015 McVey also started appearing at Hammerstone's in Soulard and at the Venice Cafe.

Across the street from BB's is the third point of the Broadway triangle -- **The Beale on Broadway**, a double venue with inside and outside stages. Opened in 2000, here is the most recent in the trio of clubs in the downtown just south of Busch Stadium. The schedule is the most stable of the three, just about every night held down by a regular band or two.

Bud Jostes is the owner. He named the place to make a connection with Memphis (the self-proclaimed "home of the blues") but has in his lineup more blues bands in a week than Beale Street can muster in a month.

In fact, looking at a recent *USA Today* list of the Ten Best Bars on Beale Street in Memphis, one finds an Irish bar featuring dueling pianos, an Elvis imitator bar, a country bar, a hotel piano bar, three places that feature no music at all, a place with karaoke five nights a week, and BB's Blues Bar, which features the same group -- B.B. King's Blues Club All-Star

Band -- four nights a week. Thankfully, there's also Mr. Handy's Blues Hall, with bands every night.

Compared to BB's 14 different bands a week and BOB's 10 to 12 a week, already there's a wide distance between St. Louis and Memphis, both in quantity and quality.

Now add The Beale -- another nine shows a week, in 2014 with the regulars: Kim Massie (Tuesday and Thursday), Miss Jubilee (Tuesday), Roland Johnson (Wednesday and Saturday), Ground Floor Band (Thursdays and Friday); the Soul Reunion (Sunday) and a Monday jam. Beale's also has out of town bands headlining Friday and Saturday (from Oklahoma City and Chicago in November 2014) as well regular stints by Jeremiah Johnson, Marquis Knox, Mike Aguirre, Al Halliday and Skeet Rogers in the Friday, Saturday and Sunday slots.

Jostes arrived in St. Louis in 1989 after spinning blues platters on a college radio station in New Mexico. He was surprised to find people like Bankhead, Sain and Townsend playing the bars of his new city.

After several years as booker then owner of the Soulard Ale House he began gazing at an empty building across South Broadway from BB's. He financed it on a shoestring and got three homeless men to help him renovate what is now the inside portion of the venue. He said that even now nothing in the club's construction is level.

But his blues are pure, played on the level. To wit:

-- **Kim Massie:** An East Sider in her late forties, Massie is cut from the Etta James/Aretha Franklin mold. She's big and brassy, tender and pure of note. She's confident and cool, able to talk directly to an audience, even in concert settings like the Sheldon Theater or at the Missouri Botanical Garden summer series.

But it's at The Beale where she is most frequently seen and appears most at home, whether it's rendering a heartfelt "At Last" or convincing the tourists to drop a dollar in the tip jar.

-- **Roland Johnson:** A true pro, with a voice straight out of a soul music greatest hits collection, Johnson moves with the ease of a cat and can also charm a crowd out of all its loose change. He makes James Brown, Bobby "Blue" Bland and Otis Redding come alive week after week, twice a week down by the river on South Broadway.

His band is all-star quality, an example of the kind of sidemen who flesh out that St., Louis thing. They include Eugene Johnson, vocals, bass; Lew Weiner III, sax, vocals; Steve Martin, guitar; and Al Lawrence, drums.

As the songs slide by -- "Georgia," "A Little Bit of This, A Whole Lot of That," "Heart of the City" -- the crowd eases down in a glow of lights and feeling.

-- **Ground Floor Band:** The group is the vehicle for another East Sider, Charles Hunt, a clever singer and full-blown bluesman who's seen most everything in his life, including a long stint as half of the recording duo Ross & Hunt.

Hunt takes some time to let me in on his life before one of his sets:

> I was born April 6, 1950, in East St. Louis. I started taking lessons on guitar when I was 11 or 12 -- after about five or six years I got into a band, Little Soul, playing at a music store. Then I got started in a band called the Corvettes with a guy named Big Bud.
>
> That's how I met Ross, James Ross; we used to call him Catman. He had a hit record back in the early sixties and he traveled with Albert King. They went all over of the world. Albert wanted me to go with him, too, but I had a job.
>
> St. Louis closed in those days at midnight or one o'clock but Brooklyn (on the East Side) stayed open till six in the morning. Down there in the seventies me and Ross started playing. We started getting a lot of gigs, but I still had my day job.
>
> I worked for 33 years. I was a maintenance mechanic at a chemical plant -- a zinc plant -- Amax Zinc. Then came Big Rubber Zinc. I worked all day and played all night. That zinc plant was interesting work. I loved what I was doing. I'd get dirty, but I'd love it. I learned a lot of stuff. I learned how to weld, how to pipe fit, how to work with pumps, a lot of stuff.
>
> I played with Ross up into the eighties. We did an album in 1975. *Rosebush.* The Ground Floor Band came together in the eighties, over on the North Side. Then, over there, disco slowed it all up. I got into a place called Molly's over in Soulard. Played there every Thursday for almost 10 years until they closed it. It was real nice. When I first started in Molly's there weren't nobody in the place. In six months we started packing up that place. We got going from there.
>
> After it closed up I still always had a place to play. I tried to sound like other musicians. But I never could. So I just developed

> my own style. I just can't play like nobody else. I tried and tried but I just can't do it, so I put my own style on the guitar and that's what I play. If like it, you like it, if you don't, you don't.
>
> I'm lucky to be still playing. I retired from the zinc two years ago (2010.) I like playing here (Beale's.) It's steady. It's easy. I'm still learning.

-- Jeremiah Johnson and the Sliders: I happen to catch Jeremiah on his first gig at The Beale, backed by a rhythm section and two horns -- Jim Rosse and Stu Williams. Rosse plays a trumpet, Williams the sax. They've toured with Little Feat, Johnnie Johnson, and Bob Weir of Rat Dog

The band is greeted by a full house, a group made up of mostly young locals particularly fond of pounding their beer glasses on the wooden tables. Jeremiah is dressed in his cowboy costume -- white shirt, black hat, but he's a blues man all the way, a young blues man whose touch is pure and whose sound is like the ring of the liberty bell.

He does all originals, a three-set show running past two o'clock in the morning. Jeremiah's songwriting shows a working class attitude.

The blues came from people who held jobs and this cat works outside five days a week year round. He sings about women, known and imagined, old and new, about work, about life.

Of particular note is his song "Southern Drawl," introduced with some kind words about his grandmother, a woman who came from the Kentucky tobacco country and raised him for most of his childhood. The song breaks through the laughter of the crowd, the conversations stop, the bartender doesn't pour. We become transfixed in the spell. The words ride through on the waves of guitar, trumpet, sax, flute, bass and drum.

"There ain't nothing wrong with a little southern drawl," he sings. "Watch a baseball game -- it's a crackerjack night. Let the home runs fly. Listen to a little Johnny Cash -- Go to church on Sunday -- bust my ass on Monday -- There ain't nothing wrong with a southern drawl."

Born in 1973, he grew up on the South Side and wanted to play an instrument when very young.

> Both my parents were hippie types, My father was two terms in Nam, came back, grew his hair long, beard long and was into what was then modern rock and roll, what you'd call classic rock now.

My mother didn't have enough money to even rent me an instrument. We were pretty poor. I remember drinking powdered milk. I wouldn't have had an instrument at all if wasn't for school. My father and mother were divorced when I was six. I would just see him every other weekend.

He lived out in West County. My mother lived in a mostly black area. Every other weekend I was brought out into a hard-core white racist environment. My father and my grandfather -- that's what they learned. They didn't know any better. So it was a weird deal, balancing that. So I was out there with whites racist against blacks and going to school where the blacks were teaching their kids to beat me up because I was white.

But through it all I didn't really get upset or mad about it. I just assumed this is how it is; deal with it. When you grow up in St. Louis . . . you know, I think that's why it continues on. You just sort of accept it. This is the way it is. I didn't know why people were the way they were. My best friends when I grew up were all black kids. There were only a couple of white kids around and I didn't care who anybody was as long as they were cool to me.

-- **Marquis Knox:** Marquis got his early lessons from Henry Townsend and Big George Brock and started playing clubs in 2006, age 15. John May, the BB's owner, saw a star in the making:

> The big question is always the future of blues. All the innovators are dying out and the future of blues is in danger of becoming white rock 'n' roll. Right now this kid should be on at every blues festival in the country.
>
> He's got a big voice like Muddy Waters, and he's got that machismo. He's really stunning when you hear him. He's rough and raw, and he's pure.

Knox adds:

> I listen to hip-hop, but blues is exciting. I don't care what nobody thinks. I got some friends who like the blues. There's a lot a young people that like the blues, but they don't want to say they like it. They want to make sure their name's kept up. They don't want everybody to know what else they like, because they want to make people think they're big and bad with the hip-hop. That's not where it's at. All that stuff fell down from the blues.

Marquis first performed in fourth grade during a Black History Month celebration. By age 20, he released his third record. He's opened for B.B. King, played Europe and by 23 is a mainstay at the St. Louis festivals and clubs around town.

"I got a whole bunch of tricks lined up," he said. He adds that people never believe when he tells them his age. They can't believe someone so young "can sing the blues in a traditional way, that I'm not changing it up, keeping it the way (early blues performers) did it."

Big Mike Aguirre and the Blu City All Stars -- Another of the young players, this one seeped in the East Side, in Albert King, Stevie Ray and Magic Sam. He got started at age 19 with John May's old band, the Crying Shame, playing both the electric lead and acoustic solo.

After some coaching from Big George, David Dee and Boo Boo Davis, Mike founded the Blu-City All-Stars in 2010. He's developed into a mainstay, playing frequent weekends at the three South Broadway clubs, making festival appearances and packing the Blues City Deli.

He nailed down the Sunday slot at The Beale in the fall of 2014, where Marquis Knox is a frequent guest. In 2013, he was the St. Louis representative in the national blues competition in Memphis.

Al Holliday and The East Side Rhythm Band -- Another band from Illinois, only this one has more to owe Ike and Tina then Albert King. Funk is the word here. Old school uplifting soul. An *RFT* critic heard a little Joe Cocker in the mix, maybe some Fats Domino.

Holliday is also fond of horns and deploys the St. Louis sound to good effect, latching onto the river bottom whenever given the opportunity. This band hasn't been around long, but is snagging gigs downtown and working on a second CD.

The Bottoms Up Blues Gang -- A feast of seasoned fare. The sound ranges from twenties bromides refreshed with the zip of a kazoo, a well-spoken Ani DeFranco or a snappy original you might have heard before. The core of the band is the singing of Kari Liston and the guitar of Jeremy Segel-Moss, but on any given night, the gang of players expands.

The band developed in the shadow of Bennie Smith, Townsend, Sain and the other giants. Liston and Segel-Moss listened carefully and can now bring that St. Louis thing to the table night after night. The crowds, like the band members, change with the various venues. The core -- band and crowd -- is always in the mood to party. As the gigs roll by -- three to four a week -- there doesn't seem to be a let down in energy. They are infused with the spirit.

Liston was born in South County, May 27, 1977. She went to school with Brian Curran, another St. Louis musician, "whose father had a recording studio in his basement, his dad had this stuff. He also had a pool and we'd have pool parties, playing and jamming and making up songs on the fly. That was my first introduction into singing live around people."

The band came together at The Beale, starting after Kari, Jeremy and Adam Andrews, a young harp player, found themselves one Monday night as the only people sitting at the bar. Kari remembers:

> Brian called me up to sing a couple of songs and then he brought Jeremy up and Adam up and then he introduced us all to each other. We didn't know each other at all. And we started talking. Six months later we were a band and a year later we had a CD. It just all kind of happened.
>
> Jeremy dubbed us the Bottoms Up Blues Band because all we did was drink and play blues. One day we were sitting around and I go "how many people are there in the band?" And we started counting people up and there's maybe eight. And so I go, "that's not a band, that's a gang."' So that was the joke and when we got our first gig we were going "what will we call ourselves?" And so we went with Bottoms up Blues Gang.

In 2014, the BUBG opened for B.B. King before close to 3,000 people at the Peabody Opera House and issued its fourth CD. The band plays about one-third of its gigs on the road with frequent appearances in New Orleans and Colorado.

Beyond the downtown triangle and the juke joints, the clubs spread around the city, gathered in districts like Soulard and the Delmar Loop, the Grove and Mid-Town. Here, as well as at private parties, public events and various festivals and holiday celebrations, the musicians fan out on a variety of schedules. Here are some of the performers we've come across.

Brian Curran -- A blues singer-guitarist of the traditional inclination, from the same South County area as Kari Liston. At 13, he heard an old bluesman playing some old songs. The singer was John Lee Hooker and Curran was hooked.

"I fell in love with the sound. It was just one voice and a guitar, and that was haunting to me," Curran says. "I was captured. (Hooker) had this thing nobody else has. That appealed to me, and I searched that out."

He has been studying and playing blues, beginning in his father's basement, for nearly 20 years.

Pokey LaFarge -- "What is America without swing or ragtime?" Pokey asks, thinking about the history of music in St. Louis. "What is the South or Chicago without the blues; what are any of us without jazz?" He added that he plays for "people out there who haven't heard real American music."

> I like being from St. Louis because it's an underdog city -- people are very humble. Being that I've always been a world traveler, I've kept my Midwestern roots, and it has helped people start talking about St. Louis. And that's what we want.
>
> We're very proud that we didn't have to move to New York City or Los Angeles or Nashville or Austin or Portland or Seattle to say that we made it, you know? We stayed right home in St. Louis. I think St. Louis weeds out the weak.

LaFarge was born in 1983 as Andrew Heissler in Bloomington, Ill., halfway between St. Louis and Chicago. His grandfather supplied his first guitar. He heard blues in Normal, Ill., on a pizza parlor CD player. He read Kerouac. He listened to the old-timey music of cartoonist R. Crumb. Upon hearing country star Bill Monroe at age 16, he traded his grandfather's guitar for a mandolin.

He graduated high school in 2001 and hitchhiked west. He took up the name Pokey LaFarge, a childhood nickname from his mother. He met Ryan Koenig and Joey Glynn of The Rum Drum Ramblers while playing on a street in Asheville, N.C. Adam Hoskins joined Glynn and Koenig to form the South City Three, which joined up with Pokey in 2009.

On July 16, 2013, Pokey landed on the David Letterman television show, a rare network appearance for anybody from St. Louis. Fans around town pulled up a chair or a barstool for the broadcast. A Pokey watch party was hosted at the Royale, a South Side bar where a packed courtyard of fans gathered.

Royale owner Steven Smith, said:

> There's a certain level of cooperation that you have to get to in this town to get to an understanding. He's got it. He understands it. And it doesn't hurt that he's very hard working and talented as well. It's a musicians' kind of city here.
>
> Despite the fact that we don't really recognize that it is, that's how we are recognized around the country and around the world. So, he gets it. And he's been able to take it to the next level. And it's kind of fun watching when a local boy does good.

On the TV, LaFarge makes his thirties move on the big-headed microphone saying, "We're gonna take you back to St. Louis now." Into "Central Time" he goes, a joyful little swinger about life in the Midwest. His hair is buzz cut above the ears, the sharp navy suit flows right down to the black-and-white spats.

In November of 2014, Pokey signed with Rounder Records, the Nashville label of Robert Plant, Bela Fleck and Son Volt. LaFarge plays St. Louis regularly. In 2014, he also touched down in New Zealand, Australia, India and Europe, where he played the Moulin Blues Festival in the Netherlands. But he ended up the 2014 at home, playing a free New Year's Eve show before the shivering multitudes at Grand Center.

There was also no stopping him in 2015, playing everywhere from Zurich to Birmingham, Ala.; from Dublin to New Orleans.

Rum Drum Ramblers -- A string band led by Mat Wilson falls into the young/experienced category that evolved from punk rock and mohawks. The group moved more toward blues in 2014, playing clubs like Off Broadway and the Blues City Deli, sometimes helping raise money for Local Harvest, a market featuring homegrown produce.

Wilson is a standout on the scene, singing in a distinct style and rattling away on his loaded guitar, often playing with the Kansas City transplant, Little Rachel.

Dawn Weber -- Her website proclaims: "Jazz infused, Funk inspired, Electronica Injecting, Classical Cool, Soulful Siren! Singer, Songwriter, Trumpeter, Composer, Arranger, Dancer, Entertainer!"

She left home at 16 to study trumpet in the North Carolina School of the Arts in Winston-Salem. There she took jazz and classical trumpet classes and lessons for four years. The NCSA band toured during school breaks including an appearance at Carnegie Hall. She studied classical trumpet under the principal trumpet player of The Cleveland Orchestra.

In 1998, she moved to the confluence and things began to swing, namely Vargas Swing, a legendary group that put out a CD called *Fire* with all original Weber compositions. The group toured for two years from the West Coast to the Keys. Next was the Urban Jazz Naturals -- House Music, Drum and Bass, Trip Hop, and Hip Hop. She was the songwriter on two CDs. She did two more discs with Mo Egeston as *Remix Project -- Vol. 1 and Vol. 1.5.*

Weber is also fully engaged on the scene, popping up with the Bottoms Up Blues Gang, playing a Saturday afternoon at the Blues City Deli, or playing in a duo with a keyboard, singing her originals. She's also in Electro Funk Assembly, a spinoff from the Jazz Naturals, high-energy house style.

Tommy Halloran's Guerrilla Swing -- His website lists "Influences: Billie Holiday, Louis Armstrong, Lester Young, Chet Baker, Charlie Parker, Leon Redbone, Fats Waller, Duke Ellington, Jack Teagarden, Nat King Cole, Miles Davis, Nina Simone, Thelonious Monk, Warne Marsh."

He's another guy -- like Pokey -- who wears a suit to work. "I'll play 300 times this year," he says. "So it's a job. But gigs are only four hours a night. That still leaves 20 hours a day for leisure." This includes solo, in a duo with a violinist and with his three-piece Guerrilla Swing band, playing the hits from 1920 to 1945.

His parents played classic jazz and blues around the house and Tommy has been out there performing for 20 years, making eight records (with Tom Maloney and Kari Liston among many others) in the process. He says his love of swing came from a teenage ska band called graHm in 1993, age 16.

He started playing full time out of high school: Ambiguous, Rowdy Cum Lowdies, Jon Bonham & Friends.

He calls the music he's evolved toward simply jazz. "I call it jazz, but serious players can get bent outta shape. And I don't go down to BB's and say I'm a bluesman. It's a netherworld where I like to hang out."

"And I thought it would be possible in St. Louis to make it work if I put myself out there, made enough phone calls, and hustled enough. And it's really worked out. To make it work for me, I need to play five to six times a week – that's the magic number.

Thus, we find him listed on Stag Night at the Livery, a dive bar on Cherokee Street, and at Jazz at the Bistro, the swank new Grand Center jazz club. Stag Night also celebrated an anniversary in 2014, 10 years on Cherokee, three bands, $5 cover, ice cold Stags in the can, a buck each.

In 2015, Halloran took up a regular residency at the Bistro and in 2016 became a fixture at the Venice Café Tuesday jam led by Jeremy Segel-Moss.

Mellissa Neels -- Her inspiration comes from Chuck Berry, Bonnie Raitt and Patti Thomas of the St. Louis group Patti and the Hitmen. Neels' experience is from two decades of club dates and festivals. Add in 14 years building minivans on the Chrysler line in Fenton and it all adds up to a St. Louis blues singer.

Born in Oakville in South County, July 13, 1974, Neels heard a lot of Joplin, Cream, Delany & Bonnie and Ray Charles on her mother's record player growing up. But it was a tape of Chuck Berry's "Greatest Hits" played on family trips to the Lake of the Ozarks that got her going.

"I thought, man, I want to learn how to play guitar like Chuck Berry." Eventually, in 2003, she opened for Berry at his regular Duck Room gig.

> I was so star-struck. He signed the card that had my name and Chuck's name on it -- he was really nice. We were told not to talk to him unless he spoke to us. But he wanted to meet me and say hi -- it was just a great experience.

Neels had met another hero far earlier -- in the late eighties when she was 15.

> It was sophomore year in high school. Bonnie Raitt came to the Muny Opera stage that summer.
>
> Before the concert my mom says I should write her a note -- tell her you are into her music, you admire her and she's a big influence on you. I go, "Mom, we are never going to meet Bonnie

> Raitt." We go to the concert. We send the note back to her and it got to the right person and she sent out two backstage passes for my Mom and I.
>
> She told me to keep playing those blues. From then on I was determined to do something with the guitar.

By 1998, she formed a band through an ad in the *Riverfront Times.* All this came at the same time she held down her day job at Chrysler building Dodge Caravans on the assembly line, a job that started in 1995. In 2005, she had to stop playing to work the night shift. She stayed with Chrysler until 2008 when the company ended her career as an autoworker by closing the plant, a facility that once employed 8,000 people.

By 2014, the current Melissa Neels Band was on the rise, more gigs, more places. Also, she was part of the all-women blues/rock band The Pie Tarts.

Nelly -- The undisputed king of hip-hop in St. Louis.

Since his debut solo album, *Country Grammar,* in 2000, he'd sold more than 20 million albums, had nearly a dozen Top 10 singles (including 2012's "Just a Dream") and was rated the No. 3 overall artist of the decade 2000-2010 by *Billboard* behind Eminem and Usher.

Starting in 2007, he's held an annual Black & White Ball -- first at the plush Chase Park Plaza Hotel, then, in 2013, moving over to the equally swank Four Seasons, entertaining an invited list of music and city bigwigs in dress clothes colored black and white.

"With the Black & White Ball I wanted to start something to celebrate St. Louis," Nelly said at the 2012 gala. "Nice dinner, nice evening, nice time, nice night of music and entertainment. It's a chance to give something back, I thought that was a hot thing to do."

He rarely plays St. Louis outside of surprise appearances in places like Blueberry Hill in University City, the neighborhood where he grew up. But he spreads his money throughout the community, opening a recording studio and helping young musicians.

Nelly was born Cornell Haynes Jr. in Austin, Texas, on Nov. 2, 1974, and moved to St. Louis when he was in grade school, starting the hip-hop group St. Lunatics in 1993, age 19. He signed a national record deal in

1999 and exploded onto the charts in 2000 when the single "Country Grammar" notched 8.4 million units.

He followed up the album *Country Grammar* with two more No. 1 hits from *Nellyville* in 2002 and did the unheard of -- a simultaneous release of separate albums, *Sweat* and *Suit*, in 2004. They sold over 700,000 combined in the first week. In 2008 he made his fifth studio album, a disc that featured the rising star Ashanti on *Body on Me.*

"My career has gone phenomenal," Nelly beamed as he looked across the room full of splendidly dressed St. Louisans that night at the Chase. "My music is about growth -- to me 10 years at anything is a blessing."

But in 2013, a new disc, *M.O.,* showed how fickle the fates of the music industry can be, selling just 15,000 units in its debut week. By 2015, his style had changed to a more funkified sound and his gigs had moved into small venues.

Also in 2015, Nelly had finished a second season of his reality show on television. Like the album, it's called *Nellyville* and fits a family-friendly formula of such shows, this one on BET, the black channel. He was also reported to be working on an eighth studio album.

Most of the show centered on St. Louis and the Nelly family and musical friends, shot in St. Louis, at his suburban and city recording studio.

Other rappers: Beyond Nelly, the St. Louis hip-hop scene is deep and wide, with dozens of artists recording, presenting stage shows at venues like the Pageant, the Ready Room, FUBAR ("F---d Up Beyond All Recognition") and The Gramophone, and at house parties and small club venues on both sides of Delmar. One of the rappers is **Tef Poe**, an artist whose reputation is of someone who tells the story of St. Louis.

Poe's rating of 50 St. Louis rappers include **T. Prince, Doorway, Aurelius the Saint, Legend Camp, Thi'al, OOOPS, Prince Ea, and Tag Team**. Their shows are way underground, but they are there to be found by fans of the music.

Ryan Spearman Band -- Running a little late, we catch the folkie Spearman on the grassy hill at the band shell of the Missouri Botanical Garden. Spearman and his somewhat country band kick into "Cripple

Creek," the dedication going to John Hartford, the St. Louis cousin of Tennessee Williams and winner of Grammies in three different decades.

Spearman starts into a story about a guy in the crowd who complained -- too many originals. "'Play something I know so I can tell if you are any good,'" the guy said. "That's what good old 'Cripple Creek' works well for," Spearman added.

He does B.B. King and Prince, a song about fishing, an original off his new album. He says he actually does little fishing. "I prefer to read about fishing, then write a song about fishing."

He has performed professionally and conducted instructional workshops in countless cities across 18 states in many settings including festivals, clubs, concert halls, elementary schools, square dances, barn raisings, weddings, house concerts, and everything in between. For New Year's Eve 2014 he and his new band Aching Hearts landed the coveted slot at Sheldon Concert Hall.

Spearman teaches at The Folk School of St. Louis -- claw hammer banjo, old time and bluegrass fiddle, guitar, old time ensemble performance. He also offers a "30-day online banjo course delivered to your email inbox every day for a month" and "inspiration, tips, and practical guidance for aspiring folk musicians."

He's also done what is perhaps the most local of all local records, *Get Along Home,* using found and recycled instruments, written, engineered, mixed, mastered and designed in St. Louis.

Ptah Williams -- A jazz pianist who was on the keyboard at age 4. His work was heard for years in the powerhouse jazz trio Tracer. After 2012 he became more of a solo show. He plays an electric keyboard, synthesizer as well as a rollicking acoustic piano. In all the years he played every Wednesday on Delmar, fans were never sure what they were going to get on any given night. He can easily run from Gershwin to Beethoven, from "The St. Louis Blues" to "Stardust."

Williams got a new weekly gig in 2015, appearing at a jazz club in Grand Center, the Dark Room.

Sarah Jane and the Blue Notes -- A retro band -- twenties through the sixties -- hot jazz and St. Louis blues. Sarah Jane's sound comes out of the "red hot mama" tradition of the blues that goes right straight back to Bessie Smith and even further back to Mammy Lou. This bunch can be found at the Venice Cafe, the new West End club Nathalie's and elsewhere on weekends.

Miss Molly Sims and the Bible Belt Sinners -- One of the younger of the performing St. Louisans, she got her start at age 14, acting older and jumping into jams, singing and playing acoustic guitar. She's played with harpist Eric McSpadden, the drummer Marty Spikener and the veteran bass man Eugene Johnson, learning her trade from those who know.

As she reached her early twenties her gigs multiplied, her music became more original and she dove into all kinds of styles, the whirls and swirls of the Mississippi waters coursing through her veins.

"People really need to be moved and see a great show to be impressed," she said of the St. Louis audience. "I think our music resonates well with folks because we have lots of energy at our live shows and we want them to be part of the show. We're tossing back PBR (beers) right along with them and having just as much fun."

The Rattlesnake -- The youngest of the young, a protege of the oldest of the old, a new player on the scene. Born in 1997, the kid called Rattlesnake started on guitar at 11, began listening to Stevie Ray Vaughan at 12, began to absorb Albert King, BB King and Freddie King in one manic gulp.

Big George, Jeremiah Johnson, Rich McDonough and Aaron Griffin have all helped get the young man get off the ground. He's played at Fair St. Louis, BluesWeek, Molly's in Soulard, Beale on Broadway and sat in at various gigs, always welcomed as a rising member of the music tradition.

Sleepy Kitty – At the opening act of the 3rd LouFest, an alt rock festival in the Central Fields grasslands of Forest Park Paige Brubeck is all gussied up for the show -- her sunglasses black and fifties, her waist band white, wide and spangled and her skimpy kitty shorts showing lots of leg. The songs are of the Veruca Salt, grrrrl rock persuasion, not surprising given that she and drummer partner Evan Suit are from Chicago. They have relocated in St. Louis and were one of the few locals bands hired for the festival.

Son Volt – Here we find another LouFest 2012 entry, led by St. Louis singer/songwriter Jay Ferrar. Originally from the East Side, Ferrar's commentary on St. Louis in his songs rings through the years. At LouFest, an afternoon rainstorm has cooled and wet down the field. A crowd 500 strong watches as the stage crew does its mop up, hoping nobody will be electrocuted.

The band starts with "Down to the Wire" from the 2009 record *American Central Dust,* a song that reveals Ferrar's apocalyptic vision of our modern world, from Biddle Street near the St. Louis waterfront up to the football Jones Dome where the "intrigues of the new royalty" are performed on the field, "playing out the legacy of long dead industry titans and haters of men.

"Plastic grocery bags fly from trees," he sings. He sees the city as a place of "proud symbols of a cavalier progress. Memories and landscapes in triage."

The crowd knows this source of this band from its days as Uncle Tupelo, a band that started out at Cicero's on the Delmar Loop. The band later split in three -- Son Volt, the Bottle Rockets and Wilco, all of which built successful acts. Wilco relocated in Chicago and has pumped out hit alt-country records for 20 years under the guidance of Jeff Tweedy, Ferrar's former partner from Belleville, Ill.

Son Volt has stayed closer to home, playing regular gigs at the Pageant while keeping up a national touring schedule in such venues as the Living Room in Brooklyn and the Lancaster Roots and Blues Festival in Pennsylvania.

Chuck Berry -- Playing at Blueberry Hill, Berry is resplendent in his sequined flaming red shirt, the long, long sleeves flying over the stage, that big guitar held high, like a hillbilly player would do. In person, close up to the stage, Berry's hands are tree roots in a rain forest. The long, long fingers look for that sweet spot on the fret, the one that makes the crowd jump.

"I'm glad to be here. At 85, I'm glad to be anywhere!"

"Take a picture of me. Anything can happen. What should I play?" He's the Joker in a captain's cap.

At the end he invites "the ladies" up on the stage.

Once about 15 women get up there, Chuck sits down and plays his riff. Chuck Jr. and Darlin' Ingrid step up and Bob Lohr gives it the Johnnie treatment with the piano trill and boom! The show is over and the ladies get down from the stage and form up in a line, waiting for their after-show autographs. Chuck disappears.

Two shows at The Pageant:

El Monstero: Pigocalypse -- A cast of thousands: Jimmy Griffin, vocals. guitar; Mark Quinn, vocals, guitar, Dave Farvar, sax; Kevin Gagnepain, bass; Bryan Green, guitar; John Pessoini, drums; Bill Reiter, keyboards; Jake Elking, keyboards; Erminie Cannon, Tandra Williams and Mindy Mierek, backup vocals; plus a groupie, three policemen, a headmaster and several pole dancers and aerialists.

The show starts with Quinn riding a podium 30 feet above the stage, moves on with the invasion of a squad of pig fascist cops and builds into a wild evening of tricks, flames and spectacular effects -- all to the tunes of Pink Floyd's visionary albums, played with precision and emotion.

The show is a St. Louis Christmas tradition, seven nights with six sell-outs at 1,800 people a night. Lasers, symmetrical poles draped with dancers, a ballet dancer, a pig on stilts, the aerial contortionist Meg from Circus Flora, and a table top walk by saxophonist Farvar keep pace with the music to make this far more than a tribute show.

The performance had its start at Mississippi Nights in 1999 and has built up more shows each year since moving to the friendly confines of the Pageant. The act also performed on Art Hill in 2014 as well as in Chicago. For the dedicated followers of the contrary attitude.

Mama's Pride - Pat Liston and his brother Danny sell out this show every year. A nostalgiathon that draws a tightly niched crowd of all-white, 50 to 60 year old fans, many who live in St. Louis County and see one music show a year. This is a wanna-be Allman/Skynyrd band that had a brief shot at stardom.

At Cicero's, up the Loop from the Pageant, it's **Jake's Leg,** one of a number of the city's Grateful Dead/jam bands. Another is **Swag**, seen often at the Venice. **Pepperland** is a Beatle cover band that sometimes includes Kari Liston up front.

Arthur Williams – A longtime Delta harp player who in his late seventies still makes the occasional performance here or there. He was born in Tunica, Ms., in 1937 and moved to Chicago when he was a child. He relocated to St. Louis in the seventies after stints with Muddy Waters and Elmore James and became a frequent collaborator with Larry Griffin. Williams also recorded and toured with Big Bad Smitty. His harmonica work on a 1966 album with the Arkansas bluesman Frank Frost remains notable, as is his 2001 CD *Midnight Blue.*

Elsie Parker and the Poor People of Paris. -- At the St. Louis Art Fair in a big parking lot in Clayton this unique outfit performs in French, bringing the streets of Paris to the confluence. The band caught on quickly at the new Nathalie's in the Central West End in 2015. The group has released four CDs. A special show late in 2015 celebrated the 100th birthday of the French star Edith Piaf.

While all those mentioned in this musical safari were alive and performing (at least up to the end of 2015), one artist no longer with us deserves a mention before we go home to get some sleep before tomorrow night's shows start. And that would be John Hartford, who died in 2001.

Hartford was the city's most popular folk musician. As well as being related to Tennessee Williams, Hartford was a descendent of American revolutionary Patrick Henry. Hartford's grandfather was a founder of the Missouri Bar Association and his father a doctor. Born Dec. 30, 1937, the folk singer lived in St. Louis until 1965, when he moved to Nashville.

He recorded a catalog of more than 30 albums, was on TV with the Smothers Brothers and Glen Campbell. In 1967, he wrote and sang one of the most popular songs of all time, "Gentle On My Mind," covered more than 300 times. Glenn Campbell's version got 5 million airplays in 1968. Hartford once told a reporter:

> I went to see the movie *Doctor Zhivago* the night I wrote it. Everyone's made a whole lot out of that. I know it gave me a feeling that caused me to start writing, but as far as saying it came from that, I don't know. It just came from experience. While I was writing it, if I had any idea that it was going to be a hit, it probably would have come out differently and it wouldn't have been a hit. That just came real fast, a blaze, a blur.

Hartford worked the Mississippi River during his youth, getting a real job at age 16. Hearing Earl Scruggs on the radio led him to the three-string banjo. By 13 he played fiddle, guitar and mandolin. In his high school, the upper-end John Burroughs School, Hartford formed a bluegrass band.

He spent four years in a Wash U commercial arts program learning calligraphy, but didn't go much of anywhere with his art degree, spending the early sixties rattling around the city's music scene, DJ, banjo player, making the occasional bluegrass single.

After he left in 1965, he kept in touch with the city even as the fame grew. When he died, Hartford left behind a large collection of model boats and river artifacts, including antique steamboat parts, photos, and more than 1,000 books, many having to do with the Mississippi River. They were all donated to St. Louis Mercantile Library at UMSL.

And there is a footnote before we leave the clubs and the theaters and the festival fields: the sad saga of the St. Louis Bluesweek Festival, once the premier outdoor festival in all St. Louis, run out of downtown, chased into suburban Chesterfield, then killed altogether, at least for 2015.

This event was the direct descendant of the 1st Fest put on in 1986 by what was then called the St. Louis Blues Club (not called Society yet). With the exception of one year, the show went on downtown for free.

Under the management of Mike Kociela, a promoter and musician who for over a decade worked to solidify a highly regarded festival in the home of "The St. Louis Blues," it grew and prospered.

As recently as 2012 and 2013 Bluesweek (the latest name of the fest) drew big crowds of people (50,000 and 60,000) downtown to see live music. Vendors did well, sponsors lined-up. The delicate break-even that kept free admission was achieved and the fest lived to play another year. Kociela had a vision and made it happen.

Then rumblings came from City Hall. The parking law was changed and the Fest-goers would no longer get free parking. Even worse they would have to feed two-hour meters to go hear the music. The city also pulled the sewage pickup and trash clean-up contracts. This all added up to a far more expensive festival, one that could no longer be free.

In April 2014 the Board of Aldermen brushed off vocal opposition from musicians and music fans and passed a bill giving exclusive concert rights to downtown venues to ICM, an L.A. booking agency. Most of its clients were TV or movie actors. The company also managed television productions and set up author book tours. The city gave exclusive rights to an ICM spinoff called Summer Rocks to put on annual concerts Memorial Day and Labor Day downtown, starting in 2015. It had never organized a single such show before.

One city official said the new contract "would put us on the music map for our country," something apparently not accomplished by hundreds of shows a month, major venues all over town, world class blues, innovative country, jazz both smooth and free, dozens of world renown performers and a history that includes songs such as "The St. Louis Blues," "Stagger Lee," and "Frankie and Johnny."

Summer Rocks said initially it would present a country festival in May and a rock festival over Labor Day. No blues, no jazz, no funk, no R&B. The events were touted as drawing residents throughout the South and Midwest to the area around downtown's Soldiers Memorial and was approved by a 21-4 vote by the Aldermen and signed by Mayor Slay.

The pending invasion from L.A. sent Kociela scrambling for a new venue, landing 25 miles to the west in Chesterfield. The suburban venue was cleaner, more comfortable, less diverse, less urban, less interesting. The quality of the music was as usual, but it somehow wasn't the same without the echoes of the buildings downtown. Attendance was down sharply. It lasted just one year.

And, just as the blues community had predicted, by November 2015 Summer Rocks had failed to come up with either new show downtown. The city shrugged, the aldermen who passed the bill shrugged, the music fans had another round of drinks and a few "I told you sos" and went on to the next page.

Kociela helped get the National Blues Museum, co-founded with Dave Beardsley, off the ground before moving San Diego.

Despite the trouble with BluesWeek, Segel-Moss, the new president of the St. Louis Blues Society, retained his optimism:

> It continues to be a disappointment that the city from the top down does not see our culture, our food, our music and our history as an economic commodity. It's worth endless amounts of money, jobs and pride. St. Louis has, hands down, one of the

> most important musical heritages in the world. But we continually decide on corporate money, instant money, from out-of-town people.
>
> And that just doesn't work. I'm hoping that, now that this ICM festival is out of the way, the city will find a way to seed new festivals and embrace them for a long time.

Segel-Moss later became music director at the Blues Museum and in the summer of 2016 announced a new look for the old Big Muddy Festival in Laclede's Landing. He booked into the event an all-local lineup of 46 blues acts, large and small, that included all the top names in the city.

The museum opened a new venue as a side stage to the facility with a separate entrance and a state-of-the art sound system. A highlight of its opening shows featured a classic blues trio of Ron Edwards, Bob Case and Johnny Diamond. Edwards presented a comprehensive look at country slide blues ala Tampa Red and talked fondly of his days with Henry Townsend. Case, a veteran who carries one of the city's most underrated singing voices, has a welcoming stage presence and sang several originals. Diamond showed off the tradition of the wailing St. Louis harp blues, ala Keith Doder. The new museum venue provided an afternoon's worth of entertaining history and was crowded for the show, bringing cheers from people from Australia and Portland, (Oregon and Maine)

In 2014 the celebration of the city's 250th anniversary proved disappointing. Nothing created by the city came close to matching previous celebrations such as the 1914 Pageant and Masque history play staged on Art Hill for the 150th anniversary, an event that combined drama, poetry and music with the new, progressive politics.

For the 250th anniversary of Laclede's founding in 1764 there were a number of events tagged with a history sticker, but generally these were events that would have been held anyway. Official events included a lame reenactment of the founding down by the river, some Fourth of July fireworks, and a cocktail party at the History Museum.

The museum also staged an exhibit of the usual crew of famous St. Louisans. A series of coffee table books were issued with glossy pictures and text. A fund-raising drive was launched to clean up the park near a downtown statue of Laclede, but few visitors were sighted in the tiny park.

A ceremony was held at City Hall where speeches were given recounting the founding. Attendance was scant.

Perhaps the most successful feature of the anniversary celebration involved cakes. These were 250 cardboard anniversary cakes, short and squat, scattered around town advertising sponsoring businesses. Some were an artistic success; others had enough humor painted on them to draw a smile from the curious passerby. They were popular with people who felt the need to point cell phone cameras at them or those who had a desire to take another smiley selfie. Outside of Facebook, however, the cakes left virtually no mark.

Kociela's company, Entertainment St. Louis, had the best idea, a Burnin' Love Festival of music, food and arts on Art Hill on the February anniversary date. An untimely ice storm, however, forced a delay in the event, keeping a shivering crowd small.

But no matter how exciting the anniversary could have been, there is no doubt it would not have been the biggest historical moment in St. Louis in 2014. And, no matter how good the music was or how good the Cardinals played, the biggest story of the year was destined to spring from another element of that St. Louis thing -- the city's seemingly endless struggle with questions of race.

And that story was easy to locate and easy to sum up in just one word: Ferguson.

Chapter Thirty-Five
Ferguson: White and Black at High Noon
1993-2016

Michael Brown's death had highlighted a racial divide in a city where blacks are now in the majority, while municipal institutions remain dominated by whites. This divide will only grow with the decision of the grand jury, particularly because city officials were unable to convince with their arguments so far.

-- *Le Monde,* Paris, France, 2014

Until the end of 2014, Darren Wilson worked as a police officer for the town of Ferguson, a North County suburb once the first station stop outside St. Louis on the Wabash railroad going west. The nineteenth century town grew to 21,000 people by the time Wilson came to work there, a city best known as the headquarters of Emerson Electric Co., a Fortune 500 firm that generated nearly $25 billion worldwide.

Wilson changed that reputation forever when he fired his Sig Sauer P229 semi-automatic pistol 12 times on an August afternoon in 2014, killing an unarmed black teenager.

A strapping 6-foot-4, 210-pound white man, Wilson was born May 14, 1986, in Fort Worth, Texas. Blonde and fair-skinned, he grew up to favor the buzz cut, military look of the Iraq War generation. By the time of his November 2014 resignation he had let his hair grow out a little during three months of paid leave, but his look remained very much that of a young white male in the twenty-first century.

His parents divorced in 1983 and he, his mother and stepfather moved first to St. Peters then to St. Charles County on the far western edges of the metro suburban sprawl. Wilson entered St. Charles West High School in 2001. St. Charles, a Missouri River city founded just a year later than St. Louis, in the twenty-first century was a growing white suburb with a historic downtown.

During his first year in high school Wilson's mother, Tonya Durso, admitted to crimes that involved stealing her neighbor's mail, opening credit cards to take out high-dollar loans she did not pay back. She pleaded guilty and was sentenced to probation. She declared bankruptcy. Two months later she died, age 35, from what officials described as natural causes. Wilson was a sophomore in high school and became his stepfather's responsibility.

When told that Wilson was a police officer in Ferguson, a former neighbor of the officer and his mother said, "I'm surprised Wilson passed the background checks to become a policeman. People can change, but that was a bad home. His mother was a serial con-woman."

Wilson attended police academy and in 2009 was hired onto the force in Jennings, a high-crime suburb of 14,000 people, like Ferguson, one of the majority black towns in North St. Louis County. Wilson was a rookie cop on a force of 45. There were two black police officers in Jennings, a town 89 percent African American.

Two years after Wilson joined, the Jennings department was ripped apart and closed entirely over a series of corruption charges ranging from excess use of force by white officers to misuse of grant money on a check-writing fraud.

"You're dealing with white cops and they don't know how to address black people," a black city council member said of the Jennings situation.

"He didn't go above and beyond," a superior officer said of Wilson, "and he didn't get in any trouble." Others described him as low-key, reliable.

After the Jennings force was dissolved, Wilson, then 25, landed a new job -- patrolman in Ferguson, another small-sized, majority black town, about four miles northwest of Jennings. Wilson married and moved into a house in Crestwood, 20 miles away from Ferguson along I-70 in South St. Louis County. Crestwood, a town of 12,000, had a black population of 2 percent. A neighbor described Wilson as tall and slim and said she would see him walking his dog. She had no idea her neighbor was a police officer.

In 2014, nearly 67 percent of the population of Ferguson was African American, much of it located in low-income housing. Fifty of the 53 town police officers were white.

Wilson had little trouble in his new department until Aug. 9, 2014, a sunny Saturday summer day when the white cop saw two black teenagers walking down the middle of a street near one of the housing projects.

His friends called him Big Mike and Michael Brown was big, a 6-foot-5, 290-pound black man, called a "gentle giant" by those who knew him. He was born May 20, 1996, in Florissant, Mo., another North County suburb. In the summer of 2014, he was 18, a newly minted high school graduate hanging out with his friends, waiting for the next turn of the page.

The night before he was killed Brown was in a good mood, writing on Facebook: "Everything happen for a reason. Just start putting 2 n 2 together. You'll see it." He had recently been talking excitedly with relatives about having a religious experience where he told them he saw an angel.

Brown's parents, Michael Brown Sr. and Lesley McSpadden, were teenagers when they conceived their first child. Michael grew up with his parents, his father's parents and later a younger sister.

He took up the drums with the help of his father. The house eventually broke up and he lived mostly with his mother. But the father and numerous uncles, aunts, cousins and grandparents all lived near one another, several in Ferguson.

Reporters digging into Brown's life after the shooting found an accusation of stealing an iPod when he attended school in Florissant, a charge dropped when McSpadden arrived at the school with the receipt for the purchase. He bounced around until his junior year in high school when he started to attend Normandy High, one of the numerous underperforming schools in the St. Louis area battling to stay open.

Even though his mother moved out of the district and the school was threatened, Brown settled into classes there, his goal to graduate on time. He did. He was described by teachers as reserved, not a high-achiever, a slightly low average student. He continued to be surrounded by family, living with his paternal grandmother so he could remain at the school, but sometimes also staying with his maternal grandmother.

He posed for his graduation picture in March. Normandy had only enough funds to buy just two gowns for the pictures. The graduates, taking turns sitting in front of the camera in pairs, used the same two gowns. Brown had been accepted to a downtown trade school and was looking forward to a job as a skilled worker, perhaps in electronic repair.

Brown's friends said that at school he was a peacemaker who tried to avoid confrontation. His relatives warned him about contact with the police, giving him advice on how to respond. He had never been arrested. He knew the low-income area well; several members of his family had lived in the federally subsidized Canfield Gardens over the years. He also knew what the racism was like in St. Louis County, how quickly things could happen.

His autopsy found THC in his blood, giving rise to theories that he was out of control, high on marijuana at the time of the shooting. But grand jury witnesses later said there was no way to tell how THC would have affected Brown in his confrontation with Wilson. THC was not the cause of death.

The cause of death was a bullet that hit Brown's head, the 12th time Wilson fired at Brown that day on Canfield Drive.

The indirect cause of Brown's death was the history of St. Louis and America. On that street the long and often bitter conflict between races slammed together across 152 feet of hot asphalt on an early afternoon in August.

Not long before the shooting, the town of Ferguson had been enjoying something of a surge. There was a new fire station and a new community center. Police headquarters had been updated. The Ferguson Brewery Co., a microbrew, opened in 2012 and was praised for its burgers and fresh beer. Other small businesses had taken hold including a wine bar and a popular bakery featuring homemade cupcakes.

Emerson Electric had been headquartered for 70 years on a grassy campus just off Ferguson Avenue. Founded in St. Louis in 1890, it was financed by John Wesley Emerson, a Civil War veteran who saw a future in electric motors. The company made its fortune quickly with a Gilded Age invention -- an electric ceiling fan that gained popularity after being shown at the World's Fair of 1904.

By 1938, as the Second World War approached, the company had moved out of the city into suburban Ferguson, about three miles northwest of the city line. That year the firm hired an up-and-coming businessman, Stuart Symington, who had been running a stainless steel company in Rochester, N.Y. Symington built Emerson into the world's largest manufacturer of airplane armaments. During the war, Emerson ranked No. 52 on the list of most military contracts.

Symington went on to become the Secretary of the Air Force and in 1953 won the first of four terms as a U.S. Senator from Missouri. He ran for president in 1960, backed by former President Truman. He was the early favorite against the neophyte John Kennedy and the Texas arm-twister, Lyndon Johnson, but the Democratic Party nomination slipped through his fingers.

Symington, unlike either of his rivals, suffered because he refused to speak to segregated audiences. He also failed to see the importance of the party primaries; losing the nod at the convention to the delegates Kennedy had rounded up in those contests.

Meanwhile, Emerson continued its growth and by 1973 was spread around the world in 82 plants with 31,000 employees and $800 million in sales. David Farr took over as CEO in 2000 and as chairman since 2004. By 2013, the company generated $24.7 billion and Farr was making $25 million a year.

Farr was president of Civic Progress, the council of St. Louis tycoons who have been making the major decisions in the city for half a century. Emerson had long been active in Ferguson, especially through its encouragement of students to attend Ranken Technical College on the North Side. In 2014, 1,300 people worked at Emerson in Ferguson.

Michael Brown thought maybe someday he could become one of those workers.

Brown's Ferguson neighborhood, however, was stacked against him. Canfield Gardens' median income was under $27,000, making it the eighth-poorest census tract in the state; 95 percent of Canfield residents were black.

Here, like nearly everywhere in the St. Louis metro area, the number of arrests of blacks in the community far outstripped the percentage share of its population. In Ferguson, with its 67 percent black population, police statistics showed that during traffic stops from 2012 to 2014 African Americans made up 85 percent of the stops, 90 percent of the tickets and 93 percent of the arrests.

Once stopped, black drivers were more than twice as likely to be searched than whites even though the statistics showed the blacks were 26 percent less likely to be carrying illegal substances. Blacks also accounted for 94 percent of the "failure to comply" charges and 95 percent of "walking in roadway" arrests. Black made up 92 percent of the warrants issued by the Ferguson Municipal Court in 2013. The court, a leading source of income for the town, employed a system the Justice Department later found unconstitutional and unduly harsh.

A quarter century previously, in 1990, Ferguson was a middle class suburban town three-quarters white. But black flight north from the city in the nineties changed the racial mix to half and half. Poverty was not intense with just 5 percent unemployed in 1990. That number jumped to 13 percent by 2000 and the number of residents in poverty doubled.

Things only got worse after 2008 when the Great Recession grew the income gap between rich and poor even more. In 2012, the most recent figure, black unemployment in Ferguson was nearly twice as high as white.

The town administration, the courts and the police came to rely more and more on a strategy of using arrests to fund the town's operating costs through fines. In January 2013, an email from the police chief to the city manager noted that court revenues from fines had passed $2 million a year for the first time. The city manager responded, "Awesome! Thanks!"

The tally from the court in 2013 was up even more to $2.5 million, an 80 percent increase from only two years prior. The collected fines represented one-fifth of the total operating budget for the town.

This intense ticketing aimed at the black population led to relentless conflict between the police and the town's economically distressed

African-American population. Justice Department investigators found this policy of "policing to raise revenue" included "harsh" and "aggressive" police practices that undermined "community trust, especially among many African Americans."

This was the context in which the shooting of Michael Brown was imbedded. Brown's apparent crime was initially "walking in roadway." Wilson felt severe distrust when he confronted Brown.

In grand jury testimony, Officer Wilson described Brown as a "demon."

> When I grabbed him, the only way I can describe it is I felt like a 5-year-old holding onto Hulk Hogan. Hulk Hogan, that's how big he felt and how small I felt just from grasping his arm.
>
> (Later, as Wilson fired at Brown) it looked like he was almost bulking up to run through the shots, like it was making him mad that I'm shooting at him. And that face that he had was looking straight through me, like I wasn't even there, I wasn't even anything in his way."
>
> (Wilson said Brown made) a grunting, like aggravated, sound. I've never seen anybody look like that, for lack of a better word, crazy. There was nothing he was seeing.

Lesley McSpadden, Brown's mother, said she tried to mitigate against the community distrust of the police through a network of family and friends, including a retired juvenile officer, to make sure Michael got through his teenage years unscathed in the environment of racial and economic division.

His uncle, Bernard Ewing, remembers talking about how to interact with police officers: "I let him know like, if the police ever get on you, I don't care what you doing, give it up. Because if you do one wrong move they'll shoot you. They'll kill you."

The white and black chasm in Ferguson reflected the chronic division all over the area, a division that went back and back. Missed opportunities were seen in the thirties, the fifties, and again in the sixties and seventies. There was again little change in the eighties, but the nineties brought yet another new hope for those who wanted to see an end to the divisions. In 1993, a black mayor was finally elected in St. Louis.

Other big cities with large black populations -- Cleveland, Washington, Newark, Cincinnati, Detroit, even Seattle -- all had black mayors before St. Louis did.

African Americans in the River City won office in the local wards beginning in the mid-thirties when Jordan Chambers switched from Republican (the party of Lincoln) to Democrat in support of Franklin Roosevelt's New Deal. Chambers became known as the "Negro mayor of St. Louis," but his influence was never citywide and never extended much beyond his 19th District stronghold. The black population was too small to win an at-large vote until the sixties when depopulation changed the balance.

The first black to hold a citywide office was Benjamin Goins, a protege of Chambers who became active in North Side politics in 1956. In 1968, he was appointed license collector. Goins was backed by a lobbying effort of South Side ward power Francis R. Slay, who held the 23rd District committeeman seat for 45 years and was father of four-term mayor Francis G. Slay.

More importantly was the election, also in 1968, of William Clay to the U.S. House, a task made easier by new boundary lines that made the North Side a unified electoral bloc. Clay, a bus driver raised in Mill Creek Valley, had won election to the Board of Alderman in 1959 and engineered passage in 1961 of the public accommodations measure that outlawed racial discrimination in restaurants, hotels, recreation facilities and sports stadiums.

But North Side unity didn't last. In the 1972 Democratic primary, Clay and Goins each sent out slates of six candidates for ward slots on the Board of Aldermen. Clay gained the upper hand in close races. In the 19th Ward his ally, activist Jet Banks, was the winner by just 23 votes. The depth of division in Chambers' former stronghold grew worse as both sides threw hardball charges at each other, alleging cases of people voting early and often. Each reported threats to election officials as well as to the voters standing in line.

The 1972 contest had a ring of familiarity to the days in the early twentieth century when voters were intimidated by Boss Butler's repeaters, his gangs of "Indians" and various ballot stuffing techniques. Clay, the veteran of the Jefferson Bank fight, called the Goins faction "a cadre of black hustlers who think it's more important to socialize with white bigots than to represent black interests."

Goins was appointed sheriff and the rivals squared off in 1978 for the House of Representatives seat. But during the campaign Goins was convicted in federal court of accepting bribes from vending machine operators. Clay was easily reelected.

Black voting rolls continued to increase in terms of percentage of city voters in the seventies and eighties as whites left the city faster than blacks. But no black candidate was able to break through to the city's highest office until 1993, when Freeman Bosley, Jr., succeeded Vincent Schoemehl, who had once been a great hope for the black community.

In his election in 1981, Schoemehl had carried all but one of the city's wards, winning overwhelming support in the black community with his pledge to keep Homer G. Phillips Hospital open. But closure of the hospital and Schoemehl's concentration on developing the central corridor soured black voters, dropping his support to 30 percent in his 1989 victory. He left the mayor's office in 1993 to make an unsuccessful run for governor.

Bosley Jr. was part of a prominent black family with deep roots in St. Louis. His grandfather, Preston Bosley, was born in 1898, the son of a slave who migrated from Little Rock, Ark., who retired in 1964 after working for more than 50 years as a mail clerk for the Missouri Pacific Railroad. He lived on until 1993, until age 94.

During his retirement, Preston Bosley helped found the Yeatman Community Development agency, a group of investors who tried to halt the decline of the North Side, especially in what is now called Near North or Old North. Bosley's group also started the Yeatman Health Center that had a leading role in the seventies exposing cases of lead poisoning.

Preston's son, Freeman R. Bosley, Sr., became alderman from the 3rd Ward in 1985 and was still serving in 2016, elected to his ninth four-year term in 2013.

During the eighties the North Side continued to deteriorate. Under Schoemehl the percentage of black workers in the city work force declined sharply, led by the closure of Phillips hospital. There was also a 63 percent drop each in black sanitation and community development employees. Overall, between 1979 and 1990, black employment in the city work force dropped 57 percent.

In the 1993 Democratic primary the favorite in the race was Thomas Villa, the president of the aldermen who had Schoemehl's support. Another white candidate was Tony Ribaudo, a state representative from the Italian section backed by the powerful family of Francis R. Slay.

Bosley Jr. announced his candidacy with considerable fanfare in Forest Park. He was elected circuit clerk three times and was head of the Democratic Party committee. He was a graduate of the St. Louis University School of Law who ran on a platform that linked the city's major problems -- housing, crime, jobs and schools – to racial divisions.

He had been a quiet law clerk in his 12 years in the court system, but once on the campaign trial he came alive, running on a unity message his father was fond of: "It takes white and black keys to sing the 'Star-Spangled Banner.'"

Bosley was all but ignored in the campaign by the two white candidates, who were not worried about a 38-year-old upstart from the North Side. The white candidates beat each other up, running negative ads on television, touting their endorsements.

Bosley had two new weapons in the race: members of the newly energized environmental movement and a young army of pro-choice women fighting for abortion rights. Adding to these new activists were veterans from the civil rights movement and the black business community who supported his father. Bosley Jr. conducted a door-to-door blitz not unlike the one Schoemehl deployed in his first run for mayor.

Bosley held back his television ads until late in the race, then came out with a positive message. His speeches grew boisterous and impassioned, adopting the sixties rhetorical style of Martin Luther King and the black clergy. He landed a surprise endorsement from three-term U.S. Sen. Thomas Eagleton, who said Bosley was the best campaigner he had ever seen on the St. Louis mayoral stump.

He didn't exactly sweep into office, but his message of racial inclusiveness went over well enough with white voters in the central corridor to pull in 44 percent of the vote in the primary, defeating Villa (36 percent) and Ribaudo (12 percent.) His total in the final was 66 percent.

Bosley's inauguration was a celebration a long time coming for the black community. After an open-air swearing in ceremony cut short by a drenching April rain, the festivities moved to the new Cervantes Convention Center where a pair of giant piano keyboards flanked the stage, representing the black and white keys of racial unity.

There, before 6,000 cheering Bosley supporters, the 13-piece Ralph Butler Band blasted off with James Brown's "I Feel Good, I Got You," entertaining one of the most racially diverse crowds in St. Louis history.

Bosley gripped Butler's hand and shouted, "What's going on, St. Louis? You look really good. We're going make St. Louis the No. 1 city in the country."

The city's first black mayor started with a rush, determined not to miss the opportunity to cross the racial chasm. He pushed programs to strengthen neighborhood schools. He obtained funding and built new city housing on the North Side, generally in low-rise homes that looked like suburban subdivisions and still dot city blocks north of the Delmar Divide.

He made possible a new master plan for Forest Park, using both private and public funding and drawing in his environmental allies. He pushed through an increase in the city tax to help shore up the budget. He threw himself into attracting the pro football Rams from Los Angeles in time for the 1995 season. He also played a role in a $70 million bailout of TWA Airlines at Lambert Airport.

And Bosley led the city in its battle against the Great Flood of 1993, which came just four months into his new term. The flood, propelled by drenching rain, rolled all down the Missouri and Mississippi rivers in the summer. The water consumed farmland and small towns along the river, reaching the confluence in late July and putting the city on high alert. The city put its hopes on its 11-mile concrete levee wall, built to protect riverfront factories beginning in 1959.

The river climbed ever higher up the 52-foot wall, reaching the 49-foot level as residents held their breaths. But breaks in levees upriver on both the Mississippi and Missouri rivers brought down the water in the river as it rushed past the city just six feet below the foot of the Arch on Aug. 2.

In Chesterfield, west of the city, a levee broke, leaving the suburban town swamped. South of St. Louis, the Illinois town of Valmeyer was flooded as were farms in a 20-square-mile area nearby.

Most of the danger in St. Louis was to the southern part of the city, beyond the reach of the wall, especially where 51 propane tanks were threatened. Bosley ordered the evacuation of 9,000 people who lived near the tanks. The containers held their moorings.

Meanwhile, thousands of people gathered to gawk at the water near the Arch. A floating Burger King was torn off its mooring at the levee but a nearby McDonald's held fast.

Overall, the flood caused $15 billion in damage, the most costly in U.S. history. Nine states were affected and 50 people died as the floodwaters moved from North Dakota through Missouri. At least 15 million acres of farmland were swamped and 75 towns were completely under water.

Bosley, however, passed his first test as mayor. He was given credit for strong, calm leadership during the crisis, but two years later the political waters of the city's divide began to swamp his administration.

He thus became a one-term mayor. The trouble began when his police chief, Clarence Harmon, the first black chief in the city's history, quit on Dec. 5, 1995, not long after the midway mark of Bosley's term.

Schoemehl named Harmon chief in 1991. But he grew tired of outside meddling by the city's arcane police board, a governor-appointed body that forced Harmon to rehire a staff member he had fired. The board also blocked an officer's transfer, overruled promotions of staff and even told the chief what copy machine he could buy. There were also political alliances that led to conflicts with Bosley and distrust by blacks on the board that led to a distrust of Harmon on the North Side.

Once out of the chief's seat, Harmon decided to try to upset Bosley's plans for a second term.

Bosley became an increasingly easy target during his second two years in City Hall. One major mistake involved the central corridor of the city, an area of crucial Bosley support where half the white voters supported him in 1993. The issue was cell phones, the portable communication device that became widely available in 1988 with the introduction of time division multiple access (TDMA), the digital format that allowed large increases in data to flow from the mobile system.

St. Louis was an early area of cell phone use and Bosley spread the phones widely through his administration. Suspecting misuse of the new phones, which were most popular in the central corridor, the *Post-Dispatch* and KSDK-TV filed a suit that forced city workers to disclose records of use, records that showed numerous personal calls on the portable phones, calls that were much more expensive than regular lines, making the calls appear to be a waste of city money.

There was also the Midnight Basketball scandal. Bosley established basketball leagues supported by corporate donations and city funding that caught on in the central corridor and the North Side, but several of the people Bosley hired to administer the leagues proved corrupt, putting money in their pockets. Bosley fired the director but the scandal spread to several other people the mayor recommended. Several employees were indicted.

There were also conflicts of interest involving unpaid parking tickets by the mayor's mother and a deal arranged through a city agency that benefited his father's mattress factory.

With race always a factor in St. Louis politics, these scandals fed the fears of whites who voted for Bosley. The mayor put a number of inexperienced black staffers into city jobs, prompting one politician to sum up that Bosley's appointees "got too greedy too quickly."

As Bosley's standing slipped, Harmon's rose. The powerful business organization Civic Progress had supported Tom Villa in the 1991 election but was soon sitting around the meeting table at an exclusive Ladue golf club with the city's first black mayor. Bosley said he was blunt at these meetings, a situation one millionaire called "high-risk."

Enter Harmon, the African American whose police credentials appealed to white voters. His support among black aldermen was virtually nil, but his appealed to whites on the South Side was solid. To them, Harmon was someone akin to Colin Powell, the black general who was head of the Joint Chiefs of Staff. In 1990, Powell ran the military during the invasion of Panama and during Operation Desert Storm, the massive U.S. invasion of Kuwait. His political capital soared and gave whites a black politick figure they could get behind.

But while the white establishment rallied around Harmon as a St. Louis version of Powell, black activists and civil rights officials called him an Uncle Tom.

Born in 1940, Harmon was older than Bosley and did not have the urban style of "street-cred" of the flamboyant mayor. Harmon's father was a racehorse groom and railroad cook. His mother was a nurse at Homer G. Phillips Hospital. He was a paratrooper in the Army then got a master's in criminology from Webster. He became a police officer in 1969, rising to chief by 1991.

Harmon ruffled a few feathers in his time as head of the department, introducing pepper spray, promoting his son ahead of more experienced officers, and instigating the arrest of two officers who had been shaking down motorists. He also remained at odds with the police board throughout his term. Crime in the city came down slightly under his leadership, homicides down from 260 to 204, total violent crime from 14,076 to 12,452.

He was charged by the NAACP with showing favoritism to white officers. Harmon also tried to fire of the head of the black police officers organization.

Following his resignation from the force he got a job as an executive at United Van Lines but was quickly urged by Civic Process and South Side politicians to make a run for mayor. Slay and Eagleton remained loyal to Bosley but the white vote in the central corridor swung to Harmon in the primary.

Harmon had launched his campaign with a hard-hitting attack on Midnight Basketball, a commercial he dubbed "Night Shade." The campaign turned ugly as blacks made an issue of Harmon's marriage to a white woman. Bosley's father called Harmon "a rented Negro."

The vote came in heavily for Harmon, 56 percent to 43 percent. Only a few blacks attended Harmon's victory celebration. He promised to reverse the city's population decline, provide better housing on the North Side and offer a more open administration.

But Harmon made only a slight dent on the city. None of his announced goals were achieved. By the time he ran for reelection in 2001, he could only muster 5 percent of the primary vote. He portrayed himself as a non-politician, but he lived in a very political environment.

He was never a cheerleader for the city and seemed content to watch as the national economy improved without St. Louis. The city population continued to fall, dropping 12 percent between 1990 and 2000, from nearly 400,000 down to 350,000.

Outside of a hotel development very little changed in the downtown during his four years. He waffled on issues such as Metro transit expansion and saw little development anywhere in the city. A new flood of immigrants took over much of the housing that had emptied on the South Side. Survivors of the Bosnian War in Europe arrived. People from Latin America and Asia also came, drawn by some of the lowest housing prices in the nation.

Harmon's appointments were mainly from the military and the police department, leaving politicians on the sidelines. He failed to show up at fundraisers. He didn't buy a season ticket at Busch Stadium and wasn't there the night Mark McGwire hit his 62nd homer in 1998. The sign on his desk at City Hall read, "There's nothing honorable about politics."

This inaction gave both Civic Progress and the Democratic Party a cold chill. The door was left wide open for Francis Slay, who became the first four-term mayor in St. Louis history beginning with his victory in 2001. Both Bosley and Harmon ran against Slay but stood little chance. Bosley spent his time apologizing for past mistakes. Harmon's campaign staff deserted him.

Slay won 53 percent of the primary vote to Bosley's 41 percent, defeating the former mayor in the crucial central corridor 8,342 to 5,415 and offsetting Bosley's 23,000 advantage on the North Side with a 31,000-vote margin on the South Side.

Harmon took a job teaching public administration at Southern Illinois University in Carbondale. He admitted his low-key approach didn't work. "I was an administrator, not a mover or shaker," he said in 2002.

Bosley returned to a law practice and became part owner of a concrete supply company called United Materials. He got into trouble in 2001 for an apparent attempt to get minority funding when the company was mostly white-owned and again in 2014 over allegations of mishandling a lawsuit.

The 2010 census showed more decline, with the population of the city down another 8 percent over 10 years to 319,294 people. Blacks were the largest racial group at 49 percent with the white population making up 44 percent. The Delmar Divide was shaper than ever, 94 percent black in North City. South of the line, African Americans made up 35 percent in the central corridor and 26 percent of South Side residents.

Hispanic and Latino was 3.5 percent of the population. The Asian population included concentrations of Vietnamese and Chinese making up a little over 2 percent of the total city population. The rest of the city was Native American, Alaskan native and mixed race.

The influx of Bosnian refugees in the nineties brought some 70,000 mostly Muslim Bosnians to the city and county. The concentration was the largest outside Europe. The transition was surprisingly easy.

These refugees were accepted by residents, churches and businesses, hired in skilled jobs, bought cars, then homes, and saw their children graduate from American high schools, then colleges. In less than a generation three mosques were built, a Chamber of Commerce formed, restaurants and stores built in the Bevo Mill area on the South Side. Bosnians also moved to South County where they found affordable housing.

St. Louis County population, which reached the 1 million mark in 2000, slumped slightly in the first decade of the twentieth century, down to 998,954 in 2010, but was back up to just over a million again in a 2014 estimate.

Population in the St. Louis metro area was a different story. This category counted the sharp growth in the far suburban areas of St. Charles County, and also added four more counties on the Missouri side of the river and five in Illinois.

Greater St. Louis, putting all the areas together, had added 8.3 percent between 1990 and 2000 and another 3.3 percent by the 2010 census, up to a total of 2,787,701. Of this total 77 percent were white and 18 percent African American.

What about crime? In 1915, St. Louis city police reported 74 homicides. In 1921, there were 138 homicides, a rate of about 14 per 100,000 residents.

Starting in the fifties, overall crime and homicides began to rise. The total number of homicides in the city topped out in 1970 with 309 killings (a rate of nearly 50 per 100,000.) The highest rate was in 1993 at 69 homicides per 100,000 people.

In the Greater St. Louis area overall, homicides peaked in 2007 with 266, while the highest rate per 100,000 people was in 2008 at 8.3 per

100,000. In St. Louis County there were 34 homicides in 2013, a rate of 3.4 per 100,000 residents.

In 2014, there were 159 murders (about 53 per 100,000) in St. Louis city, the highest yearly tally since 2008, and the highest per 100,000 in the nation, fitting the city's "murder capital" stereotype. The rates were skewed, however, by the decline in population inside the city and growth in the metro area. Putting the city and county together showed a rate of about 12 homicides per 100,000, lower rate than Ingelwood, Calif., or Little Rock, Ark.

Using the Greater St. Louis figures the homicide rate for 2012 was 7.3 per 100,000.

Police Chief Sam Dotson said domestic violence and arguments between people who knew each other caused a majority of the killings. Many also had drug and gang overtones, with most victims showing a criminal record and the killings concentrated in a few neighborhoods.

In 1994 Morgan Quinto Press (now CQ) began distributing rankings of cities as "most livable," "smartest" and other categories including "most dangerous city." St. Louis was named No. 1 "most dangerous city" three times since, the most recent was 2010, adding to the national reputation as a crime-plagued city.

City officials, along with the FBI, the American Society of Criminology, and the U.S. Conference of Mayors have consistently questioned the rankings. The criminology society said the rankings were based on faulty methodology where separation of St. Louis city from the surrounding area (St. Louis metro) made the ranking meaningless.

"These rankings represent an irresponsible misuse of the data and do groundless harm to many communities," the society said. The Conference of Mayors pointed out odd disparities in the methods used for the rankings as well, such as giving homicide and auto theft the same statistical weight in the final tallies.

Criminologist Rick Rosenfeld said that in St. Louis, "If you're heavily involved in crime, you run a strong risk of being killed. If you're not, your risk is much, much lower."

Francis G. Slay was born March 18, 1955, into a political family on the South Side, the second of 11 children. His father, Francis R. Slay, was the long-time committeeman in the 23rd Ward. He lived for 83 years until his death in 2011, becoming the dean of St. Louis Democrats, a restaurant owner and power broker.

Francis R. Slay stayed mostly behind the scenes of St. Louis politics. His father, Joseph R. Slay, a Democratic alderman from 1946 to 1950, was a Lebanese immigrant who started a restaurant, the first of three eateries in the family.

The most popular was Slay's Restaurant on Hampton Avenue, one of the few places on the South Side where blacks were served during the sixties. The future mayor worked there as a young man, tending bar or greeting people at the door.

Francis R. Slay was first elected Democratic committeeman in 1964 and went on to two terms in the Missouri House. He returned to St. Louis in 1970 and became City Recorder of Deeds, but resigned to run the restaurant in 1977. He moved back into his slot as 23rd Ward committeeman, where he remained until 2008.

His power base was a church banquet hall at St. Raymond's Catholic Church just south of downtown. Every Wednesday for decades Slay smiled and slapped backs at the city's unofficial power lunch. He maintained a glass-enclosed office where he discussed local issues. There he paved the way for his son's rise to the mayor's office and celebrated three of his victories with celebratory runs around the dining room.

Prior to being elected mayor, Francis G. Slay served as an alderman for 10 years, then as president of the Board of Aldermen from 1995-2001. He earned his law degree from St. Louis University School of Law. Slay's administration has been generally bland, quietly working with Civic Progress to help revitalize downtown and the central corridor.

His first term saw a new baseball stadium built downtown and in his third term the Ballpark Village development finally filled the parking lot where the second Busch Stadium stood. Slay also supported the redevelopment of the Washington Avenue Loft District, which struggled through all his years in office. The Old Post Office on Market Street was saved but an adjacent historic office building was demolished for a parking garage. The ornate walls of City Hall, in dire need of a facelift, were left untouched and Union Station remained devoid of regular passenger service.

The Central West End saw the biggest change, adding numerous restaurants and shops, becoming more upscale, its rents the highest in St. Louis. The central corridor had something of a building boom, with a new IKEA furniture store, a Whole Foods supermarket and high-tech development with the Cortex Innovation Community leading a movement of "start ups." Over Slay's term many single young people were drawn into the city but all over the core of the region empty blocks still stood, scattered with broken brick and garbage.

Another proud achievement for St. Louis was the new Stan Musial Bridge across the Mississippi to Illinois, a modern structure of striking beauty built just north of the Arch, where a major reconstruction of the grounds and museum was underway. Also near in the Arch the new National Blues Museum opened, aimed at drawing music fans to the River City.

But the nearby to these new developments the Jones Dome stood empty after St. Louis lost its football team to Los Angeles. And Laclede's Landing, perhaps the most beautiful architectural area in the city, remained forlorn, ill-used and cut off from the pulse of the region by a monster highway system and a dominant casino.

Despite Slay's efforts, the city schools seemed to defy improvement, perhaps the chief legacy of the decline in population and the fear of crime. There were sparks of bright lights here and there in a charter school program backed by the city, but overall the educational level of public schools remained low. In scores revealed in August 2014, St. Louis was one of just 3 percent of state school districts below the accredited threshold.

And on the North Side, outside of the struggling Old North development, little progress was made over Slay's years in office, the housing gradually crumbling in old neighborhoods that slowly, family by family, emptied. Brick was stolen, city services dwindled and stores disappeared. The destruction of an area seven miles long and five miles wide continued year after year.

Slay, or course, was not alone in failing to deal with the giant ghetto that covers nearly half the city's geography. Through all the administrations of all the mayors since 1972 -- Cervantes, Poelker, Conway, Schoemehl, Bosley, Harmon and Slay – the demolition of the Pruitt-Igoe housing project hung in the air over St. Louis. The image remains thicker than the coal dust or the industrial blight along the waterfront, a vision of collapse and despair.

The land where the 33 buildings of the giant housing project stood remained empty all that time, over 40 years the project has remained as the national icon of urban waste, 74 acres just two miles northwest of the Gateway Arch. The land returned to forest, dominated by a canopy of fast-growing trees above a tangle of underbrush that hid broken glass and old tires. The cover of forest made it a popular drug market.

Large concrete warehouses lined the southern end of the property. The east side was fenced-off by St. Stanislaus Catholic Church. To the west and north was an area that was once saw a flourishing neighborhood of a single- and multi-family homes built of St. Louis brick in the late nineteenth and twentieth centuries. Newer urban renewal projects were scattered in these neighborhoods built at far lower density than was once present.

The only use of the site was the Gateway Schools complex, three interconnected buildings located in the southwest corner of the project where Pruitt Homes once stood. The schools were opened in 1995, one and two-story brick buildings facing a courtyard that included a shelter, playground and vegetable garden.

A variety of plans have been proposed for the area -- they include a business park, a 9-hole golf course surrounded by housing, a 33-acre retail mall with new housing next door and a "bee sanctuary" to harvest the honey from the bees that populate the woods. None of the plans were ever fully developed.

But a major interested party emerged in 2014 -- the federal government, looking for a place to move and expand its National Geospatial-Intelligence Agency (NGA) to a new facility that would replace its current western headquarters south of the Anheuser-Busch brewery. In 2016, after heavy lobbying by Slay and the city, the top-secret agency, which maps support systems for U.S. military operations around the world, selected the Pruitt-Igoe site for its $1.75 billion new location.

Part of the reason for the selection was President Obama's desire to use federal funding help "blighted" urban areas. Hope for development of the area near the NGA building was high, with potential for stores and services badly needed all through the North Side. But there were immediate concerns that the site would add few jobs beyond those for constructing the facility and that because of high crime in the area employees would simply drive in and out from the suburbs to the new building and leave again without setting foot in the depressed neighborhood.

The NGA selection was also criticized for its connection to a far larger proposal for the embattled area -- namely the ambitious two-square-mile NorthSide Regeneration plan. That idea, pushed by millionaire developers Paul and Midge McKee, was put on the drawing board in 2003, envisioning a host of housing and retail developments, including a three-bed emergency hospital in an area totally devoid of hospital beds.

McKee owned most of the land on the proposed NGA site and late in 2015, even before the facility was awarded to St. Louis, the Board of Aldermen passed a resolution giving the city the right to use eminent domain to seize property from 37 owners within the 100-acre parcel.

By year's end the city -- represented by the St. Louis Development Corporation -- made a complicated deal with McKee for his property on the Pruitt-Igoe site, but not with McKee directly.

The city's Land Clearance for Redevelopment Authority already made a $5 million foreclosure purchase in August, buying up nearly a quarter of the NorthSide Regeneration property from an entity called Titan Fish Two. This was essentially a debt-relief plan for McKee who was being sued by Titan, which said McKee owed $17 million in notes.

A city official told St. Louis Public Radio in December that the lawsuit would be dropped once the deal with McKee was finalized.

Titan Fish Two foreclosed on McKee in June 2015 and under the deal with the city would be paid another $2 million if the NGA decided to build on the North City site. The three-bed hospital scheme would be folded into the new deal.

Titan Fish is an LLC organized in Kansas.

When originally proposed, McKee's North Side scheme envisioned total investment of $8 billion in the project.

> (It would create) a self-sustaining neighborhood of people, culture, economic opportunity, secure environment and education for our children with the infrastructure and capitalistic growth to support key, necessary services for the community.
>
> The whole idea is to get the economic wheel of the North Side going again after it's been blighted for 70 years.

McKee's mother grew up in The Ville, the once thriving center of the North Side. He was raised in South County and lives in Huntleigh, one of the wealthiest suburbs in the area, home of the Busch family.

He is a founding member of BJC HealthCare, operators of Barnes Jewish Hospital and the area's largest employer. He also developed the corporate home of Express Scripts, a pharmacy benefit management outfit that had risen to the nation's 20th largest company in the United States with 2013 revenues of $104.62 billion.

By the end of 2014 McKee's company, McEagle Property, had bought up 2,200 parcels of land, 47 of them what became the NGA site. McKee, one of Slay's major political supporters, had the mayor's blessings for the North Side idea. Slay's chief of staff called the plan bold and visionary.

But after over a decade of talking, about the only thing tangible McKee has built was a Website and a lot of scale models. He set a schedule to break ground in the fall of 2014 on a convenience store, small neighborhood market and recycling center but the shovels remained still as attention turned to the discussions over the NGA proposal.

Opposition to the overall McKee North Side initiative centered on fear that McKee was too powerful and did not have the interests of the community in mind.

At a 2014 city hearing on the issue one resident summed up the feeling of about 200 local opponents who packed the meeting to try to stop the progress of McKee's plan. James Meinert moved to the North Side in 2000:

> I moved into the neighborhood because I wanted to be a part of it. I did not move into this neighborhood to have another white man from the suburbs come in and tell us what's best for us, and to do it for us, and for the city to give him the money that should be coming to the people that are here.

Michael Allen, a Washington University architectural historian and preservationist, said:

> Clearly, for the last decade McKee's dream has cost the Near North Side hundreds of residents who have moved out of houses and apartments sold to (McKee's) shell holding companies.
>
> Who knows how many people fled as they saw the NorthSide Regeneration properties torched, brick rustled and otherwise left

> to rot. Blockbusting need not be intentional, after all. Myself and others have counted how many irreplaceable architectural treasures have been lost to the scheme.

Perhaps the North Side will be regenerated by the NGA and help blow away some of the clouds over the national image of St. Louis, clouds that became considerably thicker and darker during the anniversary year of 2014, a year not good for those who touted the often hidden treasures of the city at the confluence.

The storm blew in from just a little beyond the North Side this time, from a few miles north and west into North County where the tempests of race and police aggression produced thunderous weather following Officer Darren Wilson's killing of the teenage Michael Brown in Ferguson.

The shooting took place just a few minutes after noon on Aug. 9, a hot, humid summer Saturday in suburban St. Louis. Michael Brown and a friend were walking east in the middle of Canfield Drive, in front of an open development of 450 apartment units located in low-rise buildings not far from the main street of Ferguson. Brown's grandmother lived in a nearby complex.

As the two teens walked along, a Ferguson police SUV driven by Wilson, working alone, pulled up in the street in front of Brown and his friend, parking at an angle to block their path. Wilson stayed in the SUV. Brown stood by the window. Angry words were exchanged, words overheated by issues of race. There was a scuffle at the door. Twice Wilson tried to fire his pistol, on the third try it worked. Two shots were fired from inside the SUV, one of them grazing Brown's thumb.

Brown turned and ran back down the street. Wilson got out of the van and raced after Brown. Brown stopped and Wilson stopped. Brown moved toward the officer. Wilson fired 10 shots at the teenager. The final shot went into Brown's head, killing him.

Brown was found to be unarmed, his body riddled with shots to the chest and arms as well as the head.

Wilson suffered a bruise to the side of his face.

This narrow account takes its facts from a later grand jury proceeding. Many, many versions of what happened were presented after the killing. The story of the shooting is like that of the old party gag where one person whispers a story to the next person and they whisper it to the next and so on until the last person in the circle repeats it out loud. By then the facts have disappeared.

The incident was not televised. There was only one living participant. Everything else came from witnesses, people who saw many things in many ways.

Take just one example of the confusion, from five people all riding on Canfield in a minivan, a husband and wife, their two daughters and the children's grandmother. All five told different stories. The wife said Wilson was in a police car not an SUV. All five disagreed on where Brown was when he was shot and what he was doing as Wilson chased him.

Another witness said Brown charged the officer. Another witness said he heard a shot from and saw "Big Mike on his knees with his hands in the air." Another said three officers were chasing the teenager.

Some witnesses said they didn't really witness the shooting. They may have gotten information from television. One admitted she lied; others were found to have poor eyesight, suffered from bouts of memory loss or couldn't hear.

The fact was that Brown's dead body lay in the street in the August sun for over four hours. For a while blood streamed onto the pavement as horrified residents in the nearby apartments tried to keep children away from the scene. Others posted cell phone video on the Internet.

The lengthy delay in removing the corpse was a major reason why the killing quickly expanded from a local police incident to a national story about race relations in America, a shooting that drew the attention of the world's press and the president of the United States.

Patricia Bynes, a black committeewoman in Ferguson who had worked against Slay's reelection, said, the delay was "disrespectful to the community and the people who live there." It also sent the message from law enforcement that "we can do this to you any day, any time, in broad daylight, and there's nothing you can do about it."

Shortly after the killing, as is routine in major cases, St. Louis County Police took over from the local Ferguson force. County patrol officers reached the scene almost immediately. But it wasn't until 1:30 p.m., more than an hour after the bullets were fired, that homicide detectives arrived and at least another hour before a county forensic examiner was on the scene.

A white sheet was tossed over the body about 12:15, but Brown's feet stuck out from under the sheet and blood pooled on the pavement. He lay face down.

Chaos ensued. Brown was well known in the community. Relatives, friends and passersby clogged the roads and pressed against the yellow police tape stretched around the scene. Brown's uncle ducked under the tape but was grabbed by an officer before he could view the body.

Cell phone cameras snapped. Twitter accounts buzzed. Gunshots were heard in the distance, frightening the onlookers. Officers struggled to conduct an investigation.

A county police spokesman said detectives couldn't conduct their usual tasks "right away because there weren't enough police there to quiet the situation."

Sometime around 4 p.m., Brown's body, by then covered with a blue tarp, was loaded into a black van and driven to the county morgue, six miles away. The corpse was checked in at 4:37 p.m.

Brown's stepfather, Louis Head, said Ferguson police had "executed my son."

St. Louis County Police Chief Jon Belmar made an early statement that said Brown was killed after he assaulted an officer.

A makeshift memorial started and protests began.

Shops were looted. Fires were set in the streets.

The national media descended. A barrage of news began. One-story news coverage quickly took over cable television. For days it was Ferguson, Ferguson, all day, all the time.

The *Post-Dispatch* ran daily headlines in giant black capital letters across the front page above lurid, blurry photographs of smoke and fire. *The New York Times* ran front page banner headlines of the like reserved for wars and presidential elections.

Television broadcast images of police in full military regalia as they arrived to stop the protests.

Every one of the 100 or more reporters on the scene within a day or two started filing. Most sent out information many times a day, each time trying to find a new wrinkle, throwing more and more data into the dump. Blogs, Facebook and Twitter posts, wire copy, newspaper copy, radio and television feeds – all had to be pumped onto the insatiable Internet, usually without a second look at what was sent out, always with little chance of making a change if somebody in the pack of 100 journalists got something wrong.

Armored personnel carriers once used in the Iraq War rumbled into the streets of the town. Police in military body armor aimed assault rifles at crowds in the streets. Looting and burning continued to flare during nightly demonstrations. Rubber bullets and tear gas flew. Local police walked around in full riot gear.

Belmar praised his forces for "a remarkable amount of restraint. If there was an easy way to fix this, we would have already solved the problem."

Justice Department investigators waded in on the Tuesday after the killing, promising a full investigation of the shooting. By Wednesday President Obama was briefed on the situation.

"Hands up, don't shoot," protestors sneered in the streets as police lines pushed forward, the faces of the officers hidden by black plastic masks. The Black Lives Matter movement, born during an earlier shooting of a black in Florida, came into national focus.

Missouri Gov. Jay Nixon remained away from the scene, saying he was monitoring events. St. Louis County Prosecutor Robert McCulloch said details would not be released until later, promising everything would eventually be put in the hands of a grand jury. Calls for a special prosecutor went unheeded. Nixon said he had faith in McCulloch, a white county prosecuting attorney since 1991.

Protest leaders pointed to McCulloch's long record of family ties to police. His father was a St. Louis cop killed by a black man in the line of duty when McColloch was 12. His brother was an officer in the St. Louis PD, his mother was a clerk and other relatives were also officers.

McCulloch, too, would have been a policeman but a leg was amputated in high school. "I couldn't become a policeman, so being county prosecutor is the next best thing," he once said. His record as prosecutor included at least two controversial cases where police were cleared by a grand jury. Only a few officers had ever been indicted under his watch.

Ferguson Police Chief Thomas Jackson at first refused to identify the officer who did the shooting, citing death threats. Jackson said the officer had been injured in the incident and was "very shaken."

On Wednesday, reporters from the *Washington Post* and the Huffington Post were arrested and then quickly released on orders from Chief Jackson.

By then, four days after the shooting, the national glare was fully felt. Ferguson had become the biggest civil rights story since America elected a black president in 2008. The images reminded a nation of the marches and battles of the sixties. Protest leaders evoked Martin Luther King, demanding justice, demanding that the officer who did the shooting be indicted.

Into the fray rode one of the nation's veteran civil rights leaders, the Rev. Al Sharpton, who arrived at the scene Tuesday and spoke to 1,000 people at a church just half a mile from where Brown's body had laid.

Sharpton, an Obama adviser and national radio talk show host, urged peaceful protest and said protestors should be ready for a long fight. Another national figure, Rev. Jamal Bryant from Baltimore, added, "St. Louis is bearing witness for America. All of America is seeing the open wound of racism."

Defiant demonstrators began using a slogan from the sixties anti-war movement, chanting "The Whole World is Watching" as police lobbed tear gas into crowds near the Ferguson police station. Another of the protestors stood in a smoky street holding a sign reading, "A Good Night for a Revolution."

Nixon finally stepped forward the day after Sharpton left town, ordering the Missouri State Patrol to take over command of the forces trying to contain nightly demonstrations. This move defused some of the tension. Officers under state control put aside military-style gear and pulled back the fearsome armored vehicles, responding to a wave of national comment comparing images in Ferguson to those in the Iraq War.

But the next night, crowds, now including protesters who had been arriving from around the country, clashed with police again, this time leaving 31 arrested.

Missouri Highway Patrol Capt. Ronald Johnson said a few people determined to cause trouble had pulled the crowd along. Bottles and

Molotov cocktails were thrown at police, two fires were set and random gunfire was heard. Even so, there had been no one killed or seriously injured in the aftermath of Brown's death in the street.

"This nation is watching each and every one of us," an angry, emotional Johnson said at a news conference in the riot zone at 2:30 a.m. Johnson lectured reporters at the scene, charging them with interference, warning them to "not glamorize the acts of criminals."

Over 200 press credentials had by then been issued at the scene, including many bloggers and social media commentators now sending play-by-play accounts. Politicians, pundits and protestors poured out words that justified their views and promoted their agenda. Facts were scant, rarely in the way of a new feed.

The nightly demonstrations kept up and on Aug. 18, nearly two weeks after the shooting, Nixon called up the National Guard.

Guard troops remained largely in the background as state and county forces used tear gas to disperse the protestors. An armored vehicle was deployed again, this time met with a group of clergy who locked arms and helped police move demonstrators away from direct confrontation.

President Obama, meanwhile, condemned both sides of the conflict, telling demonstrators to act peacefully and warning police against the use of "excessive force." He urged Americans to "heal rather than wound each other." He said he would send Attorney General Eric Holder to Ferguson to meet with FBI investigators, but made no mention of any plans to visit the stricken suburb himself.

"We have all seen images of protesters and law enforcement in the streets," the president added.

> It's clear that the vast majority of people are peacefully protesting. What's also clear is that a small minority of individuals are not.
>
> While I understand the passions and the anger that arise over the death of Michael Brown, giving into that anger by looting or carrying guns, and even attacking the police only serves to raise tensions and stir chaos. It undermines rather than advances justice.

Appearing on ABC television, Brown's mother, Lesley McSpadden, was asked how peace could be restored. She said the only answer was to arrest Officer Wilson, who was identified six days after the shooting and placed on paid leave at an undisclosed location.

All the national attention, official calls for various reforms and the announcement of a date for Brown's funeral led to another period of calm. Nixon pulled out the Guard on Aug. 22 after three nights of quiet. The county police said over 200 people had been arrested in the two weeks of protest since the shooting.

Still, only one person had been killed in Ferguson in connection with the incident, a teenager by the name of Michael Brown.

Sharpton was back in town for the funeral Monday, Aug. 25, held before 2,500 mourners, nearly all black, at the North Side's biggest church, the Friendly Missionary Baptist. He led a howling, tearful crowd in the packed pews of the plush auditorium, calling for a national lament for young African-American men killed in cities around the United States.

McSpadden stood before her son's casket, still in shock. Another relative, Bernard Ewing, the man who broke police lines to get near the teenager's body shortly after he was shot to death, broke into tears standing on a stage. Nearby lay the coffin, covered with red roses, a Cardinals baseball cap sitting at the head of the casket. Brown was a lifelong Redbird fan.

"I love you, Mike. That's all I've got to say," Ewing said.

To many, the service, like the shooting, went beyond the last rites for a slain teenager.

Chris Gray, a 29-year-old who came from Minneapolis for the funeral, told the *Los Angeles Times,* "A lot of people feel they could be next. There's a historic possibility here for young people to take ownership of a new civil rights movement."

"Nobody is going to help us if we don't help ourselves," Sharpton said, adding that it was time for blacks to stop "sitting around having ghetto pity parties. A movement means we've got to be here for the long haul and turn our chance into change, our demonstration into legislation."

A 33-year-old woman who lived in nearby Jennings brought her two young children to service, saying, "I've got these two young boys to look after. This is a wake-up call for our young black men. I don't want them to be victims."

Among the others in church were the Hollywood film director Spike Lee and the actor Wesley Snipes as well as relatives of other black victims, including the sixties civil rights worker Emmett Till and those of Trayvon Martin, the teenager shot in Florida in 2012 by a white neighborhood watch guard.

The last rites for Michael Brown lasted three hours.

The church choir, one of the best in the nation, belted out stirring gospel songs to the beat of tambourines shaken by mourners. Men, women and children, all dressed in their very best, tears running down their faces, hands raised and heads thrown back, swayed to the rhythms, filled with the spirit, sending their gentle giant away, hoping his death could change America.

After the funeral the demonstrations died down, the Guard was removed, the television trucks rolled out of town, journalists packed their laptops and returned to their home bases in the east and west, in Britain and France. A simmering boil remained, as the wait began for officials to make their reports, all eyes on the St. Louis County grand jury that was meeting in Clayton, the county seat.

During the hiatus, a "national conversation" on race bubbled. A state Ferguson Commission was appointed. A federal Justice Department investigation continued. The town prepared for the decision on Wilson. Clergy held prayer meetings. Supporters of the police issued statements and held rallies. The new movement, Black Lives Matter, grew on social media.

The story remained at the top of the news locally with each wrinkle reported against televised repeats of the footage of tear gas bombs and military vehicles, the shots of flames on the main street and looters running from the police.

Across the region, in bars and restaurants, around kitchen tables and during walks in Forest Park, residents debated the issues raised by the startling events. Race discrimination was certainly not new in St. Louis, seen at every stage of the city's history -- going back to its founding 250 years past, when the first slaves landed with Pierre Laclede the day he arrived to settle the city.

The race issue was there at the 1904 World's Fair. It was there as African Americans were hung from lampposts in East St. Louis in 1917, in the disparity of treatment during the Depression and again in the economic discrimination in the World War II factories.

It was there in the destruction of Mill Creek Valley, in the rise of poverty and crime on the North Side, in the clearance of black neighborhoods for freeways during the sixties and seventies. And it was there in that moment when the white policeman shot the black teenager in the suburb of Ferguson.

In this, St. Louis was by no means unique. To paraphrase sixties radical H. Rap Brown, racism is as American as apple pie.

The growth of the American civil rights movement in the fifties and sixties had been slowed first by the assassination of Martin Luther King in April 1968 and by the election of "law and order" candidate Richard Nixon that November. The movement was further crippled by the shift in the Supreme Court with the appointment of Clarence Thomas in 1991, and weakened again by the growth of the religious right in the Republican Party during the nineties. A deadlock in the House of Representatives in the twenty-first century made progress virtually impossible even with a black man in the White House.

Nixon had given FBI Director Herbert Hoover full right to attack organizations like the Black Panther Party nationally and the Black Liberators in St. Louis, leading to the killing of Panther leader Fred Hampton in 1969 and opening the COINTELPRO infiltration of the civil rights movement throughout the early seventies.

Thomas, one of the most conservation black jurists in the nation, replaced Thurgood Marshall in what was called the "black seat" on the court. Marshall, architect of the Shelley housing desegregation suit in 1948 and a lifetime champion of African-American rights, had served on the high court from 1967 until Republican President George H.W. Bush named Thomas in 1991, an appointment that shifted the majority to favor a conservative view that, according to another justice, could "not be overstated."

Under the centrist presidency of Southerner Bill Clinton in the nineties, the attacks on the black community continued. Clinton adopted policy approaches started by Nixon and continued by the conservative Ronald Reagan, who revived Nixon's "war on crime" in the eighties, a war that sent more police and FBI into black communities. Despite his cool demeanor and professed love of civil rights, Clinton championed "three strikes" laws, expanded sentences for drug crimes, and pushed through billions of dollars for prisons and police during the nineties, especially a $16 billion crime bill in 1994.

George W. Bush continued the law-and-order trend while president from 2001 until 2009. Then disgruntled American voters sent a black man into the presidency. But Barack Obama was slow off the mark and lost his House majority in 2010. He passed a compromise version of a landmark federal health care plan that eased the medical burdens of millions of Americans but was unable to slow the massive accumulation of wealth at the top of the economy. Rapid consolidation by the richest corporations created a new Gilded Age that dwarfed the excesses of the late nineteenth century.

Indeed, the situation in the black community in St. Louis and elsewhere looked much the same in 2016 near the end of the Obama presidency as it had when Bill Clinton took office in 1992. In the quarter century where the apparently civil rights-friendly Democratic Party had been in the White House most of the time, manufacturing had collapsed, globalization had triumphed, urban ghettos remained strewn with broken glass and trash, the education system and job availability were still tilted toward whites.

A study by the Institute for Policy Studies in 2015 showed that the top 100 wealthiest Americans were worth as much at the nation's 42 million African-Americans combined. Blacks were more than six times more likely to be jailed than whites.

These conditions increased anger in the public and pushed forward two outsiders in the presidential campaign of 2016, a socialist senator, Bernie Sanders, and a Republican real estate mogul, Donald Trump. Sanders pointed to a "rigged economy" for the wealthy and Trump excited people who feared immigrants. Both surprised the establishments in their political parties (including the wife of Clinton and the brother of Bush) by promising drastic changes in the government.

In the 1,217 deadly police shootings reported nationally from 2010 to 2012 to the FBI, black males, age 15 to 19, were over 20 times more likely to be killed than white males of the same age. Another analysis showed that between 2006 and 2012 there were an average of 96 cases each year of a white police officer killing a black person in circumstances deemed justifiable. That's almost four times a week.

Police shooting statistics in St. Louis and St. Louis County showed that prosecuting an officer in any shooting was rare. In the city, 39 people were fatally shot by police officers from 2003 and 2012. Only one officer was indicted and he was acquitted.

In St. Louis County the numbers were harder to sort out. St. Louis County Police patrol only areas not included in the 90 jurisdictions serviced by the individual small town governments in the county. County police recorded 14 killings in the decade between 2004 and 2014. No officer was ever indicted. Statistics from the 90 municipalities, which have 60 different police departments, were unavailable.

Other figures showed wide discrepancies between the number of black officers and the black population. In the 14 municipalities with more than 50 percent black population, only half had more than 50 percent black officers. In the 31 towns and cities with more than 10 percent black, more than half had fewer than 10 percent black officers.

Only in University City was there an even balance, with 42 percent of the police African American compared to 41 percent of the population. St. Louis city had a 48 percent black population with 34 percent black officers.

Ferguson's population of 21,000 in 2014 was 67 percent black, its police force 7 percent black, one of the widest discrepancies in the area. The biggest difference was in Riverview, a North County town along the Mississippi not far from the North Side, where there were no black officers patrolling streets where 70 percent of the residents were black.

Other areas that gauged wellbeing in the region, rated the sixth most segregated in the country, also saw wide differences. Statistics from 2012 found blacks lagging far behind in home ownership, 57 percent to 22 percent. Black unemployment was nearly 13 percent; white was 5 percent. The infant mortality rate was nearly 16 percent for blacks; just 4 percent for whites. The overall poverty rate for blacks was 30 percent, for whites 9 percent. Among the 16-to-19 black male age group unemployment stood at 63 percent compared to 23 percent for whites.

As the statistics were hashed over, as politicians mulled reforms, as newspapers and bloggers diced and sliced the information and the misinformation, the grand jury met in the county seat of Clayton. It alone would decide the fate of Officer Darren Wilson.

The grand jury was made up of nine whites and three blacks.

Finally, on Monday, Nov. 24, three and a half months after the shooting, county prosecutor Robert McCulloch, a graying white man wearing a business suit, a somber tie and a starched white shirt, stood before a room full of reporters from around the world to announce the decision.

A few days earlier Nixon declared a state of emergency and called National Guard units back to St. Louis. He arrived in person for the decision.

Schools closed. Plywood was nailed to shop windows in Clayton and Ferguson. Streets emptied. Malls closed early. Clayton, a town of 16,000 people with 77 percent white, was a ghost town.

Miles away, protesters gathered in Ferguson, listening to radios and watching smartphones outside police headquarters. Officers from state, county and city forces braced.

Since August, Wilson had remained out of public view. He testified before the grand jury shortly after it began considering whether he would be indicted for a crime in the shooting. His testimony filled 90 pages of transcript but boiled down to one salient allegation -- he said he thought his life was in danger when he shot the unarmed teenager.

The majority of his testimony was a description of the initial struggle at the door of the police SUV, what Wilson said was a fight for his gun after he told Brown and a companion to get out of the street. Brown, according to Wilson, failed to get the gun and runs away. Wilson chases him up the street. Brown turns and comes toward the officer.

> As he was coming toward me I keep telling him to get on the ground, he doesn't. I shoot a series of shots. I don't know how many I shot, I just know I shot it.
>
> I know I missed a couple, I don't know how many, but I know I hit him at least once because I saw his body kind of jerk or flinched.
>
> I remember having tunnel vision on his right hand, that's all. I'm just focusing on that hand when I'm shooting.

> Well, after that last shot my tunnel vision kind of opened up. I remember seeing the smoke from the gun and I kind of looked at him and he's still coming at me, he hadn't slowed down.

Wilson testified that he kept shooting and Brown kept coming toward him. He said he thought Brown was reaching for something under his shirt, at his waistband. Until finally:

> I remember looking in my sites and firing. All I see is his head and that's what I shot.
>
> I don't know how many, I know at least once because I saw the last one go into him. And then when it went into him, his demeanor on his face went blank, the aggression was gone, it was gone, I mean I knew he stopped.
>
> When he fell he fell on his face.

In October, Wilson married a Ferguson police officer.

By November, the Brown family had made numerous public appearances at demonstrations, meetings and on the streets of Ferguson. Brown's mother, Leslie McSpadden, recently returned from Geneva, where she met with United Nations officials. Over the weekend, before the decision was announced, Brown's father handed out turkeys to needy families and urged demonstrators to remain calm.

McCulloch waited until darkness had fallen over the region that Monday night before he stepped behind a lectern in the county justice center. He slowly read a long statement detailing the importance of physical evidence. He discredited many witnesses whose accounts of the shooting varied from that of Wilson, then finally, after keeping the reporters, the families and the demonstrators waiting for over 20 minutes -- he uttered the words "no true bill."

The 12-member grand jury, nine whites and three blacks, had spoken. There would be no charges against Officer Darren Wilson.

In front of the police station in Ferguson, Leslie McSpadden stood on the hood of a car and screamed "They wrong!" Her face cringed in new grief, "You all know you all are wrong!" pointing at the police.

"Everybody want me to be calm," she cried, "but do you know how those bullets hit my son? Do you know what those bullets did to his body?"

A man fired four shots in the air in front of the station. Others hurled rocks and bottles at the line of police.

The officers, about 40 in number, responded with flash grenades, smoke bombs and tear gars. There was no sign of the National Guard.

The tear gas sent the crowd, numbering in the hundreds, wheeling away north from the station on South Florissant Road, a main business street that had seen no rioting in August. This time, a pizza parlor and a drug store were set on fire.

At Canfield Gardens a crowd got the news from car radios. They began to chant "No justice, no peace" and joined the other groups of demonstrators who had stormed west from about a half mile away on West Florissant, another of Ferguson's main business streets. There, protesters began smashing store windows, setting fire to a meat market, a storage facility, a used car lot, torching 10 businesses along the street.

The Ferguson Market and Liquor Store was looted. At McDonald's windows were smashed. Fires billowed out of trashcans up and down the street. Two empty police cars were torched.

The police stayed near its station. The Guard remained at its command post. Nixon said later he made a decision not to confront the looters, fearing there would be loss of life. No one was killed in the riot and only about 20 people were arrested.

By the next night, police and Guardsmen sealed off West Florissant. On South Florissant at the police station, concrete barriers were erected during the day and more Guardsmen backed a line of police.

Not long after dark Tuesday, officers swarmed the streets and when a group of demonstrators tried to burn a police car the area was immediately cleared in a cloud of tear gas. Several people were arrested and the rioting in Ferguson stopped.

The night of the decision and during the next day dozens of demonstrations broke out around the nation.

Close at hand, in the Shaw neighborhood near downtown St. Louis, a group of about 250 people expressed solidarity with the Ferguson protest by breaking windows along South Grand Boulevard and blocking lanes of an Interstate highway.

Twenty-one people were arrested near where another black teenager, VonDerrit Meyers, had been killed by a white off-duty officer working in uniform for a neighborhood watch group on Oct. 8, two months after the Brown killing.

Police said Meyers, 18, had fired at the officer and that Meyers' gun had been recovered. No charges were filed against the officer in a case that was quickly resolved by the city. Meyers' family said witnesses said Meyers had no gun and was trying to give up when he was shot.

Rallies sparked around the country in New York, Washington, Chicago, Seattle and Philadelphia. Protesters blocked streets and denounced the decision that cleared Wilson.

In downtown Los Angeles, traffic on the Highway 101 freeway was stopped. Police in Portland, Ore., fired pepper spray and made arrests. In Chicago, about 100 protesters gathered for a 28-hour sit-in outside Mayor Rahm Emanuel's office.

President Obama, who had still not visited the scene of the shooting, issued a plea for peaceful protest and restraint" from police.

"We have made enormous progress in race relations over the course of the past several decades," Obama said in a rare late-night statement at the White House. "But what is also true is that there are still problems, and communities of color aren't just making these problems up."

That Saturday, less than a week after the grand jury decision, Wilson quit the department. "It was my hope to continue in police work, but the safety of other police officers and the community are of the paramount importance to me," he said.

His lawyer, Neil Bruntrager, said Wilson made his decision because he was told of "credible threats" to the department. The lawyer said Wilson had no concrete plans for the future. He said Wilson felt "elation" and "relief" when the announcement was made, but also felt "profound sadness" by the response in Ferguson.

Ferguson Mayor James Knowles said that because the officer resigned he would get no severance pay or benefits from the force and that the city had "severed ties" with Wilson.

Benjamin Crump, the Brown family lawyer, said it would consider "every legal avenue" available. A civil case was later filed but was dismissed.

Crump said that the family was not surprised by Wilson's decision, calling the police officer "cold as ice." He added that the family wanted "the killer of their unarmed son held accountable."

Brown's parents issued a statement saying they felt "profound disappointment." They asked supporters to "work together to fix the system that allowed this to happen."

There was, of course, no final word.

Protests, meetings and kitchen table arguments continued. St. Louis Rams football players held their hands up as they ran onto their stadium field in the "Don't Shoot" position. The plywood on the windows that replaced broken glass in Ferguson and along Grand Boulevard was painted over. Marchers walked across the state for seven days from St. Louis to the state capital in Jefferson City.

Demonstrators entered the Missouri Botanical Gardens singing protest lyrics to the tune of Christmas carols. Students at several high schools walked out of class. Protests continued in California, especially in Berkeley and Oakland.

New protests flared when a grand jury in New York City failed to indict police who were captured on videotape crushing an unarmed black, Eric Garner. Two police officers there were later shot and killed by a man who said he wanted to "kill pigs" in retaliation for the Brown and Gardner cases.

Protesters continued to march in St. Louis, one day closing the Gateway Arch, another filling Union Station. By year's end the protests had continued without pause for nearly five months, right up to New Year's Eve when a dozen protesters tried to stage a lie-in at Police Headquarters.

The Brown protests had by then become one of the longest civil rights campaigns in U.S. history. Speakers vowed that the demonstrations would go on to build a new era for civil rights reforms.

In Ferguson, businesses filed their insurance claims and accepted donations. Several closed their doors, perhaps forever. A white policeman hugged a black child. A campaign to send paper hearts to Ferguson school children resulted in bags of mail from around the world.

McCulloch and Nixon deflected criticism and vowed to work toward the betterment of the county and the state. A new county executive, Steve Stenger, a 42-year-old former prosecutor, was elected with the support of McCullough. He replaced the first black to the head the county government. He said he would against a north-south MetroLink line.

County police said they would start using body cameras on officers. Senators in Washington agreed that the surplus military gear dispensed to local police was out of control. Obama ordered some of the equipment be returned to the federal government. The Ferguson City Council said it would trim the fines on traffic tickets and warrants. Mayor Slay said he had located enough money in the city budget to add 160 new police officers.

The Justice Department in 2015 issued its report. It described through a series of examples and statistics how Ferguson used its police force and courts to fund the town. *The New York Times* summarized the federal findings as describing Ferguson as "a place where officers stopped and handcuffed people without probable cause, hurled racial slurs, used stun guns without provocation, and treated anyone as suspicious merely for questioning police tactics."

Attorney General Eric Holder said investigations revealed the root of the rage that brought people into the streets. He said the city had until Dec. 8 to file a plan on how to deal with its racial problems. He added:

> Seen in this context — amid a highly toxic environment, defined by mistrust and resentment, stoked by years of bad feelings, and spurred by illegal and misguided practices — it is not difficult to imagine how a single tragic incident set off the city of Ferguson like a powder keg,

The St. Louis County court system had long been a prime example of race conflict in the metro area. It was a system that punished an inordinate number of lower income people, hitting hard at the black population. Multiple fines for routine stops led to no-shows in court that in turn led to more fines, warrants, license suspensions, more no-shows. People lost their cars and their jobs. High-speed chases resulted. Shootings were another result. Statistics showed that 21 municipalities obtained over 20 percent of their general revenue from municipal court fines.

Even before the Brown shooting a group of lawyers, the ArchCity Defenders, released statistics showing how the municipalities depended on the small courts for basic city services. ArchCity subsequently sued seven towns, followed by 13 more suits filed by the state attorney general.

Across St. Louis County there were 81 separate town courts that dished out 216,000 warrants in 2013.

Court reform legislation was passed by the state legislature and signed by Nixon in July 2015. The immediate result was an amnesty program officials said would result in dismissal of thousands of warrants and failure-to-appear charges. The most important aspect of the law changed the cap on the amount of money collected by the town courts, lowering the cap down from 30 percent to 12.5 percent of a town's general operating budget.

Two high profile towns -- Ferguson and Jennings -- were among those that decided on early amnesty by throwing out old cases and clearing warrants.

But the law and the amnesty was complicated. To cite just two of many examples:

The revenue cap only applied to fines collected from "minor traffic tickets." Thus the failure-to-appear cases could only be applied to those stemming from such traffic ticket charges. That excluded from the reform hundreds of thousands of other warrants that came from underlying housing code violations, shoplifting, "walking in roadway" and other minor violations.

The bill set a cap on traffic fines at $300 per ticket, but that fine was rarely levied on a single violation. Also more than one fine per person couldn't be added up under the law, multiple violations were all treated separately. So someone with ten tickets, all under $300, still faced big problems. Nothing was done to deal with officers who wrote several tickets during one traffic stop.

Tom Harvey of Arch Defenders was disappointed:

> They've shown for at least 50 years that without real supervision they'll violate the Constitution and jail poor and black people . . . they make our point ... the real solution is abolishing those courts.

Court reform was also on the agenda of the Ferguson Commission, a group set up by Nixon prior to the grand jury decision. The group, including 16 members, was established to promote the conversation on race. The commission was an answer from Nixon to criticism for his slow state response in the immediate aftermath of the shooting, especially his unwillingness to put the state police or the National Guard into the mix of police units at the scene. He was also criticized for staying away from the area for several days.

The governor said the commission would seek solutions to "social and economic conditions. Maintaining the status quo was simply not acceptable."

Members included nine blacks and seven whites; there were clergy and business leaders as well as community and protest leaders. One of the members, 19-year-old Rasheen Aldrige, was sworn in wearing a T-shirt that read, "Demilitarize the Police." Another was Patrick Sly, manager of the Emerson Electric charitable trust, and third was a former black chief of the St. Louis police.

The group's first meeting attracted a large group of citizens, some who had lined up two hours early at the Ferguson Community Center. A three-and-a-half hour introductory period tried the residents' patience until finally several people shouted down the commissioners, arguing that the group didn't represent the community.

"We're hurting!" yelled a black woman, pointing her finger at the chairman of the group, Rev. Starskey Wilson, CEO of the Deaconess Foundation, a North Side charity that helps inner city children's health.

"You're killing our babies," the woman yelled. "You're disrespecting us as people. We're tired."

"I understand," Wilson said. "I'm hurting too, sweetheart."

When the St. Louis police chief took the microphone he was booed down and one speaker suggested the commission get out of the building and ring doorbells to find out what was really going on.

The commission's final report, a 198-page document of findings and recommendations for future action, was released in September of 2015, long after the protests had died down. Meetings, a total of 17 in all, became calmer as time went on. Shouting sessions lessened as an uneasy consensus was reached.

Not surprisingly, the commission painted a stark picture of race inequality in Ferguson and the St. Louis area. Using a litany of statistics it broadened the race issue to the whole state, showing, for an example, that black motorists in Missouri in 2014 were 75 percent more likely to be pulled over for traffic stops across the state than whites. Another example came from St. Louis County, where in a mostly African American Kinloch, the average life expectancy was more than 30 years less than in the mostly white suburb of Wildwood.

The commission's action plan called for reform of police departments and consolidation of the courts -- the two givens in all the protests and proposals that arose from the events in Ferguson. The commission went beyond these issues, however, also calling for ways to address underlying issues.

For example, the commission called for school-based health centers, support of early childhood education and a revision of the school accreditation system. It recommended an end to "predatory lending" by banks, the creation of family development accounts, job training programs, affordable housing, an increase in the minimum wage and the expansion of Medicaid eligibility.

The response from protestors was tepid. St. Louis alderman Antonio French said the report "has just put into written form what so many people have already voiced for years about change that needs to happen in the St. Louis region, but identifying a problem and fixing it are different."

Another politician turned protestor, the Democratic state senator Maria Chappelle-Nadal, said she was afraid that after the commission's the commission's findings were announced "we're just going to hear crickets, crickets, crickets."

Meanwhile, several Ferguson officials stepped down after the Justice Department report, including Police Chief Tom Jackson, City Manager John Shaw, Judge Ronald Brockmeyer, and Court Clerk Mary Ann Twitty.

The man hired as interim chief also quit earlier than expected. Mayor James Knowles III remained.

A Dec. 8 deadline for a town reform plan set by the Justice Department passed quietly. But negotiations with Knowles and the city persisted and a settlement that would limit the use of stun guns, established training programs for police and tightened probable cause regulations for traffic stops was reached.

It came as no surprise, however, that a new civil rights group emerged from the protests in Ferguson. Black Lives Matter begun as a Twitter hashtag in 2013 after the shooting of a black teenager in Florida, then burst into the national spotlight in Ferguson. Since then it was active in numerous protests of the deaths of African Americans, especially those from police aggression in Baltimore, Chicago and Cleveland.

A survey by *The New York Times* in December 2015 saw the group as including 26 chapters, each organized by local leadership. Activists have marched and shouted, have organized meetings, have disrupted presidential candidates.

One internal group, Campaign Zero, issued a detailed policy platform on preventing police violence and increasing police accountability. Another, Black Lives Matter Political Action Committee, started by a St. Louis radio host, proposed raising money for voter education.

The group was also prominent during an October protest at the University of Missouri, where a hunger strike over racism led to the resignation of the president and chancellor.

Others in the community spoke out. At the end of 2014, Nelly held his annual Black & White Ball. He had Ferguson on his mind.

He looked ahead. His vision was that the youth of today would be swept up by education and would someday return to Ferguson to create a new community where things would be different.

"Sometimes it takes a movement to wake people up," he said, "not for the worse but for the better for generations to come together and I think that's what this is."

He saw in the future a different kind of police exchange than the one that took place on Canfield Drive that August noon.

> It's not just "hey you, get out of the street."'
>
> It's 'hey, Michael, come on y'all, move out the way' or 'hey, Timothy, y'all move out the way. I know your mama and I'm calling your mama as soon as I get back to the station.

Nelly continued his years of good works in the community with a scholarship in the name of Michael Brown to the trade school Brown planned to attend, the downtown Vatterott College.

In August 2015 Darren Wilson was found by the *New Yorker* magazine living "on a nondescript dead-end street on the outskirts of

St. Louis. Most of the nearby houses are clad in vinyl siding; there are no sidewalks, and few cars around." He held his baby daughter, born in March 2015.

He told the magazine he had tried and failed to get police work after the grand jury's decision and said that even though he hadn't read the Justice Department reports on the incident the numbers regarding racism in Ferguson were "skewed. You can make those numbers fit whatever agenda you want."

He didn't talk about the incident that led to the killing of Brown, saying he was afraid of the "spin" this words might take in future lawsuits. He showed off a drawer full of police patches sent to him by other officers.

He said he and his wife lead a secluded life, occasionally going out to local restaurants.

"We try to go somewhere. How do I say this correctly? With like-minded individuals. You know. Where it's not a mixing pot."

Late in March 2016, Slay said he would run again for mayor, ready to seek a fifth term. Then in April, just two weeks later, he did a spin, called a news conference and announced he would not run, opening the door to a dozen or so hopefuls for the top city job.

He said that while he was in office "the city has slowly won back some of its swagger" and that he was proud of landing the new NSA facility for the North Side. He also said his health was good and that he hadn't ruled out a run for another office.

The river continued to roll past the Arch and the city seemed much the same as it was before Ferguson.

Gunfire continued to crackle on the North Side. Construction jangled the nerves of residents in the central corridor. The Blues City Deli started selling pizza from a new addition. Rockin' Jake drew raucous cheers from a crowd at 1:30 a.m. at BB's. Consolidation of the city and county appeared no closer than it was in 1876.

Bill McClellan, the columnist at the St. Louis P*ost-Dispatch,* asked the question a few months after Ferguson: "Can we learn much from history?" His answer, "Probably not. Things seem to have gotten better. But just below the surface, maybe not."

Chapter Notes
Volume Two

Chapter 19: The Forties

Lead quote: "Virginia Irwin Arrives With Roar of Battle Still in the Air," P-D, May 8. 1945

Lion of the Valley, James Neal Primm, 1998

Population statistics here and throughout are from *St. Louis City/ County Demographics 1772-2000*, transcribed by Scott K. Williams from U.S. Census Data in "History's Time Portal to Old St. Louis," from St. Louis Room, St. Louis Public Library; U.S. Census Bureau, city, county and state quick facts, 2014

Missouri, The WPA Guide to the "Show Me" State, Walter A. Schroeder and Howard W Marshall, eds,, 1941; "St. Louis Mayors Brief Biographies," Charles H. Cornwell, 1965

Lynching: NYT; Federal Protection of Constitutional Rights during World War II, Dominic J. Capeci, Jr., *The Journal of American History,* March 1986; *Lynching in America: Statistics, Information, Images, 1882-1968*; Archives at Tuskegee Institute

War contracts: P-D; *Grassroots at the Gateway: Class Politics and Black Freedom Struggle in St. Louis, 1936-75, Clarence Lang, 2009;* Greater St. Louis Air & Space Museum website; *Five-Year Review Report for the Former Weldon Spring Ordnance Works,* US Army Corps of Engineers, Kansas City District, 2005; "Fighting for Democracy in St. Louis: Civil Rights During World War II," Patricia L. Adams, published June 1988, reprinted in *St. Louis from Village to Metropolis: Essays from the Missouri Historical Reviews, 1906-2006,* Louis S. Gerteis, ed.

"Carl Ichan," *Forbes Magazine,* September 2013; American Railcar Industries website; "Carter Carburetor Site in St. Louis, Missouri," Environmental Protection Agency; William K. Bixby, Missouri History Museum website; Performance Marine website, Bolton Landing, New York, 2014; *St. Louis' Big League Ballparks,* Joan M. Thomas, 2004

T*he Spirit of St. Louis: A History of the St. Louis Cardinals and Browns,* Peter Golenbock, 2000; *Only the Ball Was White,* Robert Peterson, 1970

Detroit: "The summer of '43: Race riot still reverberates, six decades later," *Detroit Metro Times,* June 18, 2003; "A race riot there will be: The View from a Polish Ghetto. Some Observations on the First One Hundred Years in Detroit", Thaddeus Radzialowski, *Ethnicity,* 1974; NYT

Becker: P-D; NYT; St. Louis Mayors: Will Dee Becker, St. Louis Public Library file

St. Louis at War, Betty Burnett, 1987

Delivered from Evil, Robert Leckie, 1987; *The Fall of Berlin*, Anthony Beevor, 2002; "She Got to Berlin,: Virginia Irwin, War Correspondent," Anne R. Kenney. *Missouri Historical Revie*w, 1985

No Ordinary Joe: A Life of Joseph Pulitzer III, Daniel W. Pfaff, 2005; *Pulitzer: Joseph Pulitzer II and the Post-Dispatch: A Newspaperman's Life,* Daniel Pfaff, 1991

Gellhorn: A Twentieth Century Life, Caroline Moorehead, 2003; *Beautiful Exile, The Life of Martha Gellhorn,* Carl Rollyson, 2001; St. Louis Walk of Fame website; *Hemingway and his World*, A.E. Hotchner, 1989; John Burroughs School website

Hadley, The First Mrs. Hemingway, Alice Sokoloff. 1973; *The Paris Wife,* Paula McLain, 2011; Hemingway-Pfieffer Museum website; Pfizer website

"A.E. Hotchner," St. Louis Walk of Fame; *Harper Collins* website; Washington University website

Five Days in August: How World War II Became a Nuclear War, Michael D. Gorsin, 2007; Source List and Detailed Death Tolls for the Primary Megadeaths of the Twentieth Century, Twentieth Century Atlas, especially figures from *Britannica,* 15th ed., 1992 printing, Atomic Bomb Museum website

"Roosevelt Facts and Figures," FDR Library website; The Funeral of Franklin Roosevelt, 1945, Eyewitness to History website; "Why Churchill Lost in 1945," BBC, Feb. 17, 2011

Chapter 20 -- Shelley to Fairgrounds Park

Lead quote: *The Fairgrounds Park Incident: A study of the factors which resulted in the outbreak of violence at the Fairgrounds Park Swimming Pool on June 21, 1949, an account of what happened, and recommendations for corrective action.* Conducted for the St. Louis Council on Human Relations. St. Louis, Missouri, George Schermer, Director, Mayor's Interracial Committee, Detroit, Michigan, July 27, 1949, Missouri History Museum Collection

St. Louis American; P-D; NYT; G-D

"Opening he Gates: Segregation, Desegregation and the Story of Lewis Place," *Gateway magazine*, fall 2005, Missouri Historical Society

Shelley v. Kraemer, 334 U.S. 1 (1948), U.S. Supreme Court decision, Find Law website

The Warmth of Other Suns: The Epic Story of America's Great Migration, Isabel Wilkerson, 2010; Lewis Place, City of St. Louis Census website; "Residents of historic neighborhood still waiting for help," *Reuters*, March 12, 2012; Lewis Place Historical Preservation website

Author interview with Pam Talley, March 2012

Winston S. Churchill: His Complete Speeches 1897-1963, vol. VII, 1943-1949, Robert Rhodes James, ed., 1974; Green Lectures, Westminster College website; *The Iron Curtain: Churchill, America and the Origins of the Cold War,* Fraser J. Harbutt, 1986; *Our Supreme Task: How Winston Churchill's Iron Curtain Speech Defined the Cold War Alliance,* Philip White, 2012; History of the CIA, CIA website

Victory Without Violence: The First Ten Years of the St. Louis Committee of Racial Equality (Core) 1947-1957, Mary Kimbrough and Margaret W. Dagen, 2000; *Stepping Over the Color Line: African-American Students in White Suburban Schools,* Amy Stuart Wells, Robert Crain, Robert L. Crain, 1999; *Politics*, Stein

St. Louis Politics: The Triumph of Tradition, Lana Stein, 2002

Behind Ghetto Walls, Black Family life in a Federal Slum, Lee Rainwater, 1970; "Why the Pruitt-Igoe Housing Project Failed," *The Economist*, Oct. 15, 2011; "Why They Built the Pruitt-Igoe Project," Alexander Von Hoffmann, Joint Center for Housing Studies, Harvard University, 2002; "Ladue Found," Charlene Bry, Ladue website, 2011; "Wendell Oliver Pruitt," Mound City of the Mississippi website; Wendell O. Pruitt and E, William Igoe, Urban Renewal STL website, March 17, 2002

"Top 20 of the 20th Century," *St. Louis Commerce Magazine*, December 1999

Civic Progress list from *St. Louis Politics*, Stein, quoting from list compiled by William A. McDonnell

"Tenth Year of Looking At St, Louis' Doctor Martin Luther King Drive," Urban Review St. Louis website; "Paul McKee's St. Louis Saga Continues: The North Side Story Turns a Page," *St. Louis Magazine,* April 11, 2013

Author interview with Larry Griffin, October 2012

Chapter 21 - Clark Terry and Miles Davis

Lead quote: "Jazz in America," John-Paul Sartre, *Saturday Review of Literature*, 1947

The Autobiography of Clark Terry, Clark Terry with Gwen Terry, 2001

The Autobiography, Miles Davis with Quincey Troupe, 1989

Biography, Discography, Recordings, Clark Terry website; "The Great Lakes Experience: 1942-45," Samuel A. Floyd, Jr., *The Black Perspective in Music,* Vol. 3, No. 1 (Spring, 1975); *Duke's Diary, Part 2: The Life of Duke Ellington 1950-1974;* Ken Vail, 2014; "Octojazzarian profile: Clark Terry," Arnold Jay Smith, jazz.com website

So What: The Life of Miles Davis, John Szwed, 2002; *Milestones: The Music and Times of Miles Davis,* 1998 (org. 1983-1985); Miles Ahead session details, Feb. 16, 1957; Peacock Alley Lounge, St. Louis MO, KSTL-AM radio broadcast; Miles Ahead: The Miles Davis website; *Making of a Kind if Blue: Miles Davis and his Masterpiece,* Eric Nisenson, 2000

City of Gabriels: the History of Jazz in St. Louis, 1895-1973, Dennis Owsley, 2006

The Birth of BeBop, Scott Deveraux, 1999; *Nothing But the Blues, The Music and the Musicians,* ed by Lawrence Cohn, 1993; *Jazz: A History of America's Music,* Geoffrey C. Ward and Ken Burns, 2000; *A Blues Life*, Henry Townsend, as told to Bill Greensmith, 1999

Jazz on the River, William Howland Kennerly; *The Rolling Stone Jazz & Blues Album Guide,* John Swenson, ed., 1999 2005; *The illustrated Encyclopedia of Jazz*, Brian Case and Stan Britt, 1978; All Music website.

St. Louis Symphony Orchestra Principle Musicians -- St. Louis Symphony website; "A Trip Through the Holton Factory," catalogue,

1920; "Miles' Mouthpiece," Trumpet Heralds website; Alabama Jazz Hall of Fame, website

The Miles Davis Quintet at Peacock Alley, Soulard Entertainment, St. Louis; *The Music of Miles Davis: The Box Set Series, 2009*; *Kind of Blue*, Miles Davis Quintet, 1959; *Basic Miles: The Classic Performances of Miles Davis, 1955-1962,* Miles and Coltrane, (1955-58), 1988

Chapter 22 - Ike Turner

Lead quote from lyrics of "Rocket 88," Jackie Brenston and His Delta Cats, 45, Chess Records, 1951; quote is from Tom Maloney, author interview 2013

Author interviews with Greg Edick and Larry Griffin, 2013

P-D, NYT, RFT

Takin' back my name : the confessions of Ike Turner, Ike Turner with Nigel Cawthorne,1999; *Ike Turner : King of Rhythm,* John Collis, 2003; *Room Full of Mirrors: A Biography of Jimi Hendrix*, Charles R. Cross, 2005

"Ike Before Tina," J.C. Marian, JammUpp Issue No. 38, E-Zine, website; "East St. Louis," All Music website; "The Devil and Ike Turner," Donald Fagan, Dec. 17, 2007, website

Devil at the Confluence, Kevin Belford, 2009

I, Tina, Tina Turner, with Kurt Loder, 1986

Tina Turner: Break Every Rule, Mark Bego, 2003; "Tina Turner: the Woman Who Taught Mick Jagger to Dance Is On the Prowl Again," *People Magazine*, Dec. 7, 1981; T*he Rolling Stones: An Illustrated Record*, Roy Carr, 1976

Ike and Tina Turner, 2 CD, Madacy, 2006; G*reatest hits, Ike and Tina Turner,* Curb Records, 1990; A*bsolutely the Best Live, Ike and Tina Turner,* Fuel, 2011; *Nutbush City Limits*, Ike & Tina Turner, LP, Capitol, 1973; T*ina: The Collected Recordings, Sixties to Nineties, Tina Turner*, 3 CD, Capitol, 1994; *Tina: All the Best, Tina Turner*, 2 CD, Capitol, 2004; I*ke and Tina: Blues*, Ike and Tina Turner, Fuel, 2013; *Private Dancer,* Tina Turner, Capitol, 1997; *Risin' with the Blues*, Ike Turner, ZOHO, 2006

Stacy Johnson interview with author, 2013

Rock 'n' Roll: "One O'Clock Jump," Count Basie, YouTube, 2014; Rock and Roll Timeline 1877-1956 website; *What Was the First Rock and Roll Record?* Jim Dawson and Steve Popes, 1992; "Saturday Night Fish

Fry," Louis Jordan, 1949, YouTube; *Before Elvis: The Prehistory of Rock 'n' Roll,* Larry Birnbaum, 2013; "Corn Bread," Hal Singler .1947, YouTube; *The Roots of Rock and Roll: The Savoy Sessions,* Double LP, Arista, 1977

Bill Haley: The Daddy of Rock and Roll, John Swenson, 1983; All Music website; Rolling Stone Guide; *Billboard* charts, from website 2014 and *The Billboard Book of Top 40 Hits, 1955 to present,* Joel Whitburn, 1983

Encyclopedia of Rhythm & Blues and Doo-Wop Vocal Groups, Mitch Rosalsky, 2002

"That's a Wrap: Technisonic Studios Go Dark," *St. Louis Business Journa*l, Aug. 1, 2010: Technisonic Studio, Minot website

The lesser lights: Most the following entries include information from *Mo Betta: St. Louis R&B 1956-66,* CD, Red Lightnin', liner notes by Bill Greensmith, 1997; St. Louis Blues And Jazz Hall Of Fame website; *Confluence;* Discography for Bobbin Records, Global Dog website, 2005

Benny Sharp and the Sharpies: "Benny Sharp & the Sharpies," Barrett Braun, *BluesLetter,* St. Louis Blues Society, No. 7, January 1990; "The Sharpies," *The Virgin Encyclopedia of R&B and Soul,* 1998

Clayton Love: *Blues Who's Who: a Biographical Dictionary of Blues Singers,* Sheldon Harris, 197; "Clayton Love," Dave Beardsley, *BluesLetter,* October 1997

Billy Gayles: "Spreading the Rock and Roll Gospel," *Riverfront Times,* Jan. 28, 1987; I*'m Tore Up, Ike Turner's Kings of Rhythm*, LP, Red Lightnin', 1976

BB's and Blues City Deli versions, author attended shows, 2012

Art Lassiter: "Art Lassiter, Charismatic Singer," *Seattle Times,* Aug. 10, 1994

Andrew Odum, "Little Aaron": *Earl Hooker: Blues Master,* Sebastian Danchin, 1995

Billy Davis Jr., El Torrors, Fred Green: "El Torros," Doo-Wop Biographies, Groups and Discography website, Fifth Dimension website, Billy Davis, Jr./Marilyn McCoo website

Johnny "The Twist": Chess Records website

Piano Slim: "In Memory of Robert T. Smith," Officer Funeral Home, East St. Louis, Dec. 30, 2011

"Screamin'" Joe Neal: "Inside St. Louis: Blueberry Hill," Antiques Warehouse website, Tom Maloney interview

Little Milton: "Little Milton's 'Second Home;" East St. Louis, P-D, no date; Blues Who's Who; "Little Milton," Voice of the Blues: Classic

Interviews from *Living Blues Magazine,* Jim O'Neal and Amy van Singel, eds, interview by Lynn S. Summers, 1974; "Feature Artist: Little Milton Campbell," Jeff Collier, *BluesLetter,* May 1989

Erskine Ogelsby: "Erskine Ogelsby," *BluesLetter,* October 1997

Tommy Bankhead: "Tommy Bankhead," Joel Slotnikoff, *BluesLetter* September 1989; "Tommy Bankhead -- Messenger of the Blues," *BluesLetter* January 2001; "Benefit & Tribute Concert for Tommy Bankhead," *BluesLetter* May 1997, "Mr. Tommy Bankhead, interview by Dave Beardsley in same issue; Memorial Program from Eddie Randle & Sons Funeral Home, Dec. 22, 2000

Big George Brock: "Artist Profile: Big George Brock," Jeff Collier, *BluesLetter,* April 1989

Bennie Smith: "Bennie Smith," Joel Slotnikoff, *BluesLetter,* November 1989; "Masters of Their Domains: Hometown legend Bennie Smith joins other blues greats at the "Guitar Master 2002" show," *Riverfront Times,* Dec. 18, 2002

Author interviews: Mike King, Sharon Foehner, Jeremy Segel-Moss

Ace Wallace: "Ace Wallace," Joel Slotnikoff, *BluesLetter*, July 1989

Gabriel: "Blowing some horn for Gabriel." *St. Louis Beacon*, Aug. 5, 2010; "The Flock Rocker on Planet," That's All Right Mama website, 2012; "A voice in the night: the incomparable Gabriel," KDHX website, Aug. 1, 2010

Doc Terry: "Doc Terry," Joel Slotnikoff, *BluesLetter*, 1989; Blues Who's Who; "Blues Man, 'Doc' Terry gave up his day job, but not his music," *East Side Journa*l, no date

Big Bad Smitty: "Artist Profile: Big Bad Smitty," Joel Slotnikoff, *BluesLetter*, July 1989; Big Bad Smitty News, Club handout, May 1993; "Big Bad Smitty," Blues World website; "Big Bad Smitty," *The Virgin Encyclopedia of R&B and Soul,* 1998,

Chapter 23 - Chuck Berry and Johnnie Johnson

Lead quote: Joe Edwards interview

Brown Eyed Handsome Man: The Life and Hard Times of Chuck Berry, Bruce Pegg, 2002

Father of Rock & Roll: The Story of Johnnie "B. Goode" Johnson, Travis Fitzpatrick 1999

The Autobiography, Chuck Berry, 1987

"The Chuck Berry House," United States Department of the Interior National Park Service, National Register of Historic Places Registration Form, Aug. 28, 2008

Spinning Blues Into Gold: The Chess Brothers and the Legendary Chess Records, Nadine Cohodas, 2001; *Before Elvis,* Birnbaum; *Life,* Keith Richards, 2010; "Keith Richards Remembers Johnnie Johnson: Stones guitarist reflects on friend, idol Johnson," *Rolling Stone,* April 15, 2005

Maybellene: "Chuck Berry," SiNG365 website: "Roll Over Beethoven," "School Day" lyrics; Rolling Stone Guide; Billboard charts; "Johnnie Johnson," "Chuck Berry," *The Big Book of Blues,* Robert Santelli, 2001; "Charles Edward Anderson Berry," Blues Who's Who; Praguefrank's Country Music Discography: Chuck Berry, website

"Go Johnnie, Go, Go, Go," *St. Louis magazine,* April 1986; "Meet Johnnie: A Big Part of Rock's Beginnings," Rockabilly Hall of Fame interview, 1991; "Fame eluded rock pioneer until later in life: Johnnie Johnson 1924-2005," P-D, April 14, 2005;" "Johnnie Johnson, 80, Dies; Inspired 'Johnny B. Goode," NYT, April 14, 2005

Author interviews: Tom Maloney, Frances Johnson, Stacy Johnson

City of Fairmont, website

Hail! Hail! Rock 'n' Roll, DVD, Delilah Films, Taylor Hackford, director, 1987

Chapter 24 - Mill Creek Valley, Gaslight Square

Lead quote: *Gaslight Square: an oral history,* Thomas Crone, ed. 2004

Also from Crone: Interviews of Jack Parker, Joe Pollack, Bob Reuter, "Smokey" Joe Cunningham, Art Dwyer, Bill Christman, Pete Rothschild, Billy Peek, Ron "Johnny Rabbit" Elz, Jeanne Trevor, Cheri Ann Schear, Joe Edwards

NYT, P-D. Star-Times, G-D, RFT

Mill Creek Valley: The Soul of St. Louis, Ron Fagerstrom, 2000

The Fourth City, 1764-1909, Volume 1, Stevens, 1911; Lion; Grassroots; Comprehensive City Plan, Saint Louis, Missouri, City Plan Commission, Harlan Bartholomew, Engineer, 1947; City Ordinance 47245, Library File

"Site of huge new redevelopment project, Mill Creek Valley, was showplace of early St. Louis," *Union Electric Magazine,* Spring 1958

Rebel Without Applause, Jay Landesman, 1987

Ted Flicker Biography (1930-) Film Reference website; "Inside the Nervous Set" Scott Miller, New Line Theater website; "The Premier Hotspot of St. Louis: Gaslight Square, O'Connell's History," Missouri History Museum website

"Gaslight Square," *Spotlight Missouri,* Spring 1962; "The City: No Squares on the Square," *Time*, May 18, 1962

"Jay Landesman: Founder of Gaslight Square's Crystal Palace," *St. Louis Beacon*, March 2, 2011; "Crystal Palace was a popular cabaret theater in Gaslight Square," *West End Word*, Jan. 29, 2014

Desolate Angels, Dennis McNally, 2003

Allen Ginsberg's 'Howl' and the Paperback Revolution, Bill Savage, 2008; *Mania*, Ronald Collins and David Skover, 2013; *The Town and the City,* Jack Kerouac, 1950, *On the Road,* Jack Kerouac, 1957; *And the Hippos Were Boiled in Their Tanks,* Jack Kerouac and William S. Burroughs, written 1945, pub. 2008

Author's experiences with Lucien Carr in the UPI newsroom, New York City, 1978-1986

Academy of American Poets website 2014

"LaClede Town: Impressions of a Native Son," Dominic Schaeffer, blogpost, retrieved 2014; "Swinging LaClede," *CITY Magazine*," (reprinted in P-D, Jan 9, 1968;) "An Urbane Humane Stew," *Newsweek Magazine,* (reprinted in P-D, March 30, 1968); "Laclede: An Experiment in Ethnic Harmony," *Dallas Morning News*, Nov. 30, 1997

"Arch Timeline," P-D Reference Department, Oct. 17, 2005; "Eero Saarinen," "Gateway Arch" National Park Service website

The Gateway Arch: A Biography, Tracy Campbell, 2013

Author interviews: Tom Maloney, Joe Edwards

Chapter 25 - Sixties civil rights movement

Lead quote: *Ain't But a Place: An Anthology of African American Writings about St. Louis,* Gerald Lyn Early, ed., 1998

Grassroots; St. Louis Politics

P-D, G-D; NYT; *St. Louis American,* RFT

"Raymond Tucker," "Alfonso J. Cervantes" St. Louis Mayors, St. Louis Public Library file, 2005

Civil Rights Movement Veterans website; *The Sixties, A Black Chronology,* Norman Harris, 1990; 'I Have A Dream," the Rev. Martin Luther King Jr. at the March on Washington, 1963, text from national Archives website

"Remarks of the President, McDonnell Aircraft Corporation, Lambert Field, St. Louis Missouri", John F. Kennedy Presidential Library, Sept. 12, 1962; *McDonnell Douglas v. Green,* 411 U.S. 792 (1973), U.S. Supreme Court decisions, May 14, 1973, Justia website; James Smith McDonnell (1899-1980) Biography, Boeing Co. website

"Reaction to Liberation: Official Response to the Black Liberation Struggle in St. Louis, Missouri," *Gateway Heritage magazine*, vol. 23, no. 4, Spring 2003, Missouri Historical Society.

Chapter 26 - Black Artists' Group

Lead quote: Trio Tres Bien Music website

Point from which Creation Begins: The Black Artists' Group of St. Louis, Benjamin Looker, 2004, portions first published in *Gateway Heritage*: The Quarterly Magazine of the Missouri Historical Society, Vol. 22 No. 1 (Summer 2001).

Gaslight Oral History; Gabriels; Jazz.com website; Rolling Stone Guide; All Music Guide, website; Blues Who's Who; *Discovering African-America St. Louis, John Wright, 1994*

P-D; NYT; G-D; RFT

Oral history T-0034 interview with Singleton Palmer, interviewed by Irene Cortinovis, jazzmen project, Nov, 9, 1971,"*Oral History Collection* (S0829), The State Historical Society of Missouri"

David Sanborn website 2014

"Clea Bradford, 67; Jazz Singer Was Known for Her Versatility," *Washington Post,* Sept. 3, 2008; "Remembering Clea Bradford," *Blues Art Journal,* September 2008

"Kittrell reflects on her lengthy career," *The Edwardsville Intelligencer,* Feb. 4, 2012

Chapter 27 - Albert King, Oliver Sain

"An Interview With Albert King," Alan Paul, *Guitar World Magazine,* 1991

Author interviews: Gus Thornton, Tom Maloney, Marsha Evans, Jeremy Segel-Moss, Larry Griffin, Rich McDonough

"Albert King," *Blues Singers: Biographies of 50 Legendary Artists of the Early 20th Century*, David Dicaire, 1999, New Rolling Stone Guide; Rolling Stone Jazz and Blues Guide; Confluence; A Blues Life; Who's Who: NYT; P-D; RFT; G-D

Albert King with Stevie Ray Vaughn In Session, Concord Music, recorded 1983, released 1999 (Stax album), 2009 (Concord DVD); *The Big Blues*, Albert King, King Records, 1962; Billboard, Top 40

Bill Graham Presents: My Life Inside Rock and Out, Bill Graham, 1992: *The Legendary Lonnie Johnson: Music and Civil Rights*, Dean Alger, 2014

Johnnie, Fitzpatrick; Blues, Cohn; Blues Hall of Fame website; History.com website; "Gus Thornton," Jeremy Segel-Moss, St. Louis *BluesLetter* 2006; "Gus Thornton: Heart of the Blues," Bruce Olson, *BluesLetter,* August 2013

Bob Kuban: *My Side of the Bandstand*, Bob Kuban, 2002; bobkuban.com, 2014; "Bob Kuban and the In-Men," The Metro St. Louis Live Music Historical Society Web site, 2014

`"Oliver Sain Obituary," Memorial service, New Cote Brilliant Church of God, Nov. 2, 2003 "Oliver Sain," *Virgin Encyclopedia of the Blues,* "Colin Larkin, 1992; "Tribute to Oliver Sain," Michael Kuelker, *BluesLetter*, October 1997; "Oliver Sain (1932-2003)," *BluesLetter* November 2003; "The Man With the Golden Horn -- Oliver Sain," *BluesLetter* interview, 2000

"Two sides of Fontella Bass, the late, great St. Louis soul singer," *Los Angeles Times,* Dec. 27, 2012; "Fontella Bass,1940 to 2012," Bruce Olson, *BluesLette*r, February 2013; "Rhythm In the Family," G-D, April 1967; "Fontella Bass," *Virgin Encyclopedia*; *No Tired Ways*, Liner notes, RPM Records, 1994; "Honoring the Life of Legendary Soul/Gospel Singer Fontella Bass," Shalom Church, City of Peace, 2013

"Barbara Carr," *BluesLetter* interview, 1996; "Catfood Records sings soul/blues singing sensation Barbara Carr," Mark Pucci Media, June 1, 2012; author conversation, 2013

Bonnie Bramlette website

In Concert: KSHE and 40+ years of Rock in St. Louis, John Neiman, 2009

Mississippi River Festival: "Dylan Joins the Band Onstage at Mississippi River Fest: The troubadour surprises Edwardsville crowd at the Band's headlining set," *Rolling Stone,* Aug. 9, 1969; Expecting Rain website, 2013-2014; SIUE Archives -- Mississippi River Festival, website

"The Night That Modern Live Sound Was Born: Bob Heil & The Grateful Dead," *Performing Musician Magazine,* December 2008; Mississippi River Fest website virtual museum

Chapter 28 - Baseball: Blacks, Browns and Birds

Lead quote: Only the Ball Was White

Baseball Encyclopedia: The Complete and Official Record of Major League Baseball, 5th ed., Joseph Reichler, ed, 1982; *The World Series, Complete Play-by-Play of Every Game 1903-1978,* Richard E. Cohen, David S. Neft, 1979; *Rob Neyer's Big Book of Baseball Legends: The Truth, the Lies, and Everything Else,* Rob Neyer and Bill James, 2008; *Primitive Baseball: The First Quarter-Century of the National Pastime,* Harvey Frommer, 1988; Sportsman's Park, Ballparks of Baseball website

Even the Browns, William Mead, 1978; *Spirit of St. Louis,* Goldenbock, 2000; "Where's the Strike Zone?" NYT, Aug. 19, 1951

"Barnstorming Aces Satchel Paige and Dizzy Dean," Larry Tye, *American History magazine,* reprint online April 1, 2010; *Satchel: The Life and Times of an American Legend,* Larry Tye, 2010; *Cool Papas and Double Duties: The All-Time Greats of the Negro Leagues,* William F. McNeil, 2001; *The Negro Leagues Chronology: Events in Organized Black Baseball, 1920-1948*, Christopher Hauser, 2006; *The Integration of Major League Baseball: A Team by Team History*, Rick Swaine, 2009; Black Baseball, website

The Gashouse Gang: How Dizzy Dean, Leo Durocher, Branch Rickey and Their Colorful, Come From Behind Baseball Team Won the World Series and America's Heart During the Great Depression, John Heidenry, 2007; ""Dizzy" Dean (1910–1974) aka: Jay Hanna Dean," The Encyclopedia of Arkansas History and Culture website; "1934: St. Louis Cardinals 11, Detroit Tigers 0," Frankie Frisch as told to Ken Smith," *The Baseball Reader*; "Stan Musial, Gentlemanly Slugger and Cardinals' Stan the Man", Dies at 92," NYT, Jan. 19, 2013; "Beyond Bunning and Short Rest: An Analysis of Managerial Decisions That Led to the Phillies' Epic Collapse of 1964;" Bryan Soderholm-Difatte, *Baseball Research Journa*l, Fall 2010

My Greatest Day in Baseball: Exciting Inside stories told by and about today's top stars and the all-time greats of the past,: Bob Gibson, as told by Jack Orr, Stan Musial as told to Bob Broeg, 1968

October 1964, David Halberstam, 1994; *The Yankees: The Four Fabulous Eras of Baseball's Most Famous Team,* Dave Anderson, et al.. 1980; *The Tigers of 1968: Baseball's Last Real Champions,* George Cantor; 1997; *El Birdos: The 1967 and 1968 St. Louis Cardinals;* Doug Feldman, 2007

Game accounts: P-D, G-D, NYT

Notes Chapter 29: Cervantes, Schoemehl

Lead quote: "Loss of Corvette a turning point for St. Louis manufacturing," P-D, July 10, 2011

Lion; St. Louis Politics; P-D; G-D; NYT, RFT; *St. Louis American*

Mr. Mayor, A.J. Cervantes, A. J. Cervantes, 1974; *St. Louis to Me,* Howard Baer, 1978; Bill Clay: A *Political Voice at the Grass Roots, Bill Clay,* William Clay, 2004

"A Two-Fisted Crime Fight in St. Louis," *Life,* May 29, 1970

"The Hoffa Files: A Deathbed Confession, KLAS TV Las Vegas, Nov. 14, 2006

"My View From the Balcony" St.. Louis Mo., Theatre Timeline, website; 1964 World's Fair 1965 - Attractions - Spain," NYWF64 website; "The Jewel of the Fair: LIFE visits the Spanish Pavilion," *Life,* Aug. 7, 1964; "A World's Fair Pavilion Hides in Plain Site," After the Fair website, Nov. 10, 2011; "The Cosmopolitan Spanish Pavilion," Ballpark Hilton file

Egan's Rats: *The Untold Story of the Prohibition-Era Gang That Ruled St. Louis,* Daniel Waugh, 2007

"Morris Shenker, 82, Ex-Dunes Owner," *Los Angeles Times*, Aug. 10,, 1989 "The Leisures and Trupiano -- The St. Louis Crime Family," Crime Library website; "Authorities call Paul J. Leisure longtime underworld enforcer," P-D, April 17, 1983; "Law and Disorder," *St. Louis Magazine*, June 5, 2007; "St. Louis: A Gangster History," Gangster Inc., website

History of St. Louis Neighborhoods, St. Louis Community Development Agency, 1980; *St. Louis Landmarks*: A Guide to the City, St. Louis Community Development Agency, 1977 "Soulard Restoration Plan," St. Louis Community Development Commission, 1975; "Soulard Historic District: The New Must Exist With the Old," *Subject to Change Magazine*, Oct. 26, 1978; "Soulard Neighborhood Historic District," National Register of Historic Places Inventory - Nomination Form., May 1972

Author interview: Bernie Hayes, 2012

"Re-examining The Team Four Plan," Bernie Hayes blog, Aug. 21, 2009; *St. Louis: A City and its Suburbs,* Barbara Williams, 1973

Crabgrass Frontier: The Suburbanization of the United States, Kenneth T. Jackson, 1985; "Reagan's Recession," Pew Research Center; Dec. 14, 2010

"Mayor's Power of Persuasion Boosts Support For Tax Plan,;" *South Side Journal,* May 9, 1984; "Schoemehl Promises Better Days for St. Louis," *South Side Journal,* April 17, 1985; Feb. 16, 2012; "Why Was Homer Phillips Killed?" *Ebony Magazine*, September 1977; Homer G. Phillips Hospital, National Register of Historic Places Inventory Nomination Form, March 1982

"The Life and Death of Great St. Louis Malls," Joe Huber Development & Preservation website, Dec. 5, 2012; "How St. Louis turned less into more: Never mind an exodus of population and jobs unmatched among large U.S. cities. Thanks to daring business leaders -- and to tax breaks and a stable economy in the suburbs -- downtown is vibrant once again," *Fortune Magazine*, Dec. 23, 1985.

Chapter 30: The Clubs

Lead quote: author interview with Joe Edwards

Other author interviews: Bernie Hayes. Gene Norman, Marsha Evans, Jimmy Hinds, Tom Ray,

Leo's Five -- Direct from the Blue Note Club, Bill Greensmith, 2008, liner notes, CD, Ace Records; Leo's Five, All Music website; "The History of KWK -- The Soul of the City," KWK106 website; "Hayes, Bernard (1935-), Papers, 1961-1989," 16 Folders, 2 Audio Tapes, State Historical Society, UMSL

P-D; RFT; G-D

"Clubs," St. Louis Music Yesterday's website; "Chambers Park," St. Louis City Talk website

Confluence; Gabriels; St. Louis Politics; "James DeShay"," STLBlues website; *Groping Toward Democracy: African American Social Reform in St. Louis, 1910 - 1949,"* Priscilla Dowden White, 2011; Blues Life

"Silvercloud," *BluesLetter,* March 1990 "Little Walter," All Music website; "Keith Doder," STLBlues Net website, "School for Fools," The Band website; "Memphis Slim," All Music website

"When Joe Edwards came home he found a shabby St. Louis, but his entrepreneurial vision helped make it vibrant again," *Christian-Science Monitor Weekly*, Dec. 17, 2012; "The Elvis Room: A Lasting tribute," *Spotlight,* August 1995; Blueberry Hill menu, 2014; "Favorite Concerts at Blueberry Hill, Elvis Room," Joe Edwards handout; Blueberry Hill Darts Tournament, May 9-11, 2014, Blueberry Hill website

"City Hall Plaza Historic District," application National Register of Historic Place," April 1975; T*he Siege of University City: The Dreyfus Case of America,* Sidney Morse, 1912: "Edward Gardner Lewis and University City," University City Public Library website; *The Bold Humor Of Davey Bold At The Celebrity Club,* Norman Records, 1961

"BB's Jazz Blues and Soups," STL Blues Reviews, STLBlues.net; "Livin' the Blues," *St. Louis Magazine*, 1993, from STLBlues.net website, 2014; "A Bigger, Better BB's," *St. Louis Magazine*, Oct. 23, 2007

"Best of Mississippi Nights," *52nd City Magazine*, January 2007; The Urge.net website; The Urge on WikiLou Webpage, 2014; "Venue Songs," They Might Be Giants, News and Downloads webpage

Chapter 31- The First Annual Blues Festival

Lead quote: "The First Blues Society Fest at Mississippi Nights," Art Dwyer, KDHX history, KDHX website

RFT; P-D: NYT, G_D

Performance Schedule for the Blues Festival, 1st Annual St. Louis Blues Festival, "A classic afternoon and evening of Blues," Produced by the St. Louis Blues Club, 1986 poster

Author Interviews: Ron Edwards, Rich McDonough, Marsha Evans, Tom Ray and Lew Prince, Sharon Foehner, Joe Edwards, Jeremy Segel-Moss, Tom Maloney, Larry Griffin,

"Construction never stops at Venice Cafe," *St. Louis Beacon*, March 29, 2012; "Not Fade Away: St. Louis Piano Blues," *BluesLetter,* 2003

"James Crutchfield," All Music website; Hellbent and Blue, video recording, Mound City Pictures, James Mann and Matt Schneider, 2000

Tom Hall Music website; "A Conversation with Tom Hall," *BluesLetter*, July 2014, "Encore: Geyer Street Sheiks, Tom Hall and Alice Spencer play it again," *St. Louis Beacon*, May 16, 2013; "Tom Hall and Alice Spencer: Otherwise Known As T&A," *St. Louis Magazine*, March 25, 2014

McCoys: *Encyclopedia of the Blues*, Edward Komara, 2006; Nothing But; "On the Road Again- Adelphi Records," Big Road Blues Show, April 14, 2014; "Bonnie McCoy At Garden House Country Blues Series in Seattle," Washington State Blues Society website, Nov. 12, 2012

Big George: "Big George Brock," *BluesLetter* 1989; StlBlues.net website; Album liner notes from Cat Head website; "Big George Brock;" Ponderosa Stomp-New Orleans, program notes, 2011; "Big Brock's 'blues bus' hits highway to Mississippi Delta," Hopson Plantation Blog, 2009; "Big George Brock, Beltholder," *Living Blues Magazine,* May 2005; "The man who beat Sonny Liston, the man who knew Muddy Waters on a plantation when they were both kids, the man who gave Albert King his first big break," AOne Blues.com interview, 2014; *Hellbent and Blue,* James Mann, et. al., VHS tape, 2000.

Piano Slim: STLBlues net website; All Music website; "Robert Smith," *Belleville News-Democrat,* Jan. 4, 2012; "Robey, Don Deadric," Texas State Historical Association website

"The Roots of Leroy Pierson," *BluesLetter,* 1999; Leroy Jodie Pierson website

"Clayton Love," *BluesLetter,* October 1997

"Keith Doder: the BluesLetter interview," *BluesLetter,* March 2001

Soulard Blues Band website; "Artie 'Bigfoot' Dwyer," *BluesLetter,* August 1996; "Third Set Blues: The Soulard Blues Band keeps Mondays moving into Tuesdays, every week of the year at Broadway Oyster Bar," *St. Louis Magazine,* December 2001; *Trickle Down Blues*, liner notes, King Solomon Records, 2004; *Live at Stuggart* liner notes, 2000; Best Blues Band Awards, RFT, 1985 - 2005; "Tops in Town Poll - Best Blues Band," *Spotlight Magazine,* Issue No. 143, 1996; "Blues Soulard Style," *Spotlight,* 1988

Silvercloud: *BluesLetter* interview, March 1990

Tommy Bankhead: *BluesLetter* interview, May, 1997; *BluesLetter,* Sept 1989; "Tommy Bankhead -- Messenger of the Blues (1931-2000)," *BluesLetter,* January 2001; "In Loving Memory of the Late Tommy Bankhead," Eddie Randle Funeral Home, Dec. 22, 2000

Billy Peek: Performance at Bluesweek 2012; All Music website; Billy Peek Facebook page, "About" 2014; Bob Lohr interview, STLBlues.net, 2014

Rondo: *BluesLetter* interview, 1989; "Rondo: Blues Power Deluxe," *Spotlight,* December 1990; *Shack Pappy's* liner notes, Rondo Blues Deluxe,

Blueberry Hill Records; "Rondo: The Roots of His Blues," *BluesLetter*, September 2006; "Rondo: The Roots of His Blues, Part 2," *BluesLetter*, November 2006; "Rondo Leewright was among St. Louis' greatest blues singers," RFT, Sept. 22 2011; Rondo Blues Deluxe, All Music website

Oliver Sain: see Chapter 27

David Dee: All Music, Soul Blues Music website, Webster Groves performance 2012; David Dee and the Hot Tracks website

Bennie Smith: Bennie Smith interview, *BluesLetter*, 2006; Bennie Smith, Blues World website, 2005; All Music website; "Passing of a Legend," Associated Press, *Southeast Missourian*, Sept. 13, 2006; "Bluesman Bennie Smith dies at age 72," St. Louis Public Radio, Sept. 10, 2006

The Myrkin Papers, Lorenzo Milam, 1969; "KDNA 102.5 mHz," *St. Louis Journalism Review*, October 1997; "A Change of Tune," *St. Louis Magazine,* Aug. 30, 2010; *Rebels on the Air: An Alternative History of Radio in America,* Jesse Walker, 2002; KDHX website; "Encore: KDHX'S last dance on Magnolia Avenue," *St. Louis Beacon*, Oct. 10, 2013

Chapter 32 - Johnson v. Berry

Lead quote: Case No. 4:00CV-01891 *Johnson v. Berry*, U.S. District Court for the Eastern District of Missouri, filed Nov. 29, 2000

Author interviews with Frances Johnson, Tom Maloney, Joe Edwards

The Father of Rock & Roll: The Story of Jonnie "B. Goode" Johnson, Travis Fitzpatrick, 1999

Life, Keith Richards, 2010

Hail! Hail! Rock 'n' Roll, DVD, Delilah Films, Taylor Hackford, director, 1987

See also Chapter 23

Author attendance at New Orleans Jazz and Heritage Festival, 1995

Johnnie "B. Goode," stakes his claim in music history from partner Chuck Berry," press release, Johnnie Johnson legal team, Nov. 30, 2000; Johnnie Johnson Blues and Jazz Society website

P-D; NYT

"Judge Dismisses Chuck Berry Royalty Suit," *Billboard,* Oct. 23, 2002; "Pianist Johnnie Johnson Dies," *Billboard,* April 13, 2005; "2010: The Year of Johnnie Be Good?" *BluesLetter*, January 2010

Author coverage of Berry statue: "Controversial Chuck Berry statue approved in St. Louis," Reuters, July 29, 2011

"Chuck Berry Praises Obama, Laments Fading Health," Rolling Stone, Oct. 27, 2012; "Chuck Berry Collapses Onstage in Chicago," Reuters, Jan. 11, 2011

Chapter 33 - Baseball 1968-2014

Lead quote: "HBO's Gumbel questions La Russa's Hall of Fame worthiness," P-D, July 25, 2014

Spirit, Golenbock; *The St. Louis Baseball Reader,* Richard Patterson, ed., 2006: *Busch Stadium, the First Season,* St. Louis P-D, 2006: *Baseball: An Illustrated History,*_Geoffrey C. Ward and Ken Burns, 1994

Expanding the Strike Zone: Baseball in the Age of Free Agency, Daniel A. Gilbert, 2013

Stats: Baseball-Reference Web Site, MLB.com, ESPN.com, Baseball Encyclopedia, 1982; List of St. Louis Cardinals Seasons, chart by Wiki Encyclopedia website

NYT; P-D; RFT

"How Budweiser Went From 'King of Beers' To Court Jester, "Business Insider Web Site, May 7, 2012 "The Top Ten Beers in the World Aren't What You Think," The Grid, Bloomberg website

Grant's Farm Features New Attractions for 60th Season, St. Louis Front Page, website, May 23, 2014

"Flood fought player reserve clause," ESPN website; "How Curt Flood Changed Baseball and Killed His Career in the Process," *Atlantic Monthly,* July 12, 2011; *The Curt Flood Story: The Man Behind the Myth,* Stuart L. Weiss, 2007

You're Missing a Great Game, Whitey Herzog, 1999

"Tony La Russa says that steroid cheats should be let in Baseball Hall of Fame -- with asterisks," *New York Daily News,* July 26, 2014; "Mark McGwire remembers baseball's Olympic boom in 1984," Olympic Talk NBC, Aug. 7, 2014; "McGwire & Steroids," *ESPN Magazine,* 2014; "Childhood friends of Tampa native Tony La Russa knew something special was in store," *Tampa Bay Times,* Nov. 1, 2011

"Stepping away helped Freese reach apex," MLB.com, Oct. 8, 2011; "Meramec alum Freese makes major league debut with Cardinals," St.

Louis Community College website, April 7, 2009; "Down to his last strike: David Freese overcame his own indifference, injuries and three brushes with the law,," *ESPN The Magazine*, Dec. 16, 2011; "Cards owners worth $4 billion: Investments include Arby's, Churchill Downs, plantation resort, Pulitzer and Tribune publishing," *St. Louis Business Journal*, May 6, 2001

Games: P-D, NYT

Chapter 34 - The Bands Today

Lead Quote: *Hidden Assets: Connecting the Past to the Future of St. Louis,* Andrew Scavotto, 2006

Author interviews: Brian Casserly, Matt and Nikki Hill, Vinnie Valenza, Rockin' Jake, Aaron Griffin, Rich McDonough, Marsha Evans, Charles Hunt, Melissa Neels, Tom Maloney; brief interviews with band members

Author articles from *BluesLette*r 2012 - 2014

Performances from author reviews, 2012 - 2015

Band websites

RFT; P-D; *USA Today;* NYT

Chapter 35 - Ferguson

Lead quote: "France cites segregation," P-D., Nov. 26, 2014

The majority of the material in this account of the incidents revolving around the shooting of a black teenager in Ferguson, Missouri., Aug. 9, 2014, comes from coverage Aug. 9 to Dec. 31, 2015: P-D, NYT, *St. Louis American, Washington Post, Los Angeles Times, USA Today,* BBC, Salon.com, *Newsweek, Mother Jones.* Also *St. Louis Magazine, Riverfront Times, BluesLetter* 2014; *New Yorker magazine*, Sept. 1, 2014, Dec. 8, 2014; *Eleven* magazine, September 2014

State of Missouri vs. Darren Wilson, transcript of Grand Jury, Vol. VI, Sept. 23, 2014

The Ferguson Report, United States Department of Justice Civil Rights Division, 2015

"The Cop," *New Yorker*, Aug. 10, 2015

Forward Through Ferguson, The Ferguson Commission, Sept. 3, 2015

For other topics see also P-D; NYT; RFT, *St. Louis American* (especially for McKee)

U.S. Census Bureau for population and race statistics

Emerson: "$60 million in data centers coming online at Emerson," *St. Louis Business Journal,* Aug 31, 2008;' "Stuart Symington," Biographical Directory of the United States Congress website.

United States of America v. Benjamin L. Goins, Appellant, 593 F.2d 88 (8th Cir. 1979)

For Clay see Chapter 25

"Eminent Domain, NorthSide Regeneration and the St. Louis American," Michael Allen on Preservation Research Office website, Dec. 16, 2012; "What's next for McKee's NorthSide Regeneration?" *St. Louis Business Journal,* April 9, 2014; St. Louis Public Schools website; "Paul J. McKee Jr.," Readers Want Walkability and Long-Term Jobs at NorthSide Regeneration," Urban Review website, April 16, 2014; "Paul McKee's St. Louis saga continues: The North Side turns page," *St. Louis Magazine,* April 11, 2013; McEagle Properties website

For Bosley and Harmon see P-D and G-D news accounts

Acknowledgements

A final thanks goes to my partner, companion and editor, Marilyn Ciafone Olson. And a raise of the glass to Roger Hudson for consistent support and insight.

Also to the music community, especially Jeremy Segel-Moss, Art Dwyer, Larry Griffin, Marsha Evens, Joe Edwards and Bernie Hayes for guidance beyond the call of duty.

And to the librarians at the St. Louis Public Library, especially those in the St. Louis Room and the Charing Cross Branch.

Index

C

D

E

F

G

H

I

J

K

L

M

N

O

P

Q

R

S

W

Y

Z

Made in the USA
Middletown, DE
05 March 2020

85898057R00357